REGISTERS OF THE CONSISTORY OF GENEVA IN THE TIME OF CALVIN

Volume 1, 1542-1544

REGISTERS OF THE CONSISTORY OF GENEVA IN THE TIME OF CALVIN

Volume 1, 1542-1544

General Editor

Robert M. Kingdon

Edited by

Thomas A. Lambert and Isabella M. Watt

with the assistance of

Jeffrey R. Watt

translated by

M. Wallace McDonald

WILLIAM B. EERDMANS PUBLISHING COMPANY
GRAND RAPIDS, MICHIGAN / CAMBRIDGE, U.K.

THE H. H. MEETER CENTER FOR CALVIN STUDIES
GRAND RAPIDS, MICHIGAN

First published 1996 in French under the title
Registres du Consistoire de Genève au temps de Calvin
by Librairie Droz.

English translation © 2000 Wm. B. Eerdmans Publishing Co.
255 Jefferson Ave. S.E., Grand Rapids, Michigan 49503 /
P.O. Box 163, Cambridge CB3 9PU U.K.

Published in collaboration with the
H. H. Meeter Center for Calvin Studies
at Calvin College, Grand Rapids, Michigan

Printed in the United States of America

05 04 03 02 01 00   7 6 5 4 3 2 1

Library of Congress Cataloging-in-Publication Data

Registers of the Consistory of Geneva in the time of Calvin, volume 1 /
edited by Robert M. Kingdon.
p.   cm.
Includes bibliographical references and index.
ISBN 0-8028-4618-1 (pbk.: alk. paper)
1. Court records — Switzerland — Geneva.
2. Ecclesiastical courts — Switzerland — Geneva —History — Sources.
3. Reformed Church — Switzerland — Geneva — Discipline — History — Sources.
I. Kingdon, Robert McCune, 1927-
II. Eglise nationale protestante de Genève. Consistoire de Genève.

KKW9983.37.R44 2000
262.9′84249451 — dc21
99-462186

Contents

Translator's Preface

The translation of this volume involved a number of problems beyond those normally encountered in translating a modern text. As the editors explain in the introduction, the text itself is very difficult, containing many incomplete and self-contradictory sentences. The French it is written in, besides exhibiting the expected differences from modern French found in any text 450 years old, frequently contains words and expressions drawn from the local Suisse-Romande dialect of Geneva, which require checking with dialect dictionaries as well as dictionaries of archaic French. Even so, some expressions remain impossible to interpret reliably. This may be due to errors in transcription, which the editors admit is sometimes uncertain, but it may also be due to mistakes made by the scribe in writing things down, and in some cases to the use of words that have escaped the compilers of dictionaries. Where a translation is uncertain or conjectural I have added a note to point this out, or have at least flagged the place with a question mark (?), as the editors did in the original for uncertain passages. I have also added a number of explanatory notes for matters likely to be obscure to English-speaking readers. Even so, the meaning of a passage is sometimes less certain than it appears to be in the translation, due to the necessity of making *some* interpretation of its meaning in order to translate it. Scholars, of course, will consult the original French.

In style I have generally tried to preserve the flavor of the original. This means that a great many words that would be expected in normal English prose are omitted, just as they were in the original. It must be remembered that these registers are of the nature of a set of lecture notes or rough drafts of case reports, not the sort of verbatim transcripts expected in modern trial reporting, and certainly not a set of well-digested reports such as one would find in a newspaper. They were set down on the spot by the secretary of the Consistory and in most cases never revised again. Therefore it is often necessary to read between the lines to understand their meaning. The style of this translation, in consequence, is often difficult, but I hope comprehensible.

The translation includes all the mass of notes provided by the original editors, with the exception of most of the notes on points of French usage and obscure French words, which would be of no interest to an English reader. An attempt has been made to translate all possible words into English, but some terms have necessarily been left in French. These include coins, weights and measures, names of offices, and some legal terms which have no real English equivalents. A glossary has been provided explaining these, when they are not explained in the notes. Personal titles have been translated when there are good English equivalents, except for "Monsieur," which I have used instead of "Mister," since it is usually preferred today for Frenchmen. "Seigneur" I have translated by "Lord," but the titles "Egrège" and "Discret," in use in Geneva for some persons, I have left untranslated; they both mean roughly "The Honorable." Another title was "Don," equivalent to the modern "Dom," and used mainly for former priests and monks who had renounced their vocations. "Donne," the corresponding title for women, seems to have been used only as a general honorific, like "Madame." Geographical names, especially names of towns, have all been converted into their modern form. This has made the geographical glossary included in the original edition unnecessary; those wanting to know where the places mentioned are can consult modern maps. Names of churches and other buildings I have converted into their English equivalents: St. Peter's, not St. Pierre. District names, on the other hand, I have left in French, an arbitrary procedure that leads to the result that, for example, the church of St. Gervase is in the quarter of St. Gervais. Personal names have been left in the form they were found in in the original, so that the wide variations of spelling allowed at the time remain evident; thus the name "Boisson," for instance, can also be seen as "Bosson," "Buisson," "Bouson," and so on. Latin forms of names were also still occasionally in use. The resulting confusion can be resolved by consulting the index. Family names, while widely used, were still far from compulsory, and many people were known alternatively by their occupation, their place of birth, or some descriptive nickname: Jean the butcher, Jean of Avignon, or Antoine Wooden-Feet. This means that it is often hard to tell whether Jean Le Boucher, for example, had the family name Le Boucher or was a butcher. I have translated nicknames when I am sure what they mean and occupation names when they appear to be such and not personal ones.

In one other respect I have followed English rather than French usage. Modern French names that include more than one given name, and names of places that are more than one word, are written with hyphens: Jean-Paul Sartre, Château-Thierry. This is not usual in English and was not done in the sixteenth century, and I have avoided it in this translation, except for names of modern persons. Passages in Latin, of which there are several, are given in the original, with an English translation following in brackets: *sic* {thus}.

I would especially like to thank Thomas Lambert for his help with this translation. He went over the entire translation carefully, both correcting my (all too frequent) errors in French and suggesting better ways of saying things in English. Although I did not always agree with his suggestions, there is no question that the result of his work is a better final text. Any remaining errors, of course, are my responsibility, not his.

W.M.

Preface

We are happy to present the critical edition of the first volume of the Registers of the Consistory of Geneva in the time of Calvin. These registers are of capital importance for all those interested in the history of discipline in the Reformed churches produced by the Protestant Reformation of the sixteenth century in Europe. The concept and the practice of discipline were fundamental for these churches, so fundamental that they often employed this term as a mark of the true church of God. The Roman Catholics of the sixteenth century evolved some fifteen *notae* or marks by which the true church of Christ could be recognized among all the competing ecclesiastical institutions of the period. The first Protestants, the Lutherans, always reduced this list to only two: the pure preaching of the Gospel and the proper administration of the sacraments. This is the formula found in the Augsburg Confession, the most important summary of Lutheran thought. But the Reformed churches, influenced by the thought and the example of John Calvin in Geneva, from the beginning found this formulation insufficient. They believed that good Christians not only have the duty of believing in true Christian doctrines; they also have the duty to live according to the principles of their religion. Calvin himself did not change the Lutheran formula in his *Institutes*.[1] But in their confessions Calvin sometimes and his dis-

---

1. See John CALVIN, *Institution de la religion chrestienne,* IV, I, 9, ed. Jean-Daniel BENOIT, Paris, 1957-1963 (hereafter *I.R.C.;* all citations are to this edition): "Because wherever we see the Word of God purely preached and heard, the sacraments administered according to the institution of Christ, there there is no reason to doubt that there is a church." For complete citations of works cited in abbreviated form, see the bibliography below. Richard Stauffer, however, following Jaques Courvoisier, says that Calvin "some-

ciples often believed it necessary to add a third mark of the true church: good discipline.[2]

In order to establish this discipline, to promote this Christian manner of living, each Reformed community tried to establish institutions to oversee the mores of all members of the community.[3] Among these institutions the oldest, the most successful, and the most admired everywhere in the Reformed world was the Consistory of Geneva. The institution was created under the auspices of Calvin himself at the time of his return to Geneva in 1541 after three years in exile. Its form was described in the Ecclesiastical Ordinances he drew up for the government of Geneva only a few days after his return. The Consistory was established as a new tribunal, with about twenty-five members: twelve elders, elected each year, and, *ex officio,* all the pastors of the city.[4] Its president was always one of the four syndics, the magistrates at the peak of the political hierarchy of Geneva. It also had an "officer" with the duty of summoning people before the Consistory and a secretary whose task was to transcribe the minutes of its weekly sessions. These minutes compose the registers which we are now editing. They were preserved faithfully through the centuries by the authorities of the Reformed Church of Geneva. They are now deposited in the Geneva State Archives. The Council of the National Protestant Church of Geneva has authorized us to publish this edition.

These manuscript registers give very detailed records. They have the advantage of containing only three *lacunae* between the beginning of the series and the death of John Calvin.[5] For the period of Calvin's ministry, 1541-1564, there are twenty-one volumes. They form a very rich source for

---

times tends to make discipline a third mark" (Richard STAUFFER, "L'apport de Strasbourg à la Réforme française," in *Strasbourg au coeur religieux du XVIe siècle. Hommage à Lucien Febvre*, Strasbourg, 1977, pp. 287 and 293, n. 23, hereafter STAUFFER, "L'apport"). In his letter to Sadoleto, for example, Calvin wrote: "The health and strength of the church consists principally in three things, that is: doctrine, discipline and sacraments" (cited in *I.R.C.* IV, p. 20, n. 4).

2. See Robert M. KINGDON, "The Church: Ideology or Institution?" *Church History* 50 (1981), pp. 84-88.

3. For a collection of examples drawn from various communities, see Raymond A. MENTZER, Jr., ed., *Sin and the Calvinists: Morals Control and the Consistory in the Reformed Tradition* (Sixteenth Century Essays and Studies 32), Kirksville, Missouri, 1994.

4. Depending on the period there were between nine and twenty-two pastors.

5. There are the following gaps for the period of Calvin's life: July 3, 1544–November 5, 1545; October 18, 1548–February 16, 1550; August 10, 1559–October 5, 1560. See Auguste CRAMER, "Coup d'oeil sur les registres du Consistoire de l'église de Genève," *M.D.G.* 9, pp. 30-63.

our knowledge of the daily life of the Genevans in this key period at the beginning of the Protestant Reformation. Although open to all researchers, these registers have never been employed systematically. The reason? They were written rapidly, during the sessions of the Consistory themselves, in handwriting very difficult to read. Only those experts trained in paleography and with plenty of patience can read them. Most specialists in the history of Calvinism have never had such training. For them, these registers remain unreadable. In the nineteenth century a skilled Genevan, Frédéric-Auguste Cramer, prepared a draft of a transcription of the Registers of the Consistory of Geneva between 1542 and 1814. These transcriptions were still in manuscript, but much more legible than the originals. Cramer distributed copies of his transcriptions by means of a lithographed edition prepared in 1853. It is Cramer's transcription which almost all later specialists have used. Thus the extracts from the Consistory registers in the *Annales calviniani,* edited by Baum, Cunitz, and Reuss for the *Opera Calvini,*[6] are drawn from Cramer's transcriptions. The best detailed history of the period of the Reform, by Amédée Roget, also depends on Cramer's transcriptions.[7] The references to the registers found in the monumental biography of Calvin by Emile Doumergue[8] are likewise drawn from Cramer's transcriptions. Again, the chapter concerning Geneva in the very erudite study of all the disciplinary institutions of Switzerland and southern Germany by Walther Köhler[9] is based on Cramer's transcriptions. But depending on these copies poses serious problems. Although Cramer had a profound knowlege of the Genevan archives, he nevertheless sometimes gives false readings, and he often leaves troublesome gaps when he cannot read a word or sentence. Worse, Cramer transcribed only five percent of the texts from the time of Calvin, and the cases he chose for his transcriptions were often the best known, the strangest, the most complicated. The ordinary, everyday cases involving plain people are not often found in Cramer. The picture of the Consistory and its work which emerges from the transcriptions of Cramer is therefore inevitably falsified. The great bulk of the registers (ninety-five percent) remained unknown to most modern researchers. It is to fill in this considerable gap in the study of the Genevan Reformation that we have undertaken this edition.

6. *C.O.* XXI.
7. ROGET II, p. 23, n. 1.
8. DOUMERGUE in the bibliography.
9. Walther KÖHLER, *Zürcher Ehegericht und Genfer Konsistorium,* 2 vols. (Quellen und Abhandlungen zur Schweizerischen Reformationsgeschichte 7 and 10), Leipzig, 1932-1942.

Permit me now to recount the history of our edition. The H. Henry Meeter Center for Calvin Studies at Calvin College and Calvin Theological Seminary of Grand Rapids, Michigan, made it possible for us to begin work toward an edition. Among the treasures found in the library of the Center are microfilm copies of many Genevan manuscripts of the time of Calvin's Reform. Among these microfilms are copies of much ecclesiastical correspondence, of the Registers of the Company of Pastors (since published), of the Registers of the City Council, and of the Registers of the Consistory. In 1986 I proposed to the governing board of the Meeter Center a complete transcription of all the Registers of the Consistory in the time of Calvin, using their microfilms for a beginning, which they agreed to. We cordially thank the members of the board, especially the then president, Professor Fred Klooster, and Professor Richard Gamble, who was almost at the same time named director of the Meeter Center. It was thanks to them that we could begin this project, and we have often profited from their good will during the years since.

We began our work in the summer of 1987. First Jeffrey Watt, who had just finished his doctorate in history at the University of Wisconsin-Madison, went to Grand Rapids. Dr. Watt had learned French paleography in Neuchâtel while working for two years in the cantonal archives with their present director, Maurice de Tribolet, and his assistants on his dissertation, since published under the title *The Making of Modern Marriage: Matrimonial Control and the Rise of Sentiment in Neuchâtel, 1550-1800* (Ithaca: Cornell University Press, 1992). I myself followed Dr. Watt to Grand Rapids in the summer of 1987. During the fall Dr. Watt continued the work of transcription, using copies of the Meeter Center microfilms brought to Madison, Wisconsin. Together we prepared a complete draft of the first volume of the registers, a draft which serves as the basis for this edition.

During the winter semester of 1987 I went to Geneva, thanks to a research grant from the Research Committee of the Graduate School of the University of Wisconsin-Madison. In Geneva I discussed our project with Genevan scholars, specialists in editions of this sort. Above all I consulted Gabriella Cahier, learned co-editor of several volumes of the Registers of the Company of Pastors. She carefully examined the first pages of the draft prepared by Dr. Watt and myself, collating them with the original manuscripts in the Geneva State Archives. She showed me all the problems to be overcome in preparing a finished edition, ready for printing. She also prepared an example of the first manuscript folio, with all the notes necessary for the full comprehension of the text.

During the following years Dr. Watt and I trained others in French paleography. Dr. Watt taught this skill to his young wife, Isabella Maurilli Watt, who also completed a course of study in Neuchâtel. She began the transcription of the second volume and worked almost full-time on this project until 1992, when the transcription of the twenty-one volumes of the period of Calvin's ministry was finished. The bulk of this work was subsidized by the Meeter Center. For my part I gave lessons in paleography to three students in history at the University of Wisconsin-Madison, all candidates for the doctoral degree there: Glenn S. Sunshine, David J. Wegener, and Thomas A. Lambert. After this training they were appointed part-time "project assistants" at the University of Wisconsin-Madison, employed on research for this project under my supervision. This work was paid for by research funds assigned to the Hilldale Professorship to which I was appointed by our university in 1988. This team of three project assistants accomplished the transcription of several volumes. With Mrs. Watt they finished the complete transcription of the twenty-one volumes of the Registers of the Consistory of Geneva in the time of Calvin in 1992.

We deposited copies of this transcription in several libraries. There are copies on computer diskette and bound copies in the Speer Library of the Princeton Theological Seminary, Princeton, New Jersey. Similar copies are deposited at the University of Wisconsin-Madison. Copies, partly printed and partly on diskette, are at the Meeter Center in Grand Rapids. Copies on disk only are found at the Institut d'Histoire de la Réformation in Geneva. There are also copies of the first few volumes at the University of St. Andrews in Scotland.[10]

Mr. Lambert subsequently chose as the subject of his doctoral dissertation the religion of the people of Geneva at the beginning of the Reformation, that is, the remnants of Catholicism and the beginnings of the knowledge of Protestantism among the Genevan populace. For this subject the first volume of the Registers of the Consistory of Geneva is an excellent source.

When our transcription was finished and we decided to undertake a critical edition of these registers, we turned to Mr. Lambert and Mrs. Watt. The present edition is principally the result of their work. The draft by Dr. Watt and me was improved a little by Mme. Cahier and David Wegener during a stay in Geneva, but only for the first few pages. It was above all Mr. Lambert and Mrs. Watt who together went over, corrected, and perfected this draft. It was also they who prepared all the very rich annotation found here.

---

10. Used by William G. NAPHY for his thesis, later published, *Calvin and the Consolidation of the Genevan Reformation,* Manchester and New York, 1994.

Mrs. Watt prepared notes especially on the frequent communications between the Consistory and the Council of Geneva, working on the microfilms of the Registers of the Council for these years lent by the Meeter Center. Mr. Lambert collated the entire text with the original in the archives of Geneva and wrote almost all the notes based on manuscript sources found there and on printed sources from the libraries of Madison and Geneva. The bulk of the notes on the very interesting linguistic usages found in the text are also the work of Mr. Lambert. [Translator: These notes, as well as the glossary of archaic French words mentioned below, being of value only to a French reader, are omitted in this English edition.] Mrs. Watt oversaw the page make-up of the final edition, except for some hundred pages prepared by Mr. Lambert. Mrs. Watt prepared most of the index. Mr. Lambert edited the glossaries and the appendices. They both corrected proofs and verified the notes. We also had the help of Wallace McDonald of Madison in the final stages, in preparing the bibliography and in making some final corrections and verifications. Finally, Christian Grosse, *doctorant-assistant* at the University of Geneva, very graciously verified many references in the notes in the manuscript sources in the Genevan archives. The learned editors of the Librairie Droz aided us greatly at every stage. We must above all thank Alain Dufour, who with Mr. Lambert compared a large part of our final transcription directly with the original text. Finally Max Engammare read the whole again, especially to correct errors and expressions foreign to the French language, written into the notes by editors whose native tongues were not that of Calvin and his Genevan disciples.

Our thanks also go to many others who helped us in our work: Richard Gamble and his colleagues at the Meeter Center for Calvin Studies; Catherine Santschi, director, Jean-Etienne Genequand, and their assistants in the Geneva State Archives; Francis Higman, director, and all those who work at the Institut d'Histoire de la Réformation in Geneva; Olivier Fatio, his assistants and colleagues in the Faculté autonome de théologie protestante of the University of Geneva. We can also add other friends and researchers who have encouraged us: Wilhelm Neuser and the other members of the International Congress on Calvin Research; Heinz Schilling and his team of researchers (who invited me for periods of research in Germany, first in Giessen, later at Humboldt University in Berlin, in order to examine parallels between their studies of the Consistory of Emden and our studies on Geneva); Bernard Roussel and his staff at the Ecole pratique des Hautes Etudes, IVème section, in Paris; Andrew Pettegree of the University of St. Andrews in Scotland, his friends and his students, who compose a very active band of researchers in the United Kingdom studying the history of Calvinism. We thank all these colleagues for the encouragement they have lavished on us over the years. We sincerely hope that these people and all those who work on the history of the Calvinist reform will find our edition useful and interesting.

Robert M. Kingdon
University of Wisconsin-Madison

Introduction

The picture of Calvinism held by the general public is characterized above all by a doctrine and a manner of life. Certainly the doctrine of predestination (or, among those who know the history of the Reformation, of double predestination) plays an important part in Reformed theology. However, some fall into excess in trying to reduce the thought of Calvin to this doctrine alone. Similarly, it is possible to exaggerate the importance of regulation of morals, of Puritanism, among the Reformers. At the same time, discipline is without doubt an essential pillar of Calvin's ecclesiology. For him ecclesiastical discipline is to the church "as the nerves are in a body, uniting the members and keeping each in its place and its proper state. "[1] This discipline depends above all on the practice of excommunication. Although in theory the right of excommunication in Geneva always rested in the Seigneurie, which regularly restated its authority, in practice the instrument of excommunication in Geneva was the Consistory.

The privileged position of ecclesiastical discipline in Calvinist thought tends to give importance to the study of the institution designed to impose that discipline. This permits us to see what Calvin meant by discipline. But the interest of the Consistory for Genevan history manifests itself in many other ways. What may be called demographic issues are also significant: the Consistory usually summoned from five to seven percent of the adult population each year. Already in its first 24 months of activity it summoned almost 850 persons, from a total population of less than

---

1. *I.R.C.* IV, XII, 1.

13,000.[2] It goes without saying that the number of people thus affected by this body, if one counts the friends and families of those summoned, greatly exceeds this figure. This is an enormous percentage, when it is considered that the Consistory functioned thus year after year.

Is it not clear that an institution with such a position in society merits the attention of historians? The editors of the published works of Calvin responded in the negative. They state: "The sessions of the Consistory were for the most part filled with correctional affairs no longer of great interest."[3] This prejudgment is not found only among these modern scholars; the perception that the Consistory occupied itself only with fornicators goes back to the very beginnings of the Consistory.

On the contrary, speaking of the article concerning fornication in the ordinances for the discipline of rural churches of 1547, J.-F. Bergier wrote: "By virtue of this article, the Consistory had to examine numerous cases that are recounted in the Registers of this institution and form the best source for a history of manners, indeed a social history of Geneva."[4] In fact, if these registers recorded only the history of sexual deviancy, we would not have taken the trouble to edit them. Nevertheless, we agree with Bergier: the minutes of the Consistory prove particularly rich for the study of many aspects of daily life.

Certainly, the Consistory saw the pursuit of *"paillards"* — from simple fornicators to repeat adulterers — as an integral part of its work; in its origin, it was inspired by the tribunal matrimonial of Bern and replaced the bishop's

2. During the first twenty-seven months of the functioning of the Consistory, including three when it did not sit (therefore 24 months net), the Consistory summoned 843 persons, of whom only 142 were witnesses (86) or plaintiffs (56). According to Alfred PERRENOUD, *La population de Genève du seizième au début du dix-neuvième siècle. Etude démographique*, M.D.G. 47 (1979), pp. 37 and 41, the population of the urban area in 1540 probably ranged between ten and eleven thousand, not reaching thirteen thousand until 1550-1552. Nevertheless, we must also take account of the rural population, relatively small compared with that of the city. E. William MONTER, "The Consistory of Geneva, 1559-1569," *Bibliothèque d'humanisme et Renaissance* 38 (1976) (hereafter MONTER, "Consistory"), p. 484, estimating that adults (or rather communicants) formed only half the population, calculated that in 1569 almost one adult in fifteen, that is nearly seven percent, was summoned before the Consistory. If, with Monter, we assume that adults comprised only half the population, we find that during our period the Consistory summoned between six and seven percent of the adult population each year. It must be said that these figures have only a comparative value; Perrenoud (p. 82) points out that it is absolutely impossible to reconstruct age profiles and, therefore, to estimate the percentage of adults in Geneva at the time, given the high rate of immigration.

3. *C.O.* XXI, col. 187-188.

4. *R.C.P.* I, p. 18, n. 2.

courts, which occupied themselves with questions involving the sacraments, particularly marriage. Therefore, the Consistory was expected above all to determine the validity of promises of marriage.[5] As throughout Europe, the Genevans of the sixteenth century customarily had sexual relations immediately after the promise of marriage, before the ecclesiastical ceremony took place. Pregnancy often resulting, the promise had special importance in law. If one party complained that the other had not held to its word, the Consistory held a hearing to decide whether there was a broken promise, in which case the parties were generally required to marry, or a promise falsely claimed, in which case they were guilty of fornication. In the latter case, these minutes teach us about clandestine sexuality in Geneva; in the former, they furnish us with fascinating information about the manner of choosing a spouse, even among the lower levels of society which are often so difficult to examine. Already, the first pages of this volume depict for us a precious scene where, according to Pernet Du Puys, he and Clauda Du Bouloz had gone walking on the Mont du Salève, near Geneva. In descending, agreeing well together, they stopped to drink in the village of Collonges-sous-Salève. The young man affirmed that, satisfied with their day together, they drank a glass "in the name of marriage," in this period a widespread method of exchanging promises of marriage. The woman, however, admits that she drank a glass, but not "in the name of marriage," because she did not have the consent of her family.[6] They appealed to the Consistory to determine whether the marriage should take place or not. This is a typical example where the testimony of the two parties gives us interesting information about the method of courting and the formation of couples in the sixteenth century.

From its first days, the Consistory investigated a gamut of cases much more varied than merely promises of marriage and sexual crimes. Throughout the period of John Calvin's ministry, beginning already in the period contained in the present volume, the Consistory investigated drunkards, blasphemers, usurers, wastrels, beggars, dancers, singers of "improper songs," healers, magicians, gamblers, and other "evil livers." As we read the whole of these registers, an entire canvas of popular culture unrolls before our eyes. Clearly it is most often concerned with deviant behavior of a commonplace sort. Even when it involves more unusual behavior, the reactions of those involved give us a detailed image of what was perceived as normal. In short, as Bergier affirms, it is an excellent source for the study of society.

5. See below, "Prehistory of the Consistory."
6. To find cases mentioned in this introduction, look in the index under the names mentioned.

There are, however, some aspects that merit fuller treatment. For the historian of religion, these minutes of the Consistory are particularly useful. This is not because they clarify the thought of Calvin. If the spirit of the great reformer permeates these registers, his voice is never heard; their interest resides elsewhere. If, however, one is interested in the religion lived by ordinary people and in the reception of the Reform among the populace, he will find here a veritable treasure-house. The Consistory was charged with repressing the practices and beliefs of the old faith and introducing those of the Reform. To this end the Consistory examined those suspected of attachment to the church of Rome as well as those who neglected their duties — principally those whose attendance at sermons did not demonstrate an ardent zeal for the Reformation.

Genevans accused of "papist" sympathies manifested an astonishing diversity of practices and beliefs of the old church during the first years of the functioning of the Consistory.[7] It is seen that they continued to pray to the saints and the Virgin Mary, that they prayed for the dead, that they fasted on Friday and during Lent, that they refused to take Reformed Communion, that they read Books of Hours and, sometimes, took advantage of the proximity of Catholic districts to leave the city to attend Mass. Sometimes the persistence of Catholic beliefs stemmed from deliberate and informed refusal to accept the Reform; sometimes it is only ignorance that speaks. But for whatever reason, in the course of years the strength of both causes dims, and one finds fewer and fewer recidivist Catholics before the Consistory. In this first volume, however, such cases form a great part of the work of the Consistory. The recidivists most devoted to the old faith — people such as Jane Bonna called Pertenne, Jaques Symond, and Bartholomée d'Orsières — make only brief appearances. More numerous are people like Pernete Du Pain, who reported having said the Ave Maria "sometimes through ignorance."[8]

All this, it can be objected, informs us only about a minority. On the one hand, we could answer that it was always an important minority during this first period. On the other hand, the Consistory did not limit itself to investigating inveterate recidivists, but interrogated hundreds of persons about their prayers, their attendance at ceremonies, their understanding of preaching, and their knowledge of Reformed doctrines. And since they posed such questions to almost all who appeared before the Consistory, not merely to those accused of offenses of faith, this gives us better access to the general

7. For persistence of Catholic ideas in Geneva, see LAMBERT, "Cette loi."
8. See below, April 5, 1543.

population than one would think at first glance. Thus, besides those neo-Catholics who, despite their protestations, despised a Communion where the bread did not change into flesh, one finds Genevans like Pierre Rugoz. This poorly taught shearer could pray only in Latin and said that "sometimes he invokes Our Lady." However, he insisted "that God does not come in the hands of priests. And that he does not have great devotion to feasts [or] the abuses of candles or of foods or of invocation of saints."[9]

This is only one example drawn more or less at random from this first volume, which is full of information about Genevan piety in the first period of the Reformation. It is this which distinguishes this period most in comparison with the registers from twenty (or even five) years later; the hundreds of interrogations on the subject of the prayers of the Genevans already disappear almost entirely in the second volume of the Consistory registers. The decrease in accounts of such interrogations is possibly due to the increase of knowledge in the populace. However, the break is so clear, so clean that we are inclined to think that the change in secretary after the first volume also plays a role, because in the last analysis it was the scribe who decided what details merited recording. For whatever reason, the present volume is particularly useful for the study of popular piety.[10]

We have mentioned that besides questions touching the reception of the Reform, the Consistory occupied itself with disputed promises of marriage. The Consistory also watched over the private life of couples. The best-known cases are those where there is a question of adultery. The Reform introduced an innovation, divorce with permission to remarry. The first well-documented divorce, that of Pierre and Benoîte Ameaux, began before the Consistory during our period.[11]

Less celebrated but much more common are the investigations of couples who did not desire a divorce but got along badly together, who had a "bad household," as one said at the time. The complaints of the husband and the wife, as well as the testimony of the servants and neighbors, say much about the behavior of couples and also about the expectations of society.

Besides problems in the bosom of the family, the Consistory concerned itself also with discord in society. In Geneva, as in France and Scotland, the Consistory (the kirk in Scotland) wished to eliminate ill will from

9. See below, February 1, 1543.

10. See for example Jeffrey R. WATT, "Women and the Consistory in Calvin's Geneva," *Sixteenth Century Journal* XXIV/2 (1993), drawn almost entirely from this first volume.

11. For this divorce, see KINGDON, *Adultery*, pp. 31-70.

society not only from fear of social disorder, but also to avoid profaning Communion.[12] Thus the *dizainiers,* men assigned to watch over a quarter of the city, were required "to know those in their *dizaines* who bear ill will against each other, so that they can be reconciled before receiving the Holy Communion of Our Lord."[13] Genevans who feared to present themselves for Communion with a troubled heart often abstained without the intervention of the authorities rather than put themselves in danger of inviting the wrath of God. If their absence was noted, the Consistory summoned them to learn whether some anger troubled them. If so, the Consistory tried to reconcile them.

Naturally, these disputes occurred not only between husband and wife, but also between father and son, father-in-law and son-in-law, mistress and maid, and among brothers, sisters, friends, neighbors, business associates, etc. For the historian, the role of the Consistory permits us to examine the social fabric over a remarkable range. Certainly, these are not peaceful relations, at least at the moment when we observe them. Nevertheless, the complaints of the parties and the decisions of the Consistory furnish us with a very rich picture of what was expected of a neighbor, a friend, or a family member. It must be added that the Consistory showed itself effective in these matters. Even inveterate enemies like the brothers Curtet or Pierre Tissot and his family ended by being reconciled in a more or less formal ceremony where the parties swore to forget all resentment and shook hands or, sometimes, embraced.[14]

Arbitration of disputes, surveillance of morals, repression of the vestiges of the Catholic cult and introduction of a Reformed mode of living, resolution of matrimonial cases: this is a general sketch of the activity of the Consistory between 1542 and 1544. In conclusion it must be added that in

---

12. For consistorial reconciliations in France, see Raymond A. MENTZER, Jr., "Le Consistoire et la pacification du monde rural," *B.S.H.P.F.* 135 (July-September 1989), pp. 373-389, especially p. 385; Janine GARRISON, *Les Protestants au XVIe siècle,* Mesnil-sur-l'Estrée, 1988, pp. 197-199; for Scotland, Michael GRAHAM, "Social Discipline in Scotland," in *Sin and the Calvinists: Morals Control and the Consistory in the Reformed Tradition,* ed. Raymond A. Mentzer, Jr., Kirksville, Missouri, 1994, pp. 129-157, especially 152-155.

13. Below, August 31, 1542.

14. The reader can follow the cases of Jehan and Claude Curtet and of Pierre Tissot and family by checking the references in the index. These two cases are relatively well-known, both being recounted in Robert M. KINGDON, "The Geneva Consistory in the time of Calvin," in *Calvinism in Europe, 1540-1620,* ed. Andrew Pettegree, Alastair Duke and Gillian Lewis, Cambridge, 1994, pp. 26-31, and that of Pierre Tissot and family is found in ROGET II, pp. 27-28.

outlining these generalizations, one passes by in silence many interesting cases, such as that of Jana Bossey. After having overturned a bottle of oil, she tried to drown herself out of fear of her husband's anger and, apparently, worry over certain debts. Her deposition gives us a rare doorway into the mental processes of a depressed woman of the sixteenth century.[15] Or likewise one can study a particular profession, the way of dating events of one's life or remembering them, the extent of the social network of servants, or some other question that the editors have not thought of and do not even know how to pose. Indeed, the editors have been inspired by precisely this possibility — that researchers could use this text for purposes not yet imagined. We hope that reading it will transmit to them a little of the satisfaction and pleasure we have had in preparing this edition.

The Prehistory of the Consistory

The Consistory of Geneva, as the reader will find it in the present volume, is an institution still in its infancy. Nevertheless, the reader is not present at the creation of the Consistory or in its first days: the minutes of the first nine sessions are missing. The Consistory has, therefore, a prehistory which deserves to be briefly recounted.

We leave the discussion of Calvin's doctrine of ecclesiastical discipline and of the Consistory to the specialists in Calvin. We content ourselves here with pointing out that for Calvin the origin of the Consistory is lost in Christian antiquity.[16] But this is a question of theory, of the Consistory as an ideal. In practice, the origin of the Genevan Consistory can be fixed at a much more recent date. The seed was planted at latest in 1537. The "Articles concerning the organization of the church and cult of Geneva, proposed to the Council by the ministers" on January 16, 1537,[17] with-

---

15. Below, October 25, 1543.

16. See, for example, *I.R.C.* IV, XI, 1: "This power of jurisdiction will in sum be nothing other than a body instituted to maintain spiritual discipline. And to this end the ancient churches established certain companies of governors who had supervision over morals, corrected vices, and used excommunication when there was need."

Also *I.R.C.* IV, III, 8: "In the beginning each church had as it were a council or consistory of good honest men, sober and of holy life, who had the authority to correct vices, as will be seen later. And experience demonstrates that this institution was not merely for one age. It is therefore necessary to hold that this office of discipline is needed in all times."

17. *C.O.* X, col. 5-14.

out doubt written at least under the direction of Calvin, proposed to introduce ecclesiastical discipline, that is, the practice of excommunication, to Geneva. The articles require the election of men "of good life" and of good reputation, not easy to corrupt, "distributed through all quarters of the city, having their eyes on the life and behavior of everyone." Those chosen should denounce evil livers to the ministers, who would exhort them "fraternally to correct themselves." In case of obstinacy, the minister would denounce the guilty person publicly at the sermon and, if he did not improve, he would be excluded from Communion and "the other faithful be ordered not to converse familiarly with him."[18] The articles do not specify who would have the authority to excommunicate. Additionally, but separately from this institution, the ministers proposed that the Seigneurie elect some of its number to judge matrimonial cases in consultation with certain ministers.[19]

This disciplinary system already includes certain elements found in the Consistory, but the differences are significant. There is no proposal here of a body of elders and of all the ministers to sit in judgment over cases. The men described in this text more resemble the *dizainiers,* who act only within their own quarter with the eventual agreement of a minister, than the elders, who assemble to examine cases from the entire city and who are not necessarily delegated from each quarter.[20] Moreover, those assigned for marriage cases seem to be independent of those having the authority to begin proceedings leading to excommunication. Although there can be seen here a first essay at introducing ecclesiastical discipline, it was not exactly the same thing as the later Consistory. In any case, regarding discipline these articles remained a dead letter; Calvin and Farel were banished in April 1538 before putting in place any disciplinary body.

During his stay in Strasbourg (1538-1541) Calvin had occasion to observe the German church and its disciplinary system. In Strasbourg excommunication had been instituted in 1534, but the right of applying it remained in the hands of the magistracy and of the *kirchenpfleger,* who were officers more of the city than of the church and who did not always apply themselves to the task with energy. Calvin adopted more or less the same system for the French church. Although it was possibly applied with more rigor,

18. *C.O.* X, col. 10.
19. *C.O.* X, col. 13-14.
20. In fact, the Ecclesiastical Ordinances of 1541 specify that the elders should represent all the quarters (see extracts in the appendices), but we do not see any concern with observing this rule as in the case of the *dizainiers* or the members of the Great Council.

it still left more to be desired, Calvin undoubtedly wanting the church to have the power of excommunication.[21]

In 1540 the Bernese put pressure on the Genevans to create a "Consistory in which spiritual matters should be judged."[22] The Small Council, who had in fact some knowledge of the Consistory of Bern,[23] told the Bernese that there was no need for such a body because their state was small and "the councillors have spiritual knowledge themselves, being old." They thought that in consultation with the ministers they had the knowledge, the means, and the authority to judge every matter that could arise without the help of any consistory.[24] It must be explained that, although the name is the same, the Consistory of Bern that had existed since 1528 was something other than the institution finally created in Geneva. The former was what Louis Aubert describes as a *consistoire seigneurial*. Although some pastors participated in it, it was a civil institution, and by general agreement the right of excommunication rested with the Seigneurie, as in Zürich and Neuchâtel.[25] Speaking of the Bernese consistories sitting in Gex and Ternier, Amédée Roget insists on the point that they "were without doubt entirely dependent on the authority of the *baillis* and had no other similarity than that of the name to the institution Calvin established in Geneva."[26] Here, as in 1537, the germ of the idea of the Consistory is seen, but apparently the proposal was for an institution more in the style of the Bernese Consistory.

In October 1540 the Council of Geneva asked Calvin to return to Geneva and Calvin agreed, but he could not come immediately. He first rep-

---

21. See François WENDEL, *Calvin, sources et évolution de sa pensée religieuse,* Paris, 1950, p. 38; Richard STAUFFER, "L'apport de Strasbourg à la Réforme française," in *Strasbourg au coeur religieux du XVI⁰ siècle. Hommage à Lucien Febvre,* Strasbourg, 1977, p. 289; Amy Nelson BURNETT, *The Yoke of Christ: Martin Bucer and Christian Discipline,* Kirksville, Missouri, 1994, pp. 71-72 and 173-207. BURNETT (p. 206) and STAUFFER (p. 289) make direct comparisons between the Consistory of Geneva and the system of *kirchenpfleger* in Strasbourg. See also DOUMERGUE V, p. 166. In his *Vie de Calvin, C.O.* XXI, col. 31, Theodore Beza recalls that in Strasbourg Calvin "set up a French church, establishing ecclesiastical discipline there, something which the Germans have not been able to do for their church even to the present time," but WENDEL (p. 38) doubts that Calvin ever had the right of excommunication in Strasbourg.

22. R.C. 34, f. 21 and f. 26 (January 12 and 13, 1540).

23. This is the *Chorgericht* of Bern, called in Genevan sources the Consistory of Bern. See for example C.O. XXI, col. 237-238 (October 5, 1538, from R.C. 32, f. 66v).

24. R.C. 34, f. 21 and f. 26 (January 12 and 13, 1540).

25. Louis AUBERT, in *Guillaume Farel, 1489-1565,* a collective work published by the Comité Farel, Neuchâtel, 1930, pp. 599-605; Richard FELLER, *Geschichte Berns,* Bern, 1946-1960, II, pp. 246 and 249. See also HERMINJARD II, p. 245, n. 1; VI, p. 346, n. 6.

26. ROGET II, p. 4, n. 0.

resented Strasbourg at the Diet of Worms and at the Regensburg Colloquy, which occupied him until the end of July 1541. Meanwhile, and by the advice of the Strasbourg ministers, he advised the Genevans to ask Pierre Viret to come to Geneva. The Bernese authorized Viret, then under their jurisdiction, to go, and he arrived in mid-January 1541.

On April 5, 1541, the Council, undoubtedly inspired by Viret, ordered:

> Since it is necessary to give many remonstrances to many who live evilly, and also in marriage cases, ordered that there be erected a Consistory which should meet every Thursday, and that there be present two from the Small Council, two from the Great [Council] and a secretary. And there were appointed Messieurs Hudriod Du Mollards and Henri Aubert, [Ami] Porralis and Emoz Des Arts, and for secretary [François] Beguin.[27]

Nevertheless, the final decision was delayed until another day to allow discussion by the Council of Two Hundred. The ministers were impatient; three days later in Council "the preachers stated that it would be most desirable to establish a Consistory for marriage cases and matters that are not civil," but again the Council put off the decision to another time.[28] The ministers tried again on April 23, but the Council opposed the wording of the ordinances for the Consistory, saying on the contrary "that one should experiment first, and then depending on how matters turn out the said ordinances can be made and established."[29] Finally, on May 17, the Council decided to delay the decision "on the erection of the Consistory" until the return of the ambassadors who were then negotiating with the Bernese in Basel.[30] This was the last time the Consistory was discussed until Calvin's arrival in September.

In the attempts of Viret and his colleagues to create a Consistory, Amédée Roget sees the work of Calvin:

> Now [he wrote], considering that the ministers were then directed by Viret and that the latter was in active correspondence with Calvin, there is no doubt that this step of the pastors was inspired by the man who was then dividing his vigilant attention between the solemn deliberations of the Diet of Regensburg and the interests of the Genevan community.[31]

27. *C.O.* XXI, col. 277, from R.C. 35, f. 145v.
28. R.C. 35, f. 148 (April 8, 1541).
29. R.C. 35, f. 173 (April 23, 1541).
30. R.C. 35, f. 207 (May 17, 1541).
31. ROGET II, pp. 2-3.

However, nothing in Calvin's letters of March and April 1541 suggests that he pushed Viret to form a Consistory. In any case, Calvin having certainly already communicated his ideas on this matter to Viret, he had no need to renew such proposals.[32] Moreover, the form of Consistory proposed resembled much more closely the Bernese model than that of Calvin. The provisional institution set up on April 5 was a small coterie of councillors without any minister. Viret being at this time still a Bernese minister lent to Geneva, it is possible that he had simply renewed the Bernese proposal of the preceding year, or that he had acted on his own initiative, following the principles which he shared more or less with Calvin. After this agitation for a Consistory there followed a period of calm in which there was no more discussion of it, at least before the Council.

If Calvin did not write to Viret to ask that he form a Consistory, it is certain that Calvin had thought about it before quitting Strasbourg. Martin Bucer, in the name of the pastors of Strasbourg, wrote to the Council of Geneva on September 1, the day of Calvin's departure:

> Hear him [Calvin], or rather Jesus Christ in him, in order before all things to establish and put in order the discipline and doctrine of Christ and the state of the church, according to his advice and counsel and that of other brothers.[33]

From the arrival of Calvin on September 13, 1541, things again began to move on the subject of the Consistory. At the very moment when he presented himself to the Council to announce his arrival, Calvin also asked "to establish order in the church, and that this be set down in writing." The Council answered, "regarding ordinances for the church and Consistory, resolved that they should be drawn up," and assigned six of its members to accomplish the work.[34] In his *Vie de Calvin*, Nicolas Colladon relates:

---

32. In fact, part of the correspondence between Viret and Calvin being without doubt lost (see HERMINJARD V, p. 65, n. 11, regarding a letter of Viret from this period supposed lost), it is always possible that Viret was responding to a request from Calvin, but it is not necessary to assume this in order to explain his actions.

33. This is an autograph translation of Viret's transcribed by Herminjard. The original reads: "*audite eum, vel potius in eo Christum, ut imprimis disciplinam Christi, ejus et aliorum fratrum sententia, constituatis et servetis. . . .*" The two versions are in HERMINJARD VII, p. 232.

34. *C.O.* XXI, col. 282 (R.C. 35, f. 324). The six deputies were Claude Pertemps, Ami Perrin, Claude Roset, Jean Lambert, Ami Porral, and, strangely, Jean Balard, one of the Genevans most hostile to the Reform.

> Now to show how Calvin behaved [on his return to Geneva], at his first entry into the city he announced that he would not accept the direction of this church unless a Consistory was established, with suitable ecclesiastical discipline. . . . Thus, by the command of the government, he immediately established a system of ecclesiastical discipline.[35]

The drafting of the ordinances was quickly completed. On September 26 the ministers and deputies presented a set of proposed ordinances, and on the 29th the Council voted to accept some articles of the ordinances and reject others.[36] On November 20, 1541, in the General Council "the ordinances for the church were passed without opposition."[37] The next day the Council ordered the final drafting of the ordinances, deputing Calvin, Ami Porral, Claude Roset, and Jean Balard for this purpose.[38] On November 24 this draft was read in Council and accepted, and the next day it was resolved to read the ordinances to the preachers and the members of the Consistory.[39] The ordinances of 1541 being so important for the government of the church and the formation and functioning of the Consistory, we reproduce some long extracts in the appendices to assist the reader.

First Days, Composition and Procedure of the Consistory

It can be held that these ordinances served as a sort of constitution for the Genevan church in general and for the Consistory in particular. However, they did not describe the whole government of the church or of the Consistory. The ordinances, for example, do not designate the president of the Consistory, and, apart from some very general remarks about "fraternal corrections," are silent on the procedure to be followed from week to week. Thus when the Consistory met for the first time on December 6, 1541, there remained many details to be settled.

According to the ordinances the Consistory was composed of twelve councillors from the different councils of the city and of all the ministers. No indication of precedence is given. A little after the first session of the Consistory it was decided that "one of the lords syndics should attend, and Lord

---

35. *C.O.* XXI, col. 64.
36. *C.O.* XXI, col. 283, from R.C. 35, f. 339 and f. 346.
37. R.C. 35, f. 406, cited in *R.C.P.* I, p. 1, n. 1.
38. *C.O.* XXI, col. 287, from R.C. 35, f. 408.
39. *C.O.* XXI, col. 287, from R.C. 35, f. 410v and f. 412.

Syndic [Domaine d'] Arloz[40] was assigned." The Council did not say so, but as the most influential magistrate, it was clear that from then on a syndic would preside over the sessions of the Consistory. From then on the syndic, rather than the councillors and ministers, posed questions and interrogated those appearing, although the ministers, especially Calvin, interceded from time to time. The minutes of the Consistory were recorded by a secretary, who is not mentioned in the ordinances either, but it will be remembered that already on April 5, 1541, when the provisional Consistory was formed, the Council named François Beguin as secretary. We have no record of the election of the secretary for the first nine sessions, but it was Ami Porral who was dismissed from the post when he was elected syndic in February 1542.[41] George Maillet was named in his place; he was a notary, a member of the Council of Sixty, and also clerk for the court of Premières Appellations in 1542. In addition, in accordance with the ordinances, from the first days of the Consistory there was also appointed a *sautier,* an officer of the city charged with summoning people before the Consistory. Claude Vovrey, called Bisard, was the first *sautier* of the Consistory and held this office until his retirement in 1557.[42]

The minutes of the Consistory are composed of summaries of interrogations. From rare details found in the registers themselves and by analogy with other Genevan judicial bodies, it appears that the interrogations were conducted as follows: the syndic, informed of the facts, begins the interrogation. He poses questions, listens to the answers, and poses new questions. Sometimes one of the elders or ministers also intervenes, but in principle this is the task of the syndic. Sentences are often found in the minutes whose ends contradict their beginnings. Where they are not simply scribal errors, such contradictions are due to the summary nature of the minutes. While the scribe wrote, the syndic continued the interrogation, asking whether the witness wanted to change his mind. Often the minutes, although they omit the questions and answers, bear the imprint of this form of procedure, the contradictions between the beginning and end of a sentence reflecting the variations in the responses of the witnesses.[43] After the interrogation the Consistory sent the witness back and called other persons linked to the case, each in turn, into the hall of the Consistory, in the former cloister of the canons of the cathedral of St. Peter. When the Consis-

40. R.C. 35, f. 423 (December 8, 1541).
41. R.C. 35, f. 492 and f. 494v (February 8 and 9, 1542).
42. For Maillet and Vovrey, see the notes at the beginning of the text in this volume.
43. See the questions proposed for the interrogation of Claude Moyron in Appendix 3, October 4, 1543.

tory found contradictions in the depositions, it confronted the two parties with each other in order to detect the liar (people lied shamelessly before the Consistory[44]). If there was not enough evidence the case was remanded to another time while witnesses were searched for who could clarify the facts. If on the other hand the Consistory arrived at a judgment, it could impose three different sentences. First, in almost all cases, the Consistory, usually through the voice of Calvin, gave severe admonitions, even when the accused had not been convicted of any crime. In more serious cases it excommunicated the guilty. Finally, if the case merited even more severe punishment, pecuniary or corporal, the Consistory sent the parties before the Council. On March 24, 1542, the Council resolved to take up cases sent by the Consistory only on the following Monday, and this remained the usual rule.[45] Later the Consistory also acquired the right to demand public apologies before the whole congregation, but this came only toward the end of the 1540s and was employed above all for apostates after the beginning of the Wars of Religion in France.

The next question to decide was that of the wages of the members of the Consistory. Already on December 12 it was resolved that those attending the Consistory should receive two sous per day and that the secretary should draw this money from the fines paid by the guilty.[46] Similarly, on January 5, 1542, the *sautier* Claude Vovrey "prayed [the Council] to consider giving and establishing some wage for him in exercising the said office." The Council "resolved that when guilty persons are punished with a pecuniary penalty, that the said Vovrey participate in it."[47] This is an interesting detail: although the Ecclesiastical Ordinances order that the "ministers have no civil jurisdiction and use only the spiritual sword and the Word of God," and although the most severe penalty the Consistory could impose was excommunication, denunciation to the Consistory could produce a civil fine on the part of the Council. It appears that the Consistory had a certain participation in these fines.

Finally, the week before the beginning of this volume, the Consistory was established in the form seen below. That is, on February 8 and 9 the elections were held for syndics, councillors, and other magistrates of the city, including the members of the Consistory and the secretary Maillet. On February 14 Calvin asked the Council in the name of the ministers to provide them

44. See LAMBERT, "Cette loi," note 5.
45. R.C. 35, f. 536 (March 24, 1542).
46. R.C. 35, f. 430v (December 12, 1542).
47. R.C. 35, f. 451v (January 5, 1542).

with "the articles for the Consistory, in order to proceed according to them," but the Council put him off again and "resolved that the said articles be read again in Council and afterwards delivered to them." There is nothing more heard of these articles, and their content is entirely unknown. As for the sequel, it is well known: the present register begins with the session of February 16, two days after Calvin's request.[48]

Nature of the Text

At the beginning of this introduction we spoke at length of the interest produced by these minutes of the Consistory. The question then arises why they were not edited earlier. In part, this is due to the text itself. The editors of the *Calvini opera*, so pessimistic with regard to the value of these registers, explain:

> We should, however, state that more than one case, which might have merited being transcribed in our records, had to be neglected because we found it absolutely impossible to decipher the frightful scribbling of the secretary. In his company the secretary of the Council of State could pass for a calligrapher.[49]

48. In a letter to Myconius on March 14, 1542, Calvin recounts one aspect of the struggle for the Consistory which is not found in the public documents: *"Cum de erigendo Ecclesiastico judicio cogitaremus, atque id nobis Senatus detulissent, boni isti viri coràm assentiebantur: quia scilicet contradicere in rebus tam apertis pudebat. Postea seorsùm circumire, et prehensare singulos Senatores, ne quod haberent in manu ad pedes projicerent (sic loquebantur), ne potestate quam illis Deus contulissent, se abdicarent, ne darent occasionem seditioni: et ejus generis permulta. Dissimulanter transire hanc perfidiam nullo modo licebat: et tamen dedimus operam, ut id sine contentione transigeretur. Nunc habemus qualecunque presbyterorum Judicium et formam disciplinae, qualem ferebat temporum infirmitas. Sed ne putes id nos sine maximo sudore fuisse consequutos* {When we first thought of erecting an ecclesiastical court, and the Senate took the idea from us, those good men assented openly, since of course they were ashamed to oppose it in open proceedings. Later they went about and seized separately on individual Senators, asking whether they would throw what they had in their hands under their feet (as they put it), whether they would abdicate the power which God had given them, and give occasion to sedition, and many things of that sort. It is not possible to exceed their perfidy in dissembling; but we went so well to work that the business was driven through without contention. Now we have such a court of ministers and form of discipline as the infirmity of the times would bear. But do not imagine that it was obtained without the greatest effort.}" (HERMINJARD VII, pp. 439-440).

49. *C.O.* XXI, col. 187-188.

The biographer of Calvin, Emile Doumergue, speaking of the minutes of the Consistory, asserts also that "the yellowed paper (that of the beginning) is covered with a handwriting particularly difficult to decipher."[50] The reputation of these registers has since deterred many researchers from reading them. E. William Monter, for his article on the Consistory, refused to read the relatively easy registers written by Pierre Aillod.[51]

Nevertheless, the registers of the Consistory are legible, the present volume being the proof. We would say in fact that their reputation is greatly exaggerated.[52] At first glance even the text of Maillet, the first and by far the most difficult of the consistorial scribes, appears legible. Even so, the reading of Maillet's text does pose problems. First, his small and irregular handwriting, although generally easy to read, is sometimes very difficult. Often this is merely a question of whether to read *"saint"* or *"sainct,"* but sometimes our knowledge was not sufficient to decipher one or two words. We have at least tried to inform the reader when we have found a word whose reading escaped us, either with an explanatory note, or by placing a question mark between parentheses, thus: (?). Also, Maillet's text is a "raw" text of minutes which no one has taken the trouble to rewrite as a fair copy. Maillet had a habit of using half-sentences and of changing subject in mid-sentence. Sometimes, even when the reading is easy and clear, the meaning of a sentence remains obscure. It is often necessary to guess at the meaning of a sentence which is not completed.

It appears that Maillet recorded the minutes on loose sheets which were bound after the redaction of the text, possibly in the nineteenth century. A note in a modern hand at the head of the first volume of the registers of the Consistory informs us: "This volume was put together by combining several notebooks; since there is no pagination, it cannot be determined whether it is complete." However, there is no gap due to loss. The only nota-

---

50. DOUMERGUE V, p. 189.

51. MONTER, "Consistory," pp. 467-468 and p. 471, n. 12.

52. Cornelia SEEGER, *Nullité de mariage, divorce et séparation de corps à Genève au temps de Calvin*, Lausanne, 1989, p. 19, gives a much more moderate and, to our mind, reasonable appreciation of these registers. She says "that it is quite possible to get accustomed to their handwriting [the clerks of the Consistory and of the Council]; nevertheless, the names of places and of persons sometimes pose difficulties that remain insurmountable." She also echoes (pp. 19-20) our views on the relative difficulty of reading the handwriting of the scribes of the Consistory: "In our textual citations, we have given preference to the best-written passages and those easiest to understand; thus, the consistorial minutes in the hand of the clerk Pierre Aillod, who worked from 1558 to the end of our period, occupy a prominent place in our notes at the foot of the page because they are often particularly clear and detailed."

ble gap in this volume results from the plague summer of 1543, when the Consistory sat only rarely.

Rules of Transcription and Principles of Annotation

[Translator: Parts of this section, being of no value to the English reader, have been omitted.]

To the extent that the text permits we have applied modern rules with regard to punctuation and capitalization. We have not taken account of the separation (or lack of separation) of words in the original. The arrangement of paragraphs and the make-up of pages are generally a compromise between the practice of the scribe and ours to render the text more accessible to the reader. Very often a new paragraph marks a change in persons before the Consistory, but this is not in any case a rule.

The manuscript includes numerous words and sentences struck out. We do not transcribe them except for those which clarify the reading or are of a certain interest. Marginal additions are integrated into the text without being noted if it is clear where they belong. Otherwise the marginal passage is put in a note so the reader can reconstruct the text. Finally, the folio number in the original is given in brackets, without further marking for recto pages and with a "v" for versos, thus: [123] and [123v].

The notes are of various sorts. A large number are notes on the text, informing the reader of incomplete sentences, illegible words, contradictions, etc. Otherwise, the notes attempt to complete the information given in the register. Thus, when a case begins before the lieutenant or is sent before the Council, we attempt to furnish the reader with useful details regarding the case drawn from Genevan documents or printed sources.

For each person mentioned in the text, we have also tried to give some biographical details. For well-known persons who have been the subjects of modern biographies, we have generally contented ourselves with mentioning the biography and making a few general remarks. For some celebrated persons, such as Calvin, Viret, Farel, and Marot, it has appeared superfluous to give bibliographical references. We have also done our best to identify persons called by their title, their profession, or their nickname, such as Roland the pastry-cook, or the castellan of Peney. These identifications are hypotheses for which we have each time tried to give the reader an idea of the degree of probability.

Often we are involved with obscure men and, it goes without saying, obscure women. If the researcher is lucky, he finds a simple reference to an act of *embourgeoisement,* a death, or a recognizance. In any case, we have searched only in the Genevan archives and in printed sources. We could perhaps have increased our knowledge by consulting other archives, but thinking that the results would be meager, we decided otherwise. Even for natives of Geneva we have not always been able to find the least trace of their lives. They may be persons mentioned in the documents frequently, but without useful precision. Sometimes they are completely unknown to us. Some of those we have not been able to identify are certainly more or less known. We also fear confounding persons of the same name. We have tried to distinguish all the Pierre Bauds, for example (there are at least three in this volume), but it is difficult to be certain of each identification. The prudent reader will exercise a certain skepticism, but we hope that our biographical notes will put him on the right track in his further researches.

The volume also includes some historical notes. We have tried chiefly to clarify references which are obscure to modern readers — who do not necessarily know the date of the War of the Bésoles or of Chandeleur, or who do not know that the school of La Roche was a center for the training of priests in the sixteenth century.

Biblical notes are very limited. We give biblical references only when a person makes explicit reference to the Bible: "As Our Lord tells us. . . ."

We hope this annotation will be useful. Certainly it is not complete, and never could be. However, we offer it to our readers in the hope that it will prove useful and that this edition will aid them in recovering the texture of Genevan society in the beginning of Calvin's ministry.

T.A.L., I.M.W.

*   *   *

I do not know how to thank all the people who have helped me to complete this work. Professor Kingdon, in his preface, has already thanked many people, and I participate in this recognition. It is necessary to add that, during the academic year 1992-1993, a grant from the Commission Fédérale des Bourses pour les Etrangers made possible my stay in Geneva. I was able to prolong my stay thanks to Professor Oliver Fatio of the Faculté autonome de théologie protestante of the University of Geneva, who hired me as a half-time assistant and allowed me much more time than he needed to for work on this edition. During the summer of 1991 a grant from the Newberry Library (Chicago) permitted me to study paleography and the principles of editing in Chicago with Professor Bernard Barbiche of the Ecole des Chartes.

Professor Kingdon has already thanked Mme. Santschi's staff; I have also enormously profited from the knowledge of numerous researchers whom I have encountered in the Archives de l'Etat in Geneva and at the Institut d'Histoire de la Réformation. I should also thank Professor Kingdon for his exceptional support and above all for having associated me with Mrs. Isabella Watt, whom I cannot thank enough for her collaboration (and patience!). Finally, many of these people and many others have become my friends. I set out on a session of research, and although my research has profited me greatly, the friendships I have formed have enriched me much more.

T.A.L.

*   *   *

For my part I would like first to give my recognition to Professor Robert Kingdon for having made it possible for me to participate in this project. My gratitude also goes to Thomas Lambert for having made our work together so agreeable and for having facilitated our communications by his skill in E-mail. Thanks go also to Gabriella Cahier, Max Engammare, Isabelle Engammare-Malaise, Barbara Roth-Lochner, and Robert Roth, for their help, their friendship, and their gracious hospitality during our periods in Geneva. A particular thanks goes finally and above all to my husband, Jeff, who with infinite patience taught me the secrets of the art of transcription, and after having involved me in this paleographical adventure, introduced me to a taste for archives and historical research.

I.M.W.

Glossary

This glossary is intended to contain all technical terms that have been left in French in the text because they were difficult to find translations for, along with a few that were translated into obsolete or unusual English forms. Since most of them involve either government offices or coins, I include below a brief description of the Geneva government of the period and a summary of its monetary system.

The Geneva city government was fairly typical for the period. There was a General Council, consisting of all male citizens and bourgeois, that met only occasionally, to ratify acts of the other councils and formally to elect officials. There was a Council of Two Hundred that met annually for these same purposes and occasionally to decide important matters. There was a Council of Sixty which met more often, being consulted on important decisions. Finally, the Small Council, sometimes called the Narrow Council, of twenty-five members carried out the day-to-day business of government. This was presided over by one or more of the four syndics, the chief magistrates of the city. The separate agencies of government — justice, defense, charity, and so forth — were managed by subcommittees of these councils, of which the Consistory, with one syndic, two members of the Small Council, and nine members of the Council of Two Hundred, was fairly typical (it was unique in that it also included all the pastors of the city). Each of these committees had one or more secretaries to record its actions. Moral offenses and religious cases were dealt with by the Consistory. Criminal cases were under the authority of the lieutenant's court, with the procurator general as prosecutor. All decisions about punishment ultimately rested with the Small Council. The areas around Geneva were governed by castellans appointed by the Small Council, assisted by their *curials* and courts composed of local notables. Beyond Genevan authority were the *bailliages* governed by *baillis* appointed by Bern.

Geneva's coinage was based on the traditional copper-silver-gold system. Twelve copper deniers made a sou, or *"sol"* as it was more often called at the time; this was nominally a silver coin, but in practice the Geneva mint coined only florins and larger pieces in silver, and only écus in gold. The livre, or pound, worth twenty sous, was only a money of account. Twelve sous made a florin, and sixty an écu, both of which were in use as basic measures of value. Other coins were defined in terms of these.

With respect to weights and measures, it should be remembered that many of these were still determined by "rule of thumb," and standards varied greatly.

assistant: one of those "sitting" (the literal meaning of the word) in a court, whether of a castellan, the lieutenant, or the Consistory; a member of a court.

auditeur: one of the members of the lieutenant's court.

bache: a copper coin of German origin *(batzen)*.

bailli: a local governor, originally a representative of the king of France. Those around Geneva were appointed by Bern, which ruled large areas near Geneva.

bailliage: the area governed by a *bailli*.

berlingue: a copper coin worth ten deniers.

bichet: a unit of measure for grain, varying from about .4 to .6 bushel.

bosset: a cask, usually for wine, of widely varying capacity, from 25 to 125 gallons.

castellan: the governor of one of the territories under the rule of Geneva, appointed by the city council; also a similar governor elsewhere.

chambre des comptes: the finance department of the city, and also the committee in charge of the department.

coupe: the usual standard measure for wheat or other grain; about 1.2 to 2.2 bushels.

curial: clerk or assistant of a castellan.

denier: a copper coin, twelve of which made a sou.

dizainier: the supervisor of a *dizaine,* literally a "tenth," a quarter of the town.

écu: a gold coin worth sixty sous.

enseigne: a company of soldiers; literally, a flag or standard, but used to mean the body of soldiers who followed the standard.

florin: a gold (or silver) coin worth twelve sous.

fort: a copper coin worth 1½ deniers.

franchises: areas near Geneva under its authority and protection; most of them were expropriated property of religious houses or of the Bishop of Geneva.

gros: a one-sou coin.

hospitalier, hospitalière: the actual operating director of the hospital, working under the procurators, and the woman who supervised the women in the hospital.

lieutenant: the judge of first jurisdiction in all criminal cases in Geneva.

magister: a schoolteacher; specifically, the teacher employed for the children in the hospital.

mandement: a district or territory, usually that surrounding a small town.

monnayeur: one of the chief workmen at the city mint; see note on f. 74v in text for details of their duties.

official: the chief judge in an ecclesiastical court, usually under a bishop.

officier: see sautier.

parpaillole: a nine-denier copper coin.

petit poids: troy weight; used for coins.

pose: a unit of land equal to about ⅔ acre.

Premières Appellations: the lower court of criminal appeal in Geneva, above the lieutenant's court and below the *Suprèmes Appellations.*

procurator fiscal: the chief prosecutor in an ecclesiastical court, such as the bishop's court before the Reform.

procurator general: the chief prosecutor of the city.

procurators of the hospital: otherwise "deacons," four members of the Council appointed to supervise the hospital under the Calvinist regime.

quart: (1) a copper coin of three deniers' value, therefore a quarter-sou; (2) a fourth of a *coupe* of grain, or about .3 to .6 bushel.

quarteron: a unit of volume, usually for wine; a little less than 2.4 quarts.

sautier, officier: an agent of the Council, with power of arrest; one was assigned to the Consistory to summon persons before it.

secrétaire de la Justice: recording secretary for the city courts.

secrétaire d'Etat: secretary for the Council of State, or the Small Council when acting in that capacity. (It should be noted that this does not mean what "Secretary of State" would mean in a modern government; the office mainly involved recording decisions, not making them.)

secrétaire en Conseil: secretary for the Small Council.

Seigneurie: the governing authority of a city-state, such as Geneva.

setier: a measure of volume, usually for wine; a little under two gallons.

sou: the basic silver (or copper) coin, worth twelve deniers, or $\frac{1}{12}$ florin.

Suprèmes Appellations: the final court of criminal appeal in Geneva.

syndic: one of the four highest magistrates of Geneva, elected annually.

teston: a silver coin worth two florins.

Sources and Bibliography

A.F.W.	A. TOBLER, E. LOMMATZSCH *et al.*, *Altfranzösisches Wörterbuch*, Stuttgart, 1915-present.
A.G.S.	*Almanach généalogique suisse (Schweizerisches Geschlechterbuch).*
Arch. Hosp.	Archives hospitalières, A.E.G.
BABEL, *Histoire économique*	Antony BABEL, *Histoire économique de Genève des origines au début du XVIe siècle*, Geneva, 1963.
BALARD	Jean BALARD, *Journal du syndic Jean Balard ou relation des événements qui se sont passés à Genève de 1525 à 1531*, ed. by Jean-Jacques Chaponnière, Geneva, 1854, separately and in *M.D.G.* 10.
BALKE	Willem BALKE, *Calvijn en de Doperse Radikalen*, Amsterdam, 1973; English translation by William J. Heynen, *Calvin and the Anabaptist Radicals*, Grand Rapids, Michigan, 1981; German translation by Heinrich Quistorp, *Calvin und die Taüfer*, Minden, 1985.
Baudichon	*Procès de Baudichon de la Maison Neuve, accusé d'hérésie à Lyon, 1534*, ed. by J.-G. BAUM, Geneva, 1873.
B.C.	Jean-François GILMONT and Rodolphe PETER, *Bibliotheca Calviniana* I, Geneva, 1991.
VAN BERCHEM, "Prédication"	Victor VAN BERCHEM, "Une prédication dans un jardin," in *Festschrift Hans Nabholz*, Zürich, 1934, pp. 151-170.
BERGHOFF, *Bonivard*	Joseph Ernst BERGHOFF, *François de Bonivard: sein Leben und seine Schriften*, Heidelberg, 1923.

BERGIER, "Amblard Corne" Jean-François BERGIER, "La démission du trésorier Amblard Corne: quelques problèmes de l'administration financière de la Seigneurie de Genève après la Réforme," *M.D.G.* 40 (1961), pp. 447-466.

BERGIER, *Genève* Jean-François BERGIER, *Genève et l'économie européenne de la Renaissance*, Paris, 1963.

BÉTANT E.-A. BÉTANT, *Notice sur le collège de Rive*, Geneva, 1866.

B.H.G. *Bulletin de la Société d'histoire et d'archéologie de Genève.*

BINZ, "Le Diocèse de Genève" Louis BINZ, "Le Diocèse de Genève des origines à la Réforme (IVe s.–1536)," in *Helvetia Sacra* I/3, *Archidiocèses et diocèses, le diocèse de Genève, l'archidiocèse de Vienne en Dauphiné,* by Louis Binz, Jean Emery, and Catherine Santschi, Bern, 1980.

BLAVIGNAC J.-D. BLAVIGNAC, "Armorial genevois, recherches sur les armoiries, les bannières et les monnaies de Genève," first part, *M.D.G.* 6 (1849), pp. 163-383.

BLONDEL, "Auditoire" Louis BLONDEL, "Le Temple de l'Auditoire, ancienne église de Notre-Dame-La-Neuve," *Genava*, new series 5 (1957), pp. 97-128.

BLONDEL, *Faubourgs* Louis BLONDEL, *Les faubourgs de Genève au XVme siècle, M.D.G.* series in quarto, v. 5 (1919).

BONIVARD, *Chroniques* François BONIVARD, *Chroniques de Genève,* ed. by Gustave Revilliod, Geneva, 1867.

BONIVARD, *Police* François BONIVARD, *Advis et devis de l'ancienne et nouvelle police de Genève,* ed. by Gustave Revilliod, Geneva, 1865.

BOREL, *Foires* Frédéric BOREL, *Les foires de Genève au quinzième siècle,* Geneva, 1892.

BRIDEL Philippe Sirice BRIDEL, *Glossaire des patois de la Suisse romande*, Geneva, 1970 (reprint of the edition of Lausanne, 1866).

B.S.H.P.F. *Bulletin de la Société de l'histoire du protestantisme français*

BUISSON Ferdinand E. BUISSON, *Sébastien Castellion, sa vie et son oeuvre (1515-1563),* Paris, 1892.

CAHIER-BUCCELLI, "Ombre" Gabriella CAHIER-BUCCELLI, "Dans l'ombre de la réforme," *B.H.G.* 18 (1987), pp. 367-389.

CARTIER, "Arrêts" Alfred CARTIER, "Arrêts du Conseil de Genève sur le fait de l'imprimerie et de la librairie de 1541 à 1550," *M.D.G.* 23 (1888-1894), pp. 361-566.

Catéchisme français Jean CALVIN, *Le catéchisme français de Calvin publié*

	en 1537, ed. by Albert Rilliet and Théophile Dufour, Geneva, 1878.
CATTIN	Paul CATTIN, *La justice dans l'Ain sous l'ancien régime*, Bourg-en-Bresse, 1993.
CHAIX, *Imprimerie*	Paul CHAIX, *Recherches sur l'imprimerie à Genève de 1550 à 1564*, Geneva, 1954.
CHAPONNIÈRE, "Bonivard"	J.-J. CHAPONNIÈRE, "Notice sur François Bonivard, prieur de Saint-Victor, et sur ses écrits," *M.D.G.* 4 (1845), pp. 137-304.
CHAPONNIÈRE, "Léproseries"	J.-J. CHAPONNIÈRE, "Des léproseries de Genève au XVᵉ siècle," *M.D.G.* 1 (1842), pp. 101-134.
CHOISY, *G.G.*	Albert CHOISY, *Généalogies genevoises: familles admises à la bourgeoisie avant la Réforme*, Geneva, 1947.
CLAPARÈDE, "Alinge-Coudrée"	Théodore CLAPARÈDE, "Les seigneurs protestants d'Alinge-Coudrée," *Étrennes religieuses*, 1874, pp. 168-178.
CLAPARÈDE, *Savoie*	Théodore CLAPARÈDE, *Histoire de la Réformation en Savoie*, Geneva-Paris, 1893.
C.O.	John CALVIN, *Joannis Calvini opera quae supersunt omnia*, ed. by G. Baum, E. Cunitz, E. Reuss, Brunswick, 1863-1900.
CORBAZ	André CORBAZ, *Un coin de terre genevoise: mandement et chastellenie de Jussy-l'Evesque*, Geneva, 1916.
Corpus Juris Civilis	*Corpus Juris Civilis, Codex Justinianus*, ed. by Paul KRUEGER, Berlin, 1892.
COTGRAVE	Randle COTGRAVE, *A Dictionarie of the French and English Tongues*, Columbia, South Carolina, 1950 (reprint of the edition of London, 1611).
D.A.C.L.	*Dictionnaire d'archéologie chrétienne et de liturgie*, ed. by Fernand CABROL and Henri LECLERCQ, Paris, 1907-1953.
DECRUE, "Complôt"	Francis DECRUE, "Le complôt des fugitifs en 1563," *M.D.G.* 20 (1881), pp. 385-428.
DEMOLE	Eugène DEMOLE, *Histoire monétaire de Genève de 1535 à 1792*, Geneva, 1887.
DEONNA, "Hôtelleries"	W. DEONNA, "Recherches de M. A. Cahorn sur les hôtelleries genevoises et leurs enseignes," *Genava* 13 (1935), pp. 330-341.
D.H.B.S.	*Dictionnaire historique et biographique de la Suisse*, Victor ATTINGER, Henri TÜRLER, Marcel GODET *et al.*, Neuchâtel, 1921-1934.

D.H.G.E.	*Dictionnaire d'histoire et de géographie ecclésiastiques,* ed. by Alfred BAUDRILLART *et al.,* Paris, 1912-present.
D.H.L.F.	*Dictionnaire historique de la langue française,* Alain REY (Robert), Paris, 1992.
DOMINICÉ	Max DOMINICÉ, "Les locaux successifs du Consistoire et de la Compagnie des Pasteurs," *La vie protestante,* Geneva, Easter 1952.
DOUMERGUE	Émile DOUMERGUE, *Jean Calvin, les hommes et les choses de son temps,* Lausanne, 1899-1927.
D.P.N.	W. PIERREHUMBERT, *Dictionnaire historique du parler neuchâtelois et suisse romand,* Neuchâtel and Paris, 1926.
D.S.	A. CONSTANTIN and J. DÉSORMAUX, *Dictionnaire savoyard,* Paris and Annecy, 1902.
D.T.D.A.	*Dictionnaire topographique du département de l'Ain* (Dictionnaire topographique de la France), ed. by Édouard Philipon, Paris, 1909.
DU CANGE	Charles DU FRESNE, sieur DU CANGE, *et al.,* *Glossarium mediae et infimae latinitatis,* Paris, 1937-1938.
DUFOUR, "Notice bibliographique"	Théophile DUFOUR, "Notice bibliographique sur le Catéchisme et la Confession de foi de Calvin (1537) et sur les autres livres imprimés à Genève et Neuchâtel dans les premiers temps de la Réforme (1533-1540)," in *Catéchisme français (q.v.),* pp. xcix-cclxxxviii.
DUMONT, *Armorial*	Eugène-Louis DUMONT, *Armorial genevois,* Geneva, 1961.
DUVAL, *Ternier*	César DUVAL, *Ternier et Saint-Julien,* Geneva, 1977 (reprint of the edition of 1879 in Geneva and Saint-Julien).
E.C.	État Civil, Morts, Baptêmes, Mariages, A.E.G.
Encyclopédie de Genève	*Encyclopédie de Genève,* ed. by Catherine SANTSCHI *et al.,* Geneva, 1982-1994.
Farel	*Guillaume Farel, 1489-1565, biographie nouvelle ècrite d'après les documents originaux par un groupe d'historiens, professeurs et pasteurs de Suisse, de France et d'Italie,* Neuchâtel and Paris, 1930.
FATIO, *Céligny*	Guillaume FATIO, *Céligny: Commune genevoise et enclave en Pays de Vaud,* Céligny, 1949.
FENOUILLET, *Seyssel*	F. FENOUILLET, *Histoire de la ville de Seyssel (Ain et Haute-Savoie),* Annemasse and Seyssel, 1891.
F.E.W.	Walther von WARTBURG, *Französisches etymologisches Wörterbuch,* Bonn and Basel, 1922-present.

FORAS, *Armorial*

E.-Amédée de FORAS, *Armorial et nobiliare de l'ancien duché de Savoie*, Grenoble, 1863-1910, and supplement by the Comte de Mareschal, the Comte de Viry, and the Baron d'Yvoire, Grenoble, 1937.

FRANÇOIS, *Meigret*

Alexis FRANÇOIS, *Le Magnifique Meigret . . .* , Geneva, 1947.

FROMENT

Antoine FROMENT, *Les actes et gestes merveilleux de la cité de Genève*, ed. by Gustave Revilliod, Geneva, 1854.

G

Frédéric GODEFROY, *Dictionnaire de l'ancienne langue française*, Paris, 1881-1902.

GALIFFE

J.-A. GALIFFE et al., *Notices généalogiques sur les familles genevoises*, Geneva, 1829-1908.

GALIFFE, *Ameaux*

J.-B.-G. GALIFFE, *Nouvelles pages d'histoire exacte, soit le procès de Pierre Ameaux . . .* (Mémoires de l'Institut national genevois 9), Geneva, 1863.

GALIFFE, *Genève historique*

J.-B.-G. GALIFFE, *Genève historique et archéologique*, Geneva, 1869, and supplement, Geneva, 1872.

J.-A. GAUTIER

J.-A. GAUTIER, *Histoire de Genève*, Geneva, 1896-1914.

L. GAUTIER, *Hôpital*

L. GAUTIER, *L'Hôpital général de Genève de 1535 à 1545*, Geneva, 1914.

L. GAUTIER, *Médecine*

L. GAUTIER, *La médecine à Genève jusqu'à la fin du XVIIIe siècle*, M.D.G. 30 (1906).

GEISENDORF, *Annalistes*

Paul-F. GEISENDORF, *Les annalistes genevois du début du dix-septième siècle: Savion, Piaget, Perrin. Études et textes*, M.D.G. 37 (1942).

GENEQUAND, "Satigny"

Jean-Étienne GENEQUAND, "Satigny," *Helvetia Sacra* III/1^3, *die Orden mit Benedicktinerregel, Frühe Klöster, die Benediktiner und Benedikterinnen in der Schweiz*, ed. by Elsanne Gilomen-Schenkel, Bern, 1986.

GINSBURGER, *Juifs*

E. GINSBURGER, *Histoire des juifs de Carouge, juifs du Léman et de Genève*, Paris, 1923.

GONTHIER, "Obituaire"

J. F. GONTHIER, ed., "Obituaire des cordeliers de Genève du XIVe au XVIe siècle," *Mémoires et documents publiés par l'Académie Salésienne* 27 (1904).

GORISSEN, *Stundenbuch*

Friedrich GORISSEN, *Das Stundenbuch der Katherina von Kleve, Analyse und Kommentar*, Berlin, 1973.

G.P.S.R.

Glossaire des patois de la Suisse Romande, Louis GAUCHAT et al., eds., Neuchâtel and Paris, 1924-present.

GRIVEL, *Syndics*

A.-C. GRIVEL, "Liste chronologique des syndics et secrétaires d'État de Genève jusqu'à l'an 1792 . . . ," *Bulletin de l'Institut national genevois* 9 (1859), pp. 1-89.

GROS, *Dictionnaire*	Adolphe GROS, *Dictionnaire étymologique des noms de lieu de la Savoie*, Belley, 1935.
H	Edmond HUGUET, *Dictionnaire de la langue française du seizième siècle*, Paris, 1925-1967.
HAAG	Eugène and Émile HAAG, *La France protestante ou vies des protestants français*, Paris, 1846-1858.
HERMINJARD	A.-L. HERMINJARD, *Correspondance des réformateurs dans les pays de langue française*, Geneva/Paris, 1866-1897.
HEYER	Henri HEYER, *L'Église de Genève*, Geneva, 1909.
HEYER, "Marot"	Théophile HEYER, "Le séjour de Clément Marot à Genève" (letter), *B.S.H.P.F.* 19-20 (1870-1871), pp. 285-287.
HOFFMANN-KRAYER	E. HOFFMANN-KRAYER and Hanns BÄCHTOLD-STÄUBLI, *Handwörterbuch des deutschen Aberglaubens*, Berlin and Leipzig, 1927-1942.
JAMES	R. JAMES, *A Medicinal Dictionary*, London, 1745.
JOANNE	Paul JOANNE, *Dictionnaire géographique et administratif de la France*, Paris, 1890-1905.
Jur. civ. R1	Juridictions civiles, R1 (causes matrimoniales), A.E.G.
JUSSIE	Jeanne de JUSSIE, *Le levain du calvinisme, ou commencement de l'heresie de Geneve*, ed. by A.-C. Grivel, Geneva, 1865.
KINGDON, *Adultery*	R. M. KINGDON, *Adultery and Divorce in Calvin's Geneva*, London and Cambridge, MA, 1995.
KINGDON, "Consistory Discipline"	R. M. KINGDON, "Calvin and the Establishment of Consistory Discipline in Geneva: The Institution and the Men Who Directed It," *Nederlands Archief voor Kerkgeschiedenis* 70 (1990), pp. 158-72.
KINGDON, "Deacons"	R. M. KINGDON, "The Deacons of the Reformed Church in Calvin's Geneva," *Mélanges d'histoire du seizième siècle offerts à Henri Meylan*, Geneva, 1970, pp. 81-90.
KINGDON, *Wars*	R. M. KINGDON, *Geneva and the Coming of the Wars of Religion in France, 1555-1563*, Geneva, 1956.
LAFRASSE	Pierre-Marie LAFRASSE, *Étude sur la liturgie dans l'ancien diocèse de Genève*, Geneva, 1904.
LAMBERT, "Cette loi"	Thomas A. LAMBERT, "Cette loi ne durera guère: inertie religieuse et espoirs catholiques à Genève au temps de la Réforme," *B.H.G.* 23 and 24 (1993-1994), pp. 5-24.
L.B.	Alfred COVELLE, *Le livre des bourgeois de l'ancienne République de Genève*, Geneva, 1897.

LESCAZE	Bernard LESCAZE, *Genève et ses monnaies aux siècles passés*, Geneva, 1981.
Livre d'Or	*Livre d'Or des familles vaudoises*, ed. by Henri DELÉDEVANT and Marc HENRIOUD, Lausanne, 1923.
LULLIN, "Évêché"	Paul LULLIN, "Rapport sur l'Évêché," *M.D.G.* 1 (1841), pp. 1-14, 204-221.
MARTIN, *Genève*	[Paul-E. MARTIN, ed.], *Histoire de Genève des origines à 1798*, Geneva, 1951.
M.C.L.	*Extraits des manuaux du Conseil de Lausanne*, edited and annotated by Ernest CHAVANNES, *Mémoires et documents de la Société d'histoire de la Suisse romande*, 1ᵉ série, v. XXXV, XXXVI and 2ᵉ série, v. I (all without date). Cited as *M.C.L.* I-III respectively.
M.D.G.	*Mémoires et documents de la Société d'histoire et d'archéologie de Genève.*
MESSIEZ	Guillaume MESSIEZ, "Petit mémorial du notaire Messiez," ed. by Théophile Heyer, *M.D.G.* 9, pp. 20-29.
MISTRAL	Frédéric MISTRAL, *Lou tresor dou Felibrige ou dictionnaire provençal-français . . .* , Avignon, 1878.
MOTTAZ, *Dictionnaire*	Eugène MOTTAZ, *Dictionnaire historique, géographique et statistique du canton de Vaud*, Lausanne, 1914-1921.
MOTTU-WEBER, *Économie*	Liliane MOTTU-WEBER, *Économie et refuge à Genève au siècle de la Réforme: la draperie et la soierie (1540-1630)*, *M.D.G.* 52 (1987).
MOTTU-WEBER, "Femmes"	Liliane MOTTU-WEBER, "Les femmes dans la vie économique de Genève, XVIᵉ-XVIIᵉ siècles," *B.H.G.* 16/4 (1979), pp. 381-401.
Mss. Galiffe	Mss. Galiffe, A.E.G.
NAEF, "Bezanson Hugues"	Henri NAEF, "Bezanson Hugues, son ascendance et sa postérité, ses amis fribourgeois (Notes et documents inédits)," *B.H.G.* 5 (1931-33), pp. 335-573.
NAEF, "Conquête"	Henri NAEF, "La conquête du Vénérable Chapitre de Saint-Pierre par les bourgeois," *B.H.G.* 7 (1939), pp. 34-127.
NAEF, *Origines*	Henri NAEF, *Les origines de la Réforme à Genève*, Geneva, 1936-1968.
NAPHY	William NAPHY, *Calvin and the Consolidation of the Genevan Reformation*, Manchester and New York, 1994.
NAUERT	Charles G. NAUERT, *Agrippa and the Crisis of Renaissance Thought*, Urbana, IL, 1965.
Notaires	Notaires, A.E.G.

OPIE and TATEM	Iona OPIE and Moira TATEM, *A Dictionary of Superstitions*, Oxford, 1989.
PALFI, "Tête Noire"	Véronique PALFI, "La Tête Noire: histoire d'une maison et d'une parcelle," *Revue du Vieux Genève*, 1995, pp. 6-16.
P.C.	Procès Criminels, A.E.G.
PERRENOUD, "Calendrier"	Alfred PERRENOUD, "Calendrier du mariage et coutume populaire: le creux de mai en Suisse Romande," *Population* 38/6 (1983), pp. 925-939.
PICCARD, *Thonon*	L.-E. PICCARD, *Histoire de Thonon et du Chablais dès les temps les plus reculés jusqu'à la Révolution française*, Annecy, 1882.
PITTARD	J.-J. PITTARD, "Observations au sujet de la teneur en or des cours d'euz du canton de Genève (note préliminaire)," *Compte Rendu des séances de la Société de Physique et d'histoire naturelle de Genève* 50/3 (August-December 1933), pp. 232-234.
PONCET, *Châtelains*	André-Luc PONCET, *Les châtelains et l'administration de la justice dans les mandements genevois sous l'ancien régime (1536-1792)*, Geneva, 1973. Also published under the title *Châtelains et sujets*, Geneva, 1973.
Les .XV. joies de mariage	*Les .XV. joies de mariage*, ed. by Jean RYCHNER, Geneva and Paris, 1963.
RAVANAT	Albert RAVANAT, *Dictionnaire du patois des environs de Grenoble*, Grenoble, 1911.
RAYNOUARD	François RAYNOUARD, *Lexique roman ou dictionnaire de la langue des troubadours . . .* , Paris, 1844.
R.C.[1]	Registres du Conseil, A.E.G.
R.C.	*Registres du Conseil de Genève*, ed. by Émile RIVOIRE, Victor VAN BERCHEM, and Frédéric GARDY, Geneva, 1900-1940.
R.Consist.	Registres du Consistoire, A.E.G.
R.C.P.	*Registres de la compagnie des pasteurs au temps de Calvin*, ed. by Robert M. KINGDON and Jean-François BERGIER, Geneva, 1962-1964, 2 vols. English translation by Philip C. HUGHES, *The Register of the Company of Pastors of Geneva in the Time of Calvin*, Grand Rapids, 1966.
R.C. Part.	Registres du Conseil pour les affaires particulières, A.E.G.

1. The citations of the printed edition take the form: *R.C.* XII, p. 45. The manuscript registers, on the other hand, are cited: R.C. 36, f. 45.

REBORD, *Complément*	Charles-Marie REBORD, *Complément du dictionnaire du clergé*, Annecy, 1921.
R.G.S.	*Recueil généalogique suisse, première série: Genève*, by Albert CHOISY, Louis DUFOUR-VERNES, *et al.*, Geneva, 1902-1918.
RILLIET, "Premier séjour"	Albert RILLIET, "Notice sur le premier séjour de Calvin à Genève," in *Cathéchisme français (q.v.)*, pp. v-xcviii.
ROGET	Amédée ROGET, *Histoire du peuple de Genève depuis la Réforme jusqu'à l'Escalade*, Geneva, 1870-1883.
ROGET, "De La Rive"	Amédée ROGET, "Girardin de la Rive ou un syndic genevois au XVIe siècle," *Étrennes genevoises* 1 (1877), pp. 85-98.
ROGET, "Porral"	Amédée ROGET, "Ami Porral, le patriote eidguenot," *Étrennes genevoises* 5 (1881-1882), pp. 147-180.
ROGET, *Suisses*	Amédée ROGET, *Les Suisses et Genève*, Geneva, 1864.
ROSET	Michel ROSET, *Les chroniques de Genève*, ed. by H. Fazy, Geneva, 1894.
R. Publ.	Registres des cries et publications du Conseil, A.E.G.
S.D.	*Sources du Droit du Canton de Genève*, ed. by E. RIVOIRE and Victor VAN BERCHEM, Aarau, 1927-1935.
SCRIBNER, *Popular Culture*	R. W. SCRIBNER, *Popular Culture and Popular Movements in Reformation Germany*, London, 1988.
SORDET, *Dictionnaire*	Louis SORDET, *Dictionnaire des familles genevoises*, manuscript (A.E.G., Mss. hist. 445).
THOMAS, *Religion*	Keith THOMAS, *Religion and the Decline of Magic*, New York, 1971.
Titres et droits	Titres et droits, A.E.G.
T.L.F.	*Trésor de la langue française*, ed. by Paul IMBS *et al.*, Paris, 1971-1994.
TURRETINI and GRIVEL	F. TURRETINI and A.-C. GRIVEL, *Les archives de Genève: inventaire des documents contenus dans les Portefeuilles historiques . . . de 1528 à 1541*, Geneva, 1877.
VUILLEUMIER	Henri VUILLEUMIER, *Histoire de l'église réformée du Pays de Vaud sous le régime bernois*, Lausanne, 1927-1933.
WIECK	Roger S. WIECK *et al.*, *Time Sanctified. The Book of Hours in Medieval Art and Life*, New York, 1988.

Other Abbreviations

A.E.G.	Archives d'Etat de Genève
CC	Two Hundred (Council of Two Hundred)
F	France
FR	Fribourg
GE	Geneva
H.-S.	Haute-Savoie
LX	Sixty (Council of Sixty)
VD	Vaud

REGISTERS OF THE CONSISTORY OF GENEVA
IN THE TIME OF CALVIN

1]   The tenth Consistory, held in the year 1542 on Thursday, February 16, which was held and observed in the Chapter House[1] after the creation of the new Lords Syndics Nobles Amied Porral, Claude Pertemps, Amblard Cornaz and Claude Rozet, appointed by the Council of Two Hundred.[2]

Those attending the said Consistory:

Lord d'Arloz[3] for Noble Claude Pertemps, appointed to the Consistory, ab-

1. In the cloister of the chapter of the cathedral of St. Peter in Geneva. See DOMINICÉ, pp. 1-7.

2. The minutes of the first nine sessions of the Consistory are lost. This is the tenth session, which followed the election of the four first magistrates of the city, the four syndics mentioned here. The election had taken place on Sunday, February 5, 1542. The next Thursday, February 9, the usual day of the Consistory, there was no meeting because the Council assembled to name the new syndic to preside over the Consistory for the next year, and also the new secretary of the Consistory. Claude Pertemps, second syndic, was named to head the Consistory. Georges Maillet, member of the LX, became the new secretary in place of Ami Porral, who gave up the place because of his election as syndic; see R.C. 35, f. 442v (December 23, 1541), ff. 485, 489 and 494v (February 5, 7, and 9, 1542). On February 14, two days before the tenth session of the Consistory, Calvin had presented himself in Council to ask permission to communicate to the Company of Pastors the articles concerning the Consistory. The Council asked him to wait until they could be read again (R.C. 35, f. 499v, *ad diem*).

After working for a period in France as a schoolmaster, Ami Porral returned to Geneva in 1518 and became a notary. He was elected syndic in 1532 and took part in almost all the great events of the struggle for Genevan independence until his death on June 3, 1542. After his death, Calvin wrote to Farel: "*Ipsius vero mortis species ut nonnihil mihi solatii attulit, ita ex adverso mihi dolorem auxit, dum cogito quantum in eo homine perdiderimus* {Truly the sight of his death gave me considerable solace, although on the other hand it increased my sorrow, since I know how much we have lost in this man}" [*C.O.* XI, col. 408 (letter 402, June 16, 1542); ROGET, "Porral," pp. 147-180].

Claude Bonna, called Pertemps, had been a councillor since 1535, syndic in 1537, and became captain general in 1544. He was also treasurer (1535-1536) and served in various functions at the Mint (CHOISY, *G.G.,* p. 121; GALIFFE I, p. 431; DEMOLE, pp. 15 and 17).

Amblard Corne (*ca.* 1514-1572) was syndic every fourth year between 1542 and 1570 as well as lieutenant (1548, 1557) and treasurer (1544-1545). See BERGIER, "Amblard Corne," with a short biographical account, pp. 452-454. See also SORDET, *Dictionnaire,* p. 290, and DEMOLE, pp. 15 and 17.

Claude Roset, father of the chronicler Michel Roset, was secretary of the Council (1533-1538 and 1549-1555), councillor in 1541, procurator general in 1544 and syndic again in 1546. He died in 1555 (CHOISY, *G.G.,* p. 388; see also Henri Fazy's introduction to Roset's chronicle).

3. Domaine d'Arlod was one of the first Genevans to adhere to the Reform. He was lieutenant in 1540 when the Council named him syndic to replace the fugitive syndic Etienne Dada. D'Arlod was subsequently elected syndic four times between 1541 and his death in 1556. On December 8, 1541, the Council decided that a syndic should participate in the meetings of the Consistory and named Domaine d'Arlod, who replaced Claude

sent on the business of the city.[4]

Calvin, Viret, Champereaulx, Bernard, Henri Mara.[5]

Rages, Frochet, Britillion,[6] the officer Vovrey.[7]

Pertemps, syndic and president of the Consistory for 1542 [R.C. 35, f. 423, f. 466, and f. 494v (December 8, 1541, January 24 and February 9, 1542); FROMENT, p. 4; ROGET I, p. 320 and V, p. 55; SORDET, *Dictionnaire,* p. 321; GALIFFE I, p. 311].

4. During the preceding years Claude Pertemps, syndic for the Consistory for this year, had often been sent by the Seigneurie as ambassador to the towns of Switzerland (see TURRETINI and GRIVEL).

5. These are the ministers present at the session. It would be useless to discuss the first two, the famous reformers John Calvin (1509-1564) and Pierre Viret (1511-1571). Aimé Champereau, pastor in Geneva from 1540 to 1545, was deposed in 1545 and later became pastor in Gex (HEYER, p. 437). Jaques Bernard, formerly guardian of the friary of Cordeliers in Rive, was minister in Geneva during the absence of Calvin, then in Satigny from April 1542 until his death in 1559. Henri de La Mare, minister in the city from 1536 to 1543, was transferred to Jussy in 1543 and deposed in 1546. According to the *D.H.B.S.* (II, p. 647), La Mare was from a Genevan family, but HERMINJARD (IV, p. 61, n. 4) thought he was more likely a native of Rouen. For Henri de La Mare, see also NAPHY, pp. 59-68.

6. The three "elders" present at the meeting, of whom only two figure in the list of the members of the Council of CC, otherwise incomplete, for 1542: Pierre de Rages, later *hospitalier* from May 1543 until his death in July 1550, and Pierre Britillion, purse-maker, of St. Gervais; he died in 1569 at the age of 100 [Arch. hosp., Aa 1, f. 48 (May 2, 1543); E.C., Morts 1, p. 16 (July 28, 1550); KINGDON, "Deacons," p. 90; R.C. XIII, p. 455 (February 22, 1536); E.C., Morts 9, p. 92 (June 19, 1569)]. Jean Frochet, cobbler on the Rue des Peyroliers, was also a member of the CC. He died on September 28, 1571 [see *R.C.* XIII, p. 455 (February 22, 1536); R.C. 35, ff. 489v-490 (February 7, 1542); R.C. 37, f. 11v (February 9, 1543); E.C., Morts 11, p. 21, *ad diem*]. In a criminal proceeding in January 1542 Roz Monet complained about the nomination of Frochet to the Consistory, saying to Ami Porral "that Frochet knew nothing and understood nothing [that would qualify him] to be this," and that he would have preferred Pierre Coster or Jean Montagnier [P.C. 2ᵉ sér., 527 (responses of January 14, 1542)].

The salary of the elders was decided by the Council's order of December 12, 1541: "Since they have raised the question what wage they should have for the pains of their attendance: resolved that an account should be kept of the fines of the guilty, and that these should be received by the treasurer and put in a box, and from this money should be paid to each of them two sous per day of attendance, and besides this the secretary should be paid for the copying" (*C.O.* XXI, col. 289).

7. Claude Vovrey, called Bisard, sometimes described as Claude Bisard, called Vovrey, often employed as a messenger for the Seigneurie between 1538 and 1541, was the first *"officier"* or *"sautier"* of the Consistory from its beginning until his retirement in 1557 because of old age [see R.Consist. 12 (July 29 and October 28, 1557)]. His role was to summon those persons ordered before the tribunal. On January 5, 1542, Vovrey had asked the Council to pay him for his office, and the Council had decided that whenever the Consistory condemned anyone to pay a fine, part of the sum should go to the officer (R.C. 35, f. 451v, *ad diem;* TURRETINI and GRIVEL).

Jane, daughter of Loys Gerod[8] of Geneva, wife of Jehan Mermecs.

The servant of the Persian Tower.[9] She replies that she has done her best to find her husband, but she has not been able to find him, and he left her because his father did not want him to complete their marriage. She was remanded to the Consistory. Resolved that she be chaste and responsible. And meanwhile one will learn from the preacher of Thonon[10] where her husband could be in order to learn where he can be found.

New marriage case.[11] Loyse Du Bioley[12] has appeared against Egrege Pierre Magnin, citizen of Geneva.[13]

Presented a supplication, and requests what is contained in it. The said Magnin has been summoned and has not appeared. Egrege Pierre Magnin has not appeared because he has not been found. And remanded to be summoned for Thursday.

8. Louis Gerod, called Jaquet, of Petit Saconnex.

9. Concerning the inn of the Persian Tower, situated on the Rue des Allemands (today the Rue de la Confédération), where Farel and Saunier stayed in 1532 at the beginning of their preaching, see DOUMERGUE III, pp. 195-199.

10. Christophe Fabri (or Libertet). Fabri went to Thonon with Guillaume Farel in 1536 after the Bernese conquest and remained there ten years, first as pastor and then as dean. Fabri always maintained his contacts with the town and church of Geneva, and one reads in the register of the Council on May 24, 1541: "Master Cristofle, preacher of Thonon. For the pains he has taken for the town, ordered that he be given 3 écus" (R.C. 35, f. 217). See VUILLEUMIER IV, pp. 575, 663-664. See also CLAPARÈDE, *Savoie*, pp. 101-102.

11. The Ecclesiastical Ordinances of 1541 provided: "Concerning differences in matrimonial cases, because this is not a spiritual matter, but concerns politics, it will remain with the Seigneurie. Nevertheless we have decided to leave to the Consistory the task of hearing the parties in order to report their advice to the Council. To pronounce judgment, good ordinances should be established, which will be followed thereafter" (*S.D.* II, p. 386). The marriage ordinances, for which Calvin worked from 1545 on, were not approved and put in force until 1561 (*C.O.* X, 1ᵉ partie, col. 34-43).

12. Loyse Du Bioley was a servant at the house of Pierre de Sales in Genthod [R.C. 36, f. 53v and f. 58v (June 26 and July 3, 1542)].

13. Apparently Pierre Magnin had left Geneva at the time of the war of 1536, because in 1539 he is found asking to be readmitted to Geneva, which was granted on his payment of a fine of 18 florins (or of a quantity of lime) for the fortifications, "considering that he has done various services for those of the city." Despite his title, he was not admitted (or readmitted) to the number of sworn notaries of the city until 1544 [R.C. 33, f. 120 and f. 170v (May 13 and June 17, 1539); R.C. 38, f. 183 (May 1, 1544)].

[f. 1v]   *New case of Pernet, son of the late Robert Du Puys of Corsier,*[14] *versus Claudaz,*
daughter of the late Loys Du Bouloz, carpenter, conceived by Maurise Talluchete,
widow of the said Loys Du Bouloz.[15]

Said that about two years ago he and the said Claudaz were on Mount
Salève and walked together, and on returning the said Claudaz asked the
said Pernet to owe the capon.[16] And the said Pernet did not understand
what this was about. Also, later when they were in Collonges, they drank
together in the name of marriage,[17] as will be made to appear by good witnesses. And he understands that she drank with him in the name of marriage in returning from Collonges while descending the mountain. And the
said Claude denies his whole statement except that she drank with him in
the company of others, and not in the name of marriage. And she does not
believe that she has consented or done anything else, because this was not
with the consent of her relatives or her mother. And she has given an account of her faith[18] and creed. Maurise, her mother, said that she does not
understand that the said Claude, her daughter, consented at all to the marriage of the said Claude her daughter. And she could not give an explanation of her faith and creed. The Consistory remanded them to next Tuesday
before our superiors.

14. Probably Robert Du Puys, of Puplinge (GE), near Corsier, admitted to the
bourgeoisie on January 26, 1543 (*L.B.*, p. 224).

15. For Maurise Talluchete and Loys Du Bouloz, see below, December 28, 1542.

16. The meaning here is not clear. Possibly there was a custom of giving a capon to
the lord of the place on the occasion of a marriage.

17. In his projected marriage ordinances of November 10, 1545, Calvin wrote:
"That all promises of marriage be made honestly and in the fear of God, and not in
profligacy, nor in frivolous lightness, as in merely offering a glass to drink together,
without having previously agreed in sober statements. And that those who do otherwise
be chastised: but at the request of one of the parties who claims to have been taken by
surprise that the marriage be rescinded" (*C.O.* X, 1ᵉ partie, col. 36; see also *R.C.P.* I, pp.
30-32).

18. Translator: The word *"foi"* ("faith") is used in a variety of senses in this text,
and its exact meaning is not always clear. It sometimes means the Apostles' Creed, which
everyone was supposed to know. It also may mean the Confession of Faith which all inhabitants of the city were supposed to swear to. It sometimes seems to mean merely the
Ten Commandments or the Lord's Prayer. Again, it may be used in a more general sense,
when it has about the same meaning it has in English. Therefore I have simply translated
it as "faith," although it often refers to some specific formula. *"Creance,"* similarly, I have
translated as "creed," although it seems that it does not always mean a formally stated
creed.

6

New case of Jane, daughter of the late Jehan Clement of Cranves,[19] *versus Bertin, nephew of Monsieur Françoys Vulliens.*[20]

Requests as contained in her supplication. Remanded to next Thursday, and summon her supporters and Monsieur Françoys Vulliens, uncle of the said Bertin, master of the said suppliant.

*. 2]   *Master Jehan Cheys, surgeon,* habitant[21] *of Geneva, from Suze near Die, in the said diocese* [of Die] *in the Dauphiné.*

Stated that he has a wife, Felize Reniere, daughter of the late Pierre Rener, apothecary of Chabeuil, and that she promised him that she would come with him here to Geneva when he wanted to come here to Geneva. That he has stayed in this city about eleven months and she has sent to him by two, three, four, five, six persons to say that she would come here to serve him. And the last time she told him that he should marry elsewhere and that she would not live with him as long as he stayed in this city. And that if he took another wife, she would be the godmother of his first child by her. And he will make it appear by witnesses, respectable people, proposing that someone be sent there at his expense to confirm the truth of his statement. And concerning this he asks for advice. The names of the witnesses in this affair: Philibert de Lyle, hosier, *habitant* of Geneva; Noel Des Degres, weaver; Enemond Berengier.[22] The lords of the Consistory advise that the witnesses be examined. Remanded to Monday before our superiors. One has re . . .[23]

Those who have been summoned who have not come:

Gamaliel,[24] Françoys Vulliens.

19. The family of Clement of Cranves had been established in Geneva since the end of the fifteenth century (bourgeoisie on April 30, 1490; see *R.C.* IV, p. 269).

20. François Vulliens, native of Chieri (Torino), grocer, apothecary, bourgeois of Geneva since 1524, already a member of the LX in 1533 and also at the time of this case. He made his will on March 21, 1559 [see L. GAUTIER, *Médecine,* p. 448; Notaires, François Vuarrier, v. 5, ff. 174-177v, *ad diem; R.C.* 35, f. 488v (February 7, 1542)].

21. Translator: There were three legal classes of residents in Geneva: citizens, who had to have been born in Geneva and who were eligible for all city offices; bourgeois, who could hold office and vote but were excluded from the highest positions; and *"habitants,"* or "inhabitants," who had official permission to live in the city but no political rights. Since the word *"habitant"* had this legal meaning, I have left it untranslated when it refers to Genevans.

22. In 1565 there was a Jeanne, widow of Enemond Berengier, weaver, *habitant* [Notaires, Bernardin Neyrod, v. 3, f. 131 (August 23, 1565); see also Mss. Galiffe 38, p. 92].

23. Incomplete sentence.

24. Gamalier Bize was one of the first called before the Consistory. Already on December 23, 1541, the Council stated that: "Because there are many who are disobedient to

Summoned:

The two pack-saddlers, Jaques and Robert;[25] Vallentin; the wife of Jehan, brandy dealer;[26] the wife of Laurent Symond.

[f. 2v]   The eleventh Consistory.

Thursday, February 23, 1542

Lord d'Arloz for Lord Pertemps.
Calvin, Bernard, Champereaulx.
Pensabin, Frochet, Blandin,[27] the officer Vovrey.

New matrimonial case between Egrege Loys Franc[28] and Huguyne, daughter of the late Claude Dupontz.[29]

And has presented a supplication and requests what is contained in it and has presented the gold ring mentioned. And the said Loys Frant denies all this and says he never gave her the gold ring. The said Loys was asked whether he ever promised her marriage. He answered no, and that he has been in her house a few times, but nothing more. Huguyne was asked about

---

the Consistory, including Gamalliet, carter, decided that the said carter be put in prison. And concerning the others who have been summoned to appear and have not obeyed, resolved that the report of the remand and continuance be made in Council and the Council informed of the crimes, and they should then be judged and put in prison for their disobedience" (R.C. 35, f. 442). The next day (*ibid.*, f. 443v) he was freed from prison on his "submission" in order to receive the Christmas Communion. He died on May 8, 1555 (E.C., Morts 1, p. 210).

25. The two pack-saddle makers Jaques Emyn and Robert Breysson (or Boysson).

26. Probably the wife of Jean Blanc. There is also a Jean Roseta, called the brandy dealer, mentioned in the public registers. See *R.C.* XII, pp. 292-293, 305, n. 1, 331 (June 17, July 2 and 22, 1533); NAEF, *Origines* II, pp. 420f.

27. Jean Pensabin and Mermet Blandin. Jean Pensabin, member of the CC, was an apothecary and citizen of Geneva. Roz Monet opposed Pensabin's nomination to the Consistory "because he was not here during the war" [KINGDON, "Consistory Discipline," p. 164; R.C. 35, f. 490 (February 7, 1542); P.C. 2ᵉ sér., 527 (responses of Roz Monet on January 14, 1542)]. Mermet Blandin, citizen, cutler, *dizainier,* member of the CC, died on May 31, 1551 [R.C. 31, f. 46v (August 23, 1537); R.C. 35, f. 20v and f. 218v (January 18 and May 27, 1541) and f. 490 (February 7, 1542); E.C., Morts 1, p. 37].

28. Noble Louis Franc, Seigneur du Crest, six times syndic between 1557 and 1577, son of Noble Domaine Franc, syndic in 1526 (GALIFFE III, p. 223).

29. For Huguine Dupont (Depontelaz), see the note concerning her below, on April 20, 1542.

frequenting sermons and about her faith and creed; she gave a reasoned explanation. The Consistory remanded both before the Council for next Monday and [directed] that she present her proof before them.[30]

3] *Jane, daughter of the late Jehan Clement, versus Bertin Vulliens.*

The said Bertin says that she induced him to have knowledge of her, which he had and does not deny, but through frailty; that he knew her carnally in the month of November. And that there was a teacher there who left four months ago. And the said Jane says no, and that he gave her a ribbon and a sleeve, and that he knew her last July, or about St. John's Day. The said Bertin says in answer to her supplication that he gave her 12 sous for her wedding gift and that what he said is true, and he offered to do whatever the Seigneurie decided, and that she strove for it more than he. The said Jane says that if it is not as she says that they should take her head, and that she would rather carry the child to all its teeth than give it to him if it was not his. And that she has never known any other than him. Remanded before the Council, which will examine them better and learn the truth better from the parties on Monday. And afterwards on their return from the Council they will be admonished further.[31]

30. Two days before, on February 21, 1542, the Council had summoned Domaine Franc "to admonish him to complete the marriage of his son," but, unless this is an error, they were talking about his son Claude, who also had worries about a marriage as well as difficulties with his father (R.C. 35, f. 505). In the case of Loys Franc and Huguine Dupont, the Council decided to free the two parties from this promise of marriage after hearing a sworn declaration by Loys Franc in which he affirmed that he had never proposed marriage to Huguine Dupont or given her anything in the name of marriage [R.C. 35, f. 509, f. 515, and f. 531 (February 27, March 3 and 20, 1542)]. According to GALIFFE (III, p. 223), his first wife (1552) was Michelle, daughter of Noble François de Martine, Seigneur de Burjod and De Pailly.

31. On February 27, 1542, the Council ordered that Bertin Vulliens "should assist the said Janne and support the child and when she has arisen he should give her five sous for a pair of shoes and, for punishment, he should be imprisoned three days on bread and water. And he has been freed from the marriage, and the said Janne has sworn that the child she bears belongs to the said Berthin" (R.C. 35, f. 509).

Normally the Consistory sent offenders before the Council for reprimands and final fines and penalties. The Council returned them to the Consistory, which gave them their final "remonstrances." Like many practices of the Consistory, this one was later put in question. On March 25, 1547, the Council had the edicts concerning the Consistory read and decided that "by these it does not appear that this return should be ordered." It decided that the lords of the Council should have the "power to return them when they see they are obstinate, and the repentant should be freed according to the resolution of the Council." On March 29 Calvin insisted that this interfered with the good discipline of the church, but the Council stood firm, insisting on its part that the repentant should be left "in peace" (R.C. 42, f. 68, ff. 70v-71).

The wife of Laurent Symont.[32]

It was reported by Monsieur d'Arloz that there was a disturbance at St. Gervase on the Sunday of the marriage of the wife of Pesmes. She [Symont's wife] answered concerning this that it is true that she was at St. Gervase the said day at the evening sermon and that she laughed at a man who was behind her and the others, and that man said that there was someone who carried a clock. And at that he said that if that man carried relics, people would kiss them after the sermon.[33] And that she heard nothing else wrong except as she has described, and that she did not want to mock the Word of God, and knows nothing more. And she asked Monsieur Bernard, preacher, to see if she had laughed or done anything else. Monsieur Bernard said many other things, as he would repeat to you, [but] this would be tedious. [f. 3v] The Consistory admonished her to be more steady in the future and not mock the Word of God any more and have the fear of the Lord and not scorn the Word of God in this way, and that she not do thus again and that she not trouble the church again, and to honor the Word of God.

New matrimonial case of George Jaquemoz of Coinsins and Mye, daughter of the late Mermet Rosat, habitant *of Geneva.*

And says he swore faith to and promised the said Mye about two or three years ago and they drank together in the name of marriage, producing the examination and letters written concerning this. And the said Mye says that she reserved the consent of her parents. The Consistory is of the opinion that the said marriage take place and that they be remanded before the Council for Monday,[34] and meanwhile someone will speak to Monsieur Pi-

---

32. Laurent Simond, called the Picard, member of the CC, former Dominican friar at the friary of Palais in Geneva, left the city when the monastic houses were closed. In 1538 he asked permission to return to Geneva without paying the contribution for the fortifications normally required of those who had left the city in time of war. He excused himself by saying that his father had sent him out of Geneva, "and later when he had learned the truth he returned to the city." He married Anne Perrin, sister of Ami Perrin, as his first wife, and as his second a certain Toynette who died after him on October 17, 1553. It was probably Anne Perrin who appeared here before the Consistory [R.C. 32, f. 119, f. 126, ff. 127-127v (August 9, 20, and 21, 1538); R.C. 35, f. 489v (February 7, 1542); NAEF, *Origines* II, p. 211, n. 1; E.C., Morts 1, p. 125 (October 17, 1553)].

33. Translator: This sentence is rather confused. The word used for "clock" is *"reloge,"* and that for "relics" is *"reliques,"* and it may be that there is a play on words here.

34. Struck from the text: "as well as the depositions of the witnesses examined by the Council in 1539."

erre d'Orsieres.[35] She was asked about attendance at sermons and about her faith and gave a good explanation, and says she goes to the sermons and is a servant of Monsieur Pierre Mallagnod.[36] Monday.

Master Jaques Emyn, pack-saddler.[37]

We have been informed of the management and course of his household and of his guests, muleteers, merchants and others from distant countries and of the words they use among themselves. He answered . . .[38] Remanded to learn his faith and creed before coming to Holy Communion, and ordered to come recite them here before taking it. Here in three weeks. He did not know the creed, "I believe in God the Father," or the Lord's Prayer.[39]

4] *Master Robert Breysson, pack-saddler, bourgeois of Geneva.[40]*

As with the other, in three weeks.

Anthoyne, daughter of the late Master Anjoz, bookseller.

Asked if she is married. She says no, but that she is pregnant by Pierre who lives at the glass-blower's, and that she has already had two children, one by Monsieur Jehan Cornuti and the other by Pierre d'Orbaz, gelder. And that the said Pierre has had knowledge of her several times for about two years. And she begs mercy of God and of justice and says he has given her only one

---

35. This refers to the criminal proceeding brought against Mye Rosat in 1539 because of a child born out of wedlock. According to the deposition of her sister, Saturnin Rosat, Mye had had a child by Pierre d'Orsières, having slept with him in Claude Chateauneuf's house, where she was a servant. Saturnin Rosat said also that D'Orsières had promised to marry Mye, "and once the said D'Orsiere wanted to agree with her parents for 50 florins, which 50 florins her said sister had obtained by means of Master Pierre of the hospital." She slept in D'Orsières's house at mid-Lent, but the child was already dead at the time of the 1539 proceeding. Pierre d'Orsières was castellan of Peney at the time of this Consistory case. He was a councillor in 1556 and died in 1559 [P.C. 2ᵉ sér., 451 (May 31–June 14, 1539); R.C. 37, f. 18 (February 15, 1543); GALIFFE I, p. 181; SORDET, *Dictionnaire*, p. 541].

36. Pierre Mallagnod was a councillor from 1541 to 1555 without interruption.

37. Jaques Emyn, pack-saddle maker and evidently innkeeper, often called Jaques the pack-saddler, from Dauphiné, bourgeois on June 9, 1506, member of the LX for the *dizaine* "vers la Corratery" in 1535. He was often summoned to the Consistory, and on May 15, 1542, the Council admonished him because he did not present himself in Consistory when summoned [*L.B.*, p. 157, *ad diem*; R.C. XIII, pp. 146 (February 12, 1535) and 454 (February 22, 1536); R.C. 36, f. 14v, *ad diem*].

38. Incomplete sentence.

39. Struck from the text: "And that he should buy a Bible and have it read."

40. Robert Breysson, called Robert the pack-saddler, bourgeois of Geneva, native of Saint Pierre de Bressieux [*L.B.*, p. 210 (June 23, 1534), under the name of Robert Boysson].

fort. And she knew well how to say her creed. The Consistory admonished her to appear next Thursday and ordered that the said Pierre be made to come that day.[41]

Pierre the glass-blower;[42] Pierre the currier on the Bourg du Four;[43] the widow of Mabuet;[44] the wife of the currier who lives in the house of Monsieur De Coudree, who lives in Morges.[45]

[f. 4v]   The twelfth Consistory.

Thursday, March 2, 1542

Lord Syndic Pertemps.
Viret, Henri.

41. Anthoyne, called Bourgnye. Her father is called variously Master Anjoz, bookseller [above and in P.C. 2ᵉ sér., 555 (July 10 and 14, 1542)], Master Anjoz, barber [R.C. 36, f. 68 (July 11, 1542)], and Master Martin, barber [R.C. 33, f. 284 and f. 287v (September 16, 1539)], but he is not in the list of barbers in L. GAUTIER, *Médecine,* pp. 468-501, or in the list of printers and booksellers in CHAIX, *Imprimerie,* pp. 140-230, or in CARTIER, "Arrêts." Anthoyne's accomplice, Pierre Rolet, tower-keeper, from Combes, parish of Saint Germain de Joux (Ain), was admitted to the bourgeoisie on August 4, 1547 [see below, March 2, 1542; P.C. 2ᵉ sér., 555 (July 10, 1542); *L.B.,* p. 233].
The priest Jehan Cornuti was the father of Anthoyne's first child, a son named Jehan, dead at age two, born before the Reform: "the first was not from the time of the reign of the Holy Gospel" (P.C. 2ᵉ sér., 555). In 1539 she had a son named Claude by Pierre Quicouz of Orbe, surgeon, who was still living in 1542 [*ibid.,* and R.C. 33, f. 284v and f. 287v (September 16, 1539)]. Finally, she had a daughter named Serpaz by Pierre Rolet, also living at the time of the case in 1542. On June 2, after the delivery, the Council decided that in the absence of Pierre Rolet the secretary Beguin, his guarantor, should give Anthoyne five florins *petit poids* and find the child a nurse within eight days. On July 14 she was banished from the city for a year and a day under penalty of being whipped "for having already committed fornication three times" [R.C. 36, f. 29, f. 63v, and f. 68 (June 2, July 7 and 11, 1542); P.C. 2ᵉ sér., 555].
42. As in the previous week, these are people summoned who have not appeared. Pierre the glass-blower was in fact Pierre Rolet, tower-keeper, who lived at the glass-blower's.
43. Pierre Poyent, currier.
44. This may be Thomasse, widow of François Mabuect, later married to André Jordan of Choulex; see below, April 5, 1543, and March 6, 1544. She could also be "la Mabuectaz," implicated in a case of fornication with Pierre Bertet, called Tallabard; see below, March 16, 1542.
45. "The wife of the currier" is Françoise, wife of Tyvent Bochot. Monsieur de Coudrée is probably Pierre d'Alinges, Seigneur de Coudrée. For the family of Alinge see CLAPARÈDE, "Alinge-Coudrée", pp. 168-178, especially pp. 168 and 174.

Du Molard,[46] Pensabin, Blandin, Tacon,[47] D'Orsieres, Frochet, the officer Vovrey.

Pernete, wife of Master Robert the pack-saddler.[48]

Asked about the discipline and fashion of living in her household according to the Word of God, about songs, sermons and her faith and her servants and maids. And she gave a sound explanation of her faith and creed. The Consistory gave her proper remonstrances to buy a Bible to put before her people to read instead of game boards, cards, songs, and to eschew all dice.

Tevenete, wife of Master Jaques Emyn, pack-saddler.

She was sufficiently admonished. First given proper admonitions concerning attendance at sermons, her faith, the manner of living in religion and her foreign guests. And she could not say her creed, at least the confession. She was admonished that within a month she should learn to render a better account of her creed and that she buy a Bible to show to the guests in her house. Also that she have good servants and maids and that God not be blasphemed or offended in her house.

Pierre Poyent,[49] *currier, from Pertuis in Provence.*

He has been in this city two years, and a fortnight ago he swore faith to a wife, and his wife is the daughter of Furjod du Molard, tanner. And concerning his faith and creed and attendance at sermons. He was admonished by the Consistory to continue to live well according to the Word of God and the Holy Scriptures.

f. 5]   *Emoz Burin, day-laborer of Geneva.*

Because of a certain child which he says someone gave him and which he has kept for himself, and he is married, which is against the command-

---

46. Hudriod Du Molard, syndic five times between 1535 and 1552. He "renounced his bourgeoisie on April 25, 1556, because the communal banner of the city had been taken from him for no reason" (GALIFFE I, pp. 231-232).

47. Aymé Tacon, purse-maker, member of the CC for the *dizaine* "sus la Pont." He is found in the list of "Lutherans" drawn up by the procurator fiscal for the bishop on August 10, 1534 [*R.C.* XIII, p. 147 (February 12, 1535), p. 455 (February 22, 1536), and p. 591, *notes complémentaires; R.C.* 35, f. 489v (February 7, 1542); see also GALIFFE I, p. 34, and SORDET, *Dictionnaire,* p. 1219].

48. Robert Breysson, pack-saddle maker.

49. Pierre Poyent (Payent), from Pertuis (Vaucluse), was admitted to the bourgeoisie on November 28, 1541 (*L.B.,* p. 222). Apparently he left Geneva for a time, because he was readmitted to the bourgeoisie on January 19, 1557 (*L.B.,* p. 254).

ment of God. And it was at Collonges sus Belle Rive in a barn, and for this he asked mercy of God and of justice. The Consistory remanded him before the Council for next Monday and admonished him. The mother is named Mermaz de Herchant,[50] and it is three weeks since she saw him, and the child is named Claude. He was asked about his faith and creed and could say nothing about it.

Pierre, son of Jehan Rolet, tower-keeper, of Saint Germain de Joux, versus Anthoyne, daughter of Anjouz, bookseller.

To whom the statement of the said Anthoyne was read. He denied the statement of the said Anthoyne. It is true that he knew her once last March. And if the child is his he wishes to take it, but the said Anthoyne first induced him to do wrong, not he her. And he gave an explanation of his faith. The said Anthoyne answered that she never had the company of any other in the last two years except him and that the child is his and he should support it, and it was about Michaelmas that she had his company. The said Pierre was urged to tell the truth. He says it is true that he did not want to give himself, that he only knew her once, and that she came to find him in the shop and asked for a *fort* or a *quart,* and he gave her oil worth a *quart.*

The said Pierre present. And the said Anthoyne answers that this was to buy plums and this was the season for plums, and he never knew her later. And she told him she was pregnant by him. And that he had already known her when she bore the other child and that she would swear readily that it was as she said and reported. She said that the said Pierre made her support the child that she bore then and that she was at that time in the service of the secretary Monsieur De Archa.[51]

The Consistory remanded them both to next Monday before the Council and resolved that both should be put under oath. If she can prove that she was elsewhere at the time in March that he says he knew her, let her profit by it and produce her proof on Monday. Advised concerning the other two children that she . . .[52]

---

50. That is, Mermaz from the commune of Herchant (probably Archamps [H.-S.]).

51. Michel de L'Arche; named *secrétaire de la Justice* in 1540, and syndic for the first time in 1550, he was a member of the LX in 1542 [GALIFFE II, p. 28; R.C. 35, f. 489 (February 7, 1542)].

52. Incomplete sentence.

[5v]   *Francese, wife of Tyvent Bochot, currier.*

Asked if she is married. Answers yes, 13 years ago, and that her husband lives in Morges. Asked why she is not with him. Answers that her husband has no business here and that she lives here making candles and that she is not separated from her husband and that it was not long ago that he came here, and that she has a daughter by her husband. Asked about her faith, of which she could give no explanation. The Consistory remanded her to return in three weeks to repeat her faith and creed and ordered that she strive to get her husband to come here or that she go to find him, and to come render an account of his faith.

Reymond de Veyrier.[53]

Said and reported that he swore faith to Aymé, daughter of Loys Pyaget,[54] sheath-maker, and that the thing was done in a proper way and that she consented to him and they drank together, respectable people being present, and he gave her a silver image and he swore faith to her and he truly wants her.

The said Loys, father of the said Aymé, said that the said Reymond did him great dishonor in swearing to his daughter. And the said Ayma said that she swore faith to the said Reymond one Wednesday and that she reserved the approval of her father and mother and that he gave her . . .[55] at the house of a baker who pressed her so much that she consented to the said Reymond. And that she will never marry him unless her father and mother consent. The said Loys, the father, says that he holds by the edict of the Council that children should not marry without the approval of their fathers and mothers,[56] and that he did not intend the said Reymond to have his daughter.

53. Reymond de Veyrier, citizen, host at the priory of Satigny in 1544 when he asked to be named a forest guard [R.C. 38, f. 274 (July 4, 1544)].

54. "Ludovycus Marthe, alias Pyaget, filius quondam Glaudii, de Barma prope Thonum [La Baume, H.-S.], gueynerius, par. Sti. Gervasii" {Ludovicus Marthe, alias Pyaget, son of the late Glaudius, from Barma near Thonum, sheath-maker, parish of St. Gervase} [L.B., p. 174 (November 18, 1511)]. He had a son also named Louis Piaget, born before 1511, member of the CC (1535), but the first child of Louis the son was born about 1546 (GALIFFE VII, pp. 423-424).

55. Words omitted.

56. It is not clear what edict is referred to. A "draft of ordinances concerning marriages" was produced under Calvin's direction in 1545, but the Council did not promulgate these ordinances until they were inserted in the ecclesiastical ordinances of 1561. Nevertheless, it is possible that the first article of the 1545 ordinances was based on an earlier edict when it stipulated "regarding young people who have never been married, that none, son or daughter, having a father still living, should have the power to contract marriage without the leave of his father, unless he has attained the age of legitimacy: that

Also the said Reymond said that the said Aymaz told him another time: "They want to give me a husband that I do not want, because despite them I will never have another than you." True that he reserved the consent of his father. She says she knows nothing and that she reserved nothing the last time.

[f. 6]

The wife of the said Loys, mother of the said Aymaz. And she complains of the household and of those who have taken her daughter and that she does not want her to be married and that she will be a girl whom he will never have. Asked why she does not want this marriage to take effect. Examined on her faith, which she could not say.

The resolution of the Consistory is that they be remanded before the Council and, considering the reservation of the father and mother, that the marriage be denied its effect and that efforts be made to get them to consent. And that the baker and those who have meddled be admonished on Monday. The said Reymond was asked about the reservation, if her father and mother did not consent what he would have done about it. Answers that he would have said that they should have patience and that he did not want to go against the will of her father and mother. The father and mother were asked about their attendance at sermons and how they serve God and about the Word of God and the holy commandments. The said mother was remanded to come here in three weeks to recite and explain her faith.[57]

George Jaquemoz, boatman, versus Myaz, daughter of Jaques Rossal.[58]

The Consistory remanded them as before to next Monday. The lords syndics have the accounts of the said marital dispute.[59]

Pernete, daughter of the late Jaquemoz Maystre, of Sauverny, versus Pierre Rapin, carpenter, formerly servant of Jacob in Versoix, where she was a maid.

And that he swore faith twice in the presence of her brothers, Mauris Maystre being present, and that it is public knowledge that this is so, and their mistress was present. And that he married another and that she had a child by him and that he gave her a piece of money in the name of marriage,

---

is, 24 years for a son and 20 for a daughter" (*C.O.* X. 1, col. 33-34). For the history of these ordinances, see *ibid.,* n. 1 and *R.C.P.* I, p. 30 and note (this last gives the same text with some variants). See also *S.D.* II, p. 338 (June 4, 1537).

57. This case was discussed in Council and the marriage contract was annulled because the girl had not made it with the approval of her parents [R.C. 35, f. 531 and f. 534 (March 20 and 23, 1542)].

58. Identified above (February 23, 1542) as the daughter of the late Mermet Rosat.

59. On March 20, 1542, the Council confirmed the validity of the marriage of George Jaquemoz and Mya Rosat and decided that it should "go into effect" (R.C. 35, f. 531).

which is a three-sous piece of Savoy which she has presented here, and that it was four or five years ago. And he married his wife in St. Gervase. [f. 6v] And that she has lived in this city two years on the Charriere des Peyroliers and that she did not know when he published his banns. And that he was never in her room and that he last slept with her about a year ago during the fair of Saint Peter's[60] and he has always said he truly wanted her. Inter . . .[61] The Consistory resolves that the said Pierre Rapin be summoned for Thursday at the customary time. And inform the Council on Monday.

The thirteenth Consistory.

Thursday, March 9

Lord Pertemps.
Calvin, Viret, Champereaulx.
Gerbel,[62] Du Molard, Britillion, Tacon, Pensabin, Frochet, Amed Darsemaz[63] for Vovrey.

Franceyse, daughter of the late Loys Reys,[64] promised wife of Pierre Berthoz,[65] coppersmith, from Machilly.

Says that she swore faith to him about two months ago, six weeks after Christmas, and that he left her two months ago today because she did not give him any money and she only had lands. And she says he went to Lyon.

---

60. The fair of the Chair of St. Peter fell on February 22 and was also called the Carnival fair. The Council register of February 22, 1549, speaks of "the fair of St. Peter, which is today . . ." (R.C. 44, f. 26), but apparently one spoke also of the four fairs of St. Peter: "each St. Peter's, that is four times a year" [*S.D.* II, p. 482 (June 22, 1546)]. The fair of Saint-Pierre-aux-liens, the only one of the four great fairs of Geneva to draw its name from St. Peter alone, began August 1 and lasted about fifteen days, and the fair of Peter and Paul took place about June 29 (BOREL, *Foires;* BERGIER, *Genève,* pp. 238-240).

61. Incomplete sentence.

62. Antoine Gerbel, councillor since 1537, syndic in 1540, lieutenant in 1543, and first syndic in 1544 and, according to SORDET, *Dictionnaire,* p. 676, "devoted to the Reform" [R.C. 36, f. 167 (November 10, 1542); R.C. 37, f. 275v (November 18, 1543)].

63. Amed Darsina, called Callameta, cobbler and watchman, died suddenly of a fall on March 1, 1546 [R.C. 37, f. 16v (February 13, 1543); R.C. 41, f. 33v (March 2, 1546); Mss. Galiffe 38, pp. 12 and 394].

64. Louis Reys died before June 25, 1534, the date when his widow, "Joyosa relicta Ludovici Regis," appeared in Council (*R.C.* XII, p. 567).

65. Pierre Favre, called Berthoz, from Machilly (H.-S.), admitted to the bourgeoisie gratis on January 22, 1538, at the request of the syndic Pernet Des Fosses, his master (*L.B.,* p. 217).

And that she did not consent to his company in consummating the marriage. And she says their banns were proclaimed. Joyeuse, her mother, says that they did not contract the said marriage in money and there was only real estate. The Consistory resolved that they strive to find him and send to ask what he means to do and that he do his duty.

[f. 7] *Pierre Boysson, point-maker.*[66]

Says he is married to a living wife who is at home and he has a son who is in Germany and that he is of the Gospel. And he was asked if he has known any other woman besides his wife. It is true that it is said that there is a poor Mermete, daughter of Glaudaz Jappaz, and that she has already had a child and is pregnant by one called Michel the tailor in the Tour de Boël. The Consistory admonished him to improve always and to assist those whom he knows who do not travel the road well.

Pernete, daughter of Jaquemoz Maystre, appears against Pierre Rapin, her sworn husband.

And remanded to Thursday, as she has already been remanded.

Fourteenth Consistory.

Thursday, March 16, 1542

Lord Pertemps.
Calvin, Viret.
Gerbel, Frochet, Pensabin, Britillion, the officer Vovrey.

On the reading of the answers of Pierre Rapin to Pernon, promised wife of Pierre Rapin.

The advice of the lords preachers Calvin, Viret.[67]

---

66. Translator: That is, a maker of "points," the laces men used to fasten their hose to their doublets.

67. The advice of the two ministers is not recorded, but this affair was also discussed in Council [R.C. 35, f. 530 (March 18, 1542)]. Pierre Rapin, of Thyez (H.-S., sometimes Thiez), was condemned to public whipping "carrying a miter on his head" and to banishment "from the city, lands and *franchises* . . . under penalty of the gibbet" for having engaged himself to two women and having "consummated marriage with both." The two wives, Anthoine, daughter of Master Thivent Des Gaignieurs, called Du Mollard, and Pernon (Pernete) Maystre, received permission to marry again [R. Publ. 1, f. 71 (March 18, 1542)].

[. 7v] *Anthoyne Servoz, from Vienne, cobbler, living on the Rhône Bridge in the house of Glaude Humbert.*[68]

If he is married and if he has children. Answers that he is married and has one child. And if he goes to sermons. Answers yes, sometimes when he can. Answers that his son is only three and cannot yet understand them. Asked about his faith and creed. Answers that he does not understand it well. Said the Lord's Prayer, but did not know the confession. Given proper admonitions to attend the sermons more often and to see that he learns to say his confession. Asked when he last heard the sermon and who preached and what the preacher said. Answers that it was four days ago at St. Gervase, he does not know what day. He has a Bible. He heard Master Farel[69] preach at St. Peter's, he does not know when or on what day. The Consistory admonished him to come within two weeks to render an account of his confession, and his wife and family, and to frequent the sermons both on Sunday and the day of prayer.[70]

Donne Dominique de Ulmodaz.[71]

Asked what quarrel she has with P[ierre] Costel[72] her son-in-law and where her husband is. Answers touching her son-in-law that she does

68. Claude Clement, called Humbert. An Humbert Clement was admitted to the bourgeoisie in 1490. From this time a Claude Clement, called Humbert, cutler and armorer from Cranves (Cranves-Sales, H.-S.), is often found in the public registers and is probably the same person admitted to the bourgeoisie under the name Humbert Clement. In 1525 the brothers Claude and Jean Humbert, citizens and armorers and cutlers, had a lawsuit pending against Pierre Taccon concerning a house on the Rhône Bridge. Claude Clement was elected to the CC for the Pont du Rhône in 1541 [*R.C.* IV, p. 269 (April 30, 1490); *R.C.* V, p. 64 (October 20, 1492); *R.C.* X, p. 20 (February 28, 1525); *R.C.* XIII, pp. 129 and 306, n. 1 (January 15 and September 11, 1535); *R.C.* 35, f. 56v (February 9, 1541)].

69. Guillaume Farel (1489-1565), the famous reformer of French Switzerland, was minister in Neuchâtel, but at the time of this session of the Consistory he lent his services to the Genevans, staying in Geneva from Monday, February 27, to Thursday, March 23, 1542 (R.C. 35, f. 508v and f. 533).

70. On November 11, 1541, the Council ordered that there should be common prayer one day a week. The Council chose Wednesday only for the first week, but that day remained from then on the official day of prayer (R.C. 35, f. 385).

71. Dominique de Vaulx, widow of Mermet de Ulmo (de l'Olme), bourgeois, notary (without minutes in the A.E.G.) (Mss. Galiffe 38, p. 278).

72. Called also Pierre Coster, he could be the Pierre Coster, lawyer, who was elected to the CC for the *dizaine* of the Rue Saint Léger [*R.C.* XIII, pp. 253 (June 29, 1535) and 455 (February 22, 1536)]. He could also be the Pierre Coster accused of murder who appeared in Council on January 11, 1541 (R.C. 35, f. 8): "Master Jullian Boccard in the name of the said Coster of Rochier has asked that the said Coster be allowed to defend himself

not know why unless it was for her son's wedding, because he swore that he would never drink with her and that he did not want to be present. And that her husband is away on business. Because P[ierre] Coster was not found she was remanded to Thursday; meanwhile the said P[ierre] Coster will be summoned, and also Philipaz, her daughter, wife of the said Coster.

Solit(?) {As usual (?)} VII

[f. 8]   *Pierre Gonet versus Macarde's maid.*

He has presented a discharge issued by two vicars. The Consistory is of the opinion that one learn from Macarde how the discharge was made and also from the one who was with her then and from the neighbors. And remanded to Monday before the Council, and he before the Consistory;[73] for Thursday Noble Amed de Fernex.[74]

Pierre Bertet, called Tallabard, from Valleiry, armorer.

Asked how long he has lived in this city. Answers that it was 15 years since the pardon of St. Claire[75] and that he fell into fornication, which

---

outside prison against the charge of having killed Loys, innkeeper. Having heard the evidence, ordered that he make his defense from prison and that if he does not wish to appear that he be proceeded against in accordance with customary law." In the testimony of his wife, Philippaz (below, March 23, 1542), there is a reference to his stay in prison. See also DECRUE, "Complôt," p. 396, n. 4.

73. The maid in question was named Glaudaz, daughter of Monet Preudon. She had served at Macarde's, but "at present she lives in Cuisia with the son of the said Macarde" [R.C. 35, f. 531 (March 20, 1542)]. The Council therefore transferred the case to the *official* of Bourg. Macarde is probably the wife of Noble Guillaume Macard [see P.C. 2ᵉ sér., 862 (July 15, 1550)]. This case was resumed in Consistory on May 25, 1542. Gonet also presented himself in Council on May 26, 1542 (R.C. 36, f. 23), requesting "a divorce . . . between him and Macard's maid." The Council decided to "pursue justice" and to give him the "letters and writs necessary." He was at last recalled to the Council on June 5, 1542 (R.C. 36, f. 31), where he was "separated with liberty to contract [marriage] elswhere" because Macard's maid "lives in adultery with the said Macard."

74. We have not found any Amied de Fernex in Geneva at this period. GALIFFE (II, p. 197) says in his habitual anti-Calvinist tone that a branch of this ancient noble family remained in Geneva after the Reform, "but despoiled of its ancient rural properties . . . deprived of all influence to the profit of foreign zealots . . . it fell little by little into a state of bourgeois mediocrity."

75. This probably refers to the great Jubilee announced by Clement VII in 1524 and begun in 1525. It was extended to 1526 (see NAEF, *Origines* II, p. 319), but apparently the Poor Clares continued to offer indulgences in 1527; on March 19, 1527 (*R.C.* X, p. 329),

made him unhappy, and that his wife had no child, so that he looked to see whether he could have one elsewhere. And he begs mercy of God and of justice, and says he did it to spare his wife, who is old. Asked if he knew why his wife had no child, because when he first made her pregnant she did not want him to reveal that she ruptured her womb. Answers that she said it was not for that reason that she was ruptured, etc. Remanded by the Consistory to Monday before the Council, and meanwhile that he . . .[76]

8v]   The fifteenth Consistory.

Thursday, March 23, 1542

Lord Syndic Pertemps.
Calvin, Henri, Champereaulx.
Gilbel,[77] Britillion, Rages, Tacon, Pensabin, Blandin, the officer Vovrey.

---

the Council prohibited the Clares from issuing indulgences: "*Fuit prohibitum dominis Sancte Clare ne habeant publicare eorum indulgencias, quia stantibus periculis non permictetur quempiam intrare hanc civitatem, et quod easdem indulgencias faciant suspendere usque ad unum aliud tempus.*" {The nuns of Saint Claire were prohibited from publishing their indulgences, because in the present emergency no one can be permitted to enter this city, and that the said indulgences be suspended until another time.} See also *ibid.,* p. 330, *ad diem.* Speaking of another indulgence, the Poor Clare Jeanne de Jussie wrote that in 1531 a general pardon was proclaimed "through the countryside. The poor people came there [to the convent of St. Claire] in great devotion; but the Genevans closed the gates of the city . . . by which the poor people were greatly troubled, because they came there from afar" (JUSSIE, pp. 26-27).

76. Incomplete sentence. On January 27, 1542, the Council ordered Pierre Bertet put in prison for three days for having made a woman pregnant who was not his wife (R.C. 35, f. 470v). On March 29, 1542, after this session, he was "freed from his penance of nine days that he has stayed in prison for fornication" (*ibid.,* f. 541). The woman by whom he had this child was probably Thomasse, widow of François Mabuecta (see below, July 5, 1543). Bertet, already established in Geneva in 1532, was banished for a year in 1538 for having said "that the lords syndics at present are only named to restore the fornicators" [R.C. 32, f. 65v and f. 76v (May 27 and June 7, 1538), cited also in ROGET I, p. 119; Notaires, de Compois, 7, f. 159 (June 25, 1532)]. He also presented himself in Council on April 1, 1544, asking to "be admitted to the number of bourgeois gratis and to be admitted among the officers of St. Victor." The Council "orders that he be told that the said offices are filled, and as for being a bourgeois, that he should come another time" (R.C. 38, f. 146v). He was finally received into the bourgeoisie on August 15, 1547 (*L.B.,* p. 234).

77. Antoine Gerbel.

Robert the pack-saddler.[78]

Asked by Monsieur Pertemps why he did not appear and present himself last Thursday when he should have and about his charge and how he had carried out his charge and why he did not present himself and do his duty. Answers that he did what he could and attended the sermons. He could say nothing of his faith. The Consistory is of the opinion that he be given a longer term to instruct himself better in the faith and that he come every Thursday to show how he has profited and that he come every Thursday before Communion. And that he be given more severe [admonitions] and that . . .[79] Asked what profit he has made and how he has profited from the sermons since his last appearance. Says he listened every Sunday and that last Sunday he heard the sermon at St. Peter's and he does not know who preached, or what he said, and that it was at vespers and that it was Faret[80] or another, and that he has not been there on Wednesdays. He said that he preached on the commandments. The Consistory remanded him to present himself every Thursday from now until Easter, and after Easter until he is fully instructed in the fear of God, to give an account of how he has profited day by day; otherwise the Council will not be content with him. The lords preachers have given him just admonitions.

[f. 9] *Jaques Emyn, pack-saddler.*

Interrogated like the former. He has always been at the sermons on Sunday. Said the Lord's Prayer fairly well; was present in the morning and at vespers. Remonstrances and admonitions as given to the former and remanded like the former, and told to buy a Bible to instruct his people and guests in the Word of God. He is Master Jaques. Also the said Jaques offered that if someone sent him a young child or any other that would teach him to say his faith and creed, that he would be well contented and would spare no effort with him, which was granted him.[81]

---

78. Robert Breysson, pack-saddle maker.
79. Incomplete sentence.
80. Guillaume Farel.
81. Written in the margin of folio 8v: "He is Master Jaques . . . Which was granted him."

Philipaz, wife of Pierre Costel, daughter of the late Egrege Mermet de Ulmo.[82]

Asked what conflict there was among her, her husband and her mother. Answers that she has no grudge against them. Asked if her husband is angry with her. Answers that the anger her husband bears her mother is because he did not want her brother, Just,[83] to marry and that he would not be at the wedding if the said Dominique her mother was there, that he would leave. And she knows nothing more. Asked if she supports her mother or her husband. Answers that when her husband was in prison, she spoke to her mother and told her that if she wanted to go see Pierre Costel, her husband, she should. And she did not want to go. And therefore she took care to comfort him. And it was another time that her brother's marriage was in question. The Consistory, having heard the said daughter, resolves that both should be called and confronted with each other, having given them proper admonitions to make peace with each other. That the mother and daughter should not be in discord from now on, but live in peace with each other. And that a respectable man be provided who will report how they have made peace. He will inform Monsieur Calvin and Monsieur Gilbel[84] and the said Costel together. [f. 9v]

Pernete, widow of Pierre Puvel.

Asked about the frequenting of sermons. Said that she was at St. Peter's last week in the morning and at vespers, and that Master G[uillaume] Farel preached in the morning; at vespers she does not know. And if she has remembered the Word of God at all times as the Word of God requires. And

82. The history of a house sometimes parallels the history of a family. The curé Jean de L'Olme and his brother Mermet, father of Philippaz, owned a house together. Mermet de L'Olme, who had made his will in 1525, was already dead when his brother made his will in 1532 and in 1537, naming as heirs the sons of his brother, Antoine, Mermet, and Just, whose marriage is the subject of the dispute discussed in this session of the Consistory. Just de L'Olme, who was later an elder of the Consistory, left a son, Michel, dead without issue. The brothers of Just, as well as his sister Clauda, being dead without issue, the house passed to Philippa de L'Olme and later to Julian Costel (Coster), son of Philippa de L'Olme and of the late Pierre Coster, named sole heir in his mother's will in 1561. Some of these documents are lost, but they are mentioned, with the date and the name of the notary, in the bill of sale of the house by Julian Costel on November 27, 1568 (Notaires, Jean Ragueau, v. 10, pp. 503-510). See also Notaires, François Vuarrier, v. 3, f. 167 (August 5, 1532), will of Jean de l'Olme.

83. Just de L'Olme was an elder of the Consistory from February 15, 1543, to February 15, 1546. He was 25 or younger on February 24, 1542 [R.C. 35, f. 506v ("he is not 25 years old")]. See also the previous note.

84. Antoine Gerbel.

she does not know the Lord's Prayer and is dissatisfied because she cannot say it. And other matters. The Consistory advises that she come every Thursday to give an account of her faith, considering her great ignorance, and that she learn her faith and continue every Thursday and that every day she frequent the . . .[85]

Myaz, wife of Claude Cherrier.

Says that she has lived 30 years in Geneva and that she was at the sermon on Sunday twice at St. Peter's. Remanded like the others.[86]

Pierre Costel.

Presented himself and was admonished about quarrels and anger. Replies that this was for the marriage of his brother-in-law, the son of Donne Dominique, and that he was not at the wedding because his mother-in-law had said that she would not be there if the said Costel was and that it was better that he should be absent than the mother, because the mother is closer than others. And he said that he bore no grudge against his mother-in-law. And remanded as stated above with the others, including his mother[-in-law].

[f. 10]   *Loyse, daughter of Claude Bozonet of Vessy in Troinex, who is a maid of the curial of Peney.*[87]

And that she promised herself to one Thibaud, crossbowman,[88] and Jehan the miller, son-in-law of Jehan Curtet, was present, and it was last St.

85. Incomplete sentence. Pernete Puvel was probably the widow of Pierre Puvel the father, former *dizainier* and member of the CC, dead before June 16, 1535, but there was also a Pierre Puvel the son, citizen [*R.C.* XIII, pp. 139-140 and 243 (February 5 and June 16, 1535)].

86. See "Charriere" below, March 30 and April 6, 1542.

87. The R.C. says that his father, Claude Bossonet, was dead [R.C. 35, f. 562 (April 18, 1542)]. The *curial* of Peney at this time was Aymé de Muro, who had replaced Pierre Bally in 1538. The Council decided to dismiss him in 1542 because he "has erred in a decision made in the court of Peney," but he was again *curial* in 1543 [R.C. 31, f. 199 (February 19, 1538); R.C. 35, f. 553v (April 10, 1542); R.C. 37, f. 90v (May 14, 1543)]. The *curial* was the representative of the castellan's court who administered justice in the countryside. Elected by the Small Council, but before 1551 chosen from the people of the place, the *curial* had the duty of registering all legal documents in his jurisdiction. See *S.D.* II, pp. 345 (April 5, 1538), 490-499, 505, 508 (February 14, May 16, August 10, 1547); see also PONCET, *Châtelains*, pp. 81-91.

88. Thibaud Gauthier, son of François Gauthier of Grand Saconnex, crossbowman. He was admitted to the bourgeoisie on June 21, 1546 [R.C. 35, f. 562 (April 18, 1542); *L.B.*, p. 226].

John's Day and that she drank with the said Thibault and her mistress. And she made no reservations [about the marriage], nor he either, until at last they had supper at her master's house. And she did not want to give him up and she would be given five florins if she gave him up. And she never wanted to give him up and she never wanted to take the money and she did not seek for it or ask it.

Thibaud, son of . . . ,[89] says that he went to play skittles and held the stakes and she gave him drink and she drank without saying anything else. And the other young men told her mistress that her maid had drunk in the name of marriage and told her: "May you be happy." And he did not understand that this was in the name of marriage and says that she was later satisfied with 60 sous; that her father had not consented and if . . . .[90] Jehan Morce, Claudet Roguet[91] and Claude the Droblier[92] and Francey the blanket-maker were present when they made these [promises], and she did not want the said five florins for giving him up, and her master George was present.

Jehan Morce says that he was at the house of the said Loyse's master; they drank there and told the said Loyse to drink with the said Thibaud, and Symond the miller and Jehan Thesiez[93] were also present when they drank.

Claudet Roguet said that he saw the said Loyse drink with Thibaut and someone said to her: "May you be happy." And this was at a late lunch they had at her master's. [f. 10v] The lords advise that the other witnesses be heard, and they are summoned for next Thursday.

89. Name omitted by the scribe. This is still Thibaud, son of François Gauthier.

90. Incomplete sentence.

91. On July 10, 1534, "*Claudius filius quondam Petri Roguet de parrochia de Pers, charreterius, habitator Gebenn., parrochie S. Gervasii, fuit constitutus et admissus in burgensem* {Claude, son of the late Pierre Roguet of the parish of Pers, carter, *habitant* of Geneva in the parish of St. Gervase, was constituted and admitted as a bourgeois}" (*R.C.* XIII, p. 6). He was elected *monnayeur* in 1542 [*R.C.* 36, f. 48ᶜ (June 21, 1542)].

92. Claude Loup (Lupi), le Droblier, or "the Knave," from Dombes (Ain), admitted to the bourgeoisie on January 3, 1514 (*L.B.*, p. 177). He was a butcher, living on the Rhône Bridge [*R.C.* XIII, p. 178 (March 23, 1535)], but he is also called once "Claudius Lupi, *patisserius et burgensis* {baker and bourgeois}" [*R.C.* XII, p. 547 (May 24, 1534)]. He died before August 10, 1542, the date when his widow Françoyse Loup, called the Drobliere, appeared in the Consistory; see below *ad diem*.

93. Probably Jean Theysier, miller (see below, April 10, 1544). There was also a Jean Theysier, apothecary (*"pouldrier"*), citizen, who lived on the Rhône Bridge in 1549 [P.C. 2ᵉ sér., 800 (July 12-23, 1549), regarding a fight between Anthoine Darbey, baker, citizen, and Jean Theysier, on one side, and Pierre Mestrazat, watchman, on the other].

[Michel Bossu].[94]

He says he has sworn faith to a girl from St. Claude named Susanne Rosset, daughter of . . . ,[95] inhabitant of Saint . . . ,[96] widow of Master Jehan de Cabanis, painter(?). And he asks advice, because he cannot publish his banns in St. Claude because of the papistry.[97] The lords are of the opinion that the said marriage should be made, and remanded to tomorrow before the Council, before their lordships.[98]

Thursday, March 30, 1542.
Postponed to Friday, the next day, last of March.

Lord Egrege Porralis.
Calvin, Viret, Henri, Champereaulx.
Gerbel, Rages, Pensabin, Tacon, Frochet, Britillion, Blandin, the officer Vovrey.

Jaques Emyn.

Summoned to render an account of his faith. He responded that he had made a little progress and said the Pater, "Our Father, etc.," and a few words of the creed. The Consistory advise, having given him proper admonitions, that he find a teacher who will instruct him in the faith and explain what the words mean and make him understand what concerns God. And that he be admonished a little later to go every day or more often to the preaching for his better profit. [f. 11] And that he come close to the pulpit to hear the Word of God better and that he be refused Holy Communion unless he acquits

94. Michel Bossu, cutler; his name has been omitted by the scribe. This case was treated in Council on March 24, 1542 (R.C. 35, f. 536), when it was decided "that the marriage contracted between them should take effect when the three banns have been published."
95. Name omitted.
96. Name of the place omitted.
97. Translator: The word in French is *"papisterie."* In Geneva it meant both the doctrines of Catholicism and, more frequently, the Catholic territories surrounding the city. I have translated it throughout as "papistry," although in English this word usually meant Catholic doctrines, while "Popedom" was used for Catholic territories. Both words are obsolete, however.
98. The day after this session of the Consistory, Friday, March 24, 1542, the Council ordered that "the cases commenced in the Consistory when remanded should be remanded to Monday" (R.C. 35, f. 536, printed in *C.O.* XXI, col. 292).

himself otherwise. And that he be given a respectable teacher, and if he does not render a better account of his faith before Easter . . .[99]

Jaquemaz, widow of Claude Camparet.

Asked about frequenting of sermons, etc., and about the child her son has had by her maid. Answers that she has put the child out to nurse. Asked about her faith, she says the Pater in the new Reformed manner, but does not know the Credo. And that she has nursed her husband six years in illness and that her son . . .[100] And that she was at the sermon Sunday morning and that she believes it was Monsieur Calvin. And that she does not know about her son. The Consistory ordered her to frequent the sermons and . . .[101]

Master Tyvent Laurent, called Echaquet, citizen.[102]

Asked about the wizard he had in his house and why. Answers he never had one, except a man from Challex who attended his wife[103] who was sick, and he said he would cure her. And that he often came to his house and would give him herbs to dissolve in wine, which was not done at his house. And that the man owed him money and that he came for no other reason. And he goes to the sermons when he can and gave an explanation of his faith and creed, Pater and Credo, and says he wants to live and die in the Word of Our Lord. The lords preachers having given him proper admonitions and given him leave, he was asked about those who go to his house for. . .[104] They are Michiel Du Mur[105] and Aymé Tacon and others.

99. Incomplete sentence.
100. Incomplete sentence.
101. Incomplete sentence.
102. The cobbler Tyvent Laurent, called Exchaquet, still in the CC in November 1529, had left the city during the war of the Gentlemen of the Spoon [translator: a name the "Peneysans" gave each other because they swore mutual fealty at a banquet]. Because of the measures taken against the Mamelus, Laurent was at risk of having his goods confiscated for having left the city in time of war. Therefore he returned to Geneva in December 1530 and, although put in prison and threatened with the loss of his bourgeoisie, he was reestablished on paying 20 écus [*R.C.* XI, p. 335 (November 7, 1529); *ibid.,* pp. 501, 512, 513 (November 8, December 6 and 9, 1530); R.C. 30, f. 77 (October 27, 1536); see also MARTIN, *Genève,* pp. 187-190].
103. Possibly "Jane, widow of Tivent Laurent, bourgeois of Geneva, living on [the Rue du] Peron . . . dead of a long illness, aged 60 [E.C., Morts 5, f. 98 (December 8, 1562)].
104. Incomplete sentence.
105. Michel Du Mur, cobbler, from Landecy (GE), admitted to the bourgeoisie on June 8, 1535 (*R.C.* XIII, p. 235). He was a member of the CC, *curial* of Peney in 1542 and died before March 23, 1567 [Mss. Galiffe 46, f. 49; E.C., Morts 7, p. 65 (*ad diem,* death of Janne, his widow)].

[f. 11v] *Donne Jane Pertennaz.*[106]

Asked about her faith and why she has not received Holy Communion and whether she has heard and gone to Mass every year. And she said her faith and that she believes in one God and wants to live in God and the holy church and has no other faith. And she frequents the sermons on Sunday. She recited her Pater in French: "I believe in God the Father, omnipotent, etc." Answered that Our Lord knows our hearts and that she believes as the church believes. Asked what that is. Answers that she does not . . .[107] except as the church believes. Asked if there is a church in this city. Answers that she knows nothing; she believes that the Word of God is . . .[108] And that she wants always to live as a Christian and that there is only one God. And whether the sacraments of Our Lord are administered. Answers that it is preached and that Communion is taken, and she believes in Holy Communion as God said: "This is my body, and do this in my memory."[109] And that where the Word of God is, God is, and that she conforms to the Word of God and that the Word of God is here. And she said she wanted to live and die in it, and it has the administration of the sacraments according to the Word of God and nothing else. Asked why she is not satisfied with the Communion celebrated in this city but goes elsewhere. Answers that she goes where it seems good to her. And that there is talk of princes who are not in accord in what they do openly, but they must be obeyed. And that Our Lord will not come here well-clothed or shod[110] and that where His Word is, His body is [f. 12] a word [sic]. Our Lord said that ravenous wolves would come, and therefore she does not know who these ravenous wolves are or where there are false prophets and . . .[111] Remanded as outside the faith and to appear day by day. And she did not want to renounce the Mass.

Puvellaz.[112]

Said that she prays to God and recommends herself to God and the Holy Spirit. Said the Lord's Prayer in a general way, with various errors, but not her creed or confession of faith, as last time, and could do nothing else.

106. Jana, mother of the syndic Claude Bonna, called Pertemps, widow of Jean Bonna, called Pertemps, and later of Claude Tornier [*R.C.* XI, pp. 130 and 236 (October 6, 1528, and April 8, 1529); see also Mss. Galiffe 40, f. 77].
107. Word omitted by the scribe.
108. Incomplete sentence.
109. Luke 22:19.
110. Reference to Matthew 11:7-8 or Luke 7:24-25 (same text).
111. Incomplete sentence. She cites Matthew 7:15.
112. Pernete Puvel, widow of Pierre.

Remanded to Monday before the Council and at the request of the lords preachers to Thursday.

Charriere.[113]

Said her Pater fairly well, the creed very little. Remanded to Thursday.

The sheath-maker's wife.[114]

Said she has a daughter who knows her faith better than she, and she did not know it except in Latin as in former times, and in the French language she could not say her creed; in Latin in a general way. And she does not know it in another language and does not understand it otherwise, and as for the sermons she has not frequented them. And that she could not come last Thursday because she had to look after someone in childbirth. The Consistory remanded her to Thursday.

Thibaud versus and [sic] De Murro's maid.

Remanded to Monday to bring his witnesses.[115]

12v] *Mermeta Jappaz.*

Said she is pregnant by the son of Berthelomier Fouson, named Bezanson,[116] and she already felt the child at Christmas, and this was at the said Fouson's house. And she did not say her Pater well, and she goes to sermons on Monday and other days not. And she wants to give it to its father, and her mother knows nothing, and she has had another child. And the other child was put to nurse and died. Remanded to . . .[117] The Consistory

---

113. Myaz Cherrier.

114. The wife of Louis Pyaget.

115. Thibaud Gauthier and Loyse Bozonet. On April 18, 1542, the Council ordered: "Concerning the statement that marriage had been contracted between Tybaud and Loyse, the consent of the said Tybaud's father was always reserved, as is shown to us by the confessions of both parties. Also at the said marriage the parents of the two parties were not asked, of whom François Gauthier, father of the said Tybaud, has said in person he does not want to consent to such an affair. Concerning this we have ordered the said marriage to be held null and invalid, freeing both parties respectively from it with license to contract marriage elsewhere when it seems good to them" (Jur. civ. R1, f. 1; see also R.C. 35, f. 562, *ad diem*).

116. Besanson Fouson was the son of Peronette and Barthélemy Fouson. The father was an apothecary "of Monreale, received bourgeois on August 31, 1509, member of the LX in 1527, councillor in 1531. He left Geneva in 1535 because of his attachment to Catholicism, returned in 1536 and died on September 6, 1550" (*R.C. XII*, p. 127, n. 3; L. GAUTIER, *Médecine*, p. 447; also *ibid.*, p. 20).

117. Incomplete sentence.

advises that she abstain from taking Communion because of her serious fornication. Remanded to Thursday.

To be summoned:

Tallabard[118] and Bezanson Fouson; Françoys Gerin's maid;[119] Arthauda and her daughters on the Bourg du Four; Aymo Lemballioz; Catherine from the Molard; the barber on the Molard;[120] Pierre Baud to know why he does not send his people to the sermons; Jana, maid of Jehan Tacon[121] the haberdasher.

[f. 13]

Tuesday, April 4, 1542

Lord Porralis.
Calvin, Viret, Champereaulx, Henri.
Du Molard, Pensabin, Girbel, Frochet, D'Orsieres, the officer.

Donne Janne Pertennaz.

Recalled and asked why she displays no efforts to admonish herself and lead herself to the faith. Answers that she has not taken the Host. The said Janne asks if the Holy Scripture has now fully arrived. Lord Calvin admonished her from the Word of God. She said it was true that last Sunday there were some Germans who spoke to her maid, and there was one who came to the said Donne Jane, a respectable German, who asked her [in marriage], saying he wanted her very much. And she told him she was married. And the said German asked how she prayed. She answered that here they do not want you to say the "Virgin Mary, pray for us." She answered that she went nowhere at Christmas because she was ill. Asked what faith she held toward God. Answers that she keeps the faith in good earnest and believes there is one God. Said that the lords preachers should know better than she what concerns God, and that she puts all her reliance on God. Said that Our Lord, by the merit of his passion, will pardon

118. Pierre Bertet, called Tallabard.
119. Possibly Jana Bouvier. Françoys Gerin, saddler, was elected to the CC for the Rue du Boule from 1539 on, and died before 1551 [R.C. 37, f. 11v (February 9, 1543); Mss. Galiffe 38, f. 430; E.C., Morts 1, p. 36 (May 19, 1551, death of Pernette, his widow)].
120. He was named Pierre.
121. Jean Guenet (Guinet), called Taccon. There were two, father and son, both haberdashers. Jean the son was elected to the LX for the Poissonnerie, and it was probably he who was a member of the CC at this time [R.C. XIII, pp. 147 (February 12, 1535) and 455 (February 22, 1536); R.C. 35, f. 490 (February 7, 1542)].

her and that she has given her heart to God and that he will guard her from all dangers. And that she will never follow another than God and that she is not a cleric like them and that there is no other God for her than God. [f. 13v] She was asked in what manner she takes Holy Communion. Answers that she does not want to be an idolater or hypocrite; she leaves the faith as it is. Said that the Virgin Mary is her advocate. Said the Virgin Mary is a friend of God and that the Virgin Mary is the daughter and mother of Jesus Christ. And she understands that no one will be damned if it pleases God and that she does not know anything about the church. Said her faith is good and she does not know whether the faith of others of others [sic] is good. And that she never had another faith than the faith of Jesus Christ and that Our Lady is a gentle woman and that God is our advocate before God the Father and that none can pardon except Our Lord, and that she wants to live in the faith of the holy church, and she said that if the lord syndic was a heretic she would not want to be one.

The Consistory advises that she be made to speak once more to learn her will; afterwards that she be remanded before the Council or corrected in an evangelical manner, or remanded to another Thursday, and depending on what is found that she either be remanded to Friday before the Council or forbidden Communion, so that she will not go elsewhere to worship idols. And that she be admonished to go to the sermons every day. She says she is subject to the Seigneurie of Geneva.

Asked if she believes. She believes that everywhere where the Word of God is, she believes in that. Remanded to Thursday to learn first if she is united with us in Holy Communion. That there is only one mediator God, Jesus Christ; as for the saints, that one should do like them. Secondly whether she does not believe that Jesus Christ is our advocate and whether the sacraments administered in this [city] are from God or not and whether Jesus Christ is [or] is not in the Holy Communion and that we have no other advocate than Jesus Christ before God the Father. [f. 14] Believes that Jesus Christ is in heaven; has heard that God sees all and is all. Also always has and always will believe as she has said. Remanded to Thursday to respond firmly without doubt. Answered that she wanted to give for the love of God on Maundy Thursday and that on such a day he made his Communion, and that Our Lord fasted 40 days.

We declare that she cannot be received at Communion and we deprive her of it from now until the Lord touches her heart, and she is declared outside the church. Answered that in the time when the Jews were expelled from this city, that the time was coming when the Jews would be throughout the city.[122]

122. In the Middle Ages the Jews of Geneva lived in a quarter at the bottom of the Rue des Granges and of the Grand Mézel which in the sixteenth century was still called

Catherine, from the Molard.

Said that she believes in God and that he is our advocate and in Jesus Christ. The Pater and the faith she knows little or not at all. And that she received Communion last Christmas at St. Peter's. The Consistory having learned her poverty has given her leave to learn the faith and receive Communion.

Noble Donne . . . ,[123] wife of Noble Jehan de Pesmes.

Said that she was at the sermon on Sunday. She came to this city about six weeks ago. And [asked] if she believes as in the past in the papal ceremonies, that it is great idolatry and that the Mass is abominable, and if she believes in Holy Communion. Answered that she has received Communion and believes in the Gospel and intends to receive it like others according to the Reformation and . . .[124] The Consistory admonished her to frequent the sermons. Said that she knows how to read and has a Bible. And at this given leave.

[f. 14v] *Arthaudaz from the Bourg du Four.[125]*

Said that she wants to live according to God and that she has no other faith than in Jesus Christ and that she has no rosary or Ave Maria and receives Communion and goes to sermons when she can. She could not say the Pater well, and the creed even less. Admonished to abstain from songs and other things that are not proper and to instruct her daughters honorably, and that they should not insult one another as they do and have done, and at this she departed. And to frequent the sermons and learn the faith.

---

the Juiverie. Under the influence of a preacher, the syndics decided on December 23, 1490, to expel the Jews of Geneva: "*vellent omnes Judeos ab hac civitate expellere secundum doctrinam moderni predicatoris*" {they wish to expel all Jews from this city, according to the doctrine of a recent preacher} (*R.C.* IV, p. 321). They demanded that the Jews quit the city within ten days [*ibid.* (December 28, 1491; n.s. 1490)]. See also GINSBURGER, *Juifs,* pp. 1-2; GALIFFE, *Genève historique,* pp. 164-167.

123. Name omitted. This is probably Donne Jeanne, daughter of the late Noble Etienne Nycoud of Gex, wife of Noble Jean de Pesmes. Jean de Pesmes was 36 in 1534, was elected to the LX in 1535, and died on November 3, 1552. He was the brother of the Mamelu Percival de Pesmes. Already in the fifteenth century the Pesmes were one of the most illustrious families of Geneva [GALIFFE III, pp. 397-398; NAEF, *Origines* II, p. 402; MARTIN, *Genève,* p. 70; *R.C.* XIII, p.146 (February 12, 1535)].

124. Incomplete sentence.

125. She was a *hospitissa* {innkeeper} on the Bourg du Four in 1531 [*R.C.* XII, p. 21 (September 4, 1531)].

Monsieur Pierre Baux.[126]

Concerning frequenting of sermons by him and his family. Answered that he wants to live according to the Reformation and the sacrament of Communion. Said that he knows the Pater, but the Credo only in Latin. That he would teach it to his family in the current mode. And at this he departed. That he instruct his family.

Pierre, the barber on the Molard.

Answered that he goes to sermons, and that he was there Sunday morning and believes that it was Calvin, and that he preached from St. John; and after dinner he does not know who, but he preached from John. He said his Pater; the faith he could not say, nor the commandments of God. Believes that the Word of God is here and that we have only one God. Admonished to frequent the sermons and instruct his family in the Word of God; otherwise . . .[127]

François Mermiez, from Choully, and his wife. Thursday.
Jehan Du Nant, host of the Stag.

15]   **For Thursday, April 6, 1542**

Lord Syndic Pertemps.
Calvin, Viret, Henri, Champereaulx.
Gerbel, D'Orsieres, Britillion, Pensabin, Blandin, Frochet, the officer Vovrey.

Besanson Fouson.

About his foolish acts throughout the city, also about the woman he has made pregnant, called Mermetaz.[128] Answers that he knew her about St. John's Day and said that Furbi's boy[129] and Foy's valet have also been with her; therefore he says that the child is not by him.

126. One of the most common names in Geneva at this period. This is probably Pierre Baud, son of Jean (syndic in 1519 and 1523). Pierre Baud was a citizen, an ironmonger, a member of the CC in 1529 and of the LX in 1535. He died in 1558 [GALIFFE I, pp. 44-47; SORDET, *Dictionnaire*, pp. 74-75; E.C., Morts 2, p. 43 (July 26, 1558)].
127. Incomplete sentence.
128. Mermetaz Jappaz.
129. Jaques Furbi.

Mermyez's wife, from Choully.[130]

Why for a long time they have done nothing but beat each other in their quarrels. It was about five years ago that he took this position, and when her husband takes it into his head nothing stops him, and it is by the will of God. And they frequent the sermons when they can. Said the reason why Pierre Bon[131] has a respectable wife is that . . .[132] About her faith: neither Pater nor Credo, neither in Latin nor French. The Consistory orders that she be admonished to frequent the sermons, and touching Communion that she be admonished first that if there is friendship between them they be reconciled; otherwise we will proceed farther; and that her husband also be reconciled with those who will be sent to them before taking Communion. And to learn her faith and creed.

The sheath-maker's wife.[133]

Said that she was at the sermon on Sunday; the preacher spoke of a lantern, that Our Lord finds His way easily without a lantern. Said her Pater fairly well, and the confession of belief very little. The Consistory is of the opinion that she be left to her own [f. 15v] good will, continuing always to the end from good to better, and that she has profited and holds no grudge against anyone, and that before receiving Communion she come to be reconciled to the preacher of St. Gervase, and Monsieur Britillion with him, to reconcile them before Communion, and she should frequent the sermons in order to profit more and more to the honor of God. That she go to Holy Communion. That she go to the sermon tomorrow with her husband and the baker of St. Gervais and that they be reconciled, and also the daughter of the said sheath-maker's wife, tomorrow after dinner at St. Gervase. Tomorrow after dinner the aforesaid sheath-maker's wife, her husband, her daughter and the baker to be reconciled after dinner, and Reymond.[134]

And similarly: Charvetaz,[135] Jehan Roman[136] and his wife.

130. The wife of Françoys Mermiez (see below, April 13, 1542).
131. A Pierre Bon, "carpenter, bourgeois of Geneva, living near the City Hall," died on July 2, 1558 (E.C., Morts 2, f. 37).
132. Incomplete sentence.
133. The wife of Louis Pyaget, sheath-maker.
134. Reymond de Veyrier.
135. Charvetaz apparently kept an inn or tavern of some sort in St. Gervais in 1541. In 1544 she was authorized to open an inn under the sign of the Golden Falcon [R.C. 35, f. 341 (September 27, 1541); R.C. 39, f. 30v (November 7, 1544); see also P.C. 2ᵉ sér., 707, col. 7 (March 31, 1546)].
136. Jehan Roman, from Greny (Ain), miller, admitted to the bourgeoisie on January 26, 1524, living then in St. Gervais (*L.B.*, p. 200).

Magdalen.

Tappunier and Vernaz[137] who are angry, that they be summoned to-morrow to the Magdalen after dinner at 12 o'clock, the preacher Monsieur Viret and Monsieur Girbel being present.

Saint Gervase.

Charvetaz, Jehan Roman and his wife, Claude and Jehan Curtet, Claude Voland[138] and Jehan Curtet, Mabuectaz's brother and Tallabard, by resolution of the Consistory.

Tallabard.

That he has not done what the Council commanded after his detention. He was admonished to be more sensible than he has been in the past.

Aymoz Foural, host of the Three Quail.[139]

He was asked who summoned him here. Answers that it was not he, but his wife,[140] who cannot come, and he wants to respond for her and also himself. Asked about the frequenting of [f. 16] sermons. Answers that he goes when he can, and Monsieur Calvin preached Sunday morning. And said his Pater and creed fairly well. Said that his wife was ill. Afterwards said that he should not be summoned more than others and that he had done more and that he wants to know what is wanted from his wife. The Consistory orders that he bring his wife at once, and he was admonished to go to sermons and not tell lies any more.

137. Claude Tappunier (Tapponier, Tappugnier), iron-monger from Presilly (H.-S.), admitted to the bourgeoisie on January 29, 1521. He died on May 17, 1561, at age 70 [*L.B.*, p. 191; E.C., Morts 3, p. 109; SORDET, *Dictionnaire*, p. 1221]. Vernaz, named here, could be the wife of Pierre Vernaz, elected to the Consistory from the Council of CC for the years 1543 and 1544.

138. There were a Claude Voland, bath-keeper (see below, July 5, 1543), and an "Egrege Claude Voland, agent for Noble Pierre d'Alinge, Seigneur de Couldree" [R.C. 38, f. 83v (February 22, 1544)]. Claude Voland, wife of Jean Voland, was summoned to the Consistory on December 13, 1543.

139. Aymoz Foural, baker, from Thuet near Bonneville (H.-S.), bourgeois on September 2, 1530 (*R.C.* XI, p. 474). In 1537 he was forbidden to post the sign of the Three Quail, but the sign was returned to him [R.C. 30, f. 180v (February 22, 1537)].

140. Anthoyne Foural.

Master Robert.[141]

Asked how he has advanced in the Christian faith. Answers that he has learned his Pater, which he said, and that he was at the sermon on Sunday and Master Pierre[142] preached and he remembers nothing of the sermon or very [little]. The Consistory orders that he continue the sermons every day and that he not be left alone until he knows all his faith as he should and that he not come to Communion, that he be given sharper admonitions, that he be forbidden Communion until he can recite it well, and that he have a Bible in his house.

Franceyse, wife of Claude Bellet.[143]

Asked about the sermons. Answers that she goes on Sundays and that she has a child to watch and cannot go to sermons and that she has to earn a living because her husband has earned nothing since the grape harvest. Said her Pater and confession fairly well. The Consistory admonished her to frequent the sermons.

Bernardaz.

Asked where her husband is. Answers that he lives in Les Bornes and she has two children by him and he gives her no help, and she has lived in this city 20 years and she struggles hard to live and goes sometimes to sermons and does not know her faith. She was . . .[144] [f. 16v] to live with her husband. The Consistory advises that if her husband does not want to live here, she stay, considering that she says she wants to live according to our law and that she . . .[145] and to frequent the sermons. And why it is that they are not together.

141. Robert Breysson, pack-saddler.
142. Pierre Viret.
143. This may be Claude Du Villard, called Bellet; see below, January 24, 1544. Claude Villard (Villario), currier or dyer, from Sappey (H.-S.), was received into the bourgeoisie in 1550 [*L.B.,* p. 143 (s.d. 1500); *R.C.* XII, p. 554n]. A Claude Bellet was named in the list of "Lutherans" made on August 10 and September 23, 1534, by the bishop's procurator fiscal [*R.C.* XII, p. 609, and *R.C.* XIII, p. 592, *notes complémentaires*]. In 1537 it was reported in Council that Claude Bellet lived in fornication and he was ordered to marry the girl, possibly this same Franceyse. In 1540 Claude Bellet presented himself in Council and "since he is insane, without a means of living, he prays that he be given some office, which he will exercise with a good heart." He also complained that "he cannot properly feed either his wife or his son." Not being fit for any office, he was granted a gift of four *coupes* of wheat [R.C. 34, f. 119v and f. 123v (March 2 and 8, 1540)]. We think all these are the same person, but possibly he is sometimes confounded with Claude Bellet, late husband of Colletaz (see below, March 20, 1543).
144. Words omitted. Probably "admonished."
145. Words omitted.

Venturinaz, wife of Sollier.

Asked about frequenting of sermons. Answers that she goes when she can and she was there today and Master Viret preached. Said her Pater and very little of her faith and confession. The Consistory advised her to frequent the sermons and learn to know her faith better than she does.[146]

Charriere.[147]

As above, she presented herself as knowing her faith better than last time. Said her Pater, but still cannot say the Credo, and was at the sermon Sunday and does not know what was said because she cannot hear well, because she is a little deaf. The Consistory orders that she be admonished to do better and frequent the sermons and that she be remanded for a month to learn a better explanation of her faith, and that she not be let off yet.

Anthoyne, wife of Aymo Foral, host of the Three Quail.

Because of songs, games and other acts that are not proper. Answers that they do not follow a bad course and that they do not disobey the Seigneurie. And said her Pater; the Credo she knows hardly anything of. And she frequents the sermons. The Consistory admonished them both to live honestly in their house and with their guests and household, that they not follow a bad course in their house and that they obey justice. Named the wife of the *dizainier* something [sic] and that she be summoned for Thursday.[148]

Furbi's son[149] should be summoned for Thursday.

f. 17]   *Besanson Fouson.*

The Consistory advises that he be forbidden to receive Holy Communion because of his fornication and remanded to Thursday until it is evident that he has improved, and that he frequent the sermons. Yesterday he named

146. Venturine was the daughter of Claude Butin (Butini) of Collonges (Collonges-Bellerive, GE). Her husband, Antoine Revilliod, called Sollier, was received into the bourgeoisie on January 30, 1540; he was innkeeper of the Golden Rose (to which he joined the Crescent and the Crown) on the Molard (GALIFFE IV, pp. 289-90; *L.B.*, p. 220; DOUMERGUE III, pp. 215-216).

147. Myaz Cherrier.

148. Probably Philiberta, wife of Claude Magnin, *dizainier* of St. Christophe (see below, April 13, 1542).

149. Jaques Furbi.

Jaques Furbi's son and Thibaut Tissot, Nantermetaz's son[150] and Foy's valet for Thursday, who knew the said Mermete as well as he.

The proposed ordinance for Holy Communion made in Consistory.[151]

For St. Peter's for the two Communions: Lord Girbel, Mychiel Varod,[152] D'Orsieres, Jehan Coquet,[153] Pierre de Rages, Checand.[154] For reader . . .[155]

For St. Gervase: Lord Hudriod Du Mollard, Monsieur Pierre Britillion, Blandin, Loys Dufour,[156] Emoz Tacon, for reader the procurator general.[157]

For the Magdalen: Jehan Pictiod,[158] Fontannaz, *hospitalier,*[159] Pensabin.

150. Thibaud Tissot, son of Noble Nantermet Tissot, often called Lantermet (councillor in 1519), and of Noble Marguerite Maillard, daughter of the late Noble Jean Maillard, widow in 1527 [GALIFFE I, pp. 509-510; R.C. XI, p. 329 (October 17, 1529)].

151. On December 23, 1541, the Council ordered that Communion "should be celebrated and administered on Sunday in three places, that is St. Peter's, the Magdalen, St. Gervase, and that the lords deputies of the Consistory should distribute the wine" (R.C. 35, f. 442v).

152. Michel Varo, apothecary, bourgeois, member of the CC in 1535, was among the Genevans who supported Courault, Farel, and Calvin in 1538. Varo was probably assigned to distribute Communion because he was a procurator of the hospital [R.C. XI, p. 481 (September 19, 1530); ROGET I, p. 88; GALIFFE III, pp. 479-480; DOUMERGUE II, p. 131, from FROMENT, pp. 95-97; KINGDON, "Deacons," pp. 88-89].

153. Jean Coquet, councillor in 1526, syndic in 1527, 1533, 1539, and 1543, died suddenly on September 29, 1546 (GALIFFE II, pp. 172-173; CHOISY, G.G., p. 61).

154. Antoine Chiccand, syndic six times between 1531 and 1551 and ardent Calvinist, died on July 10, 1554. He was also *hospitalier* from June 1540 until his dismissal in November 1541 (GALIFFE II, p. 160; KINGDON, "Deacons," p. 90; L. GAUTIER, *Hôpital,* p. 22).

155. The phrase "for reader" is found on a separate line in the manuscript, and it is therefore unlikely that Checand was the reader. This sentence is treated as incomplete.

156. Noble Louis Dufour, merchant, Seigneur de Bossey, admitted to the bourgeoisie on October 14, 1524 (L.B., p. 201), councillor in 1531, 1533, 1534, died in 1561 at age 81 or 82. He was sent to Strasbourg to bring Calvin back in 1540 (GALIFFE II, p. 151).

157. Thomas Genod, procurator general 1541-1542.

158. Jean Chautemps, called Pitiod, businessman, miller, councillor in 1541, elder of the Consistory in 1555, syndic in 1556, and "one of the most active partisans of the Reform in Geneva since the time of the first preaching of Farel" (R.C.P. I, p. 39, n. 7). He made his will on December 5, 1569, when he was over 80 (CHAIX, *Imprimerie,* p. 160). See also the biographical notice concerning him in CARTIER, "Arrêts," pp. 432-438, and KINGDON, *Wars,* pp. 94, 122-123.

159. Jean Fontanna, former priest, member of the LX and *hospitalier* from December 21, 1541, to May 2, 1543. After some months the Council complained about his treatment of the poor, and finally he was deposed because he "does not do his duty in his office and is not charitable to the poor," and because "Fontannaz and the procurators of the hospital cannot agree" [R.C. 35, f. 489 (February 7, 1542); R.C. 36, f. 80 (July 28, 1542); R.C. 37, f. 78 and f. 82 (April 30 and May 2, 1543). See also L. GAUTIER, *Hôpital,* p. 22].

And throughout a lord syndic. And enter the pulpit at 4 o'clock for the first and for the second at 7:30.

Thursday, April 13, 1542

Lord Syndic Pertemps.
Calvin, Viret, Champereaulx, Henri.
Pensabin, Frochet, the officer Vovrey.

Claude Magnin, called Goudoz.[160]

Presented himself for his wife, saying she is at home with some people. Asked about the behavior of his household. Answered that he has made an oath to the city that he would live according to the commandments of God[161] and that he did not want to permit anything improper in his household. And that he is the *dizainier* of St. Christofle and will not permit anyone to do anything improper.[162]

The daughter of Joyeuse.[163]

Concerning her promised husband who left, and she has not sent to the place where he is because she has never learned where he went, and asks that she be separated. The Consistory advises that someone be sent to Lyon to inquire. And after the fair,[164] depending on the report, provision will be made.

160. Claude Magnin, from Belley (Ain), innkeeper on the Bourg du Four, admitted to the bourgeoisie on July 4, 1531. He was *hospitalier* from August 1538 to June 1540 [*L.B.*, p. 208; *R.C.* XIII, f. 571 (May 16, 1536); KINGDON, "Deacons," p. 90; L. GAUTIER, *Hôpital*, p. 21; see also GALIFFE III, pp. 310-311; FROMENT, p. 44].

161. Claude Magnin is probably referring to the oath of 1537, which he had been obliged to take as a *dizainier*. It was in that year that Calvin and Farel asked the Council to require all bourgeois and *habitants* of Geneva to swear to the Confession of Faith of 1536. See DOUMERGUE II, pp. 219-223 and 236-251; ROGET I, pp. 35-37 and 47-48; *Farel*, pp. 356-358; RILLIET, "Premier séjour," pp. lviii-lxx. For the text of this confession of faith see *Catéchisme français*, pp. 101-122. However, he may be referring simply to the oath normally taken by *dizainiers* (see next note).

162. The *dizainiers* were obligated to take arms against the enemies of the city, reveal all plots against the city, oppose all sedition and riots, "maintain good peace and union" and "stop all dissoluteness and insolence, and in general everything that is contrary to order and discipline in the city" [*S.D.* II, pp. 415-416 (January 28, 1543)].

163. Françoyse, daughter of Loys Reys and of Joyeuse, and Pierre Favre, called Berthoz.

164. Since 1420 the Easter fairs in Geneva and Lyon coincided. J.-F. Bergier tells us: "It will be seen that at the end of the fifteenth century the dates of the fairs of Geneva

And that she do her best to find out, and afterwards provision will be made. Her mother is present. And she was given proper admonitions always to persist in doing better and better, and remanded until after the fair.

Françoys Mermiez of Choully.

Said that he could not come last Thursday and that he had gone to his father who was ill. And why he does not live in peace in his house with his wife and has been very quarrelsome and combative for a long time with those in the village of Choully. And [f. 18] answers that three weeks ago his wife fought with some other women and he did not want to believe it and he struck her, and that he did not take up a stick to hit her, but for another purpose, and that she does nothing but fight with other women. And that four years ago he was a servant at the priory of Satigny,[165] and that he has not beaten her except the time that he described. The Consistory advises that he be given appropriate admonitions and remonstrances and that he be made to give an explanation of his faith in intelligible language. And whether he knows how to pray to God and whether he frequents the sermons. Answers that he never misses a sermon and cannot say his Pater except in Latin, which he did. And he said the Ave Maria in Latin, and also the Credo in an unintelligible manner. And that he present himself here in one month.

Jaques, son of Furby.

Asked about his bad behavior concerning the pregnant woman Mermete.[166] And once about a year ago, being with Fouson's son, the said Besanson opened the door to him and said to the said Furbi: "Stay a little." And meanwhile she entered, as though he had consented to what he did to the said Mermete.

Thibault Tissoctz because of the said Mermete. Answers that he knew the said Mermete about a year ago in the clock-tower of the Corraterie.

The Consistory advises that all three be held, that they not be released,

---

were regularly delayed two to three weeks, to avoid coincidence with those of Lyon" (BERGIER, *Genève,* p. 239).

165. The priory of Satigny, possibly of the Order of St. Benedict at first, is better known to historians as a priory of Augustinian canons between 1134 and the Reformation. In 1541 the tavern attached to the priory was suppressed in order to lodge the pastor of the place there. See BINZ, "Le diocèse de Genève," p. 36; GENEQUAND, "Satigny," p. 1437ff.; *D.H.B.S.* V, p. 728; GALIFFE, *Genève historique,* p. 255, also the supplement, *ibid.,* pp. 116-118, with a print of the "remains of the former priory of Satigny."

166. Mermete Jappaz.

because of the child of the said Mermete, and that they be remanded before the Council in order that young people not ruin themselves thus; and that they be admonished that fornication is forbidden by the commandment of God. And that it would be good to drive such fornicators from the city to avoid such scandals and so they would not abuse themselves with fornication. Present were the said Besanson Fouson and all three. They were given proper remonstrances. Remanded to Monday before the Council. Foy's servant did not present himself.[167]

18v]   *Philiberta, wife of Claude Magnin, called Goudon, from the Bourg du Four.*

Asked by the lord[168] about the management of their house as an inn. Answers that they do nothing reprehensible and about their behavior and that she knows nothing of the pregnant woman spoken of. And why she jeered at her neighbor, the hunchback's wife, who presented herself to the Consistory.[169] And if she knows any neighbors who do not behave well according to the Word of God. And she knows nothing of bad behavior. The Consistory gave her proper remonstrances.

It is necessary to give the names of those who do not appear in the Consistory on the days recorded above. Also to consider those members of the Consistory who do not appear on Thursdays in the Consistory, to advise that action be taken.[170]

For Monday, April 17, 1542. The names of those who have confessed having knowledge of Mermetaz Jappaz, who is pregnant with a child.

First Jaques, son of Furbi, Thibault Tissoctz, Besanson Fouson and Foy's servant who did not appear. The Consistory advised that all three be held, that they not be released because of the child the said Mermete bears, and that they be remanded before the Council on Monday in order that young people not injure themselves thus. And that they be admonished that fornication is forbidden is forbidden [sic] by the commandments of God, and that it would be good to drive such public fornicators from the city to

---

167. Implicated in the case discussed above, Foy's servant was summoned several times to the Consistory without ever appearing.

168. That is, the lord syndic who presided at the sessions of the Consistory.

169. Anthoyne, wife of Aymo Foural; see her testimony above, April 6, 1542.

170. From the beginning those who were refractory in presenting themselves in Consistory were put in prison. Only three days before this session the Council decided to free Jo. Brouge from prison, "considering his long detention" for having refused to appear before the Consistory, which intended to reconcile him with his wife [R.C. 35, f. 553 (April 10, 1542)].

avoid such scandals and to keep them from abusing themselves by fornication. And that they be admonished.[171]

[f. 19]   *Those who do not appear in Consistory when summoned.*

The widow of Pierre Puvel;[172] the said Mermete Jappaz; Pierre Claret;[173] Brectaz; the wife of Jaques the pack-saddler;[174] Jehan Du Nant, host of the Stag; Foy's servant.

Also to advise concerning those who are assigned to serve on the Consistory who do not appear on Thursdays.

That orders be given and that they be persuaded to come there every day that the Council orders it be held.

Those who should be summoned for Thursday, April 20, 1542.

Master Michiel the saddler on the Molard[175] and Mermet his nephew, who have been in conflict a long time; the widow of Falcoz, who left Saturday without leave from the Council, because of Holy Communion; Bellengier the archer; Jehan Du Nant the goitered, cobbler, *dizainier,* and his wife,[176] who live on the Rue de la Poissonerie; Aymoz Cortagier and his wife;[177] Jaques Carre; Uguynaz Depontelaz and the bastard daughter of Monsieur Jehan Amyci;[178] Jana, formerly maid of Françoys Gerin, who lives by the wall below the Bishop's Palace[179] near the church of the Magdalen.

171. On April 17, 1542, the Council considered Mermeta Jappaz's fornication: "Jaques Furbi, Thibaud Tissot, Bezanson Fouson, who have committed fornication with Mermetaz Jappaz so that she is pregnant: resolved that they be put in prison for three days on bread and water, and that the one who is found to be the father of the child should support the child at his expense, relieve her, and give her five sous for a pair of laced shoes." Regarding Mermetaz: "When she has delivered the child, ordered, because it is the second time, that she be whipped." On April 28, 1542, Bezanson Fouson was recalled to Council (R.C. 35, f. 572) after having been "detained for having committed fornication: resolved that after being admonished in Consistory he be freed from prison after meeting the expenses of the woman's delivery and take the child, and five sous to the said female fornicator . . ." (R.C. 35, f. 559v).

172. Pernete, widow of Pierre Puvel.

173. Pierre Reclans, called Claret, baker.

174. Tevenete, wife of Jaques Emyn, pack-saddler.

175. Michel Julliard.

176. As always, Jehan Du Nant and Clauda his wife.

177. Aymoz Cortagier, citizen. Jeanne Bertherat was his second wife; see GALIFFE I, p. 450.

178. Huguine Amici.

179. On November 23, 1535, the old episcopal palace near the cathedral became the prison of Geneva. For a detailed description with plans see LULLIN, "Évêché."

Thursday, April 20, 1542

Syndic Porralis.
Calvin, Viret, Bernard, Champereaux, Henri.
Molard, D'Orsier, Britillion, Blandin, Tacon, Pensabin, Frochet, the officer Vovrey.

The advice of the lords preachers concerning the problem of banns for those being married in the papistry, because of Megerandi's daughter[180] *who has promised herself to a husband from La Roche called De Grangia.*

The Consistory advises that marriages not be obstructed or banns be published here unless the government makes such a law. And that they be given an affidavit.[181] Summon the girl and her parents here and admonish them.

Concerning the other, the teacher who affianced the daughter of Master Bastien.

That the banns may be published, since there is good testimony and no deceit.[182]

---

180. Actually this is Jane, the sister and not the daughter of Pierre Migerand; see below, later in this session.

181. Underlined in the manuscript: "The Consistory . . . an affidavit."

182. This entire paragraph is struck out in the text, from "concerning" to "deceit." It concerns not the daughter of Sébastien Castellion, but his sister Etiennette. Concerning this marriage the Council register says on April 17, 1542 (R.C. 35, f. 559): "Here it was stated that a marriage was contracted between Master Pierre, teacher in the said schools, and the sister of Master Bastien, who decided to espouse themselves in the congregation of the faithful. Nevertheless, since they are both foreigners, there was some doubt about signing their banns. Resolved that this be sent to the Consistory." On April 21 (R.C. 35, f. 565) the Council ordered: "Concerning the marriage contracted between them, having had sufficient testimony and information about them, ordered that their said marriage should take effect." This marriage was then contested in Consistory by Tevenon Nycod; see below, May 2, 1542. Etiennette Castellion's husband was named Pierre Moussard and was a native of Charité-sur-Loire (Nièvre). He made his living as a teacher in Geneva and later in Ville la Grand and Morges. He was admitted to the bourgeoisie of Geneva on June 8, 1553, and died between 1560 and 1563. The Moussards had eight children, the first of whom, Anna, was born on May 1, 1543 (BUISSON I, pp. 181-182).

Sébastien Castellion (ca. 1515-1563), native of Saint Martin du Fresne (Ain), became a regent of schools of Geneva in 1541, but was deposed in 1544 because of conflicts between him and Calvin. He continued to be an adversary of Calvin, especially during and after the Servetus affair, and is also known as a translator of the Bible and advocate of religious tolerance.

Monsieur George Poutex, De La Verchiere and Mychiel Morand, religious from Satigny, appeared.[183]

And asked about their duty to God and how they serve the church and why they do not want to read the passion during Communion. Answer that no one gave them the book and they do not have it and do not have a New Testament, and that they are poor. And how they instruct their people in the faith. And they said the Pater, and the confession in a general way. Monsieur George said the commandments in Latin poorly. Monsieur Verchiere similarly; he said the commandments well in French. Monsieur Morand said . . .[184] and could not say the Ten Commandments. [f. 20] The preachers gave them proper admonitions that the Council has been advised to admonish them. Admonished whether they have any scruples about the present law of the Reformation. Answer that they have not. All three were enjoined to get books and the commandments of God and the New Testament, so there will be no more bad reports about them.

Pierre Reclans, called Claret, baker.

Asked where his wife is and why she does not live with him and how long ago she left him. Answers that it was a year ago at Christmas and that she is in Veigy and that he has not seen her for three years and that she [sic] had a daughter by her. And that she left him of her evil will and that she destroyed his goods and that he would indeed love her except that she does not behave well. And said that he would do what the Council commanded

---

183. Poutex, Verchiere, and Morand had been canons of the priory of Satigny before the Reformation; concerning this priory see the note above under April 13, 1542. They had already been summoned to Council for having persisted in the Catholic faith. Georges Poutex was imprisoned on May 12, 1536, for having said Mass (*R.C.* XIII, p. 569). On August 29, 1541, the Council reproached all three for their absence from sermons and encouraged them to live "according to God" under the threat of removing their prebends [R.C. 35, f. 297 (August 29, 1541)]. At the same time Verchiere was accused first of concubinage, then of adultery with his maid [*ibid.* and R.C. 35, f. 308 (September 2, 1541)]. In 1543 Verchiere and Morand were named foresters at Peney [R.C. 37, f. 87 and f. 90v (May 8 and 14, 1543)]. On February 13, 1544 (see below *ad diem*), Verchiere became a warden of the church of Satigny, and was one still in 1550. He was still living on October 3, 1560 [R.Consist. 5, f. 13 (March 27, 1550); R.Consist. 17, f. 156]. On February 21, 1545, George Poutex was beheaded for having raped a poor 12-year-old girl (CAHIER-BUCCELLI, "Ombre," p. 384). [Translator: I have used the word "warden" to translate the French "*garde.*" The *gardes* of the churches were mainly concerned with supervising the morals of the parishioners and reporting deficiencies to the local castellans and ultimately the Consistory. Their duties were not much like those of English churchwardens, but "guard" would not be a very good translation either.]

184. Words omitted.

him. And if the Council would like, he prays that it send to the *bailli* of Thonon[185] to send her back, and he would take her back. And he did not know his faith or his creed in Latin or in French. Said also that his wife bought many goods and he believes with his money, because he had 12 *bossets* of wine and she took the money. The Consistory advises that he go to seek his wife if he can get her, or if not they will write to the *bailli* of Thonon to have her come here to the Consistory, and that she live with her husband, and that he come to catechism at St. Peter's to learn his faith with the others.

Robellaz Falcaz.

To know where she received Communion and why she limps. Answers that her husband sent to seek her on the eve of Easter and that she fell on the Arve Bridge and hurt herself, so she limps. And that Lord Syndic Rozet gave her permission to go there. And she did not take Communion or hear Mass, either in Machand or elsewhere, and she submits to losing her head and being banished from the city [sic]. [f. 20v] Said her Pater and faith[186] in French according to the new Reformation, and has never spoken any evil of the Word of God or the preachers or the Gospel, and this is under the same penalty.[187] She was given proper remonstrances; if she does otherwise the Seigneurie will attend to it.

Master Michiel the saddler and his nephew.[188]

Why he and his nephew have been in conflict for a long time, and various other questions. Answers that he pardons his said nephew although he

185. Nicolas de Diesbach was *bailli* of Thonon from November 1537 to July 1543 (HERMINJARD IV, p. 314, n. 1, and IX, p. 168, n. 1). The Bernese created six *bailliages* in their conquered territory in 1536, one of which was Thonon. The courts of the *baillis* "were composed of the castellan of the district and *assistant-jurés* chosen from property-holders of the district approved by the Bernese administration. There was an appeal from this court to the *bailli,* from the *bailli* to the *boursier [général]* and from him to the *commissaires-députés*" (DUVAL, *Ternier,* pp. 87-88).

186. This folio begins with a passage struck from the text: "The lords preachers are of opinion that those who depart outside the territory of the Gospel should not be proceeded against. And that she should send to Lyon where he lives, and if she can have him, she should have him. And that she should live decently and should have news of him and of her also." This probably concerns the case of Françoyse Reys (see above, April 13, 1542). The passage which follows, commencing with "she said her Pater and faith," again concerns Robellaz Falcaz.

187. That is, banishment.

188. Michel Julliard, saddler, from Jonzier (H.-S.), received into the bourgeoisie on June 10, 1502 (*L.B.,* p. 148), and member of the CC for the Poissonnerie [*R.C.* XIII, p. 455 (February 22, 1536)]. His nephew, Mermet Julliard, also from Jonzier and also a saddler, was admitted to the bourgeoisie on April 30, 1543 (R.C. 37, f. 78).

has caused him much pain, and that he will never be in his company, and that he has not taken Communion three or four times because of this quarrel, and that he took it last time. The Consistory, the preachers having given the said Michiel strict admonitions, exhorted him to pardon his said nephew entirely according to the commandment of God for the offenses his said nephew has committed against him for the honor of Jesus Christ. Answers that for the love of God he pardons him entirely for the injuries he has done him. And also that he go to the sermons, and answers that he can hardly go there because he is ill.

The nephew was asked what grudge or resentment he has felt against his uncle for a long time, and other things. Answers that he carries no hate against his uncle and that he does him all the favors he can, but that he is not pleased with him and does not care about him, and that he does him all the honor he can and has begged mercy on his knees from his [f. 21] uncle and that he wants to pardon him also, and promises that he will never give any displeasure either to him or his aunt. And they pardoned each other and embraced and expressed love for each other and left together.

Aymoz Cortagier.[189]

Because of the faith and frequenting of sermons and other things involving the Reformation of the church and whether he has any scruples.[190] Answers that he has no scruples and that he goes to sermons and makes his daughters learn the evangelical faith and takes them to the school,[191] and that he wants to live according to the evangelical Reformation. Remanded to persevere in serving God, and having his . . .[192]

Noble Pierre Mygerandi[193] *and Jane, his sister.*

Because of the marriage mentioned above, having explained why and responded. Jane answers that she swore faith to and promised her husband two

189. Aymoz Cortagier, citizen, died on January 5, 1560, at age 50 (GALIFFE I, p. 450; E.C., Morts 3, p. 3).

190. Translator: That is, whether he has no doubts about following Reformed practices. This question of "scruples" recurs frequently, and is regularly stated in this way.

191. According to Liliane Mottu-Weber: "Girls had to wait a long time for public instruction in Geneva; during the period we are treating only a few small local schools, replaced for boys by the Collège, were open to them. They learned to read the Bible, to write a little and, if possible, arithmetic" (MOTTU-WEBER, "Femmes," p. 391).

192. Incomplete sentence.

193. Pierre Migerand, member of the CC in 1538, sworn as notary on April 25, 1545, syndic in 1556, 1560, and 1564, lieutenant in 1562, died in 1566 (SORDET, *Dictionnaire*, p. 920; ROGET, lists of councillors; R.G.S. I, p. 165).

years ago. Asked if it pleases her brother that the affair should proceed as she claims. Asked whether she has received Holy Communion and why. Answers that it is for the love of Our Lord. The said Pierre says it was about five or six years ago that they promised themselves in marriage and that he was not there. She was admonished to strive to serve God and that she not go looking for her damnation, considering that she has received and confesses having received Holy Communion. And that she not renounce Jesus Christ to go worship idols, not to do otherwise and turn aside, because the Consistory forwards it [to the Council]; that the Seigneurie will not consent to it, according to the edicts enacted. And between now and tomorrow their lordships will examine the matter in Council, and may God help her to turn to good counsel.[194]

21v] *Uguynaz Depontelaz and the bastard daughter of Monsieur Jehan Amyci.*

Whether they go to sermons and serve God and how they recommend themselves to God. Answer that they go to sermons. The Bastard answers that she had a child by Monsieur De La Bastie[195] and that she had it nursed by La Coquete(?) and that she paid 12 florins per year and that Monsieur Jehan should pay the rest at his cost and from his money. And that Monsieur De La Bastie gives her nothing and expelled her from his house. And how they live, because there is evidence of their bad behavior, and they will be led through the city in miters if they do not govern themselves more decently than they do. And that many young men go to them both by day and night at all hours, and as fornicators they will be driven from the city dishonorably. The Consistory exhorted them to frequent the Word of God and to avoid such gallants, who should not enter into their uncle's house. And that they serve God and recommend themselves to the Lord, living decently according to God and his commandments.[196]

194. The Council had decided to return the Migerands to the Consistory in its session of April 17, 1542 (R.C. 35, f. 559). Following the advice of the Consistory, on April 21, 1542, the Council refused to publish the banns in Geneva "because they should be published in La Roche in the papistry" (R.C. 35, f. 565).

195. François Champion, Seigneur de la Bastie [R.C. 34, f. 142v (March 19, 1540); R.C. 36, f. 118v (September 12, 1542)].

196. Huguyne Dupont was the daughter of Claude Dupont and niece of the two Amici brothers, both of whom were former priests of Geneva and both of whom were named Jean. The second Huguyne, also called "the Bastard," was the daughter of one of the two Jean Amicis. The two brothers lived in one house and, although Jean Amici the younger was known for his amorous adventures before the Reform, there is nothing to establish which of the two was the father of the "Bastard" (see NAEF, *Origines* II, p. 311, n. 1, and p. 352; FROMENT, p. 157).

In her deposition the Amicis' maid, Françoyse Perrod, states that Jean François

Jaques Carre in the dizaine of Longemale, merchant of this city, bourgeois of Geneva, dealing in merchandise such as salt, wheat, iron and other things.[197]

And he goes to sermons. And he is from Vandoeuvres and married and has children. Four years ago he married a girl from St. Gervais. And he goes to the sermons here at St. Peter's and the Magdalen. And knows his Pater in the Reformation. And that his wife goes, but she cannot go there because of the child she is nursing, and she knows only the Pater. And that he knows about broken bones, dislocations and fractures and says that his father was a surgeon like his father, and that he makes plasters from virgin wax and certain herbs and uses wax to draw bad humors from illnesses and that he never uses talismans or charms. Says that he has used them to cure [f. 22] fractures,

---

Ramel had slept with both the Huguynes, but more often with "the older," that is Huguine Dupont, niece of the Amicis. In 1550 Huguyne, daughter of Claude Dupont, wife of Pierre Rosset, became pregnant during the absence of her husband, who had then been living in Strasbourg for seven years and who said he had not seen his wife for two years. She denied the charge and admitted that she "was accused of having slept with Jean Françoys Ramel, but it was not true and was never proved or could be proved." Rosset asked for a divorce, but without going to England he could not prove that he had not slept with his wife. The cost of the voyage being too great for him, he lacked proof, and the divorce was not granted. Nevertheless Huguyne Dupont was banished, but she returned "every day" to see her lover Jean Maillard. In September 1551 she was readmitted to Geneva, and already on October 14 the Council reported that men "go to the said Huguyne's house to fornicate" [P.C. 2ᵉ sér., 924 (January 26-28, 1551); R.Consist. 5, f. 84, f. 92v, f. 106v (December 4 and 23, 1550, January 22, 1551); R.C. 45, f. 235 (March 26, 1551), R.C. 46, f. 1v, f. 117v, f. 287 (July 6, September 17, October 14, 1551)]. In 1558 the Council granted her permission to remarry, having been abandoned by Pierre Rosset, but a little later she was banished again for having stolen a piece of linen. As usual she denied the charge [R.C. 54, f. 257v (August 15, 1558), P.C. 1ᵉ sér., 798 (February 14-24, 1559)].

The younger Huguyne was the daughter of Jean Amici. The maid Françoyse Perrod said that "the younger Hugyyne already has had a child, which she has seen in the house," probably the child of M. de La Bastie mentioned above. She said that Jean Villiet, gilder, slept with the younger Huguyne, and that the son of "Jehan Pictiod" (Jean Chautemps called Pitiod) and Joffrey Levin, called Joffrey Franch [R.C. 36, f. 3 (May 2, 1542)], also visited both Huguynes, but that "the said two uncles knew nothing" [P.C. 2ᵉ sér., 547 (May 2, 1542)]. The Council condemned the two Huguynes and their lovers to prison (R.C. 36, f. 3, *ad diem*). The register says that "the niece of Don Amici" was freed on May 9 (R.C. 36, f. 8), but this is more likely the Bastard, because she is identified as the mistress of Jean Villet and because on May 19, 1542, Huguyne Dupont, *i.e.,* Jean Amici's niece, was freed (R.C. 36, f. 17v).

197. Jaques Pichard, called Carre, from Bonvard (GE), was admitted to the bourgeoisie on April 9, 1540 (*L.B.*, p. 220). He was dead at the time of the death of his daughter, then three weeks old, on November 8, 1566 (E.C., Morts 7, p. 23).

but that he has never used them with any other charm, and he submits to punishment if anyone finds otherwise. And that he has never used charms, and what he has done for his patients is for the love of God. And he could not say his Pater or anything else. The Consistory ordered him to learn the Lord's Prayer and his faith and creed so he can teach his children. And that he, his children, his wife and his household go to catechism on Sunday with the others.

Those who did not appear last Thursday, April 20.

Puvel's widow;[198] Mermeta Jappaz; Brectaz; the wife of Jaques the pack-saddler;[199] Jehan Du Nant the host of the Stag;[200] Foy's servant.

Those summoned for today who did not appear.

Jehan Du Nant the goitered, cobbler, *dizainier,* and his wife from the Poissonerie; Cortagier's wife;[201] Jane who was a maid of François Gerin.[202]

Those summoned for Thursday, April 27.

The maid of the mistress of the girls on the Rhône Bridge;[203] Jehan and Claude Curtet; the servant of Master Michiel the saddler on the Molard and the wife of the said Michiel the saddler;[204] Villieta's son[205] and the son of Jehan Loys Ramel the younger.[206]

f. 22v]

Thursday, April 27, 1542

Lord Pertemps, syndic.
Calvin, Viret, Bernard, Champereaulx.
Britillion, D'Orsiere, Frochet, Tacon, Blandin, Pensabin, the officer Vovrey.

---

198. Pernete Puvel, widow of Pierre.
199. Tevenete, wife of Jaques Emyn, pack-saddler.
200. His name is struck from the text.
201. Jane Bertherat, wife of Aymoz Cortagier.
202. Possibly Jana Bovier; see below, May 11, 1542.
203. Marguerite Vignon. The following passage is struck from the manuscript: "The maid of the mistress . . . the wife of the said Michiel the saddler."
204. Michel Julliard, saddler, his wife Claudaz, and his servant Jean de la Pierre.
205. Jehan Villiet.
206. Jean François Ramel, son of Noble Jean Louis Ramel the younger, member of the CC in 1546, grandson of Jean Louis Ramel, first syndic in 1523, 1527, and 1532 (GALIFFE I, pp. 459-460).

Claudaz, wife of Master Michel Julliard the saddler.

Asked to give an explanation of her faith and about the quarrel between her husband and Mermet, their nephew, and why she has a grudge.
Answers that the said Mermet said vicious things to her but that she wishes
him no harm and that she wishes him no harm [sic] and pardons him
freely. Said the Lord's Prayer in her native tongue not very well, and says
she knows the confession in Latin, and that she always takes Communion
for the love of God. The Consistory advises that she be reconciled with her
nephew Mermet. And touching the faith, that she frequent the sermons and
come to catechism on Sunday with the others. And that she be admonished
about the hypocrisy of her peace with her nephew Mermet. And that Monsieur Pierre Viret, Britillion and Frochet be assigned to reconcile them and
that they be remanded to Monday after the sermon at the Magdalen so they
can live in peace together.

Mauris Chastel of Cruseilles.[207]

Has submitted a supplication and asks as contained in it. Said many
words. The supplication begins: "Respectable . . ." The said Laurence[208] answers concerning his request that she did not know him and does not know
what this is, because the letter of marriage that Vulliodi received . . .[209] And
she said [f. 23] that he married another wife three years ago and that information should be obtained about this and many other words that would be
tedious to write down. Responded that the contract of marriage was made in
Presinge and that he never wanted to help her with anything and that she
married him. The said Mauris has often called on her to go live with him and
that he has many women at his command. The said Laurence answers that he
came when he wanted and then left for a long time and then returned and
that he never wanted to bring her to his house in Cruseilles and that she always received him when he came to her and that he always wanted the goods
she had. When separated from the said Mauris the said Laurence said that
the said Mauris is detested and that he wanted to have another wife and that
three years ago he espoused another and that she does not consider him her
husband because he never did her any good. The advice of the Consistory is
that inquiries be made to determine whether the said marriage should continue and that she be remanded to Thursday to bring her witnesses to justify

207. Called later Mauris Du Chastel and, in a Latinized form, nobilissimum
Mauricium de Castro; see below, May 4, 1542.
208. Laurence Viongiere.
209. Incomplete sentence.

her testimony and that the said Laurence bring her proofs that he married elsewhere. And that the said Laurence obtain the truth about the other wife and that she follow him, since the marriage was long ago. And that she have certification that he is married to another wife and bring her witnesses and some affidavit. That both be remanded to Thursday.

Summon:

Brodiose;[210] Sobreta; Nycolas Porat. Should summon Jehan, who has made pregnant . . .[211]; Jaques Combaz; Jaques the pack-saddler.[212]

23v] *The officers of Peney: Pierre Baud, Claude Joly from Malval, Claude Dufour from Bourdigny, and Claude Poutex from Choully, and Claude Dufour, officer, called Cachevallie, and those sitting in the court of Peney.[213]*

Concerning the knowledge of God, because they are to do justice, whether they fear God and have received Communion. The lieutenant said

210. Possibly Reniere, wife of Jean Veillard, embroiderer, often called simply "the embroiderer."

211. Name omitted by the scribe. Jehan is probably Jehan Benez, vine-dresser for Jean Du Mollard; he had made Jana, daughter of Aymon Grenier, pregnant; she was also a servant of Jean Du Mollard. See below, later in this session.

212. Jaques Emyn, pack-saddler.

213. These are the *assistants* and the officer of the court of the castellan of Peney, having jurisdiction over the villages of Malval, Bourdigny, and Choully. According to the *Encyclopédie de Genève:* "in the Genevan lands, the castellan opened criminal cases, arrested and interrogated suspects, transmitted the dossier to the Small Council of the city. In minor cases, where the crime only merited a fine, the castellan judged the case himself." "The castellan administered justice surrounded by a tribunal composed of a 'lieutenant' and of several assessors called 'assistants.' While the castellan was normally a citizen of the city, the lieutenant and the *assistants* were rather inhabitants [of the *châtellenie*], chosen from the principal notables of the place. They were named by the government of the city." The "officer" was "the local chief of police, who . . . cited the accused and the plaintiffs to appear in court, made arrests, functioned on occasion as jailer" (*Encyclopédie de Genève* II, pp. 72-73; see also PONCET, *Châtelains,* pp. 92-105).

The names Dufour, Baud, and Poutex being very common in these villages, it is impossible to identify these individuals with certainty. A Claude Poutex was curé of Satigny and also of Peney before the Reform. The warden of the church of Satigny was also named Claude Poutex in 1550, and this may be the same man. See CAHIER-BUCCELLI, "Ombre," p. 384, and R.Consist. 5, f. 13 (March 27, 1550). Apparently the two Claude Dufours had some office in 1537, and possibly the same under the Bernese (they were called to attend at the exchange of the arms of Bern for those of Geneva at the priory of Satigny). In any case, Claude Dufour, called Cachevallie, became officer of Peney in 1540. Pierre Baud and Claude Dufour of Choully were again *assistants* in 1543. See R.C. 30, f. 223 (May 3, 1537); R.C. 34, f. 123 (March 8, 1540); R.C. 37, f. 87 and f. 90v (May 8 and 14, 1543).

that he goes to the preaching of the sermon when he can. And the senior said that he did not receive Communion this Easter because he was in a bad location because he is a long way from the place where Communion is given because of the Allondon.[214] And he said the Pater in Latin. The others went to the sermon and took Communion and said the Lord's Prayer and the Credo and Pater in the vulgar tongue. The Consistory resolves that they do their duty better so that God may be honored, considering that they are officers of justice, to show an example to others. And that they learn their faith, and be remanded in three weeks to see how they have profited in religion, and that they go to catechism when it is held, and that wardens[215] be sent to make them come and that they all be made to attend preaching.

Marguerite, daughter of Aymoz Vignon, maid of the mistress of the girls from La Sémine in Quincy.

Asked why she does not believe her mistress and mistress [sic] and does not bother about God or his Word and does not frequent the sermons. Answered that she was at St. Peter's last Sunday and it was Champereaulx, and said her Pater in the vulgar tongue and her creed fairly well. Given proper remonstrances that she go willingly to the sermon and the catechism at St. Gervase every Sunday with the others.

[f. 24] *Jehan de La Pierre, saddler, servant of Master Michiel Julliard, saddler on the Molard.*

Why and for what reason he and the said Michel, saddler, are in conflict and what he . . .[216] Answers that he is always forced to make peace between them and that he does not want to believe him and that he does not know their desire or their will and that the said Michiel sent to him to come live here with him to serve him and that they are at peace with each other at this time. The Consistory remanded him to appear with his said master and mistress and the said nephew on Monday at the Magdalen after the sermon.

Jehan Curtet, butcher.

To know why he and his brother do not live together in peace. Answers that he wants to live like respectable people and does not want to do otherwise.

214. The Allondon, a small river in the Genevan countryside that issues into the Rhône near Russin.
215. The wardens of the church, charged with enforcing the ordinances for the discipline of the rural churches; see *R.C.P.* I, pp. 14-21.
216. Incomplete sentence.

Claude Curtet, cutler, concerning the said conflict, why he did not appear in the congregation the Sunday before Easter with the others at St. Gervase. Answers that he does not love his said brother and that they are at law before the lieutenant and that he has a great hatred for him. And that his brother blamed him severely because their mother was a respectable woman and [that] I [sic] was the cause of the loss of Vétraz[217] and that he did so much against Monsieur François Goyet[218] that he had an affidavit against him. And he did not receive Holy Communion last Easter and does not say his Pater because he wishes harm to his brother and when he sees his brother he thinks he sees his hostility. The Lord Syndic admonished him to make an agreement with his brother and that they pardon each other and behave as respectable people should and submit themselves to the judgment of respectable people. Answers that touching the criminal case he will do nothing, and as for other matters he would indeed want it if he wants to live in the fear of God. [f. 24v] The Consistory advises that they be reconciled in amity by respectable people and that Lord Bandiere,[219] captain general, name them. And they declare him to be outside the union of the faithful, and considering this the preachers do not hold him as belonging to religion, and in view of his bad heart that he be proceeded against more rigorously by the Seigneurie. And that men be assigned to reconcile them, as otherwise there would be great scandal. And was admonished to expel all his rage from his heart. Nevertheless he agreed to do his duty and that their difference be examined into and that his honor should always be maintained with respect to the Council and that he will do what he ought to.

Jehan Curtet said of the said injury that he was associated in the administration of Vétraz and that Monsieur François Goyet drew him up a re-

217. The seizure of the *mandement* of Thyez (H.-S) by the king of France, Vétraz being a village of the *mandement.* The king of France having seized "without justification" certain "vineyards of Rive, being in Vétraz" on August 31, 1540, the Seigneurie sent Pierre Vandel to Chambéry to plead their case. On December 20, 1540, Vandel reported "that he could not obtain justice" (R.C. 34, f. 414v and f. 565v). In the end the Seigneurie sent Jean Ami Curtet to the king's court, again without result (see J.-A. GAUTIER III, p. 205; ROGET I, pp. 198-201). Claude Curtet had been rent farmer of Vétraz [R.C. 35, f. 76v and f. 100v (February 15 and March 4, 1541)].

218. François Goyet, canon of the chapter of the cathedral of Geneva, withdrew to Annecy with the other canons at the Reform. On May 1, 1536, the Council ordered that "the affidavits against Claude Curtet made in Annecy in the case of Vétraz be dismissed" (R.C. 36, f. 1). For Goyet see NAEF, *Origines* II, pp. 85 and 402.

219. Noble Amied Bandières, councillor in 1532, captain general in 1534, 1540, 1543, 1544, syndic in 1535 and 1541; he died in 1544, and according to Galiffe was "one of the most zealous defenders of liberty" (GALIFFE I, p. 22; J.-A. GAUTIER III, pp. 96, 163, and 214).

cognizance for 100 écus. Ordered by the Consistory that the syndic open proceedings and bring him here for Tuesday and concerning this investigate whether there was an injury or not.[220]

Jehan Du Nant, host of the Stag.[221]

Why he does not appear as often as he is summoned. And touching frequenting of sermons because he keeps an inn, and that God is not honored in his house and that he is like the others in the papistry. Answers that he has nothing to do with the papistry and will not permit it and there is no gaming in his house. Said his Pater in French not very well and his creed like his Pater, little and rather badly. The Consistory gave him proper admonitions to teach service to God in his house and to frequent the sermons and to learn his faith better and that his family, servants and maids go to catechism on Sunday at the Magdalen with the others. [f. 25] Claudaz, wife of Jehan Du Nant, treated as her husband was above.

Jane, daughter of Aymoz Greniez, of Prégny.

Whose is the child she bears and whether she has had any other. Answers that it is by Jehan, who lives at the house of Monsieur Jehan Du Molard,[222] and she has been pregnant since last August, and he is a sufficiently honest man to perform what he promises. And that he dresses vines for the said Du Molard, and that it will not be more than six weeks [to the birth], and that she has had no other, and he gave her drink in the name of marriage and gave her a silver ring. Remanded to next Tuesday in the Consistory, and summon the said Jehan.

220. The case of Claude and Jehan Curtet was examined in Consistory several times. The Curtets were called to Council because of their dispute on September 20, 1541 (R.C. 35, f. 332v), and May 1, 1542 (R.C. 36, f. 1). The Council tried to reconcile them by means of "remonstrances." Jean and Claude Curtet were sons of Jean Curtet, called Mauboys, butcher, who died before October 22, 1535 (*R.C.* XIII, p. 329). Claude was elected to the Council of LX for the *dizaine* "sus le Pont" on February 22, 1536 (*R.C.* XIII, p. 454), and in 1540 was banner-carrier for Claude Salaz, captain of Saint Gervais [R.C. 34, f. 368 (August 4, 1540)]. Jehan Curtet, member of the CC for St. Gervais, a butcher like his father, died in 1552 [R.C. 30, f. 194 (March 20, 1537); R.C. 35, f. 489v (February 7, 1542); E.C., Morts 1, p. 259 (October 24, 1552)].

221. There was a Jehan Corajod, called Du Nant, cobbler and *dizainier* in the Poissonnerie or Mollard (the same quarter) like the Jehan Du Nant here. However, he was the host of the Golden Lion and the husband of one Jana, and not the host of the Stag and husband of Claudaz like this Jehan Du Nant. For Jehan Corajod see below, August 3, 1542.

222. Jehan Benez of Cranves. He appeared again in Consistory on July 13, 1542, but on that occasion the register says that he lived at the house of Monsieur Hudriod Du Mollard, Jean's brother. For the Du Mollards see GALIFFE I, p. 231.

Pernete Gremire.[223]

Andrea, daughter of Jehan Janin of Cologny.[224]

Touching the Pater. Answered satisfactorily.
The others summoned were remanded to next Tuesday.

About the quarrel of Monsieur Coquet with Don Hugoneri.[225]

That Monsieur Calvin and Monsieur Hudrio Du Molard and D'Orsieres be assigned to bring them to an agreement.

[f. 25v]   **Tuesday, May 2, 1542**

Syndic Pertemps.
Calvin, Viret, Bernard, Henri, Champereaulx.
D'Orsieres, Pensabin, Frochet, the officer Vovrey.

Amyed Darnex of Bourdigny, living in Satigny.

Because of a child kept six years without baptism. If he has a child.
Answers that he has two sons and two daughters, one daughter about six
years old called Claudaz who was baptized last Sunday, and she was still
named Claudaz. And he was sorry because a woman had baptized her, and

223. Incomplete sentence.
224. Speaking of Jean Collognier or Cologny, called Janin, Henri Naef says: "'young
and of small stature, a maker of pikes, lances, javelins and arrows,' the armorer surren-
dered himself to intense proselytism. He was a Genevan and seems to have had as a family
name, or actually a name of origin, Cologny or Colognier, Janin being only a diminutive
to distinguish him from his father, whose first name was Jean like his. Colognier was accused [in April 1533] of various impertinent actions. He was heard, during one of the
Lenten sermons, to criticize moderately the Dominican from Auxerre . . . Another time
Janin contradicted the religious 'in the very pulpit, in the church of the Jacopins'" (NAEF,
Origines II, p. 416). Janin was also accused of anabaptism; see BALKE; also GEISENDORF,
Annalistes, pp. 416, 421, 426; J.-A. GAUTIER II, pp. 427, 528.
225. Jean Coquet, member of the party of independence and of the Reform, member
of the LX in 1519, councillor in 1526, syndic in 1527 and 1533, first syndic in 1539 and 1543,
died suddenly on September 26, 1546 (GALIFFE II, pp. 172-173). Jehan Hugonier, former
priest, rallied to the Reform and was one of the first priests to marry (with Marie Bertherati)
[*R.C.* XII, p. 557 *(notes complémentaires)* and *R.C.* XIII, pp. 461-462 (February 23, 1536)].
The dispute between Coquet and Hugonier may go back to 1537 or even earlier: on January
22, 1537, "Jehan Hugonier and at his request Noble Jehan Coquet promised to follow the law
and do what will be decided in the case of the goods of Don Guillaume de Vegio, between
him, Jo. d'Arlod, the wife of Piard and others with an interest" (R.C. 30, f. 155).

the preacher told them the said baptism had not taken place.[226] And that he did it from ignorance and that the mother died, and the woman who baptized her was named Clauda. The Consistory advises that he be put in prison to learn more from him and that he make a public apology and be admonished. Also it would be good, if there are others, to identify them, and to announce that if there is any child to be baptized it should be brought for baptism, and proclaim these rules,[227] and that he be remanded to Thursday and that he frequent the sermons. Asked if he knows or has heard about any other child at his house who is yet to be baptized. Answers that if he knew of any others he would tell the Seigneurie. And that he frequents the sermons.

Jehanete, widow of Jehan de Thouz, Pernete wife of Claude Darnex of Bourdigny, Mayaz wife of Jehan Darnex[228] of Bourdigny were asked why the aforesaid girl was kept so long. Answers that the said Amyed told her about it, and she told him that he must baptize her, which he did, and spoke to the preacher about it, and she was godmother of the said Claudaz. Said her Pater [f. 26] in the French tongue and the confession fairly well. They were admonished to frequent the sermons.

Roletaz Falliodaz, wife of George Bovagnie, baker.[229]

Asked about the unhappiness of her daughter. Answers that she bears her no ill will and that she did the best for her that she could. Said her Pater in French and the creed rather badly. The Consistory advises that the daughter be summoned and that the mother admonish her daughter. And remanded to next Thursday.[230]

---

226. Encouraged by Farel, the Council prohibited baptism by midwives in 1537. The ordinances for the discipline of churches in the countryside of 1547 added that "if the midwives usurp the office of baptism, they should be recalled or punished appropriately to their crimes, and it [the baptism] held as null, considering that the authorization is not given to them," a principle already applied here [*S.D.* II, p. 333 (January 16, 1537); *R.C.P.* I, p. 16 (May 17, 1547); also in *S.D.* II, p. 502].

227. These rules are not found in the public registers. The Consistory, like the Council and all the town governments of Europe, always feared the anabaptists and, therefore, all unbaptized infants. On October 26, 1541, the ministers had "revealed that in Geneva there is a girl of the age of five who is still not baptized," and the Council resolved to inquire about it (R.C. 35, f. 370). For the anabaptists in Geneva, see BALKE.

228. There was a Guillaume Darnex, son of the late Jehan, from Bourdigny, farm laborer, admitted to the bourgeoisie on November 26, 1562 (*L.B.*, p. 273).

229. George Bovagnie, from La Mura (H.-S.), admitted to the bourgeoisie on December 3, 1535 (*R.C.* XIII, p. 370).

230. "And remanded to next Thursday" is struck from the manuscript.

Jehan Villiet.[231]

Because of the fornication at Monsieur Jehan's house. Answers that he has not been there in over a month and that he has not been there since he went there with a relative of his. The Consistory advises that he be proceeded against more sharply, since he does not tell the truth, and that he be admonished and remanded to the Council to learn the truth. Said that he never slept there and never touched anyone and would not deign to do it.

Master Pierre, teacher.[232]

Because of a woman who has denounced him about her banns. Answers. Remanded to next Thursday.

The quarrels of the Curtets.

The syndic reported that the Council was in disagreement over whether the lawsuit should be stopped, and that they be reconciled with regard to other matters and brought to agreement if possible.[233] [f. 26v] Claude Curtet appeared. Was admonished to live in union with his brother Jehan. Answers that as for money matters, he wants to agree with his brother if he can. And as for the question of dishonor pending before the Seigneurie, he wants to do nothing and would be pleased to pardon his brother, and that the suit should take its course. Remanded to Thursday with his brother.

231. Jehan Villiet is here accused of having had sexual relations with Huguyne Depontelaz and Huguyne, bastard daughter of Jean Amici; see above, April 20, 1542. After Villiet had been imprisoned with Jehan François Ramel, accused of the same crime, the Council resolved on May 4, 1542, to require Villiet and Ramel to answer the charges (R.C. 36, f. 4). They were freed on May 8, 1542 (R.C. 36, f. 6v), after paying fines of five écus for Ramel and three for Villiet. The money was sent to the Consistory.
232. Pierre Moussard, schoolteacher; see below the case between him and Tevenon Nycod.
233. The previous day the Council had resolved to try to reconcile the brothers Curtet, to punish "the offender" (Claude Curtet) "for a time," and to return them to the Consistory for admonitions. Finally, the Council had ordered that "the case between them pending before the lieutenant should be delayed and the affidavits against Claude Curtet made at Annecy in the case of Victra should be dismissed." It appears here that the Council changed its mind (being "in disagreement") and decided that the case should continue [R.C. 36, f. 1 (May 1, 1542)].

Tevenon, daughter of Pierre Nycod[234] the bootmaker, living in Rive on the Rue Verdaine.

Because of Master Pierre the teacher of the school whom she . . .[235] That he do as he promised and take her in marriage. And that a long time ago when he came to keep the school a man, Master Estienne,[236] advised her to defend herself against the said Pierre. And that she had a child by Anthoyne who lived at the hospital and had other children by brother Ensis,[237] a religious of Rive. And the said child died during the Masses,[238] and she bears one in her belly who is by the said Master Pierre. And that she had the said Master Pierre told that if he wanted her to give him anything she would not refuse. And he answered that he would do what would be commanded. Asked whether there is any promise of marriage with the said Master Pierre and whether she [is] pregnant, and since when. Answers that the said Master Pierre promised her to do what a respectable man should do. And that there is no other promise and he did not give her anything, or to drink, and that she slept with him four times and that she has felt the child. And that the child she bears is his and that he should take it and nurse it and that she was pregnant by him from All Saints' Day to Christmas. The Consistory advises that she wait until there is more evidence of a child and that then Master Pierre do his duty by the child and that Master Pierre's marriage run its course. And that she be remanded until there is a stronger appearance of the child.

[f. 27] *Jana, wife of Cortagiez.*[239]

Because of frequenting of sermons. Answers that she was at the sermon on Sunday and Monday at St. Gervase and does not know what the preacher

234. Probably Pierre Nycod, alias Garnier, cobbler, admitted to the bourgeoisie on September 17, 1504 (*L.B.,* p. 154).

235. Incomplete sentence. Pierre Moussard was, with Estienne Roz or Roph (mentioned below), one of the schoolteachers supervised by Sébastien Castellion [R.C. 35, f. 521v (March 9, 1542)].

236. Estienne Roz, schoolteacher in Geneva since June 20, 1541 (R.C. 35, f. 240v, and below, July 13, 1542).

237. Egidius Ensis, guardian of the friary of Rive in 1527 [*R.C.* X, p. 523 (December 19, 1527)]. According to Abbé Chavaz he was a doctor and already guardian of Rive in 1518; see the list of guardians presented by Chavaz in GONTHIER, "Obituaire," pp. 237-238. Ensis was still living in Geneva in 1534 [*R.C.* XII, p. 476 (February 15, 1534)].

238. That is, before the suppression of the Mass in Geneva on August 10, 1535.

239. Jane, daughter of Pierre Bertherat and Péronette Pecolat, wife of Aymoz Cortagier (GALIFFE I, p. 450).

said. And that she has learned her faith and Pater as said now, and said the Pater in French and the Credo very poorly. She was admonished.

Those remanded for Thursday, May 4, 1542.

Marriage of Noble Mauris Du Chate[l] of Cruseilles and Laurence Vyongiere, his wife; Master Pierre, teacher of children in Rive; Jehan and Claude Curtet; Jana,[240] mother of Percevaud, for the sermons; Myaz Santousaz. Remanded by Alexan[dre] the watchman.[241]

Those who must be summoned for Thursday.

Jehan, the vine-dresser of Monsieur Du Molard,[242] who has made pregnant Janne, daughter of Aymoz Grenier, from Prégny, living in Saint Gervaise; Jaques Combaz; Jaques the pack-saddler;[243] Pierre the cobbler who lives near the Molard;[244] Guilliama, widow of Bertheracti; the tailor Martin, near the Molard; the widow of Richardet;[245] Guilliama, wife of Jehan Jaquet, laborer; Myaz,[246] daughter of Falliodaz; Bellengier the archer; Jane, maid of François Girin;[247] Jane Tabarie in the Fusterie.

27v]

Thursday, May 4, 1542

Lord Syndic Pertemps.
Calvin, Viret, Henri.
Pensabin, Frochet, Blandin.

Master Pierre Clerc, cobbler.[248]

Because of the Pater, because Master Robert the pack-saddler[249] said in Rumilly that he did not know how to say his Pater and that . . .[250] Answers that he found two men in Rumilly who asked him about our law, and he an-

240. Jana, called below Pernon, widow of François Bovier (see below, May 4, 1542).
241. Probably Alexandre Davonex, watchman.
242. Jean Benez of Cranves, vine-dresser for Jean or Hudriod Du Mollard.
243. Jaques Emyn, pack-saddler.
244. Pierre Clerc, cobbler.
245. Bartholomée d'Orsières, widow of Claude Richardet.
246. Myaz de Bars, daughter of Roletaz Falliodaz.
247. Possibly Jana Bovier.
248. Pierre Clerc, from Contamine-sur-Arve (H.-S.), admitted to the bourgeoisie in 1514 (*L.B.,* p. 180).
249. Robert Breysson, pack-saddler.
250. Incomplete sentence.

swered that our law was better than theirs, and he said his Pater and confession fairly well. The Consistory admonished him to be careful what he says another time and to frequent the sermons and teach his children the evangelical doctrines carefully.

Johan Constant from Poitou in France, tailor, about . . .[251]

Answers touching muttering at the sermon that he says the passion, and that he can read and understand it in Latin and that he is more attached than he ever was to the Gospel and that he knows the Pater in Latin and the Ave Maria and his office of Prime, Terce, etc. The Consistory advises, considering his hypocrisy, that he come every Thursday to give an account of his faith and go every Sunday to catechism and that he be admonished more sharply and that he abstain from the sacraments until he is better informed.

[f. 28]   *Laurence Viongiers presented an affidavit.*[252]

Mauris Du Chastel appeared, who was asked if he had espoused another wife named Anna, daughter of Coppier,[253] of Crusilles, and he kept her two years and then she died, and that about three years ago it was announced here at the Magdalen why he could not do without a wife. He asks that he be freed from what Laurence put on him and that he earlier denied having espoused her. The Consistory advises that they be remanded to the Council, considering his falsity and great lies.

Resumption.[254]

Loyse asked as in her supplication. Pierre Magnin appeared and said that it is not so and that he did not promise himself to her, and she has had a child and he does not believe it is his, because she did not carry it the full time[255] and had it eight months ago, so it is not so. Loyse appeared and asks and tells him that he swore to her to . . . ,[256] and it was at the house of Monsieur Pierre de Sales in Genthod[257] at the hour of vespers, and then she came with him into this city.

---

251. Incomplete sentence. In the margin: "Morning."
252. For the copy of the affidavit see below at the end of this session.
253. Anna, daughter of Noble Aymon Coppier.
254. This concerns the matrimonial case of Pierre Magnin and Loyse Du Bioley, presented in Consistory on February 16, 1542.
255. *I.e.,* she had it less than nine months after they had sex.
256. Word omitted.
257. Noble Pierre de Sales, master of Loyse Du Bioley, was the husband of Georgea, daughter of Amé de Langin, Seigneur de Vigny. At the time of the Battle of Coppet in October 1535 Pierre and Georgea de Sales were made prisoners by the partisans of the city to

And he was Langin's receiver and she was a young lady in Langin's house, and they wanted to give him another but he refused her, and it was about two years ago on St. Maurice's Day. Pierre answers that one evening after supper they made some promises together, and she has had the child about a year, and he had her company on October 4. The said Loyse says that she has never had his company since he knew her on the said occasion and that she has carried it in her belly since Michaelmas or two days earlier or later. And he knew her in Genthod the morning after the swearing. And she had the child two days after St. Claude's Day in the month of June, Tuesday the eighth day of the month of June 1540. And he put the child to nurse and she paid the nurse and he contributed something and he gave her 18 *gros* when she . . .(?) [f. 28v] and she was badly advised to have done it before the ceremony. The Consistory having given proper admonitions, he consents by the will of their lordships of the Consistory to take her and marry her as God has ordered and that their banns be published.

The teacher of the school.[258]

The Consistory advises . . .[259]

Myaz Santouzaz.[260]

Answers that she was married to a husband who died, and François Perrissod of Contamine lived with her and promised and swore faith to her and gave her a *parpaillole*. And this was at the beginning of Lent, and she never knew him carnally because he never asked it, and he is a tailor. And the said François says he lives at Cortagier's house and that he did not promise her and did not give her the coin and there was no one there but the two of them. And that he has a brother who was ill and she nursed him in his illness and that this was after the promises, and they did not drink together in marriage. And said the Pater in our Reformed manner. The Consistory advises that she come next Thursday and that she go to the sermons.[261]

---

be exchanged for those Genevans taken by the Gentlemen of the Spoon. On March 21, 1536, Pierre de Sales asked to be "freed to withdraw to Genthod, considering that he is our subject and has sworn fidelity, and that he has no power whatever for the liberation of our said prisoners" [*R.C.* XIII, p. 501; see also *ibid.,* pp. 323-324 (October 11, 1535); TURRETINI and GRIVEL, pp. 132-133; FORAS, *Armorial* III, p. 236].

258. This may be the case between Tevenon Nycod and Pierre Moussard, school-teacher in Rive; see above, May 2, 1542.

259. Incomplete sentence.

260. Myaz Du Boule, called Santousaz.

261. On June 5, 1542 (R.C. 36, f. 31), the Council remanded this case to the next Monday, June 12, but there is no further trace of this affair.

Noble Bartholomie, widow of Richardet.[262]

Because of the sermons and the rosary, and that she always has fever and cannot go to the sermons and has had it for a year, and knows how to say only the Pater and not the confession. She was given proper remonstrances.

[f. 29] *Guilliama, wife of Bertheractie.*[263]

Has [fever?] like the preceding and said the Pater. Like the preceding.

Jana, widow of Jehan, farm laborer.

Did not acknowledge the rosary, and [said] that a woman named Jana Crosetaz had it and someone thought it was she. And said her Pater and confession in the form of the new Reformation in a general way, and goes to sermons. Like the preceding.

Pernon, widow of François Bovier,[264] *from Arenthon,* habitant *of Geneva, mother of Percevaux.*

Because of the sermons, faith and other things concerning the creed. Said her Lord's Prayer, and does not know the confession.

Jaqueminaz, daughter of Fore, wife of Estienne de La Combaz.

Asks and prays that means be provided for her to send her children to the said Jaques, father of the said Estienne. Jaques de La Combaz, purse-maker, father of Estienne de La Combaz, purse-maker,[265] says it is a month since he saw her and that he keeps a bastard daughter of the said Estienne for her. He

262. Bartholomée d'Orsières, daughter of Pierre d'Orsières the syndic, sister of Pierre d'Orsières, elder of the Consistory. She had been the wife of Claude Richardet, syndic and first lieutenant of Geneva in 1528 and again in 1537. After his death she married Jean Achard, Sieur de Rosey, who died apparently without issue. According to Galiffe: "She wanted to remarry in 1557, when she was 70 years old, with a young man of 26, but this was prohibited. She made her will on December 1, 1564" (GALIFFE I, pp. 180 and 530; BONIVARD, *Police,* p. 37; ROGET I, p. 318). Bartholomée Richardet belonged to the minority of Genevans who refused to renounce the old religion; see below, March 1, 1543, and R.Consist. 5, f. 29v, f. 32, and f. 32v (May 15, 20, and 22, 1550); R.Consist. 11, f. 37v (July 2, 1556).

263. Guillauma, widow of Egrège Pierre Bertherat, notary, daughter of the late Yvonet Contant, bourgeois. She contracted marriage again with Conrad de la Palle (translation of Conrad Schüffelin) in 1543 [GALIFFE I, p. 355; *R.C.* XII, p. 322 (July 12, 1533)].

264. Pernette, widow of the carpenter François Bovier, died on January 30, 1550 (E.C., Morts 1, p. 4).

265. Jaques de La Combe from Saint Blaise, near Cruseilles (H.-S.), admitted to the bourgeoisie on January 8, 1524 (*L.B.,* p. 199).

was exhorted to take the children of his son that she has, three small children. Answers that he will do what he can if he has the power and that he will help her.

Guilliamaz, wife of Jehan Jaquet,[266] farm laborer, living at the Grand Pernon's house in the Fusterie.

About frequenting of sermons. And goes willingly to the sermons, and Master Henri[267] gave the sermon and said that one should retain nothing from the other people. And could not say the Lord's Prayer except in Latin, not in French.

The Consistory advises:

That from now on those who are brought here because of Christianity all be made to go to catechism every day and that their names be given to the lords preachers and that they learn to pray to God and that they all be summoned for Thursday before Pentecost.

29v] *Jana, wife of Tabary.*

Said that the preceding did not go as often as she said. Said the Pater in the proper form and not the confession. Thursday before Pentecost.

Jaques Pernod, from La Muraz, boatman.

Asked if he is married. Answers yes, and that he married in La Muraz and has lived in this city since Christmas. And his wife is named Tevene, above St. Gingolph in Vallais, and the banns were published in Rolle and he married her in La Muraz. And that he has the certificate of the preacher before whom they were married, and the banns were published three times. And that he has been married twice besides this time, and that the last died in Rolle at Christmas and the other went to the wars. Says that no one asked him whether if the first had died, whether he should not marry. And because no one wanted to marry him in Rolle his wife went to La Muraz. The Consistory advises that he bring an affidavit by next Thursday that he married the said Tevene. Tevene the wife of the said Jaques, from Novel above St. Gingolph in . . . ,[268] daughter of Jehan Curdi, living above the wall by the Magdalen in the house of Maria the watchman,[269] swore faith at the house of

---

266. Guillauma Jaquet died on May 20, 1555 (E.C., Morts 1, p. 211).
267. Henri de La Mare, minister.
268. Word omitted: "Valais."
269. Claude Michallet, watchman, called Le Maria. See E.C., Morts 1, pp. 31 and 158 (January 19, 1551, May 6, 1554; death of the children of Claude Michallet).

the late Andrier Mermouz of Rolle and was married in La Muraz about three weeks ago. She presented an affidavit from Novel above St. Gingolph signed by Johannes de Ponto on October 13, 1541, and an affidavit from the vicar of La Muraz signed by Aguiellerii on October 20, 1541, and certain banns without a signature, and has lived [here] two years and makes coifs.

Myaz, daughter of Falliodaz, widow of F[rançois] de Bars.[270]

Says that her mother has given her only a *pose* of land and not a hundred florins as she says. The said Myaz holds the said land and begs the Seigneurie to give her a room to live in; otherwise she will be forced to go serve a master. And her mother never gave her the hundred florins that she says, but only a hundred florins that Monsieur De Bonmont[271] gave her when [f. 30] she was married and another hundred florins that Monsieur Guilliame de Gingin, bastard of Monsieur Bonmont . . .[272] And prays that her mother may give her a room elsewhere than where she lives. Remanded to Thursday, and the said Falliod her mother.

Stephane de Baptista, watchman.[273]

Asked if he knows where his brother is who swore faith to the daughter of Joyeuse, and that he has not been arrested yet and . . .[274] The advice of the

270. Myaz, widow of François de Bars, cobbler, citizen of Geneva (*R.C.* XII, p. 298, and *R.C.* XIII, p. 106). She was still living on October 26, 1559 (R.C. 55, f. 134v).

271. Aymon de Gingins (1465-1537), abbot of the Cistercian abbey of Bonmont. He became a canon of Geneva in 1481, apostolic protonotary and abbot of Saint Marie de Bonmont in 1485. In 1513 he was elected bishop of Geneva by the Chapter of St. Peter, but at the instance of the duke the Pope gave the miter to Jean de Savoie. Henri Naef wrote of Aymon de Gingins: "Much loved by the bourgeois to whom he had rendered more than one service, he inclined to the party of liberty" (NAEF, *Origines* I, p. 77). For a good biographical notice see NAEF, *Origines* I, pp. 75-81. On the episcopal election of 1513 see ROSET, pp. 67-68, and MARTIN, *Genève*, pp. 171-173.

272. Incomplete sentence. According to Naef, Guillaume de Gingins, bastard of Aymon de Gingins (see the preceding note), was a "rather bad subject" who wounded "a woman seriously with his rapier" in January 1524, and in 1535 he was put in the episcopal prison of Geneva for unknown reasons. He had been a canon of Lausanne since 1526, but never became a priest. Finally, "Guillaume, having returned without difficulty to civil life after the Reform, was still living at the château of Charansonay in 1544" (NAEF, *Origines* I, p. 80).

273. Stephane de Baptista, from Avenches (Vaud), admitted to the bourgeoisie gratis on May 29, 1537, died on May 24, 1561, at age 50 (*L.B.,* p. 217; E.C., Morts 4, p. 1; GALIFFE V, p. 333).

274. Incomplete sentence. This is the matrimonial case between Françoyse Reys, daughter of Joyeuse and Louis Reys, and Pierre Favre, called Berthoz.

Consistory is that the Council write to the said husband within a month. And Monsieur Fosses[275] will see that the letter the Council will write says that he should come do his duty as he promised.

For Laurence.[276]

Ego subsignatus curatus ecclesiae parrochialis Olleriarum per presentes actestor dud.(?) fuisse contractum matrimonii et in facie Sancte Matris Ecclesiae sollempnizatum inter Nobilum Mauricium de Castro de Crusillia ex una et Nobilam Annam filiam Nobilis Aymonis Copperin[277] parrochie Olleriarum ex alia partibus, et quostquomodo Maricium et Annam disponsam sollempniter in facie Saincte Matris Ecclesiae. Feci cumque ante ipsam disponsationem tres annunciationes sine denunciationes publicas. Et in quoquomodo matrimonio nullum inveni impedimentum prout ita actestor teste signeto meo manuali(?) hic appendio in testimonium promissorum, die tercia mensis maii anno domini millesimo quingentesimo quadragesimo secundo. Idem Aymo de Barali. {I the undersigned curate of the parish church of Ollerius [Les Ollières] by these presents attest that there was a contract of marriage solemnized in front of the church of the Holy Mother between Noble Maurice de Castro of Crusillia [Cruseilles] on one part and Noble Anna daughter of Noble Aymon Copperin of the parish of Ollerius on the other part, and in this manner (?) I married Maurice and Anna solemnly in front of the church of the Holy Mother. And also before this marriage I made three public announcements without objections. And I found no impediment whatsoever to the marriage, as I thus attest. Attested by my sign manual, which I append in testimony of the promises, the third day of the month of May, year of Our Lord 1542. The same Aymo de Barali.}[278]

For Thursday, May 11, 1542.

Myaz Santousaz; Françoys Perrissod of Contamine, her promised husband; Jaques Pernod, who should report how he espoused the said Tevene.

---

275. Pernet Des Fosses, councillor at this time and syndic six times between 1528 and 1563 (GRIVEL, *Syndics*). He was the master of Pierre Favre, called Berthoz, in 1538 [*L.B.*, p. 217 (January 22, 1538)].

276. Laurence Viongiere.

277. Anna Coppier of Crusillie.

278. Aymon de Barali, curé of Les Ollières (H.-S.) since at least 1517, served until possibly 1565 at the latest (REBORD, *Complément*, p. 335).

[f. 30v]

Thursday, May 11, 1542

The said Thursday, May 11, the Consistory moved the Consistory that should have been next Thursday to next Wednesday because of the ceremony of the Ascension.

Lord Porralis, syndic.

Calvin, Viret, Bernard, Champereaulx, Henri.

Du Molard, Pensabin, Britillion, Blandin, Frochet, the officer Vovrey.

Nota: the secretary and the officer were paid, the others are to be paid another time.

Jana Crosetaz.

Touching the rosary that was turned in by François Girin's maid.[279] Says that once at the sermon, and this woman who wore the rosary, and she told her that it would be taken away, and she gave it to the *dizainier,* and she does not know [anything more].

Marriage case.

Gervayse has presented a supplication and was asked whether she married.[280] Says no, but only swore faith, and Master Claude Sallia[281] and Estienne the weaver were present. And he gave her a *teston* in the presence of those above and he held that the Council would not want to publish their banns, the mother and her sister. The Consistory advises that the Council be told that she can marry, considering that she has no news of him. Also that she is not bound to him and that the truth be learned from the Magnifico[282] whether his servant sent to tell her that she could marry someone else. Remanded to Monday before the Council.

279. Jana, maid of François Gerin, could be Jana Bovier. See below, May 11, 1542.

280. Gervayse, daughter of Anthoyne Bochu. In her supplication she asked to be freed from the promise of marriage she made to an ex-servant of Laurent Meigret, called the Magnifico.

281. Claude Sala of Saint Gervais, then councillor [R.C. 35, f. 486v (February 6, 1542); *R.C.* XII, p. 209 (February 11, 1533)].

282. Laurent Meigret or Maigret, called the Magnifico, a French gentleman who arrived in Geneva at the beginning of the Reformation and became an important person there. See FRANÇOIS, *Meigret.*

Roletaz Falliodi, wife of George Bovagne, and Myaz, her daughter, widow of François de Bars.

Proper remonstrances. And the said Myaz requires that her mother give her a room. The said Rolete answers that the house is not large and there is no room, only enough for her and her husband, and that . . .[283] should not be done, considering that her said husband . . . ;[284] also the whole house is falling in ruins and it should not be granted(?) [f. 31] for her husband. Remanded to next Wednesday.[285]

Monsieur Jaques Symo[n]d.

Touching the Word of God and the Holy Gospel and frequenting of sermons. Answers the exhortations made to him; answers that he does not despise the Word of God. Said the Pater and confession. Also said that it was proper to pray to God and the Virgin Mary, because he was in great danger from brigands when he called on Our Lord and the Virgin Mary. And is still in this error and asks advice about it and still believes that it is good because of the angelic salutation that descended from heaven. And he does not understand that it is idolatry, and has received Holy Communion. And he did not understand that it was idolatry to invoke the Virgin Mary, and he was in this error a long time. And he considers the Mass not good and abominable. Asked if he is certain about the holy sacrament of Holy Communion. Answers that he believes as is now believed among us, as is announced to us among us, and the custom of the city. The Consistory gave him proper admonitions.[286]

Françoyse, daughter of Biollesi, and Philiberte, her sister.

Answers that she is married and does not know where her husband is, and was in the Vaud district with Monsieur De Mastignin,[287] and that she

---

283. Words missing.
284. Words missing.
285. Roletaz Falliodaz and her daughter Myaz were summoned to the Council on May 19 and 30, 1542 (R.C. 36, f. 17v and f. 27), and July 28, 1542 (R.C. 36, f. 81). The Council decided to settle their dispute by arbitration.
286. Jacques Symond, called the Picard, son of Laurent Symond, also called the Picard, member of the LX in 1533, treasurer in 1539-1540. See *R.C.* XII, p. 46 (December 6, 1531), p. 208 (February 11, 1533); ROGET I, pp. 319-320; SORDET, *Dictionnaire,* p. 1194. For the beliefs of Jaques Simond, see LAMBERT, "Cette loi."
287. The manor of Mategnin was bought by Jean Lect in 1528 and sold by Barthélemy Lect in 1547. We assume that at the time of this consistorial case the lord of Mategnin was Jean Lect the younger, or possibly Anthoine Lect the younger. R.C. 33, f. 183 (April 29, 1539); Notaires, Jean Duverney, v. 5, f. 9-f. 10 (February 1, 1542) and fo-

has been in this city two weeks, and she came here on the way to Chambéry to a sick relative, and that she was not at the sermon because she was ill. And that she did not say that she had no use for going to the sermon, and that she wants to go there and does not want to live here.

Philliberte answers that those who come to their house, it is not to do wrong, they are not such people, and they never did any wrong to do wrong. Said the prayer and her creed. [f. 31v] Proper admonitions to govern themselves well.

Vincent Gabornaz of the town of Alais in Languedoc.

Has stayed two weeks because of a marriage between him and Gonyne Levracte of the village of Saconnex. Four years ago she espoused Master Jehan Burgnet, and it took place in Avignon, and he is a purse-maker, and he only lived with her three weeks, and she does not know where he is, except that someone told her she [sic] was in the papistry. And his wife asks that they be separated.

To this Andree, wife of Jaques Portier, of Esserts, living with the Sageys near Mornex, answers that she has a daughter named Gonyne and that she is in Mornex, and that she does not live in this city and she does not know where she is and does not know whether she is her daughter. And the said Vincent says that he brought his said wife to her mother's house. And why she did not recognize her. Answers that her husband did not want her. And why she does not want to give her said daughter to her said husband here present, and that she say what the reason is. Answers that she does not know anything. And that she came to her house the other day and stayed only two hours and went to Saconnex where she lived with her neighbors, one [day] with one and another day with another. And that she leases her property from the castellan of Saconnex,[288] and is in Esserts at her father's house. Asked whether she has not lived a year in this city. Answers not so long, and that she does not know except that she lives with her father in Esserts.

The Consistory advises that they be remanded before the Council for Monday,[289] and that she make every effort to get her said daughter to live

---

lios 97-100 and 103 (May 11 and June 6, 1545); R.C. 41, f. 21 and f. 58 (February 23 and March 26, 1546); Titres et Droits, Pa 619, f. 564 (June 17, 1545) and f. 483v (December 1, 1546); Choisy, *G.G.*, pp. 202-214 (although our research makes us think that this genealogy includes some errors).

288. The scribe probably meant the castellan of Genthod, who had jurisdiction over Saconnex. In 1542 the castellan of Genthod was François Lullin [R.C. 37, f. 18 (February 15, 1543)].

289. "The Council for Monday" is struck from the manuscript.

with her husband and to bring them together. Answered that she would make her come one of these days, but that he would support her; otherwise that they should be separated. Answered that if he had his said wife he would take her to his own country, and he has his goods and his profession, and asks that he be given time, because he has no money and has already waited four or five days.

32] *Jana, daughter of Jehan Bovier.*[290]

And was never married. Acknowledged the rosary and that she carried it in her belt and that she picked it up. And has served masters, and she was brought young to this city. Has served three or four masters, and has always lived in this city. Said her Pater and confession of faith. She does not know whether it is good to pray to the Virgin Mary and does not know whose the said rosary is, but she picked it up and it is not hers, and that she wanted to take it to Decompesio's house[291] to be burned. She was remanded to Monday before the Council, or whenever she will be summoned. Conriousaz, living by the wall, saw her when she found it between the inner and outer doors at St. Peter's at the chief sermon about three weeks ago, and again at the small door of St. Peter's, and they were taken out of her hand while saying the Pater at the morning sermon. Admonished to speak the truth.

Pierre Favre, son of Glaude Favre, glass-blower, living on the Bourg du Four at the house of François Mercier,[292] glass-blower, versus Bernard the servant of Master Jaques the mason.[293]

Because of an insult. Says he was in a . . .[294] and they pardoned each other and shook hands.

290. This could be Jana, François Gerin's maid, already summoned several times by the Consistory, but who never appeared. One or several Jean Bouviers are mentioned in J.-A. Gautier and Galiffe, but none who is definitely linked to a Jana. See J.-A. GAUTIER II, p. 203; GALIFFE I, pp. 33, 344, 464, and 554.

291. This is probably the *dizainier* Claude de Compois (Compesio in Latin), notary.

292. François Mercier, from Regny, received into the bourgeoisie on January 9, 1537 (*L.B.*, p. 216).

293. Possibly Jaques Mercier or Messiez, mason, bourgeois, who in 1537 rented a house on the Rue Saint Christophe (the Porte de Saint Christophe was at the foot of the Rue des Belles Filles) [R.C. 30, f. 246 (June 1, 1537); Notaires, Jean Duverney, v. 5, f. 75 (February 12, 1544)].

294. Word omitted by the scribe.

Jaqueline Marronne, daughter of Master Jehan Marron, from the town of Bourg, diocese of Viviers, in Languedoc.

Presented a supplication and asks a decision on it. The Consistory advises that the Council send to the place to get a letter from there, to have a proper basis to act in her favor from the country she is from and where she married.[295]

[f. 32v]   *Debet totum nunc.* {All is now owed.}

Wednesday, May 17, 1542

Lord Syndic Porralis.
Calvin, Viret, Bernard, Henri, Champereaulx.
D'Orsieres, Britillion, Pensabin, Frochet, Blandin, the officer Vovrey.

Jaques Emyni, pack-saddler.

Syndic Porralis has had a report from the Council because he has not been obedient, saying he should go to prison and was therefore not released and that he did not hold the said master more than six days. Asked what progress there has been in his faith and creed since his last appearance and what his teacher has taught him. Answers, and said the prayer and his confession very poorly. Admonished to do better than he has; otherwise he will not be received into the holy congregation. The Consistory resolves that he be remanded every Sunday to the catechism with the others and examined like the others, and every day at the sermons, and that he be constrained more sharply; otherwise that he appear at every Consistory.

295. Jaqueline Marron presented herself in Council on May 15, 1542 (R.C. 36, f. 13v), to ask for a letter addressed to the vicar of Uzès to find out whether her husband intended to take her back and treat her "decently as his wife." If not, she wanted to be separated from him. The Council granted her such a letter on May 19, 1542 (R.C. 36, f. 18), "in order to deal with this, considering that her said husband persecuted her because of the Gospel." She returned to the Council to plead her case on October 5, 1543 (R.C. 37, f. 235v), and was again in Consistory on October 18, 1543. On October 22, 1543 (R.C. 37, f. 249), the Council, after hearing the accusations of infidelity and concubinage presented by Jaqueline against her husband, decided that before granting her a divorce it was still necessary to obtain "good evidence on the behavior of her husband." In 1546 the Council gave her a grant, "considering that she has lived in Geneva a long time and is old" and because her daughter was in Geneva, the widow of the *sautier* Petremand Falquet [R.C. 41, f. 56v (March 23, 1546)].

Loys Savarin, tailor.[296]

Answered that he believes in God the Father and no other, and said the Pater, and has not carried a rosary for three years or heard Mass. Said the confession fairly well, and cannot read or write, and knows nothing else, and has still not been to catechism. He thinks his wife knows how to pray to God.

Falliodaz and her daughter.[297]

Remanded before the Council.

33] *Jana Conriousaz.*

Answered that she saw something picked up, and she does not know what it was, and the others told her it was a rosary.[298] And touching the girl who lived at Monsieur Ramelli's,[299] she is somewhat of a fornicator and thief. Said the prayer. She is Janetaz from the Rue du Bouloz. Admonished to frequent the sermons.

Claude Arthaudaz, hosier, citizen of Geneva.

Asked when he came to this city. Four years ago, and he lived in Lyon. And he bought the decorated collar from a cobbler, and it cost him 15 sous. And he goes to sermons and says the prayer, the confession. He wants to live in the faith of Jesus Christ and in the Reformation, and he will frequent the sermons.

Concerning Gervayse.[300]

The lords preachers of the Consistory should inform the Council.[301]

---

296. Louis Savarin, tailor, was named *dizainier* of the *dizaine* of the Maison de la Ville in 1543. He died in 1554 [R.C. 37, f. 196v (August 17, 1543); E.C., Morts 1, p. 159 (May 16, 1554)].

297. Roletaz Falliodaz and her daughter, Myaz, widow of François de Bars.

298. This refers to the case of Jana or Janetaz Bovier.

299. Either Jean Louis Ramel, son of the former syndic Jean Louis Ramel, or possibly Jean Ramel, son of the same, former priest of Geneva. See GALIFFE I, pp. 459-460.

300. Gervayse Bochu.

301. On May 19, 1542 (R.C. 36, f. 18), John Calvin and Pierre Viret appeared in Council to maintain the validity of the promise of marriage between Gervayse Bochu and Jehan, ex-servant of Laurent Meigret, who had withdrawn to France. Before considering this question the Council decided that it was first necessary to find this man.

Those remanded to next Thursday because of Holy Communion at Pentecost.

Jana, wife of Tabari, for religion; Guilliama, wife of Jehan Jaquet, farm laborer; Myaz Sanctousaz[302] because of her promised husband.

Those who must be summoned for next Thursday.

Françoys Dupra, blacksmith in St. Gervais; Mermaz, wife of Bernard the boatman, living at Monsieur Ramelli's; Janeta, daughter of Jehan Bovier; Claude Falquaz; Roland Du Verney, millstone-cutter; Noble Jehan Goulaz; Roud Monet; Jehan Favre, called D'Orbaz; Philipe Pellouz;[303] Pierre Veyron; Uguynaz daughter of Depontelaz;[304] the bastard daughter of Monsieur Jehan Amoyci.[305]

[f. 33v] *Debet totum.* {All is owed.}

Thursday, May 25, 1542

Lord Rozet, syndic, for Lord Pertemps.
Calvin, Viret, Henri, Champereaulx.
Girbel, Rages, Pensabin, Blandin, Frochet, Tacon, the officer Vovrey.

Noble Jehan Goulaz.

Admonished whether he plans to receive Holy Communion and live according to religion and the Reformation. Given remonstrances. Answers that he does not want to do otherwise and that he wants to behave like one of the faithful.[306]

302. Myaz Du Boule, called Sanctousaz.
303. This is actually Petremand Pelloux, summoned to Consistory with Jean Goulaz, Roz Monet, Jean Favre, and Pierre Veyron. See below, May 25, 1542.
304. Huguyne Dupont.
305. Huguyne Amici.
306. This case is linked to the four following cases of Roud (or Roz) Monet, Petremand Pellouz, Jehan Favre called D'Orbaz, and Pierre Veyron called Sermod, all notorious persons in Geneva. They were accused of seditious words and a dissolute life. In particular, on the day of Christmas Communion they stayed at the house of Goulaz drinking and banqueting. Goulaz then gave them "hose all of the same kind" to go to Communion, and Roz Monet said that they would be appropriate, like four syndics and a *sautier*. Moreover, Jean Favre called D'Orbaz was accused of having said *"clistoyre"* (enema) or *"constenayre"* (consternary?) in place of *"Consistoire"* (Consistory), among other "insolences." They were put in prison, and later freed on May 13, 1542, on condition of not leaving Geneva without permission for a year and of asking pardon of justice

Roud Monet.[307]

Admonished like the preceding, and also that he criticized the holy sacrament of Holy Communion he last received and that he avoid scandalizing the church. Answers that he has never been found in a place where evil was spoken of the Consistory and that he is not a traitor because he has a trouble in his heart, and that he will not receive Communion this time, because he is troubled in his heart.

[P.C. 2ᵉ sér., 526 (January 12-April 22, 1542); P.C. 2ᵉ sér., 528 (January 12-April 21, 1542); P.C. 2ᵉ sér., 531 (February 14-May 9, 1542); R.C. 36, f. 12 (May 13, 1542)]. Goulaz, Pelloux, and D'Orbaz, along with Denis and François Hugues, were accused a little later of having sung and spun about in derision of the ministers one evening at the Porte de Rive, the ministers coming from supper at the house of Jaques Bernard [P.C. 2ᵉ sér., 553 (July 17, 1542). According to BONIVARD (*Police*, p. 93), Pelloux, D'Orbaz, and Monet were all "chamberlains of Perrin" at the beginning of the 1540s. Noble Jean Goulaz, procurator general in 1536, syndic in 1537, and lieutenant in 1541 (elected November 14, 1540), was one of the first and most ardent Reformers. In 1539 he renounced his bourgeoisie, but he was forced to swear it once more. Goulaz was often reprimanded and imprisoned over the years. See FROMENT, p. 4; J.-A. GAUTIER II, pp. 349, 353, 547; *ibid.* III, pp. 99, 113, 155 and note; GEISENDORF, *Annalistes*, pp. 400, 446-447, 487; and the extract from a letter from Farel to Guérin on November 18, 1532, cited in *R.C.* XII, p. 164, n. 1.

307. This continues the interrogation of Jehan Goulaz and his companions. At this time Roud Monet was still on good terms with the Perrinists and particularly with Philibert Berthelier ("they were two bodies with one soul," says Bonivard). But by receiving the post of secretary to the lieutenant Monet alienated Berthelier, who also wanted it. Later, in 1549, he boasted of having saved Ami Perrin from torture and, fatal error, of having had the favors of the wives of Perrin and of Pierre Vandel. The ministers and their party were evidently already hostile to Monet and, deprived of every supporter, he was executed, although Bonivard was convinced of his innocence. Calvin wrote to Viret: ". . . *Rodolphum Monetum hodie demum in carcerem fuisse conjectum. Alia illi scelera impunita erant, nisi comicum Caesarem [Perrin] iactasset sua opera e furcis ereptum, illius et Vendelini uxores a se fuisse subactas. Mirum itaque erit si furcas ipse effugiat. Ego inter varios motus qui in utramque partem concitantur sileo.*" {Today Rodolphus Monetus was finally thrown into jail. His other crimes would have remained unpunished had not his actions disturbed the comic Caesar [Perrin] stolen from the gallows, whose wife and that of Vendelinus had been suborned by him. It will therefore be remarkable if this one escapes the gallows himself. I remain quiet among the various emotions that are stirred up on both sides.} See ROGET III, pp. 112-116; J.-A. GAUTIER III, pp. 383-386; BONIVARD, *Police*, pp. 101-104; *C.O.* XX, col. 407 (letter 4162, 1549, dated *a coena, sponsalium die* {at dinner, day of betrothal}).

Jehan Favre, called D'Orbaz.[308]

Admonished like the others because of remonstrances on the Holy Communion which he last took last Christmas, and on the respect it should be held in, because he has scandalized the church. Answers that he will correct himself and avoid offending and scandalizing the church.

Petremand Pellouz.[309]

Like the other preceding. Answers that he will not take Holy Communion because his heart is charged against someone who has done him great injury, by whom he was wounded, and he cannot earn his living or that of his family, and he prays God every day to remove this hate from his heart. And that he wants to be one of the children of God, if it pleases Him. The Consistory . . .[310]

[f. 34]   *Pierre Sermod, called Veyron.*[311]

Was admonished because of the Holy Communion taken at Christmas, with friendly remonstrances. Answers that he will do his duty and means to receive Holy Communion next time and that he has no grudge against anyone.

308. The interrogation of Jehan Favre, called D'Orbaz, is also linked to that of Jehan Goulaz above. Jehan Favre was the bastard son of Pierre Favre of Echallens, admitted to the bourgeoisie gratis on November 12, 1537, "considering he has always been a good servant." He apparently lost his bourgeoisie in 1538 for having "committed various insolences for which he deserves to be ousted from his bourgeoisie." On November 4, 1545, the Council authorized him to keep an inn under the sign of the Griffin, and re-admitted him to the bourgeoisie. In 1554 he was an officer [*L.B.*, p. 217 (November 12, 1537); R.C. 31, f. 161 (January 16, 1538); Mss. Galiffe 38, f. 360; E.C., Morts 1, p. 178 (September 28, 1554; death of his wife Pernette)].

309. This interrogation is also linked to the three preceding. Petremand Pellouz, bourgeois of Geneva, native of Viry (H.-S.), was then rent farmer of Peissy, and later became host of the inn of the Green Head. He died on November 12, 1569 [SORDET, *Dictionnaire*, p. 1000; R.C. 38, f. 18 (December 28, 1543, R.C. 38, f. 121v (March 11, 1544); E.C., Morts 10, p. 6].

310. Incomplete sentence.

311. Like the preceding cases, that of Pierre Sermod is linked to that of Jehan Goulaz above. Pierre Sermod, citizen and butcher, was elected a member of the lieutenant's court in 1539. He died on November 12, 1561, at about age 60 [R.C. 33, f. 341 and f. 344 (November 14 and 16, 1539); E.C., Morts 4, p. 65].

Claude Falcaz, millstone-cutter.[312]

Admonished about the grudge he has against Roland the mill-stone-cutter,[313] and carries a grudge against him. Answers that he does not wish him harm and that they are in accord and he wishes him no harm and that it is the fault of their wives.

Roland Du Verney because of the hate he has for Claude Falcaz. Answers that he wants to live according to God and that he has nothing against him that keeps them from being at peace, and that it is a good thing to live in peace with others. The two were confronted with each other so they could receive the next Holy Communion. And they agreed together before the Consistory and shook hands as a sign of friendship.

Claude Arthaud.

Because of talking too much to the dishonor of the church, that the lords preachers should not order people to go to sermons, and because of the perjury he committed concerning the decorated leather collar he wore that he had bought and afterwards said in a public place he had not, and that he did thus and mocked God and the church. The Consistory admonished him not to return again to such actions, because the Council would not be content with his doing so.

34v] *Uguynaz, illegitimate daughter of Monsieur Jehan Amyci.*

Because of fornication, because she swore before the Seigneurie, and to receive the next Holy Communion of Our Lord, and she mocked the Council and dishonored God and religion. Answers that she did not dishonor the Seigneurie. The Consistory advises that she be admonished, that she refrain from taking the next Holy Communion, and that she be chastised more rigorously, and frequent the sermons.

Uguynaz Depontelaz.[314]

Like the other, given admonitions and remonstrances about her faults and the lies she told the Council and to take care not to return to her faults again. The Consistory advises as for the preceding.

312. Claude Falca, from Chavanod (H.-S.), was admitted to the bourgeoisie on November 5, 1532 (*R.C.* XII, p. 158; *L.B.*, p. 209).
313. Roland Du Verney.
314. Huguine Dupont.

Handsome Jehan Cler, cobbler.[315]

About a certain conflict he and his wife have with Sollier's wife,[316] and whether he knows what conflict there is between the two women. Answers that he knows nothing, and ordered to make his wife come with him tomorrow at one o'clock.

About the marriage of Macarde's maid.

The Consistory advises that a summons be issued before the *official* of Bourg[317] and issue letters of subpoena. The names of those who brought the said maid to Bresse: first Tyvent Perier of Feigères, servant of Macard's wife; Jeny Lombard of Avusy.

Jehan Villiet.[318]

Because of fornication and rebellion, that he did not appear at the Consistory after his punishment, and evil life, and because of the next Holy Communion, and because of the lies he told the Consistory last time. The Consistory advises that he abstain from receiving Holy Communion and frequent the sermons.

[f. 35]   And note those to whom Holy Communion was refused on . . .[319]

For Thursday, summon:

The two children of Dominique Franch;[320] Jehan Cru.

For the ordinance of Communion at Pentecost, May 28, as last time.[321]

---

315. Probably Jean Clerc (Johannes Clerici) from La Contamine-sur-Arve (H.-S.), cobbler, *habitant* in the parish of the Magdalen, admitted to the bourgeoisie on June 11, 1535 (*R.C.* XIII, p. 239). There was also the wife of a Jean Clerc, banished in 1514 for having led "a lewd life" (NAEF, *Origines* I, p. 227), but we do not know whether she is the same as the wife of Clerc mentioned here. Jana, wife of Handsome Jehan Cler, appeared in the Consistory later, on May 26, 1542.

316. Venturina, wife of Antoine Revilliod, called Sollier, innkeeper on the Molard. See the note above, April 6, 1542.

317. This is the *official* of Bresse, who sat in Bourg and Pont de Vaux. According to Paul Cattin: "The *official* exercised the ordinary jurisdiction of the bishop, whom he replaced." Cattin also explains that "the archives of the *officialité* of Bresse seem to have disappeared" (CATTIN I, p. 537).

318. The proceedings against Jehan Villiet are connected with those against Huguyne Amici and Huguyne Depontelaz; see above, April 20, 1542.

319. Incomplete sentence.

320. Louis and Claude Franc.

321. For the ordinance for Easter Communion, see above, April 6, 1542.

Friday, May 26, 1542

Lord Claude Rozet, syndic, for Lord Pertemps.
Calvin, Viret, Champereaulx, Henri.
Britillion, Pensabin, Rages, Blandin, D'Orsieres, the officer Vovrey.

Aymoz Peronet the day laborer, habitant *of Geneva.*

Asked about certain medicines and about curing many ill people, and certain magic words which are forbidden by God, and what words he uses in these affairs and whether he wants to live according to the Reformation. Answers that in fractures and dislocations he does as his father did; that he does not use talismans or magic words; otherwise he submits [to a penalty]. He makes plasters of pitch, wax and heated butter, and combines them and makes plasters. He lived once in Lyon, in Aiguebelle, and is from Megève, and once lived in this city. And he uses no other words except that he always says in the name of the Father and of the Son. And says he wants to live according to the Lord and the lords of his country and he lives according to the place where he is. Asked if he goes to the sermons, says yes, and has not taken Communion because he was not here, and it is 18 years since he lived in this city, and has lived in Jehantin(?) with François Gache and another who was from Burgundy. And wants to live and go live at his father's house, and does not mean to use spells. And asked a decision before Sunday, and intends to take the next Communion at Pentecost. And no one wanted to grant this, because he is not a proper person to want to receive Communion, and that he go to sermons.

[f. 35v] *Dominique Du Gerdy.*

Asked about the Reformation and the church and the Mass and the laws of this city. Answers that he has not heard Mass for four or five years, and he sometimes goes to see to his property, but he does not go to hear Mass, neither he nor his family, and he wants to live here according to the Reformation. Told to frequent the sermons.

Pernet, wife of Dominique Du Gerdi and Claudaz,[322] *her chambermaid.*

Proper admonitions about papal ceremonies. Answers that she was at the sermon and her mother took her by the hair and did not let her go, because someone had preached that he would say Mass, and she could not leave, and she heard this Mass. And her maid stayed with her. And said the Pater, and the chambermaid, and they want to live according to the Reforma-

---

322. Claudaz Blandet.

tion. The chambermaid said she has lived three years in this city, and she said the Pater and her creed. The Consistory advises that they go to catechism on Sunday and frequent the sermons, that they promise to live according to the Reformation and not be permitted to hear Mass.

Loys Gajouz.

Asked why he has hardly profited from the sermons, and about the conflict he has with his brother, and about blaspheming God. Answers that touching his brother, he keeps a whore in Petit Saconnex, and that is why he has kept away from his brother, because he does not know whether he has married this woman. Asked if he has received Communion, answers yes, at St. Gervase, against his duty, since he wishes harm to his brother. The Consistory advises that he be forbidden Communion this time and remanded for Thursday, and Colin Gajoz and his wife and Loys Gajoz's son be summoned, and he go every day to the sermon and pray Our Lord to remove this spite from him.

Hostess of the Three Quail.[323]

Because of her chambermaid. She did not appear, and remanded to Thursday.

[f. 36] *Guigoz Veilliard, son of Jehan, embroiderer.*[324]

Because of his father, to whom he is rude. Answers that he is persecuted more by his father than by anyone else, and considering that he brought his children here to live with him and drank and ate and has not mistreated him. And he has risked his profits, and he never does anything but quarrel with him, and he came to his father to receive the Word of God, and he will be forced to withdraw, and his wife and children, and do the best they can. And he came by the command of his father, and he cannot see him; therefore he does not know what to say or do, and he came from Tours since Easter. The Consistory advises that he be remanded to another time with his father.

323. Anthoyne, wife of Aymoz Foural.
324. Guygo Veillard, member of the LX [*R.C.* XII, p. 167 (November 29, 1532)]. His father, Jean Veillard, embroiderer from Combloux (H.-S.), was received into the bourgeoisie on November 29, 1502 (*L.B.*, p. 149), later became a *dizainier* and member of the LX for the Rue de la Poissonnerie, and was one of the first "Lutherans" in Geneva. The father made his will on June 13, 1543, leaving a house to his wife and another to his son, both in the Poissonnerie (Notaires, Michel Try, v. 5, folios 98-101). See also NAEF, *Origines* II, pp. 370, 445, and 456; *R.C.* XII, pp. 211 and 475 (February 12, 1533, and February 13, 1534); *R.C.* XII, pp. 599-600, *notes complémentaires* (May 7, 1533); J.-A. GAUTIER II, p. 384; GEISENDORF, *Annalistes*, p. 408.

Reniere, wife of Jehan Veilliard,[325] mother-in-law of the said Guigoz, because of the quarrel her husband has with his for . . .[326] Answers that one Sunday he said to his father that he wanted to sell his house and his property in Saconnex, and swore that he was not his father. And that he would call himself a Boytet[327] and not a Velliard, and that the said Guigoz called her a fornicator, and that she would make what she said appear, because when they dined together the said Guygoz began to cast insults.

The said Guigoz answers that he never told him that he would never love him, and that the argument came from his said mother-in-law, and that his father brought him back when the said Guigoz had some money, and when they had his goods they drove him away. Says he does not know whether he said she was a fornicator, or whether that was of another female fornicator who goes about with her. The Consistory advises that if they if they [sic] are not reconciled that they be forbidden Communion, and that the said Guigoz be made to honor his father and mother-in-law. And to exhort the father that all three be reconciled, and tomorrow let respectable people be assigned to speak to the father to reconcile them, namely Master Pierre Viret, Pensabin and Pierre de Rages.

f. 36v] *Françoys Dupra.*[328]

For the sermons, and other admonitions on his and his wife's great anger and rage. Answers that he does nothing he should not do, and he cannot enjoy his wife[329] and must punish her. And that he goes to the sermons, that his wife does not profit him, and she does nothing he commands her, and her parents do not give her a dowry. And that he is a native of Lausanne and

---

325. Reyniere, daughter of Anthoine Puthod, bourgeois, married Jean Veillard on January 31, 1528 (Notaires, de Compois, v. 7, f. 162). She was one of Froment's first converts on his first visit to Geneva in 1532-1533 (FROMENT, p. 18). She remarried, with Claude Moret, saddler, bourgeois. On February 28, 1549, Guigo Veillard had to give up the house he had inherited from his father to pay "the marriage [portion] due to Rigniere, widow of the said late Vellard" (Notaires, Michel Try, v. 7, f. 41).

326. Incomplete sentence.

327. Guigoz Veillard probably thus took his mother's family name. On August 14, 1543, Guigo Veillard presented a supplication in Council, asking them to "induce his father to deliver him the goods that pertain to him from the Boytet side, without wasting them" (R.C. Part. 1, f. 82v). FROMENT (p. 13) says that he taught at first "in the chief room of the Boytet house, near the great square of the Mollard . . . at the sign of the Cross of Gold" (near the Poissonnerie where the Veillards lived).

328. François Dupra, merchant of Lausanne, son of François, was admitted to the bourgeoisie on June 8, 1535 (*L.B.*, p. 212).

329. Pernete Martin. [Translator: "Enjoy" here means "have sex with."]

brought his sister to serve in his house and was forced to send her back. Remanded to tomorrow after the sermon at St. Gervase to reconcile them, and her parents;[330] Champereaulx and Britillion.

Sollier's wife.[331]

Because of the quarrel she has with the wife of Handsome Jehan Clert, cobbler. Answers that she had a quarrel with his wife and that she blamed her, and she does not know why or how. And that she insulted her, saying she was a returned(?) lewd woman, and that she never insulted her, and Camilloz and XXX Coste(?)[332] the cobbler and a dyer live there, and she has no quarrel except with her.

Jana, wife of Handsome Jehan Cler, cobbler, touching the said Sollier's wife, said that she was fearful of fire, and the said Sollier's wife and her husband insulted her greatly, and the said Jane insulted them also, and that she answered back and told her that she, the said Jane, had merited being put in a galley to be whipped. The Consistory advises that they be admonished to be reconciled and to live in peace from now on. And they made peace together before the Consistory for all offenses.

[f. 37]

Thursday, first of June, 1542

Lord Claude Rozet, syndic, for Lord Pertemps.
Viret, Bernard.
Pensabin, the officer Thoni Regis.[333]

Myaz de Bouloz, called Santousaz.

Presented a supplication, and asks as in it.[334] The said François Perressodi, tailor, says that there is nothing to the said supplication and

330. Guigo Martin.

331. Venturina, wife of Anthoine Revilliod, called Sollier.

332. Possibly "Trentecoste." The reading is not clear. It could also be Christophe Coste ("χρ," like the abbreviation for Christ, followed by "x" for etc.), but this seems an extremely chancy reading. We have not been able to identify this person.

333. Thoni Regis, otherwise called Anthoine Rey, was an officer and watchman of the city. He became a watchman on July 1, 1539 (R.C. 33, f. 189v). He should not be confused with another Anthoine Rey or Regis, executed for theft [R.C. 36, f. 21 and f. 22 (May 23 and 24, 1542)], against whom the officer Anthoine Rey had once testified [P.C. 2ᵉ sér., 467 (September 24-27, 1539)].

334. For a copy of the supplication presented by Myaz Du Boule, see below in this session of the Consistory.

that he never had anything to do with her, except that she served him for a week in an illness, and he paid the said Myaz nothing for his illness, and he never knew her carnally, and although she served him he did not ask her to, and he never had anything to do with her. The Consistory advises that if there is no testimony it does not appear that there is a marriage, and that they be remanded before the Council to Monday after the sermon.

Nycolas Baud of Peycier,[335] concerning the official letter of the castellan of Peney.[336]

Asked whether his wife[337] who was brought to bed of his child which she carried, where it is. Answers that he had a woman come to his house and another woman, and that the child died immediately and that his son carried away the said child dead and it was not baptized. And he carried it to Seyssel, and he says that Our Lord takes all to mercy without being baptized.

37v]   Son of the said Nycolas Baud[338] about the answer of the said Nycolas his father concerning the child last mentioned. Answers that his mother was delivered of a son about a month ago, and he took it away and she did not know where he had it, and he took it to Seyssel over the Seyssel Bridge in front of the chapel of the said bridge, in front of the Chapel of Our Lady[339] who does miracles, and it was baptized in the said place and later buried, because Brother Jehan Bourgeoys said so. And that no one commanded him, and if it had been buried he would have dug it up to carry it off. And it was buried there in Seyssel, and he did not have money to have Masses said. And he believes God is a light(?) for all the world and that this was his belief and that he is excitable, and begs mercy from God and the Seigneurie, and claims that he is a cleric.

In the presence of the father strict admonitions were given them. The

---

335. The Bauds being so numerous in Geneva at this time, we cannot determine whether this is the same Egrège Nicolas Baud who acknowledged in Peissy on November 24, 1546, or the same who testified against Guy Furbity in 1534. A Nicolas Baud, from Meyrin, was admitted to the bourgeoisie on January 16, 1543 (Titres et Droits, Pa 619, ff. 329-335v; NAEF, *Origines* II, p. 498; *L.B.*, p. 223).

336. Pierre d'Orsières, castellan of Peney. See R.C. 35, f. 560 (April 18, 1542), and R.C. 37, f. 18 (February 15, 1543).

337. Amblarde Baud.

338. Pierre Baud.

339. Probably the church of the Benedictines in Seyssel, dedicated to Notre Dame du Tinet or Tinel (FENOUILLET, *Seyssel*, p. 43).

Consistory advises that they be remanded before the Council.[340] The others are all remanded to next time because of the absence of the elders.

The contents of the supplication of Myaz Santouzaz against François Perrissod.

My magnificent and most honored Lords, your humble servant Mya, daughter of the late Amyé Du Boule, called Santousaz, humbly informs you that it is true that below La Côte d'Hyot one named François Perrissol gave me a piece of silver of three *quarts* current in the name of marriage. I, thinking of the love I have for him who espoused me, and moreover I nursed him for three weeks in the house of the Cortagiés and paid for him at my expense and paid the money myself; I assure you I believed that he would do for me what he had promised. However, I see the opposite; therefore, magnificent Lords, may it please you to take this into consideration, [f. 38] very humbly recommending myself to your benign grace, because for my part I will not renounce the marriage gift, praying you that it may please you to maintain her in her right, and she prays God for your prosperity, which may God long preserve. Amen. Magnificent Lords, he will tell you plenty of lies, but do not believe him.

Thursday, June 8

Because of some matters that came up the Consistory was not held this day.[341]

---

340. Nycolas Baud was summoned to Council on June 5, 1542 (R.C. 36, f. 31), for having had his son Pierre carry a child to Seyssel to be baptized and buried in Catholic territory. The Council ordered the castellan of Peney to put them in prison.

341. We do not know what matters the register refers to, but the Council did not sit either this day. The syndic Ami Porral had died on June 3, but the Council functioned normally. On June 6 the Council was disturbed because of a "great number" of Swiss troops who were then staying in Geneva, and it feared the arrival of another ten *enseignes* the same day. The Council ordered that "the artillery be ready and the people armed in their homes, and that good guard be kept." On June 10 the Genevans asked a band of Italian or Lombard soldiers to leave the city. Finally, in the evening of June 12, there was an *"emotion"* between the people and the soldiers of the Grisons. The next day the captains made their excuses, and they probably left the city the day after (R.C. 36, folios 32v, 36v, 38, 38v).

Thursday, June 15, 1542

Lord Syndic Cornaz.
Calvin, Veret, Bernard, Henri, Champereaulx.
Girbel, Britillion, Frochet, Blandin, the officer Vovrey.

Tristant and Madeleine Pecollate.

She asks that action be taken according to the resolution of the Council of their lordships, and asks testimonials. And the said Tristant says that if she had sent to him to return her ring that she had given him, she would have broken off with him. And that his heart is not in her, because he would not know how to earn a living for her and him. And that he knows of nothing in her that would not make her a respectable woman, and that the ring is lost, and he returned ten écus to her in compensation. [f. 38v] The Consistory advises that it be learned how the marriage should be dissolved, considering the promises. And that they be read the last decision made and asked why the said marriage should not be carried out. The last decision read. The said Magdeleine answers the preachers' question. Says that if it does not please the said Tristant that what he does will not displease her, and she will leave him. And that he gave her 100 écus when he was engaged to her and he is a wastrel and will not keep his promise to her. And concerning the 500 florins that she promised him, that she has no support and she begs from her neighbors. The said Tristant says that because she did not keep her promise he can do nothing and that he has nothing to live on. The case comes from her side because he does not know what to do and he has no heart in her and he cannot support her. On the other side the Consistory advises that they be remanded to Monday before the Council and that such a marriage should not thus be broken or dissolved because of the consequences. And that they be remanded to Monday before the Council.[342]

342. The matrimonial case of Madeleine Cornille, widow of Estienne Peccollat (GALIFFE I, pp. 132-133), and of Tristan de Branges from Château Thierry (Aisne) was discussed several times in Council. The promise of marriage seems to have been made before December 8, 1541, before Claude Bernard and Guillaume Le Franc and Guillaume Du Bosco. Tristan de Branges maintained that Madeleine Cornille had promised him a dowry of 500 florins and that for his part he had promised her 100 florins if he died before her. She admitted having promised to marry him, but denied having offered such a dowry [Actes Privés, Contrats de mariage 4, n. 6 (December 8, 1541)]. On June 19 (R.C. 36, f. 44) and July 31, 1542 (R.C. 36, f. 82), the Council ordered that the witnesses present at the contract of marriage be examined. On August 7, 1542 (R.C. 36, f. 88), the Council decided that the marriage should take place, but when Branges refused he was impris-

Loys Franch.

Because of his marriage, which has waited so long before having the wedding, and this . . .[343]

The hostess of the Three Quail.[344]

Because of her chambermaid who fornicated in her house, and afterwards went to have the child outside Geneva in Ternier, and to know where the child is. Answers that she has no maid at her house who has fornicated and that she has only decent girls for servants, and that she paid off a maid who left, and she knows nothing else, and this was about a year ago on St. John's Day. And that she has had neither girl nor servant who left pregnant with a child from her house, and that she knows nothing else, that there is nothing else. [f. 39] The Consistory advises that an affidavit be obtained from the Consistory of Ternier and that she be remanded to Thursday before the Council.[345]

Jana Tabarie.

Because of frequenting of sermons, her faith and creed. Answers that she knows only the prayer and confession, no more than before. Since she has not profited, that she frequent the sermons and present herself here the Thursday before the next Communion and go to catechism every Sunday and work hard to learn the faith and creed.

Jehan Cru.

Did not appear and has left. The Consistory advises that it would be good to visit his wife because of the other thing done to her, which is terrible; that the Syndic report to the Council tomorrow and that the Council decide to do justice.[346]

---

oned. On August 10, 1542 (R.C. 36, f. 91v), Branges was finally freed after having consented to marry Madeleine Cornille.

343. Incomplete sentence. This is probably the matrimonial case between Loys Franc and Huguyne Dupont, presented in Consistory on February 23, 1542. On Tuesday, June 20, 1542, the two brothers Claude and Loys Franc were admonished to marry the girls they were engaged to within three weeks following. The day after this session of the Consistory, that is on June 16, Claude Franc was also reprimanded in Council for the "conflict" between him and his father, Domaine Franc (R.C. 36, f. 45v and f. 43).

344. Anthoyne Foural, hostess of the Three Quail.

345. On June 19 the Council decided to write "to the Consistory of Ternier to learn the truth about this case" (R.C. 36, f. 44).

346. He was spoken about in Council under the name of "P. Cru, living in St.

Concerning the affair of Monsieur Coquet and Hugonery.

Monsieur Jehan Hugonery concerning the said conflict between the two of them because of certain company and money lent because of a lease that the said Coquet drew entirely to himself, and that the said Coquet had told him that the said Hugonery wanted to kill him and sought his death, which he had never thought of. Nevertheless he submits to have the matter arbitrated and is content with that.

[f. 39v] *Jeneta, widow of Amy Julliain.*

The woman because of the stole[347] which was on the ground in the square, that she says that she joked that the Mass must be going to come. She was ordered to frequent the sermons and the catechism.

Report of Bechod in the case of Porralis and Chavanel.[348]
Friday.

For Thursday, June 22.

Calabri the mason;[349] the writing master of St. Gervais;[350] Jaques the pack-saddler;[351] Robert the pack-saddler;[352] the mother of Lord Pertemps;[353] the Triumphant.[354]

Gervais." It says there: "for the insolences he has committed against his wife, resolved that he be punished" [R.C. 36, f. 42 (June 16, 1542)].

347. Translator: *I.e.,* a priest's stole, dropped there somehow.

348. The syndic Ami Porral died on June 3, 1542 [R.C. 36, f. 30 (June 5, 1542)]. Bechod's report seems to have been presented to the Council the next day, as the Consistory states here. The Council register says: "Offenses committed because of the death of the late Lord Syndic Porralis. Because there are some who committed various insolences and mockeries of the death of Lord Syndic Porralis, ordered that accurate information be obtained, and that they be punished accordingly" [R.C. 36, f. 42 (June 16, 1542)]. We have learned nothing more about this affair.

349. Pierre Calabri of Corsinge, received into the bourgeoisie on January 5, 1525 (*L.B.,* p. 204). In December 1541 he was working on the walls of the city [R.C. 35, f. 443v (December 24, 1541)].

350. Anthoyne Dordotz Goyti.

351. Jaques Emyn, pack-saddler.

352. Robert Breysson, pack-saddler.

353. Jane Pertemps, called Pertennaz.

354. Jane, wife of Claude Thorens, called the Triumphant.

Thursday, June 22, 1542

Lord Syndic Pertemps.
Calvin, Viret, Henri, Bernard, Champereaulx.
Girbel, Blandin, Frochet, the officer Vovrey.

Colin Gajouz from Petit Saconnex.[355]

Said he has a wife named Loyse from Crepon near Ballaison, and that his brother Loys and he do nothing but fight because of this wife and are always at odds. And he has not taken Communion for two or three years, and he married his wife in a house in Rive, and Don Guynand of St. Gervais married them, and Jehan Marcoz[356] recorded the contract, and he bought the banns from the said Don Guynant and gave him 8 *gros,* and this was at the time when they removed the churches,[357] and that the wedding was in Rive. [f. 40] The Consistory advises that the wife be heard, that he do his best to get his letter of marriage, and that they be reconciled on Thursday.

Loys Gajoz concerning the said conflict answers that his brother keeps a whore, and he does not know how he keeps her, and he does not know whether he has married her or not, and he did not receive Communion the last time or at Easter, and that he has no neighbor who says she is his wife. The Consistory advises that the two brothers be reconciled as above and that all three be brought together and that they do their best to make the said marriage clear, and by testimony, and that he bring his witnesses to testify, and that all three be summoned, and the wife of the said Loys Gajoz.

Donne Joyeuse and her daughter.

Asked that [a message] be sent and she be delivered from the promise made with her promised husband.[358] *Vide ibi retro signo* {See there on the back at the sign} #.[359]

355. A Colin Gajouz or Gaige, farm laborer, died on November 23, 1566, at age 60 (E.C., Morts 7, p. 30).
356. Jean Cohendoz or Cuenod, called Marcoz, was *secrétaire de justice* and later procurator general during the detention of Procurator General Jean Lambert by the Mammelus in 1535 and 1536 [*R.C.* XIII, pp. 337 and 356 (October 26 and November 19, 1535) and p. 483 (March 9, 1536)]. He was also a notary (without minutes in the A.E.G.) and, in 1541, *auditeur* in the lieutenant's court (Mss. hist. 145, p. 39).
357. That is about August 10, 1535, the date of the suppression of the Mass in Geneva, the period when most of the ecclesiastics left Geneva.
358. This concerns the matrimonial case between Françoyse Reys and Pierre Favre, called Berthoz, presented in Consistory on March 9, 1542.
359. For the continuation of this case, see below in this session of the Consistory.

Anthoyne Dordotz Goyti, native of Bajovve, Bajovve [sic].[360]

Has been in this city about three years, and has had a license from the Council to hold a writing school in the house of Amed Gervays.[361] And he makes a living where he can and he has lived with the son of the executioner, Janin the executioner, and that he has not been forbidden to be near his wife.[362] And that he did not say that there is no cat who, when he finds the pot uncovered, will not take something, and that he never thought about the woman. Said that Monsieur Britillion was in his house, he told him to leave, and that he asked the said wife of Janin for a blanket, he came to a child and he took what he wanted to cover himself. The Consistory advises that Britillion and the said teacher be summoned for Thursday, and that he be forbidden to go again with the said woman or hang around her and that information be obtained.

40v] *About the affair of Magnin and Loyse Du Bioley.*

That he have the banns published and that he look after the woman and the child and that the marriage go into effect and that he take and support the child. The mistress of Loyse[363] appeared with Anthoyne Charvet[364] to ask that the said marriage be carried out.[365]

360. Struck from the text: "Thotefeu(?)."

361. Noble Ami Gervais, apothecary, member of the Fifty in 1527, councillor in 1535, and *dizainier* in 1537. Died on August 13, 1553, on the Rue de Saint Gervais [GALIFFE III, p. 233; *R.C.* XII, p. 45 (December 3, 1531); R.C. 30, f. 167v (February 7, 1537)].

362. These are the wife and son of the executioner Janin Navetaz, son of the former executioner of Geneva, Jean Navetaz (the post did not pass directly from father to son). Like almost all the executioners of Geneva, he lived in the St. Gervais quarter. He was already executioner in 1526, and became a member of the CC in 1527 at the latest. He was also for a time gatekeeper of the Porte de la Corraterie [*R.C.* III, p. 144 (June 23, 1480); *R.C.* X, pp. 108, 240, and 420 (September 17, 1525, September 14, 1526, July 12, 1527); *R.C.* XI, p. 105 (August 4, 1528); Notaires, Louis Mestral, sole volume, f. 5v (June 23, 1509)].

363. Georgea de Langin, wife of Pierre de Sales.

364. Anthoyne Charvet, draper of Chambéry (Savoie), admitted to the bourgeoisie on July 9, 1532 (*L.B.*, p. 209), member of the CC in 1541, in 1544 living "on the Rivière dessous" (Rue basse du Marché, near the Molard). See GALIFFE III, pp. 124-125, and MOTTU-WEBER, *Économie*, pp. 33-34, 114, and 117, n. 110.

365. On June 26 and July 3, 1542, the Council ordered Magnin to take charge of the child and marry Loyse Du Bioley under the threat of being sent to prison (R.C. 36, f. 53 and f. 58v). Finally, on November 24, 1542 (R.C. 36, f. 177v), the Council ordered that Magnin be "freed from prison if he marries the woman he has sworn faith to."

François Boulatz.

Was married in this city. Says it was a year ago that he had a woman whom he made pregnant and has the child with him and keeps it in the district of Gex and asks mercy. The Consistory advises that he be remanded to Tuesday before the Council and that the woman with whom he has fornicated be made to come on Thursday.[366]

About the affair of the chambermaid of the Three Quail.[367]

Vide superius {See above}, the affair of the daughter of Joyeuse under this sign #.[368]

The Consistory advises that she continue to strive to get news so as to be freed from the said marriage. Considering that she has made efforts and the said husband has not come here, it would be good for her to write to him one more time to have better evidence for a separation. And that he come make an end of the said affair and of her promise, and if he can come here an end will be made of the said affair within two weeks. And afterwards, depending on the information, he will be remanded before the Council, which will make a clear decision. Two weeks to get an answer.

The contents of the letter sent: "To Françoyse, widow of François Curt,[369] living on the Rue de Saint Gervais in Geneva. Françoyse my friend, I commend myself to you and to your mother. Know that she is the cause, by the words she said, that I am thus in another [f. 41] country; we would not have had the quarrel we had if I had thought when I started the affair. I think indeed that you are as unhappy as I; nevertheless we must have patience and commend ourselves to God, because I hope for one pain we will have fifteen joys.[370] I pray you to give news of yourself to the present carrier, because he will surely bring it to me afterwards. When I have news of you I will send you more ample news of me. At the moment I am well, thanks be to God, wishing the same for you. Commend me to your brother Claude, his wife, etc. I write

---

366. Boulatz was later imprisoned for fornication, and on September 11, 1542, the Council resolved that he be "made to answer" (R.C. 36, f. 117).

367. See above, June 15, 1542. Struck from the text: "For Thursday, June 29, in Consistory."

368. Continuation of the case of Françoyse Reys versus Pierre Favre; see above in this session of the Consistory.

369. Possibly François Curt, son of Claude, from Champfromier (Ain), admitted to the bourgeoisie on November 19, 1538 (*L.B.*, p. 218).

370. *Les quinze joies de mariage* is an anonymous satire of the Middle Ages on marriage, the title of which is taken from the prayer of the fifteen joys of the Virgin. See *Les .XV. joies de mariage.*

nothing else for the present, except may God give you the accomplishment of your desire. From Lyon, the first day of May, 1542, by him who is and will be yours, Pierre Favre."

For Thursday, June 29, 1542

Those who have not appeared.

Colin Gajoz's wife and Colin Gajoz, having been remanded; Loys Gajouz and his wife; Jaques the pack-saddler.[371]

Those who will be summoned again.

The mother of Syndic Pertemps;[372] the Triumphant;[373] Pierre de La Tablaz, butcher;[374] Jehan Desboys, carpenter in the Fusterie, *dizainier;* Jehan, the servant of Jehan Tacon; Robert the pack-saddler;[375] Calabri the mason;[376] the hostess of the Three Quail and her husband.[377]

The said day, Thursday, June 29; because of certain obstacles the Consistory was not held on this day; postponed to July 6.[378]

41v]

Thursday, July 6, 1542

Lord Syndic Rozet.
Gerbel, Molard, Britillion, D'Orsieres, Rages, Blandin, Frochet, the officer Vovrey.

371. Jaques Emyn, pack-saddler.
372. Jane Pertennaz.
373. Jane, wife of Claude Thorens, called the Triumphant.
374. Pierre Durand, called De La Tablaz.
375. Robert Breysson, pack-saddler.
376. Pierre Calabri, mason.
377. Anthoyne and Aymoz Foural.
378. On this day the Council received a letter from Basel "saying that the lords of Bern refuse the friendly settlement offered in Basel of the differences between the two seigneuries of Bern and Geneva." The Genevans resolved to send ambassadors to Basel to show their good will, then to discuss the matter in the Council of Two Hundred the next Monday. On Monday, July 3, they elected Claude Pertemps ambassador and named Jacques Des Arts "to keep him company" [R.C. 36, f. 55 (June 29, 1542); f. 59v, f. 60v and f. 61 (July 4, 1542)]. However, we do not know whether this is the reason why the Consistory was not held on June 29.

Because the lords preachers were not in the city[379] the parties and elders left, and put off until next Thursday, July 13.

Thursday, July 13

Lord Syndic Rozet.
Calvin, Viret,[380] Bernard, Henri, Champereaulx.
Girbel, Britillion, Pensabin, Orsieres, Blandin, Frochet, the officer Vovrey.

Jehan Desboys, carpenter, dizainier of the Fusterie, for various reasons.[381]

Answers concerning religion and his office that he was not thus instructed, and that he will be diligent in regulating his *dizaine* in religion and that he will make those women, children, servants and maids whom he can go to catechism.

The writing master of St. Gervais,[382] *named above because of the executioner's wife.*[383]

Asked whether since his last appearance he has been in or frequented the executioner's house; whether he has frequented the said executioner's house and whether he was not forbidden to go there again. Answers that he is married in his own country, that he has sent for [his wife], and that if there is anyone who has seen him enter any part of the said house he wants to be hanged and strangled, except into the shop to ask for some [f. 42] money that the said executioner owes him and to ask him for his money. And says that he was not

379. Calvin appeared in Council on July 4 and 10 (R.C. 36, f. 61 and f. 65v), without mentioning any absence or other business that prevented the ministers from attending the Consistory in the meantime.

380. This is the last time that Pierre Viret attended the Consistory before his departure for Lausanne. The decision was taken on July 10, 1542: the ministers "have proposed through the mouth of Master Calvin, our minister, that Master Pierre Vyret, because of the great necessity in the church of Lausanne, should travel to the said Lausanne . . ." (R.C. 36, f. 65v). *Ibid.,* f. 72 (July 7, 1542), it says that in the General Council "Master Pierre Vyret took leave of their lordships, to the great regret of the Seigneurie at his departure, and he was given proper thanks, and it was ordered that he be given twelve écus." On June 7, 1542, the council of Strasbourg wrote that the recall of Viret was "very troublesome for Monsieur John Calvin, because everything may not yet have been restored to good order around him, and Monsieur Calvin himself, because of his poor health, cannot do everything" (HERMINJARD VIII, p. 53, translated from German).

381. Jean Desboys (de Nemoribus), from Machilly (H.-S), bourgeois and member of the CC [*L.B.,* p. 113 (December 28, 1490); R.C. 37, f. 10 (February 9, 1543)].

382. Anthoyne Dordotz Goyti.

383. The wife of Janin Navetaz.

there except to ask for a blanket, and Monsieur Britillion came there. And denied that he wanted to drink, but he walked through the room. And Monsieur Britillion told him that he found him with the cloak, and they were ready to drink. Says and answers that it is not so, although the said Britillion told him that he should not be there with another man's wife without her husband being present. Also, being in St. Claude, at someone's instigation he agreed to come to Geneva for his bitches. And various good admonitions. Answers that he will enlarge on the things he did and that he has sent for his wife. The Consistory advises that he be given leave and told to depart the city because of the scandal about him because he does not have his wife with him, and that he be remanded to Monday before the Council. And that he go get his wife and that it be known who he is, where he is from, and that he be given a sufficient term to go seek his said wife and that it be known when she comes and that good information be obtained. And that he cease to go into the said house where the said executioner lives in Monsieur Britillion's house. Note that he has asked a woman in this city to be his wife, Palligotz' widow.[384] And denied it and wants to be punished, and that someone wanted to give him the maid of the mill, and he did not want to marry.[385]

Estienne Roz, teacher in the school.

Complained of a woman who insulted him, named Estienne, daughter of the late Pierre Nycod called Du Puerchoz, who was pregnant by Master Pierre.[386]

The said Estienne appeared. Says that once she came to the said [teacher] Estienne, that she went to tell Monsieur Calvin that Master Pierre, who was married, was then in the school, and that she had told him that she was pregnant by Master Pierre. And then he said that she should take counsel of Monsieur Calvin, and Monsieur Calvin remanded her to the Consistory.

Also the said [teacher] Estienne said that she was spiteful without reservation before the Seigneurie, and denied. The Consistory advises that they be admonished that peace should be made between them, because it is not a serious thing, or that the said Master Estienne should be given a discharge. And

384. The Pelligots, originally from Veigy, were too numerous in Geneva to permit us to identify this woman.

385. Anthoyne Dordotz Goyti seems to have finally recalled his wife to Geneva. On September 20, 1550, Jaqueme, his daughter, died, probably very young, in the Tour de Boël (E.C., Morts 1, p. 23).

386. Estienne (or Tevenon) Nycod opposed the banns of marriage between Pierre Moussard and Estiennette Castellion, claiming that Moussard had already promised to marry her and that she was pregnant by him. See above, May 2, 1542.

that they be reconciled here and that she be punished and that the Council be informed. And both were remanded to Monday before the Council.

[f. 42v] *Donne Jane Pertennaz.*

She was admonished because of certain crosses and darts in her hemp-field.[387] And has received Holy Communion where she was ordered, and that she has obeyed the Seigneurie where she is and lives and that she puts her faith in God. And that she has not put out the crosses or darts, and much more. Answers that she always believed in God and His Word, and where the holy Word of God is, she believed.[388] And that she always has faith in her God and that she is not excommunicated and separated from the church, and she opposed this, and no one will ever know her faith but God and herself. Presented a certain paper on which were certain Gospel words in the Latin language[389] which someone gave her. And that she should know who gave it to her. Answers that it was a village woman and she does not know her name. Remanded at once to the City Hall because of her rebelliousness.[390] The Consistory advises that she appear every Thursday at the Consistory, or otherwise, and every day at the sermons until her profiting is apparent, and that she be remanded before the Council, which will admonish her more sharply, and that she confess who gave her this Gospel paper. Or, before she is remanded before the Council, that she be summoned once a week for remonstrances to see whether she can be converted to the Holy Gospel, and that someone be assigned to admonish her, and that she go to catechism, and that she come here Thursday.

Pernete, wife of Guillaume Bocherens.[391]

Why they do not live together. Answers that last Sunday they returned together and are together. She and her husband remanded to Thursday. Thursday, Bocherens and his wife to Thursday [sic].

---

387. Translator: This is what the text appears to say. The meaning is not very clear, but possibly she was accused of some sort of magical practice to protect her hemp crop.

388. Struck out in the margin: "and that it is the word of Jesus Christ."

389. These were probably some prayers taken from the Bible which she carried with her and read in the manner of a small book of Hours.

390. There are hardly any minutes of the Council for this day, the Council having considered only the case of fornication between Jehan Benez and Janne Grenier (R.C. 36, f. 68v); see below.

391. Guillaume Bocherens, butcher, from Ballaison, was admitted to the bourgeoisie on November 17, 1517. His wife Pernette died on September 29, 1553, in Longemalle, already a widow (*L.B.*, p. 186; E.C., Morts 1, p. 120).

43] *Jane, wife of Claude Thorens, called the Triumphant.*

Because of the sermons and her faith. Said the prayer and the confession. Answered that since this law came things have never gone well in this city, and it was at the time when the mercenary soldiers passed by here.[392] The Consistory ordered her to frequent the sermons and her . . .[393] and the catechism on Sundays.

Jehan Benez, from Cranves, farm laborer, living sometimes here and sometimes in Cranves and at the house of Monsieur Hudriod Du Mollard.

Jana, daughter of Aymoz Grenier, from Prégny, says she had a child by him and it is six weeks old and has still not been baptized and that he should do for her what he promised her and that he swore faith and was engaged to her, and he denies the child. He asks for a copy [of the testimony] and time to respond. The Consistory advises that he take the child and that it be baptized and that he be admonished.

Also asked whether he had knowledge of her. Answers once in a meadow, that she came to meet him in the said meadow once. And he repents it, but the child is not his, and if she gives it to another he will be more able to support it than he. Nevertheless if she gives it to him on her conscience he will take it, but only if she swears to it. He believes that the child is rather by another than him and that he never promised himself to her. The Consistory . . .[394]

Pierre Favre, coppersmith, and Franceyse, daughter of Joyeuse.

Asked why he did not complete the said marriage. Answers that he came to complete the said marriage and that he went outside [the city] to earn some money. The said Françoyse was asked whether he mistreated her, why she does not want to marry him and why he should not go. Joyeuse, her mother, said that he is a liar and that he said that he would only go for four days, and he has lived in Lyon until now. [f. 43v] The said Piere was asked why he left and how long it has been since he left. An-

392. This probably refers to the passage of the Bernese soldiers, come to the aid of Geneva against the Duke of Savoy in February 1536. Although not likely, it is possible that Jane Thorens refers to the first stay of the Swiss allies in Geneva in 1530, when the Reform was preached in the cathedral for the first time (in German). See *R.C.* XIII, pp. 419 and 446 (February 2 and 16, 1536); FROMENT, pp. 211-217; NAEF, *Origines* II, pp. 256ff.

393. Word omitted.

394. Incomplete sentence. This case was discussed in Council the same day without adding anything (R.C. 36, f. 68v).

swers that it was two weeks after Christmas and that he wanted to get an advance to put up a shop. And they only wanted to give him a *quart* of wheat and four *quarterons* of wine and wanted to burden him with supporting four people with him, and because of this he left. He was given many admonitions and remonstrances. The mother and daughter said that the daughter would never marry him and that he was a man who would never be in their house. The Consistory advises that all three be remanded to next Thursday.

Thursday, July 20, 1542

Lord Syndic Cornaz.
Calvin, Ph[ilippe] de Ecclesia, Pierre Blanchet,[395] Henri.
Girbel, Rages, Pensabin, Blandin, Frochet, the officer Vovrey.

Andrier Piard, notary.[396]

Asked whether he goes to the sermons. Answers that he goes to the sermon and to Holy Communion every day, on Sundays. Said the Pater and the Credo in Latin, and in French the faith and confession very poorly, and said that Sunday morning before dinner Master Viret preached. The Consistory advises that he be commanded to bring the books in which he studies the Word of God immediately. *Vide* *.[397]

395. Pierre Blanchet and Philippe de Ecclesia were presented to the Council by Calvin and approved for the ministry on July 10, 1542, and presented to the Congregation [of the Company of Pastors] on Sunday, July 16, 1542 [R.C. 36, f. 65 and f. 72 (July 10 and 17, 1542)]. De Ecclesia was transferred to Vandoeuvres on July 28, 1544. On February 15, 1549, the Company of Pastors censured him because he "held in the Congregation some propositions that were not for edification and posed useless questions . . . and even erroneous doctrines" (*R.C.P.* I, pp. 47 and 56-58). He was deposed on January 27, 1553, for usury, mistreatment of his wife, and talking to Jérôme Bolsec, Calvin's adversary (*R.C.P.* I, pp. 76, 134, 144-45, 148, 151). Blanchet went to the plague hospital to minister to the poor on May 11, 1543, and died there about June 1 (R.C. 37, f. 89 and f. 110).
396. Probably the son of Andrier Piard, hosier, made a bourgeois on December 31, 1501 (*L.B.,* p. 145), died before July 7, 1535 (*R.C.* XIII, p. 271). Andrier Piard the son was probably already working as a notary in 1528, or in 1533 at the latest [*R.C.* XI, p. 402 (December 7, 1528), and XII, p. 186 (January 7, 1533); no minutes in the A.E.G.]. Apparently either the father or the son shared a house with Aymoz Cortagier, who follows below [*R.C.* XII, pp. 401-402 (December 12, 1533)]. Piard was condemned to have his head cut off for "falsity" on September 20, 1544 (R.C. 38, f. 380v).
397. Continue below at this sign: *.

Aymoz Cortagier.[398]

Because of the sermons. Answers that he goes to the sermons, not every day, and that he has a lawsuit in Collonges sus Belle Rive, and he goes on Mondays and Thursdays. He was given admonitions and remonstrances to frequent the sermons more often, and also his wife.

44]   *Nicolarde, widow of Mathieu Roland.*

Said that she has never engaged herself to a husband, unless it is one to whom she said that if he wanted to come live under the Council of Bern she would agree, and if he had come they would have made a promise. And she did not want to go live there[399] because of the Mass, and she still has not made a promise and has not done otherwise, and she does not want to marry him in the papistry. The Consistory advises that considering the case written above that she be commanded to write to the said Rolet that he should carry out his promise, and that the marriage be carried out, considering that the said Roland is not vouched for. And that she bring the answer he makes so that a remedy can be provided.

Vide*.[400]

The said Piard brought his *vade-mecum* and said that his other books are in the mountains where he put them during the war of Peney,[401] in Grandvaux in Burgundy, and he brought three small apocryphal books of no value. He was given proper admonitions to frequent the sermons more often than he has done in the past and to bring the good Bible he has in Grandvaux and present it here.

Master Pierre Calabri, mason.

Because of the sermons and the Holy Communion. Answers that he goes to the sermons on Sundays after dinner. In the morning he has business with his servants because of the walls, that he has to pay [them] on Sunday, and that he has always received Holy Communion. Said the Lord's Prayer in the French language in a general way; he did not know the confession, and excused himself strongly. The Consistory advises that he be ordered to go to

398. He shared his house with Andrier Piard (see the interrogation of Piard above).
399. Translator: *I.e.,* where he was then living, in Catholic territory.
400. Continuation of the interrogation of André Piard; see above at this sign: *.
401. The war from July 1534 to 1535 against the Peneysans, the Genevans loyal to the bishop and the Duke of Savoy, named thus for the château of Peney to which they withdrew. See MARTIN, *Genève,* p. 200.

and frequent the sermons, and that he abstain from receiving the next Holy Communion. And that he go to catechism every Sunday, and that he say who was next to him at the last Holy Communion at Pentecost. And that he come present himself before the next Holy Communion to show how he has profited before it is given to him.[402]

[f. 44v] *Mermete, daughter of Claude Bocard, called Baufri, of this city.*

Because it is said that she has promised herself to a husband. Answers no, but it is true there was one who wanted her to promise, and she answered him that she did not want to consent, and he gave her nothing, and she has many people whom she named. And she did not want to unless her father and mother[403] knew him, and that she did not want to go outside the city without the knowledge of her father and mother. And she goes to the sermons. Said the prayer and confession properly. The Consistory advises that Monsieur Pierre de Rages find out from the neighbors and . . .[404]

Guilliama, widow of Pierre de Carro,[405] and Jehan de Carro her son.

Because of the sermons. Answers that she and her son often go to the sermons on working days and Sundays, and they were there three times on Sunday. Said the prayer and not the confession. And the son said that he knows only what his father taught him when he was alive. And he has received Communion, and does not know the prayer or the faith. The Consistory advises that they be admonished and that they go every day and come here every Thursday to give an account of their improvement, and to the catechism. And that his mother teach him good morals, and that she make her other son come. The mother excused herself from going to the sermons every day because she has no one to help her.

Jana Carre, the wife of Jaques Carre.[406]

Because of the sermons. Answers that she goes to the sermons when she can, because she has three small children who prevent her. Said the

402. Pierre Calabri, from Corsinge (GE), was admitted to the bourgeoisie on January 5, 1525 (*L.B.*, p. 204). He died of plague before August 10, 1543 (R.C. 37, f. 188).

403. Guygonaz Bocard.

404. Struck from the text: "that she be remanded to Thursday."

405. Guillauma, widow of Pierre de Carro, was still living in 1554 (GALIFFE II, p. 135).

406. Jaques Carre was the brother of Jean de Carro, mentioned above, and the son of Guillauma and Pierre Pichard, called Carre.

Lord's Prayer and the faith and creed in Latin and the confession and the Ave Maria. The Consistory advises that she be ordered to frequent the sermons and that she come here every Thursday and go to the catechism on Sundays.

Andri Arnod, from Vance in the diocese of Chartres, bookseller, and Janetaz Ponarde, his wife.

Where he was married and who published his banns. And that he published his banns here and is in Cossonay, and that Champereaulx and Curteti[407] signed them. And as for the Word of God, [f. 45] answers that he cannot go to the sermons every day; when he can. The wife said the confession and the Lord's Prayer. They were . . .[408]

Monet Ramu, boatman, bourgeois of Geneva, and Humberte his wife, from this city.[409]

Answers there is hardly anything; it was today, and they go to the sermons three times a week. He said the Lord's Prayer and the creed in the French language. The wife did not know how to say it as well as the husband. The Consistory resolved that they both continue to frequent the sermons.

Robert the pack-saddler.[410]

Because of the sermons and faith and creed. And said the prayer and the confession poorly. Answers that he did not receive Holy Communion because he was forbidden to receive it. The Consistory advises that he be remanded to the Council, or rather admonished because of his poverty of understanding as a desperate man and badly disposed because of his faith and creed. To Monday before the Council, which will admonish him.[411]

---

407. The syndic Jean Ami Curtet.

408. Incomplete sentence.

409. In a notarial act concerning a loan by Conrad Vity they are identified as Monet Ramus, from Massongy (H.-S.), *habitant*, boatman, and Humberte, daughter of the late Pierre Du Cimitiere, from the parish of Pougny (Ain) [Notaires, de Compois, v. 6, f. 195 (November 18, 1527)]. Monet Ramus was admitted to the bourgeoisie on January 5, 1537 (R.C. 30, f. 144).

410. Robert Breysson, pack-saddler.

411. On July 24, 1542, the Council ordered him to go to the sermon every day until he knew how to say the Confession of Faith (that is, the Apostles' Creed) and to go to the catechism for a year (R.C. 36, f. 76v).

Jane, wife of Guyon de Montagu, goldsmith.[412]

Because of the sermons and bad words spoken by her, and she does not go to the sermons every day. Answers, and denies the infamous words, and she cannot frequent the sermons, and she excuses herself because of her household. Said the Lord's Prayer and the confession. The Consistory gave her remonstrances and admonitions to follow the sermons often.

The wife of Aymoz Cortagiez.[413]

Because of the sermons, and other admonitions. Answers that the Consistory is badly informed, and she goes to the sermons on Sundays, and when she can on the day of prayer.[414] Said the Pater and the confession, and she is sickly. Admonished to frequent the sermons more often than before.

[f. 45v]

Thursday, July 27, 1542

Lord Syndic Cornaz.
Calvin, Henri, Blanchet, Champereaulx.
Gerbel, Rages, Pensabin, Frochet, the officer Vovrey.

Bernardaz, wife of Anthoyne the haberdasher.[415]

Asked about the children she smothered. Answers that about three weeks ago a child of hers died, which made her very unhappy, and that it was not due to her. And confesses freely that two others of hers have died by the evil of someone she feared, whom she asks be examined about the events. And she fears Claudaz, purse-maker, who lives at Deleta's house.[416] The first child lived only five hours and died and was smothered. The second died under the cushion, being in the bed with it. And it is true that a neighbor called to her to go look after Abraham, her last son, and she told her that she was carrying her own, and she answered that Jesus Christ would watch her child. And when she went to the child she found it dead. And this was the wife of

412. Guydo Montagu, son of Gonin, from Besançon (Doubs), goldsmith, living in the parish of the Magdalen, admitted to the bourgeoisie on June 4, 1535 (*L.B.,* p. 212).
413. Jana Bertherat, wife of Aymoz Cortagier.
414. Wednesday.
415. Anthoyne Diard, haberdasher. Identified as the son of Jaquemette, widow of Maxime, in a criminal proceeding against François Perret [P.C. 2ᵉ sér., 267 (June 27-29, 1531)].
416. Was he Egrège Pierre Deleta, who died before April 27, 1545 (R.C. Part. 1, f. 272v)?

Claude Vullierme,[417] that God had been very gracious to her, and that she was cold in the heat of the sun, that the time was past that the witches could do any more to her, because her children had both died at the age of her last. Therefore she strongly urges that they examine the said woman. And says that she did nothing to her children that a mother should not, and she would say this even if she were before God. Also asked why she did not go to see her child that cried. Answers that she did not hear it cry. And whether her husband was ever in this city when the said three children were killed and died. Answers none of the three, but he was abroad. Her children died from negligence. The Consistory advises, considering the great scandal, that she be remanded to the Council, which should make a more ample inquiry tomorrow, Friday, July 28.[418]

46]   *Lyonard de Bouge.*[419]

About the Word of God, the sermons, and mistreatment in his household and his anger against all. Answers that he goes to the sermons when he can, but may it please them, he has so much against Savoex and others[420] that

417. Possibly Claude Vullierme, bourgeois, cobbler, living on the Rue de la Maison de la Ville, who died February 11, 1566, at about age 80. He signed a contract of marriage with Georgea, daughter of Nicod Merma, on October 19, 1543. She was still living in 1552 [*L.B.*, p. 179 (May 5, 1514); E.C., Morts 6, p. 114; E.C., Saint-Pierre B.M. 1, baptêmes, April 28, 1552; Notaires, George Maillet, v. 1, folios 148-152]. There was also a Claude Vulliermo, called Callie, son of Michel, farm laborer, identified in 1557 as "formerly farmer for the late Egrège Deleta." However, at this time he appears to have lived in either Collonges or Vandoeuvres. He was a poor man, banished several times from Geneva. His father had been executed for sorcery, and the son was also accused. It is certainly he who is found suspected of witchcraft in 1544. See P.C. 1ᵉ sér., 626 (March 10-17, 1557), and R.C. 39, f. 38v (November 14, 1544).

418. Bernardaz, wife of Anthoine Diard, haberdasher, was summoned to Council on July 28, 1542 (R.C. 36, f. 81), because "it is understood that through mistreatment three small children of hers died." The Council ordered an investigation, and on August 8, 1542, Bernardaz was freed from prison and declared innocent of the accusation of infanticide (R.C. 36, f. 91).

419. Lyonard de Bouge (de Bougier, de Bogiaco), citizen and member of the CC, heir of his grandfather, the former syndic Claude Richardet. He was a merchant and apparently an apothecary (condemned for "false powders" in 1556) [GALIFFE II, p. 57; L. GAUTIER, *Médecine*, p. 450; R.C. 36, f. 26 (May 30, 1542)].

420. This refers to a suit Lyonard de Bouge had against Claude Savoye [R.C. 36, f. 26 (May 30, 1542)]. Claude Savoye, born about 1491, was master of the mint, councillor, syndic, and first syndic. In 1539 he was imprisoned and deprived of all his offices for intrigues with the Seigneur de Montchenu, ambassador of the king of France. One of Farel's first converts in Geneva, Claude Savoye ended by renouncing his bourgeoisie in Geneva and fleeing to Bern, becoming a bourgeois of Bern in 1542 "to shelter himself from the persecutions of the intolerant party," in the always anti-Calvinist words of Galiffe (GALIFFE I, p. 225; ROGET I, pp. 142-143; DEMOLE, p. 20; SORDET, *Dictionnaire*, pp. 1172-1173).

he cannot go very often because of the quarrels he has. And that he wants to obey justice. He was admonished to go and frequent the sermons and not fail.

Mauris de La Ruaz.

Because of the treatment of his wife in his house and other things in his household. Answers that he struck his wife because she did not do what he commanded her. And that he never gave her more than four blows. Jane, his wife, for the reason above, with her husband. Answers that they have had some conflicts, but nevertheless she has not ceased to do her housework, and he struck her because she had not cleaned up in front of the house. The Consistory advises that they live together in peace as they promised God in front of the church, and to frequent the sermons.[421]

Pernete, widow of Jacques Collombet, boatman, fishmonger;[422] *Merma, widow of Franceys Plantem, fishmonger.*[423]

Because of the Word of God and the sermons. Both answer that they can rarely go because they must earn their living, and they do nothing but give themselves to the devil and blaspheme God and fight each other. Answer that they do not fight each other. Both said the Pater and confession. Admonished to live peaceably and frequent the sermons, and that they admonish the other fishmongers of the Molard and others who fight each other.

[f. 46v]   *[The maid of the Three Quail.]*

The opinion of the Consistory was that the Council be asked to write to the chief *bailli* or to the Consistory of Ternier[424] to get an affidavit from the

421. Maurys de La Ruaz, former priest of Geneva, was admitted to the bourgeoisie on May 2, 1539, "considering that he has taken many pains for the city." His wife was apparently the daughter of François Duvillard who disputed with Mauris de La Ruaz over her dowry and the *fiancement* of their marriage (the *fiancement* is a pledge given by the husband that he will manage his wife's dowry carefully). The Council resolved that "if the said De La Rue wants to have the marriage portion of his wife, he should swear to preserve the rights of the said wife and of his children." He died of plague on April 19, 1545. His wife survived him [L.B., p. 219; CAHIER-BUCCELLI, "Ombre," p. 374; R.C. 33, f. 391 (December 22, 1539); R.C. 35, f. 555 (April 11, 1542); E.C., Morts 1, supplément (carnet des morts de peste, 1545), p. 4; R.C. 41, f. 67 (April 6, 1546)].

422. Pernette Collombet died at the hospital on April 26, 1569, at age 80 (E.C., Morts 9, p. 73).

423. For Merma Plantens, see the note below on her son George on March 22, 1543.

424. The *bailli* of Ternier was then Germann Ientsch (1541-1549). See DUVAL, *Ternier,* p. 91.

maid of the hostess of the Three Quail[425] on the Bourg du Four because of her maid's fornication, about the child she had and then lost. She never wanted to say the name.

Thursday, August 3, 1542

Lord Syndic Cornaz.
Calvin, Champereaulx, P[ierre] Blanchet, De Ecclesia.
Britillion, Rages, Frichet, the officer Vovrey.

One of the guests of Jehan Du Nant.[426] *Michiel Cochet of L'Eluiset, carpenter,* habitant *of Geneva, living in the* dizaine *of Jehan Du Nant.*

Because of frequenting the sermons. Answers that he was at the sermon Sunday, and did not recognize the preacher. And asks mercy and pardon this time, and he was in Etrembières on Sunday and was not at the sermon, and he has not been to St. Peter's for a week and does not know who preached. Said the Pater and confession. Admonished to frequent the sermons.[427]

Jehan Corajoz, cobbler.[428]

Because of a child he has at the school of La Roche, a place in the papistry.[429] Answers that he does not keep the child there from any regard for

425. Antoine Foural, hostess of the Three Quail.
426. Jehan Corajod, called Du Nant, who follows below.
427. Michel Cochet and his wife Françoise were also called with other inhabitants of Jehan Corajod's house (the Golden Lion) this same day; see below. Michel returned to the Consistory with his neighbors on October 19, 1542. Finally, on May 27, 1544, Michel and Françoise were recalled to the Consistory for having baptized their child on Catholic territory.
428. Struck from the text: "Du Nant." Jehan Corajod, called Du Nant, bourgeois of Geneva, from Etrembières (H.-S.), cobbler and host of the inn of the Golden Lion. He was named *dizainier* of the Poissonnerie in 1534 and still had that office in 1541. He died on June 14, 1554, in the Poissonnerie [*L.B.*, p. 192 (December 13, 1521); *R.C.* XII, p. 566 (June 23, 1534); R.C. 35, f. 56ᶜ (February 9, 1541) and f. 490 (February 7, 1542); E.C., Morts 1, p. 163].
429. On January 29, 1537, the Seigneurie ordered "that those who have children in school should be told that they should not dare to have them elsewhere than in Christian schools" (*S.D.* II, p. 334). The college of La Roche was a good school where many Genevans sent their children (see, for example, Loyse and Jehan Bennar, below, February 1, 1543). The Consistory did not fear this school without reason, for, as the *Encyclopédie de Genève* tells us (V, p. 155): "During some decades [in the middle of the sixteenth century] only the three colleges of Annecy, La Roche and Evian provided basic instruction for future priests." Under Pierre Veillard, rector of schools of La Roche in 1529, this school produced illustrious Jesuits:

the papistry but because the school was not good here, and he has not re-turned since, and he will come whenever the Seigneurie pleases. And his wife is ill, and he believes the householders in his house are respectable people. Said his Pater; confesses that his child worships idols at the school of La Roche. Says that his wife has never missed Holy Communion, and he came here, and his wife is ill in Etrembières.

[f. 47]   *Goni[n] Laurent, butcher; Jehan Martin, butcher; Marquiot de Villa, farm la-borer;*[430] *Jehan Sautier, butcher;*[431] *Pierre Soutiez, his brother;*[432] *Jehan Gantoz;*[433] *Jehan Voland, carter,*[434] *did not know how to say the confession.*

Guests at the house of Jehan Corajoz, called Du Nant, in the house of the Golden Lion. Most said the Pater and confession rather poorly; admonished.

Loyse, wife of Jehan Martin; Ayma, wife of Claudon Sermod;[435] *Mermeta, wife of Claude Soutier;*[436] *Tevene, widow of Pierre Mossier; Perronete, widow of Henery Du Crotz; Jane, wife of Gonyn Laurent; Claudaz, wife of Jehan Volant; Pernete, wife of Marquiot de Ville; Françoise, wife of Michie[l] Cochet.*

About frequenting of sermons. Members of the household of the said Jehan Corajod. All said the Pater, whether well or ill, and the confession. Admonitions and remonstrances. Jehan Voland, carter, remanded to two weeks.

"Claude Lejay was the seventh companion of Ignatius Loyola and directed the universities of Ingolstadt and Vienna; Pierre Favre, connected with St. Francis Xavier, became the first priest of the Society of Jesus" (NAEF, *Origines* II, p. 274).

430. Marquiot de Villa was identified as a cobbler living in the Poissonnerie at the time of the death of his daughter Pernette on May 9, 1550 (E.C., Morts 1, p. 11).

431. Jean Sautier or Soutier, citizen, butcher in Longemale, died between 1563 and 1572 [E.C., Morts 5, p. 107 (December 18, 1563), and E.C., Morts 11, p. 35 (May 6, 1572); deaths of a son four months old and of his widow, Martine].

432. There was a Pierre Sautier, farm laborer, who died on September 19, 1555 (E.C., Morts 1, p. 118).

433. According to Sordet (*Dictionnaire*, p. 661), Jehan Gandoz came of a bourgeois family that had lost its bourgeoisie. He was rehabilitated in 1545, became a member of the CC in 1557, and died in 1572. However, it may be that Sordet confuses father and son; a daughter of the *late* Jehan Gandoz died on June 11, 1552 (E.C., Morts 1, p. 65).

434. Jehan Volland, called Gentil, carter, was admitted to the bourgeoisie on June 11, 1535 (*L.B.*, p. 213; see also below, December 13, 1543).

435. A Claude Sermod, citizen and butcher, is found in a list of butchers in 1559, and lived in Longemale in 1566 [R.C. 55, f. 160 (December 19, 1559); E.C., Morts 6, p. 152 (June 2, 1566), death of his child].

436. Mermeta, wife of Claude Soutier, citizen, butcher in Longemale, died on September 23, 1553 (E.C., Morts 2, p. 60).

Thursday, August 10, 1542

Lord Syndic Cornaz.
Calvin, Henri, Blanchet, Champereaulx.
Orsieres, Blandin, Britillion, Rages, Frochet, Pensabin, the officer Vovrey.

Matrimonial case of Pierre Mamburier of Bons.[437]

Stated that . . .[438] Pernete, daughter of the late Jaque Aubrier, from Sallanche, *habitant* of Geneva, said [that] the said Pierre had promised himself to another wife and published the banns twice and that . . .[439] And the said Pernete said that he swore faith at the house of Master Pierre Vallet,[440] carpenter, and his son named Tuppin. And the said Pierre gave them to drink together, when she said and understood that it was in the name of marriage. And the said Pierre denies it and says that it is not so.[441] Pernete: the said Pernete was asked whether she had his company. Answers yes, twice, and that it was not at night. Claude, son of Pierre de Vallet, carpenter, called Tupin, his master, Françoyse his wife, the mother of the wife of the said Tuppin, the wife of Gervex were present when they drank together.

The said Pierre was asked why he does not want to complete this marriage. Answers that he has never had her company, and denied it vehemently. Asked about the said promise of marriage, denies the said marriage; denies everything repeatedly.

Confronted with each other, the said Pernete said that she had his company once or twice, and it was at the house of his master Pierre Vallet at night and that he promised her that he would never have another wife than her. And she would prove it, and how they drank together, by his master and others when it was necessary. The Consistory advises that she be asked if she was induced to say what she did and when and at what time it was. The said Pernete answers that the lieutenant[442] urged her to go to the Consistory and that no one advised her to say such words, except God who advised her. [f. 48] And that the said Tuppin told her she should complain, and it was

---

437. Pierre Mamburier, son of Claude, from Bons, was condemned to prison for fornication [reference to a session of the Consistory whose minutes are lost, in P.C. 2ᵉ sér., 809 (January 2-6, 1550)].

438. Incomplete sentence.

439. Incomplete sentence.

440. Pierre Vallet, carpenter from Vigny (H.-S.), admitted to the bourgeoisie on January 16, 1515 (*L.B.*, p. 181).

441. Struck from the text: "and the wife of Gervays was present and . . ."

442. Then François Philibert Donzel.

over a year ago. And that the said Pierre was a servant and earned wages in a carpenter's shop. And says he gave her nothing, the said Piere, in the name of marriage. The Consistory advises that both be remanded to Monday before the Council and that the said Pernete bring her witnesses before the Council.[443]

Noble Pernete, widow of the late Michiel Du Pain, apothecary.[444]

Asked how long she has been in this city. Answers three months, and she has not been able to go to the sermons because of her clothes, and they are pawned in Evian and she does not have anything to redeem them. And that her children should remove this debt from her. And that Amblard never helped her at all, and Pierre Paule did her good, and she lives in his house. Aymoz, her son, who is with a master, has never helped her in anything. And Amblard has offered her his house, but she does not want to go there. Answers concerning the sermons that she has not been there in the last three months except this week, and she wants to go there.

Amblard Du Pain, her son, was asked why his mother does not go to the sermons and why he does her no good. And that he has encouraged his said mother to frequent the sermons, and it is not due to him that she does not come live with him. And because he went to get her clothes. And said if she wants to live with him he will support her at the price. The Consistory advises that he and the other children be admonished; that she love the said Amblard like the others and come to the sermons, and that the children confer on going to get her clothes, and that the three children be made to come here Thursday, and that they pay her pension. The children should be summoned for Thursday: Pierre Pauloz, Amied and Amblard. The said three brothers were remanded to tomorrow at the Magdalen after the sermon to be reconciled. 280 florins. Her clothes are pawned for the sum written above.

443. According to the depositions of the two parties and the witnesses, the Council determined that they had drunk in the name of marriage, and because of the oath taken by Pernette the Council ordered "that the said marriage should go into effect" [R.C. 36, f. 95 and f. 99 (August 15 and 21, 1542)].

444. Pernette Roget, widow of Claude Mareschal and of Michel Du Pain. The latter, bourgeois and apothecary of the city, was condemned as a Mammelu (partisan of the Duke of Savoy) in 1527 and died in 1535. Of the three sons mentioned below, Amblard and Pierre Paul at least were apothecaries like their father [L. GAUTIER, *Médecine*, p. 445; GALIFFE I, pp. 155-156; E.C., Morts 1, pp. 150 and 275 (January 10 and February 25, 1554)].

Aymoz, son of the late Egrege Nycod de Prato, tailor.[445]

Because of the sermons. Answers that he has not been since last Sunday and that he cannot go there because of working at his trade, and that he cannot well go except Sunday and Wednesday. Said the prayer [and] the confession. Denied that he told his sister that if she were not pregnant he would shove a sword into her belly and that she called him vicious and a traitor. The Consistory advises that both be remanded here in a week and that his sister come here.

Vincent de Villa, hosier.[446]

Because of the Word of God and papistry and whether there is any doubt of the Word of God. Answers that he believes in the Word of God and loves to hear it and the Pater and that he would like to know more if he could. Said the prayer and the confession and that the Old Testament was past, consumed, because Jesus Christ came to the world. And that he did not say that one could add as much to the Holy Scripture as the priests, that the preachers of today could also change it. And that if he said it, this was from ignorance. The Consistory advises that he be admonished to go to the sermons and frequent them often and that he not turn again to lies and go every day to the sermon. And for this time he was pardoned, and that he refrain from evil speech.

Loys Agniol, purse-maker from . . .[447] *in Picardy.*[448]

Asked if he was married. Answers yes. Denied that he laid hands underneath on a girl in the public street, and that it was a scandal if it was done and that he did not intend any harm. And asked about the sermons. Answers that he goes and said that he knows the prayer and the confession. Given proper remonstrances.

445. Nycod de Prato, notary, became procurator fiscal for the bishop in 1528. After having been implicated in a plot against the city on July 30, 1534, he withdrew from Geneva and became one of the chiefs of the Peneysans. In November 1536 he was taken prisoner by French soldiers, who returned him to Geneva, where he was executed as a traitor on December 5, 1536. Hardly anything is known of the son, except that in 1543 he had to offer his father's protocols as security for a debt of seven florins [NAEF, *Origines* II, p. 136; J.-A. GAUTIER II, pp. 421-422 and 524; ROGET, *Suisses* II, pp. 115-117; R.C. 30, f. 43v (November 18, 1536); R.C. Part. 1, f. 17v (March 6, 1543)].
446. The tailor Vincent, bastard son of the notary Vincent de Villa, was admitted to the bourgeoisie on June 22, 1535 (*L.B.*, p. 214).
447. Word omitted.
448. A Loys Agnet, purse-maker, died on June 23, 1553 (E.C., Morts 1, p. 106).

[f. 49]   *Pernon, wife of Mermet Chienballiard, on the Bourg du Four.*

About the honesty of her house, because of certain young men who come and go in her house, as in fornication. Answers that no one follows an evil course and that she lives at the house of a respectable woman and that no one frequents her house except her husband's nephew and her first husband. And that she has always lived with her, and if she is shown those who say this, they can do what they wish with her. And that she has no neighbors who wish her any harm. And if someone has spoken against her this has been due to malevolence, and they should proceed in this affair, because she does not intend to be like that. She was admonished to refrain from doing so any more and to be sensible, and for this time she is pardoned, and not to return here again; this is for the last time, otherwise we will proceed further.

Guygonaz, wife of Claude Bocard, called Baufri.

Because of the Word of God and the sermons and squabbles. Answers that she says nothing, except when she sells her fish she goes and swears loudly in selling her fish, and she goes to the sermon. And today she was at the Magdalen, and she does not understand what the preachers say because she is deaf, and she has been there three times this week. Said the prayer very poorly, and nothing of the confession. Admonished to frequent the sermons and that she punish the others and . . .[449]

Mermet Cathon.

Said that he is married and that his wife went to Germany to roam the world, and he does not know why she went, and he has not heard of her, and it was two months before last Christmas that she left, also his son. And that he speaks well and has taken Communion, and he went to seek his wife three times, and she came with him, and this was in Evian, and she is married in Yverdon to another. [f. 49v] The Consistory advises that he be commanded to go seek his wife or go live with her, and if she wants to come whether he will take her back. And that he write to his wife to return and strive to get her to return, and that he bring her back within two weeks. Answers that he has no means to pursue this or energy or good, well attested information.

Françoyse, widow of Claude Loup, butcher, called Droblier.

Because of frequenting of sermons and other things, swearing and blaspheming God. Answers that the officer Vovrey went to find her at the

---

449. Incomplete sentence.

sermon at St. Gervase. And says the Mass is not good and that she did not go there often except when she had leisure. And goes to the sermon twice a week, and it was last Wednesday, yesterday, and cannot say anything of the sermons that she heard, and does not know how to pray to God except after the preacher. And said the Pater in Latin, and could not say the Credo. She cried much and her hands shook in Consistory before their lordships. Remanded here to Thursday to learn to pray to God and retain what the preachers preach.

Jehan Collomb, butcher, and his wife.[450]

Because of the Word of God and frequenting of the sermons. Jehan answers that he goes when he can. Asked about dissension with Conscience[451] and his wife, that they insult his wife, calling her fornicator. Said the prayer, and does not know the confession. Asked whether he wants to be in accord with Conscience and his wife. Answers yes.

Claude Mestra, butcher; Henriete, his wife.

Because of the quarrel between the aforesaid Jehan Collombz and his said wife; they want to be in accord with each other. All were admonished together for their dissension. All with one accord pardoned each other and said they would not return to this dissension. Also about the child of the said Collombi and that they should frequent the sermons and the catechism.

[50]   It was proposed that the Council be informed about the songs that are sung at night until 10 o'clock in the streets and elsewhere and also on the Bourg du Four, and especially in front of the Parrot.[452]

Claudaz, wife of Jaques Panchaud, barber,[453] and Jane Recameysaz.[454]

Also mention those summoned to Consistory who do not want to obey.

Also those remanded to another day who do not appear again.

About those summoned several times who have not come.

450. There was a Jean Collomb, son of André, butcher, living in the parish of the Magdalen, admitted to the bourgeoisie on October 12, 1520 (*L.B.*, p. 190), but many people of this name are found in Geneva at this time.

451. Conscience is probably a nickname for Claude Mestra, who appears below with his wife because of a quarrel with Jean Collomb and his wife.

452. The Parrot: a Genevan inn kept by Louis Du Bouloz. See DEONNA, "Hôtelleries," and GALIFFE III, p. 283.

453. Clauda, wife of Jaques Panchaud, was among the "baker women appointed to make bread and sell it in the square in front of the City Hall" on July 16, 1545 (R.C. 40, f. 184).

454. The rest is missing.

To increase the wages of the officer Vovrey; he has great difficulty and labor almost every day.

Thursday, August 17, 1542

Lord Syndic Pertemps.
Calvin, De Ecclesia, Blanchet, Champereaulx.
Girbel, Rages, Pensabin, Blandin, Frochet, Britillion, the officer Domeyne.[455]

Guillaume Bocherens, butcher.

Presented himself because of the quarrel between him and his wife.[456] Answered that they are reconciled and are at peace and that he is sorry for what was done. Said the prayer and the confession.

Jehan Bornand, granary worker, called Callaz.

Warned about frequenting the sermons and other papistical things. Answers that he goes to the sermons and does not profit at all because he cannot retain the words of the sermons. [f. 50v] Said the prayer all backwards and the confession even worse than the Lord's Prayer.[457] The Consistory advises that he make his wife come on Thursday and that he frequent the sermons and go to catechism on Sundays, and that he be admonished also for profanity he uses in selling his merchandise, and that he should learn the prayer and the confession, also his household and his son and wife.

Andrier Piard, notary, bourgeois of Geneva.

Because of rebellion and words spread against the Word of God and justice, and why he has been summoned so often and has not come to obey. Answers, may it please the Seigneurie to hear him; he has never spoken against the lords preachers, and would like to know those who have heard him, and he wants to obey the Seigneurie. And asks that he be given in writing the manner in which he should help himself and live, and he will do it under penalty of the indignation of his superiors. And he believes in God like the others. Said that someone wants to do him an ill turn. The Syndic

455. This is probably Domaine Guex, officer of the city; see for example R.C. 36, f. 173v (November 20, 1542). On March 20, 1538, he was identified as a citizen of Geneva, 30 years old (P.C. 2ᵉ sér., 401).
456. Pernete, wife of Guillaume Bocherens.
457. In the margin: "Thursday, and his son. Three weeks to come show his improvement."

asked him what he was thinking, if the Council is known to do injury to none. And that Monsieur Calvin was not his superior and he would not obey him. Was highly rebellious against the Seigneurie and the members of the Consistory. And said that certain women told him not to go, because someone would do him an ill turn. And he was put in prison for his great rebelliousness. Remanded to the Council.[458]

Jaques Emyn, pack-saddler.

Because of his remand at his last appearance, and how he has profited from the Word of God, and about Holy Communion, which he was forbidden. Answers that he has learned a little, and said the prayer well, and has profited a little, also the confession as above, fairly well. The Consistory advises that he come before taking Communion, the Thursday before the next Communion, and that he be admonished to frequent the sermons and catechism and to buy a Bible.

Benoyte, wife of Pierre Amyaulx.

Because of the quarrel she had with her husband. And the Consistory wants to know what quarrel there is between them. Answers that she would like to know the truth. [f. 51] And the lord syndic asks about the quarrel, and what is the cause. Answers that her husband gets angry all the time because of a certain ward he has, and he beats and strikes her and is very angry. And she does not know why he does this, and he is not content with anything she does. The Consistory advises that she be admonished to live in peace and union with her husband and to frequent the sermons.[459]

Tevene, widow of Pierre de Bour, who had a child after the death of her said husband and has kept it from baptism three weeks, and it is not baptized.

Answers that it is not so and that she be given a term to respond. Answers that the child is in a village, and she does not know where it was bap-

---

458. Accused of rebellion against the church and justice of Geneva, Piard was imprisoned. On August 21, 1542 (R.C. 36, f. 99v), the Council decided to leave him in prison for having "blamed the Seigneurie and the preachers," and particularly for having maintained that Calvin "was a foreigner, and he would not obey any foreigner without the license of the Council, and that he would not govern him." The Council also ordered that "because he is not fit, he is forbidden to meddle again with the art of the notary." The next day Piard's son presented a supplication to the Council asking that his father be freed, which was refused [R.C. 36, f. 101 (August 21, 1542); P.C. 2ᵉ sér., 561 (August 25, 1542)].

459. The conflicts between Benoyte Jacon, wife of Pierre Ameaux, and her husband ended in a divorce studied in detail in KINGDON, *Adultery,* pp. 31-70.

tized. And the father is Master Jehan Cheys, surgeon, and he has never had her company since she had the child. And she does not know the village where he put it to nurse, and she hears it is very agile and . . .[460] The Consistory advises that she be admonished vigorously and told to abstain from the next Communion and that she be remanded to Monday before their lordships in Council, and to frequent the sermons.[461]

Jehan Tevenyn, pin-maker.

Because of hanging around a house where he goes too much, more than being a relative would justify. Answers that he does not go to do wrong as far as he knows, and that he has no quarrel with his said relative, his mother's brother. The Consistory admonished him to refrain from going to this house again with the said wife of his said relative.

[f. 51v]   *Mermet Verdon.*[462]

Because he does not live in marriage as he should and live in peace. Answers that her mother forbade him to . . . ,[463] and he presently lives with his wife, although he kept away for a while, and that he would condemn another who did thus, and that he is in good accord with his wife. And asks that he be given an account of what he is owed for the marriage of his wife and that he be given what he is owed. And he does not want his wife to live with her mother while he lives elsewhere. The Consistory advises that he have his rights and live with his wife. As for what he asks, that he go ask for justice from the lieutenant.

Claude Gindro, from Brens, and his wife.[464]

Because of their marriage, that they do not live together in peace and union. Answers that the other day he beat his wife because she was fighting with other people. And they both said the prayer and the confession not very

460. Incomplete sentence.
461. On August 21, 1542, the Council ordered Jehan Cheys and Tevene de Bourg (or Du Bourg) imprisoned for fornication. The next day the Council heard the responses of Jehan Cheys and again ordered the imprisonment of Tevene de Bourg (R.C. 36, f. 99v and f. 102v).
462. Mermet Verdon, carter, "raised in Geneva," was received into the bourgeoisie on May 21, 1540. He died in St. Gervais on March 30, 1562, at age 80 (*L.B.*, p. 220; E.C., Morts 4, p. 108).
463. Word(s) omitted.
464. Claude Gindre (Gindro) was admitted to the bourgeoisie gratis on May 1, 1543, "because he served in time of war and was taken prisoner" (*L.B.*, p. 224). His wife, Jovenon Brand, died on April 17, 1550 (E.C., Morts 1, p. 9).

well, and he cannot always go to the sermons, and he goes when he can. Proper admonitions that they live in peace and frequent the sermons, to the catechism, and that he refrain from swearing and blaspheming and learn the prayer and to pray to God.

Mama Buctin, Claudaz his wife, and the wife of Claude Soutiez, named Martinaz, because of the Word of God.

The said Mamad answers that he cannot come because he has work to do, and that he goes to the sermon, and his wife, when they can. And he has such a thick head that he can retain nothing of the preaching. And he was there Sunday and Master Calvin preached. His wife answers that she was at the sermon Tuesday and retained nothing. Said the prayer and the confession. The said Mamad said the prayer and the confession, the confession poorly.

52] The said Martinaz, wife of Claude Soutiez, butcher, was asked when she got a bad eye and who did it. Answers that fully four months ago her husband beat her so much that she lost an eye and can see nothing with it, that the barber who treated it cut off a thread, and she was struck with a broom, and the blow was struck thus. And she asks mercy, and did not dare to say it because of her husband who, if anyone opposed him at all, would go away and leave behind his wife and children and her mother. Then she said she was wrong and asks that he might be pardoned so he will not go, because he will leave great misery in his household.

The Consistory advises that he be given remonstrances of correction, and at his wife's request that nothing be done to him and that he be remanded to Monday before the Council and that he promise not to get angry or beat his said wife, have any anger between him and his wife.

Touching the said Mamad and his wife, the Consistory advises that he be made to learn his creed and appear on Thursday before the next Holy Communion to give an account of his faith, and go to catechism on Sundays and frequent the sermons when he can.

Touching Martinaz, the Consistory is of the advice and opinion that she always be obedient to her husband, and let them live in peace with each other.[465]

465. On August 22, 1542, the Council resolved that Martina and Claude Soutiez should be summoned to Council to be admonished to live in peace (R.C. 36, f. 99v).

Jana, wife of Jehan de Genevaz, fishmonger.[466]

Because of blasphemy between some and others, also frequenting of the sermons. Answers that she was at the sermon yesterday, and Monsieur Calvin preached. Said her prayer and confession poorly and the . . . ,[467] and she never fought with anyone. Admonished like the others preceding and told to abstain from the next Holy Communion and appear the Thursday before, and otherwise like the preceding.

[f. 52v] *Françoyse Drobliere, widow of Claude Loup.*

Because she was a little beside herself last Thursday, to learn whether she has profited from the Word of God. Answers that she goes to the sermons and learns to pray to God as much as she can. Said the prayer as she did last time and has not profited from the Word of God. The Consistory ordered her like the other to abstain from the next Communion and come the Thursday before, and to treat her son-in-law well.

Thursday, August 24, 1542

Lord Syndic Pertemps.
Henri, De Ecclesia, Blanchet.
Rages, Pensabin, Frochet, the officer Vovrez.

Jaques Carre and his wife.

Asked about frequenting of sermons and about some charms. Answers that he goes willingly to the sermons, he was there today, and that he does not use charms and he wants to live like a Christian, and he knows the commandments, like the Pater and confession, poorly. His wife said the prayer and the confession. The Consistory advises that the husband be admonished to be more diligent and frequent the sermons and learn the prayer and confession, and go to the sermons every day before Communion, and that he come here Thursday to give a better explanation.

466. Jana, widow of Jean de Geneve, "living on the lake at the Golden Cross," died on May 26, 1558; her husband had died on April 18, 1554, in the Poissonnerie. In 1548 they were hosts of the Three Sheep on the Cité [E.C., Morts 1, p. 156; E.C., Morts 2, p. 26; R.Consist. 4, f. 5 (March 1, 1548); BONIVARD, *Police*, p. 49].
467. Word omitted.

Franceyse Callaz, wife of Jehan Corajod, granary worker.[468]

Because of the Word of God and the faith. Answers that she does not know how to pray to God except in the Latin manner. Said the prayer fairly well, and of the confession two or three words.[469] [f. 53] The Consistory advises that she be admonished to frequent the sermons and appear here Thursday before Communion to learn how she has profited. And every day until Thursday and to catechism on Sundays.

Jaques Bornant, called Callaz, cobbler.

Because of the sermons and wasting time in gambling games. Answers that he goes to the sermons on Sundays. Said the prayer and the confession and does not know the commandments. The Consistory advises that he be admonished to cease to gamble to give an example to others, and to frequent the sermons.

Claude Sermo, butcher.

Because of evangelical instruction and whether he knows how to pray to God and ever goes to the [sermons]. Answers that he was at the sermon on Sunday. Said the prayer and the confession in a general way. The Consistory: That he be given good remonstrances to frequent the sermons and not to gamble and to strive to learn to pray to God and to live in peace with his wife and his household.

Was decided to hold the Consistory Tuesday, and Thursday it was not held because of the absence of the lord syndic.

[f. 53v]

Thursday, last of August, 1542

Lord Syndic Rozet.
Calvin, Henri, De Ecclesia.
Pensabin, Frochet, Blandin.

468. Françoise Callaz was the wife of Jean Bornand, called Callaz, granary worker. Her husband, here called Corajod probably in error, had been summoned to Consistory the week before (August 17, 1542).

469. On a leaf interpolated between folios 52 and 53 there is a note not evidently connected with any other proceeding of the Consistory, of which the part in Latin is struck out: "*Etiam fuerat remissus ad se presentandum jovis ante cenam proxime [sic] lapsam ad docendum de diligenter instructionis verbi domini.* {And was remanded to appear on Thursday before the next Communion to be taught diligently about the Word of God.} Was remanded to frequent the sermons and on Wednesdays and Sundays the catechism and appear before Holy Communion, and whether he knows the prayer."

The officer Vovrey was not paid, nor the three written above. *Debet totum.* {All is owed.} To pay the scribe.

Pierre de La Tablaz, butcher.

About his refusing to appear six times and about the knowledge of Our Lord God. Answers that he appeared and could not always be here. And concerning a child that was baptized in Peney that a woman of Peney attributed to him, thinking to have him for a husband. And that he was the widower of his wife. She had to remove it elsewhere and, because she had not received a promise of marriage, she had nothing to live on. The child she had was named Maurise,[470] and the woman was Loyse, living at the house of Couvaz[471] on the Bourg du Four, a servant. She was delivered in Troinex, and his wife took her there to be delivered. And he says the child is not his and that the said child was by Boniface Compte,[472] who went to the wars. And as for his faith and creed, he said the prayer in Latin and could not say it otherwise, and also the Ave Maria in Latin. He goes to the sermons on feast days when he can. And he has married since the birth.

That he abstain from receiving Holy Communion until Christmas and that he learn his faith and creed and not swear and go to the sermons every day and learn the commandments [of] Our Lord, and also on Sundays to catechism. And remanded to Monday before the Council.[473]

Jaques Carre.[474]

As to his faith, said the prayer and the confession as he did the first time. The Consistory is [of opinion] that he frequent the sermons often and

470. The name "Maurise" is struck from the text.

471. Pierre Brune, called Couva, citizen [R.C. 36, f. 111v (September 4, 1542); *R.C.* XIII, p. 629 *(notes complémentaires)*; Notaires, de Compois, v. 8, f. 62 (March 22 and April 20, 1530)].

472. Boniface Comte, a *"libertin"* in the manner of Philibert Berthelier the younger, saw himself condemned at the time of the defeat of the Perrinist party. He escaped from Geneva, always remaining in contact with such other Perrinist fugitives as the brothers Balthasar and Michel Sept [P.C. 2ᵉ sér., 543 (April 24-June 6, 1543); P.C. 2ᵉ sér., 737 (December 22, 1546); P.C. 1ᵉ sér., 774 (October 21-December 1, 1558)].

473. Pierre de La Tablaz was mentioned in Council under various names. "Pierre Durand called the Bavouz" was detained for fornication on July 3, 1542. Later, on September 1, after this session of the Consistory, the Council ordered Pierre Couva's maid and "Pierre Grandchamps, called De La Tablaz, butcher" put in prison. On September 8 he was freed "considering his long detention." He died of plague on May 1, 1545 [R.C. 36, ff. 59v, 111v, and 115; E.C., Morts 1, supplément (carnet des morts de peste, 1545), p. 6].

474. Jaques Pichard, called Carre.

not attempt anything with the medicines he knows touching dislocations or fractures, and if anyone is in any danger that he leave them to those who know more. That he frequent the catechism.

Carro's widow.[475]

On the progress of her faith, frequenting of sermons and the Word of God. Said the prayer and the confession correctly. Admonitions as last time to frequent the sermons and catechism and to serve God constantly. And her son has gone to the village, and that he come back. Here Tuesday.

[f. 54] *Guillaume Jehan Banit Rebete of Lausanne, cobbler, living at Part's house.*

About the Word of God and praying as one should pray and frequenting of the sermons. Said the prayer and the confession; he attends the sermons when he can find leisure. Is married to Claude Cuvat's daughter and has two daughters.[476] And he wishes harm to no one and pardons everyone. Admonitions that he not gamble any more and that he go to the sermons.

The Consistory should be summoned next Tuesday and Thursday.

Also that the *dizainiers* be told to find out those in their *dizaines* who bear ill will toward each other so they can be reconciled before they come to receive the Holy Communion of Our Lord.

Tuesday, September 5, 1542

Lord Cornaz.
Calvin.
Orsieres, Pensabin, the officer Thoni Regis.

---

475. Guillauma de Carro, widow of Pierre Pichard called Carre and mother of Jaques Carre, mentioned above.

476. The contract of marriage "of Guillaume Blant, otherwise Ribitel, bourgeois of Lausanne, cobbler, *habitant* of Geneva," on the one part, and of Pernette, daughter of Egrège Glaude Cuvat, notary, citizen of Geneva, on the other part, was signed before the notary Claude de Compois (Notaires, de Compois, v. 12, folios 224-224v) on October 28, 1539. There is no record of the bourgeoisie of Ribitel, but before 1544 "to enjoy the rights of bourgeoisie [at Lausanne] it was sufficient, apparently, to possess a house in the city or live there more than a year and a day" (*Livre d'Or,* p. lxx). However, a certain Humbert Blan, alias Rebitel, was a bourgeois of Lausanne in 1537 (*M.C.L.* II, p. 12). Pernette Cuvat signed a new contract of marriage with Michel Guichon, boatman, on April 4, 1569, but they were married sometime earlier "without the said marriage being in any way reduced to writing" [Notaires, Aymé Santeur, v. 2, f. 129; minute of the same act, v. 3, f. 223v *(ad diem)*].

Robert the pack-saddler.[477]

To learn his progress for Holy Communion. Answers by saying the prayer and the confession fairly well. The Consistory advises that he has profited a little, that he be given Communion with admonitions to profit more and more by the Word of God, more than before.

Henriete, seamstress.

Asked about her fashion of living, often in hidden fornication, and that . . .[478] Answers that she has not known a man for 21 years, although she sometimes fornicated with certain men who are dead, and never since. And she refers to her son-in-law and her daughter,[479] who have always lived with her. [f. 54v] And she asked mercy of the Consistory for that occasion, and will never again return to it. About the past, asked to tell the whole truth, whether she has ever made an agreement with another and how long it is since she fornicated. Answers that she has not fornicated for 20 years and that she is not able to do it because of her illness, and she has no power to have knowledge of a man. And that she has been blamed because certain persons have sometimes come to live and drink with her. And said that Monsieur Rozet had investigated whether she was what she was said to be or not. Remanded to next Thursday here.

Thursday, September 7, 1542

Lord Syndic C[ornaz].
Calvin, De Ecclesia, Blanchet, Henri.
Gilbel, Blandin, Tacon, Britillion, Pensabin, Frochet, the officer Regis.

Master Jaques Emyn.

To know his progress in the faith and to be eligible to receive Holy Communion. Said the prayer and the confession as in former times. The Consistory advises that he receive the next Holy Communion under the condition that he always profit more than he has, and that he be admonished to have a Bible to keep in his house.[480]

---

477. Robert Breysson, pack-saddler.
478. Incomplete sentence.
479. Humberte. See below, September 7, 1542.
480. In the margin: "That he can receive the next Holy Communion."

Noble Jehan Gringallet, merchant.[481]

Because of frequenting the sermons and his faith and confession. Answers that he goes to and frequents the sermons as well as another, but because he has lawsuits he cannot go there. Said that he goes sometimes in the morning, and if he has failed in the past he will do better in the future. Said the prayer and the confession. The Consistory advises that it be learned whether he is on good terms with his wife[482] and whether he is always of the faith, and his family, and that he make his wife come, and that he be admonished. Answers as is written above and that they are in good accord, as good as any person here. And his son is in Lyon to learn [f. 55] some good trade to earn his living honestly. And that his son's wife is kept and supported where he pleases. And why the marriage is not accomplished, and that there is no obstacle, considering that she is a young girl. Touching the obstacle of the girl, whether the Lamberts[483] want to make him support her. Concerning the conflict with Claude Savoex, if he wishes him any harm that he not receive the Holy Communion of Our Lord, and that he asks nothing of him. And that they be reconciled and that he appear tomorrow at the Magdalen after the sermon, and that the said Savoex be summoned tomorrow morning after the sermon.

Guygnome, wife of Loys Meyniez, from Gex.

Because of frequenting the sermons and living according to religion, and she hides when she goes to the sermon. Answers that she goes willingly to the sermon and does not live in papistry and has small children that she . . . ,[484] therefore she cannot go every day, but when she can. And does not know the prayer; her husband is teaching it to her. She said it in Latin, and the Ave Maria in Latin, and every day the Pater and Ave Maria. And that she learn it within two weeks and come give an account [of it] and frequent the sermons, and that she not receive Holy Communion unless she knows it by next Saturday.

481. Jean Gringallet, citizen, elected to the LX in 1537 for the quarter "vers la place du Pont." He was a member of the LX in 1542, and became *dizainier* for the Rue de la Cité in 1545. He died on July 12, 1553 [R.C. 30, f. 166v (February 7, 1537); R.C. 35, f. 489 (February 7, 1542); R.C. 40, f. 303v (November 26, 1545); E.C., Morts 1, p. 108].

482. Peronette de La Rive, widow of Pierre Magistri, daughter of Pierre Anthoine de La Rive and Marie Lambert. The two spouses were in conflict over the wife's dowry. Gringallet claimed the payment of the dowry in Council several times [CHOISY, *G.G.*, p. 40; R.C. 36, f. 119 and f. 184v (September 12 and December 5, 1542), f. 214v (January 16, 1543); R.C. 37, f. 282v (November 30, 1543); R.C. Part. 1, f. 30v (March 30, 1543)].

483. His wife's family. See the preceding note.

484. Word(s) omitted.

Donne Jane Troctiere.

And frequenting the sermons and why she does not live with her husband.[485] Answers that she cannot support him here, because she has two children, and she has much difficulty supporting them and herself also. And goes to the sermons on Sundays. Said the prayer and the confession. And she has not done anything to her husband that would make him not live with her, and he prospered hardly at all in this city. The Consistory advises that she write to her husband, and that either he come here or she make every effort to do her duty by him within three months. And that she frequent the sermons more often, and make her son come from Lyon to live here. Touching her son who is in Lyon and who married in the papistry, answers that she knows nothing and that he did this without her leave. And that his wife is said to be in this city, and is named Andriaz, widow of Claude Magnin.

[f. 55v] *Gonyn Floutet.*

Because of games and frequenting the sermons and games in his house. Answers that he goes willingly to the sermons and that he sold a *bosset* of wine and bread at the village fetes, and he wants to be punished if he follows or has followed an evil course or gambled. Was today and yesterday at the sermon at St. Gervase, and Master Henri preached. And he was found to be a liar, because he has not preached there for ten days. Said the prayer and the confession. The Consistory admonished him to obey the Lord.

Françoys Dupont.

Because of songs in front of his house at night and frequenting the sermons. Answers that it is not with his consent, and it was young girls, because he was asleep, and no one has sung since the last time. Said the prayer and the confession. Admonished to attend the sermons, and his wife also.

Tevenete Bocone, wife of François Dupont named above, about the Word of God and frequenting the sermons. Answers that she goes to the sermons when she can and to Holy Communion. Said the prayer very poorly,

485. On February 16, 1535, Jana Troctiere was already the widow of Egrège Claude Troctier, bourgeois of Geneva and ducal secretary. She made her will on December 24, 1558 (codicil of October 14, 1559), under the name of Janne Brasette, widow of Claude Troctier, without any mention of a second marriage. Her three children, Perceval, Jehan, and Andrée, wife of Martin Danel, were all children of Claude Troctier. Perceval, apparently the oldest, was probably the one who lived in Lyon (see below) [Notaires, de Compois, v. 9, f. 141v (February 16, 1535); Notaires, François Vuarrier, v. 5, f. 161 and f. 162 (December 24, 1558, and October 14, 1559); *L.B.*, p. 185 (March 20, 1517); see also R.C. 30, f. 140 (January 1, 1537)].

and not the confession. And she was not there when there was singing in front of their house, and she always cleans her house at night, and this was little street girls. Given proper admonitions to frequent the sermons, especially every Sunday, and other days when she can, and to strive to know her faith and creed well, and go to the prayers on Wednesday.

Pernete, daughter of Rolet Bonivard,[486] *Peycier's wife and Jaques Panchaud's wife,*[487] *all because of songs at night.*

They excuse themselves as much as they can and ask grace of God and of justice, and they sang songs in praise of God and of the Gospel. They said the prayer and the confession. They were admonished.

56] *Jaques Portier,*[488] *bourgeois of Geneva.*

Because of improper songs, and why he does not observe the proclamations. Answers that he would not deign to do it, and said the confession; neither in his house nor in the streets has . . .[489] He was admonished to fre[quent the sermons].

Jane, the wife of Jehan de Genevaz.

About her profit from the Word. Said the prayer and confession in French and Latin in the Biscay(?) manner. Said that sometimes she invokes and asks help from the Virgin Mary.

Andriaz, carter's wife, who delivers children.[490]

The Consistory remanded her to next Thursday with her husband, and that she not receive the present Communion, and frequent the sermons.

Henriete, seamstress.

Said that her son-in-law has not come, but her daughter has. And she will tell what else she knows, nothing otherwise than as she already said last Tuesday. Said she will never say anything against her honor. Humberte, her daughter, does not know where her husband went; she has not . . .[491]

486. Pernette Bonivard, daughter of Rolet Bonivard, of Vandoeuvres, baker, bourgeois, died on December 21, 1566, at age 50 [*L.B.*, p. 195 (September 19, 1522); E.C., Morts 7, p. 39].
487. Claudaz, wife of Jaques Panchaud, barber.
488. A Jaques Portier, innkeeper, died on the Bourg du Four on November 24, 1551 (E.C., Morts 1, p. 46).
489. Incomplete sentence.
490. This could be Andriaz, widow of Gonin Genod. See below, October 5, 1542.
491. Incomplete sentence.

Don Pauloz Alliod, from Russin.

Because of persevering in papistry, and a certain bowl of water. Answers that he always wants to live and does live according to the Reformation of the church.

Concerning the resolution on Holy Communion, the lords ordered as was done before.[492] [f. 56v] And the lords attending written below were assigned. And first the said seventh of September: Monsieur Girbel, Lord Hu[driod] Du Molard, D'Orsieres, Britillion, Pensabin, Tacon, Frochet, Blandin, Rages. Neither Rages, Du Molard, nor Orsieres was present, although they were summoned.

Thursday, September 14, 1542

Lord Claude Rozet, syndic.
Calvin, Henri, Blancheti, Champereaulx.
Pensabin, Blandin, Frochet, Orsieres, the officer Vovrey.

Guilliermon Moyne.

On the Word of God, because of the sermons. Answers that she goes to the sermons on Sundays, and other days when she can, and all the feasts. And she goes by herself and approaches [the chapel of] Our Lady, and goes sometimes to Confignon; when she is ill she cannot go. And that she cannot retain what the preachers say, and says that she lives in the true faith. Said the prayer in French terribly badly, against the Word of God, and also as her mother taught her in Latin. And that she is old[493] and cannot remember. And her confession, she says "I beg mercy of God," and then all wrong. She was admonished to frequent the sermons and strive to learn to pray to God and go to the house of Monsieur Henri, minister.

492. That is, the same people were assigned to distribute Communion; see above, April 6, 1542. The next day the Council ordered that Communion "be celebrated next Sunday at three churches" [R.C. 36, f. 115 (September 8, 1542)].

493. Guilliermon Moyne was the daughter of Girard Moyne (Monachi, Moenne) [*R.C.* X, p. 514 (December 5, 1527)]. Her father, received into the bourgeoisie on September 25, 1459 (*R.C.* I, p. 333), died between October 28, 1475, and June 18, 1484 [see *R.C.* II, p. 394, and Notaires, Pierre Braset, v. 2, f. 294 *(ad dies)*]. She was therefore 57 years old.

Noble Pierre de Joex.

On frequenting the sermons and anger expressed in his house. Answers that he has not been summoned three times and that he goes to the sermons on Sundays, and other days when he can, except when he goes to the village on business. Given proper admonitions to frequent the sermons.

Jehan Jalliod, of Peney, son of Henri Jalliod.[494]

Because of the woman he has been engaged to a long time. Answers that her parents have not obtained for him what they promised in the marriage, and that she has enough goods for her and me [sic], and he has nothing. And he will marry her when he is given what he was promised. And this is marrying for money. And further he answers that he should be shown the family deeds, and if she has nothing, he wants nothing. Michie, daughter of Vouchiez Gallatin, called Dufour, of Peney, is . . .[495] years old. And he swore, and has done nothing else with her, and he drank and ate with her and nothing else. And he has nowhere to take her, no house, because he lives with a master. And he is very willing to marry her, but only if she does what she should. And he asks a term to marry her. Remanded to tomorrow before the Council.[496]

Tyvent Chenu and Anthoyne de Crouz.[497]

Because of their hatred, and frequenting the sermons and other reasons, because of the Word of God. The said Chenu answers that he goes to the sermons on Sundays and is obedient, and he has lost the habit of swear-

494. Jehan Jalliod, son of Henri, acknowledged for his father's goods in Peissy on November 18, 1546 (Titres et Droits, Pa 619, ff. 369-372v).

495. The scribe omits the number.

496. On September 15, 1542, the Council enjoined Jalliod "to marry his wife" within the next six weeks (R.C. 36, f. 122).

497. Thivent Chenu, cobbler, merchant, and bourgeois, member of the CC for the Grande Boucherie in 1542. According to Galiffe he died in 1576, but this was rather his grandson, the son of Jean [L.B., p. 146 (December 31, 1501); R.C. 35, f. 489 (February 7, 1542); Notaires, Jean Duverney, v. 5, f. 65 (October 14, 1543); GALIFFE II, p. 115; CHOISY, G.G., p. 151; see also E.C., Morts 6, p. 144 (April 29, 1566) and E.C., Copies 2, January 23, 1564)].

Anthoine de Crouz, elected to the CC for the Rue des Peyroliers in 1537, was the husband of Louise, the daughter of Thivent and Pernette Chenu. Anthoine de Crouz died before August 12, 1571, the date when his widow married Jean Collonda [R.C. 30, f. 168 (February 7, 1537); E.C., Saint Pierre, B.M. 2, mariages, *ad diem*; Notaires, Jean Duverney, v. 2, folios 526-530 (February 14-15, 1535, testament and codicil of Pernette Chenu); SORDET, *Dictionnaire*, p. 380].

ing and blaspheming and lives with everyone in peace, and his neighbors do not complain of him. And as to the conflict he has had with his son-in-law, he says they are in good friendship. The said de Crouz answers that they are good friends. [f. 57v] And he is forced to go out for the maintenance of his household, and he plans to frequent the Word, and he wants to give up all evil works and think about living well. And he says he prays to God in his mind. And said the prayer. Admonished to come often to the sermons and live in peace in his house and with others.

Jana, daughter of Rolet Bonivard, because of songs, and Philiberte Biollesian.

Answer that they do not sing improper songs, only those of the Gospel, and she knows no other except a song she sings, "The other day when I was riding," etc. And they go to the sermons when they can. Admonished to come to the sermons whenever they can and to remember the doctrines of the Lord. And let the said Jane be subject to her mother and obedient, and let them go to catechism on Sundays.

Pierre Calabri, mason.

On the Word of God, and for the sake of profiting by the Word of God. Answers that he goes willingly to the sermons when he can, as often as others, especially on Sundays, and he does not know the prayer except as his father and mother taught him. And he has done his best to learn it as far as he knows it; his son is teaching him. And he will strive hard to learn to pray to God well. Said the prayer and the confession very poorly. Received the last Holy Communion. The admonitions are that he frequent the sermons, the catechism, and be taught before receiving Holy Communion, and appear when he is summoned. The next Communion at Christmas.

[f. 58] *Jehan de Carroz.*[498]

Because of the holy Word and frequenting the sermons and that he . . .[499] Answers that he did not receive Holy Communion because he could not say his Pater and the confession. And he does not know the Pater word for word, and he goes to the sermons twice a day on Sunday, and the other days sometimes when he can. The Consistory gave him a term to learn his prayer to God and his confession, within six weeks, and let him frequent the catechism on Sundays and the sermons and come to render his duty here.

498. Jehan Pichard, called Carre or De Carro.
499. Incomplete sentence.

Claudaz, daughter of Pierre Myvella, from Servonnex, maid at the inn of the Parrot.

Because of songs at night.[500] The maid of the Parrot said that her master had gone outside. Answers that she did not sing improper songs, only that called "Our Father Almighty" and another that she cannot remember. She did not change her mind about what song she sang besides that of "Our Father Almighty." And she sang "Our Father Almighty" all the time. And she says she is not mocking God or justice. Said little of the prayer, and the confession fairly well. The Consistory admonished her that she frequent the sermons and learn to pray to God and that she go to the sermon and the catechism.

Colleta, daughter of Andrier Berthier,[501] market-woman of the Molard.

On the sermons and evil words. Answers that she goes to the sermons at the Magdalen and on Sundays at St. Peter's, and she has not been for three weeks, and she was ill Sunday and could not go. And she was raised in this city and is not married and lives with a woman named Pernete. And she does not know the prayer, except the Pater as formerly in Latin, and says that she receives Communion at the Magdalen. [f. 58v] The Consistory admonished her to go every day, and Sundays to catechism, and that she learn how one prays to God within six weeks and present herself here.

Jana, daughter of Pierre Macho, market-woman called the Goitered, living near the Magdalen, selling groceries.

Because of evil words spoken in selling, and giving herself to the devil. Goes to the sermons on Sundays and does not know how to pray to God except in the way her father and mother taught her, and she goes every Sunday to the sermon. And she has received Holy Communion, and said the prayer the way God knows. She was given proper admonitions to go to the sermons and the catechism and see that she is taught to pray to God and the prayer and confession, and let her not fight with others, and present herself here within two months.

Thomas Bonnoz, citizen of Geneva.

Because of a written spell in a purse where he has 17 écus, and on frequenting the sermons and other things. Answers that he was given it in

---

500. The Consistory had already discussed the nocturnal disturbances in front of the inn of the Parrot in its session of August 10, 1542.

501. Colleta Berthier, widow of Michel Chabod, cobbler, bourgeois [*L.B.*, p. 174 (January 9, 1512); see also below, December 19, 1542].

Grenoble because he went bleeding along the road, and the *curial* gave it to him, and he has always kept it since.

Anna, wife of Amyer, farm laborer, of Jussy.

Because of Bochu's wife[502] and her daughter whom they called a witch. And she has always been an inhabitant of Geneva, and they have twice called her a witch in the street. And goes to the sermons when she can. And said the prayer, and that she learned it from Master Guillame Farel, and said the confession. Admonished to go to catechism every Sunday and to the sermons.

The lords ministers asked Syndic Rozet to convey them copies of the articles enacted for your Consistory in order to examine their contents.

[f. 59]   Those to whom one is a debtor for the whole term up to the present of the present Consistory, since May 11, 1542.

Lord Porralis I I [2][503]
Lord Roz[et] I I I I I I I [7]
Lord Cornaz I I I I I I I I [8]
Lord Du Molard I I [2]
Blandin I [1]
Gilbel I [1]
Orsieres I I [2]
Britillion I I [2]
Frochet I I [2]
Pensabin I I [2]

Thursday, September 21, 1542

Lord Syndic Cornaz.
Calvin, Champereaulx, Blanchet.
Orsieres, Pensabin, Frochet, Britillion, the officer Vovrey.

Franceyse the Drobliere.[504]

Because of improvement in her faith and creed in the Christian law. Answers leave her in peace, and that she should not be persecuted so much, and that she does not know how to say the prayer in the way it is said at pres-

---

502. Pernette Bochu.
503. The scribe evidently tallies the number of sessions each one has attended.
504. Françoise Loup, called the Drobliere.

ent, but in the papistic fashion. Said the prayer as she knew how to say it, and that she did not receive Communion, and that she did not appear on Thursday before the said Holy Communion in the fall. The Consistory gave her a term of one month from today.

Tevene, the widow of Pierre de Bourg.

Answers that she took Communion at Pentecost, being pregnant with a child, and not the last time in the fall because it was forbidden to her because fornicators should not receive the Communion of Our Lord.[505] And she asks mercy of God and of justice for the faults she has committed; and if she has committed a fault, she does not want to commit two.

59v] *Loys Du Bouloz, baker, bourgeois of Geneva.*[506]

Because of songs. Answers that he was not here when he was summoned by the officer and that he knows nothing about the songs he was summoned about and that his accuser should be brought forward. And that he has done nothing to displease justice, and he wants the witnesses who have said this of him examined, and he wants to improve. And he asked grace for the fault he committed last Thursday when he did not appear at the Consistory. The Consistory gave him proper remonstrances.

Pierre Durand, called De La Tablaz, butcher.

Because of his repentance for having offended by fornication. Answers that he begs mercy of God and of justice and that he was not married when he fornicated. And he received the last Communion in the fall. The Consistory advises that he be admonished at the sermons and on the day of prayer[507] and that he not receive the next Holy Communion, and go to the catechism. Began to pray, and did not know how to finish, or say more than two words.

505. In the Genevan liturgy of Communion of 1542 the minister excommunicates all adulterers and fornicators (see *C.O.* VI, col. 198).

506. A Louis Du Boulo, from Choulex, baker, was admitted to the bourgeoisie on January 12, 1509, living then in the parish of Saint Léger (*L.B.*, p. 163, *ad diem*). Later, on April 10, 1534, *"claves porte Sancti Leodegarii fuerunt remisse Ludovico Girodi dicto Du Bollouz, patisserio"* {the keys of the Porte St. Léger were delivered to Ludovicus Girodus, called Du Bollouz, baker} (*R.C.* XII, p. 522). Finally, according to Galiffe, a Louis Duboulouz was host of the inn of the Parrot in 1544 and "one or two Louis du Boules, on the Bourg du Four" were members of the CC in 1539 and 1544 (GALIFFE III, p. 283 and *ibid.* II, p. 71). The one cited here before the Consistory was probably the host of the Parrot, considering that he was asked about songs, while Claudaz Myvella, maid of the Parrot, had been interrogated on the same subject the previous week, on September 14, 1542.

507. That is, Wednesday.

Pernete Bochue, widow of Roland Bochu.

Did not bring her daughter because of Anne, the wife of Amy the farm laborer. Answers that when they lived in their house they damaged the chimney and the spiral staircase, which cost them 15 *gros* to repair. And she, being angry, said many villainous words to her, but not "witch." And she does not bear her any grudge, and she received Holy Communion in the fall.

[f. 60] Anne, wife of Amy the farm laborer. And Pernete Bouchue insulted her and locked her in her room, and she will prove it by Jana Bechodaz, maid of Oddet, blanket-maker. And she called her "Witch! Witch!" And that she was blamed, and four daughters she has. And if she proves that she broke stones from the chimney or the stairs she wants to be punished. Admonished whether she wants to be reconciled with the said Pernete. The said Pernete examined again on having said "witch" to the said Anne, and still answers that she never called her witch. They were confronted with each other and reconciled with each other. And that the said Pernete should return her honor to the said Anne, and let her retract her words before those who heard and were present when she insulted her. And that she holds her for a respectable woman. And they made peace together and were in accord, and let them have no reproaches between them from now on.

Jehan Collomb, carter,[508] *and Henri Giron, blacksmith.*[509]

Because of regular games in his stable on Sundays when people are at the sermon. The said Collomb answers that they gamble sometimes, and admits the practices of gamblers. The Consistory is of the opinion that they promise not to gamble, which is blaspheming God, and that they not permit the young poor journeymen to gamble, because of their household and family, nor to continue the games.

[f. 60v] *Mychiel de La Forest, from Mâcon, barber, living with Alixandre the barber.*[510]

Answers that he goes to the sermons on Sundays and has spoken only good of the lords preachers. And denies that he said that the preachers could

508. He should not be confused with Jehan Collomb, butcher, summoned above on August 10, 1542. This is probably Jehan Collomb, carter, who was elected to the CC for St. Gervais in 1541 and 1542, like Henri Giron, who appears here with Collomb [R.C. 35, f. 56^b (February 9, 1541) and 489v (February 7, 1542)].

509. Henri Giron, from Chêvres, parish of Vuillonex (GE), identified as an iron-monger on his admission to the bourgeoisie on July 7, 1534 (*L.B.*, p. 211). He was a member of the CC for St. Gervais in 1542 [R.C. 35, 489v (February 7, 1542)].

510. Alexandre Charles (Caroli), barber, received into the bourgeoisie gratis on May 14, 1543. He had killed a barber in a fight in 1522, and it was he who examined the body of the canon Werli in 1533 (L. GAUTIER, *Médecine*, pp. 477-478.

tell lies as well in this city as in their own country. And it was of another that the wife of the charcoal-burner complained, of a Frenchman who had taken a cloak from her.[511] And that he did not speak of the preachers. And that he came here ten weeks ago, and that he did not come to curse the lords preachers. And that if the contrary is proven he wants to be punished. He was given proper admonitions.

Blayse Mugnier, cobbler, from Evires en Bornes.

Because of the sermons and swearing. Answers that he goes to the sermons and that he treats his wife decently, and when he is angry he sometimes says "The devil!," and not "In spite of God!" And that he would like to be punished if it is otherwise. And said the prayer and not the confession. He was enjoined to learn his confession within two weeks and come here.

Noble Pernete de La Ryvaz, wife of Noble Jehan Gringallet.

Because of papistry and the sermons. Answers that she frequents the sermons and that she does not prevent her husband from going and goes on Sundays and Wednesdays, and other days she cannot because of her own affairs. And that she went willingly to Mass when it was said here, and because of looking after her children she cannot come to the sermons every day; she would indeed like it if she could. And that she would like to follow them better than she has in the past, and she wants to save her soul. She was given proper admonitions.

f. 61]   *Tybauldaz, wife of Glaude Martin, seller of pigeons on the Molard.*

Because of swearing in selling and buying. Answers that she sometimes gets angry, but does not swear, because one must not swear. Goes to the sermons on Sundays and Mondays; said the prayer and the confession. She was given proper admonitions.

Noble Dominique de Vaulx, widow of Egrege de Ulmo.

Because of Holy Communion, and what she is up to. Answers that she was ill when she should have received Holy Communion and was sorry that she would not receive it. And that her one son was ill and she sent her maid to look after the millet. And touching her husband, he is always away on business, and he wanted her to go with him, and she did not want to go because of the papistry, into which she did not want to come. And she lives with her children, and she does not make the sign of the cross any more.

511. Struck: "money that he owed her."

127

Myaz, widow of Egrege Illayre Richardet.

Because of the Word of God. Answers that today she was at St. Gervase and that a good man who is not here preached,[512] and she goes when she can. And that she has no scruples about the Word of God, likes to hear the sermons and does not know how to pray to God except by reading and in Latin by heart. She was given a fortnight to pray to God and to learn the prayer and the confession by heart.

[f. 61v]   *Loys Gajouz.*

Because of a quarrel he has with his brother and his wife. Answers that he wishes them no harm and that he has not talked about them and that he does not know whether she was legitimately married, and believes that the wife of his brother is a whore and that the children she will have by Colin will all be bastards.

Colin Gajoz his brother. And answered that the letters of their marriage are in the City Hall and that Marcoz[513] received them and that Don Glaude Guenant married them. And there were about three women there when he married her. And he did not receive the last Communion, and he is good friends with his brother. The Consistory advises that he be admonished that they should agree and live in peace, and if he does not want to comply that he be remanded before the Council. Remanded to Monday before the Council, which the said Loys did not want to accept.[514]

Gervayse.[515]

Said that she promised herself to a servant of the Magnifico[516] and they asked their banns of the Council, which did not want to do anything. And that she engaged herself to another, and similarly the Council refused to permit the banns. The Consistory advises that she be remanded to Monday before the Council, and that there is no obstacle wherefore . . .[517]

512. This was probably the new minister, Philippe de Ecclesia, absent from this session of the Consistory.

513. Jean Cohendoz (or Cuenod), called Marcoz.

514. Deliberating on the complaint of Colin Gajouz "that his brother, Loys Gajoz, quarrels with the wife of the said Colin," the Council "resolved to search the papers of Johan Marcoz Cohendoz to see whether the said marriage was contracted or not, and if it was not contracted, that they should marry in the congregation of the faithful" [R.C. 36, f. 129 (September 25, 1542)].

515. Gervaise Bochu.

516. Laurent Meigret, called the Magnifico.

517. The Council rejected the advice of the Consistory with regard to Gervaise

Thursday, September 28, was not held because of certain obstacles.[518]

Thursday, October 5, 1542

Lord Pertemps.
Calvin, De Ecclesia, Blancheti, Henri, Champereaulx.
Girbel, Pensabin, Tacon, the officer Vovrey.

Monsieur Pierre Baux.

On his profiting by the Word of God since his last appearance. Answers that he knows only the Pater in Latin and the Ave Maria and Credo. And he believes that the angels do the will of God and that the order of Geneva is of Christianity. And he believes in God like the others and the ministers. The Consistory advises [that] he be asked his intention and whether he wants to obey and live according to the Reformation of the church, and if he answers sharply, that he be remanded before the Council, or that he go to the sermons every day until he has become diligent. And here next Thursday to render an account of his gains. And considering that he did not observe the promise he made here last time, that he be proceeded further against and that the fierceness of his heart be broken, and that his wife and his maid come here, and his brothers. Every day and every Thursday here and to catechism. Answers that he wants to live like the others.

Nycolas Pollier.

Similarly to the last, about an order he was given to frequent the sermons. Answers that he has been to the sermon when he could and that he has been indisposed sometimes, and that he does not stay in the streets at the time of the sermon. Said the prayer in French and the confession. The Consistory advises that he be sent back with strong admonitions, since he has not done his duty, that he go every day to the sermon and be more diligent than he has been in the past and follow the command given him before, and to the catechism, and that he be held in subjection, and his wife.

Bochu and resolved, "inasmuch as she asks that her banns be published . . . that this be refused, and that she should follow her fiancé" [R.C. 36, f. 129 (September 25, 1542)].

518. The Council not sitting again this day, the nature of the obstacles remains unknown.

[f. 62v] *Andrier Piard.*

Following what he did above and following the Word of God, and whether he has profited since the remonstrances the Consistory . . .[519] Answers that he was foolish and badly advised, begs mercy of the ministers, and that he wants to live according to the Word of God, and he gives thanks for justice, and he goes to the sermons on Sundays and prays to God in Latin, since he understands it. And is always sorry that he insulted Monsieur Calvin. Also he wants to live according to the Holy Gospel and says he conforms to the church and the Reformation of the Council and retains nothing in his heart; but he has not brought his Bible, which belonged to the bishop Jehan Loys, to Monsieur De Malvenda.[520]

Andrier Bonachon, called the Gagnion, on the Bourg du Four.

Because of great and devilish disturbances in his house, his daughter and son-in-law. Answers that he is taken for another and that he has never had words with his son-in-law and that there is no disorder in his house or family. And he goes to the sermons on Sundays; he does not know who preached, and he does not remember anything of the sermon or of the Gospel, and possibly in three years he would not remember anything. Said the prayer in French, but nothing of the confession. The Consistory advises that he go to the sermons on Sundays and that he render an account of his household, whether it is well instructed in the Word of God, and on Sundays to catechism, and that he learn to say the confession of his faith, and come here in a month.

Jehan Bornant, granary worker.[521]

On the penalty that was imposed on him last time touching his profiting by the Word. Answers, and said the little he could of the prayer, and the confession fairly well. Françoyse Callaz, his wife, like her husband above, and as above on her improvement. Answers and says that she knows the Pater and not the Credo in the present fashion. Said the prayer correctly and not

519. Incomplete sentence.
520. Jean Louis de Savoie, son of Louis I, Duke of Savoy, was Archbishop of Tarentaise (1457) and Bishop of Geneva (1460-1480) (*D.H.B.S.* V, p. 740). See the severe judgment of Bonivard on this bishop in his *Chroniques* I, pp. 220-223. The family of Malvenda, originally from Valencia (Spain), arrived in Geneva in the fifteenth century. This may be André II, *official* (1471) and vicar general (1473) of Geneva, who died in 1499. There was also an André still living in Geneva in 1535 (*D.H.B.S.* IV, p. 648; *R.C.* XIII, p. 196).
521. Jean Bornand, called Callaz.

the Credo. The Consistory: that both be admonished to continue the sermons and the catechism on Sundays, that they be treated gently in view of their good will.

63] *Claude, daughter of Jaques de Pelley, from Thorens, inhabitant of Geneva, called the daughter of La Sartoz.*[522]

Answers that she is not married and has not been to the sermon and that she has to go earn a living. And she is not pregnant and has not misbehaved, and she is a good girl, and does not know who has brought this up, and that no one has engaged her in marriage, and she wants always to behave well, if it pleases God. And they have not done well who have blamed her thus, because she would tell it willingly if it were true and be punished, and she denied that it was so, and does not know how to say the prayer. The Consistory advises that she be remanded to next Thursday and that Pitiod[523] be questioned and that more be found out, and that no one should give false testimony. Such people should be punished for false accusations. And learn the prayer for Thursday.

Jehan Du Nant, host of the Stag.

Because of his wife and his older son[524] who are strongly against the Word of God; that this law would not endure. Answers that he knows nothing about it and does not believe that she said this. The Consistory advises that he make his wife come here Thursday and his son and he also, and that he be enjoined to come and his people also, and that he be examined now, and frequent the sermons. Asked whether he has learned to pray to God to pray to God [sic], about his confession. Said the prayer not very well, the confession similarly. Answers that he was at the sermon Sunday twice and that Master Calvin preached, and in the evening Master Henri. It is necessary to know whether the present law is good or not and when it should fade.

---

522. Clauda, daughter of the late Master Jaques de Pellis, farm laborer, *habitant* of Geneva, called the Short, was condemned to death as a spreader of the plague on March 25, 1545. During her trial she said that she had earned her living making coifs before catching the plague [P.C. 1ᵉ sér., 396, folios 12-19 (February 28-March 25, 1545)].

523. Jean Chautemps, called Pitiod, councillor.

524. Jehan Du Nant, his wife Clauda, and their son Amblard.

Andriaz, widow of Gonyn Genod.[525]

Because of children she delivers, that she says the Virgin Mary, invokes the Virgin Mary in aid. Answers that sometimes it escapes her sometimes [sic], and she says truly none has power but God, and asks grace, groaning and weeping. [f. 63v] And would not want to be other than a respectable woman. She was given proper admonitions to instruct women well in giving birth to children.

Gervayse Bochue, who had been remanded before the Consistory.

Asks that she be given power to publish her banns, so that something may be done for the honor of God and she may not lose her time. The Consistory advises that she be remanded to Monday before the Council, that she publish her banns and follow her husband and be given an affidavit that there is no impediment to her marrying a husband, since she wants to go to Orbe. Remanded to Monday before the Council.[526]

The officer Vovrey was paid for the last Consistory, which was not held because of an obstacle, because he had summoned the Consistory and the parties.

Thursday, October 12, 1542

Debet {Owed} 1.
Lord Syndic Cornaz.
Calvin, Henri, De Ecclesia.
Du Molard, Orsieres, Britillion, Frochet, Pensabin, Blandin, the officer Vovrey.

525. A certain Andriaz, wife of a carter, who delivered children, was summoned to Consistory for the same reasons on September 7, 1542, but this time she was asked to return to Consistory with her husband. Nevertheless it may be the same person. An Hugonin Genod, carpenter in St. Gervais, was admitted to the bourgeoisie on January 7, 1511 (*L.B.,* p. 171).

526. On October 9, 1542 (R.C. 36, f. 139v), the Council reiterated its previous decision that she should follow her promised husband within ten days or be whipped. She presented herself again in Council on August 10, 1543 (R.C. 37, f. 187v), to ask for charity. The Council gave her ten florins and admonished her again to "follow her husband."

Pierre Bezanson of Choully, Pierre Gallatin[527] of Peney, Richard Porvieu[528] of Satigny, Rener Bastard[529] of Bourdigny, Ami Du Nant[530] of Peissy.

Summoned to the Consistory to establish order in the church by watching over those who live badly in their villages and to conserve the holy church, to show a good example to those others who wish to err in the church, for the sake of the Word of God, which should be well heard. And it being known that they are honest and peaceable [f. 64] and a good example to others, that they should admonish them with the minister about the Word of God[531] and see that the others do their duty. And not spare anyone, neither their families, wives, children, servants or maids, at instruction after dinner. And that they should remand those in error to the Consistory, and those who retain papal superstitions from the former times. And give good admonitions [to] tavern-goers, blasphemers and other evil livers, also those with anger and hatred for each other and those who rebel against the Word of God and the honor of justice, as far as they can. The Consistory advises, since they are here, that they be presented to the Council to take the oath to observe what has been said to them, or that it be put off to another time, and that they be given the admonition above.[532]

527. There were one or, we believe, rather two notables named Pierre Gallatin who lived in Peney. One, "formerly a citizen of Geneva," appears to have been from Peney, and asked to be readmitted to Geneva in 1539. In 1541 he was imprisoned in Satigny "because he did not do his duty in time of war." He became a sworn notary in 1543 and came to the notice of the Seigneurie in 1546, when, as a citizen of Geneva, he refused to submit himself to the court of Peney, and as an inhabitant of Peney, refused to appear before the lieutenant and claimed the right of being judged in the court of the castellan of the place. It appears to have been another Pierre Gallatin who was summoned to attend at the exchange of the arms of Bern for those of Geneva at the priory of Satigny in 1537, when the first would have still been in exile [R.C. 33, f. 273v (September 5, 1539); R.C. 35, f. 418v (December 5, 1541); Choisy, G.G., p. 151; Titres et Droits, Pa 619, ff. 336-348v (November 20, 1546); R.C. 41, f. 46v and f. 53v (March 11 and 18, 1546); R.C. 30, f. 223v (May 3, 1537)].

528. Richard Pourvieu acknowledged for a vineyard in Satigny on November 24, 1546 (Titres et Droits, Pa 619, ff. 475-477).

529. Also parishioners of Satigny, but established in Bourdigny, Rener Bastard and his wife came to baptize a daughter on September 3, 1542. He acknowledged in his own name and that of his brothers, all of Bourdigny, on December 1, 1546 [E.C., Satigny 1, *ad diem;* Titres et Droits, Pa 619, ff. 477v-479v).

530. Like Pierre Gallatin, Ami Du Nant was among those summoned to attend the exchange of arms in Satigny in 1537.

531. The minister of Satigny was then Jaques Bernard.

532. This is the presentation of the wardens of the church of Satigny, in the *mandement* of Peney, charged with enforcing the ecclesiastical ordinances. The ordi-

Claudaz, wife of Jehan Du Nant, and Amblard their son.

Because of the sermons and their children. Other children go to the school here in Geneva.[533] It was about a month ago, and she did not say that our law will not endure, and that she adheres to this [law] here. Claudaz answers that she holds the faith and belief of the present. Said the prayer and the confession a little, and she has not sent her children to another school than in this city.

Amblard, the son, said the prayer and the confession. They were given remonstrances and admonitions to frequent the sermons and the catechism and to buy a Bible in their house and have it read.

Claude Arthaud.

Because of punishment and debauchery and waste of his goods. And has been here two other times. Answers that he was exhorted here about the things said above and that he spends money in the taverns with those for whom he has made hose. And he thus goes to taverns, and does not know that he has done worse since his last appearance. And he rarely goes about with Dolen[534] and does not much care, and does not know the commandments except by reading them. [f. 64v] Accused Dolen, who often swears by the name of God, and when he is reproved he curses even more and is angry at the one who says it to him. Promised not to return to doing wrong or wasting his time and to honor his mother and not debauch himself any more, but to follow his trade and not gamble again, and he will not return here again for any reason.

---

nances on the discipline of rural churches of 1546-47 decree: "That the castellan, assembling the soundest and best part of the parishioners (after having admonished them), shall hold an election of wardens, who should be respectable people, fearing God, then send the said wardens to the Consistory to be admonished on their office, and from there they will be sent before the Council to take the oath ... That by the advice of the minister and of his wardens or of one of them, the castellan, or in his absence one of the *assistants,* should remand offenders before the Consistory" (*R.C.P.* I, p. 19). These five were sworn before the Council the same day (R.C. 36, f. 142). The Council ordered also "that they should participate in the offices [*i.e.*, in the proceeds of the fines]."

533. Above, on August 3, 1542, Jehan Corajod called Du Nant, host of the Golden Lion, had stated that he had sent his son to the school in La Roche "because the school here [in Geneva] was not good."

534. On October 22, 1543, Claude Arthaud is found in prison with Pierre Dolen and Claude Macheret, accused of theft (R.C. 37, f. 248). Dolen was summoned to Consistory on October 19, 1542.

Blayse Mugnier, cobbler.

On improvement in his faith and creed. Said the prayer and the confession, and has not been able to go to the sermons, because he must go earn his living. He was admonished to frequent the sermons on Sundays and Wednesdays and the catechism.

Myaz, widow of Hylayre Richardet.

Said the prayer from a small paper she carries with her, and does not know how to pray except by reading, which small paper she gave to the lords ministers of the Consistory. She was admonished to frequent the sermons and the catechism at noon on Sunday, and that she go there with the others.

Noble Jana, widow of Noble Jehan Loys Ramel.[535]

Because of the sermons and faith and creed. Answers that she cannot go to the sermons every day, and she goes when she can. Said the prayer and confession, and she knows it in Latin as it was said in former times. The Consistory admonished her to profit from the Word of God and go to the sermons every day.

Anthoyne Prodom.[536]

Because of frequenting the sermons. Answers that he goes to the sermons but cannot go every day, since he has no wife and must look after his affairs. Said the prayer and the confession, and that he wants to live under the law, because he knows that it is preached correctly, and he will frequent the sermons and leave some of his personal affairs to frequent the sermons.

535. Jana Ramel was apparently the second wife of Jehan Louis Ramel, syndic four times between 1518 and 1532. Their son, also named Jehan Louis Ramel, was implicated in the affair of the Articulants, but he was again in the good graces of the Seigneurie by 1546. Jane Ramel died on March 12, 1555, on the Molard [GALIFFE I, pp. 459-460; R.C. 41, f. 8v (February 9, 1546); E.C., Morts 1, p. 203].

536. Antoine Prodhom, citizen, member of the CC in 1535 and later of the LX. An Anthoine Prodhom died on February 7, 1574 (SORDET, *Dictionnaire*, p. 1078; E.C., Morts 12, p. 80). Prodhom was the object of an inquiry in 1539 because he persisted in praying to the Virgin Mary, maintained the effectiveness of holy water, and said "by his behavior that things in former times were as good as today" [P.C. 2ᵉ sér., 452 (June 4, 1539)].

[f. 65]   *Aymé Becuel[537] from Lancy.*

Said in Consistory that it was three months ago last Tuesday that they were together, and he asked her if she wanted him in marriage. And this was after the afternoon meal, and he asked if she had promised any other husband, and she said no. Then they drank together in the name of marriage at Roud Mossu's, along with his wife Tevene, and he gave her two gold écus in sign of marriage.

Glaude, widow of Jehan Gardet.[538] Says it is not so, and he never gave her anything in the name of marriage, and she did not promise him, even if he proves it by respectable people and swears it. It was under the stairs outside the door, and he asked her what she was doing there, and she answered that she was taking the dinner into the garden, and he kept her company that far. And he asked her if she wanted him, that he would marry her gladly, and she answered no, her husband had just died and she was taking care of her child. And then he showed her some pieces of gold, some of which he gave her, and she did not want to take them. And he told her to take them for a petticoat. And she told him she would take an écu to make an apron, since she did not want it for a skirt. And said that she had drunk in his company, but did not drink with him in the name of marriage.

Becuel. And another time she came to find him at the Bochet,[539] where she asked the said Becuel, and someone went to tell him that a woman had come to seek him. And they should eat at . . .[540] house and then draw up the contract. And the said Becuel says that the said Claudaz went after him and not the said Becuel [after her]. And Tevene came to look for her.

The said Claudaz promised to speak the truth, and said that she did not give him the word of marriage, and that she went after him to buy wheat, from the said Becuel in Longemale, and did not find him. [f. 65v] And that she wanted to buy, and they found him at the host's, and he gave them money for a *quarteron* of wine for the two of them, and they ate together at the said Tevene's

537. Aymé Becuel had been a priest in Lancy or Onex [HEYER, p. 222, n. 2 (transcribed as Bethuel)]. He was summoned to Consistory again on June 26, 1550, because he always kept a missal in his house (R.Consist. 5, f. 41).

538. There were several Jehan Gardets in Geneva, including a butcher, still living in 1536, and a baker, received as bourgeois on April 26, 1493. There was also a Jehan Gardet, priest, implicated in the poisoning of Pierre Viret but declared innocent. In 1539 he was summoned by the Council with the other former priests then living in Geneva, but did not appear [L. GAUTIER, *Médecine*, p. 22; R.C. 33, f. 390v (December 22, 1539); R.C. XIII, p. 536 (April 14, 1536); L.B., p. 119].

539. The inn of the Bochet (a family name) in Rive.

540. Name omitted by the scribe.

and spoke together whether she wanted it or not, and she wanted to speak to her brother. And he wanted to give her a gold ring that she did not want to accept and the écus écus [sic] that he showed to give her. And if her brother had come he would have sent for him to La Bâtie,[541] and he should . . .[542] And he was hidden there and was there inside, and she never promised him anything and did not want to take anything and would be greatly ashamed. And if what he says is true let him make it appear, and she is content to be punished.

The Consistory advises that he bring his proofs and that they be remanded to Monday before the Council. It was decided instead that they be remanded to a week from Monday because he has to make a trip to Dauphiné to cut wood(?) at(?) Viennesin.[543] The said Claudaz was asked about frequenting the sermons. And was there last Sunday, and Monsieur Calvin preached, and after dinner Champereaulx. Said the prayer and the confession. Was ordered to hear them all.

Jehanete, wife of Perrin Falquet, and Donne Jane Myaz, wife of Master Loys, doctor.[544]

The said Johanete spoke to the Consistory against the said Donne Mye, that she is her husband's mistress and that she killed her [Johanete's] children, and she asks justice, and she was never of an evil life. The said Donne Mye denied the killing of the children and that she is reported to be a procuress and that she should know it well.

The said Donne Mye was asked whether such words are true. Answers that her husband knows this well. [f. 66] The Consistory advises that they be reconciled and be silent to each other. And if they cannot agree that they be remanded before the Council. The said Donne Jane Mye was admonished to be reconciled with the said Johanete. Having heard the admonitions and remonstrances, she was content to pardon her and cease to insult her any more for the honor of God and of the congregation, and they will be reconciled and not return again to such injurious words from now on. The said Johanete answers that, since she was insulted publicly, she should retract her

541. La Bâtie: name of several châteaus and fiefs, including the château of La Bâtie-Mellié at the junction of the Rhône and the Arve, near Lancy, the village where Becuel lived.

542. Incomplete sentence.

543. Viennois, an ancient district of Dauphiné?

544. Louis Beljaquet, bourgeois, doctor, former rector of the college (1518-1523), and member of the LX since 1536. He died on July 4, 1562, at age 80. His wife died on June 29, 1573 (L. GAUTIER, *Médecine*, pp. 22, 35-36, 424, 510; E.C., Morts 5, p. 20, and E.C., Morts 12, p. 56).

words before those who were present. And she was given admonitions and remonstrances, and they made peace together.

Noble Pierre Baux.

Reported on his profit from frequenting the sermons and other things. Answers that he has profited; said the prayer and the confession in the vulgar tongue, and that he pardons all and has pardoned everyone. Also he bears no grudge against Pensabin. Proper admonitions to frequent the sermons and to continue.

[f. 66v]

Thursday, October 19, 1542

Debet {Owed} 2.
Lord Syndic Rozet.
Calvin, Champereaulx, Blanchet, Henri.
Girbel, Orsieres, Frochet, Britillion, Tacon, Pensabin, Vovrey officer.

Pernete, widow of Jehan Du Nant, boatman.

Because of the sermons and other things. Answers that she was at the sermon Sunday at St. Peter's, and Master Calvin preached, and she does not know what he said except that it was good, and otherwise she would not know what words he said then. And that she does not hear because she is a little deaf and does not understand what the preacher says. Said very little of the prayer and cannot say the confession. The Consistory advises that she frequent the sermons and come to give an account of her gains and appear here [in] a month, and go to the catechism.

Pernete, widow of Oddet Paquet.

Because of the sermons and other things. Answers that she frequents the sermons when she can, and she sometimes has things to do in the village, and she rarely misses when she is in the city. And that she has been here all week, and named the sermons and those who preached. Said the prayer and the confession. She was given remonstrances and admonitions that . . .[545]

Jehan Corajod, called Du Nant, cobbler, of the Golden Lion.

If he has brought back his son who was in La Roche, whom he should have brought here at Michaelmas to be instructed in the Word. And his wife

545. Incomplete sentence.

is in Etrembières, whom he should also bring. Answers that his son came back from La Roche and [f. 67] he sent him to Etrembières to pick fruit, and he helped take the plow to the said Etrembières, and he will have him come when there is need. And touching his wife, she returned to Etrembières to collect her property, and when she is here she goes to the sermons. And his son will be here tomorrow. And that he will make his wife come here when she comes back from the village. Also said that Claude Sermod told him that he could not come today and would be here next Thursday.

Gonyn Laurent, Claude Mestral, Marquioctz de Villaz, Jehan Martin, Jehan Soutier, Mychiel Cochet.

Because of the sermons and frequenting them. They answer, Gonyn for the others, that they do not care for their *dizainier*,[546] that he does not admonish them well, and that they sometimes go to the sermons on Sunday when they have a desire to go. The Consistory gave them proper admonitions and commanded the said Du Nant, their host, to persuade them to frequent the sermons. And they submitted to observing this.

Pierre Dolen.

Because of wandering about and wasting time and other things. Answers that he works when he has employment, and very willingly when he has it. And that he goes to the sermons when he can, and that he has to watch the house when his wife goes to the sermon.[547]

Michiaz, wife of the late Tyvent de Jussiez, who stays at Compesio's,[548] and with Anthoyne de Jussiez, day-laborer, her son.

What course she . . .[549] Answers that she follows a good course, and that a woman who goes there goes there for an illness that her said husband, who is called Glaudaz the washerwoman, came to treat her illness and not for any

546. They all lodged at the Golden Lion, kept by Jehan Corajod, called Du Nant, *dizainier* for the Molard.

547. Some weeks later Pierre Dolen is found in quarantine for having been in contact with someone who died of plague [R.C. 36, folios 177v, 178v, 182v (November 24 and 27 and December 4, 1542)]. In 1543 he was imprisoned with Claude Arthaud and Claude Macheret for having committed thefts in several houses of those struck by the plague [R.C. 37, f. 199 and f. 248 (August 21 and October 22, 1543)].

548. Claude de Compois (de Compesio), bourgeois, member of the LX, notary (minutes preserved in A.E.G., 1504-1544), inhabitant of the Molard, died July 22, 1550 [SORDET, *Dictionnaire*, p. 375; R.C. 35, f. 55v and f. 489 (February 8, 1541, and February 7, 1542); E.C., Morts 1, p. 15].

549. Incomplete sentence.

other reason except to visit her in her illness, and she does not know of any other reason why. And she comes and goes sometimes, and not otherwise. And she went for wine and left the said Claude and him together, and the door was fully open. And she goes to the sermons when she can. And the said [C]lauda goes there to arrange the marriage of her niece to the said Estienne. And the said Mychie goes for wine and the said Claude with the said Estienne. [f. 67v] And it was last week when she was at the sermon at the hour of vespers at the signs[550] that he espoused the daughter of Glaude Marchian, and last Sunday she was at the noon sermon at the catechism, and she was not there in the morning or the evening. Said the prayer and the confession. The Consistory advises that she frequent the sermons more often than she has in the past and that she not allow the said Claude to come to her house again because of the danger of fornication, and that her life be investigated more fully.[551]

Françoys Boulat.

Because he rebelled against appearing for remonstrances. Answers that he had gone outside [the city] and would not have been here today if he had not been summoned. Said that he knows how to pray and frequents the sermons. The Consistory admonished him.

Glaudaz, daughter of Jaques de Pelley, from Thorens.

Has been accused of being pregnant. Appeared the two preceding Thursdays to protest against those who have falsely accused her.

Thursday, October 26, 1542

Debet {Owed} 3.
Rozet, syndic.
Calvin, Henri, De Ecclesia.
Pensabin, Frochet, Vovrey, officer.

Claude Sermod, butcher.

On frequenting the sermons and profiting by the Word of God and because he did not appear. Answers that he went willingly to the sermon and

550. Translator: Sic. The exact meaning is not clear.
551. On October 19 the watchman Jehan Blanc put the day-laborer Antoine de Jussy and Claudaz the washerwoman in prison without having received an order from the Council. The next day the Council freed them and opened an inquiry into the accusations of fornication [R.C. 36, f. 149 (October 20, 1542)].

that he cannot come when he is outside the city because he has to go for merchandise, and he does not gamble and attends the sermons when he can. And said that he will be saved in the way that pleases God. And has not been at the sermon for two weeks, and in the time of the Mass sometimes six weeks. [f. 68] The Consistory advises that he be admonished to go on Sunday to catechism and frequent [the sermons], and that he profit more than he has in the past. Frequent the sermons, and that he not be a gambler and promise to do what he has been told and instructed for his salvation, and also the same for his wife and children. Promised.

Claude Vuarin, called Macheret, the younger, locksmith.

Because of the Word of God and frequenting the sermons and to pray to God. Answers that he was there last Sunday, and other days he cannot go because he must work for himself and his father who is ill. And he was at St. Gervase Sunday after dinner. And he improved in saying the prayer. And he does not know what the preacher says, he understands nothing, and hopes to be saved by the commandments and by works. The rest of the sermons is nothing to him, only the prayer and the commandments. Said that because of some spite he feels against some who have given false testimony against him, that is the reason that has kept him from frequenting the sermons, and he has not said the prayer because of this spite. And that he believes in God, and does not know when he received Communion; about half a year ago. And that he already felt hatred for those who had testified against him, whom he cannot name at this time. The Consistory advises that he be remanded here and that he come in a better frame of mind than he has come here in, and that he name those who have testified against him in order to be reconciled with them. And that he come here next Thursday, and meanwhile commend himself to God.

Thursday, November 2, 1542

Debet {Owed} 4.
Lord Syndic Cornaz.
Calvin.
Orsieres, Blandin, the officer Domeyne.[552]

552. Domeyne Guex.

Guygona, wife of Meyniez, from Gex.[553]

Because she has improved in the faith. Said the prayer and the confession rather badly. [f. 68v] Answers that she has not been able to go to instruction because of her affairs. She was admonished, and it was advised that she be made to go to catechism and instruction and remember the faith well and the confession and appear here next Thursday and frequent the sermons, and present herself before the next Communion at Christmas.

Lord Jehan Favre,[554] *merchant of Geneva.*

Because of some bad words, of example to others and improper. Answers that he does not know that he has spoken so badly, unless as a joke, and he did not intend to do wrong. And that he will correct himself and will not return here again for such a reason, and that he will refrain from now on.

Jehan Mouri of Peissy. [The] curé *of Peissy, summoned by the castellan of Peney.*

Because he fornicated in this city and he is married, and other reasons. Answers that he did not fornicate and that someone puts this crime on him because he is examining the rights of the Council.[555] Although he was found in a tavern with this girl with a pot of wine and a *quart* loaf, he did not fornicate with her, because he is married, and he takes God to witness that it is not so. Admittedly he was behind this house and told the host to take him up to another room in order, he said, that the watch would not make him pay for a pot of wine. And the host took him up and he drank the said pot of wine with the said girl and the *quart* loaf and had a tart made, which he says he had made for the girl's mother, who was ill. The Consistory advises and is of the opinion that he be remanded to Monday before the Council.[556]

553. Guygona, wife of Louis Meyniez.

554. Probably Jean, son of Jean Favre and brother of the famous François Favre. See CHOISY, *G.G.,* p. 120.

555. Jean Moury, former rent farmer of the place, whose term had expired the previous Michaelmas (September 29). Here he probably accused the people of Peney of having denounced him because in investigating the rights of the Council he also tried to make them pay their feudal dues. See R.C. 36, f. 25v and f. 33v (May 30 and June 6, 1542).

556. On December 18, 1542, the Council asked the castellan of Peney to make him appear in Council to be punished for fornication (R.C. 36, f. 192). See also R.C. Part. 1, f. 8 (February 20, 1543, numbered f. 9).

Thursday, November 9, 1542

Debet {Owed} 5.
Lord Curteti, syndic.
Calvin, Henri, Champereaulx, De Ecclesia.
Girbel, Pensabin, Blandin, Frochet, the officer Vovrey.

Donne Jaqueline, wife of Anthoyne Gojon.[557]

Because of the sermons. Answers that because she is nursing a small child she cannot go to the sermon and can only go there on Sundays, so the other days she sends her maid, and thus cannot go. And she was at St. Peter's last Sunday after dinner, and at the catechism. And she has no other scruples about the law, because she did not come here because her parents did not want her to come because of this Word of God. Said the prayer and the confession.

On those not presenting themselves in Consistory, decided that if someone does not appear the third time, that they be remanded to the Bishop's Palace for the third time, and then remanded here.

Claude Du Crest,[558] *locksmith on the Bourg du Four.*

Came to excuse his wife who he says has been ill for 15 months and cannot leave or go out of the house or the shop. The Consistory advises, since she is ill, that someone go to console her and instruct her in the Word of Our Lord and that she be admonished.

Jane, widow of Tyvent Mermet,[559] *mother-in-law of the secretary Beguin.*[560]

On frequenting the sermons and other things. Answers that she serves God as she can and goes to the sermons when she can, and was there last

557. Anthoine Gojon, merchant from La Roche, was admitted to the bourgeoisie on July 19, 1538, and in 1542 was a member of the CC for the Fusterie. He died on May 31, 1551 [*L.B.*, p. 218; R.C. 35, f. 490 (February 7, 1542); E.C., Morts 1, p. 37].

558. Claude Du Crest, admitted to the bourgeoisie on July 21, 1524 (*L.B.*, p. 201).

559. Tyvent Mermet was received into the bourgeoisie on March 29, 1504 (*L.B.*, p. 153).

560. On February 4, 1541, François Beguin was proposed as *secrétaire d'Etat*, and on February 6 as secretary of the Chambre des Comptes, but both times Claude Roset received more votes. Nevertheless, on June 21, 1541, he appeared before the Council in the character of secretary in connection with a matrimonial case. He was then *secrétaire de la Justice* (there is also a sentence of 1543 against Roud Monet signed by Beguin). On June 2, 1542, he was also qualified as *secrétaire en Conseil* [R.C. 35, folios 47v, 51, 53, 241v; R.C. 36, f. 29; P.C. 1ᵉ sér., 368 (February 27, 1543)]. Beguin, a member of the LX at the time of this consistorial

Wednesday and every day. And she does not remember anything he says in his sermons and she does not know whether it is she who mutters in the sermon. And she knows how to pray to God: said the prayer, and prays God to give her the Holy Spirit; said the confession, and wants to live in the faith of God. [f. 69v] Moreover said that sometimes when children are baptized she goes apart to pray to God that he will always help her, and that she will not abstain for anyone whatever from making the prayers she has been accustomed to on her knees. And says that God is her witness that she did not say on entering here: "What devil wants me here?" And she certainly said it. The Consistory is of the opinion that she be admonished to frequent the sermons and that she be gained if possible by remonstrances and that she cease her muttering and that she be forbidden to mutter any more in the sermon.

Noble Pernete, wife of Bartholomyer Fouson.

On the Word of God, her conscience and frequenting the sermons. Answers yes, when she can, as well as she can, and that she will guard herself from doing wrong and that she prays her Creator to give her the grace to live honestly and to the salvation of her soul. And she has seen and associated with many respectable people, and she was at the sermon yesterday before dinner, and does not remember what the preacher said, and she remembers much of the sermons of former times, and of those here not much, and retains what she can. And there are preachers who are much easier to understand than others. And she prays God to help her and says her prayers and prays for her husband, for her children and not for the dead, and says her *In manus.*[561] And she remembers well the good father who said it was always necessary to have a new heart. And that she always prays in Latin. The Consistory is of the opinion that she be admonished not to mutter any more and to listen to the sermons and to communicate with someone and come here the Thursday before Christmas.[562] And that she be admonished on what she

---

case, also served as *curial* of St. Victor (1536), procurator general (1537-1540), councillor and syndic (1547). According to Sordet he was secretary until 1555. Although Galiffe says that Beguin was counted among the Perrinists incorrectly, Sordet says that, "regarded as a leader of the party of the Libertins, he was forced to depart in 1556 and renounced his bourgeoisie" [R.C. 35, f. 489 (February 7, 1542); R.C. 30, f. 62 and f. 175v (September 29, 1536, and February 14, 1537); SORDET, *Dictionnaire,* p. 82; GALIFFE, *Ameaux,* p. 86, n. 1].

561. *In manus:* prayer at Compline drawn from Ps. 30:6 of the Vulgate: *In manus tuas commendo spiritum meum.* In the liturgy of the diocese of Geneva the *In manus* "was not said except from the first Sunday of Lent until the Sunday of the Passion, and then it was also said at the fêtes; apart from this period there was no respond at Compline" (LAFRASSE, p. 296).

562. In the margin: "Tuesday; Thursday before the next Communion."

should do and that she should behave herself and pray to God before going to the sermon, and whether she knows how to pray in French, and should follow the catechism that is given on Sundays.

Jana, wife of Jaques Symond.[563]

Because of the sermons and other causes. Answers that she cannot go to the sermons; her husband rarely stays in the house and she must watch the house, and therefore it is not possible on working days. On Sundays she goes there willingly, and her husband goes Wednesdays and she watches the shop. When her husband commands her she [f. 70] will go there willingly. And she was at the sermon yesterday, and he preached about the beheading of St. John,[564] and that her children know their faith, and she also, and she hopes God will have pity on her through his passion which he suffered. The Consistory is of the opinion that she be admonished to frequent the sermons more often than she does.

Master Henri, minister of the Word of God.

Proposed last Thursday at the Consistory to their lordships of the Consistory that it would be good and laudable to make the people of Cologny, Petit Saconnex and those of the village of Champel come to the Consistory, since they do not know what the Word of God is, to give them remonstrances. And their lordships of the Consistory advised that you bring it forward next Monday, November 13, before the Council.

Thursday, November 16, 1542

Debet {Owed} 6.
Lord Syndic Cornaz.
Calvin, Henri, De Ecclesia.
Rages, Frochet, Pensabin, the officer Vovrey.

The Drobliere.[565]

Appeared because of the words she says, and does not know how to say the confession or the prayer or pray as one prays [today]. And she does not fail(?) to go to the sermon except today, when she was not there. And she was

563. On the Symonds, see LAMBERT, "Cette loi."
564. Matt. 14:8-11; Mark 6:25-28.
565. Françoise Loup, called the Drobliere.

at the sermon yesterday, and does not know what the preacher said, and has not retained the words. Her maid indeed says that she has a poor head, and she knows well that she has a poor head and would not know how to pray to God except in the manner that her father and mother taught her, and would not know how to speak otherwise. And that she does not do anything that a respectable woman should not do, and that she does not offend Our Lord in this manner, and she says she is a good Christian and that it is too late to teach her the Pater. [f. 70v] The Consistory advises that she be forbidden the next Holy Communion and that she come here to render an account of her gains and that her son be summoned for Thursday and she also.

Master Claude Convers,[566] barber, bourgeois of Geneva.

Because of an illness and letting of blood to make bleeding. Answers that the master surgeons have the herb betony which is useful in bleeding, whose aid they obtain. The Consistory admonished him to refrain from using charms and words over sick people and inscriptions and talismans.

Jehan Porrentu, furrier.

Answers that he was at the sermon today and does not know who preached or what he said. He goes to the sermons at the feasts, and working days he does not go because he has work to do, and he knows well how to pray to God, and said the prayer and does not know the confession. And . . .[567] The Consistory charged him to go to the sermons three times on Sundays and to abstain from Communion and not scoff as he has been reported to scoff and to present himself here before receiving it.

Jaques Symond, merchant.

For what reason and why his mother and his wife do not come to the sermons and what they mean by it. Answers that his mother is ill and old and his wife goes when she can, because when he goes away on business she has to watch the house, and his mother has her heart always on God. The Consistory gave him proper remonstrances and admonitions.

---

566. Claude Convers, possibly the son of Jean, also a barber and bourgeois, was "often named in the registers of the Council between 1527 and 1544, [a member] of the CC from 1533 to 1536" (L. GAUTIER, *Médecine*, p. 478). Gautier says also (*ibid.*, p. 68): "Two surgeons only, Claude Convers and Pierre Tissot, were members of the CC in this period [1536-1569]. The first was probably a citizen . . . The inferior status of the surgeons of the time of Calvin prevented them from playing an important political role."

567. Incomplete sentence.

Anthoyne Bochu,[568] blacksmith.

Because of religion and the scandal there is between him and his wife and despite the name of God. Answers that he goes to the sermons on Sundays, and the other days he stays in his house. And that he gets angry with his wife, and she must be subject to him. Also he must be subject to his trade. He was admonished to frequent the sermons and refrain from being angry at his wife in order not to scandalize the neighbors and other people.

71]   *Little Jehan Losserand, cobbler.[569]*

Because he has a grudge against his mother and is not obedient to her. Answers that he does not disobey his mother and does not want or intend to do improper things and that he is not stained with fornication and is innocent of that thing. It is true that he had words with his mother when staying up, and says that she would not buy him the hempen cloak he needed because she did not want to lend him something he had need of. Said the prayer and the confession. Admonished to live in peace with his mother.

Jana Truffeta.

Because of the sermons. Answers no to this. Says the prayer and the confession. She does not know what makes her say it in Latin unless it is God, and sometimes says the Ave Maria and Sancta Maria Mater.[570] The Consistory advises that she come present herself before receiving Communion, and go three times on Sundays to the sermon and the catechism.

---

568. Antoine Bochu, bourgeois or citizen, former religious of the order of St. Dominic in the friary of Palais in Geneva, established himself shortly after the Reform as a blacksmith. On January 21, 1546, Bochu, "detained by illness," was granted a pension because the former friar had "abandoned everything to follow the Reformation" [R.C. 40, f. 354, *ad diem;* see R.C. 30, f. 148v and f. 181v (January 12 and February 23, 1537), which shows that this concerns the same person, as well as R.C. 32, f. 5 (March 15, 1538)].

569. A Jehan Losserand, cobbler from Megève (H.-S.), son of Mermet, was admitted to the bourgeoisie on November 29, 1521. In 1537 Jehan Losserand was elected to the CC, and in 1545 he was one of the tithe collectors of the city [*L.B.,* p. 192 (November 29, 1521); R.C. 30, f. 168 (February 7, 1537); R.C. 39, f. 102 (January 15, 1545)]. A Jehan Losserand the younger, also a cobbler, son of Pierre Losserand, citizen, is found later among the criminal trials [P.C. 1ᵉ sér., 970, f. 6 (responses of August 18, 1561); see also E.C., Morts 1, p. 157 (April 26, 1554, death of his son)] and Jehan Losserand the elder, cobbler, son of Mermod Losserand [P.C. 1ᵉ sér., 1222, f. 1 (August 17-23, 1564)].

570. For the text of the Sancta Maria Mater, see GORISSEN, *Stundenbuch,* p. 232.

Anthoyne Wooden-Feet.

Because of the sermons and cursing the preachers. Answers no, and it would not please God for her to speak evil of them. And that she was at the sermon Sunday at dinner, and learned nothing except to pray to God as she was taught. And said the confession very poorly, and that she prays to God thus: "Our Father who is in Heaven," and has never said the Ave Maria since the Gospel has run here. And goes willingly to the sermons, and cannot go except on Sunday. She was given remonstrances and admonitions to frequent the sermons.

[f. 71v] *Jane Burdetaz, wife of Loys Burdet.*

Because of the feasts and that of last Saturday.[571] Answers that she does nothing about it, and does not know whether the Mass is bad or good,[572] and often heard Masses in the time when they were said here. And goes to the sermons when she can, and said the prayer very little, almost not at all, and knows the confession hardly at all, almost none. Admonitions as to the [one] preceding.

Thursday, November 23, 1542

Debet {Owed} 7.
Lord Syndic Rozet.
Calvin, Genesto, Champereaulx, Loys Trepereaulx.[573]
Frochet, Rages, the officer Vovrey.

571. The feast of Saint Martin, November 11.
572. To be noted: her husband, Loys Burdet, was summoned before the Consistory in 1546 for having supported the Mass and having persisted in saying his rosary, in giving the sign of the cross at the sermon and in praying for the dead and to the Virgin Mary. See R.Consist. 2, f. 74v (August 12, 1546).
573. Matthieu Geneston and Louis Treppereau were presented to the Small Council for the diaconate on July 10, 1542, and approved in General Council on July 16 (R.C. 36, f. 65v, f. 72). Geneston came from Geneston, in the diocese of Nîmes. He died of plague shortly before August 11, 1545 (R.C. 40, f. 212). According to Jean-François Bergier: "Louis Treppereau, originally from Artois, a refugee in Geneva, admitted in 1542 as a 'coadjuteur' of the pastors, was shortly placed at the head of the rural parish of Céligny, serving also the village of Crans, in the Vaud district, hence under Bernese control. It will be seen [in the *R.C.P.* I, p. 23] that Treppereau expressed very strongly a desire to pursue his career in Vaud. It happened that in 1553 difficulties arose between Geneva and Bern, and the latter prohibited Genevan pastors from preaching in its lands. Treppereau abandoned the service of the Seigneurie . . . [He] was later appointed to Lausanne, where he exercised his ministry for some twenty years" (*R.C.P.* I, p. 22, n. 6).

Messieurs Pierre Falcat and Nycod Moury from Jussy.[574]

Asked how long it is since they came to the place. Answer six weeks, and have been to the sermons in the town of Jussy, and do not want to live according to the Reformation. P. Falcat. Pierre answers that he has doubts about the Reformation, because he means to live and die in the law of his predecessors and would not want at all to leave the ancient law because of saying the Mass. And his schoolmasters taught him the Mass and he would like to stay with it. Asked whether he would rather follow men than God. Answers as before that he wants to live according to the law under which his father, mother and master lived. And they want to be good Christians and believe perfectly in God and in Jesus Christ and that Jesus Christ will be the judge of all the world. He would leave Christ in this fashion. And that the Holy Spirit does not inspire him otherwise than it did in the past. And his masters were Magister De Nanto, De Bonnaz, and Magister Corajodi.

Nycod Mouri. Answers that he believes in Jesus Christ, and will never renounce the Mass. And that it is said in many places. And he wants to abandon everything that is against Our Lord, and all that is in the Mass is entirely from Holy Scripture. And that there are many respectable people who have said Mass. [f. 72] The Consistory advises that they be given proper admonitions to frequent the sermons and the Word of God.

Claude Loup, son of the Droblire.[575]

Because of the sermons. Answers that he goes to the sermons, and he has had no words with his mother, although he was angry with his mother who had drunk a little too much, that it was necessary for someone to answer her. And he does not know why she does not go to the sermons, and the said Claude is married.

---

574. Falcat and Moury, both priests in Jussy before the Reform, left the lands of the Seigneurie apparently to live where they had other benefices. The Council ordered them to return to the city under penalty of losing their Genevan possessions. They several times asked for an extension of the delay granted them to wind up their affairs outside Geneva and to move there. Having often admonished them to "live according to the Reformation" or to go to the "sermons, and similarly to the lesson," the Council finally tired of these "great papists" and banished them in April 1543 and, despite the protests of their families, confiscated their possessions under Genevan jurisdiction. See below, March 20, 1543, as well as R.C. 36, folios 124, 127, and 176 (September 17 and 22 and November 24, 1542); R.C. 37, f. 43 and f. 48v (March 26 and April 2, 1543). In 1551, "inspired to leave the papal law," Falcat returned to Geneva (CAHIER-BUCCELLI, "Ombre," p. 370). On Falcat, see also CORBAZ, pp. 60, 82, 84, and 360-361, and ROGET I, p. 161. On Moury, see CORBAZ, pp. 47-48, 60, 84, 363.

575. Françoyse Loup, called the Drobliere.

The mother of Monsieur Hugoz, haberdasher.

Because of a woman who came from Annecy. Answers that she is a widow woman who lived with her nephew and that she came to this city for the Gospel. And she is named Jane, widow [of] . . . ,[576] baker. And she is a respectable woman, goes to the sermon every day, and she knows only complete respectability in her, and she makes her apprentices go to the sermons.

Wife of Master Anthoyne Bochu, blacksmith.

Because of her injurious words of monkery[577] and that they live only in ruin. Answers that she goes to the sermons when she can. Admonitions that she go to the catechism and frequent the sermons.

Roland the baker.[578]

Because of the sermons and the games in his house. Answers that he wants to recommend himself to God and he goes to the sermons as much as another, and as for the games, they play for wine. He was given proper admonitions to refrain from having games or other things and to frequent the sermons.

Nycolardaz.

Says that Versonnelle[579] sent them to her and she gave them a room she rented(?), and she is named Myaz and is not from this city but from Troys Lieuz(?) in the Gex district, and she takes no one to her room. [f. 72v] And it has not appeared that the said Myaz does anything dishonest, because she would make her go, although some of the neighbors told her that she behaves badly. And she does not know it except by the words of others, although her sister comes sometimes to see her and does not stay.

Myaz, daughter of the late Pierre Patron of Péron. Answers that she has lived in this city six years and had a child by Pierre Bonnet who is outside the city, a forester[580] of this city. And she lives by her work and she goes out to serve and get her living as she can. And she has brought no one to her room except her brother, and she submits herself to the mercy of justice. And in-

576. Name omitted by the scribe.
577. Antoine Bochu had been a religious at the friary of Palais; see the note above, November 16, 1542.
578. Roland Marquerex, baker, admitted to the bourgeoisie on May 24, 1541 [*L.B.,* p. 221; R.C. 36, f. 217v (January 19, 1543)].
579. On October 17, 1542, the Council ordered Versonelle to leave Geneva within fifteen days, without specifying the reason (R.C. 36, f. 146).
580. On the foresters of Geneva, see PONCET, *Châtelains,* pp. 122-127.

deed one came there to whom her sister had given money, and he came to put on a shirt, and he is a servant of one who is said to be respectable, and is ready to obey. And she goes to the sermons and has learned to pray to God, saying her Pater in the vulgar tongue and the confession and the grace. And her sister is named Anthoyne.

Claudaz, widow of Claude Dechallon.

Because of the sermons and the Word of God. Answers that she does the best she can and was at the sermon Sunday, at the sermon after dinner. Says that she is a poor widow woman with children, and she must work for her living for herself and her children. Said the prayer and the confession, and has four children; two are outside [the city] and the other two she teaches as well as she can. She was admonished.

f. 73]

Thursday, last of November, 1542

Debet {Owed} 8.
Lord Syndic Curtet.
Calvin, Henri, Genesto, De Ecclesia, Trepereaulx.
Blandin, Frochet, Rages, Pensabin, the officer Vovrey.

Noble Pernete Fousone.

Because of the Word of God, that she has been reluctant to go to the sermons since her first appearance. Answers that she wants to satisfy what she is required to do and that she was ill from having stayed here too long last time and that she has nothing on her conscience. Said that she would rather be admonished in her house than go here to the Consistory.

The mother-in-law of the secretary Beguin.[581]

Like the preceding, who has not frequented the sermons since her last appearance. Answers that she was there last Wednesday and last Sunday. Said that Master Henri spoke about the Pater and the daily bread. She was admonished to frequent the sermons.

Renere, wife of Jehan Veilliard, embroiderer, and Jane, the wife of Guyon.

On the occasion of a dispute they have with each other. Renere answers that she would like to settle it, because the said Guyone answered the

581. Jane Mermet.

said Renere with insulting words in such a way that they could not agree. And they received Communion and frequent the sermons and have not profited at all by the Word of God. And she said to her: "Rossaz, I have suffered seven years' bad luck with my husband." They were exhorted to make a friendly reconciliation with each other and bury all insults and pardon each other. They answer that they wish it sincerely. Guyonaz answers that she will never pardon her until she asks mercy where she blamed her publicly. They made friendly, perpetual, durable peace, all their enmity being put in the past.

[f. 73v]   *Jaques Des Vignes.*[582]

Presented himself to excuse his wife[583] who is ill and could not come, and he well knows why, because of certain words and enmity.

Tevene, wife of Pierre Des Vignes.[584] Because of certain evil words and long-established hatred against her sister. Answers that it was long ago, that it was about Mychiel Guilliet's cellar that was sold about seven years ago,[585] and her sister always hid from her and fled her company. And she received Communion after her sister. The Consistory asked whether, if her sister wanted to be reconciled with her, she would also agree to be reconciled. If not that they both be remanded to Thursday, and the men their husbands.

---

582. Jaques Des Vignes, citizen, member of the CC in 1530 and *dizainier* for the Rhône Bridge in 1537. He was a member of the CC and probably still a *dizainier* at the time of this session of the Consistory. A Jaques Des Vignes, armorer, living on the Rhône Bridge, died on September 16, 1571 [SORDET, *Dictionnaire*, p. 542; *R.C.* XI, p. 451 (June 18, 1530); R.C. 30, f. 167v (February 7, 1537); R.C. 31, f. 2 (June 15, 1537); R.C. 35, f. 56ᵃv (February 9, 1541); R.C. 35, f. 489 (February 7, 1542); E.C., Morts 11, p. 18].

583. Jeanne, wife of Jaques Des Vignes, daughter of the councillor Noble Ami Gervais, living in 1557 (GALIFFE III, p. 233). A Janne, wife of Jaques Des Vignes, living on the Rhône Bridge, died on October 3, 1571 (E.C., Morts 11, p. 22).

584. Pierre Des Vignes, brother of Jaques, cook, living on the Place Saint Gervais, died on August 27, 1551 [*R.C.* XIII, p. 31 (August 7, 1534); E.C., Morts 1, p. 248].

585. According to NAEF (*Origines* II, p. 43, n. 3), Michel Guillet, "rich banker, perpetual mayor or *mayor* [translator: his title, a local variant of the usual term, *maire*] of Crans, co-Seigneur of Monthoux, had lived in Rome and did not acquire his Genevan bourgeoisie until 1521. As early as 1526 the *eidguenots* carried him into the Council; his foreign origin prevented him from reaching the syndicate ... In 1534 circumstances threw him into the episcopal camp and transformed him into a leader of the Peneysans." He was condemned to death *in absentia,* and was still living in Savoy in 1558 (*D.H.B.S.* III, p. 699). Among the goods confiscated from Guillet were 23 *bossets* of wine, sold to the Des Vignes brothers and Claude Curtet on August 7, 1534 (*R.C.* XIII, p. 31).

Jehan Blanc, brandy dealer, and his wife.

Because of a quarrel they have with each other and frequenting the sermons. Answers that he goes to the sermon and has learned to pray to God in the French language. The Consistory gave them proper admonitions to live together in peace and amity with the others in their household.

Donne Jana Begaz, wife of Begoz.

Because of some words she spoke about the preachers, that the preachers of the past were as good as those of the present. Answers that all preaching is good, and she believes that she only said that preaching is good, and she believes in God who made all things and in Jesus Christ. And she believes that the God whom the priests show is that same God, Jesus Christ. And she prays to God the Redeemer, and does not know how to pray to God except in the manner in which her father and mother taught her to pray, in Latin; and the Credo in Latin as it was said in former times, and said the Ave Maria in Latin as in former times. The Consistory advises that she come present herself here in two weeks and frequent the sermons and learn to pray to God in her maternal tongue, and go to the catechism.

74]   *Donne Claudaz, widow of Claude Chavassu.*

Because of the Word of God. Answers that she goes to the sermons and understands well and knows how to pray to God, and that in the past the Mass was good, and that she says the prayer in Latin and in the other tongue, French. Said and sometimes says the Ave Maria in French also.

Thursday, December 7, 1542[586]

Debet {Owed} 9.
Lord Syndic Cornaz.
Calvin, Genesto, De Ecclesia, Trippereaulx.
Orsieres, Rages, Pensabin, Frochet, the officer Vovrey.

586. The former minister of Jussy, Nicolas Vandert, should have appeared at this session, but there is no mention of him: "Master Nycolas Vander. About the order that he be dismissed from his office because he did not go to visit the sick, ordered that all those complaints made against him be set apart and he be made to respond to them in the Consistory" [R.C. 36, f. 184 (December 5, 1542)].

Henriete, wife of Jehan Favre, butcher.

Because of the sermons. Answers that she goes when she can, and was there Sunday morning. And because of a little girl she has, who cannot go and does not know what the preacher says. And she knows how to pray to God; said the prayer, and does not know the confession. The Consistory advises that she be delayed from receiving the next Communion until the other at Easter, and that she know her faith and creed and refrain from swearing and blaspheming, and go on Sundays to the catechism.

Pernon Veyrona, butcher's wife.[587]

Was at the sermon Sunday at St. Peter's and after dinner at the Magdalen, and cannot say what was said by Monsieur Calvin. And knows how to pray. Said the prayer and the confession.

Jaques Des Vignes and his wife; the wife of Pierre Des Vignes.

Because of some quarrel. Jaques answers that they have settled it by legal process and they wish each other no harm. The Consistory advises that they be given a day and a place and a man to reconcile them all with each other. All four next Monday at the Magdalen.

[f. 74v] *Master Claude Regne, Guillaume Morce, Guillaume Cartier, coiners.*[588]

Because of blaspheming the name of God. Claude answers that it is not he who made a scandal when the work annoyed him and that it is not he who has vices(?).

Thursday, December 14

Debet {Owed} 10.
Lord Syndic Rozet.

---

587. Possibly the wife of Pierre Sermod, called Veyron, butcher.
588. Guillaume Morce (or Morsel) and Guillaume Cartier were admitted as *ouvriers* of the mint (therefore not *monnayeurs*, "coiners" properly speaking) on June 21, 1542 (R.C. 36, f. 48ᶜ). The register makes no mention of Claude Regne in this connection. DEMOLE (p. 33) says: "The *ouvriers* [of the mint] had the job of bringing the metal to a proper thickness, of cutting it into blanks, and of adjusting these to their standard weights. The *monnayeurs* then gave to these blanks, by means of stamps, the imprint of the mint. The distinction between *ouvriers* and *monnayeurs* was not always rigorously observed."

Calvin, Henri, Genesto, Champereaulx.

Orsieres, Frochet, Blandin, Pensabin, Rages, the officer Vovrey.

Wife of Noble Henri Goulaz, master of the mint.[589]

Because of the Word of God, whether she is instructed in the Word of God. Answers that she says her Pater in Latin and does not understand that it is wrong, and is not as resolute as she should be, but has no wish to pray to saints.

Mychie, daughter of Gallatin, from Peney.

Answers that she does not want her promised husband because he has nothing and it is better that she be with her father than elsewhere in difficulty. And that she swore faith to him and does not want him to be her husband for the reason above, and that she has not been debauched.

Jehan Jallio, promised husband of the said Mychie, on the said marriage. Answers no, because the girl does not want it. And if it pleases the Council he is ready to marry her if she wants it, and it is not his fault, and he has done nothing to make her refuse him.

The said Michie recalled. Answers when she swore faith to him he had plenty of goods, and no one tried to prevent her from doing this. Says that if she gives him her goods he will waste them, and she would not know what to do with him. Remanded to respond whether she wants it or not on leaving here, and if not that she be kept in this city until tomorrow. Asked for a term to respond and have counsel from her mother and her friends, since it pleases the Seigneurie, and to marry him next Tuesday, and they agreed to this.

[f. 75] *Pauloz Tarex.*

Because of some infamous songs sung in his house on his recent return from his illness and danger of plague, in place of praying to God. Answers, first thanking the Seigneurie, that he did not sing indecent songs but rather

---

589. Mye, daughter of Michel Nergaz, wife of Henri Goulaz. Henri Goulaz, apothecary from Chieri (Turin), was received into the bourgeoisie on April 28, 1514, became a member of the LX, and died on September 8, 1558. He had already been master of the mint of Cornavin in 1528 and became master of the Geneva mint in 1539. He was replaced in 1546, but returned in 1548, dividing the post with the brothers Berthelier until their condemnation to death in 1555. Goulaz was definitively replaced soon after [GALIFFE III, p. 338; L.B., p. 178; R.C. 30, f. 166v (February 7, 1537); E.C., Morts 2, p. 57 (September 8, 1558); DEMOLE, pp. 20-21. On the functions of the master of the mint in general, see DEMOLE, pp. 18-19].

songs of war and according to the Gospel, and not others. And that he would not want to do otherwise, offering that if he be found to have played since his cure either at dice or cards he submits to the penalty of whipping, except during the time when he was afflicted with plague.[590]

Donne Dominique de Vaulx.

For the sake of being diligent in making her husband come with her or going to him. Answers that it is not her fault, and if it had not been for the law[591] she would have gone to find him, since he indeed wanted to bring her, and she did not want to go because of the law, because she does not want to go to the other law. And she lives with her children who support her.

Mermet, son of Mermet Collomb, farm laborer on the Bourg du Four, from this city.

States that he was married and has a wife who does not behave well, but fornicates and eats his sweat and his labor. Pernon, daughter of Jehan Navatier.[592] And he asks justice and that he be dealt with by law. And he knows how to pray to God; said the prayer and confession. Asks chastisement of his wife who behaves badly, that justice found her doing wrong.

Pernete, wife of the above, daughter of Jehan Navatier. Answers that she has never been found in fornication, but says that a man was found in another room. And that it is not as her husband stated, and she [wanted] to know who had made a complaint against her. And she did not send away the girl who lived with her, and she went to sleep with a woman, therefore went

590. Paulo Tarex, merchant and citizen, member of the CC for Saint Gervais [Notaires, Jean Duverney, v. 5, f. 96 (May 6, 1545); R.C. 35, f. 489v (February 7, 1542); R.C. 37, f. 9v (February 9, 1543)]. At the time of this appearance before the Consistory, Tarex was contesting accusations that he had buried a German in the court of his house. Already at the Council session of September 27, 1542, the procurator general, Thomas Genod, presented a supplication in favor of Tarex, who had caught the plague and could not appear (R.C. 36, f. 130v). On October 6, 1542, Paulo Tarex asked without success for permission to return to Geneva before the end of the quarantine imposed by the edicts (R.C. 36, f. 138). On October 9 and 14, 1542 (R.C. 36, f. 139 and f. 144), after the death by plague of two of Tarex' servants, the Council ordered three journeymen who worked for him to go into quarantine at his expense. On October 24, 1542, the Council refused again to give him permission to return to Geneva (R.C. 36, f. 153). Having reentered the city about November 14, Tarex asked for a copy of the accusations against him, and succeeded at last in establishing his innocence [R.C. 36, folios 168, 171v, and 197v (November 14 and 17 and December 22, 1542)].
591. That is, for the sake of religion.
592. Underlined in the text: "Pernon, daughter of Jehan Navatier."

to Troinex. The Consistory advises that she be remanded to Monday before the Council.[593]

Tuesday, December 19, 1542

Debet {Owed} 11.
Lord Syndic Cornaz.
Calvin, Henri, Genesto, Trepereaulx.
Orsieres, Rages, Frochet, Blandin, Pensabin, the officer Vovrey.

Jehan de Carro.

Said the prayer and the confession poorly. The Consistory advises that he should come to instruction to know whether he will be given Communion, and before he comes to Communion he should come here Thursday and go to the catechism on Sundays and frequent the sermons; otherwise he will be rigorously punished.

Myaz, widow of Ylayre Richardet.

Said the prayer without book and the confession and has no scruples. The Consistory advises that, in view of her good will, although she is still not well instructed, that she frequent the sermons more often, and can receive Communion, and that she make the others profit.

Pierre Ballon, haberdasher.[594]

Because he leaves his wife and children without doing them any good and goes abroad often and often stays in Vevey. Answers that his children and wife are in this city, and because of some words he left. And he thought he would come sooner than he did because he cannot minister to his children as he

---

593. On December 18, 1542, Mermet Collomb asked in Council to be separated from his wife "because she was found in adultery . . . and is disobedient." The Council then ordered the imprisonment of Pernete Navatier, his wife (R.C. 36, f. 192).

594. According to SORDET (*Dictionnaire*, p. 64), a Pierre Ballon, citizen, "was a monk in the monastery of the Augustinians of Our Lady of the Arve Bridge, and embraced the Reform." However, we have no reason to suppose that he was a priest, and we find only a Jean, son of Jean Hugonier, called Ballon, among the former clergy of Geneva [see for example R.C. XIII, p. 361 (November 24, 1535), pp. 415, 461-462 (January 28 and February 23, 1536)]. We also find a Pierre Balon, a gate-keeper of Rive, who died on August 17, 1558 (E.C., Morts 2, p. 49), without being able to establish any link among these various references.

should, although he sent a *teston* to his wife. And he goes to the sermons willingly and knows how to pray to God and knows the confession. The Consistory advises that he be forbidden to look for gold any more in the Arve[595] as he does and that he follow his trade and not leave his wife and his children so often.

Françoyse, wife of Jehan Bornant.

Because of the Word of God and on her improvement since her last appearance. Said the prayer and the confession poorly as before. Was at the sermon today and remembered nothing. The Consistory is of the opinion that she frequent the preaching more often and learn better to say the prayer between now and Thursday, and Jehan Bornant her husband should come here with her and she with him. And says that he will not be able to come in time.

[f. 76] *Colleta, widow of Michiel Chabod, cobbler, [daughter] of Andrier Berthier.*

Said the prayer.

Daughter of Ratellier. Claude Macheret. Jehanete, widow of Mauris Dentant, pregnant by Glaude Macheret, locksmith.[596]

And is pregnant since Pentecost and not by any other and has not fornicated with any other, as she says, and has no child, and had his company only once at her house. The Consistory is of the opinion[597] that she appear here Thursday.

Master Jaques Enyn, pack-saddler.

Because of Communion, and whether he is better instructed than the last time that he received it. Said the prayer and the confession poorly, as last time. Has bought a Bible that the merchants read in his house.[598]

Thursday, December 21, 1542

Lord Syndic Pertemps.
Calvin, Champereaulx, Treppereaulx.
Orsieres, Rages, Pensabin, Frochet, Blandin, the officer Vovrey.

595. There is in fact a small amount of gold in the Arve (see PITTARD, pp. 232-233).
596. Jehanete Dentant, bastard daughter of Don Jean Ratellier, and Claude Vuarin, called Macheret.
597. Struck: "that he be forbidden Communion."
598. On March 2, 1542, the Consistory had ordered his wife, Tevenete, to buy a Bible for his guests "to read in place of game boards, cards, songs . . ." See above *ad diem.*

Donne Jane Troctiere.

Because of the absence of her husband. Answers that she has done her best two or three times and has not had an answer, and he is in Padua. The Consistory advises that she be admonished to use more diligence than she has and to write to him again.

Donne Jane Begaz.

Because of her creed and profiting by the Word of the Lord. Said the prayer and the confession and another Benedicite,[599] and was at the sermon Monday and at the prayer at St. Peter's. The Consistory admonished her to frequent the sermons and prayers and always profit by the Word of the Lord.

76v]   *Pierre Mercier, citizen of Geneva.*[600]

Because of the wife he promised[601] so long ago, what he is doing and what obstacle there is. Answers that he took her on condition. Said in the presence of her relatives who wanted him to marry that he was not of an age to have a wife and asked for a term to speak to his friends. And they answered him that they knew well what he was and that he was ready if he was paid as he was promised. And when he receives the amount he is ready to do his duty. And the relatives of the girl have the money and have always told him she had lots of money, and they sent him from one to the other, and no one wanted to establish the marriage, and he will not be engaged to her if he is not given the said amount. The Consistory advises that the relatives be interrogated to learn what they mean by it and that the mother and the relatives of the principals be summoned here and those who should pay for the marriage, and that it be remanded to another day. Remanded to next Thursday.

599. *Benedicite:* a canticle of Lauds and the fore-Mass, drawn from the deuterocanonical text of Daniel 3:57-88 in the Vulgate. On the *Benedicite,* its history and usages, see *D.A.C.L.* II.1, col. 660-664.

600. There were several Pierre Merciers in Geneva in the first half of the sixteenth century, including a Pierre Mercier, member of the CC in 1542 from the *dizaine* of Claude Morel (in Longemale) [R.C. 35, f. 490 (February 7, 1542); and R.C. 35, f. 399 (November 15, 1541), for the identification of the *dizaine* of Claude Morel]. This matrimonial case lasted a long time and was taken up many times both in the Consistory and in the Council.

601. Claudine Chenu.

Pierre Voland,[602] *from Ambilly, servant of Pierre Bienvenu.*[603]

He was presented a written charm, which he acknowledged having written, and says that he knew formerly that it was a charm, six years ago before he came to this city. And he asks mercy and says that he does not want its help at present and that he has had words with the wife of Master Rolet,[604] the widow of Master Rolet the baker. The Consistory advises that he be admonished and shown the said talisman and how much it is worth, and and [sic] that he be reconciled with his master's sister, Master Rolet's widow, tomorrow at the sermon. And that he valued the said talisman. He answers not at all, and broke it and tore it to pieces.

Pierre Sermod, called Veyron.

Because of dice games with the host of the Bochet, and that he lost his money. Answers that the one who is dead[605] and he played for drinks a fortnight ago with blank dice. And there were many people, about ten, and they did not play except for drinks, and he left because they were eating supper, and he cannot name those who were present. The Consistory is of the opinion that he be given good remonstrances and forbidden the next Communion until he is better disposed and worthy of receiving it and makes more improvement.

[f. 77]   *At the inn of the Bochet in Rive, those who played at dice about two weeks ago.*[606]

Pierre Sermod [called] Veyron, 6 écus. Françoys de Monte, haberdasher, living below the Magdalen at Berengier's. The said person had gained

602. "Pierre, illegitimate son of the late Egrège Claude Volland, from Ambilly," was admitted to the bourgeoisie on May 29, 1542 (*L.B.*, p. 223).

603. Pierre Bienvenu, merchant and citizen, died in 1565 at age 60. A Pierre Bienvenu, possibly his father, was syndic in 1531 [*E.C.*, Morts 6, p. 4 (January 8, 1565); R.C. 30, f. 133v (December 21, 1563); SORDET, *Dictionnaire*, p. 105; GALIFFE I, p. 429].

604. We believe that this is the wife of Master Rolet Bon, baker, often mentioned in the R.C., because on July 1, 1522, a lease was guaranteed for François Bienvenu by *(cavet per)* Rolet Bon and Pierre Bienvenu. Rolet Bon, from Challex (Ain), was admitted to the bourgeoisie on November 28, 1503 (*R.C.* IX, p. 188; *L.B.*, p. 151).

605. Françoys Deponte. See the note below.

606. Here are some traces of the affair that led the Council to start a hunt for gamesters. On Wednesday, December 20, 1542, Françoys Deponte supped with Denis Hugues at the inn of the Bochet in company with Aymé Bochu, Françoys Comparet the elder, Felix Amary, Pierre Sermod called Veyron, and others. After dinner Deponte proposed a game to decide who would pay for the meal. Having lost, Bochu accused Deponte of not being worthy of being a player and struck him with his sword, killing him. In an extraordinary session in the evening of December 20 the Council ordered Bochu's arrest. On December 22 the Council decided to take a hard line against all gamblers and jailed Bochu

the 6 écus; he played for the meal. There were about six persons at 6 sous per man. Also Françoys Comparet, baker, lost 2 florins for the meal, and he never goes to the sermons, nor his brother Claude either, and the mother and the two children must be summoned.[607]

Thursday, December 21, 1542[608]

Lord . . .[609]
Calvin.
Rages, the officer Vovrey.[610]

Françoys Comparet.

Because of games. Answers that he goes to the sermon when he can and sometimes with friends to drink, and yesterday they drank a pot of wine to-

---

and several others, including Pierre Sermod called Veyron, who "persists in gambling." Bochu was executed for murder on December 27, while Sermod remained in prison until January 10, 1543. Sermod was also implicated in another criminal case at the same time. He had quarreled with Jehan Goula while gambling: "Goula struck the said Veyron, then went to get the sword of the said Veyron and threw it to him, then put his hand to his sword and told him, 'Draw your blade, fornicator!'" This cost Goula a half year in prison chained by the leg and deprivation of all honors. See R.C. 36, folios 195a-e, 197-198, 200, and 201v (December 20-22, 27, and 29, 1542), folios 205 and 212-212v (January 2 and 12, 1543); NAEF, *Bezanson Hugues*, pp. 526-527; P.C. 1ᵉ sér., 366 (January 5-27, 1543); P.C. 2ᵉ sér., 567 (December 23, 1542-January 9, 1543).

607. These are the children and the widow of Claude Comparet, bourgeois. The mother, Jaquema, died on April 18, 1568, at age 80. A little after this session of the Consistory Claude Comparet the son, baker, had a bastard child by Mermette, daughter of Jehanton Genod. Claude Comparet died on August 31, 1571. It is François the elder who is here reprimanded for gambling. In the next session, the second session dated December 21, François the elder appeared in Consistory with his brother François the younger and not with Claude, as is indicated here (see below). The two François Comparets, bakers like their brother, became embroiled in the conflicts of 1555 and found their death there, being decapitated as traitors on July 3, 1555 [R.G.S. I, pp. 114-116 and 134; R.C. Part. 1, f. 39v (April 13, 1543); E.C., Morts 1, p. 77 (August 22, 1552); E.C., Morts 2, p. 59 (September 11, 1558); E.C., Morts 9, p. 11 (April 18, 1568)].

608. The second session dated December 21.

609. The name of the syndic is lacking, indicating that he was probably absent from this session.

610. The scribe, having left space to list the names of the Consistory members who never came to this supplementary session of the Consistory, began to write the minutes above the name of Vovrey. Therefore his name is found struck out in the middle of the following text.

gether with good company. And answers nine sous for three, and he was not there, and he lost three sous per man. And that he was at the sermon Sunday and . . .[611] preached. Said the prayer and the confession. Remonstrances just as to the other, and let him abstain from the next Communion.

François Comparet the younger, brother of the aforesaid François, in the bakery. Goes to the sermon on Sundays when he can, and they bake every day at seven o'clock in their shop and go to the market to supply the shop. And said the prayer in Latin. And it is only about six months ago that he came to this city. Was at the vespers sermon Sunday.

Camparet's widow,[612] mother of the two named above, because she does not discipline her children, who are badly taught in all good morals. Answers that other young boys lead them astray and ruin them, and they are good children and obedient, and they were not at the scandal that was made thus, and she does not know what it is. And goes willingly to the sermons when she can, and above all on Sundays. The younger son does not come to Communion. The Consistory advises that she watch out from now on, that she teach her children and frequent the sermons and the catechism on Sundays; otherwise the Council will see to her. And that the children frequent the sermons.

[f. 77v]   *Claude Macheret.*[613]

Because of the bastard daughter of Ratellier[614] whom he made pregnant. Answers that he knows nothing, although he once took a fancy to her, and it may be he knew her once about a year ago, and he does not remember the time. And she cried out to him that she wanted some sort of clothes. And let the glover's wife,[615] who knows well who went to her, be summoned. And that he believes there was one named Malliard[616] and others. And whether he will name those about whom he is unhappy. Answers that he pardons everything and means to receive Communion. Named Busmetaz because she insulted his brother, also Jehan Genod's wife.[617] Syndic Rozet knows well those who are involved.

Ratellier's daughter, because of being remanded to today for having named the aforesaid Macheret, and that she not charge someone wrongly.

611. Name omitted.
612. Jaquema, widow of Claude Comparet.
613. Claude Vuarin, called Macheret.
614. Jehanete Dentant, bastard daughter of Don Jean Ratellier.
615. Possibly the wife of Vincent Fichet, glover.
616. On the Maillards, see SORDET, *Dictionnaire*, p. 855.
617. Possibly Jeanton Genod, member of the CC and the LX, brother of the procurator general, Thomas Genod. See GALIFFE IV, pp. 226-229.

Answers that she had no man's company but his, and Malliard was there, but this was because of another who was pregnant by the said Malliard, and she died of plague. And she would indeed like to swear this is so.

The Consistory advises that they be remanded before the Council and that she abstain from the next Holy Communion because of her fornication. Remanded to a week from Monday before the Council. Touching the said Macheret who wants to receive Communion, that he should reveal the guilty and that he be forbidden Communion and that he name . . .[618] Answers as above, and pardons everyone with a good heart. It is left to his own good will whether he retains anything, and if he takes Communion with resentment, it will be by his own judgment. And he takes God to witness that he retains nothing in himself. Named only Jaque Pape,[619] the son of Taberlet,[620] remained here.[621] Ratelliere: she denies that anyone other than the said Macheret has lived with her, because those named did not.

Jane, wife of Jehan Corajod, host of the Golden Lion, cobbler.

Answers that she is of this city and of Etrembières to do the work and watch her goods and the animals of the house for profit. And has not heard the sermons because there is no sermon given, and has not heard Mass and has never been to the sermon since the last Communion was given and has not received the Host in Etrembières. And knows the prayer, and the confession does not know how to say at all. And prays to God in her heart, because the tongue does not do anything if the heart [f. 78] does not say it. And she prays God always to help her. And she keeps Lent and believes this is well done, because she has lived all her life just as her predecessors taught her. And when she receives Communion she understands that she receives it for the salvation of her soul. The advice of the Consistory: that she not receive the present Communion and that she remain longer in this city than she has done in the past and frequent the sermons and the catechism on Sundays and strive to serve God more fully than she does or has done in the past and

---

618. Incomplete sentence.

619. The daughter of a Jaques Pape, miller and citizen, living on the Rhône Bridge, was born dead on June 27, 1563. His wife died "of disease of childbirth" the next day, at age 40 (E.C., Morts 5, pp. 191 and 192).

620. A Loys Taberlet, living in Geneva in 1540, died on April 6, 1553. Pierre Taberlet, innkeeper, was received as a bourgeois on February 3, 1514, and a Pierre Taberlet, hosier, possibly the same, died on December 19, 1552 [R.C. 34, f. 524 (November 14, 1540); E.C., Morts 1, pp. 87 and 99; *L.B.*, p. 178].

621. Underlined in the text: "And takes God to witness . . . the son of Taberlet, remained here."

make a Christian confession, and that she be given good remonstrances. And that she not go any more to stay in the village, and follow the Word of God here; otherwise the Council will not be content with her. And that she not go without license from the Council.

Pierre Durant, called De La Tabla, rebels against coming.

Answers that he was not in this city, but was in the village in the Vuache, and did not know the prayer, and that he must cease from fornication. The Consistory advises that he not be given the next Communion and that he frequent the sermons and the catechism on Sunday, and that next time he come the first time he is summoned.

On Communion.

Will be celebrated on Monday, [as decided] by the stronger voice, and the ordinances like the preceding ones written above.[622]

On those rebelling from appearing in Consistory after being summoned three times.

Who are: Pierre Calabri, mason, Claude Arthaud, hosier, and the Drobliere of Saint Gervais.[623]

All those attending the Consistory were paid from today back, and the rest [will be paid] in the future, except Lord Cornaz, syndic, who did not want to receive anything for his attendance, and from this [that was due him] the money was paid for the two Consistories last preceding and down to the first upcoming, which will be January 4, 1543.

[f. 78v]

Thursday, December 28, 1543[624]

Lord Syndic Cornaz.
Champereaulx, Genesto, Trippereaulx.
Orsieres, Rages, Frochet, Pensabin, the officer Vovrey.

622. One sees here the wavering of the Genevans on the sabbatarian principle. Only two days before the Council had "commanded to celebrate the Holy Communion of Our Lord next Sunday before Christmas," that is Sunday, December 24, in place of the traditional Christmas day [R.C. 36, f. 194 (Tuesday, December 19, 1542)]. For the ordinances of the Easter Communion, see above, April 6, 1542.

623. On January 15, 1543, the Council condemned Calabri, Arthaud, and Françoyse Loup, called the Drobliere, to three days in prison for having failed to appear in Consistory (R.C. 36, f. 213).

624. It will be remembered that the new year began at Christmas in Geneva at this time.

Pierre Mercier.

Because of his marriage, as above. Answers that he is ready to do his duty and that he should be given an explanation.

Mychiel Chenu,[625] *Amy Chenuz's widow, Jehan Gringallet.*[626]

For next Thursday.

Jehan Bornand, granary worker.

Because of his improvement. Answers that he frequents the sermons. Said the prayer; the confession he does not know at all, or very little. Should frequent the catechism, and know how to pray by the next time he is summoned here.

Françoys Dupont.

Because of a quarrel he has with Maurisaz Tallichetaz. Answers that it is over the will of Orbanna Talluchetaz, aunt of the said Maurise, who is the heir of the said Orbannaz.[627]

Maurisaz Tallucheta received Communion last Monday in a state of resentment of the aforesaid Françoys and insulting words. Answers that she received Communion like the others at nine o'clock, and that yesterday she

---

625. Michel Chenu, former Benedictine of the monastery of St. John in Geneva, left his monastery and became a refugee in Bernese territory at the time of the Reform. In December 1536 he was already back in Geneva, and the Council admitted him to the bourgeoisie "at the request of Amye Bandiere, considering the services [that he] has done for the city." He married Claudine, daughter of the priest Claude Maillet the younger, before October 6, 1537, and subsequently became a merchant and, in 1542, a member of the CC. He was implicated in the famous rising of May 16, 1555, which provoked the final downfall of the Perrinist party, but apparently only by accident, and he was found innocent of all accusations. He died on May 15, 1568, at age 70 [*R.C.* XIII, p. 546 and note (April 23, 1536); R.C. 30, f. 105v, f. 111 (December 8 and 12, 1536), abridged and corrected in *L.B.,* p. 216; R.C. 31, f. 71v (October 6, 1537); GALIFFE I, p. 398; E.C., Morts 9, p. 55 (October 15, 1568, death of Claudine); R.C. 35, f. 490 (February 7, 1542); BONIVARD, *Police,* pp. 142, 145; ROGET IV, pp. 245-288; E.C., Morts 9, p. 16].

626. All those mentioned above were from the family of Pierre Mercier's promised wife. His fiancée Claudine was the daughter of Ami Chenu (bourgeois in 1523; died in 1539) and of Philiberte Gringallet, daughter of Jehan Gringallet; see the note concerning her above, September 7, 1542. Michel Chenu, brother of Ami Chenu, was the guardian of Claudine [GALIFFE II, pp. 113-114, and III, pp. 255-256; *L.B.,* p. 196 (January 16, 1523)].

627. According to Galiffe (II, p. 71): "Maurise, widow of Louis Du Boule, bourgeois, had inherited goods from Urbaine, widow of Egrège François de Léamont [syndic], otherwise called Tallichet, who possessed them in 1519."

insulted him when she was in the presence of people on the Rue de Saint Anthoine, saying that the said Françoys had made her pay 15 florins, which she had delivered to a good man; he was very angry at this. The Consistory advises that she come present herself here within two weeks to render a better explanation of her faith, and frequent the catechism, and bring her daughter. And they both pardoned each other for all evil words, and not to return under penalty . . .[628]

[f. 79] *Donne Jane, widow of Philibert de La Ryvaz.*[629]

Because of her muttering in the sermon, and whether she has some doubt of the . . .[630] Answers that she has always lived outside in the village and only recently came [to the city]. And she does not say the Ave Maria, and she sometimes says some words of the Psalms, and that it would be better for her to stay in her house than go to the sermon, considering that she has children, and she has no scruples about the Word that is presently preached.

Marguerita Benelaz.

Because of the sermons. Answers that she goes when she can on Sundays and that she has to watch the house and the merchandise. And she goes to the catechism on Sundays. Said the prayer and the confession.

George, widow of Jehan Martin; Henritaz, widow of Henri Martin; Gerardaz, widow of Passet, living at the old school in Rive.[631]

Because of the sermons, which they do not frequent. Answers that she was at the sermon at Easter, George, and did not say the confession. The said Henrietaz said the prayer and the confession, and Girardaz similarly, and all of them very little, understanding badly. They were admonished to frequent the sermons and the catechism.

628. The penalty is not specified.
629. This is most likely Jeanne Curt, widow of Noble Philippe de La Rive, also reprimanded on November 18, 1557, because of certain images found at her house [CHOISY, G.G., p. 42; P.C. 1ᵉ sér., 685 (November 18, 1557)].
630. Word omitted.
631. Due to the generosity of François de Versonay, "the Council decided to build a school above the friary of the minors [Franciscans]" in Rive in 1428. This building was replaced in 1494 by a school reputedly "marvelously built," but according to Henri Naef: "the building which replaced the first school of Versonay was not as marvelous as it was said to be, since in 1535 there was nothing more pressing than to transfer the pupils to the secularized friary of Rive" (NAEF, *Origines* I, pp. 279, 281, and 278-295, for the history of this school until the Reformation; see also BÉTANT).

Pernetaz, widow of Jehan Du Nant, in front of Rive.

Answers that she never goes to the sermon, that she cannot. Said the prayer, and does not know how to say the confession, and she takes God as her savior. Remonstrances that she frequent the catechism.

Claude Bordon, weaver.[632]

Because of the sermons. Answers that he frequents the sermons, and he never fails to go twice a week, and the other times he has to work for a living. Said the prayer and the confession. Admonitions to frequent the sermons and the catechism.

79v] *Françoyse Cosemere, from the Rue du Boule.*

Because of the sermons. Answers that she often goes to the sermons. Said the prayer and the confession in a general way. Admonitions that she persevere in the sermons and instruct her children and serve God.

Mermet Michallet, farm laborer, and Pernete his wife.[633]

Because of the sermons. Answers that he was at the sermon Sunday and when he can, and that those he works for do not want him to go to the sermons. And that he does not speak indecent words to girls or to others; he kisses them sometimes. Said that he wants to live so he will have a good reputation. Said the prayer and the confession fairly well. The said wife said the prayer like her husband. Admonitions that he frequent the sermons and not say lewd words any more to the maids and use decent words in the house.

Request to the Consistory for the wife of Jehan Corajod, cobbler, called the Goitered.[634]

The Honorable Pierre de Rages, member of the present Consistory, stated before the said Consistory that today the said Jehan Corajodz prayed the said deponent to pray the said Consistory that it might be their pleasure to give permission to his said wife to go to the village to look after their house, goods and animals. And she will come every Saturday and Sunday and Wednesday to come to the sermons and catechism until they can pro-

632. Claude Bordon, "weaver of cloth," died on March 4, 1555, on the Rue Verdaine [E.C., Morts 1, p. 202; see also R.C. 35, f. 169v (April 20, 1541)].
633. On April 6, 1563, "Mermet Mychallet, citizen of Geneva, living on the Rue Verdaine, . . . aged about 60," died (E.C., Morts 5, p. 160).
634. The wife of Jehan Corajod, called Du Nant, host of the Golden Lion.

vide a farmer who will stay there entirely and do his job as farmer and exempt the said woman from going and coming so often from the said place to look after those goods, and she can frequent the sermons better. And having heard the said request, they granted it to him as it was asked.

1543[1]

The curé of Céligny.[2]

Proposed to the said Consistory to accomplish the marriage promised by Pernet Villan of Coppet and Gasparde, daughter of Noble Jehan Bornant, of Céligny. The Consistory remanded the said affair to our superiors, syndics and Council, to deal with it.[3]

Thursday, January 4, 1543

Claude Michallet, watchman, announced having summoned Claude Vallouz, barber, and his wife,[4] Michel Du Mur and his wife,[5] by command of Syndic Rozet.

Lord Syndic Rozet.

1. The indication of the year is at the top of the page above the supplication of the curé of Céligny.

2. Jaques Baud, minister of Céligny and the only Genevan priest to retain his office after the Reformation. He was finally deposed "because he is not capable of announcing the Holy Gospel," in this case because of his wife's scandalous life. See R.C. 37, f. 227 (September 24, 1543), and FATIO, *Céligny,* pp. 69-70.

3. In the end Pernet or Pierre Villan and Gasparde Bornant were married in the Bornants' house "in the papistical form" by the priest Don Pierre Gex before July 2, 1543. In July 1543 the plague reigned in Geneva, and the priest had proclaimed that "all those who believe in the Gospel will die of the plague." Pierre Gex, Gasparde Bornant, and her mother, Gabrielle Bornant, were all put in prison in Céligny, but were finally freed on July 13. The husband seems to have left Céligny, since the mother was told to "induce her daughter to go find her husband, and to do this urgently" [R.C. Part. 1, folios 72, 73, and 74 (July 2, 6, and 13, the session of July 6 being dated June 6)].

4. His wife is identified in a *"vendicio faicta per Glaudium, filium quondam Johannis Vallodi, burgensum Gebennis et Girardum, ejus uxoram, parrochie S[ti] Gervasii"* {sale made by Glaudius, son of the late Johannes Vallodus, bourgeois of Geneva, and Girardus, his wife, of the parish of St. Gervase} [Notaires, Amédée-Bon Novel, only volume, f. 93 (September 18, 1518)]. Despite the date and the orthography, one asks whether this is not the same person who was admitted to the bourgeoisie in 1520 under the name *"Glaudius Vallens, alias Faverges, filius quondam Johannis de Vallens, de Challongio, barbitonsor, par. S[ti] Gervasii"* {Glaudius Vallens, alias Faverges, son of the late Johannes de Vallens, from Challonges [H.-S.], barber, parish of St. Gervase} (*L.B.,* p. 190). He died before February 12, 1553, the date when Robelle, the daughter of the late Master Claude Vallouz, married [E.C., Copies 7 (mariages, Saint-Gervais)].

5. The widow of Michel Du Mur died on March 23, 1567, at age 60 (E.C., Morts 7, p. 65; her first name is not given).

169

Calvin, De Ecclesia, Genesto.
Pensabin, Rages, Frochet, Blandin, the officer Vovrey.

For the marriage of Pierre Mercier.

Michel Chenu and Pierre Mercier's wife's mother[6] stated that they have sold goods to pay for the said marriage, about 150 écus,[7] and that he took goods to the value of 200 florins to hold for the rest. And the said Mercier does not want to consent to what they affirm, and it is not their fault. The mother of the girl says that she told him that there was hardly anything lacking of the sum and that he should do his duty, and that for the rest he would have two meadows to hold until he is fully paid, and this in the absence of Michiel Chenu, and that there could lack only 200 florins, which he will be paid at Easter, and that he would be given 200 écus in currency.

Jehan Chappon, furrier.[8]

Because of the sermons. Answers that he is obedient to the Gospel and does not want to drive it away and has it at heart. And that he has only three months out of the year to earn his living. He is angry at his servant and wife who are not found in the shop but go get drunk, and therefore he does not leave the shop. And he goes willingly to the sermons, except on Sundays, but on Wednesdays he is there when he can be. And because a merchant owed him money and he gave leave to the said servant. [f. 80v] And that he has not failed to go to the sermons on Wednesday except three times by accident. He was admonished to follow the sermons.

Monsieur Jehan Favre, merchant.

Because of the sermons, and whether he has any resentment. Answers that he always goes to the sermons except when he has something to do, and he cannot go every day because of the market he has charge of. And he sends

---

6. Philiberte Chenu, mother of Claudine Chenu, promised wife of Pierre Mercier.

7. According to the supplication of Philiberte Chenu before the Council the sum was only 150 florins. See below, note.

8. Jehan Chappon, furrier from Lyon, was admitted to the bourgeoisie on July 7, 1534; he was a member of the CC from 1535 on [*L.B.*, p. 210; SORDET, *Dictionnaire*, p. 232; R.C. 30, f. 167v (February 7, 1537)]. Chappon was discussed several times in Council in connection with a letter that Etienne Dada, a fugitive, had sent him, and with a house and goods left by Dada at his death [R.C. 35, f. 246 (June 27, 1541); R.C. 36, f. 50v (June 23, 1542); R.C. 37, f. 261 (November 2, 1543)].

his wife[9] when he he [sic] cannot go there. He was admonished as above . . .[10] as often as he can.

Noble François Chamoex.[11]

As above, because of the sermons and other things. Answers that it is true that he does not go there as often as he should, and he goes as often as he can.

For Mercier, about the marriage; Noble Jehan Gringallet.

Because of the marriage of Pierre Mercier and . . . ,[12] to know what is going on. Answers that he is not her guardian, and that someone wanted to beat him, and the girl's father's brother is her guardian,[13] and he is annoyed that they do not make an end and that the husband will not agree to put an end to the affair, and it is not his fault. He was admonished that he should help, and also his daughter, the girl's mother,[14] should get together to use all their power to put an end to it. And also to frequent the sermons better than he does.[15]

9. Jaquema, daughter of the syndic Louis Plonjon (CHOISY, *G.G.*, p. 120).

10. Words omitted: "to frequent the sermons."

11. François Chamoex or Chamois, lieutenant in 1540, was one of the ambassadors sent to Bern to abrogate the treaty signed by the "Articulants." Implicated in this affair, he was deposed as lieutenant. According to Galiffe it was his son, also named François, who returned to the CC in 1546 and subsequently became a councillor (1549), syndic (1551), and lieutenant (1554), "that is, if it was not the same man." Certain references in the R.C. make us lean to this last hypothesis, without in any case providing proof. Like other Articulants, Chamoex had been condemned not to leave the city without asking leave from the Council. On June 19, 1543, François Chamoex, Etienne Chapeaurouge, Claude Chasteauneuf, and Jean Lullin, "who had been restricted and named in the proceedings" three years before, asked the Council to free them "from their said restriction," which the Council granted to Chamoex, Chapeaurouge, and Lullin on June 22. Later, on February 9, 1546, speaking of Chamois, Chapeaurouge, Jean de Pesmes, and Jean Louis Ramel, the Council decided: "Because these in the past were held suspect and have not been in the Council [of Two Hundred] since 1540, when the fugitives from Geneva who are called Arthichaulx left Geneva, it is put in question whether they will be of the Great Council or not. And on this ordered that, considering that from the said time to now they have lived honestly, being obedient to God and justice, that they should be deputies of the Council of Two Hundred" [GEISENDORF, *Annalistes*, p. 487; R.C. Part. 1, folios 64v, 68, and 69 (June 11, 19, and 22, 1543); R.C. 41, f. 8v (February 9, 1546). See also BONIVARD, *Police*, p. 82; GALIFFE II, p. 110; SORDET, *Dictionnaire*, p. 226].

12. Word(s) or name omitted by the scribe. The marriage is that of Claudine Chenu.

13. Michel Chenu, guardian of Claudine Chenu.

14. Philiberte, widow of Ami Chenu.

15. There was no further discussion of this marriage in Consistory, but it occupied

Jehan Balard the younger.[16]

Because of the sermons. Answers the remonstrances given him, giving thanks for the admonitions, and that he wants to do what a good citizen should do.

Master Claude Vallouz, barber, and his wife.[17]

Answers that he was at the sermon Sunday and cannot go the other days because he has no servant to watch the shop and he has to watch the shop himself. He goes on Sundays and Wednesdays, and not the other days. His wife answers that she sends two daughters to school to be instructed in religion and a son, and that they say grace to God every time they have food.

---

the Council repeatedly during the following year. On February 19, 1543, Mercier complained of not having received Claudine Chenu's dowry. Michel, Claudine's uncle, and Philiberte Chenu, her mother, then promised to give him the promised 700 florins (R.C. Part. 1, f. 7v). In April Philiberte Chenu asked in Council that Michel Chenu be compelled to give up 150 florins that he held in trust for the children of his brother Ami. She also asked that Ami Bandière pay the 100 florins he owed, apparently for the marriage of Claudine Chenu. Bandière and Michel Chenu made a settlement with Philiberte Chenu, both asking to be freed from the guardianship and pledge of marriage. Moreover, Michel Chenu complained of Pierre Mercier, who had said, probably to his mother-in-law, "'You have done enough. You have sold out to a monk,' saying such words of Michiel Chenuz" [R.C. Part. 1, f. 46v (April 27, 1543)]. Despite the agreement between Michel and Philiberte Chenu, two weeks later she was again obliged to ask that he pay the rest of the dowry and that Mercier, on his part, complete the marriage. The Council then gave her permission to present her case before the lieutenant [R.C. Part. 1, f. 51 (May 11, 1543)]. The next week, being threatened with prison, Mercier said that he would leave the city rather than carry out his marriage. Apparently he avoided prison by promising to marry Claudine Chenu. Despite the remonstrances of the Council in June and September, he was in no hurry to keep his word. On September 24, 1543, the Council again ordered Mercier's imprisonment for still not having obeyed the order to marry his promised wife [R.C. Part. 1, folios 55v, 57v, 64, and 87v (May 18 and 22, June 9, and September 3, 1543); R.C. 37, f. 226, *ad diem*]. On November 6 Mercier was put in prison, this time for fornication, and freed six days later after asking pardon and paying a fine [R.C. 37, f. 264v, *ad diem;* f. 266v and f. 271 (November 9 and 12, 1543)]. On November 27, 1543, Mercier again asked to be paid in full for his marriage, and on November 30 Michel Chenu would have been put in prison for this reason except for the intervention of Ami Bandière (R.C. Part. 1, f. 106 and f. 107). At this point one loses track of one of the most complicated matrimonial cases presented to the Consistory in its early years. It seems that the two parties finally agreed: Claudine, widow of Pierre Mercier, was still living in 1584 (GALIFFE II, pp. 113-114, and III, pp. 255-256).

16. Jean Balard, son of the syndic Jean Balard. See the short biographical notice on the son in the introduction to BALARD, pp. xcii-xcvi *et passim*.

17. Girarde, wife of Claude Vallouz.

Du Mur produced a supplication. The said Claudz has a relative with whom he has a quarrel and some wrongly spoken words, and they do not live in peace.[18] Answers that he does not refuse to be in accord with him, but [f. 81] that his said adversary said that he would not agree unless the law ordered it. And otherwise he wishes him no harm. And the Seigneurie prayed them to agree with each other. The admonitions are that he refrain from swearing by God and frequent the sermons.

Arthaudaz.

Because of the woman she has assisted in her house.[19] She answers that she has brought her, and she is from Coppet, and she has done her all the good she could, and she asked her to shelter her to have her child, and three weeks ago she had her child at her house. Mermaz, daughter of the late Guillaume, from Lausanne, living in Coppet, widow of Claude Dupont, who lived in Coppet, and stayed with her about five years. And that she met her three weeks ago last Monday, and she never knew who she was until the said Saturday when she sheltered her until she had been delivered of this daughter she carries. And the said Arthaude gave her a place to have the child because of earlier acquaintance, and she had gone to drink there as in a tavern. And she had the child by a journeyman whose name she gave, and he is called Glaude Magnin, servant of Monsieur De Viri,[20] and he is always in Coppet or in the district, and he is from Sallanche. And she prayed the Lord to pardon her, and to hide her dishonor she came to this city to have it secretly, and she had not come before. And it was well known that she was pregnant and came to have a master to serve, and that she should tell the truth, and she would not. And she had not fooled around since the death of her husband. Arthaudaz, because she said that she had not seen her except on that Monday, and she only saw her when she had the child, since there had been a proclamation that no one be sheltered more than

18. This refers to a suit between Claude Vallouz and Michel Du Mur regarding "the sharing of a house" located on the Rue de la Poissonnerie. See R.C. 36, folios 210, 214v, and 221v (January 9, 16, and 26, 1542).

19. The Council investigated this case on January 15, 1543 (R.C. 36, f. 213), and decided to imprison Arthaudaz for having received a fornicator in her house. She was again in prison on December 7, 1543, for "rebellion against justice," and was freed after making reparation before the lieutenant, but we do not know whether there was any connection with the present case (R.C. Part. 1, f. 109).

20. Michel de Viry, baron and lord of Virey, La Perrière, Coppet, and Rolle. He was forced to sell his goods to pay his debts and died destitute in 1547 (FORAS, *Armorial* 5, p. 370). See also *D.H.B.S.* 7, pp. 150-151, and MOTTAZ, *Dictionnaire*, p. 505b *et passim*.

three days.[21] And she assisted her daughter and those who had husbands. Admonitions and remonstrances were given [f. 81v] to both on account of having brought this dishonor to Geneva by fornication. The advice of the Consistory advises [sic] that the woman carry the child to its father, and touching Arthaudaz that she should be punished according to the rules proclaimed. And remand Arthaudaz to the Council on Monday.

Colletaz de La Tientura, wife of P[ierre] Navet[22]; Tevenon Du Puerchoz[23]; Anthoyne, wife of Françoys de Pelley; and Amblarde, wife of Claude Favre.

Because of the sermons and the Word of God. Colletaz answers that they have been persuaded to believe it, and they go to the sermons, and she was at the sermon at St. Peter's Sunday morning, and at vespers at Communion. And she does not remember anything of the sermon. Answered for all the others. Admonitions that they all go to instruction on Sundays.

Claudaz, daughter of Claude Bastard[24] of Bourdigny.

Of the child she was recently brought to bed of. Answers that it is by Michiel Nergaz and that he would indeed like to be her husband or would marry her and that he would do enough to make her content with him and would do her good and would marry her, and that he took her by force. And she goes to the sermon presently, but not so much in the past. The opinion of the Consistory advises that she be admonished and remanded before the Council to Monday to be punished.[25]

21. The ordinances of 1536 fixed the delay in announcing the presence of a foreigner to the *dizainier* or captain at one day. The ordinances of 1539 modified the duties of hosts, stipulating that they should not lodge foreigners "more than three days without coming to notify the Council, under a penalty of sixty sous." The ordinances of 1536 also enjoined "that no one shelter people of evil life, such as fornicators" and others [*S.D.* II, pp. 309 and 348 (February 29, 1536, and February 22, 1539)].

22. Pierre Navet, citizen, dyer [P.C. 2ᵉ sér., 692 (February 6, 1546)].

23. Tevenon Nycod, daughter of the late Pierre Nycod, called Du Puerchoz.

24. There was indeed a Claude Bastard in Satigny, near Bourdigny, who acknowledged on November 19, 1546 [Titres et Droits, Pa 619 (Mategnin), folios 465-468], but it appears that Maillet mistook the name of the father and that this is the daughter of Henri and not of Claude Bastard (see following note).

25. On June 20, 1542, the Council ordered that Michel Nerga and Clauda Bastard should be put in prison for fornication. They were freed on June 26, 1542, on condition that Nerga "give a bond to assist the girl and support the child, and this being done she should leave the city, and he should give her five sous for a pair of shoes" (R.C. 36, f. 46v and f. 54). On November 19, 1542, the minister Jaques Bernard baptized Michel, son of Michel Nergaz, and Clauda, daughter of Henri Bastard, in Satigny (E.C., Satigny 1, *ad*

Claude Arthaud.

Appeared, but was not summoned. Asked that he be given the names of those who have so strongly inveighed against him. And that he was absent from the city and went on business to the *bailli* of Ternier to make hose.

[f. 82] *Tuesday, December 19, 1542,*[26] *Johannete, widow of Mauris Dentant, farm laborer, illegitimate daughter of Don Jehan Ratellier, was summoned because of fornication.*

Who appeared in your Consistory, having first been summoned by your officer Vovrey. She was asked by whom she was pregnant. Answers that she is pregnant by Claude Macheret, locksmith, and it was after Pentecost, and it was by no other, and she never fornicated with any other than the said Macheret. And that he slept with her only once in her house. And also that she has no child. And she was remanded to next Thursday, and the said Macheret should be summoned. The said Thursday having come, which was the 21st of the said month, the said Claude Macheret was summoned in the case of the said Jehanette, bastard daughter of the said Ratellier, of whom it was asked whether he had had the company of this Ratelliere. Answers that he knows nothing about it; it is true that he once had a fancy for her; possibly he knew her once, about a year ago, and he does not remember the time, and she cried out to him that she wanted some sort of clothing. And let the wife of the glover[27] be summoned, who knows well who went to her. And he believes it was one named Mailliard, and others named Jaques Pape and the son of Taberlet. The said Ratelliere answers, and denies that any other slept with her than the said Macheret, because [f. 82v] those named were not there, because the said Mailliair was there, but this was because of another girl who was pregnant by the said Mailliard, and she died of plague. And she would

---

diem). On November 24, 1542, the Council finally remanded Nerga and "Clauda, daughter of Henri Bastard of Bourdigny" before the Consistory (R.C. 36, f. 176). According to Galiffe (III, p. 338) this was the same Michel Nergaz who was syndic three times (1507, 1511, 1517) and "an enemy of Berthelier and the party of independence, a traitor to Geneva and banished as such," but the R.C. *(ibid.)* shows that this was the son instead.

26. This concerns a copy of an interrogation regarding the matrimonial case between Jehannette Dentant and Claude Macheret. The date of December 19, 1542, refers to the initial appearance of this case in the Consistory and not to the date of the drawing up of this document. Copied in a clearer handwriting than the usual handwriting of Maillet, the document may have been copied by another scribe. In any case, the orthography shows that it was certainly not Maillet who drew up the original.

27. Possibly the wife of Vincent Fichet, glover.

indeed like to swear that it was so. And she would not want to charge the said Macheret wrongly. The Consistory heard the parties; the said Ratelliere was remanded before the Council for the Monday after Christmas.

Those who rebel against coming to Consistory.

Being summoned several times, despising the Seigneurie and religion, who were remanded before Your Excellencies to give an explanation: Pierre Calabri, mason, and the Drobliere.[28]

Thursday, January 11, 1543

Lord Syndic Curtet.
Calvin, Champereaulx, Genesto, Trippereraulx [sic], Henri.
Rages, Pensabin, Blandin, Frochet, the officer Vovrey.

Maurisaz Talluchetaz.

Because of her faith and confession and certain words against Françoys Dupont. Answers that it was as she stated last time. And as for her confession, said the prayer and not the confession. The Consistory is of the opinion that she be remanded to another time and frequent the sermons and appear on Thursday after the creation of the lords syndics in order to give a better explanation of her faith and creed, and frequent the sermons more often. One month.

[f. 83] *Estienne Furjodz.*[29]

Because of Holy Communion and some anger and ill will. Answers that he received Communion at St. Gervase, and Jaques Symond and Françoys

28. On January 15, 1543, Pierre Calabri and Françoise Loup, called the Drobliere, as well as Claude Arthaud, were put in prison for three days for having failed to appear in Consistory (R.C. 36, f. 213).

29. Etienne Furjod, citizen, had recently asked for and received "a license to put up the sign of the Stork and keep an inn" [R.C. 36, f. 174 and f. 181v (November 21 and December 1, 1542)]. The next year he asked to be admitted as a sworn notary and "clerk of the bench," which was granted him if he "wanted to undergo the examination" [R.C. Part. 1, f. 14 (October 2, 1543)]. He became an officer in 1544 (see below, November 8, 1543) and apparently became a notary only later (GALIFFE II, pp. 323-324). A certain Etienne Furjod, more often called Thivent (but possibly the same, Thivent being only a form of Etienne), was guard of the Tour de Saint Pierre in 1537. He became a member of the city watch on March 8, 1541, and still held this office in 1549 [R.C. 30, f. 178v (February 20, 1537); R.C. 35, f. 31 and f. 103v (January 24 and March 8, 1541); P.C. 2ᵉ sér., 800 (July 12, 1549), always under the name of

Lullin[30] were present, and Master Loys Trippereaulx preached Communion, and says that he has nothing against any person whatever, and that he gambled, but it was for drinks. The Consistory advises that he be spoken to a little more roughly so he will understand his course better and that he not receive the young people of the city to spend their goods, and that he refrain from having games, and that he be given good remonstrances and proceeded against more sharply.

Françoys Dupra and Pernete his wife, daughter of Petrequin Martin.[31]

Because of the sermons and Communion. Answers that he goes to the sermons and received Communion at St. Gervase; Françoys Lullin was near him, and there preached — he does not know who preached. And his wife was not there and did not receive it because of a young child who prevented her from going there. And they live in peace together, and sometimes they get angry. The last sermon he heard was by . . .[32] His wife says that she does not know whether anyone wishes her harm, because she wishes harm to no one. The said Françoys said that she causes him lots of trouble, and he would like it very much if she would correct herself, because he has enough trouble with her. The Consistory is that someone, that her husband[33] correct her more sharply than he has done, and if she does not correct herself that she be remanded before the Council. And that she be given good remonstrances to refrain from bothering her husband and not bother him any more, but be obedient to him. And as for him, that he be admonished to frequent the sermons, since he has been reluctant to do so until now. And to the said Pernete, that she know better how to pray to the Lord the next time she is summoned.

Claude Tappugnier, ironmonger.

Because of the sermons and faith and creed. Answers that it is a long time since he could go to the sermons, because he has had business, and therefore he has not been to the sermons, and when he can. And because of the law-

---

Thivent; R.C. Part. 1, f. 322 (October 15, 1545), under the name of Etienne]. Finally, there was still another Furjod, *dizainier,* but he died before August 17, 1543 [R.C. 36, f. 225v (January 30, 1543); R.C. 37, f. 196v, *ad diem*]. See also SORDET, *Dictionnaire,* p. 644.

30. François Lullin, son of the Articulant Jean Lullin, councillor, Seigneur de Tournay, host of the Persian Tower, died before 1572 (CHOISY, G.G., p. 219).

31. Guigo Martin, called Petrequin. According to BLONDEL (*Faubourgs,* pp. 37 and 56) a certain Peytrequin, master mason, was already dead in 1535, and his widow occupied herself with various activities in the city.

32. Incomplete sentence.

33. "That her husband" added interlinearly.

suits he has in Ternier it is not possible to go there, and he received Communion at Christmas and was at the second sermon. [f. 83v] The Consistory is of the opinion that he be given remonstrances and admonitions and asked whether he has any scruples about our religion. Answers that he has none, since he would say so. That he follow the sermons, his wife and family.

Roland the baker,[34] bourgeois.

Because of the games he holds in his house and whether it is a long time since there was gambling at [his] house. Answers that there was playing last Sunday after dinner at skillets and cards, at "triumph,"[35] for drinks, and he does not know who it was. And they did not play at vespers, and he puts himself at the mercy of the Seigneurie if anyone played at night at his house, that no one could say it in truth and that no one shelters at his house. And he was at the first and second sermons on Sunday, and he did not recognize the preacher. The Consistory advises, because he has lied to the Council, that he be admonished and remanded before the lieutenant, and that he shelter no one and follow the sermons. The said Roland admitted that he had played "malcontent" and does not remember about it.[36]

George Lyonet.[37]

Because of taverns, games and other drunken acts. And who gambled with him at the said Roland's. And they played the game of "the fish merchant," Mugnier, Pierre Curt's son;[38] there were about seven after supper, and

34. Roland Marquerex.
35. Translator: "Triumph" had the same name in English, which later gave rise to the word "trump." We have been able to learn nothing about the other card games mentioned except the names, which are translated into equivalent English words.
36. On January 19, 1543, Roland Marquereux is found in prison because he "sold as in a tavern and permitted gambling. On which resolved that he be forbidden the tavern for two years and that he be commanded to go to the sermon" (R.C. 36, f. 217v).
37. George Lyonet, citizen, inhabitant of Saint Gervais, died on June 17, 1580, at age 80 (E.C., Morts 12, p. 313). See also P.C. 2ᵉ sér., 707 (March 31, 1546), and R.C. 36, f. 197v (December 22, 1542).
38. Possibly Jaques Mugnier (also called Jaques Le Mugnier) or his son and the son of Pierre Curt, called Choupin. In 1543 Jaques Mugnier, baker and bourgeois, left his red hose to Pierre Curt, called Choupin, bourgeois. Jaques Mugnier, tithe collector in 1541, member of the CC for the Rue des Peyroliers since 1537, had already been reprimanded for gambling in 1536. Ill with the plague when he made his will, he died before April 21, 1544 [Notaires, Jean Duverney, v. 5, f. 52 (July 24, 1543); R.C. 35, f. 56ᵈ and f. 250 (February 9 and June 30, 1541); R.C. 30, f. 136 and f. 168 (December 26, 1536, and February 7, 1537); R.C. 38, f. 169 (April 21, 1544)].
Pierre Curt, called Choupin, from Puplinge (GE), admitted to the bourgeoisie on

they played "triumph" this Sunday and not last. And he goes to the sermons especially on Sundays; the other days when he can. And he does not shelter anyone in his house. To the lieutenant.

Jullian's widow.[39]

Did not appear. Was remanded by the Consistory to the Bishop's Palace. Cursed the Gospel and those who maintain it.

Henri Philippe, pawnbroker in this city at the Magdalen, and his wife.

Because of mistreatment in their life together. Answers that they live together as it pleases God, although sometimes they get angry when he has lost something, and this does not last long. And sometimes they fight. He believes he lives chastely. The wife answered that she would not want to go drown herself in the lake. They were admonished to frequent the sermons and live in peace.

84]   *Claude Malbuysson.*

Because of the sermons and that he has not improved, and considering that he has been in great danger and a waster of goods. Answers that it is true that in the past he did not do his duty as he should have.[40]

Pierre Rouz, haberdasher, native of Pougny near Chancy.

Because of the sermons and other things. Answers that at his beginning he asked for alms while saying the Psalms, and since the Gospel he took to the trade of selling haberdashery, and he has a wife and children. And he no longer mut-

---

August 4, 1536, was host of the inn of the Green Hat in Longemale in 1546. The brothers Aymé and Pierre Choupin were citizens. According to Sordet they were the sons of Pierre Choupin, bourgeois in 1499, but the *L.B.* gives only a Petrus Chapuys of Vandoeuvres admitted in that year. Pierre Choupin, citizen, died on August 22, 1577 [GALIFFE I, p. 517; SORDET, *Dictionnaire*, pp. 260-261; *L.B.*, p. 216, *ad diem;* P.C. 2ᵉ sér., 692 (April 27, 1546); *L.B.*, p. 140 (1499, s.d.); E.C., Morts 12, p. 152].

39. The widow of Jullian Recouz.

40. Claude, son of Jean Malbuysson (councillor, condemned as a Peneysan). The "great danger" to which reference is made here is certainly the plague. On November 28, 1542, the Council refused permission to Malbuysson, "who formerly was infected with plague," to return to Geneva before the term established by the edicts. The accusation of "waste" was possibly connected with his wife's dowry: in December 1543 he entered into conflict with his father-in-law, Conrad de La Palle, who asked the restoration of the dowry of his daughter, Barbe de La Palle [GALIFFE I, pp. 383-384; R.C. 36, f. 179; R.C. Part. 1, folios 114v, 119, and 123 (December 28, 1543, January 18 and February 9, 1544)].

ters, and has not asked for charity except from the procurators of the hospital since he was commanded to obey the commandments. And also, meaning no harm, he has taught the feasts to those who asked him. And he has not lent money at interest, and if it is found otherwise he will give it to the Council. He was admonished to refrain and not give a bad example to others and to do better than he has in the past and not to teach the feasts any longer to people who ask.

Thursday, January 18, 1543

Lord Syndic Rozet.
Calvin, De Ecclesia, De Genesto, Trippereaulx.
Rages, Frochet, Pensabin, Blandin, the officer Vovrey.

The Droblire,[41] *who has been in prison*[42] *and was remanded to the Consistory to receive admonitions.*

She was given friendly remonstrances, which she accepted, to frequent the sermons.

Sermaz, daughter of Guillaume Moret, from Saint Julien.

And said that her daughter had gone to Tournay. She was admonished to bring her daughter on Thursday.

[f. 84v]

Thursday, January 25, 1543

Lord Syndic Cornaz.
Calvin, Champereaulx, Trippereaulx, Henri.
Rages, Frochet, Pensabin, the officer Vovrey.

The wife of Mychiel the saddler.[43]

Excused her husband, who is ill. Answers that she was at the sermon to-day, and Champereaulx preached. And received Communion. Does not know what the preacher preached. And does not know how to say the prayer except in Latin. Said that she will see that she knows it and will take pains. The Consistory advises that she be admonished to frequent the sermons, she

41. Françoise Loup, called the Drobliere.
42. See the note above, December 21, 1542.
43. Claudaz, wife of Michel Julliard, saddler.

and her husband. And that her excuses are not legitimate, and to know how to pray to God, and know how to pray before the next Communion, and present herself here the Thursday before Easter.

Mermet, saddler.[44] Answers that he wishes no harm to his aunt and owes her nothing, and does not know how to pray to God otherwise . . .[45]

Serma, daughter of Guillaume Moret, and Clauda her daughter, wife of Jehan, farm laborer.

And is married, and her husband left her, and she does not know whether her husband is dead or alive. She left him in Lausanne and has lived here in Geneva since St. John's Day. And she gave her money to her husband, which he ate up, and he left to go to the wars. And her husband did not ask the Consistory of Lausanne to be separated from her. And that she was not summoned to the said Consistory of Lausanne for bad behavior, but she was summoned for a small fault and to ask mercy of God, and she had a child, and it was not by her husband. The mother answers and says that information should be obtained from respectable people that her daughter has done nothing wrong with her body since they have been in this city, and they live in St. Gervais near the house of Monsieur Jaques Blondel.[46] She went to Prégny, to Tournay to look for hemp to spin. The Consistory advises that she be summoned again and that she be remanded to two weeks, and meanwhile news will be had from the Consistory of Lausanne, to inquire further. The girl did not want to answer anything more than she had said, and she has not misbehaved since she was in this city. They prayed to God and said the prayer and the confession, not very well. And they go to the sermons when they can.

f. 85] *Don Rolet Voland, citizen of Geneva.*[47]

Answers that the Mass is nothing, and he regards it as it is regarded here. And at the time he regarded it like the others, and he said the Mass like

44. Mermet Julliard, nephew of Claudaz and Michel Julliard.

45. Incomplete sentence.

46. Jaques Blondel, notary, syndic in 1560, and lieutenant in 1566, died March 26, 1581, at age 74 (*R.G.S.* I, p. 57; GALIFFE I, p. 405).

47. A former priest of Geneva, Rolet Voland had been summoned to the Council to abjure the Mass on December 22, 1539. In general the registers give only the response "wicked" or "did not appear," but in the case of Rolet Voland and two others, it says only "Is not there." It may be that this is some sort of abjuration of the Mass, but it appears more likely that, considering his absence on this occasion, the Consistory wanted a formal abjuration (R.C. 33, f. 389 and f. 390). He may have established himself as a butcher after the Reform; on November 11, 1542, the brothers Hugo and Rolet Voland, citizens and butchers, witnessed the will of Pierre Des Chosaulx (Notaires, Jean Duverney, v. 5, f. 40v).

the others. And he does not hold by it at all, neither the altar nor the Mass. And if it is proven that he does it, he submits himself to the mercy of justice. And he goes to the sermons when he can, because he has gout, which prevents him. Said the prayer and the confession, and that the Mass is bad and he wants to maintain that it is such. He was admonished to frequent the sermons.

Anna de Pallex, mother-in-law of De Verneto.[48]

Because of the Mass. Answers that she no longer holds at all by the Mass, goes to the sermons when she can and when she is [in] this city, and cannot when she goes outside it. And Champereaulx preached. Said the prayer and the confession a little. She was given remonstrances and admonitions to frequent the sermons and strive to learn to pray to the Lord.

Tevena Glectire from Avully, maid of Claude Du Pain,[49] *apothecary.*

Answers that she has lived five years in this city and is not married and does not know why her apron lifts itself and has not had the company of anyone except the servant of her master, Claude Du Pain, and he is named Christofle and is from Reignier. And it was five or six months ago, and she did not look for him. And she cries for mercy from God, and recognized that she had done wrong for herself. And he took her by force, and it was at the top of the house. And she understood well from the sermon that fornication is . . . ne(?).[50] And she was at the sermon at St. Gervase on Sunday morning. And she would not want to tell a lie, there is no other than the said servant Cristofle. The Consistory is of the opinion that she be exhorted to behave well and guard the fruit she carries and be sensible from now on and not return to sin again.

48. Probably Jean Duverney (de Verneto in Latin), from Arbusigny (H.-S.), apostolic notary resident in Geneva, 1502-1546 (period of activity; minutes conserved in the A.E.G.), bourgeois on December 7, 1540 (*L.B.,* p. 221).

49. According to L. Gautier, "Claude Du Pain, son of Lucain, was also strongly attached to the party of the Reformers. Councillor since 1541, then Treasurer [1551], then syndic [1546, 1550], he was dismissed from the Council in 1556 for bankruptcy. The examination of his accounts with the Seigneurie took several years, but his honor appears never to have been put in doubt, since he continued to sit in the LX until his death (1566)." Claude Du Pain was also apothecary of the city (1541-1557) and lieutenant (1555) (L. GAUTIER, *Médecine,* p. 56; GALIFFE I, p. 143).

50. Illegible words.

Bocardz, weaver, and his wife.

Because of idleness and the sermons. Answers that he goes to till the ground for his living and goes on boats on the water, and his trade is worth nothing. Goes to the sermons when he can and does not frequent taverns except sometimes on Sundays for company, and he looks for work to live.

Johannete, his wife, daughter of Betend the dyer, because of some gossip about her.[51] Answers that she does not know . . .[52] and that she is admonished. And whether she knows someone named Henri Phillipe. And he goes into her house and is her godfather, that her husband brings him [f. 85v] into their house, and she often gets angry with her husband. And he takes [property] from the household and sells it, and what is worth twelve sous he gives for six, and wastes everything and eats up her goods and her marriage [portion], and then he will leave her. And that no one has found anything wrong in her, and that she goes to the sermons only on Sundays. Said the prayer and the confession.

The said Bocard. He was given admonitions and remonstrances to work and live in his household and govern his wife wisely and live in amity with her. And he asked that his wife be told to live with him in his room and not go any more to her father's house. And he promised that he would do his best and work at his trade and that she would stay in his room.

The said wife was given admonitions and remonstrances to live together peacefully in their room and that each do his duty and live according to God and be united. And to frequent the sermons. And they formerly lived at the wife's father's house. And they both promised to live in peace together.

It is necessary to establish order at the public baths for the separation of men and women. Also of male servants and chambermaids.

Also to send to the Consistory of Lausanne to know how Serma and Claudaz, her daughter, wife of Jehan the farm laborer,[53] were at the said Consistory of Lausanne and why and get a response in order to decide on a remedy.

Necessary to look after the child of the said Glectiere,[54] maid of Monsieur Claude Du Pan, who fornicated at her master's house.

---

51. Probably Janne, daughter of François Betend, dyer, who had a child by Jehan Bandiere in 1545. Bandiere claimed that the child was not by him because "others have had her company," but he was obliged to take the child nevertheless. François Betend, citizen, died before June 9, 1550 [R.C. Part. 1, f. 309 and f. 310v (August 27 and 31, 1545); R.C. XII, p. 497 (March 3, 1534); E.C., Copies 7 (marriage of her son at St. Gervase)].

52. Struck: "who should." Incomplete sentence.

53. Serma Moret and Clauda, her daughter.

54. Tevena Glectiere.

[f. 86]   **Thursday, first day of February, 1543**

Lord Syndic Curtet.
Calvin, Henri, De Ecclesia, Champereaulx, Trippereaulx.
Orsieres, Rages, Frochet, Pensabin, the officer Vovrey.

Nycolas Baud of Peissy.

Summoned by the castellan of Peney[55] because of waste of his goods
and other evil living in his house and household. Answers to the admonitions given by Monsieur Calvin that he has a man whom he has working at
hauling stone, and he does not hold this to be badly intended or against the
edicts of the Council. Asked mercy from God and the Seigneurie. The Consistory advises that if he does not correct himself the Council will proceed
against him, and that he be admonished to treat his wife better than he does
and to follow the sermons and show a good example to his children and
make them follow the sermons, and that he be given admonitions and remonstrances not to sell more of his goods, but recover those he has already
sold.[56]

Jehan Bennar, coppersmith, and Loyse his wife, hosts of the Rock.[57]

Because of religion. Answers that his son is in La Roche at school[58] to
be taught and to remove him from being near his mother. And he does not
believe that there has been any bad report of him, and he wants to be punished if he does or says anything he should not. The advice of the Consistory
is that they be admonished to attend the sermons and give a good example to
others and that he should bring his son back here, and that they be well in-

55. Pierre d'Orsières.
56. Since Baud was "out of his senses," on April 6, 1543, the Council ordered the
castellan of Peney to "have proclaimed to the said *mandement* that no one may contract
with the said Baud without license from his guardian, whom the said castellan should ap-
point for him." Evidently Baud had not improved any when on January 4, 1544, his wife
Amblarde "petitioned that because her husband is a bad manager, she should be given her
assets of marriage." She renewed her request several times, and the Council ended by
again forbidding anyone "to buy in any way whatever from the said Nycolas" [R.C. 37,
f. 52, and R.C. Part. 1, f. 36 (April 6, 1543); R.C. Part. 1, f. 115 and f. 164 (January 4 and
June 6, 1544). See also R.C. Part. 1, folios 166v, 180v, 277v, and 285-286 (June 17, August
8, 1544, May 19, June 23, 1545)].
57. Jehan Bennar (Benna, Beina), citizen, member of the CC, host of the inn of the
Rock, on the Bourg du Four. He died on June 26, 1562, at age 60 (DOUMERGUE III, p. 354;
E.C., Morts 4, p. 84; R.C. 35, f. 56^{d} (February 9, 1541)].
58. For the school of La Roche, see above, August 3, 1542, note.

structed in religion and have a Bible to show to their guests. And when the child has come that he come here. The said innkeeper asks for a term to make his son [come] from La Roche, during next August, since the schoolmaster has received his merchandise to the value of his money. The Consistory did not consent to such a long time, but to mid-Lent.

86v] *Claude Du Chesne of Peissy, blacksmith.*

Was summoned by the castellan of Peney[59] for the sake of chastity in marriage. Answers that he broke the marriage, and cries for mercy from God and justice because his wife is very old and he cannot have a child by her. And he unfortunately fell, had a child by a girl at Jaquemoz Dufour's,[60] from Peissy, and it was after Christmas, and was baptized in Divonne. The opinion of the Consistory is that he be remanded before the Council and it make its decision, and that he be punished and support the child, that he put it to nurse, and be remanded here after his punishment on Monday and follow the sermons and come a week from Monday.[61]

Master Pierre Rugoz[62] the shearer.

Because of papal ceremonies and frequenting the sermons and superstitions. Answers that he goes to the sermons sometimes, and from avarice[63] he cannot go there. And if he had business tomorrow he would work, even though it is a feast.[64] And he wants to live according to God

---

59. Pierre d'Orsières, castellan of Peney.

60. A Jaques Dufour of Bourdigny, merchant, was a member of the court of the castellan of Peney in 1543 [R.C. 37, f. 87 and f. 90v (May 8 and 14, 1543)].

61. Without the reason being specified, on February 20, 1543, Claude, son of Paul Du Chesne, of Peissy, was condemned to three days in prison on bread and water and to pay two "gross of planks for the use of the quarry of Satigny." He asked for grace on March 13 without result, but on October 29, following a resumption of the conflict between him and his wife (see below), the Council "orders, considering the misery of the said Glaude, that he pay only one gross of the said planks, and the rest when he is rich" [R.C. Part. 1, f. 8 (numbered f. 9), f. 22, and f. 98v; see also R.C. 37, f. 234 (October 1, 1543)].

62. Pierre Rugoz, shearer, is often cited as a witness in the acts of the notary Jean Duverney [for example, Duverney, v. 5, f. 22v (March 31, 1542)].

63. Translator: The meaning of the French is not quite clear, but it seems to mean "avarice" in the sense of "greedy regret for loss of time."

64. February 2, the feast of Candlemas or of the Purification of the Virgin Mary. According to the *G.P.S.R.* (III, p. 303b), "Candlemas commemorates the Purification of the Virgin Mary, forty days after Christmas . . . Until the beginning of the twentieth century, it was one of the four great Marian feasts, of the same rank with the Immaculate Conception, the Annunciation and the Assumption of the Virgin . . ."

and His Holy Word. And is not married. The Consistory advises that he range himself with God and serve God and improve himself, and if he does not improve he will be remanded before the Council, and be asked about the Mass. And that he be commanded to go three times a week and asked whether he knows how to pray and be admonished, and whether he has any scruples about religion and whether the Mass is good, and that he know how to pray to God and come here in three weeks. Answers that it seems to him to be an abuse and false, and he has no scruples, and that God does not come in the hands of the priests.[65] And that he has no great devotion to the feasts or to these abuses of candles[66] or foods or invocation of saints, although sometimes he invokes Our Lady. And he does not know how to pray to God except in Latin, as he prayed in former times.

Jana Truffeta.

Because of the sermons and her improvement in religion. Answers that because she has had the fever she could not go to or frequent the sermons. Said the prayer and the confession. She has rarely been able to go to catechism. She was admonished and . . .[67]

Jane, daughter of the late Amyé Grenyer of Prégny.

Produced a supplication. And the said Bene[68] says and answers that he did not take her for a wife in marriage because she [f. 87] attributed a child to him, and she belongs to many,[69] because she is public to everyone. And he never promised marriage to her. And she looked for him and he received the child and had it nursed as he was told, and he never promised her marriage and had her company only once. And he constantly repents having known her, and he did not give her a ring. And that she had a child by someone from Tournay. The Consistory is of the opinion that they be remanded before the Council and that the girl verify her supplication by witnesses and produce her supplication to the Council. The Consistory admonished the said Bene

---

65. Translator: *I.e.,* He does not come as the transubstantiated bread and wine.

66. As the name indicates, candles played a central role in the customs associated with Candlemas. Candles blessed on this day conferred numerous benefits, including protection of men, women, animals, houses, and fields against sickness, storms, hail, and evil spirits. See in this regard SCRIBNER, *Popular Culture,* pp. 3, 6, and 259-260.

67. Incomplete sentence.

68. Jehan Benez.

69. Translator: The reading is uncertain in the French, but the meaning seems to be that given.

to keep his promise to the said Jane. The supplication was ordered returned to the woman.[70]

Creation of the syndics.

It should be noted that on Sunday, February 4, 1543, a General Council was held in the cloister of St. Peter's to elect and create new syndics. And of the eight [proposed] remained four, namely: Nobles Jehan Coquet, Girardin de La Ryvaz,[71] Anthoyne Checand and Hudriod Du Molard.

Election for the Consistory.

And the following Wednesday, seventh of the said month, in Narrow Council the following were assigned to attend at the Consistory next Thursday, eighth of the said month: for syndic Lord Girardin de La Ryvaz, Lord Hudriod Du Molard and Lord Claude Pertemps.[72]

Thursday, February 8, 1543

Lord Syndic De La Ryvaz.
Calvin, Henri, Genesto, Trippereaulx, De Ecclesia, Champereau.
Du Molard, Pertemps, Cornaz, Frochet, Blandin.

---

70. Jane Grenier presented her case in Council on February 19, 1544, but Jehan Benez continued to deny having drunk or sworn in the name of marriage. The Council authorized him to contract marriage elsewhere, but condemned him nevertheless to "pay that which the birth cost her [Grenier] and five sous for the shoes" [R.C. Part. 1, f. 10 (numbered f. 11) and f. 16v (February 19 and March 5, 1543)].

71. The apothecary Girardin de La Rive was a councillor in 1522, treasurer in 1525, and a syndic in 1528, 1535, 1543, and 1547. He also served as lieutenant in 1534 and 1545. Roget characterizes him as a man "moderate, calculating, skilled in business, who, in rendering service to his country, did not neglect his own interests, compromised himself as little as possible and, managing everyone, navigated skillfully among the rocks." Roget also says that De La Rive "figured meanwhile in the number of the adherents of the old religion" and was condemned to banishment in 1536 for his beliefs, but the sentence was revoked when he promised to go to the sermon with his family. He died towards the end of 1550 (ROGET, "De La Rive," pp. 85, 88-89, and 97; CHOISY, G.G., pp. 40-41. See also L. GAUTIER, *Médecine*, p. 447; DEMOLE, p. 17).

72. This is the provisional list, before the election of the new Consistory. In the end Girardin de La Rive was named to the Chambre des Comptes and Hudriod Du Mollard to preside over the Premières Appellations [R.C. 37, f. 13 (February 9, 1543)]. The presidency then passed to Anthoine Checand.

Pierre Pauloz, Amblard and Aymoz, the three brothers Du Pain.

Because of their mother[73] who does not . . .[74] Pierre Paule said that he is entirely ready to do his duty for his third part, and Amblard, and similarly Aymoz Du Pain. [f. 87v] And also for the pension due to her. Also that she should have her clothes so she will not excuse herself from going to the sermon, and that . . .[75]

Noble Pernete, widow of Michiel Du Pain, because of her pension. Answers that she wants to live with her children and in the Reformation of the Council and wants to live with the oldest. And Michel Du Pain has had her marriage [portion], and has two thousand florins without the household, and all in cash, which is in the hands of the said Michiel Du Pain, as she will make appear by her documents. And she loves one as much as another, but it would be very bad for her to change so often. Aymoz said she should content herself with 45 florins for the three.

The opinion of the Consistory is that a term of one month should be given for her clothes to be here, and as for her pension, that she have 15 florins from each of them and that they remember her in her necessity, and that the idolatry be considered. And admonish the mother and Pierre Pauloz, her son, and Paule's wife to pay the pension each ember days. Amblard proposed that it be determined what is in the coffers in order . . .[76] It was ordered that they be brought into this city, that she give the keys to Amblard and Aymo and that the coffers be brought to the house of one of the two, Aymo or Amblard, and that Pierre d'Orsieres and Blandin be present to see whether there is any foolishness of idolatry and to make an inventory. And that the keys be brought here to the Consistory and be given to the two members of the Consistory.

Noble Master Pernet Gay the shearer and Jaquemeta, his wife.[77]

Answers that he wants to live and die according to the Reformation of the Council. He cannot go to the sermons because of his affairs, and goes to the catechism, and is not a papist, and was at the sermon last Sunday, and cannot say or recite anything of the sermon. And he suddenly does not re-

73. Pernette Du Pain.
74. Incomplete sentence.
75. Incomplete sentence.
76. Incomplete sentence.
77. A bourgeois living in Geneva and already married to Jaquemette in 1534, Pernet Gay left the city during the war. He asked to be readmitted in 1536 [Notaires, de Compois, v. 9, f. 30 (June 18, 1534); *R.C.* XIII, p. 555 (May 2, 1536)].

member what was said at the sermon. Said the prayer and the confession. The wife does not know how to say it except in Latin as in former times. [f. 88] The Consistory gave them admonitions and remonstrances that they be admonished to frequent the sermons more often, and within a month, and go on Sundays to catechism and learn to pray.

Angelynaz, widow of Jehan de Crouz, and . . . ,[78] wife of Anthoyne de Crouz, son of the said Angeline.

Because of a quarrel they have with each other. Angellinaz answers. Answers that there is no great argument, but only some trivial words, without hurting each other. The advice of the Consistory is that the younger be summoned to learn what quarrel there is between the two of them. Answers that there is no great argument over evil words the said Angeline spoke against her father, because it was long ago and it is entirely pardoned and blotted out between them and they are good friends. They were given proper admonitions always to live in peace.

Thursday, February 15, at the Council of Two Hundred

The Council of Two Hundred ordered the naming of the members of the Consistory for the present year, 1543.[79]

Namely, the third one assigned in Council for the Consistory: Noble Anthoyne Checant. For members from the Narrow Council: Lords Michiel Morel,[80] Claude Du Pain. From the Council of Two Hundred: Pierre d'Orsiere, Pierre Verna,[81] Baudichon de La Mayson Novaz,[82] Jehan Du

---

78. Name omitted. Anthoyne de Crouz's wife was Louise Chenu (see the note on Anthoine de Crouz above, September 14, 1542).

79. See R.C. 37, f. 12v (February 9, 1543).

80. Michel Morel, notary, citizen, councillor in 1536, *dizainier* first in Rive, then for the district of the Maison de la Ville, finally syndic in 1544 and 1551 [SORDET, *Dictionnaire,* p. 933; R.C. 35, f. 56ᶜv (February 9, 1541); R.C. 36, f. 225v (January 30, 1543); DEMOLE, p. 17].

81. Pierre Verna, merchant and innkeeper, citizen, member of the CC in 1536, *auditeur* in 1541, councillor in 1544. He was son-in-law of this year's syndic, Girardin de La Rive, and Froment mentions him as one of the protectors of Farel in 1532. He died on October 7, 1554 (SORDET, *Dictionnaire,* p. 1281; CHOISY, *G.G.,* p. 42; FROMENT, p. 9; E.C., Morts 1, p. 179).

82. Baudichon de La Maisonneuve. According to NAEF (*Origines* II, p. 93): "Baudichon was only a patronymic nickname, probably vested in the oldest of the family;

Mollards, Laurent Symond, Jehan Pensabin, Pierre de Veyrier,[83] Justz de L'Huermoz,[84] Mermet Blandin. For scribe George Mailliet. For *sautier* Claude Vovrey.

[f. 88v]   *Those who are assigned to attend the Consistory.*

And first for syndic, Lord Anthoyne Checand. From the Narrow Council: Nobles Michiel Morel, Claude Du Pain. From the Council of 200: Pierre d'Orsieres, Pierre Verna, Baudichon de La Mayson Novaz, Jehan Du Mollard, Laurent Symond, Jehan Pensabin, Pierre de Veyrier, Justz de L'Uermoz, Mermet Blandin. For *sautier:* Claude Vovrey. For scribe: George Mailliet.

Also it was decided that every three months the members should assemble in the meeting place of the Consistory to confer on the matters that are necessary and have a reading of the articles enacted on this subject.

[f. 89]   **Thursday, February 15, 1543**

Lord Syndic Checand.
Calvin, Henri, Champereaulx, De Ecclesia, De Genesto, Trippereaulx.
Claude Du Pain, M[ichel] Morel, Jo. Du Molard, Pierre de Veyrier, Blandin, P[ierre] Vernaz, Pensabin, Just de Ulmo, the officer Vovrey.

Mathieu Gathsiner,[85] host of the Three Haberdashers.

Because of religion and the sermons. Answers that those who have talked about him are not well informed. On those of the papistry, he must give them what they ask. On the sermons, he goes on Sundays when he can. On meat, he

---

his first name was Jean. The difficulty is that it was not used." After his death this name passed to his brother Etienne, but here it still refers to Jean, one of the first Genevan "Lutherans." "His house, located on the Rues Basses near the Molard, became the headquarters of the Reformers" (*R.G.S.* I, p. 163). See also DOUMERGUE II, pp. 732-734; NAEF, *ibid,* pp. 90-94 *et passim;* and *Baudichon.*

83. Pierre de Veyrier was already counted among the "Lutherans" in 1535 according to the episcopal inquiry [*R.C.* XIII, p. 592, *notes complémentaires* (January 2-3, 1535)]. In 1543 he was a member of the CC for St. Gervais and also held the *"poys du blé"* (office of weighing grain). Ill with the plague during the year, he had to withdraw from the city with his children and find a replacement to weigh the grain [R.C. 37, f. 9v and f. 126 (February 9 and June 12, 1543)].

84. Just de Ulmo.

85. Mathieu Gathsiner (Gatzener), from "Babauzer, diocese of Augspourg" (Babenhausen über Memmingen, Bavaria), admitted to the bourgeoisie in 1532 [*L.B.,* p. 209 (September 3, 1532)].

eats it with the men who eat it in his house. And that he does not hold the Gospel in abomination and that he wants to live and die in the Gospel and Reformation and in the law and customs of the city at the command of the Council as an obedient subject. Said the prayer, and the confession he still did not know at all, except the Pater in Latin, German, and and [sic] believes in God and was baptized in the name of God. Said that he has six children and a granddaughter 12 years old. The opinion of the Consistory is that he know the confession by Easter and bring his wife by . . .[86] and his children to the instruction of children on Sundays and that he instruct his guests in religion, and be admonished to do this and to frequent the sermons. And that he have a New Testament[87] in his house, and come here before receiving Communion, and that all three of his daughters appear here, and to teach his guests.[88]

Catherine, market-woman of the Molard.

Because of the sermons and other matters. Answers that she has to earn her living and cannot go to the sermon, and hears nothing that is said there because she is deaf. And does not know how to pray to the Lord, and always says the Ave Maria. The Consistory is to induce her to fear God and not scandla [sic] scandalize anyone and pray to God and leave off all idolatries and frequent the sermons, and give good remonstrances, and that she be punished(?)[89] and to learn to pray to God, [f. 89v] not scandalize anyone by her hypocrisy. And that she be given strong remonstrances not to invoke the Virgin Mary any more.

Anthoyne Fraychot.

Because of usury, and to remain here or not, and other oaths and blasphemies of the Lord; usury.[90] Answers that he wants and intends to stay here entirely except when he is away on business, and to leave his wife here until his return, that he leaves his wife enough to live on. He intended shortly to go to Germany to look for some practice of his trade in medicine, and to leave his wife for a time until he can find out whether the country is good for him to stay there. Touching swearing, it escapes him often. On usury, there are three transactions. He lent on some gold rings to certain men of the Vuache and took a notary to record the act and did not want to take any profit and wanted

86. Illegible word.
87. "New Testament" is struck from the text.
88. In the margin: "three weeks."
89. Reading uncertain.
90. The rate of interest had been limited to five percent since 1538. See *S.D.* II, pp. 343-344 (January 17, 1538), and BABEL, *Histoire économique* II, p. 483.

his money within a month, and they wanted to give him wine if they did not pay him, and they gave him eight *setiers* of wine, which was more water than wine. The second transaction was of grain, which was then worth two florins, and he promised to pay 22 sous, and he has not received the grain. The third point of his scruples is that he bought six *coupes* of wheat paid in rent for 100 florins and wanted to recover his money and cancelled it for four *coupes* for the six, and it is not fit for acceptance. And he offers his life if any more is learned about it. And he asked his wife whether she could maintain herself until he came. The Consistory is that he correct himself for swearing and that his wife not abandon him and that he see that he does not fall into the hands of justice, and give him three or six months as a term, and not to leave her entirely, his said wife, and that he go to the sermons. And about his usury, if it is otherwise than he has said, that the Council, etc., and that he guard himself from every sort of evil. And whether he leaves enough money to his wife and whether he treats his wife well. And that he take his wife with him. Resolved that he not leave his wife; otherwise he will be attended to. And that he recover his debts if he wishes. The said Anthoyne asked license from the Consistory for three months; meanwhile he will come get his wife for the harvest and recover his debts. He was remanded to next Monday before the Council to say on oath where he is going and make submission in the hands of the Council, and to know the place he is going to, and that [f. 90] his wife be asked whether she has enough to live on during the said time.[91]

Estienne Fogasse.

Because of usury and other transactions, that he bought five *coupes* of wheat in the blade, and after the harvest had seven. Answers that he had 30 écus when he came to this city and that he bought four *coupes* of wheat at a price of 22 sous in the month of April and sold it later for three florins after harvest, and he never bought more than one *quart* at a time in the market. And that no grain will be found in his house, nor flour, and that if he has made such a transaction in which he sells the grain for more than it is worth, he wants to lose his head. And that when he came to this city he bought forty *coupes* of wheat at 22 sous and sold it, and that he sold 30 *coupes* to a baker at 38 sous the *coupe,* and since the month of July he has not sold any. The advice of the Consistory is that he be remanded before

---

91. Anthoyne Fraychot and Estienne Fogasse (see below) were summoned to Council on February 19, 1543, and accused of having lent money at usury (R.C. 37, f. 20). They were both admonished, and the Council told Fraychot that if he wanted to leave Geneva he would have to take his wife with him.

the Council[92] in order to see about the other matters, and touching some silver that he has to melt down and make alloys. And to know whether he gives out money at usury and for a week at one sou per . . .[93] And that he be admonished, and where he melted his alloy that he wanted to melt.[94]

Reminder to the Council to put another warden in Peney with the others who are there, because there are not enough of them posted there. And also to put one in Jussy.

Thursday, February 22, 1543

Lord Syndic Checant.
Calvin, Henri, Champereaulx, De Ecclesia, Genesto, Tripereaux.
Vernaz, D'Orsieres, De Veyrier, De Loermoz.

Pernete, wife of De Miribello.[95]

On papistic prayer. Answers that she does not carry a rosary and says the Pater in Latin and in French and has many children and must teach them.

92. In the margin: "to Monday."
93. Incomplete sentence.
94. Fogasse was recalled to Council with Anthoyne Fraychot on February 19, 1543, accused of usury (see previous note). On October 2, 1543, Fogasse asked for a license as a money changer "as a foreigner," which was refused him until he became a bourgeois [R.C. Part. 1, f. 91v (October 2, 1543); R.C. 37, f. 236v (October 5, 1543)]. On November 20, 1544, the Council again admonished Fogasse, "who is from the Netherlands and accumulates money and makes alloys and is not a bourgeois" that he should become a bourgeois or cease this business. The next day Fogasse (this time identified as a native of Avignon) declared in Council his desire to become a bourgeois, but said that he did not have enough money because of the scarcity of the times and preferred to wait, which was granted him. On November 24, 1544, his request for admission to the bourgeoisie was accepted at the price of 10 écus, but it was not until June 29, 1547, that Fogasse, of Avignon, was admitted to the bourgeoisie (R.C. 39, folios 46v, 47v, 49; *L.B.*, p. 230).
95. Pernete, wife of Claude de Miribello, died in 1562 at age 60. Egrège Claude de Miribello, bourgeois, was a notary in the city and in the parish of Versoix, 1517-1544 (minutes preserved in the A.E.G.). At the time of this session of the Consistory he was a member of the CC, and later, in 1544, *dizainier* for the Rue de la Cité. He died of plague on April 24, 1545; unless this was his father, who died on May 1, 1545, or his bastard *(donatus)* son, also named Claude, admitted to the bourgeoisie in 1524 [E.C., Morts 5, p. 179 (April 26, 1562); R.C. 37, f. 9v (February 9, 1543); R.C. 39, f. 5 (October 13, 1544); E.C., Morts 1, supplément (carnet des morts de peste, 1545), p. 5 (April 24, 1545); R.C. 40, f. 99v and f. 303v (May 1 and November 26, 1545); *L.B.*, p. 199 (January 8, 1524)].

[f. 90v] And that one should pray to and ask from God without ceasing, and she sometimes goes to St. Gervase, and to St. Peter's to the sermons. And she first prays to God for herself, for her husband and for her children. Said the prayer in Latin and in French and the confession. The Consistory advises that she be remanded to another time and that she abstain from receiving the next Communion, that she be admonished to pray more to the Lord in the vulgar tongue and come to present herself in two weeks, and that she be asked whether she wants to live according to the Reformation, and that her husband be summoned to learn how he instructs his wife and children, and to frequent the sermons more often.

Jullian Recouz's widow.[96]

Because of the Gospel, that she has cursed it and those who support it. Answers that she does not know what this is about, and she loves all those who honor God, and does not recognize anyone who has said such words as "The devil confounds everything" or "The other law was better than this." But if by chance she has said it she cries for mercy to God, that it was by chance, long before she was of the Gospel. And that she has been of the Gospel for about a year or two, and she is acquainted with God. "May the devil confound the Gospel and all those who maintain it." Answers again that she said it only as she said above, and she wants to have the witnesses brought forward. And she does not know how to pray to God except in Latin as in former times; said the prayer in Latin and the Ave Maria. The advice of the Consistory advises [sic] that she be remanded before the Council and that the names of the witnesses be given to the Council, that they be examined and corporal punishment be given in order to give an example to others.[97]

96. Julian Recouz, butcher, from Saint Julien (H.-S.), was admitted to the bourgeoisie on April 28, 1495. He died before May 1, 1534 (*R.C.* V, p. 256; *R.C.* XII, p. 534).

97. In the margin: "before the Council to Monday." In place of following the advice of the Consistory, the Council was content with reprimanding Jullian Recouz's widow "because of certain blasphemies against the Gospel and the preachers" and enjoining her to learn the prayers in the vulgar tongue and to live according to the Reformation [R.C. Part. 1, f. 10v (numbered f. 11; February 26, 1543)].

Guilliermeta, daughter of Jehan Martin[98] the watchman, living at the house of the host of the Fool in St. Gervais,[99] maid of the host of the Fool, whom she has promised and engaged herself to for the space of a year.

And that she is waiting for Monsieur Thibauld Toquet[100] who made the promise and this Easter should come to carry out the marriage. And they have still not published their banns. And she has never slept with the said host except twice. The advice of the Consistory advises [sic] that they both come and that someone go to get the host of the Savage immediately in order to confront them with each other.*[101]

91]   *Noble Claudaz, wife of Noble Domeyne Franch.[102]*

Because of the rosary and frequenting the sermons. Answers that she has not had a rosary since she has been with Domeyne Franc and has not had one under her apron. It is true that she says the prayer, "Our Father." She cannot go to the sermons because her husband is ill, which usually keeps her from going to the sermons, and that it will not be proven that she says her rosary. And she always goes when she can, as much to St. Gervase as to the Magdalen. She was admonished to frequent the sermons.

98. Guillermeta, daughter of Jean Martin, from Sionnet, officer, and of Jeanne Rigot (GALIFFE II, p. 240).

99. Jehan Curt, host of the inns of the Savage and the Fool *(Fou)*, called the inn of the Oven *(Four)* in his death certificate. This German, from Landau (Bavaria), was admitted to the bourgeoisie on May 17, 1541 [E.C., Morts 1, p. 283 (December 26, 1554); L.B., p. 221, and below].

100. Thibaud Tocquet (Tucher in German), bourgeois, was a "fervent arquebusier" and important merchant of a family of Nuremberg "in whose society daring conversations were held about 1526." However, the Tuchers did not play a very active role in the Reformation in Geneva, leading Naef to conclude that "the Tuchers were therefore not apostles, but crude peddlers of German ideas" [NAEF, *Origines* II, pp. 95-97; L.B., p. 208 (July 4, 1531)].

101. This sign refers to the interrogation of Jehan Curt, host of the Savage, later in this same session.

102. Clauda de Fernex, widow of Bezanson Hugues, remarried, to Domaine Franc, in 1539. The Fernex family was very rich, and despite the marriage alliance with Hugues it mainly adhered to the ducal party. She died in 1551 [NAEF, "Bezanson Hugues," pp. 335-573; on Clauda de Fernex, pp. 458-465; GALIFFE II, pp. 194-225; on her, pp. 212-213]. Despite being only a bourgeois, her husband, the merchant Domaine Franc, from Savigliano (Cuneo, Piedmont), served as syndic in 1536 in place of his brother-in-law, Jean Philippe, then absent from Geneva. He was also a member of the LX, and died in 1550 [GALIFFE III, pp. 222-223; SORDET, *Dictionnaire,* p. 536; L.B., p. 173 (August 29, 1511); R.C. 35, f. 488v (February 7, 1542); E.C., Morts 1, p. 3 (January 25, 1550)].

Monsieur Pierre Gerod, merchant, habitant *of Geneva.*

On frequenting the sermons. Answers that he goes to the sermons when he can, because he often has to go to the villages. Said the prayer and the confession. He was admonished to frequent the sermons more often.[103]

[104] Jehan Curt, host of the Savage, German, and with him Michiel the carter, his interpreter.

Asked whether he knows why he was summoned. Answers no. Asked whether he is engaged to a wife. The interpreter asked. Says no, and that he promised his maid a year ago. And whether he is married. Says no, and that he has not slept with her except a few times since they made the promises, and he is ready to marry her. And that he is waiting for a merchant who made the agreement, and he will marry her. And says that he will not wait any more. The Consistory advises that both be remanded before the Council tomorrow and that attention be paid to this because of fornication, and that the banns be published. And that they be admonished about the consequences and forbidden to fornicate, and that he be punished promptly.[105]

103. The name Pierre Gerod was very common. A Pierre Gerod, merchant draper from Ochiaz (Ain), son of Claude, lived in Geneva, but he ought to be classified as a bourgeois and not simply as an *habitant* [*L.B.,* p. 219 (October 6, 1539); MOTTU-WEBER, *Economie,* p. 40, n. 61]. A certain Pierre Gerod, called Piollat, son of Monet, from Petit Saconnex (GE), was arrested on February 5, 1543, because of gambling and on February 27 was condemned to a month in prison. He was later accused with others of having had contacts with "enemies of Geneva" associated with the Articulants of 1540, and above all of having wished "to lead certain citizens to war at the instigation of Andrier Philippe," Claude Franc and Jean Gabriel Monathon, fugitives from Geneva. After a long detention he was condemned to banishment for a year and a day on September 29, 1543, but he appears to have stayed in Geneva and was finally pardoned after paying a fine [P.C. 1ᵉ sér., 368 (February 5-27, 1543); R.C. 37, f. 5v (February 6, 1543), f. 197v and f. 198 (August 18 and 20, 1543), folios 230, 231, 232, and 233 (September 27, 28, and 29, 1543), 264, 266v, 270, and 275 (November 6, 9, 12, and 16, 1543); R.C. Part. 1, f. 91 (September 29, 1543)].

104. Here recommmences the interrogation suspended at this sign earlier in this same session.

105. The next day the Council admonished Jehan Curt to marry Guillermeta Martin within the next three weeks (R.C. Part. 1, f. 8v, numbered f. 9v). According to GALIFFE (II, p. 240) she was the wife of Guillaume Bouvier, called Chevellu, but this may have been a second marriage.

Thursday, first day of March, 1543

Lord Syndic Checand.
Calvin, Henri, Champereaulx, De Ecclesia, Trippeaulx [sic], Genesto.
Du Pain, Morel, Molard, Orsieres, Verna, Pensabin, De Loermoz, Laurent
Symond, Blandin, Veyrier, the officer Vovrey.

Pierre Des Vignies, Jehan Jaquard of the baths.

Because of a quarrel and following the sermons. Answer both together
that they are not in conflict and that they wish each other no harm, and they
go to the sermons and do not shelter any vagabonds in their houses and do
not follow an evil course. And that they cannot frequent the sermons; on
Sundays they go to the sermons, and cannot do so the other days because of
their trade. And the said Jaquard was at the sermon last Sunday at St.
Gervase, and he does not know who preached or what the preacher said. And
Des Vignes does not know what the minister said. They want to leave the
baths, since they are not properly furnished, but they are not . . .[106]

Maurisaz Talluchetat.

Because she should give an explanation of her confession and why she
did not appear last Thursday. Answers that she does not know how to say the
commandments or her Credo. Said the prayer and not the confession, except
possibly half. And last Thursday she could not come because she was selling
wine. And she was at the sermon Sunday at St. Peter's, and Master Henri
preached, and it was Genesto. The Consistory is of the opinion, since she has
made no improvement, that she appear here in two weeks and frequent the
sermons every day and the catechism. And then she be asked about the articles and other matters. Admonitions and remonstrances; otherwise she will
be remanded before the Council.

Jehan L'Oste.

Because he left his wife in Lyon. Answers that this is because he is suing
here in Geneva for some money someone owes him, and he will send for his
wife to reside in this city five weeks ago [sic]. And he is suing Goddeta. And
he was at the sermon on Sunday, and he cannot say what was said. And when
he went to Lyon he could not earn his living, and he did not receive Communion or go to Mass. And he does not swear in the name of God. He certainly
wants to settle here entirely with his wife. The opinion of the Consistory: in

---

106. Incomplete sentence.

view of his excuse, give him a term to bring his wife here, within two months or six weeks, so that he may follow the Christian religion peacefully and not lose what religion he has. Since he is one of the first,[107] that he be given strong remonstrances to follow the sermons while he is here.

Noble [Mye], wife of the master of the mint.[108]

Because of muttering. Answers when there is prayer she prays like the others, and she says her Pater and lives as the others live, and she has no scruples about religion, and it is not wrong to fast. And she has no scruples about the Virgin Mary or the saints as advocates. She was given admonitions and remonstrances.

The widow of Bertheractz,[109] *promised wife of Gonrardz de La Palaz.*[110]

Because of the rosary. Answers it is not so, because she does not mutter anything, and for this someone sent her here. And she frequents the sermons and prays to God as the Council has commanded her, and she says the Pater with good intentions and goes to the sermons and prays to God as she prayed in former times, with good intentions. And she does not keep feasts because she has no calendar, although sometimes when they are together she talks about feasts with the others. And she does not solemnize them and did not fast this Lent and has no scruples about eating meat and does not scandalize others about religion. Remanded to Monday before the Council. The Consistory is that she be asked whether she wants to marry her husband and what term she plans, before Easter or after, and according to what she answers that she be given a precise term, and admonish her to refrain from scandalizing the church because she constantly stays with her husband at suspect hours, and let them have their wedding promptly. [f. 92v] Answers the questions that she does not know whether their banns have been published or not because [sic] Monsieur Glaude Malbuisson,[111] and she means to marry next

---

107. We have found no references to him in the sources concerning the "first Reformers," but the religious Jaques Comberet, called L'Hôte, was among the first "Lutherans." See NAEF, *Origines* II, pp. 203-204 and 243; *R.C.* XIII, p. 592 *(notes complémentaires)*.

108. Mye Nergaz, wife of Henri Goulaz. Her name has been omitted here by the scribe.

109. Guillauma, widow of Pierre Bertherat.

110. Conrad Schüffelin, called De La Palle (a direct translation of Schüffelin), from Nuremberg, was admitted to the bourgeoisie in 1519. He possessed various properties in Geneva and was authorized to sell "cannon powder" in 1541 [GALIFFE I, pp. 355-356; *R.C.* VIII, p. 288 (February 4, 1519); *R.C.* 35, f. 79 (February 18, 1541)].

111. Claude Malbuisson was Conrad de La Palle's son-in-law.

Monday, and not at a suspect hour, and she left between eight and nine o'clock, and she will refrain from this if it pleases the Seigneurie. And she goes there by day and not by night, since he is ill and cannot stand, while waiting to be married in the house. Remonstrances.[112]

Noble Bartholemie, widow of Richardet, wife of Achard.

Because of superstitions and rosaries. Answers that she does not know what this is about and she always keeps the feasts because she does nothing, and she does not know what she said, and she has never said the rosary with her fingers, and someone lent it to her. And she has no images either in her house or elsewhere or blessed things, although she has a St. John that was in their chapel.[113] Monday before the Council and the procurator general.[114] The Consistory decided that she be remanded to the Council with her idol and that someone go with her to investigate her idols, and that two be assigned to visit.[115]

112. The next Monday, March 5, 1543, there was a report in Council about Bertherat and De La Palle, that "she goes to her husband's [fiancé's] house by day and night, although they are not married. Resolved that they should marry this coming Sunday in seven days" (R.C. Part. 1, f. 16v). However, the couple did not contract marriage until July 1, 1543 (Notaires, Claude de Miribello, v. 2, ff. 23-24v).

113. Bartholomie Richardet's brother, Pierre d'Orsières, appeared in Council in connection with a house located in Saint Gervais and belonging to the chapel of the D'Orsières. One can therefore suppose that this chapel was at the church of St. Gervase [R.C. 35, f. 499 (February 14, 1542)]. Bartholomie Richardet appeared in Council several times because of this house [R.C. 35, folios 82v, 100, and 143v (February 22, March 4, and April 5, 1541); R.C. 36, f. 77v (July 25, 1542)]. However, it appears that the D'Orsières family also had a chapel at the New Church of Our Lady. Louis Blondel says: "The third chapel (of this church) has on its keystone the arms of the D'Orsières; its altar must have been consecrated to St. Anthony, whose chapel is mentioned in 1436, and again in 1442, as a foundation of the D'Orsières. . . . Jean de Crose founded a chaplaincy of the Visitation there in 1502, and in 1454 it is said that it derives from a foundation of the canon Jean Symonet and of Jean d'Orsières" (BLONDEL, "Auditoire," p. 122). This Jean d'Orsières was the grandfather of Bartholomie Richardet (GALIFFE I, pp. 178-180). Finally, the Richardets also had a chapel at St. Gervase [A.E.G. Finances M 23, f. 81 (not dated, 1535-1536)].

114. Pierre Vandel was named procurator general on February 5, 1543, or a little earlier (R.C. 37, f. 4).

115. Bartholomie Richardet was summoned to Council the next day in this connection, and later, on March 5, 1543, the Council reprimanded her "because she took the paintings of St. Barbara from their chapels, which she confessed having taken, and that she did not dare restore them without the heir." She remained in prison for some time [R.C. 37, f. 25v (March 2, 1543); R.C. Part. 1, f. 16v (March 5, 1543); R.C. 37, f. 89v and f. 93v (May 11 and 15, 1543)].

Noble Denys Hugoz.[116]

Remanded by the Council because of his detention for gambling and other things, sermons and games and blasphemy. The Consistory admonished him.

Thursday, March 8, 1543

Lord Syndic Checand.
Henri, De Ecclesia, Champereaulx, Blancheti, Trippereaulx.
Morel, Du Pain, Du Mollard, Laurent Symond, Pensabin, Blandin, De Veyrier, De Loermoz, the officer Vovré.

Mathieu Gathiner.[117]

About the diligence of his faith. Answers that he has done what he could, also his older children, the younger are behind, and he will do what there is to do. Said the prayer and the confession, and has frequented the sermons, and Master Henri preached yesterday at eight o'clock, and it was Champereaulx. And he will profit as best he can from religion, and he believes he will be saved by his faith. The Consistory: that he be charged to profit better from religion before Holy Communion and that he come every Thursday until Easter to know how he has profited, and that he be given a particular day before Easter to present himself to one of the ministers and . . .[118]

---

116. Denis Hugues, son of the famous *eidguenot* Bezanson Hugues. He was host of the inn of the Bochet at the bottom of the Pélisserie which he acquired by his marriage with Jeanne Exchaquet the younger, widow of Noble Nicolas Du Bouchet. See the biographical notice on him in NAEF, "Bezanson Hugues," pp. 523-535, and DOUMERGUE III, p. 404. Here the Consistory refers to his detention following the murder of Françoys Deponte at the inn of the Bochet where he was playing dice (see above, December 21, 1542, note). Hugues was freed from prison on January 5, 1543, but he was "commanded to take down his sign and commanded to go to the sermon for a year and a day, and if he is found defaulting, he will be rigorously punished" (R.C. 36, f. 207v). On January 16, 1543, he asked the Council "to permit him to put up his sign and keep a tavern as he kept it before," but the Council decided "still to put off this request for a time" (R.C. 36, f. 215). Finally, on the eve of this session of the Consistory, the Council of Two Hundred granted him grace "in the case of the tavern" on condition that he not offend again and that he appear in the Consistory [R.C. Part. 1, f. 14 (February 28, 1543)].
117. Mathieu Gathsiner (Gatzener).
118. Incomplete sentence.

Claude de Miribello and his wife.[119]

Answers that he is teaching his wife and his children as it is proper to instruct them to pray to the Lord and not otherwise. And the wife answers that she does not carry a rosary or say it on her fingers. The husband answers that he frequents the sermons and believes in the union of religion and has no scruples about religion, and does not believe that the Virgin Mary is our advocate or in praying for the dead. The advice of the Consistory: that he be admonished to teach his wife and his children and frequent the sermons and that the wife say her Pater and pray to God, also the confession. The wife said the prayer and the confession.

Tyvent Chenu's wife.[120]

Because of muttering. Answers that she does not adore images and that she prays to God to give her the Holy Spirit, that he instruct her in His Word, and for all her family. And when she goes late to the sermon she does not understand all that was preached. Said the prayer and the confession. She was admonished.

Pernon Comtesse, wife of Mermet Ravex,[121] farm laborer.

Answers that she did not keep the last feast of Our Lady[122] and that she had no words with a woman named Donne Loyse who said to her, "Go to the sermon," and she answered that she should stay with her husband. And that she did not say to a pregnant woman, "Go away, wicked one that you are, who do not keep the feast," and that she did not say that God would inflict suffering on her before he would deliver her of the child she carried. And she does not remember it, and if she said it she begs for mercy from God and justice, that she be pardoned. This was a woman named Petremandaz to whom she says that she told her she was doing wrong and that her fruit [would be] in peril if she did not keep the feast. [f. 93v] And she was at the sermon Sunday, and she cannot say what the preacher said. Said the prayer, and did not know how to say the confession. Received Holy Communion. And she meant no harm when she said the words to the pregnant woman. And she

119. Pernette de Miribello.
120. Pernette, daughter of the late François de Vaud, called Fornier, wife of Thivent Chenu (GALIFFE II, p. 115). She made her will on February 14, 1535 (Notaires, Jean Duverney, v. 2, pp. 526-530, with a codicil of February 15).
121. Mermet Ravex died on September 20, 1571, in the parish of Saint Germain (E.C., Morts 11, p. 19).
122. Candlemas, February 2. See the note above, February 1, 1543.

begs mercy of God and justice. The woman who was pregnant is named Pernodaz, and she said that Our Lady would make her pay, and she meant no harm, although she certainly said it from bad judgment. And she has no rosary, she has none in her house. And she wants to live and die in the Gospel. To Monday. The Consistory is of the opinion that she appear here before Easter before receiving Holy Communion or be remanded before the Council, because the case is scandalous, and that she come here and frequent the sermons. She again confessed the words that Our Lady would not help her to bear her child, that she is named Perrodaz, that she is in childbed and has given birth to a son. And she cannot say otherwise.

Dominique Jerdy.[123]

Because of the Mass. Answers that he has not heard Mass for eight years and that his wife has not danced or heard Mass. And he received Christmas Communion in this city at Christmas, and his wife. Immediately afterwards his wife went to Evian, and he does not know that his wife did anything against God. And after Christmas they stayed in the village, and he forbade his wife to go to Mass. Again he said that he received Communion at Christmas, and Master Henri preached, and he did not go there on Friday before Christmas; either Monsieur Champereau or Henri gave him Communion, and he will prove it by his nephew.

[f. 94] Pernete, daughter of Pauloz Du Nant, wife of Dominique Du Gerdi. Because of the sermons. Answers that she frequents the sermons and was at the sermon Monday, and Champereaulx preached. And a fortnight ago she was in Evian, and received Communion in this city twice, at Easter and at Christmas; she was in Evian, and has not heard Mass for over a year, and was not in the church in Evian. And she went to Evian to see her father who was ill, and there was no feast, and there has been no mummery or masquerade there for a long time. Indeed she believes that many wore false faces, and she did not dance or ring bells or disguise herself. And her husband came there the day after Christmas and arrived about four o'clock, and did not dance.

Claudaz, daughter of Jehan Blandet, of Lucinges, maid of Dominique Du Gerdi. Answers that she lived two years with Monsieur Jehan Pensabin and had lived with her master and mistress only a short time on Christmas Eve, and her master stayed a week more and did not hear Mass or a sermon and was not at the church and did not hear Mass. And no one has forbidden her to tell the truth, nor has her mistress. She was never with her mistress at

123. Dominique Du Gerdy and his wife Pernete.

the church. And they had no feast or banquet that she knows of and did not dance and she knows of no instrument or mummery that she knows of, and she did not recognize those who wore false faces through the town. And they had no banquet. And she cannot say at what time her master arrived because he stayed a week longer and they stayed six weeks, in which they were never at the church, and her master and mistress did not instruct her to say this, always no. [f. 94v] The advice of the Consistory is that they be remanded until they are summoned and frequent the sermons.

Pierre Dumont, called Perriar, tailor.

Because of adultery, fornication while being married. Answers the admonitions and remonstrances given to him that he wants to live in the fear of God and obey his commandments and also justice.[124]

Brother Solliet[125] and his wife who have been in prison.

Because he hides his behavior in his house because of his wife. Answers the admonitions given him in the City Hall that he will refrain from making scandal in the church.

Mermete at Deleta's house, daughter of Claude de La Chavane.[126]

Because of rosaries, foods, fasts and vigils. Answers that she has not carried a rosary for more than three years, goes to the sermons when she can and on Sundays, and does not fast at all. Said the prayer and the confession, and does not know that she has profited by the sermon, and it is more than seven years since she heard Mass, and she believes only in Jesus Christ. She was given admonitions and remonstrances.

124. Pierre Dumont had already been reprimanded in Council for his adultery and condemned to three days in prison on bread and water and to pay a gross of planks for the repair of St. Peter's [R.C. Part. 1, f. 8 (numbered f. 9, February 20, 1543)].

125. Thivent Solliet, a former religious, was among Farel's first converts at the friary of Rive (MESSIEZ, p. 24). In 1539, at the time of the formal abjuration of the former clergy before the Council, he declared the Mass "pernicious," like most of the others [R.C. 33, f. 390v and f. 391 (December 22, 1539)]. Finding himself without a trade, he asked the Council to find him a post. The Council offered him the rent farm of the friary of Rive if he posted a bond which he apparently could not meet (CAHIER-BUCCELLI, "Ombre," p. 378). Finally, on September 18, 1542, the Council granted him a pension "like the other priests and monks" (R.C. 36, f. 121v). Thivent Solliet and his wife were accused of having had gambling at their house. His wife was suspected of fornication with Michel Nerga and Jaques Claret [P.C. 1ᵉ sér., 369 (February 15-20, 1543)].

126. In the margin: "of Vovrey, maid."

Jehan Clement.

Because of his wife, whom he sent out of his house, and why. Answers that he did not give her leave and that she was given a piece of vineyard and her children wanted her to sell it, and her nephews not. And he told his wife that she should go get her marriage [portion], that her brothers wanted to sell her assets, and that he has brought his wife back and they are both united. And they do not want to follow the letter because they pester him and they have wasted all their goods, her said brothers. And [f. 95] he frequents the sermons sometimes and is not a gambler. He was given admonitions and remonstrances.

Hugonyn de Monthouz, carpenter.

Because of gambling. Answers that it is not so, and he does not keep any journeyman, although it is true that Arthaud[127] stayed with him one night, and they are not obtainable. And he said to his mother . . .[128] And he left a rapier in his house, and he only stayed there once. And Macheret[129] and Arthaud lodged there one night, and they [usually] go to the baths to sleep. And he has no neighbors who complain of him. He was given remonstrances and admonitions.

Thursday, March 15, 1543

Lord Syndic Checand.
Calvin, De Ecclesia, Genesto, Henri, Trippereaulx.
Morel, Vernaz, Pensabin, Blandin, De Veyrier, Du Mollard, Orsierres, De Ulmo, Symond, the officer Vovrey.

Claude Corniez from Bellevaux, farm laborer.

Because of anger. Answers to the inquiries that they rarely fight, although there are people who wish him little good, but they wish each other no harm. His wife[130] is working and he has no quarrel with his wife. Sometimes he is angry with his wife. Goes to the sermons on Sunday, and the other days he cannot because he has to earn his living. Does not know how to say the prayer or the confession. Said the Pater, the Ave Maria, the Credo.

127. Claude Arthaud.
128. Incomplete sentence.
129. Claude Vuarin, called Macheret.
130. Collete, wife of Claude Corniez.

[f. 95v] He prays to God by saying the Pater Noster, as well as when he takes Communion, and he has been here seven or eight years. The advice of the Consistory is that he be admonished to pray to God and that he not be given Communion, that he be remanded to some time and that he frequent the sermons and bring his wife here within a month, and he is not qualified for Communion, and that he be admonished more sharply and given remonstrances.

Marie, daughter of the late Jehan Du Nant, called Vulliet.[131]

On the quarrel with her mother. Answers that her mother separates herself from her and there is nothing else; this since All Saints' Day, and she does not know why, and they did not separate without her command, and she committed no sin to make her mother angry. And she lives at Vandelli's.[132] And they have no grudge against each other, and she said to her mother that she should explain her grievance before two respectable women. Goes to the sermons Sunday at vespers. Said the prayer and the articles of faith. The opinion of the Consistory is that the two of them be reconciled, the mother and her daughter, after the sermon next Wednesday, and frequent the sermons.

Anthoyne de Crouz.

On blaspheming Our Lord. Answers that he does not get angry at his mother, but often at his wife, and he goes to the sermons when he can, as much as any neighbor he has. He was at the sermon at the Magdalen today, and Monsieur Calvin preached, about Joseph's departure.[133] Promised to

---

131. Marie, daughter of Jehan Du Nant, hosier, died on August 1, 1550 (E.C., Morts 1, p. 17).

132. The Vandels played a very important role in the struggle for Genevan independence and in the introduction of Protestant ideas in Geneva. This is probably either Pierre Vandel, councillor and procurator general at the time of this session of the Consistory, later twice syndic and one of the most important people on the Genevan scene until the fall of the Perrinists in 1555, or else Thomas Vandel, his brother, a former priest of Geneva. On Thomas Vandel see the biographical notice in NAEF, "Conquête," pp. 100-112.

133. Gen. 37:13-17, or at latest Gen. 38:12. According to Jean-François Gilmont and Rodolphe Peter: "A first rather vague project of a commentary on Genesis goes back to 1542. On July 28 of this year Calvin wrote to Farel: 'With regard to my remarks on Genesis, if God grants me a longer life and some leisure, I may put my hand to this work . . .' (HERMINJARD 8, pp. 80-81; C.O. 11, col. 418). In his notes Herminjard assumes that at this date Calvin was interpreting Genesis, without discussing whether it was in public sermons or lessons in theology" (B.C. I, p. 521, notice 54/8).

correct himself from blasphemy and other things. They sometimes live together, and it is not his fault. The Consistory is of the opinion that they be reconciled and frequent the sermons.

[f. 96] *Angellinaz, widow of Jehan de Crouz, mother of the said Anthoyne.*

Because of idolatrous superstitions. Answers that she has no Hours[134] and no longer holds by papistries and did not go with her son or his wife, her daughter-in-law, because of some conflict, and therefore is separated from them, and to obviate scandal did not want to live with her son and his wife, and she will do everything the Consistory commands her to do. And she has no scruples about religion.[135]

Loys Piaget, sheath-maker.

Because of superstition and other things. Answers that he has no idols in his house and his wife does not say the rosary that he knows of and they eat meat when they have it. And that he has engaged his daughter[136] and he expects the husband to marry her, that the husband has parents in La Sémine whom they are waiting for. And he has no money for the household goods. And that his brother who is in Estavayer wants to come here to help him. And that he wants to act and live like his predecessors. And he says the Virgin Mary is the mother of Our Lord, and may Our Lady help him. The Consistory is of the opinion that he be remanded to another day in order to allay the excitement he is under at present. Remanded to Thursday, and his wife.

Pierre Rugoz, shearer.

Because of his faith and creed. Answers that it is because of his Pater, and he was given a term of three weeks. Said the prayer and the confession and that he has learned from the sermons and has no scruples about religion

134. Book of Hours.

135. Anthoine de Crouz and his mother were subsequently accused by the Small Council of having "received from the sisters of St. Claire a large sum of gold and silver that should belong to the city and not to them, and it is ordered that the said De Crou, who is already detained, be made to respond to this; and as for his mother, that she be detained in the City Hall until the full truth of the case is known" [R.C. 37, f. 248v (October 22, 1543)]. On November 2 Angellinaz asked to be freed from prison on a bond of 100 écus, and a week later they were declared innocent for lack of proof [R.C. Part. 1, f. 101; R.C. 37, f. 267 (November 9, 1543)].

136. See the matrimonial case between Aymée Pyaget and Reymond de Veyrier, above, March 2, 1542.

and his sole intention is to reach God. He was is[137] that he be admonished to profit by religion more and more and frequent the sermons.

96v]   *Jaquemetaz, wife of Pernet Guex, shearer.*

To pray to God; was remanded. Said the prayer and the confession, and that five years ago the law of former times was worth as much as this one, and that since this law came we have gained hardly anything. Indeed it is true that on the eve of Our Lady of Candlemas[138] she went through the city to look for a candle at the apothecaries' to give to someone from Mornex, a charcoal-burner, and found one that cost her three *quarts,* and she wants to live according to religion, and can rarely go to the sermon because she has a child, which prevents her. And she heard the sermon at St. Gervase on Sunday. And she pardons Bernarde, who did her an injury. The Consistory: that she be given remonstrances and admonitions to refrain from drunkenness and evil words and that she be punished and guard herself from improper words and that she not keep the feasts again.

Maurisaz Talluchete.

Said the prayer and the confession down to "the Virgin Mary,"[139] and wishes no one any harm, except that she is involved in a case for which she was condemned last Friday. The advice of the Consistory is that she be given another term of a week.

Pollet.[140]

Because of the evil course he follows and what is said about his maid.[141] Answers that his maid is a decent girl and that he is innocent of this. And that it is not honest for a man who is not married to keep a young girl as a maid, and he spoke insolently. He was ordered to be more steady another time and admonished not to scandalize the people and to frequent the sermons.

---

137. Maillet confuses here two standard formulas, "He was admonished . . ." and "The Consistory is of the opinion . . ."

138. For the importance of candles at Candlemas (February 2) see the note above, February 1, 1543.

139. That is, she could recite the Apostles' Creed down to "born of the Virgin Mary," or very little of it.

140. Pierre Guillermet, called Pollet.

141. Nycolardaz Perrissod.

[f. 97] *Thibauda, wife of Guillaume Arpin, and Pernete, wife of Nycolas Torniez.*

Because of papistic ceremonies, rosaries and other things, and the sermons. Answer that they keep nothing of this, do not keep Lent or the feasts or fast. They go to the sermons on Monday, Wednesday, and other days when they can. And they pray to the Lord and not the Virgin Mary. The advice that they be admonished more sharply and remanded to the Council, and not fight each other in selling. The said Thibaudaz does not know where her husband is, and it is eight years since she had news.

Nycolardaz, daughter of the late Jehan Perrissod, servant of Pollety.[142]

Because of her master Polleti. Answers that she has lived 14[143] years with him, six years with his wife her mistress and seven years with her master Polleti, and she does not sleep with him, since he has not asked her to, and she wants to be punished if it is otherwise. And it is not possible for her to be married because she is entirely ruptured by the work done in her youth. She goes to the sermons on Sundays and sometimes during the week. Said the prayer and the confession, and that taking him for a husband, her master, was mentioned to her, and not . . .[144] And that her master has supported her for 20 years in all. She was admonished to frequent the sermons and guard herself from scandal and behave herself sensibly.

[f. 97v]   **Tuesday, March 20, 1543**[145]

Lord Syndic Checand.
Calvin, Henri, Blancheti, De Genesto.
Morel, Molard, Vernaz, Pensabin, Blandin, Veyrier, De Loermoz, Symond, the officer Vovrey.

142. Pierre Guillermet, called Pollet.
143. Written XIIII, probably meaning XIII (13); otherwise the total is not right.
144. Incomplete sentence.
145. The day before this session the Council considered a question which would hold a central place in the greater conflicts of the following years and which would not be resolved until 1555, whether the Consistory had the authority to excommunicate: "Here it was decided to see whether the Consistory will have the power to forbid those not qualified from receiving the Holy Communion of Our Lord or not. Concerning which, resolved that the Consistory should not have any jurisdiction or power to forbid, but only to admonish and then make a report to the Council, so that the Seigneurie may judge the guilty according to their offenses" [R.C. 37, f. 37v (March 19, 1543)].

Noble Lucresse Curtetie.

Because of papistic superstitions, fasts, vigils, foods and others. Answers that she lives by the law that seems better to her and has rarely been to the sermon this winter because she fears the cold, and her brother[146] has admonished her. And she believes God inspired her to do so. And she believes in God firmly and commends herself to God and to justice. And she was at the sermon for the honor of God and to hear His Word. Said the prayer and the confession. She wants to live in the law that the Lord inspires her to follow and wants to live in the Reformation of the church of this city, and says that God is all-powerful and our advocate. The Consistory is of the opinion that she be admonished to follow the sermons and the catechism, and other good admonitions, and exhorted to say whether she has any scruples.[147]

Janne, widow of Pierre Aprin, called Belletaz.

Because of papal superstitions. Answers that she cannot go to the sermons except sometimes on Sunday, and that she eats meat, poultry(?)[148] and fish and that God knows the heart of a person. And she was at the sermon Sunday and does not know who preached or what the preacher said, and she was ill Sunday, and the previous Sunday she was there and Master Calvin preached. And says that if she ate meat Friday and not Saturday it would be wrong, and she believes only in God and has no belief that the Virgin Mary will aid her and does not invoke her. And that she has no scruples about [f. 98] anything except eating meat on Fridays. And intends to live according to the Reformation. The opinion of the Consistory: that she frequent the sermons.

Colletaz, widow of Claude Bellet,[149] daughter of Tyvent Garmesoz.

Because of papal ceremonies. Answers that she goes to the sermons and has been of the Gospel since the beginning and does not say the rosary and prays to no other but God, and that she does not wish harm to any person whatsoever. Said the prayer, and the confession she hardly knew at all. She was given remonstrances and admonitions.

---

146. The councillor, elder, and future syndic Jean Ami Curtet.

147. Despite these admonitions and the efforts of her brother, Lucresse Curtet continued to fast, pray to the saints, and pay for Masses in Annecy. See R.Consist. 2, f. 77v (August 26, 1546).

148. Translator: The French word here *(cypaz)* is indistinct, and as transcribed has no known meaning, but is conjectured by the editors to mean "fish." I have emended it to cover the traditional three forms of animal food, but the translation is conjectural.

149. See the note above on Claude Bellet, husband of Franceyse, April 6, 1542.

Those from Jussy, two priests, Messieurs Pierre Falcat and Nycod Mouri.

Because of their resolution to live according to religion. Falcat answers *ut prius dix[i]t alia vicaduum(?) fuit. Ibidem* {as he said before, he was at other places in the vicinity(?). At the same time} he was at the sermons and heard good arguments. He wants to live and die in the faith of Jesus Christ and believes that no one should be adored but Jesus Christ, and that it is not for him to dispute about the Mass. He did not mean to receive Communion because it is not proper to receive it in wine.

The said Mauri answered like his companion; they believe that the Mass was made by God and he instituted it, and they keep Lent as in former times. The opinion of the Consistory is that they be remanded to the Council at some time and that they make response concerning their religion. Next Monday, March 26.

Amy Favre of Jussy.

Because of religion. Answers that he lives according to religion and that the Council pardoned the fault he had committed in taking his wife,[150] and he does not go elsewhere because he left her, and he blasphemes the Lord God as little as he can. [f. 98v] And he goes to the sermon when he can, since he has a suit with Master Henri; therefore he cannot go. And he received Communion at Christmas and does not fornicate. He was admonished.

Claude Vallodi and his wife and Michiel Du Mur.

Because of their ill will against each other. Vallodi answers that he wishes them no harm, and they are at law over some conflict. And Du Mur says similarly.

Jehan Bornand, granary worker.

Because of his improvement. Said the prayer and the confession poorly, and has improved hardly at all in religion. The advice of the Consistory advises [sic] that before Pentecost he know how to pray to God, and frequent the sermons.

---

150. Amy Favre was already in prison for adultery on September 29, 1542, the date when his father, Pierre Favre, presented a supplication in Council "asking that he (Amy) be pardoned to relieve his father." Hardly two months later Amy again asked the Council "to grant him grace for having committed adultery, for which he is deeply in great contrition and sorrow." The Council decided that "all penalties incurred should be pardoned him, and for penitence and punishment he should be imprisoned on bread and water the space of six days" in the prison of Jussy [R.C. 36, f. 133 and f. 171v (September 29 and November 17, 1542)].

Noble Jane Pertennaz.

Answers that she is always seen as in former times, and prays to Our Lord; sometimes she says her rosary, and she does not want to be a heretic. She believes that which the holy church believes. And she believes the church of Geneva is good. And she believes in good works. Asked whether Monsieur Calvin is God. The opinion of the Consistory is that she be deprived of the union of Communion and of the church and remanded before the Council and frequent the sermons. Monday, the Council.

The wife of Master Michiel the saddler.

On the anger of his nephew Mermet.[151] Answers that they are in accord and pardoned and are at law before . . .[152] And he has improved in religion. Said the prayer, and sometimes in Latin. Admonitions to frequent the sermons and know how to pray to the Lord.

f. 99]   *Guilliodaz and Jaquematz of the hospital.*[153]

Guilliodaz said that she had words with the said Jaquemaz on account of the pot, that the *magister*[154] would be angry. And she said to her: "I will give you a badly cleaned bowl, the dirtiest of them." And the said Jaquematz answered: "And this way you want to poison me." And if she said it, she begs mercy from God and the Seigneurie, and she meant no harm. The said Jaquemaz begged mercy of the said Guilliodaz and of justice.

Polletaz versus the said Guilliodaz. Says that she had no argument with the said Guilliodaz and could not go to receive Communion, and that she would never receive Communion because she had revealed that she had some goods that the Council went to look for. The said Polletaz said that she had no anger against the blind woman.[155]

151. Clauda, wife of Michel Julliard, saddler, and Mermet Julliard, his nephew.
152. Words omitted. Should probably read "before justice," *i.e.,* the lieutenant.
153. Underlined: "of the hospital."
154. Master Mathieu Malesta. Malesta was apparently already *magister* on January 14, 1543, but his nomination must have been recent, since on March 18, two days before the present session of the Consistory, it is recorded that "The procurators [of the hospital] have ordered that Master Mathieu Malesta, *magister* of the children of the hospital, be paid what the other masters are given, that is 25 florins, and to know when he entered the hospital and what he should be paid" (Arch. Hosp., Aa 1, f. 41 and f. 45). His predecessor Louis Tonyer is known to us principally for having become angry at the *hospitalière,* the reason why he was dismissed, but he had departed long before this session of the Consistory [R.C. 35, f. 297v and f. 422v (August 29 and December 7, 1541)].
155. Some days later there appeared before the procurators of the hospital "the

Gonon of the hospital and Fat Pernon, who are not content with what is given out at the hospital.

Answers no, and only complains about the bedclothes, and sometimes asks for skin when it is breaded.[156] And similarly the said Pernon.

The mother and two daughters: Jennete, widow of Amed Recouz, and Perne and Bernarde, her daughters.

Because of the disorder of their house. They live together and do not get angry with each other. They were at the sermon last Sunday. And they do not fight with anyone whatever. The two daughters know how to pray to God and the their [sic] mother not. Admonitions.

[f. 99v] *Anthoyne, daughter of Just Cristen, from La Roche, living at Abbé Tissot's house.[157]*

Is not married to Servet Sermod. Has one, two[158] children by a man from Bossey at Guilliaume Glaudi's house; the last at Michaelmas, the first at her father's house. And she was brought to bed in Presinge. The said man promised her his faith and had all her labor, and to marry her, when she lived in Curvin at the Danels'.[159] She wants to correct herself, and begs mercy of God and of justice. And has only had two children. And if she turns again to fornication she wants to be punished.

Reminder to the Council to write to the Consistory of Coppet in the case of Grillion, who is engaged to Aymoz Bochu's widow.[160]

---

wife of Cristen Jenod, blind, entirely wasted in the face, to whom is given a loaf of bread and a *quarteron* of wine, to whom was given a command to know the Lord's Prayer within a month and she would be left with her donation, and she should bring her husband here to the hospital next Sunday" [Arch. Hosp., Aa 1, f. 46 (April 1, 1543)].

156. Translator: The meaning of this French phrase, *"de l'epiderme quant on le fayt empater,"* is not clear.

157. The title of *abbé* was usually reserved to the captain general, at this time Ami Perrin. Here it possibly refers to the influential Perrinist, Pierre Tissot.

158. The word "two" is added interlinearly.

159. A family originally from Jussy, of which various branches were established in Geneva. Those admitted to the bourgeoisie are described in GALIFFE VII, pp. 92-113.

160. Françoise Bochu, who was engaged to Guillaume Grillon.

Thursday, March 22, 1543

Lord Syndic Checand.
Calvin, Blancheti, Genesto, De Ecclesia, Champereaulx.
Pensabin, Blandin, Justz de Loermoz, Symond, Vernaz, Morel, Veyrier, Du Pain.

Anne, wife of Nycod de La Ravoyre.[161]

Because of a daughter of hers recently married and that she has no cash money. Answers that because they have no money they cannot have banns published or have the wedding, and that later they would not want to carry it through. And they are not waiting until after Easter for any other reason than this.[162] And the woman who lives at the Vegios'[163] is not here and is not married and is a widow and is named Claudaz and has a daughter about three years old, and goes to the sermons when she has leisure. Says she has no form for praying to God and knows well how to pray, as she says. Said the prayer and the confession poorly. The opinion of the Consistory is that she be sent back if nothing else appears, and frequent the sermons.

100]   Jaquemaz, daughter of Nycod de La Ravoyre and daughter of the said Anne. Answers that she married someone at Bernard Prodom's[164] house and does not know why the wedding is not held. Says that she frequents the sermons sometimes. Touching the said woman who lives at Vegios', says she is not married and she does not know who goes or who comes from there except her father, who goes there sometimes in going to and frequenting the sermons. She is learning to pray to the Lord. And she was there last Sunday, and she does not know what the minister preached. And said "Our Father, etc." and the confession. She was admonished to frequent the sermons.

161. Nycod de La Ravoyre, the elder, farm laborer, from Villette, was admitted to the bourgeoisie on June 23, 1547 (*L.B.*, p. 228).

162. The Consistory feared that the De La Ravoyres were following an ancient custom of observing a time closed to marriage during Lent. The closed times of Advent and Lent are found respected in France under the *ancien régime* "in almost all parish monographs." In Geneva demographic studies show that "fifteen years after the adoption of the Reform, certain traces of religious censure can still be observed. In 1550-1559 a slight trough shows in March, but already Advent is no longer respected. A generation later nothing remains of the ancient nuptial regime, March becoming, with January, the most frequent month" (PERRENOUD, "Calendrier," pp. 925 and 929).

163. For the De Veigys see FORAS, *Armorial* 5, pp. 566-569, and DUMONT, *Armorial,* pp. 422-423.

164. Bernard Prodhom, butcher, citizen [R.C. 30, f. 194 (March 20, 1537); Notaires, Jean Duverney, v. 5, f. 78 (April 30, 1544)].

Mermet Verdon.

And says that he was summoned because he does not know all of his Pater and said only a part. Was at the sermon today and did not retain anything, unless that he recommended himself to God. The opinion of the Consistory is that since he is a mocker of the Word, that he be admonished and remanded here in two weeks, and that he profit more from prayer and make confession of his faith, and that his Communion be deferred to next time, and to frequent the sermons every day and refrain from mistreating his wife and live decently in his household.[165]

Clauda, daughter of Tyvent Joctz, from the pass of the Ecluse de Farges, who had a daughter by a married man.

Answers that she came to this city before Christmas and has been married and has been a widow for four years, and that her marriage [portion] was returned to her and her father gives her wheat, and she has a daughter three years old. The daughter she has is by a man who is near Thonon, and she does not know his name, and there is another who is named Jehan. And he has never been in this city with her. And he gave her 12 florins for the nursing of her daughter. And she rarely goes to the sermons because she is ill with fever, and she has not been for a fortnight and she does not know who preached. And said the prayer poorly, and does not know the confession. She was admonished. [f. 100v] The advice of the Consistory is that if she wants to marry in this city that she marry, and appear here and frequent the sermons, and within three weeks make the man by whom she has the said daughter appear and make the father of the said daughter appear, and learn the name and family name of the said father, and cease to receive Communion until she knows how to pray to the Lord.

Maurizaz Talluchetaz.

Touching her having been remanded. Said the prayer and the confession as the last time. The opinion of the Consistory is that she be held until another time to profit better by the Word and given strong admonitions and remonstrances and asked how long it will be before she knows how to pray to

---

165. Mermet Verdon had been in prison, probably for gambling, and was freed on January 26. On February 7 he was again accused of having gambled and having held games at his house. He remained in prison through the month of February, and was finally condemned to a month in prison on February 27 [R.C. 36, f. 222 (January 26, 1543); P.C. 1ᵉ sér., 368 (February 5-27, 1543); R.C. Part. 1, f. 10v (numbered f. 11v; February 27, 1543)].

the Lord, and that she abstain from the next Communion. She was given three weeks, and to abstain from Communion.

Pierre Calabri, mason.

Does not know why he was summoned; it is for praying to the Lord. Answers that he knows and has learned to pray to Our Lord. Said the prayer and the confession. The opinion of the Consistory: that he be admonished, that he be exhorted always to persevere in the Word and frequent the sermons.

Jehan Suchard, son of Henri, tailor, and his wife Germannaz, from La Roche.

Because of the sermons. Answers that they do their best to frequent the sermons and that Jehan Blanc[166] took away a cloak and it cost them five *gros,* and they wanted to marry, and in going to the Arve Bridge they were fined by the said Jehan Blanc, and he wanted to take his wife to La Roche, but she did not want to go there.

The said Germanaz says that they have to work for their living, and she was at the sermon Sunday morning, and they went to Villette, and she has not retained anything of the sermon. Said the prayer; does not know the confession. The opinion of the Consistory: that he be remanded until after Easter [f. 101] and frequent the sermons when he can, and that his wife someday ask one of the ministers to go to their house to give him remonstrances and lead him to religion. And tell her to use more diligence in learning to pray to the Lord.

Loys Piaget, sheath-maker, and his wife.

Because of what was said to him yesterday about his daughter's wedding. Answers that it is due to the husband, who has not made provision, and he does not hold by the papistry, and that his parents are not here because of Lent and are late.[167] And he begs mercy from God and the Seigneurie, and means well. And there is a respectable man who introduced him with good words. And he was exhorted to do what the Council has ordered, and he kept Lent and did not mean to do wrong. And he was at the sermon Tuesday and heard good words that were very agreeable to him, and Blanchet preached

166. Jehan Blanc, watchman. Others complained about fines imposed by Jehan Blanc, to the point where on July 5, 1543, the Council reprimanded him for doing "more than his office justifies, and at every turn he fines the people" [R.C. 37, f. 145. See also R.C. Part. 1, f. 209v (October 9, 1544)].

167. With regard to the interdiction of marriage during Lent, see the note above concerning Anne de La Ravoyre, earlier in this session.

about the signs(?) and baptized a child of Glaude Voland.[168] Said he has a scruple, that he was given to understand that charity should not be given to the poor for God's sake, because if he saves a little soup he does not want to waste it, and he is unhappy about this. The order is that nothing be given to the poor begging at the doors, but one should give and do good for the honor of God secretly, and one may give. And that poor beggars not go crying through the streets.[169] Said the prayer in a very strange fashion, and said the confession; the articles, almost nothing, with good intentions, through ignorance.

The wife was asked whether she has any scruples about religion or Lent. Answers that she eats what her husband eats, and they have no meat, only other foods, but not meat, eggs, cheese and others. [f. 101v] She thinks that if meat were injurious to her salvation she would never eat it, and on the other hand if she knew she would offend God by not eating it she would eat it. And at present she wants to eat it and do as she said. And she has not said the rosary for a year and not kept any feasts except those ordered by the Council. And she gives medicine to some women who are ill in the stomach with plasters, by the help of God, without words. And she believes she was made to come here from malevolence, and that God will be her witness and give her vengeance. And she worshipped idols like the others. She is angry because the other people are not all summoned here as well as she.

The opinion of the Consistory is, for the husband, that he come at the beginning of the sermon on the day of Communion, and the wife similarly, that she be seen to come among the first at the beginning and not mutter at the sermon, and remove the grudge she has against those she considers in her heart to be malevolent, and they should follow the sermons, and that both be admonished.

168. Since there were no baptismal registers at this time we cannot identify this person. An Egrège Claude Voland was agent for Pierre d'Alinge in 1544. There was also a Claude Voland, baths-house master, who died in 1552 [R.C. 38, f. 83v (February 22, 1544); E.C., Morts 1, p. 251 (January 17, 1552)].

169. The ordinances against the poor who begged publicly go back to the episcopal period. In 1492 proclamation was made that "*mendicantes et coquini vacuent et absentent civitatem* {mendicants and beggars should evacuate and depart from the city}." In 1530 and 1534 the bishop's vicar reaffirmed "that all those of this city who have the power to labor and work should be held to this and should not ask charity [publicly]." After the Reformation, in 1541, the Council ordered that a man should be "appointed to make the poor withdraw to the hospital." Later in this same year the ecclesiastical ordinances decreed that the *dizainiers* "should take care that the prohibition of begging is well observed" [S.D. II, pp. 121 (November 30, 1492), 284 (March 5, 1530), 300 (February 28, 1534), 365 and 385 (January 20 and November 20, 1541)].

Master Mathieu Gacthiner.[170]

Because of improvement in his faith and confession. Said the prayer and the confession. Admonitions to frequent the sermons and instruct his children in religion.

Jehan and Claude Curtet, brothers.

Because of their quarrel and ill will against each other. Jehan answers that he wishes no harm to his brother Claude and leaves him alone, him and his family, and that he is asking by law for his own from his brother. Claude answers that a year or four ago he asked help from his brother Jehan because of Vétraz,[171] and he joined with him and stayed four or five days. He complained because of the Italians who came against him. And they were [f. 102] taken to law, and it was the cause of his loss there. And he said that his said brother Jehan presented a false affidavit to Françoys Goyet to make him more spiteful. And he said that the said Jehan told him that he wanted to sell Vétraz and other words. And that many people wish him ill. The Consistory exhorted them to receive Holy Communion, pardoning each other, reserving the suit they have against each other. Jehan said he is ready to do all that respectable people would do. Claude said that he would leave vengeance to God, after having heard the admonitions of the lord [syndic]. They were exhorted to pardon each other. Claude having heard the holy doctrine, they pardoned each other, made peace and pardoned each other and shook hands in sign of peace.[172]

Françoyse, widow of Aymoz Bochu.[173]

Because she engaged herself to a husband. Answers that she reserved the will of her family, and he is Glaude Grillion's brother.[174] And he often

---

170. Mathieu Gathsiner (Gatzener).

171. The sense is not entirely clear; it was three years before that the king of France seized Vétraz and a year and a half later that the dispute between the brothers Curtet became known. See above, April 27, 1542, text and note.

172. Claude Curtet nevertheless remained in prison until March 30 or 31. At the time of his liberation the two brothers were again admonished "to live in tranquility from now on" [R.C. 37, f. 45 (March 30, 1543); R.C. Part. 1, f. 33 (March 31, 1543)].

173. She may be the widow of the Aymoz Bochu executed only three months before for the murder of François Deponte at the inn of the Bochet. See the note about this crime above, December 21, 1542.

174. Glaude Grillion, draper, and his brother Guillaume, subject of this consistorial inquiry, from Commugny (VD or FR), were admitted to the bourgeoisie respectively on January 24, 1533, and April 16, 1546 (*L.B.*, pp. 210 and 226).

comes to this city and even to her house, but she is never alone. And it was done through Jehan Favre, butcher. And the said Grillion, who gave her a *teston*, and Aymoz Choupin and Jehan Favre were present when he decided to make the engagement. And she truly wanted it, but only if it pleased her family, and the said Grillion wanted to have her marriage [portion] before proceeding to the said marriage. And she did not sleep with him, and she has never slept alone, because she always has a girl with her. And he will not say he slept with her, even if the canopy of the bed is set on fire.[175] [f. 102v] And she has her mother and a brother who are in Fribourg. And they did not intend that there should be a marriage if it was not the will of her family. And they did not want to complete the marriage unless she was sent the marriage [portion] before they had the wedding, or publish the banns. And she does not want it, because her family does not want to consent; it would be a great injury to her family. The opinion of the Consistory: that she not receive the said promised husband any more. And that the two transgressors be made to come Thursday, and that she be summoned next Thursday with them. Thursday the two: Jehan Favre and Choupin. And meanwhile the Consistory will investigate the said husband Grillion to take care of the affair, because she was seduced. And that she appear here on the said Thursday, and that she frequent the sermons and come when she is summoned.

Mermaz, widow of Françoys Plantens, fishmonger.

Because of papistry. Mother of George Lombard.[176] Answers that she no longer has a rosary, and she commends herself to God, who will help her. And says the prayer in French and in Latin and the Ave Maria, God before and the Virgin Mary after, and does all with good intentions. And goes to the sermon on Sundays and not on other days. And that she did not say that this

175. Translator: In other words, under no circumstances whatever. This seems to be a form of hyperbole.

176. George Plantens, called Lombard. The two sons of François Plantens, Georges and Pierre, adopted the name Lombard. This family of fishermen and boatmen certainly belonged to the bourgeoisie: in 1546 Pierre Lombard disputed with Ami de Langin, son of the late François de Langin, Seigneur de Veigy, "admonishing him that he was a bourgeois of Geneva and because of this was as noble as he." Langin replied "that there is no race in Geneva that is more noble than he" and drew on Pierre Lombard, wounding him. Georges Lombard then killed De Langin, but was acquitted by reason of legitimate defense. Georges Lombard died on January 18, 1551 [*R.C.* XIII, p. 637 *(notes complémentaires)*; *R.C.* XII, p. 268 (May 7, 1533); R.C. 41, f. 44v (March 8, 1546); P.C. 2ᵉ sér., 692 *(informations* of April 27, 1546); P.C. 2ᵉ sér., 743 (responses of March 28, 1546); E.C., Morts 1, p. 31].

law is not as good as the other of former times. And she does not know the articles of faith. The opinion of the Consistory is that, considering her malice in idolatry, she should frequent the sermons and present herself before Pentecost and present herself here to give an explanation of her confession, and abstain from Holy Communion.

Françoyse, wife of Jehan Bornand, granary worker.

To give an explanation of her religion and confession. Said the prayer and the confession. Admonitions to frequent the sermons more often.

103] *The ordinance of Holy Communion for Easter 1543.*[177]

For Saint Peter's for the two Communions: Lord Pernet de Fosses, Mychiel Varod, Pierre d'Orsieres, Michiel Morel.

For the Magdalen: Jehan Chautemps, P[ierre] Vernaz, Pensabin.

For Saint Gervase: Claude Du Pan, Loys Dufour, Blandin, Amed Gervays.

103v]
Thursday, March 29, 1543

Here the Consistory was paid for the whole past, including this [day] here.

Lord Checand, syndic.

Calvin, Blanchet, Genesto, Henri, Trippereaulx.

Molard, Vernaz, Veyriez, Delarmoz, Blandin, Symond, Du Pain, Morel, Orsieres, the officer Vovrey.

Pierre Choupin, baker.

On the affair of Bochu's widow, because of a certain marriage of someone from Coppet.[178] Answers that it was not he and he was not present, unless it was his brother;[179] unless he heard that they said if it would please the girl's relatives. And he asked him whether it would be right for them to speak together at Jehan Favre's, and he does not know what they did.

---

177. The next day the Council ordered that Holy Communion "should be held and celebrated this Easter, that is twice at the three churches, St. Peter's, the Magdalen, and St. Gervase" [R.C. 37, f. 41v (March 23, 1543)].

178. This was the matrimonial case between Françoise Bochu and Guillaume Grillion, presented in Consistory on March 22, 1543.

179. This was in fact his brother, Aymoz Choupin.

Jehan Bennard, host of the Rock.

Because [of] his child that he had brought to be presented in this city, that [the one] who carried it to be baptized is of the papistry. Answers that the one who carried it was from La Roche and a respectable man and he wanted the said man, named Justz, to be godfather, and he does not know his last name. And that he had his son who was at school in La Roche[180] come to this city. He was not in this city when proclamation was made that such godparents not be sought for children, and if he has erred, it is through ignorance. The Consistory is of the opinion that he be given chastening remonstrances and be well admonished and that he receive the admonition or be remanded before the Council, which will admonish him better, because it is against God and the proclamations, also that it is through ignorance. By resolution he was remanded to Monday before the Council.[181]

Jane, wife of Jehan Corajod, cobbler.

Because of Communion and that she still holds to the papistry. Answers that she received Communion at Easter from Monsieur Henri at the Magdalen and heard the sermon and the passion, and does not know what was said. And that she does not still say her Paternosters and pray to the Virgin Mary. And she is content, if it is wanted, not to pray any more to the Virgin Mary, and she has heard that one should not pray to another than God. The advice of the Consistory: that she be asked whether she has profited [f. 104] from religion, that she be admonished and made to say her faith and confession, and whether she has done what she was charged to do last time. And that she instruct her children in religion, and that she be admonished more harshly. And why she received Holy Communion at Easter without having asked permission and why [sic], since it was forbidden her. And that she say the prayer. Said the prayer, and knows hardly anything of the Credo and did not say it. The Consistory gave her two weeks to learn to pray to the Lord and to frequent the sermons.

---

180. On the school of La Roche see above, August 3, 1542, note.

181. The ecclesiastical ordinances of 1541 stated "that foreigners should not be received as godfathers, except faithful people of our communion, since the others are not qualified to promise in the church to instruct the children as is their duty" (*R.C.P.* I, p. 9). Jehan Bennard was reprimanded in Council for having "had his child carried to baptism by a papist from La Roche." The Council resolved "that if he swears that he did not do this from malice and evil papistic intent and that he did not know the edict and prohibition, that he be pardoned. He swore" [R.C. Part. 1, f. 33v (April 2, 1543)].

Anthoyne, wife of Rener Mauris,[182] and Guycharde Auberte, her sister, wife of Jaques Richard.

The said Anthoyne says that she has often felt hatred for her sister. And the said Auberte said that she wishes no harm to her sister and that she did not deprive her of their father's goods. And that she did not ask her to come when her daughter, the said Auberte's niece, was married. And also for the children she has had, she was not asked as sisters should ask each other. The said Anthoyne answers that her husband did not want her asked like the others. They were asked whether they did not want to live in peace with each other. They answer yes, and they want to live together like good sisters. The said Anthoyne begged mercy of her sister, and Aubberte said that she begged mercy of God and not of her. And they left good friends.

Discret Aymo Choupin.

Because of an agreement that was made for Bochu's widow.[183] Answers that she swore faith to a husband and made an agreement; that she asked him to say something and took him aside: "They want to give me a companion; Jehan Favre solicits me hard." And he told her that she should not do it unless her relatives were content and she had spoken with her uncle in Sepoenché(?). And he told her that he would not meddle further if her family were not content, and that she should ask mercy of her said uncle, that she should recommmend herself to him and ask his pardon. And Jehan Favre begged her hard to have the said husband. [f. 104v] And she took him to Jehan Favre's, and he did not want him to have her, and he swore faith to her there and gave her a *teston*. And the husband asked whether she wanted it, and she answered yes, and said very little of the reserve, only if it pleased her family. And also the said husband answered that if he knew that her relatives did not want it they would not speak further. And he is named Guillaume Grillion, the said husband, from Commugny.

Jaques Emyn, pack-saddler.

Because of superstition, and why he appeared. Answers that he has always appeared when he was summoned and that he has learned to pray, saying the prayer and the confession. And Lent, because his guests do not eat Lent-breaking food, because he has no appetite for eating meat or breaking Lent. And that it is not wrong to eat meat and is not wrong not to eat it on Fridays and eat it the

---

182. Rener Mauris, carpenter from Aire la Ville (GE), bourgeois in 1524, died in 1569. He was married to a woman named Françoise who died in 1551 [*L.B.*, p. 200 (January 12, 1524); E.C., Morts 9, p. 119 (August 23, 1569); E.C., Morts 1, p. 34 (April 7, 1551)].

183. Franceyse Bochu.

other days. And he does not believe he displeases God by eating meat. And he does not intend to displease God, because if he displeased God he would do like the others who eat meat. And that each one lives by his own whim, and that he wants to rule himself by the Word of God. And that he wants to live and die in this city of Geneva. And he does not want to scandalize his Christian brothers. And that he will be more sensible and better advised another time.

The advice of the Consistory is that he demonstrate his Christianity by works; otherwise he will be remanded to the Council. And that he be admonished to fulfill the promises he made by his works. And that he be asked about his chambermaid who left his house pregnant, and by whom. That he frequent the sermons more often, otherwise he should be remanded to the Council, and that he be admonished about all the other things, and that he live according to the Reformation of the church.

Touching his chambermaid who left his house pregnant. Answers that she left, and his father gave him another. And he does not know why, because he did not send her away and does not know that she was pregnant. That she is the daughter of his wife's daughter and he has no suspicion that she is pregnant and he does not meddle with her.

[f. 105] *Jehan Mouri, from Jussy.*

Does not know why he was summoned here. Because he did not receive Communion in Jussy. Answers that he took it here in Geneva from the hands of Monsieur Calvin because he could not go there. And he did not receive it at Christmas because he was watching the house, and had no scruple about not receiving it then. And that he wishes no harm and bears no grudge against anyone, and he was at the preaching at the first preaching at St. Peter's, and he did not understand what was said because he was by the bells and was stunned for the moment, and he received Communion at the chief sermon. The Consistory advises that he be admonished to take care to receive Communion more devoutly than he has and to refrain from blaspheming, and that he be asked whether he knows his faith and confession. He gave an explanation of his confession and articles of faith.

Claude Curtet the elder, butcher.[184]

Asked where he was at the sermon the day of Communion. Answers that he received Communion as a good Christian should. And yesterday he took a bed-pendant to go pawn it and was very angry at his wife and in his

184. Claude Curtet the elder, member of the CC for Saint Gervais in 1541, died June 9, 1580 [R.C. 35, f. 56^b (February 9, 1541); E.C., Morts 12, p. 296].

house. And he sells for a living and takes only his own, and if his wife wants to support him, he is satisfied. And if he has done wrong he begs for mercy from God and justice, and he will refrain from insulting his wife. And he does not beat her as much as it is said. And said little of the prayer, and the confession. He was given admonitions and remonstrances.

Tyvent Prodon,[185] butcher.

Because of a maid he became engaged to. Answers that he knows nothing either of Gardet's maid or any other. And he was engaged to a girl, and it will not be proven that he gave her anything. The Consistory was informed falsely about this and it will not be proven. And said that he does not know her. And touching the sermons, he cannot go there on working days, but on Sunday he goes, and he received Communion at Easter. Said the prayer and the confession. And he did not go to Mass willingly. The names of those who must be examined against the said Tyven Prodom who was engaged to Jehan Gardet's[186] maid and is engaged to another. And first Loys Gardet,[187] Hugoz at Ludriaz's(?) house, Glaude the maid of Monsieur Laurent Piquard,[188] Mermet Blandin and Tyvent Chenut's wife.

f. 105v] *Claudaz, daughter of Alexandre Rosset.*

About seven months ago she became engaged to a husband, and indeed about nine weeks, and is pregnant by her husband, because they had been ill with pox and her father died. And she is not pregnant by another than her husband, and by accident before the wedding. And does not know how long ago it was that his wife died. And she did not become pregnant by him except after they swore faith. Said the prayer and the confession. And she does not know how long she has been pregnant, and it was less than a week after he swore faith to her, and it seems to her to have been seven to eight months. And it happened at her master Darbey's[189] house. And the

185. Tivent Prodhom, butcher, citizen. He was still living in 1558 [Notaires, Jean Duverney, v. 5, f. 78 (April 30, 1544); E.C., Morts 2, p. 83 (November 5, 1558; death of his daughter)].

186. Probably Jean Gardet, son of Pierre, butcher [*R.C.* XIII, p. 536 (April 4, 1536)].

187. Loys Gardet, citizen, a butcher like Jean Gardet, living on the Grand Mézel [*R.C.* 30, f. 212 (April 15, 1537); E.C., Morts 1, p. 13 (June 17, 1550); E.C., Morts 7, p. 102 (October 17, 1567)].

188. Laurent Symond, called the Picard.

189. Antoine Darbey, citizen, baker in Saint Gervais [P.C. 2ᵉ sér., 800 (responses of July 17 and 23, 1549)]. Like Clauda Rosset's husband, Darbey was infected with plague some months earlier [*R.C.* 36, f. 178v (November 27, 1542)]. Later in the same year, like

Juggler,[190] his wife and certain others were present, and she was given a *teston*. The opinion of the Consistory is that this matter be remanded to the Council and that it determine the time she has been pregnant and await the time of her delivery. And the husband must be remanded to the Council, and it should find out about her master Darbey. And that the time be determined, and that her husband be summoned here and made to confess the truth, whether he knew her before the wedding and whether it is by him. To Thursday. And that she be released until after the birth, and afterwards remanded to the Council. The name of the husband: Amy Poentet, farm laborer, from Chézery. And she has not been engaged to anyone other than the said Amed, and she has not agreed with another husband, although it is said that her husband has become engaged to a girl at Floutiez's house. It would be good to ask her whether her husband had engaged himself to the maid at Robelle's and whether the said wife gave her money to make her give him up. The husband to Thursday: Amy Poentet.

[f. 106]

Thursday, April 5, 1543

Lord Syndic Checand.
Calvin, De Ecclesia, Genesto, Trippereaulx, Champereaulx.
Du Pain, Pensabin, De Ulmo, Vernaz, Blandin, Molard, Symond, Orsieres, Veyrier, the officer Vovrey.

Pernete, widow of Glaude Guyon.

Because of divination and ceremonies. Touching Communion, answers that she received it in Jussy and Master Nycolas[191] gave it to her; at Pentecost

---

Pierre Gerod, Darbey was accused of having wanted "to lead certain citizens to the wars at the instigation of Andrier Philippe, enemy of Geneva, for which he was condemned not to leave the city for three years without permission, under penalty of 100 écus" [R.C. Part. 1, f. 91 (September 29, 1543)]. He was also accused of having had relations with Jean Gabriel Monathon and others linked to the Articulants, banished from Geneva in 1540. On March 11, 1544, Darbey obtained the commutation of this sentence (R.C. 38, f. 120 and f. 120v). See also R.C. 37, folios 197v, 198, 226v, 230, 231, 232v, 233, and 268 (August 18 and 20, September 24, 27, 28, and 29, November 10, 1543).

190. Amyed Vulliet, called the Juggler.

191. Already on October 4, 1541, the Council asked the dismissal of Nycolas Vandert, preacher of Jussy, "who does not exercise his office well, and it is a long time since he preached in Vandoeuvres" (R.C. 35, f. 352). On November 27, 1542, he still remained in office, but the accusation was added "that he does not visit the sick and does not do the other things necessary" (R.C. 36, f. 178). Returned before the Consistory for

and Christmas she received it. On the diviner, answers that Monsieur De Maxilliez never sent her anywhere for divination. And she does not know that a golden chain was lost and was never found. And a young lady went there, and she heard it said that the said golden chain was lost. And it was the young lady who went there, and the said deponent went with her. And that the said young lady went there herself and the said woman cried out, and this was fairly near her house there nearby. And she does not know whether it was a diviner; she is a good Christian. And she found it in the fields when she wanted to go. And she consented to go there, and it was in Juvigny, and they hardly spoke to . . .[192] And the said diviner is named Comba Verchey, and she spoke to the said diviner in a field that is located near Juvigny in the place called Rosse. And the said man did nothing she did not. And on returning the golden chain was found. And he said to them: "Go there, you will find it," which was so. And she does not know how it was done or what he did or what he said to the said young lady. And she saw that they spoke together, although the said young lady had told him that she had lost a chain. And that the servant found it who gave it to the said young lady. The opinion of the Consistory is that she be admonished that the case is criminal and that she be corrected with hard words. And frequent the sermons, and that she be made to say the prayer and the confession. [f. 106v] She begs mercy of God and of justice if she has done wrong. Remanded to Monday before the Council.[193] Monday, the Council and Jehan Favre, butcher.

Noble Pernete Du Payn.

Because of Easter Communion and the sermon. Answers that she heard the sermon before dinner at St. Gervase. And she did not intend to receive Communion. And she never spoke or mocked the Communion, and had a good will to receive it. And she does not kneel to pray except to say the Pater and means no harm and to be saved. And does not know whether she said on the day of Easter that she did not know how she lived. And it is when

---

this reason on December 5 (for the session of December 7), he did not appear (R.C. 36, f. 184). He was finally replaced with Abel Poupin on April 16, 1543 (R.C. 37, f. 61).

192. Incomplete sentence.

193. On April 9, 1543, the Council decided to incarcerate Pernette Guyon and make her answer more fully for having accompanied Mademoiselle Du Crest to the diviner. Four days later "the castellan of Jussy presented the answers given in his hands against Pernette Guyon of the said place, whom he has had detained. Ordered that he should pursue the case and that he should ask about all the affairs of the house of the château Du Crest, and the child of the said woman also . . . about the other things done in this house" [R.C. Part. 1, f. 38 and f. 40 (April 9 and 13, 1543)].

she is angry at her children, who give her so much trouble. And if she said it it was through ignorance, and she asks grace of God and mercy. She was at the sermon today, and does not know what the preacher said. And in her house, with the Pater, she sometimes says the Ave Maria through ignorance. She does not know how to pray to the Lord except in Latin, except the Pater which she says she knows in the vulgar tongue. And if she has done wrong she begs mercy of God and will be better advised another time. The opinion of the Consistory is that she be made to give up her rings.[194] And in view of her hypocrisy that she be remanded here on some day before Pentecost. And that she frequent the sermons every day and learn to pray to the Lord. And that her son Pierre Pauloz be admonished to instruct his family well in the Lord and that Pierre Pauloz, her son, should have a Bible.

Nycod de La Ravoyre the elder.

Because of his daughter[195] whose banns he has not had published. Answers that [it is] because he has no money to pay at the close. And he goes to the sermons on Sundays and was at two sermons on Sunday and does not know what they said. And believes that God loves him for his good works. Said the prayer and half of the confession. And sometimes prays to the Virgin Mary that she will direct him. Admonitions.

[f. 107] *Claude Tappugnier, ironmonger.*

Because of good works. Answers that he believes that he will be saved by the mercy of God and by his good works. He believes that God causes good works and that he does good works by the grace of God. And on praying to the Virgin Mary and praying for the dead, this is his scruple and opinion that he has that the Virgin Mary has the power to pray for us. Of which doubts he was relieved by Monsieur Calvin. Remonstrances.

Jaquemaz, wife of Master Renault, quilter.

Because of anger against her husband and household. Answers that it is true, and she goes to the sermons, and it was because of a girl who deceived her, and she did not receive Communion because it was forbidden her by a preacher. And this was because of some money someone owed her, and it was at law, and this was the reason she was angry. She confesses having been very

194. On February 8, 1543, the Consistory ordered her to give up the keys of certain coffers. It assigned the elders Orsières and Blandin to make an inventory. There is also mention of "her goods [that] are in pawn" on August 10, 1542, but without speaking specifically of rings (see above, *ad dies*).
195. Jaquemaz, daughter of Nycod de La Ravoyre.

wrong and begs mercy of God and of justice. And she does not wish them harm any more. She blasphemed God vigorously for having yielded to the Gospel and in defiance of the Gospel, and has no more hatred for the women her neighbors, and begs mercy of God. The opinion of the Consistory: that she be corrected and remanded to Monday before the Council, which will give her strict remonstrances.[196]

Mermet Verdon.

Because of his progress in praying to God and frequenting the sermons. Answers that he has profited. Said the prayer very little, and said that he knows no more, nor the confession. The opinion of the Consistory: that he be given a term of two weeks to come, and the Consistory admonishes him to frequent the sermons, or otherwise he will be sent a schoolmaster.

Amed Poentet of Chézery.

Has lived here more than a year, is married to Darbey's maid, named Glauda,[197] to whom he pledged himself at the grape harvest about five months ago. And he became engaged to her at Darbey's and married her about two months ago. And he embraced her before the wedding in the room where he was then staying. And he embraced her [f. 107v] about a week after they swore faith at the house of George Plat[198] in Saint Gervais, and he has never sworn faith to another. And whether he had anything to do with some other, Floutiez's maid. And he made no agreement with her; the friends of the two parties were not there. And he did not give six écus for the said maid of Floutiez. And says that he gave four écus he had to Monsieur Thomas Genod because he had offended justice,[199] to be separated from this same Loyse, because he had sworn faith to the said girl Loyse, and he understands that the said Monsieur Thomas made an agreement to end the said marriage, and because there was some impediment. And that the two women were present, and that he had not wanted it because of an impediment, that

196. The Council repeated the admonitions to "the wife of Master Regnaut, quilter, who was angry at her husband and renounced the Gospel and those who put her under such a law" [R.C. Part. 1, f. 38 (April 9, 1543)]. Jaquema, wife of Master Renault, is also cited because of a squabble with Jean Chautemps [R.C. 38, f. 13v (December 21, 1543)].

197. Claudaz Rosset, maidservant of Antoine Darbey.

198. George Plat, tailor, citizen, living in Coutance in Saint Gervais, died on April 22, 1553 [Notaires, de Compois, v. 5, f. 132 (April 29, 1526); E.C., Morts 1, p. 264].

199. Pierre Vandel replaced Thomas Genod as procurator general on February 5, 1543 (R.C. 37, f. 4).

her mother was not of a good race. And he only gave the five écus and a cheese. And he does not know whether the said Loyse received them. The cheese was given by Anthoyne Darbey. And he borrowed three of them from Mugneri, and one that he had with him. And he was at the sermon Sunday at St. Gervase. Has learned the Pater and knows it well. The opinion of the Consistory is that the affair be remanded to the Council and that there be no appearance of an agreement and that he make(?) and from those who carried out the business, and that Loyse be examined.[200]

Thomasse, called Mabuete, wife of Andrer Jordan of Choulex.

She came to this city about six weeks ago. Said that her husband is in Thonon because he had an argument with his brother who wanted to twist his arm, and they separated for this reason, and she will make it appear by respectable people, and she brought her children here. And that she will not stay longer without going to her husband. The advice of the Consistory is that means be found for her to go find her husband. And that the children be given to someone to watch over them for the parents, and that she be remanded to Monday[201] before the Council, and that care be taken that she does not sell the house or the barn in Saint Gervais.

[f. 108]   *Petremand Pellouz.*

Because of Communion. Answers that he has not received it since he was wounded, and that he cannot earn his living or that of his wife and children. And that he feels hatred for a man, that the evil is so great to him that he cannot bear it any longer,[202] and therefore he did not want to receive Communion. Touching usury. Answers that he accommodates people to avoid great injury and so they will not sell their goods. If anyone gives him something it is to support his children, and he does no injury to anyone whatsoever. He cannot say that he has received more than a *teston*, ten sous, four sous, six sous. Was exhorted to give up all grudges and enmities and ill will. The opinion of the Consistory: that he be admonished to live in peace,

---

200. Next Monday in Council "there was discussion [of] Amyed Poentier of Chézery, who espoused Glaude, maid of Anthoine Darbey, who had already promised himself to the servant on the Rue du Moulin and later knew the said Glaude carnally before the wedding. Ordered that the procurator [general] should obtain information about the said affair from those who carried out the business" [R.C. Part. 1, f. 38 (April 9, 1543)].

201. "To Monday" is written in the margin.

202. Pelloux is speaking here of Claude Philippe, whom he accused of having wounded him. See below, July 3, 1544.

to govern his conscience and to come here before receiving the next Holy Communion at Pentecost to learn whether he has pardoned his evil will. And to cease taking interest, since the proclamation has been made.

Jehan Favre, butcher.

On the occasion of a marriage.[203] Answers that the marriage of Aymoz Bochu's widow was made at his house in the presence of Choupin,[204] who said that it was not the sale of a horse, and that the said husband said that her relatives would be displeased. And the wife did not reserve anything that he heard, and she had a letter written to send to her family, and he did not hear anything else. He gave her a *teston*, and he did not say that she returned his *teston* to him, and that she did not reserve anything that he, etc. And indeed he said that she said at that time that she did not want it. And she did not say that she had married once without her family, but that she would not marry again at this time. And Chopin said that they should consider it well. The opinion of the Consistory is that he be remanded to Monday[205] before the Council, which will have the said Favre swear an oath to speak the truth, or when it pleases the Council.[206] And he did not change his mind at all later. [f. 108v] And as for the sermons, he goes to the sermons when he can. Said the prayer and the confession.

Guillaume Villars,[207] barber.

Because of usury. Answers that he knew the Mugniers and that they owe him nothing and he will give it to the Seigneurie and does not know what this is about usury. And that he lent them money, and lent them a rose noble, and sometimes 100 florins, and they gave him something and did not give him anything [sic], or grain, and he had red wine. And he knew the Figiers and lent them 100 écus, and 15 écus against the sale of 20 *coupes* of wheat and 30 *setiers* of wine. And if it had not been to do them great benefit,

203. This is the matrimonial case between Françoyse Bochu and Guillaume Grillion presented to the Consistory on March 22, 1543.

204. Aymoz Choupin.

205. "To Monday" is struck from the text.

206. "To speak the truth, or when it pleases the Council" is underlined in the text. The Consistory did not obtain the right of making witnesses take an oath until 1556, when the Council granted it to the syndic of the Consistory "to eliminate the quarrels and injuries that arise daily from witnesses who come to the Consistory and are not given an oath, so that they do not speak the truth" [*S.D.* III, p. 32 (July 24, 1556)].

207. Guillaume Villars, bourgeois, from Douvaine (H.-S.), died on December 11, 1573 [*L.B.*, p. 200 (February 16, 1524); E.C., Morts 12, p. 76; and without adding anything, L. GAUTIER, *Médecine*, p. 478].

he would not have given it to them. The opinion of the Consistory is that he be remanded before the Council and that he bring the bonds on Monday and that they be well examined.

Rolet Viret.[208]

Because of the sermons. Answers that he goes to the sermons and knows the Pater but not the Credo and ate meat throughout Lent and did not keep the novena of St. Felix although the women urged him to do it, which he did not want to do. Said the prayer, and nothing of the confession. And that it was Ayma Du Chabloz who urged him to make a novena and give 13 deniers for a Mass to St. Felix. The opinion of the Consistory is that he strive to learn to pray to the Lord and the catechism.

[f. 109]

Thursday, April 12, 1543

Lord Syndic Checand.
Calvin, Champereaulx, Henri, Trippereaulx, Genesto.
C[laude] Du Pain, Vernaz, Veyrier, Orsieres, Morel, Pensabin, Blancheti, De Lormoz, Molard, Blandin, the officer Vovrey.

Gonyn de Soubz-le-Creste,[209] *armorer, from Collonges sous Monthou near Vétraz, living in Saint Gervais; is married.*

Because of gambling. Answers that he was in Lyon six weeks and recently came back, and he went on a whim, and some children are dead. He left his wife because she did not want him to spend his money with the other young men, and it seems to him he was at the sermon Sunday and Wednesday. Said that he will do better hereafter. Said the prayer and a little of the confession. The advice of the Consistory is that if he improves he be left alone for this time, and that he pray to the Lord and be given strong remonstrances.

Maurisaz Talluchetaz.

Because of her religion and confession. Said this as she could. Was remanded to another time to know better how to pray and the rest of her confession.

---

208. Rolet Viret, laborer, from Geneva [Notaires, de Compois, v. 7, f. 28 (October 5, 1532)].
209. Gonyn de Soubz-le-Creste was admitted to the bourgeoisie with his son Loys on March 29, 1563 (*L.B.*, p. 275).

Noble Pierre Pauloz Du Pain, apothecary.

Does not know why. Answers that meat was always ordered cooked last Lent, and that he stays quietly in his house with his household and rarely goes to taverns, except sometimes with the young men. And that he did not say that the preacher should do what he . . .[210] It is true that it was another who practiced usury. And that his wife is not a papist. And if his mother is a papist it is not his fault, because he gave her a New Testament to study. The advice of the Consistory is that he instruct his wife and his mother, that he admonish and give a good example to his household [f. 109v] and that he frequent the sermons more often and remove the books from his house so his mother will not read them. And give him good remonstrances to teach his mother to pray to God and learn her creed, and all those of his house.

Ayma, daughter of the late Tyvent Du Chabloz, wife of Pierre Du Foin.

Does not know why she does not go to the sermons. Answers that she goes to the sermons, that she treats those who have syphilis and must have had one Saturday, and she never urged anyone at all to carry out the novena[211] of St. Felix. And she learned to heal in Piedmont at a doctor's house a long time ago. And if it is proven that she promoted the novena she wants to be in prison. And she treated Buclin's scalp infection and told him that it was an ulcer and not St. Felix. And she went to visit a sick girl in Viry, and did not receive Communion at Easter because she was treating a woman and two girls. And she did not tell the said Buclin to have a Mass of 13 deniers said. Said the prayer and articles of faith. And cannot say anything else about the said St. Felix. The advice of the Consistory is that she be remanded before the Council, and to examine Buclin and his wife, who could say what happened, on Monday; and she should frequent the sermons. She changed her mind and said that the wife of the said Buclin said that he made the novena and had had the Mass of 13 deniers said.

Thomassa, wife of Michiel Chapellaz, baker.

Because of the sermons. Answers that she goes to the sermons on Sundays, and the other days she cannot because she has business in her house. And she was there Monday. Said the prayer and the confession. She was admonished.

---

210. Incomplete sentence.
211. We have found no reference to this novena, but novenas were often credited with the power to heal.

Guillaume Grillion, of Coppet.

Because of the marriage of Aymoz Bochu's widow.[212] Answers that since she does not want him, nor he her, she should return him what he gave her, and then get an affidavit from the said woman's family that they do not want it. And this was done at the house of Jehan Favre, butcher. And he promised nothing to the said Favre, butcher, at Claude Rosset's house. And he did not go there afterwards. [f. 110] And he did not give or promise anything to make the said marriage, although the said Favre asked for money for a pair of hose. And he wants to know why the said widow does not want him. And she reserved nothing, except she said that she would reserve the will of her family, and if her family did not want it she would not want it either. And she gave the said Grillion four écus which he gave to the said widow of Bochu.

The said Françoyse appeared. Said and answered that she did not want him and that she had reserved the will of her relatives. And she lent the said Grillion four écus. And he should have brought her some oats. And Jehan Favre was the first who spoke to her about the said Grillion, and he took her to supper to settle it. And she did not want to consent to marry without the will of her family. And another time he took her to dinner and wanted to marry her. And she always reserved the will of her family, and many other words being said, she agreed to swear faith to the said Grillion. And he asked her to give him money for a pair of hose. And the said Grillion gave her only a *teston*, a pair of shoes and a pair of knives that she still has. And she will show clearly that her relatives do not want to agree. And he had her write again to her family, and Monsieur Denys Besanson[213] wrote the letter for her. And also she was told to write again to her family that she was willing(?)[214] to marry, and the response to this. And that her relatives should send an affidavit, otherwise the marriage would stand. Also she said that she does not want it.

Both together were asked whether they wanted to leave each other, and both are content to renounce the said marriage. The said Grillion took back the *teston* that she gave him that he had given her. The opinion of the Consistory: that they be remanded to Monday[215] before the Council. And that Jehan Favre be summoned about the seduction of the said Françoyse.

212. Françoyse Bochu.
213. Denis Hugues.
214. Translator: Once again, a French word *(caupe)* with no known meaning; it should mean "ready" or "willing" from the context.
215. "To Monday" is in the margin.

And that no reason has been found why the said marriage should not be broken.[216]

110v] *Pierre Vernaz, son of Pierre Vernaz,[217] citizen of Geneva.*

Because of fornication in his father's house which made the servant pregnant. Answers that he knows nothing about it and does not know where she is, and that she pestered him and went to find him in bed. And he sinned with her and offended God and his father. And there is no promise of marriage. And he gave her some rings and a skirt and two écus on two occasions, and he gave it to her for her services. And he does not know where she has made her expenses since she went out of the house about two months ago. And two days afterwards he went to find her at Bonivar's[218] to drink with her and some other companions. And there is no promise or reserve.

Pernete, daughter of Jehan Groz of Loisin, a servant at Bonivard's. Answers that no one keeps her and that she was a servant at Vernaz's and she was dismissed. Does not know why except that his son promised and swore faith to her in their house, and there was no person there except the two of them. And that she did not begin and that she did not go to sleep with her [sic]. And he promised himself to her when he gave her an écu and some rings. And she does not know whether she is pregnant, and she fornicated with him. And he came to look for her in her room, and not she for him. And he promised her marriage before she had fornicated and she promised him marriage before he fornicated with her. And that this was in the kitchen.

216. The civil authorities ratified the advice of the Consistory, ordering that "having heard the answers given in the hands of the magnificent lords of the Consistory and their account, and considering that . . . the said husband and wife reserved the will of their parents . . . ordered that the said marriage be null and they be separated from one another and be freed from one another" [Jur. civ. R1, f. 2 (April 16, 1543)]. However, the marriage must have taken place: Guillaume Grillion appeared in Council on September 1, 1544, after the death of his wife, Françoise, asking to be allowed to give all her goods to the hospital, "provided that three of her daughters by her first husband are taken into the said hospital." The Council ordered him to make an inventory of all the "goods of the said daughters and that her relatives be brought forward to choose a guardian in order to avoid a burden on the hospital" (R.C. 38, f. 347). Also, already on May 14, 1543, therefore hardly a month after the present session of the Consistory, Jean Marchant asked to be released from the guardianship of Aymoz Bochuz's children, which was granted him, apparently indicating that the guardianship had already passed to Grillion (R.C. Part. 1, f. 52).

217. Pierre Vernaz, son of Pierre Vernaz, the elder of the Consistory. Although Galiffe says that Pierre Vernaz the son was counted incorrectly among the Perrinists, this association earned him the penalty of death in 1555 (GALIFFE, *Ameaux*, p. 86, n. 1; SORDET, *Dictionnaire*, p. 1281).

218. François Bonivard.

The opinion of the Consistory is that she be asked who paid her expenses at Bonivard's. Answers that it was in the kitchen and he gave her . . .[219] in the name of marriage. And she answered that her father and mother without the approval of her father and mother [sic] and that they would disapprove. And he answered her that he would see that they would be able to live together without them. And she does not have a room. And that there was only one more time, and that he did not pay her expenses and that she did not sign on again [as servant] with the said Bonivard. She asked for a little time to answer about what they did and said. Answers that everything [f. 111] he gave her was always in the name of marriage. The opinion of the Consistory: that they both be made to come together to dispute about their affair. The said Pierre denies that she [sic] ever gave her anything in marriage, either écus or *bache* in marriage. The said girl answers that he gave her the *bache* and that she did not want to take it because her father and mother would not be content, and this was in the stable. The said Pierre says that he never gave her anything in marriage and never gave her any *bache* at all, and he had already fornicated with her before he gave her anything, and the girl only said it two months ago, and it was only a week before she left the house. He told her it was not so, and that he gave everything at one time. And she answers no. And when he gave her the skirt she refused it because of his father and mother. And she wanted to return him everything. The girl was asked who are those who counsel her. She has relatives in this city: the Juggler[220] and Pierre Pauloz Tarex. They were both remanded to Monday before the Council.[221]

219. Words omitted.
220. Amyed Vulliet, called the Juggler.
221. Pernette Gros presented a supplication to the Council the next Monday, August 16, against Pierre Vernaz, "whose company she has had, requiring that he be forced to fulfill and accomplish his promise, as is contained more fully in her supplication." The Council asked her father, Noble Jehan Gros, "if he gave consent and license to make the said marriage to his said daughter, and he confessed that he knows nothing of it and did not give license. And the said Pierre Verna, father of the said Pierre, saying also that he did not consent and also does not want to consent at present, asking to be freed" [Jur. civ. R1, f. 2 (April 16, 1543); see also R.C. 37, f. 61v, *ad diem*]. A week later the Council decided, "having heard the said parties and the statements of each party summoned, and because there is no proof of any consent given by the fathers of the said parties, that is of the said Pierre Vernaz who is still under his authority, which is a thing opposed to the law of God and the edicts of our most dread Lords, that the said Pierre should swear that he did not make any marriage or promise of marriage, and having so sworn, the said Pierre and the said Pernette should be freed from the said marriage. He, being so sworn, to be freed by means of a promise and commitment to pay the cost of her confinement and five sous for twenty [sic] shoes and also to remain three days on bread and water" [R.C. Part. 1, f. 43v (April 23, 1543)].

Pierre Guilliermet from Villard,[222] *tailor, called Pollet.*

Because of the sermons. Answers that he goes twice on Sundays, and not on working days, because he cannot go. And Messieurs [sic] Calvin preached in the morning at nine o'clock. Said the prayer, and did not dare say it before the company. Said the prayer and the confession. The opinion of the Consistory: that he be given strong remonstrances to serve the Lord, because he is very avaricious, and that he be exhorted about the faith and superstitions and to go to and frequent the sermons and strive to know better how to pray, and to the catechism, and appear here before Communion to show how he has improved in religion. Remanded to two weeks.

[f. 111v] *Jehan Soutiez of this city, farm laborer.*

Because of Holy Communion. Answers that he did not receive Communion last Easter because of someone who had done him an injury, a woman who cursed him, and he fell into illness, because he had gone to stay in a house against the will of the said woman. And he was at the sermon Sunday. Said the prayer and the confession. And he repents of the evil heart he had at Easter. And he does not know the Ave Maria. Said the articles a little. He will be better advised another time, and wants to receive [Communion]. Admonitions to frequent the sermons.

Pierre Guyon of Jussy, summoned by the castellan of Jussy.[223]

And does not know why he came here. And for blaspheming the name of Our Lord. Answers that he does not swear. Has served Bezanson Dadaz[224] for about three weeks and has not seen the wife of his master Bezanson Dadaz spin the sieve[225] or divine otherwise. He did see her give some written

222. Pierre Guillermet, bourgeois of Geneva, from Villard, in the parish of Saint Martin near Yenne (Savoy), a tailor according to the Consistory register and not a belt-maker as in the *Livre des bourgeois* [L.B., p. 213 (June 11, 1535); Notaires, Jean Duverney, v. 5, f. 59 (August 31, 1543)].

223. François Paquet, castellan of Jussy.

224. Bezanson Dada, citizen, from a notable family of Milanese origin. Galiffe claims that he was a Protestant *eidguenot* who became a Philippin, but Henri Naef describes him rather as a resolute adversary of the Reform, his brother Etienne being the partisan. Bezanson Dada died in 1558 [GALIFFE I, pp. 233-234; GALIFFE, *Ameaux*, p. 85; NAEF, "Bezanson Hugues," p. 463; E.C., Morts 2, p. 99 (December 29, 1558); see also SORDET, *Dictionnaire*, p. 313].

225. "Coscinomancy," or divination using a sieve and shears, was widely used for finding lost objects. An English document of the period describes the method thus: Balance a sieve on the point of the shears with the handle of the shears to the ground. Two

spells for the fever, and he left the house because he had finished his time. And it may be that he made the servant called Glaudaz pregnant. He does not know for sure whether she is pregnant or not. And he does not keep her anywhere and has not seen her since he left and he does not know whether it was because she was pregnant, and he did not follow her to Jussy, and he had her company. The advice of the Consistory: that he be remanded before the Council.[226]

The wife of Loys Piaget, the sheath-maker.[227]

Because of papistry and prayer. Answers that she offers the prayer before Our Lord and does not want to do anything against God or against society. And says that if she has offended she asks mercy. And that she goes to the church to pray to God for all those who do her good; otherwise she does not understand how she ought to pray. She was admonished.

[f. 112]   *Françoysaz, daughter of Amyed Danel of Jussy and . . .*[228]

Answers that she does not know why she was summoned, and that she likes to go to the sermon and likes it better than the Mass. Did not receive Communion because she is badly dressed and does not dare go with the others. And she stays at home all day, and was not in Bonne the Wednesday before Easter. She has not been in Bonne or Cranves for more than six years. The advice of the Consistory: that she be admonished, and find out whether she knows how to pray to God. Said the Pater, Ave Maria and Credo in Latin. Asked for a term to learn to pray. She was given a term of one month, and then to come here to give an explanation of her confession.

---

persons hold the shears with one finger each and then "ask Peter and Paul whether A, B, or C hath stolen the thing lost; and at the nomination of the guilty person the sieve will turn round" (cited in THOMAS, *Religion*, p. 213).

226. Pierre Guyon was summoned to Council on April 16, 1543, because of the fornication committed with Claudaz, servant of Bezanson Dada. Neither he nor Claudaz appeared, and the Council had "to suspend [their deliberations] in this case until the one and the other can be apprehended" (R.C. 37, f. 62). Finally, on May 22, 1543, Clauda, daughter of François Collin, appeared and asked "that it may please the Council to force Pierre Guyon to accomplish his marriage, and also considering that she is pregnant by him, and otherwise as is contained in her supplication. Ordered that the party be heard and summoned for Friday." Despite this citation no further trace of this affair is found (R.C. Part. 1, f. 57).

227. Her first name is omitted.

228. Name omitted.

Thursday, April 19, 1543

Lord Syndic De La Ryvaz.
Calvin, Champereaulx, De Ecclesia, Genesto,[229] Trippereaulx.
Du Pain, Vernaz, Pensabin, Veyrier, Blandin, De Ulmo, Morel, Orsieres, Du Molard, the officer Vovrey.

Mesre, widow of Lambert Aymoz.[230]

Because François Conte, she and Pernete the Adventuress of the Molard met on the Molard. Answers that she did not make the [sign of the] cross, and she had a wax candle, and this was with the consent of those of the house. She and her children go to the sermons and she does not forbid them to go there, and she has not seen anyone make the cross and meant no harm. Sometimes she gets angry at her children when they waste time. Said the prayer, and does not know the confession. She was given admonitions and remonstrances.

112v] *Tyvent Paquenotz, hosier.*[231]

Because of the fornication he is said to have committed; he goes over the roofs, and it is said he is engaged. Answers no, and he does not go there, and he submits to be at the mercy [of the Consistory] if the contrary is found. And denies that his father told him that he should take this girl. And she is Perissodaz's daughter, and he often goes there because he lives nearby. And he assumes it is she about whom they are talking because some people have told him so. And those who have said it are malicious, and he will maintain them to be so. And his father will not say it. And he did not say the contrary, that his father told him to go across the roofs, and his father never told him that he was unhappy, and he goes willingly. The Consistory is that he be remanded here in a week, and that meanwhile his father be asked what is happening, and that he be forbidden to go.

229. This week the Council decided with regard to Geneston that "because he was only given two hundred florins a year and he takes many pains . . . that his wage be increased by 40 florins, and amount to twelve score florins per year *petit poid.* Also that he must advise the procurator general in his affairs" [R.C. 37, f. 60v (April 16, 1543)].

230. Mesre or Meyre, widow of Lambert Aymoz, hatter; he died before March 7, 1534 [Notaires, de Compois, v. 5, f. 254 (February 5, 1527), and v. 7, f. 380 (March 7, 1534)].

231. First written as "Amblard Paquenot," this is Tyvent Paquenot, alias Dauvin, citizen [Notaires, Jean Duverney, v. 5, ff. 53-53v (May 19, 1543); E.C., Morts 12, p. 299 (June 12, 1580; death of his widow Jaquemaz, aged 56)].

Jaquemaz, daughter of the late Jehan Perrissod. Answers that she has not sworn faith to a husband. She knew Amblard Paquenot, who lives near their house, and she had no words of marriage, since he told her that he would marry when his sister was married, and that it was with his father's consent. And her mother knows well that it was with the consent of the father of the said Paquenot. And he gave her many small things, as she will make evident, such as belts of taffeta, a purse, but not in the name of marriage, although he told her that when his sister was married he would swear faith to the said Jaquemaz. The said Tyvent answers that he went there often and gave her something, not in the name of marriage, although he had had words with her about marriage, that when his sister was married he would indeed like to marry her [f. 113] if it was with the consent of her parents. And if by chance she had said no he would have desisted, and he never spoke to the mother of the said Jaquemaz. And always when he was there, it was always in the presence of respectable people. He gave her some small things. It was a long time ago that he gave her a taffeta belt and purse, without other intention.

Nycolarde, widow of Jehan Perrisod.[232] Answers that she does not know whether there is a treaty of marriage between the said Paquenot and her daughter, although he told her that if his sister were married he would take her in marriage, and he gave her a belt and a purse, and he lives very near them.

The opinion: that Paquenot be asked as above and that all three be remanded to a week from today, and that meanwhile the father of the said Tyvent be spoken to. And that they watch out for scandal. Advised that they not cause such a thing, and that two from here ask the father of the said Tyvent what is happening, and that the mother take care that no scandal arises. Messieurs Mychiel Morel and Vernaz to ask the father whether he will consent to carry out the marriage. The said Tyvent. He was admonished and remanded to Thursday.

The said Jaquemaz. Answers that she has never promised herself to another husband in any way. And that she knew a man named Jullie, a servant of Esperit,[233] and that he wanted her for a wife. And that Master Henri did not know him and she did not make him any promise, nor her mother either,

232. A Nicolarde Perrissod was already encountered above on March 15, 1543. The scribe identified the former as the daughter of "the late Jehan Perrissod."

233. Beginning in 1555 a certain Esperit Nyelle, host of the Orange Tree, was often before the Consistory because of his arguments with his wife and his sister-in-law, but we find no reference to him earlier. See R.Consist. 10, f. 73v (December 12, 1555); R.Consist. 12, f. 125 (December 1, 1557).

and at that he went away. And that the said Jullie gave her nothing except a half-rosary. Remanded to Thursday. [f. 113v] The said Nycolarde, the mother, was given remonstrances and admonitions to make sure they are not together again, and remanded to Thursday.

Anthoyne Chappellaz.

Has three children and is married. Answers that she treats them well and does not beat them or make trouble, and that from bad judgment she beat her child as much as her husband hurt himself in the cart. And she did not cripple it, and if she offended it was from bad judgment. She goes to the sermons when she can. She says the Benedicite,[234] the confession and the prayer, which she did. She was given admonitions and remonstrances to make them frequent the sermons.

Pernon, daughter of Benoyt Bonnet, mason.[235]

Because of opposition to her marriage. Answers that she will prove it by two women, his sisters. It was about ten years ago that he went to the Low Countries and four years ago that he returned. And he said nothing to her and left her to do her will and follow her own good will. And they were together to have a pot of wine with Pollier and the two sisters of the said Robert, and they drank together twice in the name of marriage. And said that she is about 26 and is a poor girl. She says that Tevenin was asleep when they made this promise. And says that she has since refused a good offer of marriage. And she will prove it by his two sisters. And that his father and mother know nothing.

Robert, son of Legier Du Nant,[236] locksmith. Answers that he knows nothing and the girl told him that she drank in marriage with her [sic]. And he returned five years ago, and he never promised her, not a word. And he is ignorant of all she told him. She says that Tevenin was then his guardian, and they never slept together. The said Robert. That he cannot give any news of what she says, and that they were raised together [f. 114] in the street. And that he did not know her and does not remember her and that they did not

---

234. *Benedicite:* a canticle of Lauds and the fore-Mass, drawn from the deuterocanonical text of Daniel 3:57-88 in the Vulgate. On the *Benedicite,* its history and usages, see *D.A.C.L.* II.1, col. 660-664.

235. The mason Benoyt Besson, who lived by the wells of St. Léger, died on September 23, 1550. His daughter Pernette died on April 30, 1552 (E.C., Morts 1, pp. 23 and 60).

236. Robert Dunant, locksmith, citizen, witness at the acknowledgement of Pierre and Claude Gallatin on November 20, 1546 (Titres et Droits, Pa 619, ff. 336-348v).

drink together, and he is 20 years old, and that it is 11 years since he left after the war of the turnips.[237] And that he is out of wardship and has not divided with his brother. And he stayed in Avignon about six years and then returned about five years ago. And if she proves the marriage, it remains for the decision of the Council. The opinion: that they be remanded to Monday before the Council to Monday [sic], and that she bring her witnesses, to examine the said two sisters.

Boniface and Mermete, wife of Anthoyne Gex,[238] daughters of Rolete de Pary.

Because of an argument between them. Answer that they do not wish each other harm, but they are at suit with each other to divide their mother's goods.[239] The advice of the Consistory: that they be told not to cease to love each other despite the suit, and that they make an agreement through respectable people and come here in two weeks to learn whether they have agreed together, and that they put themselves into arbitration and frequent the sermons.

Anthoyne Aymoz.

Because of a sick mare that is at his . . .[240] Answers that he did not know that there was any conjuring, and that there is no need to believe it until the facts are seen, and it is still not cured. And he would not want it to be cured by a wizard or by the devil. And that this was wrongly done; he did not go there, since it was not for him, and he did not do it for evil. And if it was wrongly done he would not have been there. And it is good to be thus informed so as to

237. That is, since about March 1532. In 1534 Ami Joly, purse-maker, was banished because when he should have mounted guard "*ut ceteri cives et burgenses, . . . finxit se egrotum, prout jam in bello quod dicitur des raves fecit* {like other citizens and bourgeois . . . he pretended to be ill, just as he did before in the war called 'of the turnips.'}" Like the editors of the *R.C.* we think that this refers to the period when Joly was admitted to the bourgeoisie, April 1532, when the Duke of Savoy was not allowing food to enter Geneva. On March 8, 1532, Ami Porral and Claude Roset wrote to Robert Vandel, then in Fribourg, that Madame de Savoie "requested the duke to release the food, and in fact the next Monday Faulcon [the ducal herald] came on horseback to the Arve Bridge and said, as Rolet reported to us, that everything would be allowed to pass, except wood . . . Afterwards some baskets of turnips, onions and other small things, and charcoal were welcomed" [*R.C.* XII, pp. 94 and 95 (April 30 and May 5, 1532; *ibid., notes complémentaires,* pp. 585-586 (March 8, 1532); *R.C.* XIII, p. 29 (August 4, 1534)].

238. Anthoyne Gex, cobbler from La Roche, bourgeois [*L.B.,* p. 211 (July 17, 1534)].

239. Their mother, Rolete de Pary (Parys), appeared in Council in 1542 in connection with dividing a house [R.C. 36, f. 29v (June 2, 1542)].

240. Incomplete sentence.

guard oneself another time. Thus he said, as is in the information taken at the lieutenant's bench, because he was present at what is written there and saw it and deposed it in their hands. The advice of the Consistory is that he be admonished to guard himself from the use of enchantment.

f. 114v] *Nycolas Raviot.*[241]

Answers that he had a sick mare and put her to . . .[242] And he gave him nine *gros*, and he even . . .[243] Pierre Lossiez said that he knew well that he would cure her. And a master who came to this city looked at his mare and saw and examined it, and he held the foot when the said man examined it, and he is called Master Glaude.[244] He does not know whether he made any conjuration, and he had to turn to see whether she was cured, and he did not see what he did. And Pierre Lossier of Chêne told him that he, the said Master Glaude, would cure her easily. And Rolanda[245] came and showed the said Master Claude her leg, and he told her that if she knew the Pater and Ave Maria in the fashion of former times that he would see she was cured, and she did and said as she was told. The opinion is that he be commanded that if the said Claude comes back that he inform the Seigneurie.

Jaques Fornet, hatter.

Answers that he was not there and does not know anything about what he was asked about the things written above. Said the prayer and the confession. Rarely goes to the sermons, except sometimes when he can and on Sundays.

Françoys Du Penlouz,[246] *from Evire, remanded by the lieutenant.*

Answers that he has lived with Bernardin Perret[247] and Mygerandi[248] and comes and goes in this city to seek something. He was shown some writ-

---

241. Nycolas Raviot, son of Martin Raviot, hatter, bourgeois, was elected to the CC from the Perron in 1537 [Notaires, de Compois, v. 2, f. 216 (October 8, 1524, contract of marriage between Raviot and Joyeuse Papellier); R.C. 30, f. 168 (February 7, 1537)].

242. Incomplete sentence.

243. Incomplete sentence.

244. Claude Combaz.

245. Andriaz, wife of Roland Reymond.

246. Françoys Du Penloup, notary, received into the bourgeoisie on June 15, 1553 (*L.B.,* p. 239).

247. Bernardin Perret, apothecary, from Chivasso (Turin), received into the bourgeoisie in 1520, member of the LX in 1536, living "on the Place du Pont." According to Léon Gautier he was still living in August 1556, but was absent from Geneva [*L.B.,* p. 190 (October 2, 1520); L. GAUTIER, *Médecine,* p. 448; R.C. 30, f. 166v (February 7, 1537)].

248. Pierre Migerand.

ing that he wrote. Answers yes, and if it is good he wants to maintain it, and it is something to be established and is admitted. And he does not want to test taking of interest by Holy Scripture. And that he would not want to corrupt the Holy Scripture and did not think there was any harm in what he said or wrote on the Holy Scripture, and that he came here for religion. [f. 115] The advice of the Consistory: since he acknowledges it, he should go, and also that he has been at fault and should be careful not to write again against the Holy Scripture. And that the lieutenant be informed how he has abused the Holy Scripture, and he be remanded to Monday before the Council.[249]

Jana, wife of Gerome Aygre, cobbler, and Claudaz, wife of Aymoz Du Nant,[250] armorer.

Because the said Jane complains that the said Claude called her "whore." The said Claudaz answers that she received a blow in saying "whore" to her and . . .[251] And about an apron she ordered for three sous, and when she wanted it she did not want to pay the three sous. Said the prayer and the confession. The said Janaz received a blow in the face the mark of which still shows, and says that the said Glaudaz gave it to her. And that she is well at peace with her husband at present, although formerly they fought each other.[252] And that she goes nowhere and will always be a respectable woman and that she earned six écus as a nurse at Chenalleta's and therefore is well clothed, and if her husband would govern himself well she is ready to sell her skirt to help her husband, because it has been paid for for three months. The opinion is that care be taken and that the other, Claudaz, be summoned and admonished. And touching the other, that she retract here, since she cannot prove the insult, and they should beg mercy of God and pardon each other. And they should pardon each other here, and both be admonished and be reconciled with each other. Jana did not want to pardon her, but asked justice for her injury.

---

249. Du Penloup was summoned to Council on April 23, 1543, because he "alleged in a statement written by him that usury was according to Holy Scripture." The Council ordered him to retract all this publicly (R.C. 37, f. 68v).

250. Claudaz, wife of Aymoz Dunant, armorer, died on October 1, 1551, living then on the Rhône Bridge (E.C., Morts 1, p. 249).

251. Incomplete sentence.

252. In fact the R.C. of January 3, 1541, tells us that Aygre [Esgre] and his wife were then "greatly at odds; therefore, having heard the parties, ordered that they should stay together, living in peace, under penalty of the indignation of the Council" (R.C. 34, f. 189).

Thursday, April 26, 1543

Lord Syndic Checand.
Calvin, Trippereaulx, Genesto, Blancheti, Henri.[253]
Du Pain, Veyrier, Morel, Orsieres, Pensabin, Loermoz, the officer Vovrey.

Pierre Mercier, merchant, citizen of Geneva.

Because of usury.[254] Answers that he does not know whether it is because he gives money at interest, that he was supposed to lend 200 écus, and because someone warned him he did not want to lend it. It was Madame De Mezires. And he will give all his goods to the Seigneurie if he has done it. The advice of the Consistory is, considering that he be admonished, considering that he knew what it is, and that he be admonished.

Loysaz, widow of Tyvent Mallier.

Because of marriage. Answers that François Penlouz says that he swore faith and engaged himself to her and it is not so, since he lived with her and he said nothing at all and did not promise her or swear faith, and she did not want to marry.

The said François Du Penloud. Answers that it is true that he swore faith to her, that he came to her the first day of April, was taken away by certain of her relatives, and should have been there for supper and sworn faith; it was one named Rolet and another. And that he was given about 400 florins in return for giving 40 florins. And at this the said Loyse consented and he shook hands with her and promised faith and loyalty, and she wanted it put in writing, and he gave her an écu, and he would prove it.

Loyse answers that she has reconsidered and says he is nothing but a deceiver, and she has engaged herself to another husband, and she did not shake with him with the intention that he take her in marriage, and she never gave any appearance of marrying. And the écu is redeemed for six

---

253. On April 23, 1543, it was decided to transfer Henri de La Mare to Jussy. The day after this session of the Consistory Henri de La Mare, "according to the good will of the Seigneurie and Consistory, presented himself to obey that which he was ordered, to go serve God in the church of Jussy." At his request Calvin was charged with presenting him to the congregation, along with the councillors Jean Philippin and Jean Lambert and the new castellan, François Paquet [R.C. 37, f. 68 and f. 74v (April 23 and 27, 1543)].

254. Mercier was well known to the Consistory and the Seigneurie because of various questions of money and of marriage. In this connection the Council reprimanded Mercier in 1544 for having warned a man "not to leave Geneva without paying him a debt" [R.C. 38, f. 173v (April 24, 1544)].

quarts, her sister has it, and she does not know whether it was hers. And this was for a *quarteron* of wine, and it [f. 116] was given to a girl, and she kept it carefully and her sister has it. And she never drank with him in marriage, although they made a fricassee, and it was a night of worry(?) and she did not want to eat. And he wanted her for a wife, which she refused, although they made a man get up who was in bed to make the said marriage. And he gave her nothing in the name of marriage and they did not drink in the name of marriage.

The opinion of the Consistory is, since she denies everything, that the witnesses who were present be examined, and that they be put under oath. Rolet Du Penlouz[255] and Pierre Billiod,[256] both *habitants* of Geneva, from Evires, witnesses. The sister Legiere, sister of the said Loyse, and a girl. Remanded to Monday to the Council.[257]

On the answer that Paquenotz and the Perrissodes made to Lord Claude Du Pain, which is not sufficient.[258]

The opinion of the Consistory is that the said Tyvent be exhorted to consent to the completion of the said marriage, or if not that they be prevented from being together again, and that someone talk again to the father to see whether he wants to consent. And that he refrain from going there until the said marriage is accomplished. Tyvent Paquenot. Asked whether he wants the said marriage accomplished. Answers that he wants to take her as his wife if it is his father's pleasure and he has not promised anything else, and that when his sister is married he desires the said girl. And that he has decided to speak to his father, and if it pleases his father he will do it.

255. Rolet Du Penloup, bourgeois, came from Evires (H.-S.) like Françoys Du Penloup, but was the son of Claude and not of Jean like the latter [*L.B.*, p. 221 (September 17, 1540)].

256. Pierre Billiod, from Evires en Bornes, cobbler on the Perron, received into the bourgeoisie in 1547, died in 1566 at the age of 70 [*L.B.*, p. 228 (June 24, 1547); E.C., Morts 6, p. 171 (August 17, 1566)].

257. Having heard the witnesses, Du Penloup and "the said Loyse with her present husband Querdi," the Council ordered "that the said Loyse should be freed, condemning her to [pay] the expenses" [R.C. Part. 1, f. 52v (May 14, 1543)].

258. This concerns the matrimonial case between Tyvent Paquenot and Jaquemaz Perrissod, presented in Consistory on April 19, 1543.

Colleta Chabodaz.[259]

Because of the sermons. Answers that she goes on Sundays when she can. She sometimes goes to market. And her son is on the way and did not want to come; he is staying with . . .[260]

Donne Aymaz Charletaz should be summoned before the Council on Monday.

116v] *Andriaz, wife of Roland Reymond.*[261]

Answers that no barber is treating her leg except Martin Cusin and another who is treating the gout, that he gave her a plaster that he made for an animal and did not speak words. And he had her say the Pater and Ave Maria in the fashion of former times, which she did. And she said the Pater and the Ave Maria, and was not cured by this and still is not. And she said the Ave Maria with good intentions, and if she did it she begs mercy of God. Said the prayer and the confession, and does not know whether the said Nycolas's[262] horse was cured.

Anthoyne Chenuz, called Gurdillion.

Because of superstition. Answers that he knows nothing about it and that the Consistory is badly informed, and he said the Pater as it is said [today]. And he did not say that he said that there would be so many more ministers than priests and that they did not want to visit the sick. And those who say these words are not his friends, to be charged with this. And he does not pray for the dead and he has no doubts about religion. Remonstrances that he frequent the sermons.

Jane, wife of Gurdillion, daughter of Roland Evrard.

Because of papistry and muttering at the sermons. Answers that she holds by the faith of Jesus Christ and that she says the Pater and the Credo. Said the prayer and the confession.

259. Probably Colleta Berthier, widow of Michel Chabod. See above, December 19, 1542.
260. Name omitted. Her son, Jean Chabod, apparently lived at the house of Jehan de La Ville (see below, May 3, 1543).
261. Andriaz, widow of Roland Reymond, died on July 4, 1562, aged 90. Her death certificate says that she was the mother of Pierre Jean Jessé, several times councillor and syndic in 1555. Roland Reymond, merchant haberdasher, from Grezin (Ain), inhabitant of Saint Gervais, was admitted to the bourgeoisie on December 12, 1514 (E.C., Morts 5, p. 19; *L.B.*, p. 180; ROGET II, p. 331; IV, p. 339 *et passim*).
262. Nycolas Raviot; see above, April 19, 1543.

Tybaudaz, daughter of Glaude Le Guex, wife of Bonbrillez.[263]

Because of the sermons. Answers that she goes to the sermons, and her husband, and she was at the sermon at St. Gervase Sunday. Does not know who preached, and she was indisposed, and she was at the chief sermon at St. Peter's the previous Sunday and does not know what he said, and she recognized and names Monsieur Calvin. And it is true that she speaks about feasts, vigils, Lent and other papal ceremonies, and she knows how to pray as her father and mother taught her. Said the prayer in Latin [f. 117] and the Ave Maria all in Latin. And she received Holy Communion like the others. And she has two children, a daughter and a son. The daughter is 18, who was with Master Adam; it is three years since she left this city and went to Saint Julien, and she lives in Romont now. She does not know when she left Master Adam's, and she left without her permission, and she does not know whether she has been here since, and she did not show herself to her. And she does not know whether her said daughter is pregnant, and some people have indeed told her she is pregnant. And her son is in Lyon. And she did not deliver her daughter's child. Someone told her that she bore a child by Master Adam, her master. And she had the child she does not know where, and she has not been at her house for three years. And the said Adam took her and left the place where she lived, and she did not know the child had come, although Bonbrele, her husband, told her when it came. And she heard it from those of this city; when she has thought a little; at present she cannot say. It was Gervayse who told her.

The opinion of the Consistory: that she be given a term to learn to pray and find out where her daughter was brought to bed, and abstain from Communion until she knows how to pray to the Lord, and ask Bonbrely, her husband, by whom the child is and where it is nursed and report on this. One month.

Jehan Colin, called Pollier,[264] *farm laborer, bourgeois of Geneva, from the village of Etaux.*

Because of blasphemy and papistries. Answers that he does not know why he was summoned, and he does not blaspheme and will correct himself. Goes to the sermons and was there twice last Sunday, and Calvin preached; does not know what he said in his sermon. And he does not curse the preachers or others at all. Knows the first faith [confession] that was said in former times. He has married daughters. And he has always received Communion.

---

263. Jehan Grissaney, called Bonbrillez (Bombrille).
264. Jean Colin, admitted to the bourgeoisie on January 26, 1518 (*L.B.*, p. 187).

Said the prayer and the confession in Latin and the Ave Maria. The advice of the Consistory is that he be interdicted from Communion and that he appear here on some occasion; that he strive to learn to pray to God within three weeks.

[f. 117v]   *Richardaz, wife of Pierre Rydoz, daughter of the said Jehan Colin, called Pollier.*

Because of the sermons. Answers that she goes to the sermons when she can. She has four children, and was at the sermon on Sunday morning of last week; last Sunday she was indisposed because of a mist and was ill. Said the prayer and the confession, and is not at all papist, and has not murmured against the Gospel at all, and she is not mistress over her father. She was admonished to frequent the sermons.

Clauda de Cabanage, from near La Roche, living in this city, has two children out in the country.

Answers that she acts toward God like the others and goes to the sermons, and on Sunday was at the sermon at St. Peter's, and the husband of the woman who had the meadow preached, and she does not know what he said. Said the prayer and the confession, and is not angry with anyone. Remonstrances to frequent the sermons.

Moneta Furjodaz.

Papistical, about feasts. Answers that she does not keep feasts, goes to the sermon when she can and was there this morning, and does not fight at all except on the Molard. True that a good man who lives near her shop did not want to remove himself from over her shop. She does not believe that Lent was made by the commandment of God, and she has received Communion and means to receive it. Frequenting the sermons.[265]

Tevene, wife of Cristoble Lochet, day-laborer.

Because of blaspheming the Lord. Answers that they fight among themselves when they are together, and she does not blaspheme. And as for a boy she treats badly, this must be punished because it is a false report, and she does not let him misbehave, and he does not want to believe her. And she did not try to strike him with the stone, and she was very angry be-

---

265. It is impossible to say whether it was for her thoughts on religion, her disputes on the Molard, or another reason, but already in 1537 one finds that "Moneta Furjod said many words about which it was decided that the procurator should obtain information" [R.C. 30, f. 245v (June 1, 1537)].

cause he did not want to do it. And goes to the sermons on Sundays, but not the other days. She begged mercy of God and the Seigneurie. [f. 118] Said the prayer, and the confession almost not at all. Received Communion. She was admonished to learn to pray and to appear before the next Communion.

Andrica, daughter of Jehan de Mengoz, called the Adventuress.

Answers that her mother,[266] who was summoned instead of her, has been ill for three weeks and could not come. Said the prayer and the confession. And that she met the wife of Roz Porral[267] the mason near the Magdalen and did not make a cross.

Thursday, May 3, 1543

Lord Syndic Checand.
Calvin, Genesto, D'Ecclesia, Blancheti, Trippereaulx.
Baudichon, Vernaz, Pensabin, Veyrier, De Lormoz, Molard, Morel, the officer Vovrey.

Jehan Grissaney, citizen of Geneva, called Bonbrillez.[268]

Because of his wife's daughter who has had a child.[269] Answers that Bizatz and another went there when his wife died, who asked to see him and wanted him to give drink to Thibauda, his present wife, as a wife. And she had a son who lived in Gex, and he never saw his wife's daughter who was in Fribourg, which daughter came to touch him and said that she was the daughter of Thibauldaz, his wife. And he does not know whether the said

266. Pernete de Mengoz, called the Adventuress.
267. Roz Porral was a witness of a notarial act between Amblard Bonivard and Jehan Hugonier in 1543, transcribed in CHAPONNIÈRE, "Bonivard," p. 291.
268. The name of Jehan Grissaney, called Bonbrille, is often recorded, but without giving a precise account of this person. He was accused, apparently wrongly, of having taken part in the rising of June 6, 1540, which put an end to the power and the life of Jean Philippe and his party. In 1544 he asked to be recompensed for his vigilance in informing the Council about foreigners passing through the city. The following year he complained of a certain Lucas, from Basel, servant of Michel Varo, who had made Pernette, the daughter of Michel Chapuis, then Grissaney's wife, pregnant. He died in 1554 [R.C. 34, f. 314 (June 28, 1540); GALIFFE, *Ameaux*, p. 5, n.1; R.C. Part. 1, f. 294v and f. 306v (July 22 and August 18, 1545); E.C., Morts 1, p. 162 (June 2, 1554)].
269. It was the daughter of Tybauda Le Guex who had the child. See above, April 26, 1543.

daughter has had any child except by hearsay. This daughter is in Fribourg and serves a master near the town hall of Fribourg. And he does not know where the said child is she is said to have had, her said daughter, because the said Thibaudaz was then servant to the said Bonbrillez. And he goes to the sermons on Sundays, and one must not blaspheme; he does not blaspheme. And if his wife sheltered her daughter without his knowledge he will never live with her. He was at the wars for a long time. He is scatter-brained, and a respectable man. And numerous other words. Says that he knows how to pray to God in German and Italian and as his father and mother taught him, that is in Latin. Said it in Latin. [f. 118v] And he receives Communion like a good Christian and he lives well, and he wants to be wise because he has been foolish. The advice of the Consistory is that he be admonished to refrain from blasphemy, drunkenness, learn to pray and frequent the sermons. And that he not receive Communion until the time after next, and remonstrances, that he be given a term to [learn to] pray to the Lord.

Aymaz, daughter of Pierre Megeoz.[270]

Because she does nothing but fight with her mother, her grandmother. Answers that her grandmother commands her to do nothing she does not do and that she does not complain of her. She promises to do better. Said the prayer and the confession, weeping; said that she would do better and be obedient to her father and mother.

Donne Jana Gentiaz.

Because of the sermons. Answers that she goes when she can, because sickness and old age prevent her, because she cannot go and cannot support herself. And she no longer holds by papistries. Knows how to pray as her father and mother taught her in former times. When she prays she says the Pater and Ave Maria, keeps Lent and prays for the dead.

Claudaz, wife of Jehan Colin, called Pollier.

Because of the sermons. Answers that she does not go every day, but was there today. And she fights with no one, nor with her husband, except with her husband's daughter. Has indeed said that she sometimes falls short and is very discontented, and she has no conflicts with her neighbors. Said the prayer and the confession. Remonstrances to frequent the sermons.

270. A Pierre Mege, cobbler, became a bourgeois in 1559 [*L.B.*, p. 264 (May 9, 1559)].

Boniface and Mermete, daughters of Roletaz de Paris.

Answer that they are not in accord because of one of their husbands who have not been here. Touching Communion, if their husbands come, they will present themselves Tuesday or Thursday; otherwise they will not be received for Communion.

[f. 119]   *Jehan Chaboz,*[271] *son of Colletaz Chabodaz, of this city, living near the Magdalen, with Master Jehan de La Villa.*

Answers that he does what his mother commands him according to right and reason. He sometimes goes to the sermons. Said the prayer and the confession. He was given remonstrances and admonitions.

Tuesday, May 8, 1543

Lord Syndic Checand.
Calvin, Champereaulx, Genesto, Albert Pupin,[272] Trippereaulx.
Morel, Vernaz, Blandin, Veyrier, Molard, Pensabin, De Loermoz, Baudichon, Orsieres, Alexandre the watchman.[273]

The two daughters of Roletaz de Pari.[274]

Because of their quarrel about an agreement. Answer that they are not in agreement and that the wife of Anthoyne Gex[275] wanted to wait for the Suprèmes Appellations. The opinion of the Consistory: that they look into their consciences, that they refrain from receiving the next Communion.

---

271. A certain Jean Cherbonner, called Chabod, was executed before February 25, 1546, but no evidence permits us to identify him with this Jean Chabod [R.C. 41, f. 23 (February 25, 1546)].

272. Abel Poupin, from Seiches in Agenois, minister of Geneva from 1543 until his death in 1556 (he reentered France in 1547, but was obliged to flee in 1548). A devout disciple of Calvin, he was known for his impetuous sermons and character. On April 16, 1543, Poupin was named in place of Nicolas Vandert as minister of Jussy and "in all that may be necessary in the church of Geneva" (R.C. 37, f. 61). But after only a week Poupin was replaced in Jussy and recalled to the city because he was found "good enough to preach in Geneva," and on April 27 it was ordered that he be presented to the congregation [R.C. 37, f. 68 and f. 74v (April 23 and 27, 1543); see also HAAG VIII, p. 310; R.C.P. I and II, *passim*].

273. Probably Alexandre Davonex, watchman.

274. Boniface and Mermete, daughters of Rolete de Paris.

275. Mermete de Paris.

And admonish them to exhort their husbands to agree, and that their husbands be made to come on Thursday.

Henri Philippe, the pawnbroker on the Molard, because of the poor man of the Molard, tailor.

Answers that there is a man, a tailor, who does nothing but talk and joke, and one time he stood by this man and told him that he should not make so much noise, and he did not insult him, as an old man(?). And he was at the sermon Sunday at vespers, because in the morning he was not well, and last Thursday. And on second thought he was not there. The advice of the Consistory is that he be told to correct himself from now on and not curse as he is reported to do, and that he be admonished.

Magdeleyne, wife of Girard Le Mugnier.[276]

Because of the sermons. Answers that she goes to the sermons on Sundays when she can with the others and does not mock the preachers and does not fight with her husband. And last Sunday she was at the first preaching at St. Gervase and learned the Pater. [f. 119v] Said the prayer, and the confession she scarcely knows or very little. She was admonished to know the confession within three weeks.

Pernete, daughter of Pierre Mathieu, of the Vuache.

Answers that she has been in this city about six years, and is a servant of Françoys Bonjehan on the Bourg du Four, and has served at the houses of the syndic[277] and Françoys the doctor,[278] and that she would like to go without this, and that no one debauched her in the service of the said Master Françoys or the said Monsieur Du Molard, and she wants to be punished if she [is] at all stained with fornication.

Jehan L'Ostoz, citizen of Geneva.

Answers that he has done as he was commanded last March 1.

276. A Just Mugnyer, son of the late Girard, from Moussy (H.-S.), was admitted to the bourgeoisie in 1547 [*L.B.*, p. 234 (August 11, 1547)].
277. Hudriod Du Mollard.
278. François Chappuis, doctor.

Thursday, May 10, 1543

Lord Syndic Checand.
Calvin, De Ecclesia, Blanchet,[279] Genesto, Henri, Trippereaulx, Pupin.
Orsieres, Vernaz, Du Pain, Baudichon, Du Molard, Veyrier, De Loermoz,
Pensabin, the officer Vovrey.

Donne Aymaz Charletaz, daughter of D[omaine] d'Arloz.

Because of usury,[280] and that she is a rebel against the Seigneurie.
Begged mercy of God and the Seigneurie. Answers that she was ill and did
not lend at interest and gave her money to the merchants to use and they give
her what they choose, because she has nothing to live on otherwise and has
no other lands or goods. And that no one asks her anything or complains of
her, and she has been a widow 40 years, and then she had 300 écus and now
does not have 300 florins. And she submits herself to prison if she has ever
spoken against the Gospel, and she left the neighborhood of Faucigny to
come here to the Gospel.

279. This is the last session of the Consistory which Blanchet attended before becoming minister of the plague hospital. The danger being past, the plague hospital had
been closed the previous February 23, but already on April 20 the plague appeared again
at the inn of the Rose and the Seigneurie took measures to combat the epidemic. Soon the
Council wanted to send a minister to the plague hospital, but the rumor was "that there
are preachers who have said that rather than go to the plague hospital they would go to
the devil, and the other in Champel [where criminals were then executed]. Ordered to
find out whether this is so, and if it is proven they should be dismissed from their ministry." Finally, on May 11, Blanchet was sent to the hospital, where he died about June 1
[R.C. 37, folios 21v, 66v, 70, 82, 89, and 110 (February 23, April 20 and 24, May 2 and 11,
and June 1, 1543)]. The Council then asked the ministers to elect a minister, other than
Calvin, to replace Blanchet [R.C. 37, folios 110 and 112-112v (June 1, 1543)]. On June 2
the ministers proposed to send there a "faithful one" from France (R.C. 38, f. 113). Three
days later the ministers returned to Council and announced that "none of them has the
steadfastness to go to the plague hospital, although their office requires them to serve God
and His church both in prosperity and in necessity until death, and also it is necessary to
elect and establish another in the place of Master Pierre Blanchet." The minister Geneston
"offers himself to go there, providing the election is made according to God, and if the lot
falls on him," but the Council, after having prayed "God to give them more steadfastness
for the future," decided to accept the one presented by the ministers [R.C. 37, folios
117-117v (June 5, 1543)].

280. Already in 1525 Aima, widow of Amédée Charlet, bourgeois of Sallanches, lent
money at interest, and at least one of her acts was signed in the house of Domaine d'Arlod
[Notaires, de Compois, v. 4, f. 144 (September 13, 1525); *ibid.* (November 25, 1525)]. According to GALIFFE (I, p. 311) she was the sister (not the daughter) of Domaine d'Arlod,
which seems to us much more reasonable.

[f. 120] *Loyse, daughter of Anthone Querlaz, wife of Aymoz Marquet.*

Does not know why she was summoned, and because she fights constantly with her sister-in-law. Answers that she does not fight at all with her and has never had any dissension with her. And has no scruples about the law and lives according to God, and also goes to the sermons often. Said that she does not presently know how to say the prayer, because it is said in Evian as it was here in former times, and she does not pray to the Virgin Mary, and God is stronger. Admonitions and exhortations.[281]

Claudaz, daughter of Mauris Beau of Cruseilles, wife of Claude, son of Françoys Exerton, of Neydens.

Answers that she was abused there by her husband, and being always beaten she came here to earn her living as well as she could. And she left her husband and her children because she was always beaten and mistreated by them, and Bonivard,[282] her host, did not know her, and his wife sheltered her in her house from pity and for the love of God, and she pays them no rent or expenses, and had her wedding dress that she pawned for 20 *gros* to live, and since then the said man sold the dress. And she has not decided to have her child here and wants to withdraw to her parents. She was commanded to return to her husband.

Jehan Villiet.

Because of rebellion and other things. Answers that he could not come then because he had business. He was admonished whether he did not say here about a year ago that he swore that he was not nor knew nor fornicated at the Amycis',[283] that he called God to confound him if it was so. And he did it wickedly by his confession.

---

281. In Council the previous March 2 "there was discussion of the wife of Marquet and of Aymoz Plonjon, prisoners, because of certain words against Master Caulvin, that is that he had said that the time would come when women would go [for sex] to asses and horses, as they have answered. Resolved that they be admonished to beg mercy of God and justice and also that they go to the Consistory on Thursday, paying their expenses" [R.C. Part 1, f. 16 (March 2, 1543)].

282. François Bonivard.

283. This refers to the case of fornication involving Huguine Amici, her cousin Huguine Dupont, and various men; see above, April 20, 1542.

[f. 120v] *Noble François Paquet,[284] the castellan of Jussy, has presented the wardens for Jussy.*

First Françoys Falcaz,[285] Jehan Lullier, Bernard Dymiez,[286] Amied Milliaud. They were given the rules and manner of living according [to God] in the said place of Jussy. And sent to the Council to take the oath.[287]

Master Bastien de Villa, from Nantua, surgeon.

Answers that he was not in this city and wants to be whipped [if he was]. It was about three years ago that he promised himself to a girl at Barrachin's. And if it is proven that he espoused another. Answers that he wants, that he never married her and he wants to prove that she was married to one who lives in Versonnex at Acquenee's house. Answers that he uses no black arts, and he studied with Fossent and Agrippa.[288] And he never spun

284. Noble François Paquet replaced Noble Jean Lambert as castellan of Jussy on February 15, 1543. On February 6, 1543, the Council had decreed that castellans should serve for three years, but already on January 25, 1544, Paquet asked permission to resign. On March 21, 1544, Pierre Sommareta took his place (R.C. 37, f. 6 and f. 18; R.C. 38, f. 44 and f. 130). A François Paquet, coachman, from Collonges, was received into the bourgeoisie in 1498 [*L.B.,* p. 133 (March 20, 1498)]. See also BALARD, pp. lxxvii and lxxiii, n. 1.

285. A François Falcat was among the first in Jussy to accept the Reform. Converted by Henri de La Mare, he worked with the preacher to bring the others of his village to the Reform. Already procurator of Jussy in 1536, he lent his hand to the composition of the ordinances of reform at Jussy in 1539. He had possibly been a priest before the Reformation, but he is probably confused with Pierre Falcat [CORBAZ, pp. 60, 82, 89; HEYER, p. 226, n. 4; R.C. XIII, pp. 439, 516 (February 14 and April 3, 1536)].

286. Bernard Dimier was still warden in Jussy in 1546 [R.C. 41, f. 48 (March 12, 1546)].

287. On April 27, 1543, the Council resolved to name four subjects of Jussy "proper for . . . watching over the delinquents," but there is no reference to the oath of the wardens (R.C. 37, f. 74v).

288. Heinrich Cornelius Agrippa von Nettesheim (1486-1535 or 1536), the famous doctor, astrologer, alchemist, philosopher, jurist, theologian, and soldier who served as a model for Marlowe's Doctor Faustus. Born in Cologne and having passed through half the countries of Europe, he arrived in Geneva in the spring of 1521, took his second wife there and became the center of a circle of men of letters. Having lost his hope of receiving a pension from the Duke of Savoy, he left Geneva at the beginning of 1523. He subsequently established himself in Lyon and became one of the doctors of Louise de Savoie, mother of Francis I. He lost Louise's favor when he refused to predict the future for her, and was shown the door in 1528. He resumed his wandering, dying in Grenoble in 1535 or at latest the beginning of 1536. It is not known where Bastien de Villa encountered Agrippa. It is not certain that Agrippa was a doctor of medicine, but he was incontestably learned in this science. See NAUERT, especially pp. 10-11, 71-79, 84-101. See also NAEF, *Origines* I, pp. 309-351, but Nauert is to be preferred with respect to Agrippa's religious ideas and his relations with the Reformers (NAUERT, pp. 157-193, especially 158 and 170-174).

the sieve.[289] Gave a drink. Answered that he ate at a wedding that was prepared for him and engaged himself to her and did not marry her because of the other at Barrachin's whom he took to Gex. And that he wants to take and marry the first girl. The opinion of the Consistory is that he bring an affidavit that the other woman he married and took to Gex was married when he did it, and that he get it from the Consistory of Gex.

Jane, daughter of Mathieu Milliaud. Answers that Master Bastien swore faith to her and promised to take her and gave her a sou in the name of marriage. That he that he [sic] wanted to take her to Nantua, and letters were written, received by Egrege Martin de Deserto, and he indeed wanted to take her to his house if she would consent. [f. 121] The said Bastien said that he would indeed like her to be his wife if it was the pleasure of God, and he never knew her carnally. And he would like to marry her here and not elsewhere. And by Thursday[290] bring an affidavit of the Consistory of Gex that the other woman was married.[291]

Petremand Pellouz.

Because of the grudge he carries against Claude Philippe.[292] Answers that he pardons him according to God for his offense. However, if he came

289. On this method of divination see the note in the case of Pierre Guyon, above, April 12, 1543.

290. Added interlinearly: Wednesday.

291. Bastien de Villaz, called the Good Wizard, had been imprisoned on December 23, 1541, for having failed to appear in Consistory. He was freed the following January 10 on condition of appearing in Consistory (minutes lost) (R.C. 35, f. 442 and f. 445, *ad dies*). On May 17, 1543, he was recalled to Consistory (see below), and a little later saw himself banished from Geneva chiefly because he "uses things against God in his trade," and also because he "makes himself a doctor and surgeon, and knows nothing of the whole matter" [R.C. 37, f. 102 and f. 105v (May 22 and 25, 1543)]. L. GAUTIER (*Médecine*, p. 278) recounts that Bastien de Villaz "was several times banished under pain of whipping between 1541 and 1546. Naïve clients accused him of having made them ill in order to cure them later by magical methods."

292. Claude Philippe, son of Captain General Jean Philippe (chief of the Philippins, executed in 1540). Claude Philippe often asked the Council to permit him to return to Geneva after he was banished with his brother André. While in exile the brothers Philippe were accused of having threatened traveling Genevans. Finally, in March 1544, the two brothers were rehabilitated thanks to the intervention of the Bernese, promising to pay a fine of 500 écus, which they had difficulty paying [GALIFFE I, p. 308; ROGET II, p. 114; R.C. 37, folios 50, 53, 53v (April 4, 6, 7, 1543) and f. 145 (July 5, 1543); R.C. 38, f. 5 (December 12, 1543), folios 76 (February 15, 1544), 100v, 105v and 107, 111 and 111v, 142v (March 4, 6, 8, 29, 1544), 227 (May 30, 1544), 236 (June 3, 1544)].

across him he could revenge himself and receive Communion as a good Christian should, and since he is always threatened.

The two daughters of Roletaz de Pari and the husband of the younger, named Anthoyne de Gex.

The shearer's wife answered that she did not find anyone to go to Gex to make her husband come, and therefore has not been able to come present herself. And since they are so close they will await the sentence. They were exhorted to come to some agreement. The said De Gex said that he would like to stick with the form of the will and of the two sentences already given. The advice of the Consistory is that before they come before the Council they be made to come to some agreement by arbitration, and admonish the older separately. Anthoyne Gex: the said De Gex consented to arbitration, and they will each choose two men, and the Consistory will give them half a year from next Friday and Saturday. The said wife of the shearer consented.

Jehan and Claude Curtet, brothers.

Whether they are still good friends and that they are still good friends [sic]. Answer that they have always been good friends since the Consistory commanded them to be.

Jehan Gonyn, from Viuz, boatman living in the Fusterie.

Answers that he is married and has two children and behaves himself and does not treat his wife badly and never wanted to strike her with a knife and that he has no neighbor who complains about him and that he never wanted to strike her. [f. 121v] And that he does get angry with her, so that he once wanted to box her ear. Goes to the sermons and was there Saturday, and has not been to the sermon for three Sundays, and it has been a fortnight, and he learned to do good. Said the prayer and the confession, what he could say of it. He was given admonitions and remonstrances.

Mermet de Loermoz, citizen of Geneva.[293]

Because of disobedience to his mother and brother and idleness. Answers that he wants to be punished if this is found true, and they have not taken much trouble to find him a master, and he wants to obey their commandments and does not want to be idle, and is obedient to his mother. He was admonished.

---

293. Probably the son of Mermet de Ulmo (Latinized form of De Loermoz) and of Dominique de Vaulx, and the brother of Just de Ulmo.

Merma, the widow of George Plaintemps, called Lombard.[294]

Was remanded before Easter to appear here the Thursday before Pentecost. Said the prayer and . . .[295] She believes entirely in God. Said the prayer, but none of the confession.

Pentecost.

The ordinance for Communion: for Sunday, May 13, 1543, it was ordered as for last Easter.[296]

Thursday, May 17, 1543

Lord Checand.
Calvin, Genesto, Pupin, Trippereaulx.
Baudichon, Pensabin, Blandin, the officer.

Touching the marriage of Master Bastien de Villa the surgeon and his wife, the daughter of Mathieu Milliaud.[297]

Having seen the affidavit of the Consistory of Gex[298] brought by Jehan Becho on behalf of the said Bastien and Janne, it was decided by the Consistory that, since there is no impediment, they should be remanded to the Council [f. 122] to Monday, and the witnesses who testified to the truth be summoned for next Monday. The witnesses are Loys Barrachin and Tevenyn.

Was also proposed that for a time the said Consistory cease, unless a case of importance arises, and then summon the Consistory to attend to affairs.[299]

294. Maillet is wrong; this is Merma, mother and not widow of George Plantens, called Lombard. She had been correctly identified as the widow of François Plantens at her previous appearance before the Consistory (above, March 22, 1543). Georges Plantens was still alive at this time, and may have been married to a certain Bernardine who died a widow in 1567 at the age of 70 [E.C., Morts 7, p. 60 (February 25, 1567)].
295. Incomplete sentence.
296. On May 11 the Council ordered that Communion be celebrated and that men be appointed to administer it (R.C. 37, f. 89).
297. Jane, daughter of Mathieu Milliaud.
298. A copy of the affidavit follows at the end of this session.
299. The Consistory thus gave way to the epidemic of plague that had already reigned in Geneva for some time. The epidemic began in the fall of 1542, and after a lull it attained its peak between September 1544 and July 1545 and lasted until September 1546. L. Gautier (*Médecine*, pp. 129-130) describes the reaction of the Seigneurie: "In

Contents of the affidavit made by the Consistory of Gex, sent by Jehan Becho at the instance of Master Bastien de Ville, doctor, called the Good Wizard; case of the marriage of the bastard daughter of Mathieu Milliaux:

We, Jehan Machon, lieutenant of the Respectable Lord Ambroyse Imhoffz,[300] *bailli* and governor of the barony of Gex, Jaques Camerle,[301] Laurent Martin, Jehan Chappuis, Gracian Bel, judges and consistorial auditors of the *bailliage* of Gex, deputies for our very dread Lords and Princes of Bern. To all who see these presents, be it manifest that today, the date of these, appeared before us the Honorable Jehan Bechod, bourgeois of Geneva, in the name of Janne, daughter of Mathieu Milliot of Geneva, against Loyse, daughter of the late Jehan Du Freney of Cerdon, living in Gex, saying that about two years ago the said Loyse opposed a solemnization of marriage in the church, it being announced in the customary manner between Master Bastiain, doctor, on one part, and the said Janne Milliot on the other part, saying that the said Master Bastiain had previously promised marriage to the aforesaid opposant opposant [sic], requiring the said Loyse to declare her said opposition before your lordships, who will administer justice to her, asking her to respond. And on the other part appeared the said Loyse, who says and answers she is not at all opposed to the said proclamation and banns, although the Honorable Jehan Blanc, officer of Geneva, in her name without her knowledge or consent, as the said Jehan Blanc told the said Loyse, [f. 122v] opposed the aforesaid solemnization. To which account the aforesaid Loyse answered: "You have done wrong, since I did not command you to make and did not intend to make any objection to the said marriage." Then the said Jehan Blanc answered the said Loyse: I did it by command of Loys Barrachin, your master, who had me do this." Also confessing since the aforesaid opposition that in this town of Gex in the presence of people wor-

---

1543 and 1544 work on the fortifications was interrupted to avoid contagion. . . . When the evil became grave the exercise of lower justice was suspended, that is, the court of the Lord Lieutenant; but the Council never ceased to sit and decide criminal cases and important civil affairs. . . . As for the sermons, if their number diminished, this was only while the severity of the epidemic thinned too much the ranks of the faithful." See also *ibid.,* p. 109.

300. Ambroise Imhoff was one of the Bernese delegates sent to Geneva in 1541 to resolve questions of jurisdiction in the lands around Geneva conquered by Bern. During the 1560s he served as a Bernese ambassador and also as a member of the Small Council of Bern. We do not know when he held the office of *bailli* [ROGET I, pp. 285 and 286, n. 1 ; *M.C.L.* III, pp. 168 (February 20, 1560) and 213 (October 22, 1564)].

301. Jaques Camerle, also called Camrol, pastor in Gex since 1537 (HERMINJARD IV, p. 346, n. 26, and p. 299, n. 13; *ibid.* II, p. 181, n. 1.

thy of faith she swore to and promised as her husband the aforesaid Master Bastian, who with the aforesaid Loys Barrachin her master had given her to understand that her husband, previously espoused by her, had gone from life to death, which was not found true when later it was examined thoroughly judicially here and elsewhere. For which reason she does not wish or claim to impose an obstacle to the previously cited marriage. Which things aforesaid were stated to the said Jehan Bechod appearing in the aforesaid name, as in testimony signed by our secretary, whom we, the said lords judges and auditors, have thus commanded to seal [them] with the seal of the *bailli* of Gex; the seal nonetheless should confer faith on these, since faith was thus commanded. Mychaud Machon, s. 6 s.[302] for the copying and seals. Also to the judges and remission to the officer, 7 sous. [f. 123]

In cloister
Thursday, July 5, 1543[303]

Lord Syndic Checand.
Champereaulx, De Ecclesia, Genesto,[304] Pupin, Tripperaulx.
Morel, Du Pain, Baudichon, Orsieres, Jehan Molard, Just de Loermoz, Blandin, the officer Vovrey.

Pierre Bard,[305] *weaver, from the Vuache, Chevrier,*[306] habitant *of Geneva for six years.*

Has two maids from the Vuache, had a servant who left about six days ago who is said to have sworn faith to the sister of Julliana,[307] and the maid he swore faith to did not stay with him in his service. He goes to the sermons on Sundays and not the other days. Said the prayer. Answers that they did

---

302. Possible reading: Mychaud Machon, secretary, 6 sous, the same abbreviation being used for two different words.

303. This session of the Consistory is the first since May 17, 1543. On July 3, 1543, without other explanation, the Council asked "that the Consistory be held in the cloister of St. Peter's" (R.C. 37, f. 144).

304. On August 3, 1543, one reads that Geneston was infected with plague and had lost his wife (R.C. 37, f. 169).

305. There are few references to Pierre Bard, and we cannot establish his presence in Geneva until July 28, 1543, the date when he was ordered to "leave the house that belonged to Noble François Bonivard within ten days" (R.C. 36, f. 81).

306. That is, the neighboring villages of the Vuache and Chevrier (H.-S.). Bard had probably said that he came from the Vuache and then specified that he came from Chevrier.

307. Johanete Frilot, promised wife of Pierre Bard.

not fornicate at his house, the two servants. The opinion of the Consistory is that he be questioned more sharply and that they be summoned here on some day, that he strive to know better how to pray to the Lord and that he make his wife and family come to know how they are instructed in the Word of the Lord. He was given two weeks to learn to pray to the Lord.

Pierre Berthet, called Thalabard, from Valleiry, habitant *of Geneva, armorer.*

Answers that he is innocent, that he does not still visit Mabuectaz, and he wants to be punished if he is stained with fornication with her. And he never spoke to her but once, and let him be hanged if he returns there. Asked where he went with Mabuectaz on Sunday a week ago, and they stayed all day, from morning to evening. Answers that it was to see his boy, and a woman went with him, and Mabuectaz went with him to see his said son, and another woman with them. And another time he gave a sword to her husband to go look for a master for him. The opinion of the Consistory: since he had been forbidden it, in view of his confession he merits punishment, and that he be remanded before the Council, which will give him strict remonstrances.

Johanete, wife of Pierre Bard, weaver, daughter of Claude Frilot from Saint Simon.

Does not know why she is summoned. And a servant they had furnished a piece of cloth. And the said servant is named . . . ;[308] he had Julliannaz's sister and took her to Lyon. [f. 123v] And she does not know where they went, and they wanted to go to Viry. And she has no child, although her husband has a daughter by another wife. And she goes to the sermons on Sundays, and does not remember what the preacher preaches. Said the prayer rather badly. The opinion of the Consistory: since she is sufficiently instructed, and touching the others when they surrender. And that she instruct her children. And she was [admonished] to frequent the sermons and the catechism. And that she learn when the said French weaver comes who engaged himself to the said Jullianna.

Hieronime Aygre, from Faverges, cobbler, living in Saint Gervais.

That his wife robbed him and left him nothing, and she behaves badly with her body and many other crimes. And she is named Jana, daughter of Nycod Voland, sister of Claude Volant, bath-house keeper, and many other words. She hit him twice with a stone and took him by his member, pretend-

---

308. Name omitted.

ing she would cut it off, and did him great injury. Therefore he asks to be separated from her, considering the terrible things she did to him. And she took six écus from him that she made. She mocks him and causes him all the shame she can.

Jana, his wife, daughter of Nycod Voland, of Ballaison. Does not know why she was summoned here. That she does not live according to the Gospel and they are always at odds, she and her husband. Answers that her husband destroys her and eats all her labor and does not want to do anything and has sold all his household except two chests. And she gave him three florins to go out of the country, and when they were eaten up he returned and insulted her. And she gave him six écus, and she has now earned six écus that she gave him, and he cut her purse on the bridge, and she did not want to cut off his member. She says that the Consistory has been told lies. And that she never went over the roofs to find something, and it does not come from her but from him, that he does not want to believe, and she never left the house on the Riviere at night. Answers that she does not know what it is about; that it [f. 124] is not she. Also she gave her husband money to live that he only ate up. She says that she never took a knife to do him harm.

The opinion of the Consistory is of the opinion [sic] that both be summoned and that they live in peace and that they be admonished to agree together, or if not that they both be remanded to the Council. And that they follow the sermons, and if they do not correct themselves they will be shown by justice that . . .[309]

They were confronted with each other about the lies. She gave him six écus. The said husband answers that he was at law with De Chinalleta and that he bought her a skirt. The wife answers that he ate up 30 florins from household goods he sold. And the said husband excuses himself as to his wife. And the husband answers that he will do what the Council decides. The wife answers that he will do her a bad turn and that he will never be master of a penny she has. And she is content if he works and gets some bit of money, and she also, and he has a month to find a room and she will live with him. The advice of the Consistory is that, since they do not want to agree, that they be remanded to the Council; otherwise a term of a week for them to return together and provide themselves with a room by Thursday, and frequent the sermons every day.[310]

309. Incomplete sentence.
310. Jana Voland was condemned for fornication with Claude Rima (Rymmaz), alias Claude de La Balme, on July 13, 1543. The two of them, already detained, received fairly light sentences of a few days in prison (the sources are not in accord, but in any case neither received more than six days). Jana Voland was ordered, once freed, to beg mercy of

Thursday, July 26, 1543, in cloister.

Lord Chicand, syndic.
Champereaulx, De Ecclesia, Albert, Tripperaulx.
Morel, De Veyrier, Blandin, Du Pain, the officer Vovrey.

Matrimonial case between Laurent Prire, son of Pierre Priere, from Tagny by Désingy near Clermont in the county of Genevois, says that he espoused Rolande, daughter of the late Pierre Blanch from the Vaux de Chézery.

[f. 124v]   That about 13 years ago he espoused her in Désingy at Saint Maurice in Champagne. The father of the said Laurent was present, and many others. After the espousal he stayed at his father's house, and there was . . .[311] Says that last Christmas he gave her an écu and three sous and two bars of silver to make a dress and slept with her and received thirteen score florins that his father received for him. And he will prove it by respectable people, and he drew up a document that is in his house.

Rolandaz, daughter of the late Pierre Blanch of Chézery, living in Dardagny at the house of Jehan Tornier recently, since St. John's Day, and before that in Chézery until All Saints' Day, and before that in the village of Tagny. And she knew Pierre Perriere[312] and was brought there by one of her uncles, she does not know which, and he did not induce her to speak thus, and she does not intend to have any other husband except one that she is engaged to. And the priest is named Monsieur Anthoyne, and she did not otherwise know Laurent, and she did not stay with him that she remembers and she did not give him anything that she remembers. And she was in Chézery at Christmas and he did not give her anything, the said Laurent, and she did not give him anything. And she is engaged to the son of Jehan Tornier named Bernard. And she cannot say that she fled when the said Laurent went to her recently. And she does not know what was given for her marriage. And the said Bernard

_____

God and justice and to return to live with her husband (R.C. 37, f. 153, *ad diem;* R.C. Part. 1, f. 74v, *ad diem*). Two weeks later her husband presented a supplication in Council "asking that Claude de La Balme, who committed fornication with Janne, wife of the said Aygre, be forced to pay the expenses due from the said Janne to the jailer and officers, not the said Jerosme [Aygre], who has given the *souldan* [director of the prison] a skirt as security. On which resolved that the said Janne is a fornicator and that she did not want to live with her husband according to the orders of the Council; that she should pay the said expenses, and that when she leaves the place where she has gone to nurse that she be punished. And that the said skirt should stay in the hands of the *souldan* until she redeems it" [R.C. Part. 1, f. 78v (July 27, 1543)].
      311. Incomplete sentence.
      312. In the margin: "Priere."

gave her a *teston,* and Laurent gave her nothing that she knows of, and she was never given écus or bars or silver that she knows of. And she never slept with him, and he left her in the house of Pierre Prieres. She stayed for eight years in a house where her uncle took her then and had children in that house.

The advice of the Consistory is that the said Laurent bring more ample letters and testimony and his banns on one side and the other. And that the two parties be heard together, and to avoid scandal that the girl be remanded and exhorted . . . (?)[313] marriage [portion] of thirteen score florins [f. 125] in escrow and that they be given a command not to depart.

Both confronted with each other. Rolande did not know the said Laurent that she knows of and she has seen others. It is a long time since she saw him and he stayed at his father's, and she not ever. And she never slept with him there that she knows of, only with the small girls. The said Laurent says that he slept with her for eight years before he went to the wars. The said Rolande says that she withdrew from there when she knew and no one made her withdraw except herself, because they did not treat her as they should, and she never received anything from him. And that she never received écus from him or a ring. And that she has never slept with a husband, and she slept with a maidservant in Dardagny. And the one she is engaged to has not yet espoused her, and she does not intend to have any other than the said Bernard of Dardagny. The said Laurent showed her a ring similar to that he gave her. Answers that she did not receive it. And one of her own of wool in the fashion of Chézery, when he gave her the écu and the ring similar to one he showed her.

The said Rolande in private. Asked why. Answers that she does not believe that he swore faith to her and does not know how, and she is presently 18, and she had the said Laurent cited to the Consistory and does not know what she should ask him. She does not know where he was or stayed, and he did not beat her, because she did not know where he was. [f. 125v] Answers that she will never accept him, that the said Laurent will never be her husband. Both remanded to tomorrow before the Council. And remanded to Thibaud Bernard, who will present her tomorrow to the Council.[314]

---

313. Illegible word.

314. On July 27, 1543, Laurent Prire appeared in Council and "said that [Rolande Blanch] has been his espoused wife for 13 years, as he will make appear, to which she answers that it is not so. On which resolved that within the next week the said Laurent must justify his statement, and if he pledges the expenses, damages and interest in case of failure she will be made a prisoner, but if not she will be left in the charge of Thybaud Bornan [Bernard], who shall present her as many times and whenever she is summoned" [R.C. Part. 1, f. 79 (July 27, 1543)]. The Council considered this case again on August 3 and 10, and recognized the validity of the marriage between Laurent Prire and Rolande

Thursday, August 23, 1543, in cloister.[315]

Lord Syndic Checand.
Allex Pupin,[316] Trippereaulx, De Ecclesia.
Morel, Vernaz, the officer Vovrey.

Tevene, wife of Pierre Baud,[317] carpenter, called Grippa, habitant *of Versoix.*

Answers that her husband slept with her a fortnight ago, and on Sunday he ate with her, and goes sometimes to the sermon when she can. And her husband works at Mathieu Maly's house, and does not speak indecent words. On Sundays she [goes to the sermon] twice, in the morning and at vespers, and she wants always to live as a respectable woman. And her husband and she are respectable people, poor in the goods of the world. Said the prayer and the confession, the confession rather badly, and she wants to lose her life if she does anything dishonorable. The advice of the Consistory: that she be admonished to frequent the sermons and learn to pray better to the Lord, and other remonstrances. She answered that she gets angry at her husband when he comes because he does not bring anything, and she does not want to run after him.

[f. 126]

Tuesday, August 28, 1543, in cloister.

Lord Syndic Checand.
Champereaulx, Albert,[318] Trippereaulx, De Ecclesia.
Du Pain, D'Orsieres, Blandin, De Loermoz, Vernaz, Morel, the officer Vovrey.

Blanch and condemned the wife "to the expenses" of the trial. "And as for those who counselled her to sue her husband and who appealed to Annecy to dissolve the said marriage, that is Jehan Tornyer of Dardagny and others, resolved that the procurator general proceed against them" (R.C. 37, folios 169v and 188v-189, *ad diem*).

315. The previous Friday, August 17, the minister Philippe de Ecclesia appeared in Council, "who reported that they understand, he and the other ministers, that there are various debaucheries in Geneva, asking permission to hold the Consistory because the celebration of Holy Communion approaches. On which resolved that the Consistory be held in the cloister of St. Peter's. And as for insolence, that information be obtained about the guilty, and according to their offenses they be punished." This same day the castellan of Peney, Donzel, had reported in Council "that every day it comes to his notice that there are many suspected of the crime of heresy" (that is, of sorcery) (R.C. 37, f. 195v and f. 194v).

316. This is always Abel Poupin, of course.

317. One Pierre Baud, son of Pierre, carpenter from La Roche, was admitted to the bourgeoisie on July 4, 1547, but this name was among the most common in Geneva (*L.B.,* p. 232).

318. Abel Poupin.

Pierre Monetier, called Pechod, host of the Crane.[319]

Because of his quarrel with Jehan Mestral, called De Genesve. Answers that he wanted to drink with him in token of peace, which the said De Genesve did not want to do. And he never did him any harm, and he pardons him with a good heart. And as for the papistry, they do not give good instruction in the Word of the Lord and give a bad example to the others who lodge there, both he and his wife. Answers that he knows nothing about it, and if he did it he did wrong. And he pardons Jehan de Genesve with a good heart. Answers that he was sent papistic guests because he was thought to be papistic, and he may well have the name, but the fact no. And indeed he believes that some have written to be lodged at his house as a papist, which he is not. The Consistory: that his opponent, Jehan de Genevaz, be remanded to Thursday, and since he wishes him no harm, that they be reconciled with each other. And that the wife come on Thursday. And that he be admonished, or that they both be summoned together for Thursday.

Noble Bartholomie, wife of Noble Jehan Achard.[320]

Because of papistic superstition. Answers that she does not know why she was summoned here and that she does not instruct other people in papistry, and she would like to know as much as she can about those who speak. Answers that she does not know to whom she has spoken about papistry. The advice of the Consistory: that she be given strong remonstrances and proper admonitions for the last time, [f. 126v] and that she be reconciled with those who wish her harm before receiving Communion. Answers that she wishes harm to Ypolite[321] because he gave advice to Monsieur De la Bastie,[322] robbed her and took the écus she was carrying. She says that she pardons him for the love of God and will not do him any injury and leaves vengeance to God. And she does not wish harm to any person other than this Ypolite.

319. Some months earlier the lieutenant made a complaint about those who gambled at the inn of the Crane, without giving any more information about the inn or the innkeeper [R.C. Part. 1, f. 37 (April 7, 1543)].
320. Bartholomie d'Orsières, widow of Claude Richardet, and at this time wife of Jehan Achard.
321. Ypolite Revit.
322. François Champion.

Pernete, wife of Lyonard de Bogiaco, heir of Richardet.[323]

Does not know why. Because of the sermons. Answers that she goes to the sermons, and was in Prévessin for a month, where they preach as they do here, and did not talk about papistry, and does not know what papistry is. And she was in the village the day of Our Lady of August[324] and she did not spin because she did not have her distaff, and did not keep the feast. And she does not have faith in saints and has not spoken to anyone about papistry, and prays only to the Lord. Said the prayer, and believes perfectly in God and not in another. And she has no resentment against anyone. She was given proper admonitions.

Jane Lulliemon, wife of Guychard Recouz.[325]

Because of sermons. Answers that she holds by nothing of papistry and was at the sermon Sunday at St. Gervase after dinner, and sometimes on Wednesdays. And she was in St. Saphorin at the fair to buy skins, and offered nothing and was not in the church. And she did not like going to St. Saphorin and was forced to go, and she saw Jehan d'Avignon's wife. And she has no doubts about the sermons. Said the prayer. She was given proper admonitions.

[f. 127]   The Council has remanded Nycod de La Ravoyre the elder, farm laborer, and Anne his wife, who have several times been summoned to Consistory and have not appeared; therefore they are remanded to Friday before the Council.[326]

The reason why Monsieur Calvin sent the letter, that he knows well why, and it was before he left for Metz.[327] And they were summoned to all the Consistories held since his departure.

---

323. Pernette de Bogiaco (Bougier, Bougy), née Vuychard. Leonard de Bougier acknowledged at the hospital as his grandfather Richardet's heir in 1556. In 1544 he claimed the estate of Hilaire Richardet, his uncle. He also pursued a suit against Bartholomie, widow of Claude Richardet, which may also have been connected with Richardet's estate [Galiffe II, p. 57; R.C. Part. 1, f. 225 and f. 226 (November 25 and 28, 1544); *ibid.,* f. 35 (April 3, 1543) and f. 322v (October 16, 1545)].

324. The feast of the Assumption of the Virgin, one of the four great Marian feasts.

325. Guychard Recouz, citizen, son of the late Julian Recouz, jailed for fornication in 1540 [*R.C.* XII, p. 534 (May 1, 1534); R.C. 34, f. 148 (March 23, 1540)].

326. On November 5, 1543, after having been detained for three days for having failed to appear in Consistory, Nycod de La Ravoyre's wife was freed by order of the Council (R.C. 37, f. 262v).

327. On June 16, 1543, Pierre Viret brought to Council a letter from Farel, then in Strasbourg, saying that Pierre Caroli was preaching in Metz "against the Holy Gospel, and in the pulpit greatly blames our ministers [of Geneva], naming them, that they are nothing but

Thursday, August 30, 1543, in cloister.

Lord Syndic Chicand.
Calvin, Champereaulx, De Ecclesia, Pupin, Trippereaulx.
Pensabin, De Loermoz, Vernaz, Blandin, the officer Vovrey.

Ypolite Revitz,[328] *goldsmith.*

Because of a quarrel he has with Richardet's widow.[329] Answers that she insulted him and called him "traitor," and it is at law before the lieutenant, and he asks the repair of his honor. Otherwise he wishes her no harm and bears her no grudge except for the said insult, and he wants to maintain his honor.

Mauriza Talluchete.

Because of the prayer and confession and the sermons. Answers that she will do better than formerly. She was ordered always to persevere at the sermons and to learn to pray to the Lord.

Jehan Bornand, granary worker in Longemale.

Because of the prayer. Said the prayer; said the confession. He was given proper admonitions.

127v] *Pierre Mouchon, called Pechoz.*[330]

Appeared, and wants always to be of the number of the faithful. And his opponent Jehan de Genevaz did not appear. His wife is released this time until...[331]

---

heretics." Calvin was then sent to Bern, Strasbourg, and Metz to contradict the preaching of Caroli, with the object of an eventual face-to-face disputation in Metz. Calvin, however, seems to have remained in Strasbourg, and on August 22 the Council received a letter from Calvin reporting that Caroli did not want "to keep his promise, and in short he [Calvin] will return from here" [R.C. 37, folios 129v-130, 200 (June 16 and August 22, 1543)].

328. Hypolite Revit (Rivet), a goldsmith from Thonon, *"qui jam diu civitate incoluit & tempore bellorum cum civibus, burgensibus & incolis animo forti hostibus constanter repugnavit* {who has long lived in the city, and in time of war along with the citizens, bourgeois and *habitants* with a brave soul firmly repelled the enemy}," was admitted to the bourgeoisie on April 8, 1532 (*L.B.*, p. 208). Speaking of his detention in 1546 for rebelling against the minister who refused to give the name Hyppolita to a girl he carried to baptism, Galiffe (*Ameaux*, p. 77) describes him as "one of the most valiant champions of the war for Genevan independence." However, it may be supposed that Galiffe based his judgment solely on the act of *embourgeoisement*.

329. Bartholomie, widow of Claude Richardet, wife of Jehan Achard.

330. He had already appeared in Consistory in this connection (see above, August 28, 1543), but under the name of Pierre Monetier, called Pechod.

331. Incomplete sentence.

Jehan de Genevaz.

Did not appear for the second time.

Pierre Guilliermet, tailor, called Pollet.

Because of the prayer, and excused himself for the other times he was summoned. Said the prayer and the confession. Answers that he no longer holds papistic superstitions. And there was a time when if he had killed a preacher, he would have done well. And that he has no more scruples about the Virgin Mary or the saints. He is strongly blamed for blasphemy against God and also for the saints. Answers that he swears freely, and begs mercy of God. Since he promises to improve and frequent the sermons and not tell lies any more as he is reported to do, and also be admonished to follow the sermons, and given strong remonstrances.

Magdelayne, wife of Girard Le Mugnier.

Because of the sermons and the prayer. Answers that she has profited a little more from religion. Said the prayer and the confession a little. It is advised that she do better and be admonished to follow the sermons.

Don Guillaume Marchiand[332] and Claude de Ulmo.[333]

Because of their argument yesterday and their great quarrel and argument. The said De Ulmo says and answers that they had some words together that he wants to talk over with him, and he will do what he ought to do. And they do not live together. The said Marchiand answers that he does not complain that it was a serious charge against the said De Ulmo. Both answer that they wish each other no harm, since they have no great conflict.

---

332. Guillaume Marchand, former priest of Geneva. Like almost all the former priests living in Geneva, he renounced the Mass in Council in December 1539 and obtained a pension in 1542. Marchand died of plague on October 23, 1543, leaving the "few goods he had" to the hospital (CAHIER-BUCCELLI, "Ombre," p. 370, n. 13, and p. 379; RO-GET I, p. 157; R.C. 37, f. 251, *ad diem*).

333. Like Marchand, Claude de Ulmo, "formerly a priest," living near the Magdalen according to his death certificate, abjured the Mass in 1539 and received a pension from the city [*R.G.S.* I, pp. 204-205; CAHIER-BUCCELLI, "Ombre," p. 370, n. 13, p. 378, n. 74, p. 379, n. 80, p. 382; R.C. 30, f. 196 (March 23, 1537); E.C., Morts 1, p. 5 (February 15, 1550)].

128] *Tyvent Tondu, blacksmith, and Anthoyne, his wife.*[334]

Because of a quarrel they had the other night. And that he did not make his wife jump out of the window, which she did entirely nude through the window, because he did not do it, and he beat her. And he did not call to mind the words of the Holy Communion when he started the quarrel. And they have been married for about four years, and she was the cause of the quarrel. And they are both at fault. They say they have not had a quarrel for about a year. And the said quarrel occurred about nine o'clock at night. Answer that they frequent the sermons and are of the [true] religion. He says they quarreled because of two children she has, and they are together with his own, and they are eight persons, and they do not have enough goods to sustain the expense. He said that he would always do what a respectable man should do. And that his wife's children bring in only ten florins a year. She spoke many words of reproach to her husband. And he said he would do whatever respectable people among their relatives decided. They were given strong remonstrances.

Jehan Mestral, called De Genevaz.

Answers that he has no conflict with Pechod and never said anything worse to him than his name and has no quarrel with him. And that he did not want to drink with him to make peace, and it was because of an écu. And the said Pecho once tweaked his nose. The said Pechod says he asked him to drink with him and he did not want to drink. The said De Genevaz answers that it is true. Pechod says he never did him any harm or blamed him. And he never did anything that he does not want to maintain and speak the truth, and the said Pechoz wanted to bring him down. The said Pechoz and Genevaz say they pardon each other. They were given strong remonstrances, and declare themselves good friends from now on.

. 128v] *Pierre Bard, weaver.*

Has been at the sermons and said the prayer and the confession. Was exhorted to go to the sermons with his family.

22 florins, 6 *gros.*

---

334. Tyvent Tondu, from Chermoisy (H.-S.), bourgeois in 1532, living in Saint Gervais in Coutance, where he died in 1552 [*L.B.,* p. 209 (October 16, 1532); E.C., Morts 1, p. 254 (April 22, 1552)]. Antoine Tondu, née Deladhoy, made her will on January 7, 1553, naming among her heirs Nicolarde, her sister, wife of Jean Balard. She died on May 15, 1560 (Notaires, Jean Duverney, v. 5, f. 45; E.C., Morts 3, p. 108).

The ordinance of the Holy Communion of Our Lord for next Sunday in the fall, second day of the month of September 1543.[335]

And first for St. Peter's for the two Communions: Lords Pernet de Fosses, Michiel Varod, Pierre d'Orsieres, Michiel Morel.

For the Magdalen: Jehan Chautemps, Pierre Vernaz, Jehan Pensabin.

For Saint Gervase: Claude Du Pain, Loys Dufour, Amed Gervays, Mermet Blandin.

And throughout a lord syndic.

[f. 129] *Friday, last day of August 1543 at the temple of the Magdalen: Syndic Checand and Monsieur Calvin. Reconciliation.*

Presented themselves before them Ypolite Revit, goldsmith, on one part and Noble Bartholomie, widow of Richardet, wife of Noble Jehan Achard, on the other part. Because of insults given by the said Noble Bartholomie against the said Ypolite, calling him "traitor," "wicked" and other insults, and wanting to prove it by good witnesses. To which the said Noble Bartholomie replied she did not give such insults and she never called him traitor, although she reproached him with having acted wickedly in making her lose the écus that her late husband Richardet had given her in Bâtie-Champion,[336] at the house of Monsieur De Vauruxtren(?). And many words having been heard, they were exhorted to pardon each other so as to receive the Holy Communion of Our Lord reverently and live in peace and charity with each other. To which both replied that they were content and that they would never speak of it again and put everything in suspension, and they pardoned each other and shook hands in sign of peace from now on. The aforesaid things being done, the said Revit asked that it be put in writing so as to help in future times. And the said Noble Bartholomee said she would hold him for a respectable man and would never again say anything like the aforesaid words.

335. Because of the passage of the soldiers through Geneva Communion was not celebrated until two weeks later, September 16; see below, on September 13, 1543, note.

336. François Champion was the Seigneur de La Bâtie.

Also here afterwards the honorable women Claudaz and Jana, sisters, daughters of the late Honorable George Dentant;[337] Jane, wife of the feather dealer Rosset; and Clauda, wife of Claude Rosset Du Fossal.[338]

Because of certain words spoken by the said Claudaz against the said Jane about the selling price of certain wheat sold to the said Jane, and other things. They were reconciled with each other after admonitions and remonstrances, agreed and put into suspension all words and reproaches.

[f. 129v]   The said day, Friday last of August, the ceremony of Holy Communion was put off because of certain men of war passing through here, for good reasons. It was delayed until next Sunday, September 9.[339]

Thursday, September 6, 1543, in cloister.

Lord Syndic Checand.
Calvin, De Ecclesia, Henri, Alber Pupin, Trippereaulx.
Morel, Pensabin, Blandin, Just de Ulmo, the officer Vovrey.

Egrege Françoys de La Pierra,[340] from Jussy.

Because he was commanded to be here at the Consistory, which was by the commandment of the Council because he refuses to read the Holy Com-

---

337. George Dentant, notary from Veigy (Veigy-Foncenex, H.-S.), admitted to the bourgeoisie in 1510, member of the CC in 1538 (*R.G.S.* I, p. 219; GALIFFE I, p. 311).

338. Claude Rosset, called Fossal, citizen, merchant [R.C. 30, f. 100v (December 5, 1536); see also SORDET, *Dictionnaire*, p. 547 (Claude Du Fossal)].

339. The previous Tuesday, August 28, 1543, the Council ordered that Communion be celebrated the following Sunday. However, on August 30 "it is understood that today there should arrive eleven *enseignes* going to war for the king." The Council decided to admit the soldiers to the city if they were Swiss, but not if they were Italians. In any case the Council decided to keep the gates of the city closed and to place six guards at the gate of Saint Gervais. The next day it was decided that "because the soldiers, both Italians and Swiss, are passing through here, ordered that it [Communion] be put off until next Sunday." On September 14 it was decided to celebrate Communion the following Sunday, September 16. However, the danger was not ended; on September 17, 5000 Italian troops asked permission to pass through Geneva, which was refused, "considering the suspicion there is among the Pope, Turk and French king against the emperor, and possibly also against the Christian religion" [R.C. 37, folios 206v, 208-208v, 209, 220, 221, *ad dies,* and f. 218 (September 10, 1543)].

340. François de La Pierre replaced Amy Maistre, called Joly Clerc, as *curial* of Jussy on March 9, 1543. He was himself replaced before January 25, 1544 (R.C. 37, f. 29v; R.C. 38, f. 44).

munion, which he said was the office of Gojactz,[341] despising the Word of the Lord. Answers that it is true that for 30 years he has been out of the country as rector of schools in Faucigny, until last Easter, and he withdrew here by the command of the Council.[342] He obeyed the command, left the goods acquired by him and by his wife and the debts he lost, fleeing papal ceremonies as a good subject would. And he heard the Word of the Lord, which he has always frequented, he and his family; in truth last Sunday like a good servant. And his wife was ill; she has been from Christmas until now, and he believes she would have died if God had not given her grace when he was returning. And thus he refused to read the Holy Communion for the reason above. And then he spoke to the castellan,[343] from whom he asked a New Testament, and he forced him to be the reader and he refused [f. 130] to enter the pulpit, he not being worthy to enter the *cathedra* because of unworthiness, and he has never filled such an office. He is old and cannot read any more and is always infected in his eyes. And he excused himself, saying that he has a thick tongue and cannot do as one would wish, and he did not do it out of contempt for our said lords. *Dubitat ne dominus Henricus[344] eum mali voluerit ne feri contra eum.* {He suspects that Master Henricus wished him harm and did it against him.} Answers that he did not speak like Gojatz, also saying that Master Henri never came to console his wife, who has remained ill so long, ever since Christmas. And he does not intend any insolence. And if he has any anger against him he should say so.

Henri answers that he went to see and visit his wife once between the said time and now, and no one of the said place of Jussy ever asked him to visit the sick who were at the said place. The said De Petra answers that he spoke privately outside the church about Gojat and that he had considered coming to complain of him.

341. There was no person of this name mentioned among the wardens of Jussy (above, May 10, 1543). Gojact may have been the officer of Jussy, whom we cannot identify.
342. In the margin: "two years." De La Pierre may have meant Easter 1542, or he may have practiced the trade of notary in Jussy before he actually returned, which could explain the Council's order to go there. In any case, on March 24, 1542, the *curial* of Jussy, Ami Maystre, called Joly Clerc, complained of François de La Pierre [de Petra], who had received "various documents to his [Maystre's] great injury, and also to the prejudice of the rights of the Seigneurie" (R.C. 35, f. 535v). On November 14, 1542, François de La Pierre asked permission to receive "all documents in the *mandement* of Jussy, as he was permitted to do in the beginning when he was made sworn notary, and despite this he is molested by the *curial* of the said Jussy" (R.C. 36, f. 168v). This dispute lasted until De La Pierre replaced Maystre as *curial* [see R.C. 36, f. 200v and f. 207 (December 29, 1542, and January 5, 1543)].
343. François Paquet, castellan of Jussy.
344. Henri de La Mare, minister of Jussy.

On these words the Consistory is that he be given strong admonitions, that he be admonished not to get angry as he is in the habit of doing, since he is still a sycophant, although he has offended. And that he guard himself another time from scandalizing again, and that he be informed one or two days before, and that he inform his conscience regarding lawsuits, and that he hold in suspension all grudges he has against the said Henri and others.

George Monthiou, son of Pierre, of Jussy.

Said that he was married once, thinking that she was a respectable girl, and she is a fornicator; he does not know where she is. He has not seen her for four years. And he took her back three times and she never stayed with him, but went off. He asks to be separated from her. And she is named Jane, daughter of Collet Du Bouloz, of Choulex. And he treated her well and did not act as a go-between or beat her. And he has in writing all the results(?) of the proceedings the then-*curial* of Jussy took against her four years ago. And he thought she would return, and he would not like to take her back at this time, and he does not want another wife, and he would like to separate if it pleases Your Excellencies. [f. 130v] The opinion of the Consistory is that he be remanded to the Council to obtain all information from the *curial,* and that he obtain more evidence and never bring it here [sic] and listen to the said De Petra and the other. Master François de Petra[345] touching the said marriage of George Monthiou. He married the said girl about six years ago and kept her a year, and she was a little loose. And when he corrected her she left and wandered to the end of a year and then made an honest agreement. And later she left for another year, and he wanted to make her parents take her back, and another agreement was made and she returned to her said husband. And after three months she was debauched by someone, and he has not seen her since, for about four years. And he asks you to consider the said Jane, if it can be done justly, that he may remarry elsewhere. Remanded to examine the witnesses brought here afterwards.

Pernet Gay, shearer.

Does not know why he was summoned here. Touching Paquenot. Answers that it is true that he has a girl, Perissoda's daughter, alone with him, and they come and go together, and her mother goes outside and he stays there with her for two, three hours together. And they look at the tiles on their neighbors' roofs and make faces that are not pretty. And her mother shuts them up together for two or three hours by themselves, so he says they

345. François de La Pierra.

say they are married to each other. And Paquenot the father says she will never enter his house. And one should ask Aymoz de Thonon and his wife.

Tyvent Paquenotz on the charges given and offered against him. Answers that he does not know why he was summoned here, and he knows he has been summoned before. Answers that he does not hang around with the said girl, and those who have reported this etc.[346] And that he does not do anything improper, and it may be that he has talked to her alone [f. 131] and it is not so, and if it is truly proven he wants to be punished. And there are those who wish him harm. And he has not talked to her for nine weeks, and he has never been there when there was not someone with him. And one should ask the neighbors, and he wants to be punished, and they have still not made an agreement. And when his sister is married he planned to take her. And he has not been at her house alone and no one can say so in truth. He was remanded here in a week.

Nycolarde, widow of Jehan Perrissod. Does not know why she [was summoned] here. Answers that she remembers well what she was told last time, and it is about six weeks since they left the said place together where they were staying, and since Tuesday, and the said Paquenot was there about twice, respectably. Answers that she does not go over the roofs and she has not shut them up. And he is badly informed and does not know what he says. And if he came there he did not come there to do wrong, and they often speak together in the street. And she means to have an alliance with him through the said girl, and he wants to marry off a sister in the house that he wants to marry off, and afterwards he aims at her daughter. And she denies that she shuts them up or goes over the roofs. Remanded to next Thursday here.

Jaquemaz, daughter of François Vuagniouz, from Murcier, near Chaumont.

And her husband is dead. Does not know why she was summoned. Because she does not frequent the sermons. Answers that she must work for her living, and she goes to the sermons when she can. Said the prayer; does not know how to say the confession. The advice of the Consistory is that she be admonished to frequent the sermons and appear here in one month and learn to say the confession.

[f. 131v] *Claudaz Puthodaz, wife of Jehan de Brucelles, pin-maker.*

Because of the sermons. Answers that she goes to the sermons and has nothing to live on, she or her children. And her husband left for his own

346. Incomplete sentence.

house to see that she and her said husband . . . ,[347] and he could not live here by his trade. And said he had gone to sell his goods to live here. And says that she does not keep feasts, except Sunday she attended Mass after a vigil that was held the previous day. And if she said it, she said it only in joke and meant no harm. And she begs mercy of justice, because she meant no harm. Said the prayer and the confession. She hopes her husband will be here for Christmas. She was admonished.

Aymoz Vulliet, called the Juggler.[348]

Because of the sermons. Answers that it is rarely possible to go, since he keeps a tavern; he cannot go unless he can go there without . . . ,[349] and he goes every Sunday, and no other days. Touching his son who went to war. Answers that he employed the justices of the city and other relatives. He did not want to believe it, and as much as he can he wants to live in his house and household as honestly as he can. The wife he has, he must respond to her. He says he is a lover of good wine. He has watched 20 years. He was given proper admonitions and admonitions to frequent the sermons and behave decently in his household and not to get angry in his household any more.

[132]   **Thursday, September 13, 1543, in cloister.**

Lord Checand, syndic.
Calvin, Albert, De Ecclesia, Tripereaulx, Champereaulx.
Morel, Molard, Vernaz, Pensabin, Just, Du Pain, the officer Vovrey.

George Monthouz, from Jussy, with Egrege Françoys de Pierra from Jussy.[350]

Produced the record and decision in the affair of the said George. Produced an order and examination made of this matter and, after its reading,

347. Words omitted.
348. Amyed Vulliet, called the Juggler, from Faverges (H.-S.), bourgeois in 1523. He lived in Saint Gervais and seems to have had connections with the Philippins; as with many other suspects whose faults were not sufficiently grave to merit banishment, the Council demanded that Vulliet return to Geneva in 1540. He was also among the inhabitants of Saint Gervais who assembled to support Ami Aillod, imprisoned for having risen against Calvin during a sermon in 1546 [*L.B.*, p. 197 (September 15, 1523); R.C. Part. 1, f. 89 (n.d. [September 11-25, 1543]); Titres et Droits, Pa 619, folios 58-61 (April 4, 1547); R.C. 34, f. 515 (November 9, 1540); R.C. 31, f. 61v (March 30, 1546); P.C. 2ᵉ sér., 707 (March 31, 1546)].
349. Word(s) omitted; the word "go" is struck.
350. This is the matrimonial case between George Monthou and Jane Du Bouloz presented in Consistory on September 6, 1543.

the Consistory is of the opinion, since the wife broke her marriage and ran off three times and had promised to live like a respectable woman, that she should be summoned at three sermons as for banns, and afterwards the case be brought before the Council. And that the record and the case be remanded to Monday before the Council.[351]

Johanete, wife of Claude Du Chesne of Peissy, and Claude Du Chesne, her husband, from Peissy.

Presented a statement and had it read, the said Claude her husband being present.[352] Answers that he did not throw her out of his house. Confessed that he had fornicated in the past, and not at present. Said the prayer and not the confession. He was not paid for to the Council but ransomed.[353] The opinion of the Consistory, having heard the contents of the case: that they be remanded before the Council, or that they agree together. Remanded to Monday before the Council. And as for the confession, that he know it within a month and come here to recite and explain it.

[f. 132v]   *Amy Maystre,[354] notary, bourgeois of Geneva.*

Case of fornication. Answers that he goes to the sermons every day. And about his keeping a woman with her daughter, whom he treats badly because of the woman. And that he found Jehan de Thonon's wife, and that she wanted to sue for her marriage [portion]. And he lodged her while his said

---

351. On October 1, 1543, the case of separation between George and Jane Monthou was presented in Council. The Council decided to put off any decision until the minister of Jussy, Henri de La Mare, had announced for three Sundays at the sermon that Jane, wife of George Monthou, should appear in Council (R.C. 37, f. 234). On March 19, 1546, by advice of the ministers, the Council gave Monthou permission to remarry (R.C. 41, f. 55).

352. The text of the request presented by Johanete Du Chesne is found below at the end of this session.

353. The French is as ambiguous as the English; it says *"composé"* and *"arransoné,"* both of which mean "ransomed."

354. Amy Maystre, called Joly Clerc, notary from Petit Bornand (H.-S.), received into the bourgeoisie in 1524, member of the CC, later *curial* of Jussy (1542). On May 5, 1542, the Council returned Amy Maystre to the Consistory with P. Cathon because of insults they had exchanged (not mentioned in the minutes of the Consistory). During the summer of 1543, Maystre having been struck by the plague, the Council gave him a *coupe* of wheat to feed his children. For his problems with François de La Pierre, his successor as *curial,* see above, September 6, 1543 [*L.B.*, p. 200 (January 26, 1524); R.C. 35, f. 56ᶜv (February 9, 1541); R.C. 35, f. 535v (March 24, 1542); R.C. 36, f. 4v (May 5, 1542); R.C. 37, f. 131 (June 18, 1543)].

wife was alive, and wants to be hanged if he ever stayed with her. And Monsieur Loys Bernard[355] has spoken with him.

Guycharda Aubertaz, wife of Jaques Richard, poulterer of the Duke of Savoy.

Because of the sermons. Answers that she has no neighbors, that she never goes to the sermons because she has three small children small children [sic]. And that she never said she did not want to go to the sermons and that she would not want to go to the sermons until Communion. And that she is teaching the Pater to her son in Latin and French because she was told one must know it in two languages, Latin and French.

Pierre Du Chesne, from Petit Saconnex.

Because of the sermons, dances and songs. Answers that he was at the sermon last Sunday, and that his wife is ill and pregnant. Answers that he does not sing or dance. He does not know who they are who sing, although the girls dance the "windmill." Said the prayer and the confession. Answers that he received Communion at St. Gervase, and his wife also.

Jane, daughter of the late Jaques Janyn, from Cologny,[356] tailor.

Answers that she was in Corsier last Monday to get a *quart* of wheat for Auberte, whom she had helped to recover after the birth of a child. And she was in the Vuache twice for the threshing. And they are not angry at each other. And she was never at the sermon while helping her said mistress, and the children are small. And before she was with her she frequented the sermons. Said the prayer and the confession. [f. 133] Answers that her mistress is teaching her children the prayer in two fashions. And she stayed at La Cruche's house and knew Master Jehan the doctor and had a child who is dead. And because she was thrown out of the house she sheltered with the said Master Jehan. She was helped by another than the said Master Jehan because he had already left because someone wanted to take

355. Louis Bernard, brother of the minister Jaques Bernard and of Claude Bernard, one of the first adherents of the Reform in Geneva. Louis Bernard was the first priest to rally to the Reform and to marry. His marriage with the sister of Ami Perrin linked Bernard to the rising faction, from which Bernard seems to have profited; he became a member of the CC (1536), *hospitalier* (1536-1537), a member of the LX (1539), a councillor (1545) and procurator general (1545-1548). He died in 1548 (GALIFFE III, p. 49; L. GAUTIER, *Hôpital,* p. 21; ROGET III, pp. 26, 33, 315; JUSSIE, p. 94; GEISENDORF, *Annalistes,* p. 417; NAEF, *Origines* II, p. 361; SORDET, *Dictionnaire,* p. 91).

356. Jaques Janin, from Cologny, tailor, admitted to the bourgeoisie on November 15, 1502 (*L.B.,* p. 149).

him. And she does not know where he is, and she was helped in her weakness(?).

Contents of the request and statement made by Johannete, wife of Glaude Du Chesne, of Peissy, against her husband in Consistory.

Dread lords, it has pleased the lord castellan and *assistants* of the *mandement* of Peney to remand before Your Reverences Glaude Du Cheyne and Johannete, his wife, because the said Glaude continues in his bad behavior, as in fornication and waste of goods, so much that the said Johannete here present was forced to summon her said husband by law before the said lord castellan, as is proven by the record which is shown to you, so she may enjoy the assets of her marriage and other lands settled in favor of the said Johannete, as is proven by a document which, with the said record, she will promptly show and produce. Therefore may it please you to give an appropriate remonstrance and warning to the said Glaude, forbidding him from now on from molesting, disquieting, or obstructing the said Johannete by words or deeds from enjoying her assets of marriage or other lands settled in her favor, as is proven by the said document. And she will pray God for your long prosperity.

[f. 133v] Note that on Sunday, September 16, the Holy Communion of Our Lord was celebrated which had been delayed from the second day of the said month until the said day because of an obstacle, for good reasons.[357]

Thursday, October 18, 1543, in cloister.

Lord Syndic Checand.
Calvin, Genesto, De Ecclesia, Tripereaulx, Pupin.
Morel, Molar, Vernaz, Veyrier, Baudichon, Pensabin, De Loermoz, the officer.[358]

On the affair of Jaquelline Maronne.

Having seen the information taken and brought from her country, she asks to be separated from her husband; the Consistory ordered that counsel be taken tomorrow; meanwhile . . .[359]

---

357. The Communion that should have been celebrated on September 2 and that had been put off because of the soldiers who were passing through the city (see above, August 30, 1543, note).
358. The name of the officer is omitted.
359. Incomplete sentence.

Claudaz, daughter of Glaude Fontannaz of Norcier.

Has been in this city three and a half years years [sic] at the house of Pierre Bolliet.[360] Says that she cannot get an answer from the son of Master Amy the tailor who made her pregnant, and has no other than him. And he promised to marry her and give her enough of his goods so she would be content with him, because she was badly advised. And the said son went away and it is six weeks since she saw him. [f. 134] The advice of the Consistory is that if she has a child he be made to take the child, since he sent his son away, and that she be remanded to the Council; that the father be summoned before the Council and that he answer.

Answers that it is a long time since she began to fornicate, and she received Communion at Easter, but not this last time. Said the prayer and the confession. Answers that she committed the fault through her great . . .[361] She was admonished. She was remanded before the Council, and that she summon Master Amy, the father of this one, for Monday.

Thursday, October 25, 1543, in Chapter.

Lord Syndic Checand.
Calvin, Pupin, Tripperaulx, De Ecclesia.
Morel, Blandin, De Veyrier, Pensabin, Just de Loermoz, the officer.[362]

Jehan Renault,[363] called the Braggart, locksmith.

Because of the Mass and taverns. Answers that he did not go for that and that he heard the Mass in his own country, but he did not put his heart in it. Touching the taverns, he will remain(?) in his household. He walked through the churches and did not put his heart in them, and he prayed on his knees in praying to the Lord. And he took and asked permission from the Council of Geneva to go there for his business and for a lawsuit. And he greatly disliked seeing the idols and the Mass there. He was given remonstrances and admonitions.

360. Pierre Bolliet was elected to the CC in 1542 for the Rivière dessus la Fusterie [R.C. 35, f. 490 (February 7, 1542)].
361. Word omitted.
362. The name of the officer is omitted.
363. Jehan Renault, locksmith and cutler from Saint Bris (Yonne), admitted to the bourgeoisie on June 11, 1535 (*L.B.*, p. 213).

Françoyse, widow of Tyvent Tissot.

Does not know why she was summoned. Answers that she goes to the sermon in the morning. Answers that her boy, and they do not . . .[364] And since Easter the treasurer[365] has not said a word to her and does not speak to her. [f. 134v] And her daughter-in-law[366] did not insult her, and says that she earned the goods she has, and that someone came to find her the other day when they beat each other and cursed the children; that happened to her that time. And his wife takes no account of her and did not come. And she was badly advised to have thus cursed God for her children. And she always commends herself to God and the Holy Spirit. The opinion of the Consistory is that she be talked to more amply and that her son the treasurer be made to come at the end of a sermon so they may be reconciled. And that Jehan,[367] her other son, be summoned for Thursday. And that she be given firm remonstrances, and the treasurer, his mother and his wife after the sermon tomorrow at the Magdalen.

Jana Bosseysaz, wife of Françoys Bossey, coppersmith.

Answers that she knows the reason why. And yesterday when she went to wash a child's clothes, she took something to heart and thought of drowning herself. And then she commended herself to God with a good heart. And she was upset by some bad things she had experienced. On leaving her house she went to Eaux Vives in the Pré l'Evêque, which seemed to her to die [sic]. And she has no regret except for her folly. And she did not know why, since her husband had not threatened to beat her. And she went into the water up to her belly, a little higher, because she had spilled some oil, and she was afraid her husband would be angry, and he had bought a house that was not paid for, and he had two small children, and she was afraid they would be hurt. And the present scarcity.[368] And she frequents the sermons more than formerly, and she spoke as Lord Vandel stated here. And she said she was not upset as yesterday, only a little, and she received the last Communion. [f. 135] And she says she did not undress for any reason except to go get the clothes that were going away on the water.

364. Incomplete sentence.
365. Her son, Pierre Tissot, then treasurer of Geneva.
366. Louise Favre, daughter of François Favre, the famous head of the Favre clan (GALIFFE I, p. 510).
367. Jehan Tissot, citizen, member of the CC (1534) and the LX (1536) (GALIFFE I, pp. 508-511; SORDET, *Dictionnaire*, p. 1235).
368. On September 3, 1543, the Council forbade the making of white bread "because of the scarcity of wheat" (R.C. 37, f. 211v).

François Bossey, coppersmith of Vésenaz, bourgeois of Geneva,[369] husband of the said Jane. Does not know the reason why. Answers that he attends the sermons on feast days, and as for his wife, he does not know why this accident took her so yesterday. And it was because of because of [sic] the money they owe for the house, and he sent her to look for a woman who brought her. And she had never done it before, and he has always found her an honest woman woman [sic], and he believes she is still out of her mind. And he was not angry with her. And he has never found her out of her mind as she was yesterday.

The said Jane was given proper admonitions and went away to her small children. Said the prayer and the confession.

Marguerite, wife of Amed Falcat, farm laborer.[370]

Answers that she goes to the sermons, and yesterday to the first. Has two children and had one that died, and she is very sorry about the death. And it was a daughter, and she suddenly went and found her dead in her blanket,[371] indeed in her cradle, a week before last Michaelmas, and she is very sad. And the neighbors saw her dead, and she does not know whether she was hot or cold, and she was already a year old. And Master Guillaume's wife and Red Nevet saw her and held her, and she did not put her in the bed, and what she was afraid of happened to her. She was given proper admonitions to be more careful another time. Said the prayer and the confession.

135v] *Tevenaz, widow of Jehan Marchiand, bourgeois of Geneva,[372] called the baker of the shameful poor.*

Said that a man found her with a rosary in her hand, that it was broken to bits and she no longer has a rosary. Goes to the sermons; by day she cleans at the house of Lambert the hatter. And she says the Pater after the preacher.

369. François Bossey, received into the bourgeoisie on April 15, 1539 (*L.B.*, p. 219).

370. Amed Falcat, farm laborer from Jussy l'Evêque (GE), was admitted to the bourgeoisie on June 18, 1535 (*L.B.*, p. 214). Marguerite, his wife, was among the "baker women appointed to make bread and sell it in the square in front of the City Hall" [R.C. 40, f. 184 (July 16, 1545)].

371. Translator: Conjectural translation of the word *"lyandaz,"* whose meaning is unknown.

372. There is no mention of a Jean Marchand in the *Livre des bourgeois* after 1491, when two men named Johannes Marchiandi were admitted to the bourgeoisie (*L.B.*, pp. 114 and 115).

Friday, October 26, 1543, at the temple of the Magdalen Noble Pierre Tissoctz, treasurer, Françoyse his mother and Loyse his wife were remanded to be reconciled after the sermon.

The said Françoyse presented herself. Asked for the honor of God that someone advise her son the treasurer and his wife to be in accord with her, and Jehan Tissot, his brother, son of the said Françoyse. Because the said Pierre, treasurer, and his wife did not appear, Syndic Checand and Monsieur Calvin, minister, commanded that all four be summoned next Thursday to the Consistory.

Thursday, first day of November, 1543. Chapter.

Lord Syndic Checand.
Calvin, De Ecclesia, Pupin, Trippereaulx, Champereaulx.
Morel, De Veyrier, the officer.

Jana Bochue, daughter of the late Anthoyne Bochu,[373] wife of Jehan Guychard, merchant.

Answers that her husband is away selling merchandise, and she is staying with her mother, whom she serves, and she has a child, and they live in Saint Gervais at Burnet's house. And it is a year and a half since he left, and it is because he owes money to the merchants of this city. And as for her body she behaves well; there is nothing to reproach in her. She goes to the sermons on the feasts, and her mother the other times, and on Sunday she was [f. 136] at the sermon at St. Gervase, and the child she nursed belongs to the secretary Triane(?), here near the Magdalen. She does not know how to pray to the Lord as it is done [today], but she is not papistic or [devoted] to the superstitions. She was admonished to frequent the sermons.

Treasurer Pierre Tissoctz was informed about the case.

Because his mother was bothered by him and by his wife and complained of their . . .[374] He has honor and reverence for his mother as God has ordered, and salutes her. And she tells him, "Keep your 'good days.' May the devil put them in your belly." He offered to give his mother a better pension than my [sic] father gave her, and she is always paid her pension,

373. She may have been the sister of Gervayse Bochu. For Anthoyne and Gervayse Bochu see above, May 11, 1542.
374. Incomplete sentence.

and if she does not want his wheat he gives her money to buy other, and wine, the best he has, and he recently sent her eight écus by his servant. He paid the apothecary for medicines for the illness she had, and his wife visited her. And she did not want to eat the soup she made her, and she begged mercy of him for her illness. And as for his brother Jehan, he was forced to use all the means he could in all ways that seemed best to him to reduce the said Jehan to honor, and he did not want to be so reduced, but is still debauched.

Françoyse, his mother, present, whether she remembers what she said last Thursday. Answers that he does not pay her pension as he says.

Present the said treasurer. She says that he did not pay her pension last year and only gave her a barrel of wine that she could not drink. And as for the "good day," she says he growled at her in place of saying "Good day, my mother." And she says that she, the wife of the said treasurer, never brought her soup in her illness. And that the said treasurer is the cause of the debauching of Johan, his brother and her son. And that the said treasurer never wanted to give her a glass of his wine, except two barrels of wine she could not drink. This was last year.

f. 136v] The said treasurer said that he gave her good wine, and she put the wine he gave her in vessels that were not proper for keeping good wine. The said Françoyse attributes to him the death of her two daughters, sisters of the said treasurer, who died of plague two months ago, which the said treasurer denies, and he is as unhappy about his two sisters as about himself, and is very sorry. She answers that he still owes her three *setiers* of wine. When the said treasurer called her mother, she answered him that she is not his mother, and she has again confirmed it in the presence of the lords [of the] Consistory.

The Consistory gave them remonstrances and admonitions to give up all hatred and grudges for the whole past down to the present day and to live in peace and amity together from now on and to live as son and mother, and that the said Françoyse be paid what is due her. The said treasurer offered to do what would be enough for her and to do for his part the best that he could and better than he has done in the past. And he begged mercy of his mother for the honor of God and to let fall all things past. And she did not want to do anything.

The Consistory is of the opinion that she be remanded to Thursday[375] and that she think about her affairs and return here on Thursday, and that she be given strict remonstrances to frequent the sermons. She said she

375. In the margin: "Here Thursday, and Loyse his wife, and Jehan."

would like to pardon them for the love of God and the Seigneurie. And she pardons him for all the things he has done to her, and also Loyse, her daughter-in-law.

[f. 137]   Donne Loyse, wife of Noble Pierre Tissotz, treasurer, because of her mother-in-law, that she does nothing for her. Answers that she is not the cause of the difference between her mother and her, and they are in discord. And if she knew she had need of anything she would give it to her. And when the said mother was ill, she went to her and did her good, as the neighbors know well. And when she brought her something she wanted nothing of it, cursing her when she took her anything because she wanted to save it, if she needed to have it given her. But she does not take willingly anything that is done for her, and it is not her fault that they are not all friends with each other. She was given proper admonitions.

Jehan Bertheratz, furrier.[376]

Does not know why he was summoned here, and he is still going to the sermon today. Also answers that he no longer says the rosary. He commends himself to God and says the prayer; sometimes the Gospel in Latin. And he has a New Testament, and has no Hours. And he prays to God in Latin and in French as far as he understands it, and he was not at the sermon today because today is a feast[377] and he has to earn his living as best he can, and he has only six sous as all his wealth(?) . . .[378] And he makes no difficulty about the law and that the sermon is not given any more in the tongue of former times. He was given firm remonstrances.

Pernete, wife of Jehan Bertheratz.[379]

Because of the sermons. Answers that she was there yesterday, and all those of their house, and she has no rosary, and mutters in the streets. And she does not keep the feasts any more.

376. Jehan Bertherat, citizen, living in the Fusterie, member of the CC in 1535. Sordet says that he had been one "of the most ardent adversaries of Farel." He died on October 5, 1552 [*R.C.* XIII, p. 455 (February 22, 1536); SORDET, *Dictionnaire,* p. 99; E.C., Morts 1, p. 81].

377. November 1, All Saints' Day.

378. Illegible word.

379. On October 7, 1544, almost a year after this session of the Consistory, Pernette de La Toy, widow of Michel Girbel, finally signed a contract of marriage with Jehan Bertherat "because it is a legal practice and good custom for wives to establish marriage with their husbands." She brought a dowry of almost 400 florins (Actes privés, Contrats de mariage 4, n. 9).

[37v] *Jehan Blanch, brandy dealer.*

Because of the sermons. Answers that he goes to the sermons when he can, and that he repeats what was good from past times, like the Pater in Latin, and the other sometimes in French. And he does not pray to the Virgin Mary and he no longer keeps feasts, and he said the Confiteor. He gave it up about three years ago, and he has not said it entirely since. He was given admonitions and remonstrances.

Claude Humbert, called Clement.[380]

Because he does not frequent the sermons. Answers that he is subject to an illness that prevents him from going there, and he goes when he can and every Sunday, and he sends his people. And he does not pray to the Lord in the present manner, and he has not been in Chambéry for Mass because he has no watchman. Said the prayer and the confession very badly, and knew how to say barely half. Prayed to be pardoned.

Thursday, November 8, 1543. Chapter.

Lord Syndic Checand.
Calvin, Trippereaulx, Pupin, Champereaulx.
Jehan Du Molar, Pensabin, De Ulmo, Veyrier, the officer Vovrez.

Lancellot Baux,[381] citizen of Geneva.

Confesses that he has often been summoned several times, and that he was given leave to go harvesting. Said that his brother Pierre[382] is in the village ill with pox, and confesses that he has sinned by fornication, and begs mercy of God and of justice. And the girl with whom he fornicated is in the village of Douvaine, and he was not here when she had [f. 138] the child. And he had often told her to watch carefully the fruit she carried, which died. Touching the sermons, answers that when he goes to the village he cannot come here, and when he is here he goes there willingly. And whether the girl took medicine to make her lose the child. Answers that she always told him said [sic] that she was not pregnant and that she had carried her urine to the doctor, who had

---

380. Actually Claude Clement, called Humbert.
381. Lancellot Baud, son of Jean Baud (syndic 1519, 1523). He made his will at his house in Chilly (H.-S.) in 1562 (GALIFFE I, pp. 45-46).
382. There are four Pierre Bauds mentioned in this volume of the Consistory alone. For this one see above, April 4, 1542, and note.

told her she was not pregnant. And he is not married. The opinion of the Consistory says that, considering that the whole cannot be known because his mistress cannot be had, he should be remanded to next Monday to the Council and given strong admonitions and remonstrances to frequent the sermons.[383]

Jehan Tissot, citizen of Geneva.

Because of the taverns and gambling and spending his goods at the taverns[384] and games and conflicts he has with his brother.[385] Answers that his brother was the first who began it, and he has gambled only once or twice, and sometimes. Five. And he confesses that his conscience accuses him and that his brother is the reason he does nothing and is such a wastrel, because he does not know how to do anything, and therefore is so debauched. And he said to his brother: "Take all my goods and watch them." And if his brother had helped him he would not have wasted his time. And he has not helped him at all, except a little by command. And he goes to the sermons. He was given admonitions and remonstrances to frequent the sermons.

Jane, daughter of the late Girardin Exerton.

To know how her brothers treat her. Answers that at present they treat her well, but in the past very badly, that there were words about people of the village and therefore they beat her. And she does not know why she was beaten so, and it was Humbert[386] who beat her. And her other brother defended her, and [f. 138v] she does not know why. And the words are such as Monsieur Jehan Pensabin spoke. It is because her brothers always sent her to the mill at night, which is very far, and she met a man who asked where she

---

383. On September 19, 1543, Pierre Baud complained in Council of Nicolas de Diesbach, *bailli* of Thonon, who had summoned Lancellot Baud before the Consistory of Thonon (R.C. 37, f. 223v). This summons certainly caused the present investigation. On November 16, 1543, Lancellot Baud, then in prison for his fornication, was freed "on paying his expenses" (R.C. 37, f. 273v). This case was again discussed in Consistory on March 4, 1544, but this apparently did not satisfy the Bernese; on May 5, 1544, Lancellot Baud again appeared in Council because "the *bailli* of Thonon molests the goods he has at Chilly because he does not want to answer to their Consistory." The Council then sent "a lord of the Council at his expense [Baud's] to the said *bailli* to admonish him that the said Lancellot is of Geneva, and has been punished for the case he is charged with" (R.C. 38, f. 186).

384. Some months earlier Jehan Tissot had asked in Council to be permitted to sell his goods without the permission of his guardian. The Council refused his request and admonished him "not to associate with people who are prohibited to him, and also he should not go outside [the city] or frequent taverns" [R.C. Part. 1, f. 68 (June 19, 1543)].

385. Pierre Tissot.

386. Humbert Exerton (see below in the present session).

came from and where she was going and then he was lost from her sight. And she entered a house he entered, and it was between Vésegnin and Prévissin. And she was afraid of him, and it was before day, about two months ago, it was after harvest. Asked why she was so afraid. Answers because she saw him behind her. And touching the sermons, she would go willingly if her brother would give her permission, but her brother does not want her to go there, and she can rarely go because she always has something to do. She does not know why her brother does not let her take a partner.[387] Said the prayer and the confession. And her sister-in-law sometimes told her to go to the sermon. She was given remonstrances and strict admonitions.

Claude Moyron, from Chénex, farm laborer, habitant *of Geneva.*

And that he engaged himself to a woman[388] about six weeks ago, and he has no maid, and the neighbors should be asked, and he denies that he has mistreated his daughters. And it may be she is pregnant, and she was not his maid but was a maid at Malliard's. And it is three years since he gave a blow to his dead wife, and he did not forbid her to his daughters. He has two. And his wife died about St. John's Day, and his said wife died of plague, and his daughter remembered her during the said [time]. And his wife had a grievance because he fornicated while he lived with her. And his daughters knew nothing and his neighbors [f. 139] never gave any appearance of it. And his present wife lived at Malliard's, and when they went into the vineyard they sinned together. And one of his neighbors shut up his wife in a pest-house to treat her. And he had not fornicated for a long time. And about three months before the death of his wife he fornicated with the said maid to whom he is engaged, and he received Communion in this condition. And he intends to marry her next Sunday.

Touching the sermons, answers that he does not hear the preaching as well as he should. Said the prayer, and not all of the confession, and that his daughters know it better than he. And that he has still not recovered the marriage [portion] of [his] dead wife.

The opinion of the Consistory is that he be remanded before the Council and not receive the next Communion, and in three weeks he and his wife should both be remanded here, and that he learn to pray to the Lord as is proper within the said time.[389]

---

387. *I.e.,* get married.
388. Jana, his wife, appeared in Consistory on November 29, 1543.
389. On November 12, 1543, the Council condemned Claude Moyron to three days in prison on bread and water for fornication (R.C. 37, f. 271).

Estienne Furjodz.

Answers that he does not live with his wife, nor his wife with him. And he does not want to go look for her at her father's.[390] And she disposed of the entire household during the time he was imprisoned across the Arve,[391] and his tavern[392] went also. Answers that, as for the tavern, he meddled in nothing, since she managed everything. And it is said that he took everything to sell it and that he did not shut himself up to take the curtains.[393] And that his wife shut him out of the house and disposed of all his goods. And that it is their fault, since they are not together. Both remanded to next Thursday.[394]

390. Estienne Furjod married Bezansonne Falquet, daughter of Petremand Falquet, the first to bear the title of *"gros sautier."* According to Galiffe (II, pp. 323-324), at the time of the marriage of Bezansonne Falquet the Council gave her a present because she "is very honest, and her father is not rich." Petremand Falquet died on March 7, 1546 (R.C. 41, f. 40v). See also FROMENT, p. 29.

391. At Saconnex delà d'Arve (see below, November 22, 1543). The cause of his detention is not known unless it was connected with his father-in-law's complaint (see below, November 22, 1543).

392. The inn of the Stork (see above, January 11, 1543, note).

393. The meaning is not clear. In the local patois a "curtain" could be a loose woman (*G.P.S.R.* IV, p. 463a), but Furjod does not seem to be accused of fornication or of anything similar.

394. On June 5, 1543, Petremand Falquet complained of his son-in-law in Council, accusing him of wasting his goods. Falquet asked that a *"cureur"* be appointed, as guardians for adults were called, and the Council chose Jehan Marchant, councillor (R.C. Part. 1, f. 62v). On June 11 Falquet specified that Furjod was wasting the goods of his wife, Falquet's daughter, and that Furjod "hides and does not want to obey. Also that he is locked in his house." Falquet then asked that Furjod be put in prison, which may explain the term of detention Furjod refers to above (R.C. Part. 1, f. 64v). This case was again discussed in Consistory on November 22, 1543, without settling anything, and on April 11, 1544, Furjod presented a supplication in Council against his wife, "asking that she be made to return the movables that were at the inn of the Stork that his wife removed, and he has nothing to live on." Bezansonne, accompanied by her father, said that she could not live with her husband because he had "nothing to maintain a household with." The Council then ordered them to "live and return together in peace, and meanwhile his request remains [inactive] in hope of an agreement" (R.C. Part. 1, f. 146v; see also R.C. 38, f. 158v). The Council then offered the post of officer of the lieutenant to Furjod. The Council confirmed the nomination of Furjod on April 18 and he took the oath on the 22nd (R.C. 38, f. 167 and f. 170v).

[f. 139v] *Humbert Exerton.*[395]

Because of his treatment of his sister[396] and that he and his wife beat her and do not let her go to the sermon. Answers that touching the sermons, he often commands her to go to the sermon. And if anyone wants her he will give him charge of her and will give him all he owes her, since she was given to him by law. He was admonished to treat his sister better in the future than he has in the past and strive to get her married and not keep her as a servant. That his wife should take her to the sermon with her and that he cease to send her out at night as often as he has in the past. And he answers it is true that they send her where they have business. Lord Jehan Pensabin offered to shelter her if he is given what she is entitled to.

Thursday, November 15, 1543, in Chapter.

Lord Syndic Checand.
Calvin, Genesto, Trippereaulx.
Morel, Du Molard, Pensabin, Blandin, Veyrier, Just de Loermoz, Vernaz, the officer Vovrey.

Martinaz, widow of Jaques Richel, coiner.

Because of the sermons. Answers that she goes to the sermons on Sundays when she can. And as for the course she follows, she sells, and her daughter serves her. And her daughter's husband is in Lyon waiting until he pays some men he owes, and then he will come back. And she is not one who follows a bad course in her house. And that her daughter is nursing a child to earn her living, and as above she serves her, and they are together, frequenting the sermons as much as they can. Said that she knew the prayer, but not her confession in the form in which it is said at present. And as for usury, answers that she has [f. 140] thirty florins and has lent them to two men who have given her, one a *bichet* of wheat, and the other a *quart,* and she has received so much. And these 30 florins she has and keeps thus, and she has used them for the last eight years, and she gave 15 to Nycod Berod who will return them to her, and she cannot have anything, neither the 15 florins, nor the profit.

---

395. Noble Humbert Exerton, citizen, hosier [Titres et Droits, Pa 619, folios 543v-545 (December 15, 1546); E.C., Morts 1, p. 85 (November 12, 1552; death of his son)].
    396. Jana Exerton.

289

Loys Piaget, sheath-maker.

Because of the last Holy Communion in the month of September. Answers that he has not received it since Pentecost, and he received it from the hand of Don Jaques de Bonis[397] because he wanted to wait to hear the Passion, and when he saw it was done he asked it of the said Don Jaques who was at the back, and he intended it only in good faith and did not intend any harm. Said the prayer and the confession very poorly.

Don Jaques de Bonis, of Saint Gervais.

Does not know the reason why he was summoned, and he served at Holy Communion, and he did not have the task of giving it giving [sic]. And he does not remember giving it to anyone except to some children who asked him for it and to a woman named Chamossue. And he had them say the prayer before he gave them the bread, and not the wine. Touching his maid, said that he has had a maid a long time and she is old, and he does not intend to marry, he would rather send her out of his house, and if he were of an age to marry, being 60 years old. He was given remonstrances and admonitions.

Claude Du Bochet of Le Bouchet;[398] Claude Davaulx, living in Le Bouchet.

Do not know why they are summoned. And they are neighbors, and about the quarrel, the said Davaulx asks to be reconciled with the said Du Bochet, his neighbor, because of some words spoken, the said Davaulx saying that he was insulted by the said Du Bochet, that his wife called him thief. The

397. Piaget seems to have been suspected of preferring to take Communion from a priest rather than a minister, Jaques de Bonis having been a priest at St. Gervase before the Reform (since at least 1520). On December 6, 1535, under pressure to renounce the Mass, he asked a delay to reflect, and apparently decided to leave the city. Six months later he asked permission to return to Geneva, promising to go to the sermons and give up all papal "superstition." On returning to the city, however, he was soon jailed for having sung the Mass against the edicts. Like almost all the former priests resident in Geneva in 1539, he renounced the Mass before the Council. A little after his return Jaques de Bonis became farmer of the properties of the parish of St. Gervase along with his former colleague Don Contant, but this office does not seem to have been profitable; in April 1543 he asked the Council to "release them from the said rent farm, since they have not had any joy of it." However, he was still farmer in 1544 [*R.C.* XIII, p. 374 (December 6, 1535); *ibid.,* p. 556 (May 2, 1536); R.C. 30, f. 28 and f. 60 (July 14 and September 27, 1536); R.C. 33, f. 390 (December 22, 1539); R.C. Part. 1, f. 46 (April 27, 1543); R.C. 38, f. 263v (June 26, 1544); GALIFFE I, p. 457].

398. A rather common name (see GALIFFE II, pp. 88-89). This is Claude, son of the late Gervais Du Bochet, "from the town of Le Bouchet," who acknowledged on May 29, 1545 (below, and Titres et Droits, Pa 619, folios 634-635).

other said no, and that it is not so and he wishes him no harm, that his mistress would not call him that. The said Claude said that he wishes him no harm, and Davaulx said that the wife of the said Bochet said something that is undesirable(?). [f. 140v] The said Davaulx said that the wife of the said Du Bochet reproached him with being a sorcerer, which is a thing hard to endure. The said Davaulx was asked why he did not receive Holy Communion. This was because he was not qualified to receive it. Touching the reproach of heresy[399] that he was reproached with, he answers that information should be obtained, and if it is true appropriate action should be taken. And he should not be pardoned for the said heresy; if he is such a man justice should be done. The advice of the Consistory is that their wives and their mother-in-law be made to come on Thursday.[400]

Thursday, November 22, 1543. Chapter.

Lord Syndic Checand.
Farel, Calvin, De Ecclesia, Genesto, Pupin, Tripereaulx.
Morel, Molard, Pensabin, Blandin, Veyrier, the officer Vovrey.

Estienne Furjod and Bezansonaz, with her father, Petremand Falquet.

Because she does not stay with him. Bezansonaz answers that he has wasted all his goods and has nothing to live on. And he sold what she took to him on his return from prison in Saconnex. And he did not come to see his child when she gave birth and he never gave her comfort or aid and never wanted to come to dinner. That the godfather carried him, and he was asked to be there. The said Furjoz denies that he was told, and many words which would be too tedious to write here. The said Furjod answers that he will prove that she took it out of a house he had put it in.

The opinion of the Consistory is that his bad behavior not be regarded for the future, that his wife work and follow their admonition to go forward better and that he find a way to support his wife and his child and that they be summoned one after the other and that the intentions of the said Furjod be learned. And [f. 141] as for the fourth point, he should be remanded to the Council to learn whether he can be compensated for the goods he

---

399. That is of sorcery, normally prosecuted as the crime of heresy.
400. Thibauda, wife of Claude Du Bochet; Jaquemaz, wife of Gervays Du Bochet, mother-in-law of Claude Du Bochet; and Loyse, wife of Claude Davaulx (see below, November 22, 1543).

wasted, and the other issues they can bring before the Council.[401] And that he be given a conservator, and that he can restore the marriage, and that they be reconciled and live together. The said Furjod means to live according to God, and he will pray the Lord to assist him and will live differently in the future. Was given proper and friendly admonitions.

Bezansonnaz was given proper admonitions. She answers that she wants to be and act like a respectable woman if it pleases God, and it is very proper for a woman to live with her husband if he wants to support her as he should, and she will find the means to have her life. Both together promised to live together according to the commandment of God, and if one does not go right, the Council will have knowledge of it.

Claude Du Bochet and his wife. Claude de Vaux and Loyse his wife.

The said Loyse because of the malevolence of her neighbor. Answers that villainy is imputed to her by Claude Bochet and his wife, and they called her "vicious woman" and said she was a she-wolf. And she never said Claude Du Bochet was a sorcerer. She has been ill for four years, and she has no suspicions of the said Claude except what he gives her and does to her. And if he is evil, may God make him good. And she spoke as he spoke to her. She is ill, and she, her husband and their servants are often ill when they want to do some business. She has heard that he is unlucky, and if he gives her illness he does wrong. She has heard he . . .[402] and the medicines cost her a lot. And she hired a doctor named Bastien,[403] and he treated her successfully. And when she was ill she hired him again, and he gave her boxes of ointments that smell of pitch. And he managed her case well for a year, and someone told her he was a sorcerer. She says she does not know whether the said Claude Du Bochet is a sorcerer. And she did not receive Communion in malice but leaves everything to God. [f. 141v] The advice of the Consistory is . . .[404]

All together, Jaquemaz, wife of Gervays Du Bochet; Thibaudaz, wife of Claude Du Bochet. And the father of the said Claude Du Bochet is ill and could not come here. Claude de Vaulx said that there is no conflict among them except that spoken of last Thursday, and they come to the sermons on Sundays. The said Loyse said that the said Claude de Vaulx said "Vicious fornicator!" to her, and that the earth should not hold her up. And the said Claude said no. And the said Claude said it was not so. Claude Du Bochet says he said

---

401. See above, November 8, 1543, note.
402. Incomplete sentence.
403. Bastien de Villa.
404. Incomplete sentence.

it. And they intend from this hour on to live in amity together and in peace according to the commandment of God, and they shook hands as brothers. They were admonished not to let any reproach escape them from this hour on; otherwise they will be remanded to the Council, if they return to malevolence.

Donne Anthoyne Viennesaz.[405]

Because of the feasts and papistries, the sermons. Answers that she no longer keeps feasts. On All Saints' Day she came from Bardonnex and could do nothing that day. And she goes to the sermons, although she said sometimes she has to go to dinner when she has been to the sermon in the morning. And she does not despise the Word of God, and she will carry a bell from now on when she goes to the sermon to show that she is going to the sermon. This is in contempt of the Word of God.[406] And she was there last Sunday morning, and she does not know who preached and did not put what he said in her memory. And not this week, and she does not know what they said and did not recognize those who preached. Said that she knows how to pray to the Lord and that she has no advocate but God. She was given firm remonstrances; otherwise she will be remanded to the Council.

142]   The *sautier* stated something because of what the said Furjod imposed on Bezansone, his daughter.[407]

Robellaz, widow of Falcoz Vachon, surgeon.[408]

Because of the sermons. Answers that she goes on Sundays and not the other days and that she is fully prepared and has no one with her. And as for All Saints', she was taking care of her son the whole day, and because she is subject to gout and therefore cannot go there to the sermons. And she was there in the morning before dinner, and Calvin preached, and she retained of the sermon what she could, the Pater. And on All Saints' she wanted to take her son to the weaver for her cloth. And she thinks more about the Word of the Lord than before, and if she has some scruple about religion she will come speak to the minister before receiving Holy Communion. She was . . .[409]

405. Antoina, wife of François Viennesi, daughter of the syndic Aymon de Versonay, died on March 27, 1553 (GALIFFE I, pp. 269-270; E.C., Morts 1, p. 98).

406. "This is in contempt of the Word of God" is underlined in the text.

407. Petremand Falquet, *grand sautier* of the Council, Etienne Furjod, and Bezansonne Falquet.

408. Falcoz Vachon, barber, from Crémieu (Isère), admitted to the bourgeoisie on January 4, 1519, then living in the parish of Saint Germain (*L.B.*, p. 187).

409. Incomplete sentence.

Pernete, Jane and Oddete, daughters of Guyotz Vuydat.

Because of the sermons. All three answer that they go to the sermon every Sunday, hear all the sermons and do not sing by day or night. Considering the great poverty they are in, and information should be obtained. And on All Saints' Day they worked all day. And they got up earlier in the morning than on other days to sew.[410]

Amed Servex, from Bassy in La Sémine.

About two years ago, weaver of cloth, because of the sermons. Answers that he goes to the sermons every Sunday in the morning at St. Peter's and that as far as he knows, when he spoke he did not say "Go to the sermon if you want," and to another, "Go there, you." Said the Pater, the Ave Maria and the Benedicite in Latin, with the sign of the cross. And he does not understand what he said in Latin. Said a little of the prayer in French, and none of the confession. And does not keep feasts, except sometimes he goes to the threshing at his house. [f. 142v] The opinion of the Consistory is that he be remanded here in two weeks and know how to pray to the Lord in the way he should, and that he bring his wife and be better instructed.

Thursday, November 29, 1543, in Chapter.

Lord Syndic Checand.
Calvin, Triperaulx, Champereaulx.
Vernaz, Pensabin, De Loermoz, Blandin, De Veyrier, Domeyne, the officer Guetz.[411]

Jana, wife of Claude Moyron of Chénex.

It was about Easter that he engaged himself to her, and about three weeks [ago] he married her. And he has known her since Easter, a little before

410. The daughters of Guyot Vuydat had appeared once before in Council to ask it "to give them charity; that is to permit them to live in the house that was that of the Allardets in order that they may earn their poor living. Resolved that they may stay in this house . . ." [R.C. 36, f. 78 (July 25, 1542)]. Guyot Vuydat himself asked on May 29, 1543, for charity "for his poor living" and received a *coupe* of wheat per quarter [R.C. Part. 1, f. 60v (May 29, 1543)]. One of Vuydat's daughters had her banns of marriage with Jehan Fayet refused "because he is a foreigner and did not know the ordinances" [R.C. Part. 1, f. 177v (July 25, 1544); this refers to the edicts regulating marriages between foreigners and Genevans. See *S.D.* II, p. 338 (June 4, 1537)].
411. Probably Domaine Guex, officer.

his wife died. Answers that she repents of having behaved so and that her said husband received nothing from the first marriage of his other wife. Said the prayer and the confession correctly. Answers that her husband is not here but has gone to the village to till the soil for his poor living and for both of them. The opinion of the Consistory has, since she has some knowledge and is pregnant, that she be sent back and frequent the sermons and govern her husband's two daughters well, and that she live in peace.

Tevene, widow of Marquet Peronet.

Touching the vow she made. Answers that she was very sad when she made it. It was because of her husband who was ill, and she was badly advised and repents from her heart and begs mercy of God and the Seigneurie and the Company. And she did nothing except what she revealed to the lieutenant, a pound of wax to St. Claude. And now she knows well the fault she committed and is very unhappy about it. And she was at the first sermon at St. Peter's on Sunday, and he produced good words and arguments, and it was a handsome bearded man who preached. Said the prayer, and does not know the confession, and does not pray [f. 143] to the Virgin Mary, and prays to the Lord only and no other. The Consistory, having heard some repentance, that she be given a term of two weeks to know how to make the confession of her religion. She was admonished to bring her son here the said day, and that he be admonished. And that the said son be well instructed, and be exhorted because he wanted to break into his father's chests when he died, and she should be asked whether anyone instructed her to make such a vow. Answers that no one at all ever instructed her to make such a vow, and as above she repents from her heart.

Mermete, widow of Pierre Gerbel.

Because of the vow to St. Claude. Answers that she has not made a vow to St. Claude or to others besides God or given her husband to any saint, and she never kept it 20 hours, and she believes that it is not proper to make a vow except to God, or to any saint, because this is nothing but abuse. And she does not go to the sermons except on Sundays, and the other days she cannot go there because of her household. Nor, by her faith, did she ever think she was obliged to make vows to the saints. She said she knows how to pray. She was admonished to frequent the sermons more often than she has before.

Thursday, December 6, 1543

Lord Syndic Checand.
Calvin, Albert, Genesto, De Ecclesia, Tripereaulx.
Vernaz, Justz Ulmo, Pensabin, De Veyrier, the officer Vovrey.

Amed Servex, weaver.

Was remanded to today to know how to say the prayer and to frequent the sermons. Answers that he has frequented the sermons, and said the prayer and the confession worse than last time. And he is not a bourgeois and is from Bassy. In view of his contempt for the church he should come here in two weeks and frequent the sermons better and know better how to pray to the Lord.

[f. 143v] *Jehan Dayguenoyre[412] of this city, bourgeois, cobbler, and is married and [has] a young daughter.*

Answers that he goes and wants to go [to the sermons], and sometimes on working days, and he was urged to leave the city because of religion, which he did not want to do, and he has left his own town and country. And he was at the catechism on Sunday. Said the prayer and the confession. He was given proper admonitions.

Loysaz, wife of Pierre Joly, called Collombi, carter.[413]

Answers that she goes to the sermons on Sundays and not the other days, and was not there last Sunday. And she is not angry at the wife of the gent . . . (?)[414] Said the prayer, and does not know the confession. The advice of the Consistory is that she return in two weeks with her husband and that she attend the sermons and learn to pray to the Lord.

---

412. A Johannes de Aqua Nigra (d'Aiguenoire), cobbler, from Boëge, was received into the bourgeoisie in 1495, and according to Galiffe (IV, pp. 1-2) he was still living in 1514, but he would have been very old at the time of this session of the Consistory. Another Jehan Dayguenoire, from Boëge (H.-S.), was received into the bourgeoisie in 1539. This last was probably the Jehan Dayguenoire, cobbler, who was living on the Rue Saint Anthoine and lost a daughter in 1552 [GALIFFE, *ibid.*; L.B., p. 125 (November 13, 1495) and p. 218 (March 14, 1539); E.C., Morts 1, p. 54 (March 13, 1552)].

413. Loyse, wife of Pierre Joly, called Coullon or Collomb, carter, citizen, living on the Rue Malbuisson, died on March 29, 1562, aged 56. Pierre Joly died the following August 29, aged 80 (E.C., Morts 4, p. 108; E.C., Morts 5, p. 45, *ad dies*).

414. Illegible words.

Cugniet, currier, of Saint Gervais.

Answers that he stays he stays [sic] in his house and they live together, and he buys the bread that he eats that she sells, and she gives him the money for the said bread, which he eats. Also touching drunkenness, answers that he has not struck his wife for more than four years. And as for wine, he drinks in moderation and he does not get drunk, and sometimes he is happier than others. He promised to restrain himself from this vice from now on. He was given proper admonitions to live more soberly than he has in the past.[415]

Claudaz, daughter of Cousouz, from Vandouvres.

She has been a servant at Monsieur De Fosse's for four months and a half, and she is married, and she has not known where her husband is for four months, and she did not have the means to live with him and would like to have gone with him. And he is from Vandouvres and is named Tyvent Burnet. And she does not know where he is. And they have hardly any means to live on, and he should have pledged to her what she gave him. And because she did not want to give him any more money he threatened to pull her nose off, and for this reason she left and came to this city to serve a master and earn her living. She says that it is not her fault that they do not live together, and she would like to live with him. [f. 144] And thus she does not want him to live with her, and she is content to do what a respectable woman should do. Said the prayer and half of the confession. And her master wants her to go to the sermons and commands her to. She was admonished to try to get her husband to come so they will live together in peace.

Alexandre Davonex, watchman from Geneva.[416]

Because of drunkenness. Answers that he did not drink 18 glasses of wine at one time at Choupin's.[417] It is true that he was taken with Greloz in the middle of dinner, and he made no disorder and does not know who paid

415. A certain Cugniez complained of the minister Champereau on June 12, 1543, for having refused to baptize his child with the name "Charogne," but, as here, the register does not give his first name (R.C. Part. 1, f. 65v).

416. Alexandre Davonex and Claude Michallet, watchmen, had been imprisoned some months earlier for having "drawn [their swords] on the guard of the Porte du Pont du Rhône so that those who were on guard began to cry 'to arms.'" They excused themselves by claiming they did it merely "to know whether they were keeping a good watch or not," and they were freed by the Council [R.C. 37, f. 184v and f. 188 (August 7 and 10, 1543)].

417. Probably Pierre Curt, called Choupin, host of the Green Hat in Longemale (see above, January 11, 1543, note). See also the interrogation of Aymoz Choupin below, December 20, 1543.

the bill and does not know whether there was any disorder. And he takes the host to witness. And he drank decently with them, and testimony should be taken, and if he has committed such insolence he wants to be punished. And it happened about a fortnight ago last Sunday, and he asked mercy for the offense of the Seigneurie. He was given admonitions and remonstrances.

Jehan Caliat, from Crassy, cobbler, bourgeois.[418]

Answers that he lives well in his household with his wife and with the merchants and he has borrowed only 29 écus, and he lent them to his brother Oddet, and he gave two écus of profit for 16 of Losserand's in the market of the Taccon.[419] It is true that they ate together once and they told him he should pay for the breakfast and they would pay another time, which he did. And he does not know that he drank 18 glasses of wine and gobbled the old cheese like a wolf. And Jehan Tissot gave him the money, and he paid him an écu, and the whole banquet cost two écus. And this was at Choupin's. And he had promised to pay to pay [sic] for four or five, and the others came of their own will. He was admonished.[420]

[f. 144v]   *Colleta, daughter of Aymoz de Monthouz, parish of Reignier, wife of Amed Servex.*

Because of the sermons. Answers that she was there twice on Sunday and on Monday morning, and she has no child. And her husband has always gone twice on Sunday since she has known him. She was admonished.

The first.

Thursday, December 13, 1543

Lord Syndic Checand.
Calvin, Champereaulx, De Ecclesia, Trippereaulx, Pupin.
Morel, Du Molard, Vernaz, Blandin, Veyrier, Pensabin, De Loermoz, the officer Vovrey.

---

418. Jehan Calliat was received into the bourgeoisie on September 2, 1541 (*L.B.*, p. 222).

419. Probably Pierre or Jehan Losserand. Jehan Losserand the younger was living in the Tacconnerie in 1554 [E.C., Morts 1, p. 157 (April 26, 1554)]. [Translator: The meaning of this passage is not too clear.]

420. After having been imprisoned "because he has entertained gamblers in his house and has kept a tavern without a license," Jehan Caliat was freed by decision of the Council [R.C. 38, f. 44 and f. 49v (January 25 and 31, 1544)].

Claude, wife of Jehan Voland, carter, called Gentil.

Answers that she goes to the sermons, and three times on Sundays, because she cannot go the other days because of business. On the insults she gave in the harbor with the others, and she is reluctant(?) to answer when pressed. Said the prayer and the confession well. She was admonished to frequent the sermons and to punish her children, and let them not insult people any more.

Mermet Mouri, from Aire la Ville, farm laborer, formerly a miller.

Answers that he is married and lives in Saint Gervais and lives a quiet life. Touching him and his wife who are always at odds, and he has not gone to the taverns for 18 years, and he has never known any woman other than his wife. And he has never slept with another, except with Françoys's maid who lodged with his wife and him, and he would not be content if another man slept with his wife. And he goes to the sermon very little, and on Sundays as much as he can. When he is angry he blasphemes. And he has children. Said the prayer poorly and not the confession, and said that he knows the Pater in Latin and has said it and the confession and Ave Maria in Latin every day, and he prays to the Virgin Mary as to God, [f. 145] and he has received Communion and does not know what it is. And he was at the sermon last Sunday before dinner and does not know what was said. And he will not say the Ave Maria any more. The opinion of the Consistory is that he not receive the next Holy Communion, and afterwards that he know how to pray to the Lord within two weeks, and present himself three weeks after Communion. And that he frequent the sermons more than he has reported. And that he be given harsher admonitions afterwards if he does not correct his evil, and also others until he amends(?) his life.

Guilliama, widow of Jehan Berod,[421] *farm laborer, maid of Donne Cornaz.*[422]

It was about a year ago at Michaelmas, and she was in Lausanne with her mistress and they went together to the sermon for about three months at

---

421. We have found only one reference to a Jehan Berod, who attended Garin Muète's sermon in 1533. See VAN BERCHEM, "Prédication," p. 166; *R.C.* XII, p. 597, *notes complémentaires.*

422. Jeanne Darmeis, widow of Pierre Corne, mother of the syndic Amblard Corne. She married François Bonivard in 1544 and they led a turbulent conjugal life thereafter until her death in 1552. Bonivard's biographer, J.-J. Chaponnière ("Bonivard," p. 197), remarks ironically that after eight years of marriage Bonivard and Jeanne Corne "had lived very little and very badly together." See also *ibid.,* pp. 191-196.

Monsieur Blecheret's, and she did not see a diviner at her mistress's house. And recently a man came who stayed with the Donne to treat her, and he stayed a day and slept and made a drink for her mistress and ground spices. And the said doctor did not tell her to do anything else. And when they were in Lausanne they were nowhere else that she knows of except Trelex above Lausanne at Donne Magdaleine's. And if her mistress had not been ill in her head she would have always gone to the sermon. And the husband of the said Magd[aleine] Peaollate[423] came to get them on horseback. And she does not know whether the doctor she had in her house was a diviner or not.

Donne Janaz Cornaz was asked whether she had a doctor who was a diviner in her house. Answers that she did not have a diviner in her house when she was in Lausanne; that Monsieur Jehan Roche[424] told her she should have this doctor, and she does not know who he was, and she sent to find him in Lausanne in Le Boneret. And he answered that the moon was not good, and she should send for him and he would come to this city when it was time. And she was not in Montoie and did not know about it and she did not send for anyone other than the one the said Lord Roche told her to. She was given strong words about the *curé* of Montoie and others about the sermons and negligence of the Word of the Lord. Answers that she is not always well enough to go to the sermons because her head is troubled with an illness, and she has to rest. And it is only due to her illness, and she does not go to the sermon for the sake [f. 145v] of any saint or of feasts of the saints, because her illness affects her, although she would like to frequent the sermons. And that she believes Communion is good. And touching the Mass she answers that she is not learned beyond what she can understand. Answers that if she were a lover of Masses she would be where Masses are said, but she intends to be where the Gospel is and finish her days there. And that she did not go to or look for or find the *curé* of Montoie, nor did she make this doctor come who stayed in her house a day and a half. And Monsieur Jaques of Lausanne treated her case well for four months.[425] And she is in better health than she was before. And he did not order her a novena or a Pater or any

423. Properly "Pecollate." Tristan de Branges, husband of Madaleine Cornille, widow of Etienne Pecolat.

424. Probably Jehan Rosche (Roschyz), councillor in Lausanne since 1529, named bursar before October 31, 1545 (*M.C.L.* II, p. 96; 2ᵉ sér. I, p. 10 *et passim*).

425. Probably Jaques Blécheret, doctor of medicine and citizen of Lausanne, named municipal doctor of Lausanne on May 6 of the plague summer of 1543. He was a member of the Consistory of Lausanne and was elected to the Council of Sixty in 1553. He became deacon of Orbe in 1559 and was still living in 1564 (*M.C.L.* III, pp. 84, 137, and 208; VUILLEUMIER I, p. 584).

other superstition, and if there had been any superstition she would not have put herself in his hands. And the *curé* of Le Boneret was not there. And her daughter waited for her in the said Lausanne without going farther with her, and she would have gone earlier. And she always went to the sermon when she was in Lausanne, and she no longer says her rosary and does not commend herself to the saints, because the saints do not do miracles and will not save us. And she has no scruples about saints. She was given proper admonitions. It is necessary to write to the Consistory of Lausanne about Monsieur Jehan Roche and to know more.

Donne . . . ,[426] *her daughter, wife of Noble François Chamoys.*

Answers that she goes to the sermons on Sundays and working days. And she was four months in Lausanne and in Pailly near Lausanne, and she went to the sermons in Lausanne, and she was at the house of someone in childbirth and her husband, Monsieur Guillaume, and the niece of Monsieur Françoys Conte, and it was in . . .[427] And she was nowhere else with her mother. And she does not know who went with her. And Monsieur Jehan Roche told her where to find a doctor who would cure her. And she did not know the *curé* of Montoie and did not know him [sic]. And this doctor was here, the one whom the said Monsieur Jehan Roche suggested, and he slept here one night, and they do not know whether he is a diviner, and they would not want to divine or look for diviners. And as for the sermons, when she can [f. 146] she goes, and her husband also. And she [has] no scruples about our religion, and she has her heart on God. She does not know whether the said doctor who was in their house was a diviner or not, and she never heard that he was, and she does not know at all that he is a diviner, and she . . .[428] She was admonished to frequent the sermons more often than she has in the past.

A woman appeared against Françoys Du Molard and made him come before the lieutenant.

And the said [Du Molard] wanted to take an oath that he never wanted to ask for the keys, and he wanted to swear and swore that he never asked for the keys. Also he says the wife of Master Mychiel the saddler[429] and her servant wish him harm, and they do not renounce(?) her.

426. Name omitted. This is Philiberte, daughter of Pierre and Jeanne Corne, wife of François Chamois (GALIFFE II, p. 110; CHAPONNIÈRE, "Bonivard," p. 192, n. 1).
427. Name of place omitted.
428. Incomplete sentence.
429. Claudaz, wife of Michel Julliard, saddler.

Tuesday, December 18, 1543
Held before the Holy Communion of Our Lord at Christmas.

Lord Syndic Checand.
Calvin, Pupin, De Ecclesia.
Morel, Vernaz, Molard, Blandin, Pensabin, De Loermoz, Veyrier, the officer Vovrey.

Amed Goget, from Mategnin.

And he has stayed in this city five years and has lost his goods, which they took. Because of the sermons. Answers that he goes to the sermons on Sundays, the other days before dinner, and Monsieur Calvin preached. And about spells for curing fever, it is indeed true that he cured a tailor near the City Hall with *moretoz*[430] and consumption, and he had to be laid out as if on a cross, and he said nothing else and did nothing else. And he has no scruples about the Christian religion. Said the prayer in Latin and French and none of the confession; sometimes the Ave Maria. And he says he told the priests in former times that they abuse us. Said he would do his duty by knowing better how to pray to the Lord than he has in the past.

[f. 146v] *Tevenaz, widow of Marquet Peroné.*

That she should know better how to pray to the Lord. Said the prayer and the confession very poorly. Andrier Marquet, her son,[431] who had been admonished to serve and obey his mother, the master and mistress he might have, and not to frequent those behaving badly and to follow the sermons and to pray to the Lord and to flee games.

Thivent Mathe, from Choulex, weaver.

Has been in this city 17 years and does not frequent the sermons. Answers that he goes to the sermons on Sundays and not other days because he has to earn the living of two twins and two other small children he has, and

430. Translator: Evidently a disease, but we do not know the translation.
431. In the R.C. Andrier Marquet is found detained in October 1543 for having testified in Ternier that "Hugue Berthier was a respectable man, who is not, because he is among the condemned." His wife then presented a supplication for his liberation, but the case was remanded to the Two Hundred, where he is called Marquet Peronet. Since it appears here that the son was still young, it may be that Tevenaz Peronet had just lost her husband and that father and son were both named André Marquet Peronet, or that the father was André Marquet, called Peronet [R.C. 37, f. 253v and f. 256v (October 26 and 29, 1543)].

when one of them, his wife or he . . .[432] And he has not gambled for five weeks, and the last time he gambled was behind the Tour de l'Ecole.[433] And he never said that he never would have said in gambling that he never said [sic] that he could certainly gamble, since the preachers gamble with dice. And he gives himself up to be punished, and says that he said then that there was a preacher of Orbe who had wagered five sous for a pâté with Monsieur De Saint Victeur,[434] and he did not say that he was one of the preachers of this city. Said that the preacher asked for the cards. And that he never said it was a preacher of Geneva. And he would not recognize the preacher who wagered the said pâté on the dice. It may have been three months ago that Don Hugoneri's wife[435] said that it was a preacher and he was dressed in a long robe and carried his staff on his hip. He says he said then that he had seen a preacher who gambled with Monsieur Saint Victeur as above. And if he knew who the said preacher was he would say so, even if it was Monsieur Calvin or one of the others. And he never said that the said gambling preacher was from Geneva, and he would not recognize him, and Monsieur Voland and Monsieur Jaques de Cholex were present.

Considering his confession, one could find the contrary by the witnesses, and he should state in the place where he said such words, say that he did not say it was a preacher of Geneva. And that Gonerie be checked on and Don Hugoneri and his wife and Monsieur De Saint Victeur summoned. [f. 147] Promised to appear when he is summoned either before the ministers or wherever he . . .[436]

Monsieur Thomas Genod.[437]

Does not know why he was summoned; because he treats his wife badly.[438] And he has not made her confess anything he should not; other-

---

432. Incomplete sentence.

433. That is, behind the tower of the Collège de Rive.

434. François Bonivard.

435. Marie Hugonier, née Bertherat, wife of Jehan Hugonier (or Hugoneri).

436. Incomplete sentence. On May 12, 1544, the Council ordered the imprisonment of Thivent Mathe for three days on bread and water for never having responded to four convocations of the Consistory regarding games (R.C. 38, f. 196v).

437. Noble Thomas Genod, former *curé* of St. Gervase and one of the first priests to embrace the Reformation. After the Reformation he became procurator general (1541-1542), then a lawyer. Genod died on December 13, 1546 [GALIFFE IV, pp. 226-229; J.-A. GAUTIER III, p. 101; R.C. 35, f. 100 (March 4, 1541); R.C. 36, f. 79v and f. 126 (July 28 and September 22, 1542); R.C. 37, f. 4 (February 5, 1543)].

438. Genod's wife, Blaisine Varembert, was the only female religious of Geneva to quit her habit and remain in Geneva when the other Poor Clares withdrew to Annecy. She

wise the law would take account of it. And he does not beat nor has he beaten his wife, and he would like to bring a criminal complaint against the one who said such words. And he does not know it and he wants to be put in prison if it is so, and he has not done anything he should not do. And on the charge that he frequents taverns too much and does not live in his house, answers that he has never been a fornicator and he has been with respectable women. And if he does anything he should not he wants to be punished. And he often goes to Sermet Gallaz's house.[439] He does not do anything he should not there or elsewhere, saying that if his wife offends him, why should he not punish her? And says all those who have accused him are malicious. And the reasons were given to the said Genod. It was Monsieur Michiel Morel. Answers that he has eaten and drunk at the houses of Gallaz and Tharex,[440] and he never did anything wicked. And Monsieur Pierre Vernaz told him several things politely about selling his robes and rings. It is six months or thereabouts since he hit her, except for a couple of blows he gave her because she spoke to someone he had forbidden her to speak to in his presence. Said that his wife should be summoned here and asked whether he did her wrong or struck her except the said two blows he mentioned above; he wants to be punished.[441]

Claudaz, wife of Master Michiel Galliard,[442] saddler.

Because of knowing how to pray to the Lord. And did not know how to say the prayer. And the confession like the Lord's Prayer, almost nothing. And she wishes harm to no one. And she was at the sermon Sunday at noon.

---

married Genod on January 23, 1536, the Seigneurie paying her dowry of 200 florins, which Genod collected two months later [JUSSIE, pp. 137, 146-147, 159-161, 165-166; GEISENDORF, *Annalistes,* p. 462; *R.C.* XIII, p. 504 (March 24, 1536)].

439. Sermet Gallaz, member of the CC for Saint Gervais in 1542, host of the Cross of Burgundy in Coutance in 1553 [R.C. 35, f. 489v (February 7, 1542); E.C., Morts 1, p. 268 (August 20, 1553; death of his wife)].

440. Paulo Tarex.

441. Despite the remonstrances of the Consistory, Genod never ceased to mistreat his wife. In 1545 he accused her of adultery with Paulo Tarex and refused obstinately to observe the command of the Consistory that he be reconciled with Tarex [minutes of the Consistory lost; summarized in R.C. Part. 1, f. 310 (August 28, 1545); see also R.Consist. 2, f. 18 (December 17, 1545)]. Again in 1546 "Thomas Jeno had a good wife but he beat her hard, so she was thrown into tears" [R.Consist. 2, f. 64v (June 10, 1546)]. He was also reprimanded for "many dissipations and bad examples to the youth of St. Gervais" as well as for having spoken against "the foreign preachers" [R.Consist. 2, f. 18 (December 17, 1545)].

442. Claudaz, wife of Michel Julliard (Galliard).

Said that her servant is outside [the city] at his own house and her maid is from Onex. And she does want her servant and maid to join in marriage if they want it, and she does not know whether they do anything dishonest that she knows of. And the servant has sometimes struck the said maid, and they want to send the servant away if he does not take the said maid, and the said servant . . .[443]

147v]　　Rolete, daughter of the late Jehan Cortoys, from Onex. Has stayed in this city six years at the house of Master Michiel the saddler, who sometimes sends her to the sermon on Sundays, because he has many servants and does not prefer one to another. There are five servants. And one who gives her a blow or a scratch enjoys himself with her the most, and there is one outside [the city] named Jehan who is from Vigny, by Mount Sion. And they have never spoken together about marriage. And her mistress has sometimes been angry with her about this, and her mistress has proposed that if she wants him he should take her, because he never spoke of it, and he will not take a girl who has nothing because he is very avaricious. And she does not know that he ever kissed her, and she would not hide it, and she does not remember that he gave her a blow, and he struck her in the shop, and she never went about with her [sic], and he never gave her anything or promised anything for which she would owe him great thanks. And she would like to take leave of her master because the said servant beat her and they did not want to promise each other. Said the prayer and the confession correctly. The advice: that care be taken that her mistress watches her, and as long as the said servant remains she be remanded to know the truth more clearly, and put off the matter until the arrival of the said servant, and refrain from doing anything that will make people talk and cease associating with the said servant. And to the mistress a term of two weeks to know better how to pray to the Lord and make sure there is no scandal in her house.

f. 148]　　　　　　　　　　**Thursday, December 20, 1543**

Lord Syndic Checand.
Calvin, Albert, Trippereaulx, Champereaulx.
Morel, Du Pain, Molard, Pensabin, Vernaz, Justz, Veyrier, Blandin, the officer Vovrey.

443. Incomplete sentence.

Gabriel Curlat, from Lucinges.

Is married and has lived here since the War of the Besoles;[444] has a child and a daughter [sic] and is . . .[445] Answers that he is not a blasphemer and drunkard and that he does not blaspheme and goes to the sermons once a day on Sundays. And he has never been drunk except once, a month ago, when his candle burned out and he stumbled on some dung and hurt his nose. Says he has known how to pray to the Lord in the present fashion for about 15 years. He was given admonitions and remonstrances.

Berthe, wife of Pierre de Joex.

Because of the sermons. Answers that she does not go as often as she should because she has no servant, only on Sundays and sometimes on Wednesdays. And her husband goes there more often than she. She was admonished to follow the sermons.

Aymoz Choupin, son-in-law of Decompesio.

Because of gambling. Answers that he did not play for money and that he has rarely played for more than two or three florins and that he was not there when a man was stabbed with a knife at Denys Hugoz's.[446] And he submits to justice. And he only played for drinks and did not sell anything from his household to pay, and he paid for himself and another man. He was admonished.

Noble Françoys Bonivard, Seigneur de Saint Victeur.[447]

Because of certain games held at Monsieur Hugoneri's house. He says it is true that he played checkers as others do publicly, and he had not heard that dice games had been forbidden, and he is a foreigner[448] and

444. According to the *D.H.B.S.* (II, p. 150) the War of the Besoles was the "war undertaken by Charles III, Duke of Savoy, in 1519 to break the alliance of Geneva and Fribourg. In the patois *'besole'* means fish. The Savoyards having invested Geneva during Lent, the people of the city lived on fish."
445. Incomplete sentence.
446. Probably a reference to the murder of François Deponte, stabbed in December 1542 at the inn of the Bochet, kept by Denis Hugues (see above, December 21, 1542, note).
447. François Bonivard (1493-1570), former prior of the Cluniac monastery of Saint Victor and celebrated patriot and chronicler of Geneva. Bonivard is the subject of two good biographies: CHAPONNIÈRE, "Bonivard," and BERGHOFF, *Bonivard.*
448. Bonivard was not entirely a foreigner, but also had not really been established in Geneva for a long time. Bonivard had been absent from Geneva during his

has played with respectable people, and he will reply if anyone writes against him. And he never played with a preacher of the Word of God. [f. 148v] And he answered that he plays to pass the time a little because of his old age. And he has not played with any preacher whatever either inside or outside the city.

Monsieur Jehan Hugonerii.[449]

Does not know why; because of card games, dice, certain preachers. Answers that the person who has said this does not know the truth, and he does not keep a tavern. And once Monsieur De Saint Victeur played once, and his wife, of the said Hugoneri, went to look for a gaming table, and she had no dice. And they have never played except with respectable and lettered

---

detention in Chillon by the Duke of Savoy (1530-1536), and he then lived in Bern for a time. In a letter dated from Ambilly on November 9, 1537, and presented by Pierre Folly, Bonivard's procurator before the Council of Geneva, Bonivard thanked the Council and the syndics "for all the benefits and honors they have given me, including retaining me as their bourgeois. Despite this, because of certain factors reasonably influencing me, I cannot remain among them . . . and am not well able to support the duties of two bourgeoisies. For this reason the said Folly in my name will renounce and abandon all bourgeoisie and duty of bourgeoisie that I may have with regard to the said lords of Geneva . . ." (cited in CHAPONNIÈRE, "Bonivard," p. 274). In fact Bonivard then had difficulties with the Seigneurie and did not dare return to Geneva. After the conclusion of an agreement between Bern and Geneva in 1538 Bonivard "lived sometimes in Bern, sometimes in Geneva, sometimes in Lausanne," but mostly in Bern and Lausanne. It was not until the end of 1543 that he established himself in Geneva permanently (*ibid.*, pp. 180-182, 188-191). As for gambling, Bonivard was right in that before the Reform "games were generally forbidden in public, not in private" (NAEF, *Origines* I, p. 234). The proclamation against gambling was made on February 22, 1539 (*S.D.* II, p. 348).

449. Jehan Hugonier, like Bonivard a former ecclesiastic of Geneva. A notarial act makes it appear that at this time Bonivard and Hugonier shared a house. On December 3, 1543, Bonivard and his wife, Catherine Baumgartner, already married for some time, ratified their contract of marriage "in Geneva in the house of the said married nobles and of Monsieur Jehan Hugonier, located in front of the Magdalen" (Notaires, Jean Duverney, v. 5, folios 69-70, printed in CHAPONNIÈRE, "Bonivard," pp. 289-290). However, an act of December 22, 1543 regarding a debt of Bonivard's to Hugonier was signed simply "in the house inhabited by the said Monsieur Jehan Hugonier" (cited in CHAPONNIÈRE, "Bonivard," p. 291; original in Duverney). If they really lived together, which seems doubtful to us despite the act of December 3, this could not have lasted for long. His priory having been razed when the *faubourgs* were destroyed, the Seigneurie gave Bonivard a house on his return to Geneva, but it was confiscated in 1542 to be given to a minister [CHAPONNIÈRE, "Bonivard," pp. 187-191; BERGHOFF, *Bonivard*, pp. 109-111; R.C. 29/3, f. 21; R.C. 36, folios 42v, 63, 64v-65 (June 16 and July 7 and 8, 1542)].

people. He has not held games for five or six years and says he is ignorant of this; at one time Master Clement Marot[450] played two or three times, and they played only backgammon. And touching the pâté[451] he knows nothing. And he has not seen any preacher play, either of the city or from outside it.

Pierre Joly, called Collomb, carter, and his wife.[452]

Because of their blasphemy and anger against each other. Answers that he is not spiteful and can only do what he can and does not insult others, but rather is insulted by others. And that he prays for those who do him good, and he cannot do good to those who do him evil, and he does no harm to others, and the children of the others do it to him. And he has been called a sorcerer, and he may have given them some insult. And he goes to the sermons on Sundays; the other days he goes to his work. And he pardons his enemies. Said the prayer, and does not know how to say the confession, since he has learned(?)[453] it from the preachers. The wife answered that she does not know how to say the confession. The opinion that they be remanded to three weeks to know how to pray to the Lord and the confession, and admonish them and that they be sent a teacher. And if he wants to receive Communion that he pardon all those to whom he wishes harm.

Marie, wife of Monsieur Hugoneri.

Because of games of dice as above. Answers that she has never seen play with cards or dice in their house, except a month ago some respectable people came to their house for supper and she was not ready, she went to get a table [f. 149], and neither preacher nor preacher's wife gambled in their house. And as for the five-sou pâté, that was not a preacher. And Cholex[454] went with her to get the dice, and there were only Lord Curteti[455] and Clement Mayrot, and it was that night that Tyvent Cholex was in their house. And she borrowed dice for those two she named, Curtet and Mayrot, and the said Cholex went to find the dice with her to play for a *quarteron* of wine.

---

450. Clément Marot (1496-1544), famous poet and translator of the Psalms. On Marot's stay in Geneva see Théophile HEYER, "Marot." Heyer does not fix the dates of Marot's residence, but only shows that he was in Geneva on July 11, 1543.

451. See on this matter the interrogation of Thivent Mathe above, December 18, 1543.

452. Loysaz Joly.

453. Illegible word; this is a possible reading. There may be some words missing.

454. Jaques Cholex.

455. Jean Aimé Curtet.

Pierre Amyaux and Benoyte, his wife.

The said Amyaux stated before the Consistory that three years ago he married his wife here present, who holds opinions that are against the commandment of God. First that she can live with all men and that they are all her husbands. She answers that regarding goods of this world she would remember her Christian brothers, and says that she said that the article above is true. And the said Amyaulx said horrible things contrary to the Word of God and very scandalous about her. Answers that she always holds to her former statements. Asked what led her to this. Answers that Our Lord said that one must tell(?) what one intends to be and that God is true. And she has it by revelation and only from God, and that she told it to no one. Asked by whom it was revealed to her. Answers that Our Lord reveals without out men and that no one told it to her. And that Our Lord created marriage, and two will be one flesh.[456] Answers that a wife, that a wife [sic] is not . . .[457] Asked whether a wife is not an adulteress as soon as she fornicates with another and ought not to be stoned.[458] Answers no, because she does not know. The wife who falsifies her marriage is an adulteress. Answers that she wants to believe in the Scriptures, and says that we are all one body. And the body of Jesus Christ is not indistinct,[459] and says that . . .[460] And that she would be content to receive another man than her husband.[461] Answers yes, [f. 149v], and that all women who are not married are whores. Asked what age she was when she was married. It was 18 years ago, and she was a girl, and if women are not married when they are of age they are whores. And she does not know about the Virgin Mary. The said Amyaux prayed that, considering the scandal, asks to be separated from her. Asked if she always wants to hold this view. Answers that she wants what will please God, and that it is better to marry than to burn.[462] Questioned. Answers that we are all one and that she does not know if there is anyone else who shares this fantasy she is in. And that her husband never said any of this to her. And the Holy Spirit of God taught it to her and teaches that fornicating is not wrong. And the marriage that this makes

456. Matt. 19:5.
457. Incomplete sentence.
458. John 8:5, Deut. 22:21 and 24.
459. The Consistory, hearing her idea that we are all one body, appears to have asked for clarification to find out whether she maintained the doctrine of the ubiquity of Christ, which she denied.
460. Words omitted.
461. Underlined in the text: "and that she would . . . husband."
462. 1 Cor. 7:9.

is of God, and she would not be a fornicator if she had the company of another than her husband. The opinion of the Consistory: since there is deceit, and moreover she knows how to state her case and she wants to cover herself and fornicate, she should be remanded to the Council with her deceit, and that action be taken. And concerning the request of the said Amyeaux, that he not be refused the divorce he asks in view of the scandal of fornication, or else she be given another admonition tomorrow if she will repent. Otherwise she should be remanded to the Council as soon as possible. Answers that she wants to hold by what she has said and confirm it just as she has said it and that it is not against God; the arguments she has given. [f. 150] And it is not against God that a woman is not a fornicator who lives with another, and Adam could rightly sleep with his daughters, and the Spirit told and revealed it to her and she learned it from the preachers.

Anthoyne, daughter of Anthoyne Blanc, of Plan les Ouates.

Has lived here six years and five months at the house of Pierre Baux, and did not know the servant of Françoys Philibert Bonnaz, and she did not talk to him on Sunday. And he gave her nothing, even the value of a sponge, and never spoke with her even to this hour. And she would like to tell the truth, and he gave her nothing at all. She sometimes goes to the sermons when she can, and said the prayer and the confession, and she did not see him all this Sunday.

Claude Martignin from Briod, from Chillon, in this city about six years to serve masters, and is a servant of Jehan Philibert Bonnaz. And did not know the said Anthoyne, except that he goes to the horse in the stable, and neither Sunday nor other days ever spoke to her, and wants to have his head cut off and wants to be the judge. And he never spoke to her anywhere he knows of and did not present to her or give her money and did not know her except in passing. She never asked him for money, and if it is proven that he was with her in the stable he wants to be punished, and he never spoke to her. And about a month ago a woman came from the wars who was from Vevey, and she asked the said Claude to lend her a piece of money for her and her husband who was there, and he lent six sous to the said woman from the war.

The said Anthoyne was recalled. She answers that she did not know the said Claude and would like to tell the truth and does not know who the said young man is and does not know where he is from. It may be he lives at Bonnaz's, and she would not know whether she and he ever greeted each other, and she did not meet him, and she has seen him clearly, and, again, she has rarely stayed at Pierre Baux's house, and she again will not confess that she . . .[463] [f. 150v] And she never received a half-*teston* from him, and she wants to be punished if she ever said to the other, "pay me," and she never said it.

The opinion of the Consistory: since neither of them recognized the other and their confession is negative. And to inquire of other witnesses to verify things better. She wants to be dragged through the city if she has done anything improper. On the said oath of the said one last named above, he wants to be punished if the contrary is found to what he said. As for blasphemy, sometimes. They were admonished.

Amed Servey, weaver.

On his remand to learn to pray to the Lord. Said the prayer as last time, hardly better. Offered to learn it better.

Jehan de Le Pierra, from Vigny by Mount Sion.

Has been a servant of Master Michiel[464] four years; that he struck the maid[465] once and gave her . . .[466] He made no proposal of marriage with the maid, although he struck her once because she had not done correctly what he had given her to sew in the shop, and it had to be taken apart and done over again. And he was angry then, and he believes she is a good girl. There is no proposal of marriage between them, however, and he still does not want to marry.

151] *The ordinance of the Holy Communion of Our Lord for next Tuesday, twenty-fifth day of the month of December, 1544.*

And first, for St. Peter's for the two Communions: Lords Pernet de Fosses, Michiel Varod, Pierre d'Orsieres, Mychiel Morel.
For the Magdalen: Jehan Chautemps, Pierre Vernaz, Jehan Pensabin.
For St. Gervase: Claude Du Pain, Loys Dufour, Amed Gervays, Mermet Blandin.
And throughout a lord syndic.[467]

463. Incomplete sentence.
464. Michel Julliard (Galliard).
465. Rolete Cortoys.
466. Incomplete sentence.
467. Folio 151v is blank.

Thursday, December 27, 1544, first Thursday after Christmas.

Lord Syndic Checand.
Calvin, De Ecclesia, Pupin, Trippereaulx.
Du Pain, Vernaz, Veyrier, Pensabin, Just, the officer Vovrey.

Jane, wife of Claude Pignier.[468]

Answers about Communion that it was stated in Consistory that she should not receive it because she was held in prison in the Bishop's Palace, and her husband did not know why, and she has not done anything to be held in prison for. And it was Porralis[469] and Jehan Goulaz, and she was told she was an anabaptist. She told everyone they should give her justice, and when she was brought into the City Hall whether she wanted to live according to our religion. And she has received Holy Communion in past years, and also the last Communion before Christmas. And she did not want to receive Communion last Christmas, and her conscience did not allow her to receive it, and she does not complain of justice. And she does not know that this was justice, and she presents her body for one to do what one wants with. Concerning baptism of small children she does not know what she said when she was asked, and she wants the register of the City Hall to be examined. And she does not distrust it. Asked about Communion. It is a long time since she received it, it is about two or three years, and she received it here at St. Peter's, and she cannot well say when, what day. Said she has many children to support, and she does not know how long it has been since she received it, and no one knows her heart. And Master Viret told her that she would do much better not to receive it rather than live thus. And that one may say what one wants, and she will be quiet. She must answer. She says that the said Viret told her as above and that she was taught that it is not wrong not to receive Communion. Asked whether she intends to live according to the consent and union of the church of Geneva. She believes it, and has no scruples about baptism. [f. 152v] She believes in everything that is of God. And she does not

468. Jane Pinard or Pignier, more often called the Purse-Maker. She was imprisoned for anabaptism in 1537, and following her refusal to abjure was banished from Geneva on September 28, 1537. Her neighbors asked in Council that she be readmitted to Geneva because she was teaching their daughters, and the Council granted her grace in June 1538 [R.C. 31, f. 55v and f. 67 (September 8 and 28, 1537); R.C. 32, folios 70, 74, and 79 (June 3, 7, and 11, 1538)]. For this episode see also Balke, pp. 73-96, and for Jane Pinard, pp. 85, 87, 89f, 363f, 367 (to be noted: the edition of 1977 reprints the same index, although the last two references should be to pages 349f and 353).
469. Ami Porral.

think except as God has ordered her, and she did not say that Monsieur Calvin was a persecutor or a false prophet and she would hold by what Master Viret would tell her. And she did not say that it was necessary to preach before baptism, and it would be too long to recount what was said in the dispute, and she does not remember it.[470] Said that she was searched out as the confessors did in former times, because they said more things to her than she knew, etc. Said that she has so many children that she cannot go to the sermons and that her husband does not want to let her go to the sermons. And that not as much has been done to the others as to her. Asked what Monsieur Calvin has done to her. And that she would not want to find something that is not. And she submits to having her head cut off if she ever spoke evil of Master Pierre Viret and that this is being put upon her and there are doubts about her. And she said it was not so.

Monsieur Calvin prayed the Consistory to have her say what harm he did her. Answered that she understood that the Consistory was made for fornicators, and she is not a fornicator. Asked about the wife of Pierre Amyaulx, what words she had with her. Answers that she always wanted to talk to her and she said nothing to her. And once in going to the sermon, and she says that she told her that one must give charity to one's Christian brothers, and the Spirit had told her so, and she then, the said Jane, answered entirely the opposite, that the wife should have her husband and live according to the commandment of God, and many other words that she did not understand. And she would not tell a lie for any man whatever. Asked whether she has any scruples about this. Answers no, and she would not want to. And she is very happy that the scruple that she formerly had has been removed. And she is angry about the words the said Amyaude said to her, which are horrible.

The opinion of the Consistory is that considering that the said [f. 153] Jane is always with the said Amyaude and that she should know whether she has received Holy Communion for the last three or four years and how. And that she be given strict remonstrances that she will be admonished on Thursday whether she has understood her state then. And that she be rendered more humble. On the point she has raised, whether it is necessary to believe if the preachers say there is no water in the Rhône, whether one should

---

470. Despite the advice of the Council of March 14, 1537, that it would be better to hear the anabaptists "in the Council of Two Hundred, not dispute in public, since the thing is dangerous," Farel finally persuaded it to hold a public disputation at the former friary of Rive. On March 16 and 17 the two parties disputed "all day long." Finally, on March 18 the Council concluded the disputation, finding that "it is a thing rather engendering different and various opinions than union and rather making faith waver than be firm" (R.C. 30, folios 190, 190v, 192, and 192v).

should [sic] believe it. And since she has blamed the Seigneurie and the ministers that she either be admonished before the Council or be admonished [sic]. It would be good to write to Master Pierre Viret asking him to write on the case of this woman and the articles he knows about. And that she be examined again about Communion, since she does not want to take correction here.

The said Jane was asked about Christmas Communion. Answers that she did not receive it because she had already been summoned here last Thursday, and therefore did not receive it. And she did not know that it was necessary to receive it because of the scruple she already mentioned. Also the other times. Answers that because she had been imprisoned for last time because it has to be taken worthily, because she was believed to be an anabaptist anabaptist [sic], and she does not say that Monsieur Calvin should remember clearly why she was put in prison, and it was Farel and Viret, and those who imposed this on her did wrong. And because she was put outside the city and separated from her husband who was outside the city, and she wants to live always in the faith of Jesus Christ. Remanded to Monday before the Council.[471]

471. The next Monday, December 31, the Council gave "strong remonstrances" to Jane Pinard "because she contradicted Monsieur Calvin and has not received Holy Communion for two or three years and holds certain false opinions." The Council returned her to the Consistory (minutes lost) to "confess having spoken wrongly, and that from now on she must live like a good Christian" (R.C. 38, f. 20v).

Thursday, the third day of January, 1544

The said day the Consistory was assembled and for certain reasons was put off to the following Thursday, tenth of the said month.

153v]
Thursday, tenth day of January, 1544

Lord Syndic Hudriol Du Mollard.
Calvin, Pupin, De Genesto, Trippereaulx, Champereaulx, De Ecclesia.
Morel, Vernaz, Pensabin, Blandin, Veyrier, De Loermoz, the officer Vovrey.

Rolet Galliard, barber.[1]

Because of Communion. Answers that he was the last who received it and that he was there at the beginning of the sermon, and may his ear be cut off if he was not among the first at the sermon and if the contrary is proven. And he does not go to the sermon every day, and he said it several times. The opinion of the Consistory is that since he was seen when he entered, and to hear from Master Philipe[2] who knows he said it, and that the truth be learned, and that he go to the sermons, since he did not . . . ,[3] and be remanded to Monday before the Council.

Noble Denys Hugoz.

Because of living honestly in his house and his course regarding games and blasphemy. Answers regarding Comparet,[4] and he did not know about the games and that he said that they must not play anymore or make bets for their bill. And the lieutenant collected information. And a woman should not say that he is worthy of kissing the . . .[5] of his wife, and he would not endure or permit it. And Verna[6] and the said Denys said many words and that he would not be subject to his wife.[7] He was admonished, and asked whether he wanted to persevere, and that he do better than he has done previously, and that his wife be treated better than she is, and that he

---

1. Rolet Galliard, elected to the CC for the *dizaine* of the Boulangerie in 1537 [R.C. 30, f. 167 (February 7, 1537)].
2. The minister Philippe de Ecclesia.
3. Word(s) omitted.
4. Probably François Comparet the elder, already reprimanded for gambling.
5. Word(s) omitted.
6. Pierre Verna.
7. Jeanne Hugues, née Exchaquet.

consider his position and frequent the sermons more than he has in the past.

Vincent Brolion.[8]

Because of his fornication and his having been summoned here often and not having come. Answers that he was on the road when he was summoned here and he was going for money to pay his debts, and the officer did not tell him the day, and he is ready to answer to the Consistory. And what he did he did through ignorance. Touching his fornication he asks grace of the Consistory, and no one can hide himself from sin, and he did not intend to do wrong and he repents greatly. He asks grace, and he has not falsified his [f. 154] oath, and what he did offended God, and he recommends himself to your mercy. And the child his chambermaid had is dead, and he sent her to give birth at . . . ,[9] and he does not know where she is.[10]

Noble Pierre de Joex.

Because of disobedience. Answers that he appeared here last Thursday and the Consistory was not held. He . . .[11]

Ayma, daughter daughter [sic] of Glaude Gallaz, from La Roche.

Has lived at the houses of Syndic Curtet[12] and Vincent Brolion, hosier, and she knew him well and had a child at her brother's house in Bresse, and the child is dead and did not live half an hour. And since then she withdrew to La Roche, and it was about a month ago that she withdrew. She thinks she felt he was such a respectable man that he would content her well, and she told him he had done wrong, and he did not want to believe her when she told him. And she has not spoken to the said Vincent since she came, and she often goes to the sermons. Asked whether she has had any other child. Answers yes, another by a man whom she swore faith to, and she nursed one for Master Chupin. She answers that she was brought to bed a little before All Saints', and never embraced him

---

8. Vincent Brolion, from Pouilly (H.-S.), living in the Boulangerie. He was a blacksmith and merchant haberdasher and was received into the bourgeoisie in 1541 because he "has served Geneva in time of war." However, in the margin of the register where his admission to the bourgeoisie is recorded the secretary Michel Roset adds: "December 14, 1559, he renounced his bourgeoisie" [R.C. 35, f. 201v (May 13, 1541); E.C., Morts 1, p. 41 (August 3, 1551; death of a son); MOTTU-WEBER, *Économie*, p. 40, n. 61].

9. Name of place omitted.

10. See hereafter the testimony of Ayma Gallaz, ex-servant of Brolion.

11. Incomplete sentence.

12. Jean Aimé Curtet, syndic in 1542 and 1545.

after he was engaged to his wife[13] and never spoke to him afterwards. And she was in his house in his absence, and his wife and he were then at the Thonon fair.[14] And she never talked to her afterwards except once and never said a word to him and never asked him for her salary because he is not sympathetic enough to talk to. And she answers that she never wanted to consent to him. About the said Aymaz the opinion of the Consistory is that she be sent back to the Council and admonished. She also received Communion at Easter, Pentecost and in September. Ayma fornicated a fortnight before and after he became engaged to his wife. Touching Vincent, he should be given strong remonstrances, notwithstanding that he makes an appearance of repentance. And he conversed with her about eight months, and after he was married he sometimes went to find her in bed. And remanded before the Council; Monday to the Council.[15]

154v] *Loys Piaget, sheath-maker.*

Because of Christmas Communion, which he is said to have let fall on the ground. Answers that he received Communion in the morning, that it was about half finished, and he received it from Master . . . ,[16] and the bread he received did not fall to the ground and was found, and he wanted to drink first and had no wine in the glass, and he never . . . ,[17] and ate the bread in his mouth. And when he had received it (if it is wanted the preacher will swear it) and he was at the whole sermon. And he did what he should have done; he does not think he had been was ever [sic] an idolater. And someone showed it to him, and he did not mean to be an idolater then and he was not an idolater then, since he adored the crucifix and the other images and did not throw the bread down since that would have been wrong, and to say a Pater and Ave Maria for the dead. The opinion of the Consistory: that he be given strong remonstrances, unless the contrary of his denial can be proven, and that Monsieur Amed Gervays be asked, and he should frequent the sermons and do better than he has and that he be exhorted better and present himself

13. Brolion married George, daughter of Amied Paquelon. On February 21, 1543, Brolion signed an agreement with his father-in-law regarding the payment of George Paquelon's expenses for drugs bought from François Vulliens (Notaires, Jean Duverney, v. 5, folios 47-47v).

14. In the Middle Ages Thonon had two fairs a year, one the Thursday after Martinmas (November 11) and one after Ascension (L.-E. PICCARD, *Thonon;* see also BERGIER, *Genève,* pp. 91 and 92, n. 2).

15. On June 9, 1544, the Council condemned Brolion to three days in prison on bread and water for having committed fornication before marriage. He was freed on June 13, 1544 [R.C. 38, folios 242v, 245, and 247 (June 9, 10, and 13, 1544)].

16. Name omitted.

17. Words omitted.

here Thursday. Meanwhile information will be obtained from the witnesses, and that he and his wife frequent the sermons.

The wife of the said Loys Piaget.

Answers that she received Communion in the morning, and Monsieur Amied Gervays gave her to drink, and she received it for the honor of Jesus and did not let it fall and would not want to receive it thus. And she no longer prays to saints, and she formerly prayed for the dead, and she has frequented the sermons as much as she could. And she says she still says the Ave Maria and does not think this is idolatry, and it does not seem to her she does wrong to pray to the Virgin Mary, and she has no faith in saints but in God and in the Virgin Mary. And one may do what one wants with her. She believes the Virgin Mary is a creature, the mother of Our Lord, her son she bore. She answers that she wants to believe only in the Word of God and does not believe she does wrong by invoking the Virgin Mary. And she does not know whether any other than Our Lord should be adored. And says that if she has adored the Virgin Mary may the Consistory pardon her. The opinion of the Consistory is that since she is possessed by the devil, that for the present she be commanded to go to the sermon three times a week for six weeks, and catechism, and that she be given strict remonstrances, or remanded before the Council, and that here in a week the confession of her faith be examined, and she be admonished more thoroughly to frequent the sermons. [f. 155] And that she cease to carry or say her rosary and her knotted cords,[18] and every day for a week, and appear here next Thursday and be given strict remonstrances. Ordered to go to the sermon every day for a week.

Anthoyne, wife of Pierre Rosset.[19]

Says that Rosset is ill in bed, as she says, who was summoned with her. And it is about the life they lead in their house and also an argument she

18. Translator: Used in place of a rosary.
19. We have not been able to identify this person; there was a Pierre Rosset, butcher on the Grand Mézel, another who was a saddler on the Terraillet, a bourgeois baker on the Rue du Perron, a citizen innkeeper (of the White Horse), and still others living then in Geneva. Since he spoke with Franceyse Bocone on the Grand Mézel (Grande Boucherie; below, March 27, 1544), he may be Pierre Rosset, butcher, member of the LX for the Grand Mézel in 1537 and 1541, but this is only hypothetical [R.C. 30, f. 66v (February 7, 1537); R.C. 35, f. 26 (January 19, 1541); R.C. 36, f. 16v (May 17, 1542)]. The marriage may have occurred at a rather recent date: on May 17, 1543, the syndic Hudriod Du Mollard complained of Pierre Rosset "because the said Rosset took up for the marriage of his wife a piece of vineyard in Troinex, which he sold at auction" (R.C. Part. 1, f. 55). However, it must be remembered that these questions often persisted long after the marriage.

had with Bocone.[20] Answers that she wants to behave towards her husband like a respectable woman and does not know why he beats her, because her husband is so bad-tempered that one does not know how to speak to him, and she has a case before the lieutenant against . . . ,[21] and it is not living according to God to have arguments with each other, and she did not call Bocone a fornicator. And she goes to the sermons when she can, and she cannot go there on working days. And she named one Françoyses; she said it to the Council, which is not so.[22] The opinion of the Consistory is that she come here with her husband when he is convalescent, and that most of it is due to her husband; in a week if her husband is cured, and follow the sermons.

Aymoz Choupin, son-in-law of De Compesio.[23]

Because of his life, that he does not correct himself according to the admonitions given him here. Answers that since he was here he did not enter there, and the admonitions he was given are good, and he did not recite the words spoken to him here, and he holds them as good and true. One Sunday night he was at Denys' house,[24] and in playing "cutellet"[25] he received the point of the knife in his hand, and he was never there since, and he did not know the one who struck him. And he has never mocked things and words that were spoken to him here, although he said to Denys Hugue that he enjoyed it, and he answered that he would come himself. He was given proper admonitions.

f. 155v] *Bernard Marcer of Sciez, hosier,* habitant *of Geneva, and Pernon, daughter of Jehan Recouz, butcher.*[26]

The said Bernard stated before the Consistory and his parents here last time [that] he had espoused his present wife and had not had her company. She scratched him with her hands and feet, and he has a case against her, and she calls him "traitor," "drunkard." And sometimes when he gives her a blow she says she will put a dagger in his belly. And she never says good day to him, and she moves away as though busy at her work. And he has been

---

20. Pierre Rosset and Franceyse Bocone were accused of adultery. See below, March 27, 1544.
21. Name omitted.
22. Underlined in the text: "which is not so."
23. Claude de Compois, notary.
24. Denis Hugues.
25. Translator: Apparently some sort of knife-throwing game.
26. Jean Recouz, citizen, son of Julian Recouz [*R.C.* XIII, p. 536 (April 14, 1536)].

threatened for her by Andrier Philippe,[27] who wants to murder and kill him. And once he, the said Andrier, took her on horseback with the said Andrier Philippe and meant to kill him in Thonon, and he has often shot at him to kill him. And he always wanted the girl, his wife, to escape from him and leave him(?). And he is always threatened by the said Philippe, and he has never approached her since she spoke with the said Philippe, and he showed the marks she made on his arm, and she bit him and hid a knife in the bed; he does not know why or what she wanted to do with it. And once she hid a knife because he did not eat bread at dinner, and the knife was not found, and she had hidden it.

Answers that all he said is not true and that she found a whore with him. At Christmas she went to the sermon and he mistreated her, and she wants to be punished if what he said is true. And the investigation of Andrier Philippe; and she was once in St. Julien at her uncle's, and she wanted to ask permission of Bernar, her husband, to let him go to St. Julien, and she was a little ill, and they found Andrier Philippe and he asked them where she was going, and she answered that they [f. 156] were going to St. Julien. And a man mounted her on his horse. And she never did it, and she says her husband mistreats her and she wants to be punished, and they are not worthy of being in the present company.

The said Bernard says that she wanted to go to a fair and pretended to be ill, and this woman was ill in a house, and when the said husband wanted to fetch her she cried out that he wanted to kill her and many other hard words. And a girl told him that she would come with her, and she did not want to come with her husband, and if the said Bernard died she would have Philipe. And he said also that he would not dare to go outside this city from fear.

27. André Philippe, son of Jean Philippe (chief of the Philippins, executed in 1540). André Philippe was a Genevan patriot who went to prison twice, first when taken by the Peneysans and then, in 1538, in Paris as a "Lutheran" (GALIFFE, *Ameaux*, p. 85; ROGET I, p. 69, n. 2). However, he was disgraced on his father's fall and forbidden to leave the city without leave from the Council, which he asked, for example, on February 10, 1543, and which was not granted (R.C. 37, f. 13v). Apparently he left the city nevertheless: in September 1543 he was noted as an "enemy of Geneva" and was reported as inciting Genevan citizens to go to the war [R.C. Part. 1, f. 91 (September 29, 1543)]. Finally, in March 1544 André Philippe and his brother Claude were rehabilitated and admitted to Geneva on paying a fine (see note on Claude Philippe, above, May 10, 1543). Finding himself again on the wrong side after the fall of the Perrinists, he withdrew from the city in October 1556 and became one of the principal actors in the attempt against Geneva in 1563. See DECRUE, "Complôt," pp. 385-428, p. 389 and note, *et passim,* especially pp. 425-426, where Decrue transcribes two of Philippe's letters of 1564.

Their lordships of the Consistory are of opinion that they be remanded before the Council and that the said husband have written articles prepared and give good secret information to the lieutenant, and that she be remanded to Monday to the Council, which will make better provision. And other things that will be written on the roll the said Bernard will give to the Council on Monday.

6[28]

Thursday, January 17, 1544

Lord Syndic Du Molard.
Calvin, Geneston, Albert, Champereaulx, Trippereaulx.
Jo. Du Molard, Just de Loermoz, Blandin, Morel, Pensabin, the officer Vovrey.

Thibaudaz, wife of Bombrilli.[29]

Because of her sister's child[30] who served a preacher in Divonne[31] who had had a child. Answers that she sent to get her son who had come from Lyon, and her daughter is here ready to be heard(?). Master Adam is so good that he would not let her daughter be admonished. [f. 156v] Asked whether she was brought here to have the child and that she was taken away. She knows nothing, and she did not help her recover after the birth, and she knows nothing about it and is very unhappy. She does not know where she was brought to bed, and she will go to the Council of Bern so they will learn from Master Adam where her daughter went to have the child. The said Thibaudaz's son says that his mother's daughter is in Fribourg serving a master. The said Thibaudaz says that she will go to the Council of Bern and to Master Adam to know where the said child is and was born, and it was a year ago. Where? In Fribourg. The advice of the Consistory advises [sic] that she be given a term to send to her daughter in Fribourg to learn the truth, within a month. The boy asked for some money for going to Fribourg to know the truth of the case.

28. This is the sixth session since the last payment of wages to those attending.
29. Thibaudaz, daughter of Claude Le Guex, wife of Jehan Grissaney, called Bombrilli.
30. Actually her daughter's child (see below, and above, April 26, 1543).
31. Jaques Hugues was the pastor of Divonne in August 1544 (HERMINJARD IX, p. 321 and note).

Pierre Rosseti and his wife, Anthoyne.

Because they do not live according to God. The said Rosset answers that he does not want to live except according to God and that his wife does not want to do what he commands her. Why? Because she is angry and wants to be the master. And he does not know whether there is fornication in her, and the scandal comes only from the neighbors. The wife answers that she has already been before the lieutenant because of words she had with some . . .[32] The said Pierre says that his wife insults him, therefore he has beaten her and will beat her wherever he finds her when he has forbidden her someone's company and she goes there; he will beat her in front of everyone. The advice of the Consistory is that he make no more uproar and be admonished separately, and if he does not correct himself for the future . . .[33] And as for the wife, when someone forbids her, when she is forbidden to do something that she refrain from it. And he, that he be admonished not to beat his wife any more as he has reported having done in the past, and that they be given strict remonstrances that if he returns to it he will be punished and that she be obedient to her husband. They were given strict admonitions and remonstrances. [f. 157] The said Pierre defied all the admonitions of Monsieur Calvin and gave the lie to Monsieur Mychiel, saying he was not a fornicator and fears no person on earth and that he is a respectable man, and he gave the lie to everyone. Since he spoke offensively and is angry and he should be remanded to the Council, and meanwhile information should be obtained secretly, and he should be remanded to the Council with the report and a careful inquiry made into his fornication. Remanded to tomorrow, and that he was as respectable a man as any of the city.[34]

Pierre Joly, called Collomb, carter.

To know whether he knows how to pray to the Lord. Answers that he has striven to learn to pray. Said the prayer and the confession a little. Goes to the sermons on Sundays and not the other days because he cannot get up in the morning because of the pains he takes by day in carting. Has a term of one month to learn to pray and to go to catechism. Asked that the wife of . . .[35] be summoned.

32. Incomplete sentence.
33. Incomplete sentence.
34. Pierre Rosset was imprisoned by order of the Council and submitted to several interrogations for having given the lie to Lord Morel and for being suspected of fornication. He was freed on January 24, 1544 [R.C. 38, folios 34, 36v, 38v, and 42 (January 18, 21, 22, and 24, 1544)].
35. Name omitted.

Beneyta, wife of Pierre Amyaux.

Has been remanded to the Consistory to know whether she holds to the views she did when she was before the syndics on . . .[36] Answers that she is of the same mind, she wants to live with her husband, and she thinks it would be wrong if a married man came to claim her, it would be wrong, and it is wrong for a woman to give herself to all, and other statements. Master Champereaulx has spoken to her, and let him ask her anything. And if she has said anything wrong, she is not of the same mind; one should not fornicate and it is wrong, and she no longer holds the evil ideas she did formerly and which she stated. She says she spoke evil formerly and she repents, and it is according to God and she does not say it deceitfully and she intends to live according to God with her husband. [f. 157v] And as for the others she said were like her, she answers that God will lift them up. Answers that she knows nothing else and that the wish came to her and that the devil is the father of lies.[37] And she says it may well be that there were others, and the woman who fornicates with another is a fornicator. And she desires to be and to live with her husband. The opinion of the Consistory is that in view of her response her husband be asked, since she is reduced and repents, to pardon her for the honor of God, and that they be reconciled with each other and that he live with her peacefully, and that Pierre Amyaulx be admonished. And if their peace does not endure they will be remanded, and if she returns again to her evil will. The said Pierre Amyau appeared before the Consistory, who was asked and told by their lordships what is written above, that the church holds that he should receive his wife, and this will be according to God and reason, and that he should accept her as his wife and treat her sweetly and amiably. Answers that it should be considered whether there is any hypocrisy in her, and he will not say that he said that he would do whatever the church commanded him, and it should be considered that if she did him some other ill turn in her person the Seigneurie would be the cause. Monsieur Calvin gave them beautiful admonitions from Holy Scripture, both together, and remonstrated with the wife, using firm respectable admonitions. She said that if her husband forbids some person to her she will obey him and follow his command. The

36. Word omitted, possibly "Friday." This affair was considered in Council on two Fridays, January 4 and 11, 1544, and it was decided to free Mme. Ameaux from prison after remonstrances, but the register does not permit us to state that she appeared then before the syndics [R.C. 38, f. 24 and f. 29, as well as f. 15 (December 21, 1543)].

37. John 8:44.

said Amyau handed in a statement of laws which he asked to be read, as follows here after two leaves.[38]

[f. 158] *Jaques Bernard, mason.*

Because of . . .[39] Answers that he neither beats nor torments his wife, and he goes to the sermons when he can, and the Consistory is badly informed, and he does have a brother who does not live with his wife and is named Jehan.

Loysaz, wife of Fichet, leather worker.[40]

Because of divination in her house on Christmas day. Answers that she does not know what it is about, and they did lose things, but not on Christmas day, and they did not have a diviner come, and she submits to the penalty. And she received Communion at Christmas. And a female relative of hers had gold and silver they did not find, and the Consistory is badly informed, and they will prove that they did not bring anyone into their house to divine. And her relative showed her what was in her chest and she gave it to them, and later they did not find what she had showed them, and she would not want to have her money. Denies that she lost through divination, and the truth should be found out, and the only one she had come to her house concerning this was a man who had a letter that belonged to her daughter, and he had to bring it to her. She says she did speak to him, and he did not tell her he would find it for her; she would find her goods for her daughters. The advice of the Consistory: that since there is no response from her, that inquiry be made by the Council and she be admonished to speak the truth, and that it be learned whether there was a diviner who divined, and follow the sermons.

Vincent de Villa, hosier.

About the affair of Communion. Answers that he received Communion at Christmas at St. Peter's and did not hear Mass and is perfectly satisfied with hearing the Word of God. It may be that he did not do the contents of Holy Scripture, and he knows how to read and consider the Holy Scripture, and if there is a living man who will prove this, he wants to have his head cut off.[41] Has indeed been to Fribourg. And he heard the sermon and

38. See below at the end of this session of the Consistory.
39. Incomplete sentence.
40. Probably Pierre Fichet, husband of Loyse, who baptized their son Gaspard at the Magdalen on November 27, 1553 [E.C., Copies 7 (baptêmes, Madaleine)].
41. We think this sentence includes two different ideas. First Vincent de Villa ad-

received Communion in the morning at St. Peter's, and he thinks he would recognize the preacher who preached then. [f. 158v] And he always holds by Jesus Christ. And as for the Mass, he knew the Pater and the Gospel and the Credo are good, but as for other things it is not clear enough to distribute them. The Consistory gave him strong remonstrances.

The wife of Master Mychiel the saddler.[42]

Because of her previous remand and her Pater and prayer. Answers that she knows the Pater and the confession as last time and that she was not well. She says she sent for the servant of her house a fortnight ago and exhorted them to marry. She was given a term to the first Thursday of Lent.

Master Loys Piaget and his wife.

On their remands on Thursday. Answers that the opinion the Consistory gave of them was true and they have the attitude of a respectable man, and the root of the evil tree must be removed. And his wife similarly. And they no longer pray to the Virgin Mary or for the dead. They were given good admonitions and remonstrances from Holy Scripture. Submitting themselves regarding the Communion that they let fall to the ground. They were greatly scandalized about this, and it should be learned where it came from. And if she did it herself she cannot be tormented too much.

f. 159]   *Rolete, wife of the late Claude Couturié and native of Chénex.*

She lives in her room near the Grand Mézel. And her sister has lived with her for a fortnight, and she served at Chabod's house and then at Roud Monet's, and she does not know how she behaves, and she has not lived elsewhere than at Chabod's. And she has lived in this city and at Roud Monet's, and at that time the said Rolete was in Vandoeuvres and Etaux, and she may have had a child. And when she asked her she told her she would see it. She now knows well that she had a child, and she does not know who the father is, and she did not want to tell her mistress, Roz Monet's wife. And the one who made her pregnant promised to marry her.

---

mits that he does not live perfectly according to evangelical principles, but he says he reads the Bible all the same. Then he responds to the accusation of having attended Mass in Fribourg by saying that he would submit to having his head cut off if it is proven that he attended.

42. Claudaz, wife of Michel Julliard (or Galliard), saddler.

Berthaz, daughter of Jullian Moyron[43] *of Chénex.*

Served at the house of Monsieur Roud Monet, and did not know . . .[44] Answers that she was badly advised for the moment and was embraced by a young man who is from the lands of Mme. D'A . . . eur(?). And she has another child by Jehan Marva, and her father was from Sézegnin, and she had the child at her father's in . . . ,[45] and the child is with Our Lord, and it was the first day of last year about a fortnight ago, and she would see a fatter one,[46] and the child was buried in Copponex, and she will make it appear. The father of this last is a good man and will give her good support. And she asks mercy of the Seigneurie and of God, and will not return again [to such actions]. She goes to the sermons on Sundays. The advice of the Consistory: that she be punished and returned to the Council to punish her, and obtain an affidavit for Monday that the child is [dead], and Monday. [f. 159v] Roletaz said that she does not know where she . . .[47] The said second woman has never fornicated in this city, and she submits herself to the Consistory, and the child is . . .[48]

Insertion of the statement of laws given by Pierre Amyaux.

In the Code under title 17, *De repudiis,* law 8, the law commencing: *Consensu licita matrimonia posse contrahi*[49] {Lawful marriage can be contracted by consent}. It says in the said law among other reasons for which a wife can repudiate her husband and a husband his wife, that the repudiation can be made by one of the parties against the other when one of the parties, such as the husband, has found or known or perceived his wife to desire[50] and look for and frequent dinner parties and companies of strange men without his knowledge or against his will, or if the said wife without the knowledge and leave of her said husband or without good cause has slept or

43. Berthe Moyron died on February 11, 1555, living then on the Rue Saint Léger (E.C., Morts 1, p. 199).

44. Incomplete sentence.

45. Word(s) omitted.

46. Translator: The meaning of this clause, *"et qu'elle en verroyt ung aultre plus grosse,"* is not evident. It might be "one who is more pregnant," but that makes no more sense. It may mean that she would know if she were pregnant another time, but that is largely a guess.

47. Incomplete sentence.

48. Incomplete sentence.

49. *Corpus Juris Civilis, Codex Justinianus,* V.17.8 (v. 2, pp. 212-213 in the edition of Paul Krueger, Berlin, 1892).

50. "Appetentem" in the *Corpus Juris Civilis.*

passed the night outside the house of her said husband; he has a stronger reason, etc.

160

7[51]

Thursday, January 23, 1544

Lord Syndic Checant.
Calvin, Genesto, De Ecclesia.
Vernaz, Veyrier, Justz de Loermoz, Pensabin, the officer Vovrey.

Monsieur Vindret.[52]

Because of the sermons and that he does not understand what is said. Answers that he says the Pater and the Credo, and that he has no Hours, except *In principio erat verbum,* and that they are good, and he often prays in his fashion and he says the Gospel in Latin[53] and does not understand it, and that it is not necessary to pray to the Virgin Mary or the saints. Answers that his wife has no scruples of conscience.

Claude Du Villard, called Bellet,[54] *and Jana his sister.*[55]

Because of some argument among them, and blasphemy. The said Claude answers that he would like to agree with her and he would like to have arbiters to bring them together, and that he brought his brother from Gex, and the case is of a good 2000 florins, and she answered him: "Vicious fornicator!", and her maid beat him so he died soon after and she has all his goods. "Drunkard!" The said Jane said that he had her summoned for the third time before the lieutenant, and he, and she paid him everything he gave her and she asks him for nothing, and also he beat her. And they insulted each other in the open street. The said Claude says that she and her maid

---

51. This is the seventh session since the last distribution of wages to those attending.
52. Pierre Vindret, member of the LX, tailor and merchant draper, native of Chilly (H.-S.). He was admitted to the bourgeoisie in 1501. He served as rector of the plague hospital in 1530, was a member of the CC in 1532, and was named to the LX in 1535. He died near the Magdalen in 1551 [R.C. 37, f. 8v (February 9, 1543); *L.B.,* p. 145 (December 31, 1501); SORDET, *Dictionnaire,* p. 1298]. See also *L.B.,* p. 237 (February 4, 1552), admission of Aymé Vindret to the bourgeoisie "in consideration of his late uncle Pierre Vindret."
53. That is, he reads his book of Hours.
54. See the note on Claude Bellet above, April 6, 1542.
55. Possibly Jane Aprin, called Belletaz.

took her child to the village to rebaptize it and that they took a *bichet* of wheat that they ate. And he is quite ready to show the deeds [of his property], and someone should get them to agree. And if he is given his rights he asks for no more. And that . . .[56] And both say that they wish each other no harm, reserving the right of the said Claude to have his rights and his share of his goods. Reminder of the rebaptized child. The said Jane says she has had two maids who have served her for 22 years. The Consistory ordered that she bring the said maid here on Thursday.

[f. 160v] *Mermet Mouri, farm laborer.*

Because of his Pater and prayer. Answers that he has been at the sermons when he could. Said the prayer, and the confession he hardly knows, almost nothing. Remonstrances that he frequent the sermons and learn to pray better.

Pernete Bordaz, seamstress.

Because of the sermons. Answers that her husband goes to the sermons for her, and she when she can. The feasts she keeps more than she should. And touching Jullian Bordon[57] who passed her sneezing, she said "May God help you." Answers that she enjoyed herself with him and that the said Jullian owes her some money, and once when he passed by he sneezed. And she said "Ugly thing!" in deriding him because he had some words with her because she owes him [sic]. And she wishes him no harm, and she has a grudge because he owes her some money that he has not paid, but she wishes him no harm for that reason. And she has no more scruples about religion. As for the Virgin Mary, she still has them a little, and does not say the Ave Maria and does not pray to her any more. And she does not wish any harm to the Virgin Mary and has no scruples about saints. Proper admonitions and exhortations to be diligent in going to the sermons.

Myaz, widow of Ylayre Richardet.

Because of the sermons. Answers that there is no day when she can. That she always goes to the sermons, and she does not keep feasts of saints any more, no more than others, and she reads the prayers that are ordinarily said at the sermons, and she goes more to the sermons than her neighbors, and she does not remember the superstitions of former times any more.

---

56. Incomplete sentence.
57. Julien Bordon, son of the rich merchant draper Jean Bordon. He was Seigneur de Compois and a member of the CC in 1541. He died in 1587 at the age of 76 (GALIFFE II, pp. 69-70).

161

Thursday, last day of January, 1544

Lord Syndic Checand.
Calvin, Genesto, Pupin, Tripereaulx.
Pensabin, Blandin, Veyrier, Vernaz, the officer Vovrey.

Jehan Papillié,[58] *Pierre Devorses and Loys, his son.*

Because of a certain conflict among them over certain insults in the case of Loys, son of the said Devorsa, who had learned his trade of baker, and some insults were encountered in arguing his cause, and they were taken into consideration, and they compromised and settled it for two gold écus for the apprenticeship of the said boy, besides the copies of the examination. The said Papillié concerning usury. Answers that he did not take interest except for what he lent to Claude Malbuisson. At the request of the Consistory they settled the whole thing and the insults, for the honor of God. They were given proper admonitions.

On the supplication of Burdela's wife, leper, from Troinex.

The Consistory advises that she be remanded before the Council; the Consistory is of the opinion that she be received with the customary charges.[59]

Attendance at the Consistory from December 13, 1543, until the end of January 1544.

Lords Syndics:

Checand	VI	XII	ss.
H[udriod] Du Molard	II	IIII	ss.
His brother Jehan	IIII	VIII	ss.
Vernaz	VII	XIIII	ss.

58. Jean Papillier, son of Jean (furrier, bourgeois in 1487), living on the Rhône Bridge in 1562. He did not enter the CC until 1572, and he died the next year. He was a baker by trade, and in February 1543 was reprimanded for having made bread that was against the proclamations (*i.e.*, white bread, forbidden in times of scarcity) [SORDET, *Dictionnaire,* pp. 987-988; E.C., Morts 5, p. 3 (June 4, 1562; death of his son); R.C. Part. 1, f. 5v (February 15, 1543)].

59. On February 5, 1544, the Council received a letter from the *bailli* of Troinex asking it to accept "a female leper from Troinex into the leper colony of Carouge" (R.C. 38, f. 58v). The leper colony of Carouge "was located at the intersection of the road from Geneva to St. Julien with that from Carouge to Pinchat," according to CHAPONNIÈRE, "Léproseries," p. 131. For the leper colony and leprosy in Geneva, see L. GAUTIER, *Médecine,* pp. 75-101, especially pp. 79-80 and 99.

Blandin	VI	XII	ss.
Veyrier	II	XIIII	ss.
Pensabin	VIII	XVI	ss.
Loermoz	VII	XIIII	ss.
The officer Vovrey	VIII	XVI	ss.
The scribe Malliet	VIII	XXXII	ss.
Du Pain	II	IIII	ss.

Total 13 florins.[60]

[f. 161v]   It should be noted that on Sunday, third day of the month of February 1544, a General Council was held in the cloister of the temple of St. Peter in Geneva at which the lords syndics were created: Anthoyne Chyerbel[61] for the first. The second Pierre Tissot. For the third Jehan Philippin.[62] And for the fourth Michiel Morel. And for treasurer Noble Amblard Cornaz. And the next day, which was the fourth day of the said month, a Council of Two Hundred was held and those who were councillors of the Narrow Council before under the other syndics were created [again].

Thursday, seventh day of the said month, the Consistory was not held because of certain obstacles.[63]

The lords assigned to attend the Consistory in the present year, 1544.[64]

First, Syndic Philippin. From the Narrow Council: Noble Anthoyne Checand, Claude Du Pain. From the Council of Two Hundred: Pierre Vernaz, Jehan Du Mollars, Jehan Pensabin, Pierre de Veyrier, Mermet Blandin, Justz de l'Huermoz, Guilliaume Vellu, Jehan Donzel, Jehan Pernet,[65] the officer Vovrez, the scribe Mailliet.

60. Actually the total is 12 florins and 2 sous (146 sous).

61. Antoine Gerbel.

62. Jean Philippin, syndic in 1544, 1548, and 1552, lieutenant in 1546, sat on the council that condemned the Articulants in 1540. In 1557, possibly to make way for those more disposed to a change of regime, he lost his seat on the Small Council, but remained a member of the LX (ROGET I, pp. 246-247n, and rolls; NAPHY, p. 212).

63. The nature of these obstacles is unknown to us.

64. The members of the Consistory were named in Council on February 8, 1544 (R.C. 38, f. 67).

65. Guillaume Vellu (Velluti), member of the CC for the Grande Boucherie in 1543 and also receiver of the leper colony of Carouge in 1543 [R.C. 37, f. 9 (February 9, 1543) and f. 135v (June 22, 1543)]. See also SORDET, *Dictionnaire*, p. 1280. Jean Donzel, citizen, member of the CC for the Mollard quarter, *auditeur* in 1549, councillor in 1556, syndic in 1558, died in 1561 [R.C. 37, f. 10v (February 9, 1543); ROGET, rolls; SORDET, *Dictionnaire*, p. 539; GALIFFE I, pp. 333-335]. Jean Pernet, councillor in 1555, lieutenant in 1559, syndic in 1557 and 1561, the year of his death (ROGET, rolls).

162

Thursday, 14th of the said month of February 1544

Lord Syndic Jehan Philippin.
Calvin, Genesto, Pupin, De Ecclesia.
Checand, Du Pain, Vernaz, Pensabin, Blandin, Donzel, Vellu, Justz de Loermoz, Veyrier, the officer Vovrey.

Masters Jaques Bernard and Henri Mara.

Proposed to the Consistory and asked for the honor of God. Bernard: touching the churches, and that there should be some examination of the wardens and others because of superstition. And that the Council command the wardens to reveal those who do wrong. Henry: proposed similarly for those who go to the papistry, to Bonne, Cranves and other papistic places. And also that the castellan of Jussy be exhorted to be on guard. The Consistory ordered Honorable Pierre Somaretaz,[66] castellan of Jussy, to see that both the wardens and other people follow the Reformation of the church.

Collet Grilloz, of Jussy, Bernard Dymer, George Du Bouloz, wardens of Jussy.[67] Don Loys Verchiere, Amied de Pignet of Peissy, Martin Bastard[68] of Bourdigny, Loys Gallatin[69] of Peney, Richard Porvyu of Satigny, Pierre Besanson of Choully, wardens.

The syndic commanded them to carry out their office, to watch over the Word of God, idolatry, those who lead dishonest lives, Communion, drunkards, fornicators, beaters, blasphemers, evil livers and superstitious people. They all answered they would do their duty. Those of Peney said they have poor people, and they should be given a bell for preaching because they are far away and do not hear the bell.[70] And similarly those of Jussy, and that they should be given a pulpit.

66. Pierre Somaretta, citizen, hatter, member of the CC in 1535, councillor in 1557, died in 1560. François Paquet, the former castellan, had resigned on January 25, 1544 [SORDET, *Dictionnaire*, p. 1200; R.C. 38, f. 44 (January 25, 1544); E.C., Morts 1, p. 18 (August 11, 1550; death of his daughter)].

67. Collet Grilloz, Bernard Dimier (Dismyer, Dymiez), and George Du Bouloz were all again named wardens of the church of Jussy on March 12, 1546 (R.C. 41, f. 48). Dimier was already a warden in 1543 (see above, May 10, 1543).

68. Martin Bastard, son of the late Henri, from Bourdigny, acknowledged on November 24, 1546 (Titres et Droits, Pa 619, folios 499v-501v).

69. Louis Gallatin may be the brother of the former warden Pierre Gallatin [see note above, October 5, 1542; R.C. 35, f. 418v (December 5, 1541); CHOISY, *G.G.*, pp. 150-151]. In any case Loys Gallatin had his appointment renewed at least in 1545 and 1546 [R.C. 39, f. 124 (February 5, 1545); R.C. 41, f. 36 (March 4, 1546)].

70. There was no hurry in meeting their request; Jaques Bernard, minister of the place, had to repeat this same request thirteen years later [see *C.O.* XXI, col. 671 (August 3, 1557)].

[f. 162v] *Matrimonial case between Henri Dufour of Peissy, son of Jaques Dufour of . . . ,[71]*
and Myaz, daughter of Pierre Berthoz, and Gonynaz, her mother, from Satigny.

The mother of the said daughter asks that the said Henri take the said
Myaz in marriage, and it was done for 40 florins, bed, cushion and appurte-
nances of marriage, and they are ready to give them. And he drank in marriage
in the presence of a respectable man, and whether there is reason. The said
Henri answers that it is not so and that he does not want it, although they prepared the supper at the house of the said mother of Mya. The said Jaques says
that he did not prepare anything for him because he no longer wanted to
marry because the said girl had sworn faith to and promised another husband.
And the mother answered that the said son had sworn faith to another wife.
The said Myaz says she was quite content to pay the said marriage [portion],
and they want to prove it. The said father asked the mother of the girl whether
she wanted the said Henri to go to bed with her daughter. The father says he
would like it well if his son wanted it. And the son answers that he was not
given any écus. The opinion: that the son and the father be summoned together and that the son say how the thing happened, in order to remand them
before the Council afterwards, and that they be questioned separately.

Henri, separately, said he does not know that they ever spoke together,
and he was in Chézery when they wanted to make him drink with the said
Miaz. And that his father asked him once whether I [sic] wanted to have her.
And he came to drink because there was a tavern there, and he drank there,
although he was told that his father had been there. And he was given drink,
but he never wanted to drink either before or after, and he did not drink in
marriage. And the mother of the said girl did not offer to have him go to bed
with the said Myaz her daughter. Confessed that the mother did offer her to
him to take to bed, and this was the same day that he drank there, and his father was not there. And he often drank there just to be drinking, and he was
never given écus, nor did he ever give them to the said girl, although his father once asked him during dinner whether he wanted her, and he answered
him that he did not want her and would not take her again because she had
sworn faith to someone who did not want her, Jehan Borgeois of Malval. And
their banns were proclaimed three times. And he does not want her because
he has sworn faith to another who gave him six score florins, and it was
about [f. 163] three years ago that the other did not want her.[72]

71. Name of place omitted. See the note above about one Jaques or Jaquemo
Dufour of Peissy, February 1, 1543.

72. Actually Myaz Berthod had signed a contract of marriage with Jehan Bourgeois
(Borgey), but according to the minutes of the Council it was rather Myaz Berthod who

Jaques, the father of the said son Henri. Answers that he does not want his son to have the said Myaz since he had wanted her he was . . .[73] And that he had wanted to give her to him formerly, and this was in his house, and because she had another and he did not want her to come to his house because she is poor and the other has a larger marriage [portion] and better acquaintance than that of Myaz. And says that he does not believe his son wanted the said girl or swore faith, and that he does not bring her to his house, and he takes her elsewhere. And he would rather leave the country.[74]

Note.

Monsieur Calvin stated something about the lieutenant of Peissy,[75] who is threatening Master Jaques Bernard.

The opinion of the Consistory[76] is that if they can prove the marriage the mother and the daughter be remanded to the Council. The mother answers that they will prove it by the lieutenant and several others. One Wednesday after Christmas they wanted to prepare a supper for making a marriage, and he, the father, wanted to marry his boy to Myaz, and it would have cost him his horse, and they wanted to marry Myaz, and they wanted to give him 24 écus[77] and 40 florins and bed and cushion and furnishings for marriage. And they consented that it would be the next day, and put it off to the following Sunday. And the said father said he had robes in a chest, and she should provide the 40 florins and prepare the dinner. And when the dinner was ready they did not come. And the boy came there on New Year's Day and told them that his father had told him that he wanted him to have Myaz, and gave him drink. And she will prove it by a young man who was there. And the marriage would have been accomplished if he . . .[78] Later the said [man] came to agree with them concerning his having already promised another and wanted to give an écu for them to agree not to be an obstacle to the

---

did not want Jehan Bourgeois. Bourgeois asked in Council that the marriage "go into effect" in 1540, but Myaz Berthod alleged then that Bourgeois was "light-headed," and by the advice of the castellan of Peney the Council freed the two parties from the promise of marriage and condemned Pierre Berthod to pay the expenses of the case [R.C. 34, folios 225v, 227, and 246v (May 7, 10, and 24, 1540)].

73. Sic. Incomplete sentence.
74. This examination continues below.
75. Pierre Baud, of Peissy, lieutenant of Peney.
76. Continuation of the investigation concerning Henri Dufour and Myaz Berthod.
77. "Ecus" written with an unusual abbreviation.
78. Incomplete sentence.

other woman whom the said Henri had promised. And she does not know why, and they allege something against the said girl. The girl answers that he gave her the glass and she took it, and he did not give her anything in the name of marriage. The Consistory remanded them to Monday before the Council, and that they bring the witness who was present and all others before the Council.[79]

[f. 163v] *Jehan, son of Jehan Bornand,[80] baker.*

Because of mistreatment and according to religion between him and his wife. Answers that he never strikes his wife, and swore by God and his faith that he never hit her and she did not flee, although he told her to go to her father to get some money to live on. And when she came he shut the door on her, and she returned to her father's, and she found the door locked. And the the [sic] next day she had slept with him, and she returned to her father's and said that she would die of cold and that she had slept in the stable, which was not true, because she had slept with him, and he is very angry. And if his father-in-law wanted to pay him some money he would make a profit. And his father-in-law does not want to give him anything without his bond. And his wife is staying at her father's, and he wants his wife to return to his house, and he does not treat her badly.

Pernon, daughter of Jehan Tyvent Blanchet,[81] cobbler. Because of being mistreated by her husband. Answers that her husband threw her out, and I [sic] returned to her father's, and he fastened the bolt[82] so she would not enter his house. And the night she was angry she slept again with her husband, and she has stayed with her father since then, until the present. And her husband's father promised to establish the marriage, and the doctor was present. And she says he never beat her, and she does not know why, because her husband always keeps the door locked against her and therefore she cannot enter to him, and she wants to live with her husband.

79. This case was discussed in Council on February 19, 1544, but it was remanded until after the General Council "so it can be considered with the preachers present" [R.C. 38, f. 81 (February 19, 1544)].

80. A Jehan Bornand (called Callaz) is often mentioned in the registers (see above, August 30, 1543), but this is more probably Jehan Bornand, baker, living in Rive in 1551 [E.C., Morts 1, p. 38 (June 27, 1552; death of his son)].

81. Also called Tyvent Blanchet (below) and Jehan Blanchet (below, March 6, 1544). He may be Stephanus (or Tyvent) Blanchet, cobbler, from Grand Bornand (H.-S.), received into the bourgeoisie on November 29, 1521 (L.B., p. 192).

82. Translator: This is a conjectural translation of "couta le serralie," which means "he [somethinged] the bolt." The word "couta" should not mean "fastened," but in this context can mean nothing else.

Tyvent Blanchet for the reason above, about his daughter. Answers that his daughter was, that he did not want to complete her marriage, and Pernon came, who had slept outside in a horse stable, and when he saw her he saw she was badly bruised and did not want to go to her husband. And she told him that . . .[83] and went [f. 164] to the house of Joly Clert,[84] who sheltered her for a night, and she said her husband would treat her badly if she returned to her said husband again. And that he was ready to pay the marriage [portion], since the lieutenant had given the task of settling the matter to respectable people. And he is ready to pay the said marriage if his said son-in-law binds himself for his father Bornand, which he refuses, and he fears to lose his money if they want to establish the marriage as soon as the pledge is made. And the said Jehan's father does not want to guarantee the increase of the said marriage [portion]. And if the said Jehan's father wants to guarantee it everything will be settled. And he wants to obtain what has been ordered and decided by respectable people, in the amount of six score florins, with the terms promised and agreed between them.

The advice of the Consistory is that the father of the husband of this girl be asked why he does not guarantee the said marriage of his son, if he has promised. Otherwise that he be compelled, and that the said Jehan, husband, take his wife back in the meantime, and that they all come here Thursday, and the father of the said Jehan Bornand.

Additional marriage case between Philibert Roget,[85] Boniface Thorel the cobbler.

Thursday.

Claude Chevence, barber.[86]

Requests of the Consistory that his wife be returned to him, who has gone to Rosset's house on the Rhône Bridge, and because she sold his household [goods] and then went to live elsewhere. And it is true he wanted to hit

---

83. Words omitted.

84. Ami Maystre, called Joly Clerc, lived in Rive like the Bornands [R.C. 37, f. 11 (February 9, 1543); see also E.C., Morts 4, p. 98 (March 1, 1562)]. Moreover, he came from Petit Bornand and was admitted to the bourgeoisie in 1524, while Jehan Tyvent Blanchet, if he has been correctly identified, was from Grand Bornand and became a bourgeois in 1521. His house was therefore a logical refuge for Pernon Blanchet (see preceding notes and, for Amy Maystre, above, September 6 and 13, 1543).

85. Philibert Roget, pin-maker, living on the Rhône Bridge, died on July 8, 1550 (E.C., Morts 1, p. 241).

86. Claude Chevence is not found in the list of barbers in L. GAUTIER, *Médecine.*

her with a stone because she told him he was not her husband, and he wanted to beat her because he could not have her otherwise, and he wants her to . . .[87]

Jana Franceyse, daughter of Cristofle Poynce, his wife.

In order to live together in peace, she and her husband. Answers that it is only because she does not want to give him money to live on, because she cannot work for herself and her husband and a small child they have together. And he beat her at Rosset's. The Consistory ordered them to live together in peace as respectable people should, and to frequent the sermons and not blaspheme God as he has a habit of doing, and that he not beat her again.

[f. 164v] *Pierre Migerand.*

Because of their consumption of their goods. Answers that his brother Jaques is sowing and he does not know where he is. And if he has been badly advised he will be wiser than formerly. The Consistory gave him strict admonitions and remonstrances.[88]

Anisaz, wife of Sermod Greppon.

Because of the sermons. Answers that she goes to the sermons when she can, and she gives no offense to the Pope, and she says the Pater, and the Virgin Mary is the mother of Jesus Christ, and she does not say the Ave Maria and she has not prayed to the Virgin Mary since the Gospel was preached in this city. Remonstrances.

Thursday, February 21, 1544

Lord Syndic Philippin.
Calvin, Alber, Genesto.
Checand, Du Pain, Vellu, Donzel, Molard, Vernaz, Just, Pernet, Blandin, the officer Vovrey.

87. Incomplete sentence.
88. Pierre Migerand and his brother Jaques divided their goods on February 1, 1542 (Notaires, Jean Duverney, v. 5, folios 11-13v). Pierre then received a house on the Rue du Perron and Jaques another next to it on the east. Jaques was apparently still a minor, since the division was made on his behalf by authority of Rod Pictet Du Bouloz, his cousin and guardian. Pierre Migerand was also summoned to Council on March 14, 1544, because of his debts (R.C. 38, f. 125).

Pierre Baud of Peissy, lieutenant of Peney.

Concerning a quarrel. Answers that there were no harsh words, and about a fortnight ago some words were spoken about the marriage of Jaques' daughter[89] because he had spoken about her some and he was told that they were obstructing the marriage, and someone wanted to give the thrushes that Henri, son of the said Jaques . . .[90] And he had no other speech with Monsieur Jaques Bernard. The opinion of the Consistory is that he be questioned apart, and that neither party do wrong by speaking such evil words if they are not true. And it must not be left so, and [f. 165] that he be questioned more directly about the affair, and that the affair be more fully looked into and followed up. He was recalled and reexamined. Answers the questions that it is true that he said to Master Jaques Bernard that in coming from Satigny a young man had made statements, that Master Jaques had advised the said Henri not to take the said girl, and that he[91] was given thrushes, and they wanted to give him partridges to prevent the said marriage. And he did not say it elsewhere. And he did not threaten him with sword and dagger if he wanted to continue to put any blame on him, and they were foreigners, and he would maintain his honor against the foreigners. Answers that he did not mean Monsieur Jaques Bernard and that he never said such words to Master Jaques Bernard. And he will not gainsay his words. And he was told that the girl had blamed him. And that the person named Gonrard Du Puys knows that the said Henri wanted to have the daughter of the said Pierre Berthod, who is named Myaz. And they had no other words except those he has said here. And he was told that the girl was blamed for him. The opinion: that he be admonished and that witnesses be found who will reveal the affair better, and that the said Henri be summoned to tell what he knows, and that he make the said Gonrard Du Puis come here Thursday.[92]

---

89. This is the marriage of Mya, daughter of Pierre Berthod, and Henri, son of Jaques Dufour.

90. Incomplete sentence.

91. Illegible words in the margin.

92. The next day, February 22, the matter was considered in Council: "Having heard both parties, their statements having been read and understood together with their responses, the witnesses in the said case having been examined and all that should be having been considered, and since it does not appear to us that marriage was contracted by words of the present or otherwise between the said Dufour and the said Mye, we order and pronounce that the said Henry should be freed and we free him from the opposition and complaint of the said Mye, giving permission to both parties to contract marriage elsewhere according to God; but because . . . Jaques Dufour, father of the said Henry, was

Jaques Reclans.[93]

Says that on January 14 he was in the street and spoke to Catherine. And he said to Catherine, daughter of Vyjehan,[94] he asked her if she was married. She answered no. And he asked her if she wanted him, and she told him yes. And he wanted to pay for drinks, and he gave her a ribbon and asked her if she wanted to drink in the name of marriage. And she answered that she wanted to wait for the decision of her father and mother. [f. 165v] And the said Jaques gave her a ribbon and promised a skirt to the maid and a pair of hose to the children. And she gave him a handkerchief on which was written, "Jaques Claret, do not forget me" and other words. And when she wanted to repent of having promised he told her he would make her come to the Consistory, and he slept two nights with her brother.[95] And he has often been seen, and he spoke with her several times and gave her drink, and later knew and embraced her. And another time he took her onto the roof, and the maid found them, and she would know the skirt, and she sent her to get him from the Bishop's Palace, and she herself. The advice of the Consistory: that the maid be summoned.

Claudaz, daughter of François Milliaux, maid at the house of Monsieur Vyjehan. Answers that she did not know the one who went out, except that sometimes he came to sleep with Gregoyrel and that he wanted to have Catherine, her master's daughter. And she does not know what they do and does not know how they go on except for what the girl says, and she did not send her for wine that she knows of. And he did not stay all day. On Sunday he made sure the father had gone out and then went inside and wanted to

---

a promoter of the said marriage, which did not go into effect, and the said Mye had just cause to oppose it . . ." (not completed; probably he was condemned to pay the expenses) [R.C. Part. 1, f. 141v (February 22, 1544)].

93. Jaques Reclan, called Claret, citizen, 25 years old in 1543, officer of the lieutenant in 1545, still living in 1557 (Mss. Galiffe 38, f. 73).

94. Wigand Köln (several variants), printer from Franconia, established in Geneva since 1519, bourgeois in 1531. He printed various works, especially notable being the catechism and confession of faith of Geneva in 1537. He died between February 12, 1545, and February 9, 1546. His daughter Georgia married Jaques Bernard, the religious turned minister, and his daughter Cathérine married René Tartier of Reims and, according to Théophile Dufour, died during the current year. For Wigand Köln and his bibliography see NAEF, *Origines* I, pp. 422-441; DUFOUR, "Notice bibliographique," pp. clxiii-clxxiv; CHAIX, *Imprimerie*, pp. 227-228.

95. Gabriel, son of Wigand Köln, called Gabriel Vijean. He inherited his father's printing shop, but his equipment being old and outdated he did not prosper, and in face of the arrival of the new immigrants his production was limited to minor works and almanacs. For him see the same sources cited above for his father.

swear the girl and wanted to slap her; she did not want to let him stay inside, and he left. And she did not see him enter there several times, and he did not promise her a skirt, and she does not know anything else, and she does not know whether he dined there, and she never found her alone with him. However it is true that Sunday and one other time on the stairs she told Catherine she should be careful that her father was not told, and she answered her that she had promised another and that she would watch what she did. And she did not tell him, and she told him that Monsieur Calvin had received letters from her husband, and she would not know what else to say. [f. 166] And she does not remember that the said Catherine's skirt was dusty, and it was dirty. And the said Jaques never promised her a skirt, and she does not know whether she ever told the said Catherine that she should agree with the said Jaques, who went away angry, and slept once with Gabriel Le Fleutet. And last Sunday he wanted to swear her and wanted to hit her. She said she did not want to marry, that she had news of her husband. And she never looked for wine for him.

Catherine, daughter of Master Vyjehan. In the marriage case of Jaques Reclans. Answers first that she has no promise with the said Jaques; he told her that someone wanted her for a wife, and she answered that her husband is not dead and that she would not want it without her father's consent. And he wanted to drink with her by force, and he wanted to beat her. And that Monsieur Calvin had letters from her husband. And the said Jaques answered that Monsieur Calvin made up the letters out of his own head. And she did not eat with the said Jaques without her brother always being present, and she would not want to do anything against the will of her father and mother, and she never made a promise. And once the said Jaques told her to make a promise to him, and then she said that her husband was not dead, and he had a small gold ring that he wanted to give her, and he wanted to promise her if she wanted, and she never promised him because she should not have promised him. And he was in the house several times, but not alone, her brother was always present, and he never dined alone with her. And the maid was with her brother and he was not there. And on Friday the said chambermaid told her she should do something with the said Jaques, and she did not promise him anything or want to promise him anything. And he paid for wine and the maid went for wine, and she never stayed alone with him, and on Sunday she could not put him out of the house. And her father found him once on the stairs, and he told him he was looking for Gabriel. Asked whether the maid did not go to find her once alone on the stairs. [f. 166v] And she never promised him anything, and she should not have promised him, and he brought her one of his own for a certain woman, and she did not know with what intention. And she did not give him a handkerchief. She confesses the handkerchief, and he did not dine with her for marriage, and it will not be proven. And she never drank in the name of marriage with him, and she was in the Bishop's Palace once, and she never sent to fetch him. The handkerchief was given to him in the presence of the maid because he had given away his handkerchiefs, and it said "Jaques." And she never stayed alone with him, and she does not know whether her skirt was dusty or whether the maid knew it, and she was never again on the roof of the house. And she has no promise with him and never drank with him in the name of marriage that he can prove. And Bocone[96] had made the said handkerchief, and he thought that he had a promise of marriage, and he came to find her on the bench. And once she told him that if she did not have another husband she would want him. And once she told him to take a walk, and he talked to her her [sic] about it all the time, and whether he should mention it to her father and her brother, and the handkerchief was not with that intention. The maid answers that she knows nothing except what she said, and he gave Catherine a ribbon and a belt, and she did not go for wine for them, and she never washed Jaques' handkerchiefs. And she does not know in which wash and does not know what became of them, and she did not wash them, and she did not give him a handkerchief that was written on and does not know that she did it. She said nothing to him, and he tore up a handkerchief the day she had to swear that Jaques wanted her. And he was never with the said Catherine in the Bishop's Palace and never took her to the Magnifico's house,[97] and they did not enter the Bishop's Palace with her, and they went to the Magnifico's looking for Nycolardaz, and she did not go down.

[f. 167]   Catherine, confronted with the said maid. On the point that the said chambermaid went for wine for the said Jaques. The said maid answers that it was for Gabriel, and the handkerchiefs that she soaped in the wash, and a woman was with them in the Bishop's Palace, and they did not enter the Bishop's Palace wanting to speak to the chambermaid. The said Catherine answers that the maid did not know that this was for the said Jaques. And when the maid said once to the said Catherine that she should be careful to do what she should and that her father was not discontented, the said maid says she does not know. The maid by herself because of the skirt. Answers that she does not know about the dusty skirt, and Catherine failed to tell the truth about their being in the Bishop's Palace, which they did not do. And one can do what one pleases with her. And she did not think that the ribbon

96. Franceyse Bocone.
97. Laurent Maigret, called the Magnifico.

was given to her with that intention. And she did not find them alone, and that was when she told him she had news of her husband.

Also the said maid confronted with Jaques. The maid says that she said what she . . .[98] The said Jaques had the said maid asked whether she did not often go to find the said Catherine. Answers no, and she does not know, nor about the shaking of the skirt, except when he spoke on the stairs, and she did not say anything to him when she gave him the handkerchief, and that she should help him to make the marriage. The said Jaques says that he often gave supper to Gabriel because he took him with him, and Catherine was in the Bishop's Palace, and he will prove it if necessary. The said maid answers that the said Catherine did not want to have two husbands. And Catherine told the said Jaques, and she did not want a skirt from him for this affair. The said maid, separately, says that he can say what he wants. And the merchant who wanted her said nothing about it, and he never gave her a skirt, and she did not want it.

Catherine, separately. Asked whether Donne Fousone[99] ever spoke to her. Answers that they gamble, and that her brother had spoken to the mother and to Donne Fousone, and they never stopped talking about it, and she did not speak to him about it, [f. 167v] and she never embroidered the handkerchief and will find out who did it.

The said Jaques with Catherine. The said Jaques answers that on January 14 he went to François Bordon's[100] to get money, and she cried out and told him that he . . .[101] And she told him that she wanted him to take her, and they ate together, and when he did not go to her she came to see him in the Bishop's Palace. And because of her maid she came with Gripa,[102] who went behind the gate, and he forbade her the company of the said Gripa. And she sent him a *quarteron* of wine, and sent Gregoyre to get it. And she showed a handkerchief spotted with black which she gave him, and written on it was "Jaques Claret, do not forget me," which handkerchief he cut up before last Sunday. And she says she never touched it or spoke of a merchant they wanted to give her to in marriage, and many other words about shaking the skirt. The said Catherine answers that she never drank in the name of marriage and that Bocone, and that she said to the boy . . .[103]

98. Incomplete sentence.
99. Probably Pernete Fouson.
100. François Bordon, citizen, member of the CC in 1544 and probably Conseigneur de Compeys with his brother Julien Bordon, still living in 1557 (GALIFFE II, p. 69).
101. Incomplete sentence.
102. Tevene, wife of Pierre Baud, called Grippaz (see above, August 23, 1543, and below, March 6, 1544).
103. Incomplete sentence.

The said Catherine separately. Answers that she denies everything he said. At that time her intention was, when she gave him the handkerchief, that it was because he had given her the belt, and it was for the ribbon he had given her and had sent her by Gripa, although he gave her to drink in the name of marriage and she refused, and he did not have her company.

The opinion of the Consistory: that Gripe and the boy be summoned to inquire, and also Bocone, and that they be given strong remonstrances not to talk about the case, and that the house be forbidden to the said Jaques, and the others be remanded to Thursday. All to Thursday. Catherine did not change her mind about the things written above. She was given admonitions and strong remonstrances to frequent the sermons and remanded to Thursday with the others. [f. 168] The said Claudaz, maid, did not change her mind at all, and knows nothing about any of it.

Marriage of Boniface Thorel, cobbler; Philibert Roget; Maria, daughter of Jaques Gerbain, from Draillant.

The said Boniface says that he did not understand that he was re-manded last Thursday by Monsieur Calvin because of opposition to his marriage, and that he wants to obey justice. The said Maria says that the said Boniface promised her and gave her a sou in the name of marriage. The said Boniface found a pin-maker who told him that there was a rich girl whom he wanted to give him in marriage, and many words. What village the said girl is from. That it was not so, although he was given a sou that he gave to the said Maria. And he told her she should give him up, and she wanted a skirt, and he will prove it by these two masters, since she slept with them, and they drank together in the name of marriage in such a fash-ion. The said girl says it is not so. The said Boniface gave her the sou, saying that he would hold the marriage null if he did not obtain what he was promised.

The said Maria, separately. Answers on the words that she drank in the name of marriage, that her uncle granted her and gave her the said drink in the name of marriage two or three times, and she understood that she would have a share in the goods of her said late father and that the one who owed her three score florins, which was confessed to her by her said uncle and the said . . .[104] And she slept with her master's wife because they are poor[105] and with her said master and hardly at all. The advice of the Consistory is that they be remanded to Thursday to obtain the witnesses and that the said

104. Name omitted.
105. "Poor" is struck from the text.

Boniface be admonished, and that the said uncle be summoned, who is a debtor for the 60 florins. The girl says that her uncle will be here Saturday. [f. 168v] The said Boniface was given strong remonstrances because of his ignorance about his father.

Ayma, widow of Jehan Ripha, purse-maker.

Because of the sermons. Answers that she does not know why she is summoned, and she goes to the sermons when she is sent, and she has always received Holy Communion and has never said a bad word about the law, and she has no rosary prayers. Said that she knows the Pater of the priests(?) and says "Pater noster, etc." in Latin at length, Ave Maria. And she does not pray to the Virgin Mary and has not heard the Mass since it was said here. And she takes Communion in honor of God and receives God who is given to her, and she does not know what to say, and she believes that the bread of Communion is God. And let her be given a term of one month to learn to pray to the Lord, with strong remonstrances.

Thursday, February 28, 1544.

Because of matters concerned with the negotiations of the city of Geneva with Their Excellencies the Council of Bern the Consistory was not held this day, but the parties were remanded to the following Thursday.[106]

f. 169]

Thursday, March 6, 1544[107]

Lord Syndic Philippin.
Calvin, Genesto, Albert, Champereaulx, Tripereaux.
Checand, Vernaz, Molard, Veyrier, Just, Peronet,[108] Donzel, Pensabin, the officer Vovrey.

106. The Bernese ambassadors, Jean François Naegeli, Michel Augsburger, Jean Huber, and Jean Lando, arrived in Geneva on February 25 and signed the very important agreement called the *Départ de Bâle* on February 29 (J.-A. Gautier III, pp. 185-187). The *Départ* "established the reciprocal status of Bern and of Geneva regarding the territories taken from the former ecclesiastical lordships of Saint Victor and of the Chapter" (Martin, *Genève*, p. 213). The text of the *Départ* is published in *S.D.* II, pp. 438-460.

107. Maillet had noted the date and the beginning of the roll at the bottom of the previous folio, but lacking space, he began again here.

108. Correctly "Pernet."

Françoyse, wife of Pierre Fagniant.[109]

Because of the sermons and the marriage of Jaques Claret and the daughter of Vyjehan.[110] Answers that on working days she never goes to the sermons because she has to earn her living and that of her children. And on the marriage of Vyjehan and Claret, answers: Vyjehan's daughter asked her for a pretty handkerchief for sale and took one she gave her and sold for 3 *gros* 6 *deniers*, and she had not made it for her, and she put on the writing. And she did nothing more than was done previously, and Jaques Claret never entered her house, nor did she see them speak together. She told her once that Jaques Claret did so much in her house and said that the said Claret wanted to give Catherine a gold ring to give her in marriage and that she told him that she could not marry without the knowledge of her father and mother. And the said Catherine never told her that she [sic] would be given in marriage to the said Catherine, and she understood that they had separated. Nycod the bookseller.[111] Says that she heard from the said Nycod that they had separated. Does not know whether anything was given to make them separate.

The advice of the Consistory is that the thing not be left in this state, and to pursue the affair of Jaques Claret because of the fornication that exists; that Gripe[112] be summoned. And as for Franceyse,[113] that she be interrogated, the said Franceyse, further, and that Nycod the bookseller, Jaques Claret and Wooden-Feet[114] be summoned.

[f. 169v] *Jehan Mauris,*[115] *servant of the general hospital.*

Because of the lieutenant's niece,[116] with a great oath. Answers that he has served the lieutenant and that he knew his niece, and denies the child

---

109. Françoise and Pierre de Faignant. See below, May 29, 1544.

110. Catherine, daughter of Vyjehan (Wigand) Köln.

111. Nycod Du Chesne, called Chapella, citizen. According to Paul Chaix, Nycod Du Chesne continued "to bind and sell Catholic works despite the injunctions of the Council. Ruined and embittered, he renounced his country and joined the exiled Perrinists." Du Chesne established himself at the far end of the Arve Bridge, under Savoyard jurisdiction, but he was taken in the city in 1557, condemned to death as a traitor on August 13, 1557, and executed two days later (CHAIX, *Imprimerie*, p. 177; J.-A. GAUTIER IV, pp. 84-87; SORDET, *Dictionnaire*, p. 545).

112. Tevene Baud, called Grippaz.

113. Françoise Bocone.

114. Anthoine Wooden-Feet.

115. A Jean Mauris was accused of adultery on February 20, 1543, but we do not know whether it was the same man or the same case [see R.C. Part. 1, f. 8 (numbered f. 9)].

116. The niece of Jean Lambert. Jean Lambert, elected lieutenant on November 18,

with which the said niece is pregnant, and he has not done anything that should make him fear that this child is by him.

Roleta, son [sic] of the late Master Jaques Rosse, mason. And she lives near the Magdalen, and formerly at the house of her uncle, the lieutenant, and lived there a year. And she indeed knew Jehan, who is present; about Saint John's Day, about on Sunday, in making his bed he took her. And she is pregnant by the said Jehan, here present, and she fornicated with him only once, and with no other than him, once about Saint John's Day, about a week before Saint John's Day.

The said Jehan. Answers that she never had an affair with him and that she is not pregnant by him, and if she carries a child it is not by him, and if justice decides that it is his child he will take it, and let her be visited at his expense by midwives.

The said Rolete. Answers that she is not pregnant by another than the said Jehan, and she never did it except with him, and she hardly stayed at all afterwards. And he took her twice and did not make her a promise of marriage, and he often came to see her afterwards.

The said Mauri should be admonished on his conscience to declare the act he says he did not do. The said Jehannes answers that he knew the girl in right and honor and that he was not in this city at that time, because he had gone to Bern. And he did not do it, and never had her company. This affair was reported to him about a month ago, and he informed the lieutenant that he was given to understand that it was said he [f. 170] would be prosecuted. And he committed no act with her and did not fornicate with her so she would be pregnant by him. And she never spoke to him about it or reproved him for it. And he was at Bern on June 8 and stayed for two weeks and returned to Lausanne to his parents. And if he did it he wants to endure torments, and he did not do anything with her that would make him take the child, and he never fornicated with her. And he is ready to go to prison, and

1543, syndic in 1546 and 1555, died in 1556. He was a councillor before 1538 and castellan of Jussy in 1538, 1542, and 1543 at least (the office was normally held for three years). Lambert apparently took over the inn of the Black Head after the flight of the former innkeeper, François Rosset, in 1540 under suspicion of sympathizing with the Articulants. The Bernese ambassadors lodged there in 1541. Lambert was also the older brother of the Jean Lambert who was executed in 1539 in Chambéry as a "colporteur of vicious sermons." He also should not be confused with Jean Cusin, called Lambert, who was a member of the LX when Jean Lambert was a councillor [ROGET I, pp. 162-164 and 256, n. 1; ROSET, p. 259; R.C. 35, f. 323 and f. 331 (September 12 and 19, 1541); R.C. 36, f. 80 and f. 125v (July 28 and September 19, 1542); R.C. 37, folios 9, 18, and 275v (February 9 and 15 and November 18, 1543)]. On the Black Head see PALFI, "Tête Noire," although she does not talk about Lambert.

he did not do a thing with her or with others. And he never saw her except as a respectable girl, and she is of good parents. If he is compelled to take the child he will take it, but otherwise not, and he wants to endure it. The advice: that he be taken aside to speak in secret or remanded to Monday, and the said Roleta, and privately be . . .[117] Answers that he will not say anything else that would mean that he has done anything with her.

Nycod Du Chesne, bookseller.

Because of the marriage of Claret and Vyjehan's daughter.[118] Answers that he knows nothing, and about a week ago she was in his shop, and they sent for a pot of wine, understanding that Catherine wanted to go to the Consistory. And he heard from Jaques Claret that all this was not so. And he never heard anything except what he heard. And he said that Jaques said that they had separated, and he did not hear that he had money.

Jaques Claret, what he has done since. Answers that last Thursday he came to come to the Consistory. Said to Catherine at Nycod's: "Since you have another husband I ask nothing of you." And it was at the said Nycod's. And Michiel Nergaz and the said Jaques sent for a pot of wine that they drank together. And they had no other words, and Catherine's mother was asked whether she wanted Jaques to give her up, and she was very glad. And he asked Nycod to give him some drink, and he did not know that Catherine was there, and her parents told him to give it up. And it was never he. [f. 170v] The said Jaques answers that Catherine made Gabriel . . .[119] and that he should swear faith to Catherine, and he had to go, and he never took her elsewhere, the said Gabriel, except to the taverns and the baths, and he did not want to take her. And he did not do anything except to come take the oath. The said Catherine told him she was not married. The advice of the Consistory . . .[120]

Tevene Grippaz.[121] On the said marriage of Claret and the girl. Answers that Jaques Claret found her on Christmas Eve and bought something[122] that he wanted to give to Catherine. And another time the said Jaques told the said Gripaz to go to Catherine, to send her a *quarteron* of white wine, which

---

117. Incomplete sentence.

118. The matrimonial case between Jaques Reclans, called Claret, and Catherine, daughter of Vijehan (Wigand) Köln.

119. Gabriel Vijehan (Köln), brother of Catherine. Words omitted.

120. Incomplete sentence. The decision was evidently put off in order to hear the following witnesses.

121. Tevene Baud, called Grippa.

122. In the margin: "taffeta."

she did, and carried the said *quarteron* of wine to the said Claret, and the said Catherine entered alone into the Bishop's Palace with the said Claret. And she saw nothing else, although the said Claret told the said Grippe that the said Catherine was his wife, and if it was not she, it would be never. And the said Catherine never told her that the said Catherine had said that Claret was her husband. And she knows nothing else, except that the said Claret said that Catherine was his wife.

Catherine, for reasons as above. Answers that she never gave anything to the said Claré. And last Thursday she returned the belt that the said Jaques had given her, and she returned it in Nycod's shop. And he told her that he was unhappy that they were in conflict. And she did not eat there. And they wanted to separate, and nothing was ever promised to the said Jaques to make him give her up. And she did not know that Claret would come there. And she did not have letters written on the handkerchief that she had given to the said Claret, and she bought the said handkerchief from Bocone.[123] And no one whatever was with her when she went to the Bishop's Palace, and she did not enter. [f. 171] Also answers that Bocone asked once why Jaques Claret went so often to her house, and it could be that the said Claret wanted to give her a ring. And the boy gave the handkerchief to the said Claret, and Gripa gave her the belt, and she did not understand what it was about. And no one was involved in the agreement except as she said, that they wanted to give it up, and no one ever spoke of giving anything to the said Claret for the said business, since there was nothing to be done. And she never promised anything to the said Claret, and he was not in the Bishop's Palace.

The advice of the Consistory: if any fornication is found, let punishment follow. On the marriage, let it be abandoned, and Gripa and and [sic] Catherine must be summoned and confronted with each other.

Catherine and Gripaz together. Catherine answers that she did not have the handkerchief brought by anyone whatever, and Gripa gave her the belt, and none other. And on leaving the Magnifico's[124] she saw that Gripa went to the Bishop's Palace, and she did not enter the Bishop's Palace. Grippa says that Catherine entered the Bishop's Palace on Christmas Eve and that she saw her return immediately, and the said Teneve[125] was waiting in front of the Bishop's Palace when she brought the *quarteron* of wine to the said Jaques Claret. And if she had not known it was in marriage she would never have meddled with it, and the said Jaques was angry at the said Catherine.

123. Franceyse Bocone.
124. Laurent Meigret, called the Magnifico.
125. Tevene Grippaz (who is speaking).

The advice of the Consistory advises [sic] that in view of the lies on one side and the other that the said Gregoyre be summoned to discover the matter, and regarding the fornication, and if the boy and Gripa can be had let them be remanded to the Council on Monday, and tomorrow the boy to discover, and Jaques. Note: the boy on Friday.

[f. 171v] Franceyse Bocone touching Catherine's marriage. Answers that she never told her why it was and she never wrote on the said handkerchief, and she has only paid her 11 *quarts,* and Catherine owes her the rest for the said handkerchief. And she did not know what she wanted to do, and they were never, Jaques or Catherine, in her house, although Jaques wanted to give her a gold ring, and then the said Franceyse told him that she would not do it without the knowledge of her mother and her father.[126]

[Franceyse Bocone]

Also about her having once gone to Jaques Le Mugnier's house, and she went to Saconnex with some woman with her. Answers that she does not know about this, and once she was told that her daughter was ill and she should go to see her. And Wooden-Feet[127] told her, and she wanted to ask her husband's permission to go there, and she found the said woman, Anthoyne, who told her her daughter was ill. And she asked Mabuect's wife[128] to go with her. And they went to Grand Saconnex, and when they were there she spoke to a woman, and the other woman, Mabuet, returned. And she went to her daughter and remained there two nights, and then her husband came to get her because Jaques Le Mugnier's wife wanted to give him a dinner. And she did not mount a horse anywhere, and she would not want to do anything a respectable woman should not do. And one must not believe such foolishness, because the world is in such . . .[129]

And about a certain matter, because she was worried about a child she has. And then the horse, she did not mount a horse, and she never left her shop open; this was when she went to the said Saconnex to see her daughter.

[f. 172] Thomasse, widow of François Mabuecta. Had known the said Franceyse since her confinement and was with her in Saconnex with the said

126. In the registers of the Council it is merely noted: "Remand by the Consistory of the said Claret and Catherine, who fornicated under the pretense of marriage" [R.C. 38, f. 119 (March 10, 1544)]. The depositions on the matrimonial case between Jaques Reclans and Catherine Köln end here. The interrogation of Franceyse Bocone continues below, but it concerns another subject entirely.
127. Anthoyne Wooden-Feet.
128. See the testimony of Thomasse Mabuecta, below.
129. Incomplete sentence.

Franceyse's daughter. And she sent to her to go with her, and it was as far as Grand Saconnex, and she had no one with her at Jaques Le Mugnier's house. And she went there with the said Franceyse because she, the said Franceyse, went to get money, and she did not see any horseman there nearby that she saw. And she did not see her go with any man when she went to Saconnex, because she told her she was not taking the right road, and then the said Thomasse wanted to return. And she did not say that she saw a horseman when she went with her. And because she helped her recover from the birth of a daughter whose godfather was Laurent Perret, and he never gave her anything except one *gros*. And she does not know when the said Franceyse returned, and she left her in front of the house where she wanted to enter, and she had promised to pay her well if she went with her to the said Saconnex. And at Jaques Le Mugnier's she told the said defendant that she would accompany her to Saconnex and would go as far as Petremande's house. And she does not know that she saw any person speak to her, or any horseman, and the said Franceyse did not tell her where her said child was.

The advice of the Consistory is that she be remanded to Thursday, and let Franceyse be remanded until she is recalled. Meanwhile Monsieur Claude Du Pain will come and take information, and that it be learned where her child is being nursed.

Franceyse. Answers that it is in Chevrier, because she intended to find company in Grand Saconnex, and she would find company there and then she would return, the said Mabuecte. And if she had not found company, the said Mabuecte would have gone the whole way as far as the said Chevrier. And she went to see her daughter with a girl she found who was at Mermete's, and she would not weep for her daughter, who was ill, if she died. The said Mabuecte says that the said Franceyse did not speak to anyone whatever except a girl, and she did not see Petremande.

f. 172v] *Ayma, wife of Pierre Baux.*[130]

Answers that her maid is at her house who was pregnant by Lancellot, her brother-in-law.[131] And she had the child in this city in their house, and she and a woman were present. And she had a son, and the midwife who received him baptized him in the house, saying, "In the name of the Father and of the Son and of the Holy Spirit." And because the child was in danger they went for water and baptized him. And she has no scruples about the Christian religion, and they

130. Ayma, daughter of Jean Guynet the younger, wife of Pierre Baud, son of Jean Baud (GALIFFE I, p. 46).
131. Lancellot Baud.

349

have so much business that they cannot go to all the sermons. And she does not pray to the Virgin Mary and she always commends herself to God. And her advocate is Our Lord. She has ceased fasting and has no suspicion.

Lancellot Baux. Answers that he knew a maid about seven or eight months ago who was from Douvaine, and he goes to the sermons when he is in Douvaine, and he is not in the tavern during preaching. And about the words of the diviner; he did not reprove the preacher in the pulpit.

Jehan Roget,[132] *hatter.*

Because of the sermons and the Virgin Mary. Answers that he goes to the sermons when he can, and his mother also when she can, and on Sundays. And he is not married and has no maid and has done what he was told and commanded last time.[133] And he believes in God the Creator and not in the Virgin Mary that he knows of, and he does not say that saints should be invoked. Said the prayer and the confession.

Jehan Blanchet, father of the wife of Jehan Bornant,[134] *baker.*

Says that he is ready to do what he should do, but only if the marriage [portion] is guaranteed. And if he does not want to pledge the 20 florins, let him pledge what the father will give to his daughter.

[f. 173] *Boniface Thorel.*

He was commanded to make his party come on Thursday.

The letter from the castellan of Peney was read.

Examined Gonrard Du Puys in Satigny in the presence of the aforesaid member lords.[135] Monsieur Calvin proposed that the matter be decided and that Henri Dufor and Gonrard Du Puys be summoned.

---

132. Jean Roget, citizen, living on the Rue du Perron, member of the CC in 1537 at the latest. His mother, mentioned here, was Françoise, wife of Monet Roget, already a widow in 1542 [R.C. 30, f. 168 (February 7, 1537); Notaires, Jean Duverney, v. 5, f. 33 (May 31, 1542)].

133. This is not found in this register. However, on February 7, 1542 (R.C. 35, f. 488), that is nine days before the beginning of the present volume, he was already in prison for having said that "someone wanted to make an abbot, namely Jehan Goulaz, and afterwards he withdrew the said words." He had perhaps been admonished in Consistory.

134. Jehan or Jehan Tyvent Blanchet, father of Pernon, promised wife of Jehan Bornant.

135. The members are not in fact named above. The castellan of Peney at this time was François Philibert Donzel. The members appointed on May 14, 1543, were Claude Soultier and Pierre Baud, notaries, and Claude and Jaques (or Jaquemo) Dufour. Aymé Du Mur was *curial* of Peney [R.C. 37, f. 90v (May 14, 1543)].

Thursday, March 13, 1544

Lord Syndic Philippin.
Calvin, Albert, Jehan Ferrand,[136] Genesto, Tripperaulx, De Ecclesia.
Checand, Blandin, Veyrier, Just, Molard, Pensabin, Donzel, Vellut.

Pierre Cristin, from Evian.

Being in Lancy he wanted to make friends with the daughter of Jaques Du Crest,[137] and they said yes, and Claude Hugoz . . .[138] And after supper they gave to drink to Pernete, daughter of Jaques Du Crest, and they had talked before. And they did not want to talk with him now. He asks his rights. And he wanted to give her a gold ducat, and they drank harder, and the said affair should be settled within a week. And they were answered that the girl did not want to go to live in Evian, and she did not want to take the ducat. The advice of the Consistory is that the girl and the uncles be summoned as often and when [necessary]. If the girl is here that she be called, and that the girl's brother be summoned.

Jane, wife of Lentillie.[139]

Because of the sermons and certain other things. Answers that she only goes to the sermons on Sundays, and she does what she can and works for her living, and she was at the chief sermon and [that] at vespers. And her husband has a connection in Saint Jean de Gonville with a daughter of Claude Moyron, and since then her husband does nothing but fight with me

---

136. Jean Ferron, from Poitiers, was received as a minister of Geneva on March 10, 1544, and deposed in 1549, accused "of various careless actions of which he confessed part, and also of indecent touching of his maids" [R.C. 38, f. 118 (March 10, 1544); *R.C.P.* I, pp. 58-59 (April 13, 1549); *ibid.,* p. 58, n. 4, gives the bibliography of this affair].

137. Jaques Ducrest, draper from Evian, received into the bourgeoisie on September 11, 1506 (*L.B.,* p. 157).

138. Incomplete sentence. Claude Hugues, son of Guillaume (therefore nephew of Besançon Hugues), Seigneur de la Feuillade, member of the LX in 1537. Apparently implicated in the affair of the Articulants and forced to leave Geneva, he is found in January 1544 asking permission to return to Geneva and to be restored to the bourgeoisie. He died in Geneva on March 28, 1569, aged 60 [GALIFFE I, pp. 4-7; R.C. 38, f. 29 and f. 29v (January 11 and 14, 1544); E.C., Morts 9, p. 68].

139. This is the wife of the unfortunate Jehan Dunant, called Lentille, who died of the wounds inflicted in the course of an interrogation under torture, Lentille being suspected of being one of the principal spreaders of plague in 1545. On him and on this famous affair see L. GAUTIER, *Médecine,* pp. 138-150.

[sic], and the girl there . . .[140] said she was pregnant by him. [f. 173v] And they do not love each other as formerly. And her husband reproaches her only for the past, and he tells her she is a fool. And it is true that she has kept her child for a year and spent some money she had, and she does not know how to give any other account of herself, and he has reproached her for her past. And there is no one who has complained of her since they came from Saint Jean de Gonville. And she has employed herself as he commanded and has kept order. The advice: that her husband and she should be summoned for Thursday, and whether she knows how to pray to the Lord. Said the prayer and that she knows the confession as it was formerly, and said the Ave Maria and that the Virgin Mary must be adored.

Anthoyne Wooden-Feet, pawnbroker.

Because of certain words. Answers that she has never been outside [the city] with Bocon's wife, and that once she was at Jaques Le Mugniez's and she told a girl to go find Bocon's wife, that she should go see her daughter who was ill in Chevrier. And the said Franceyse Bocone found her and asked what she wanted, and then the said Franceyse Bocone told her what it was, and she said if she would give her a *teston* to sell [sic] a fur-trimmed dress[141] that was for sale for 8 écus. And she does not know what disagreement there may be between Rosset[142] and her, and she never heard from anyone that it was so. Answers that she never said that there was dancing all the time at Monsieur Calvin's house to the virginal, and certain preachers, but she did not enter the room, only on the stairs. She was given strict admonitions and remonstrances.

Noble Jana Corne, wife of Noble François Bonivard, Seigneur de Saint Victeur.

Because of the day of their wedding. Answers that she was ill all that week, and she got up and came to St. Peter's, and she was so cold that she did not know what to do for the cold, and she thought she would go out of the city. And there was [f. 174] a man who dined in the company, and she was . . .[143] And as for the sermons, she is not always in a state to go to the sermons, and she does not serve God as she should. She was given proper admonitions for her superstitions about food and days and to live in amity

---

140. Illegible word.
141. Translator: The French says "furred with *mainbard*," but what fur this was is not known.
142. Pierre Rosset.
143. Incomplete sentence.

with her people and in charity together, and she was exhorted about Holy Communion for Easter.

On the marriage of the one from Evian [and] the daughter[144] *of Jaques Du Crest.*[145] *Jehan Ferraz, Jaques Du Crest.*

There was a statement on the marriage of Pierre Cristin. The said Cristin stated that he was in Lancy to establish friendship with them to have the sister of the said Jaques Du Crest for a wife. And they came to dine in this city and he pleased them well, but the girl did not want to go to Evian, and then they went to Compesières to Claude Hugoz and spoke of staying here for about a year, and he gave the said girl to drink in the name of marriage. He wanted to give her a gold ducat in the name of marriage, and again he drank harder with her, and they gave him a week, and he was told he should come on Sunday. And he brought his parents here on Sunday, and they made proposals about this affair, and he asks for the girl if he may have her, and if not to be freed.

Jaques Ferraz[146] says that he told him he had a wish to have his sister, and he answered him that he would leave it until the families . . .[147] and said that the said girl would never drink with him in marriage. And they wanted to go. They were still retained for a day more, and he should complete it. And he wanted to give a half ducat because it was necessary for him to give something more. And they waited again for a week because they did not intend that the said affair should be carried out, and he should not bring his parents so there would not be great expense. And he does not think his sister drank with him in the name of marriage. And they replied to him that she did not want to go to Evian. Jehan Fera danced in the house with the said Pierre and told him that he did not know whether the girl wanted it or not and that she had told him that she did not want to consent to such a marriage outside the city. [f. 174v] And also he told him straight out that he did not intend to send his sister to the papistry. And the said Pierre answered that he wanted to prove it. He said in the absence of the said Pierre that if his sister had drunk with him she should say so. And she answered him that she did not want it because she could not stay there. And his said sister never drank with him in the name of marriage, and he did not want it completed without his uncle's

144. "The daughter" is struck from the text, probably because it is Jaques Du Crest the son who appeared here. Therefore "the daughter" would be his sister Pernette, daughter of Jaques Du Crest the father.

145. The marriage of Pierre Cristin and of Pernete Du Crest.

146. Actually Jaques Du Crest.

147. Words omitted.

knowledge, and the said half ducat he alleges having given her, this was to buy pins and was not in the name of marriage, and they wanted to ask each other's relatives.

The opinion of the Consistory: that it be settled by giving an order that the girl be made to come on Thursday and the witnesses, to learn the truth here: Claude Hugoz and his wife.[148] The said Jaques was admonished to frequent the sermons, the taverns, his insolence, and to keep good company.

Boniface Thoret and Mariaz,[149] pin-maker; Pierre Borraz, pin-maker.

The said Pierre Borrat says what he knows about the marriage between the said Boniface and the said [Maria]. Answers that at vespers [he] and her uncle spoke together while supping together, and if the said Boniface wanted, he would indeed like to give her to him. And after supper he gave a sou to the said girl, and her family should be informed, and they said it was not so. And it was done in the name of marriage, and he emptied wine from one glass into another and gave her to drink, that there was no one else for him, and he borrowed a sou to give her and she promised him 60 florins and that he [her uncle] had enough goods that he would have. And afterwards they went to her parents' house and did not find what he had said, and they became angry with them. And the promise was made between the said Boniface and [f. 175] the said girl.

Egrege Françoys Favre,[150] citizen of Geneva.

Answers that he has a child named Pierre Favre. Because of fornication. Answers that it is about a month since he was in Bonne, and he lives with his mother in this city. And when his uncle is here he goes there and lodges in his said uncle's house. Asked about a maid. Answers that it is true that there is a woman who means to give him[151] a child. He does not know whether it is his, since it was given to him, and he has given great offense to God and asks mercy of God and of justice. The advice of the Consistory is that he be given strong remonstrances and remanded to the Council. And encourage him to marry, and that the Council make him marry. Asked where the girl is from.

---

148. Antoina, daughter of Claude Mazet. See GALIFFE I, pp. 4-7.

149. Maria Gerbain.

150. Should not be confused with the famous chief of the Favre clan of the same name. The one in Consistory here was from the family of Favre called Coulavin, natives of Bonne, others of whom are found in the public registers [see for example Claude Favre, called Coulavin, from Bonne but having goods in Geneva, R.C. 37, f. 212v (September 4, 1543)].

151. Translator: That is, to attribute it to him as the father.

Answers that she is from Burliez, and it was a son she gave him, and she is in the district of Gex at Chevry, and she was brought to bed at the village below Bonne, and she gave it to him ten weeks ago. And he spoke to her in this city in Longemale near where they sell wheat, and he was never again where she is staying, and he does not want to go there again. And he fell on his knees crying "mercy" to God and the Seigneurie.[152]

On the affair of the said Boniface, of the girl and Borraz.[153]

Understood that the other witness has not come, and that he be remanded to Monday to the Council. The said Boniface confirms what the said Borraz said, that it is true that he drank with her, and her uncle, of the said Maria, told him that he would have plenty, and he gave him a sou that had been lent to him, and they wanted to have the gold ring. And he took(?) the sou and gave it to the said Maria.

Humbert Favre[154] of this city, pin-maker, witness. Answers about the marriage of the said Boniface, and he knew the said girl who had lived with Master Tyvent the pin-maker. And he knows the agreement and that she swore at his house and her uncle gave her to him and he gave a sou in the name of marriage, and he gave it to the said girl. And they promised him an ample household and from her father a hundred florins and from him three score florins, and afterwards the said girl's uncle took it all back. And Pierre Borraz knew this same man, and [f. 175v] they supped together at the said Favre's house. And Borraz spoke to Boniface, and when they drank together the said Boniface said that indeed he wanted it, but that he should get what he had been promised, and he would do everything he should do. And he drank with the said girl in marriage, and he always reserved that he should obtain what was promised. And he drank simply in the name of marriage and they drank also, and Boniface took the glass and gave the said girl to drink in the name of marriage. And Boniface took the glass back and drank with her, and he should obtain what he had been promised. And he said he would not know whether to say if in drinking he said, he does not know whether he spoke those words of reserve again; he does not remember.

The advice of the Consistory is that if he said that he would want to

152. On Monday, March 24, 1544, the Council condemned François Favre, called Coulavin, to four days in prison for fornication, and he was admonished to marry (R.C. 38, f. 132v).

153. Boniface Thorel, Maria Gerbain, and Pierre Borraz.

154. An Humbert Favre, pin-maker, lived in the Tour de Boël in 1552 [E.C., Morts 1, p. 70 (July 6, 1552; death of his son)].

drink if he obtained what was promised, the advice seems to be that there is no marriage, since the conditions were not kept.

The two witnesses confronted with each other, Borraz and Humbert. First Borraz says that the girl left Master Boniface, ate with them to make the said marriage, that the girl had a good marriage [portion] and the girl's uncle, and they claimed that she had 60 florins for the wedding and 100 florins from her father's house. And they wanted to give them to drink together, and he wanted to wait until he had some of his relatives. And they wanted the said Pierre to give to drink, and the said Boniface gave a *gros,* and the said Boniface did not want to go forward if he was not given what he had been promised. And at supper he gave to drink. And someone said: "It is your turn, let it be done, let this promise be kept." And afterwards the uncle denied everything and they became angry at each other. And because he had wasted his goods they did not want him. And a priest [f. 176] told them that the said girl had nothing in the house and the said uncle found nothing, so he went to live in Lyon. And they presented a letter to have 60 florins that the said uncle had promised them. The said Fabre says this, and that the said Boniface always reserved the promise made to him and . . .[155]

The advice of the Consistory: that the girl be summoned, and that there is no marriage in view of the reservation. The husband and the girl tomorrow before the Council.[156] The girl said she will return him what he gave her in drinking in the name of marriage.

Thursday, March 20, 1544

Lord Syndic Philippin.
Calvin, De Ecclesia, Tripereaulx, Ferrand, Genesto, Albert, Champereaulx.
Vernaz, Du Molard, Veyrier, Donzel, Pensabin, Justz, Blandin.

Cristoble Favre, son of Pierre Favre, boatman, bourgeois of Geneva.[157]

Stated before the Consistory in the case of Jehan Conte of Nyon that he does not know how to present his case unless his brother is allowed to enter.

155. Incomplete sentence.
156. On March 14, 1544, the Council declared that "no marriage was made between them, freeing them to contract elsewhere, nevertheless condemning the said Boniface to the expenses" [R.C. 38, f. 124].
157. A Pierre Favre (Fabri), boatman, was admitted to the bourgeoisie on September 23, 1522 (*L.B.*, p. 195). Christoble Favre himself is mentioned in Council on October 1, 1544, in connection with a "fraud on the tolls at Evian" (R.C. 38, f. 395).

True that once Jaques Savua, and once after supper he was told that someone wanted to talk about a girl they wanted to give him. And after supper they went walking. And Jaques Savua lent him an écu to give in marriage to the girl provided that it pleased his father, claiming that it pleased his father. And he drank in Nyon, the said Jaques Savua being present. And another time the girl's father spoke to him and the said girl, Nycolarda, who answered she wanted only the one who gave her the écu. [f. 176v] And he spoke to his father, who did not want to consent; and because his [father] did not want it, he does not want to displease his father, and he never spoke to my [sic] father, and he does not want to displease his father in this way. And his father told him that if he wanted to be his son he would not do this. The advice of the Consistory is that his witness be summoned.

Nycolarde, daughter of Jehan Conte, butcher, inhabitant of Nyon. Answers the questions. Presented and showed a coif, an écu of Geneva, three silver rings, a belt and a ribbon. Four times they were given her and he gave her to drink in the name of marriage, and the rings afterwards, and the rings all at one time; present were Jaques Savua and Jaquemaz, her mother,[158] and two maids, one of whom is married; one is named Claudaz, daughter of Jehan Gerdil, and the other Jana. And they began and I asked my family what I should do, that is my father, mother and brother, and they truly wanted it. And the said Cristofle's father truly wanted it and gave her the écu and the ribbon, and it was all, all given her in the name of marriage. And the said Cristoble reserved nothing, that his father and friends consented. And it was about half a year ago about Michaelmas, and he gave her the écu and gave her to drink, and she drank with her mother's consent. And she says that she had given him a week to consider, and at the end of the week he returned to her, and he came every week and would never give her up, as she says that the said Cristoble told her.

The advice is that the father and the mother of the said Nycolarde be made to come, and Jehan Pitiod,[159] Jehan Conte, Jaquemaz his wife (the mother [of Nycolarde]), Jehan Chautemps.

Jehan Conte answers, and speaks in the words of Jaquemaz. Jaquemaz, mother of the said Nycolarde, because she is better informed about the affair. [f. 177] Answers in this way: the boy asked the girl, and she would not dare to do it without the knowledge of her father and mother, and he would be

---

158. Jaquemaz, the mother of Nycolarde. The widow of Jehan Conte (her first name is not given) died in the Grande Boucherie on March 3, 1566, aged 80 (E.C., Morts 6, p. 122).

159. Jehan Chautemps, called Pitiod.

pleased if she were given to him, and she gave him seven days to consider and to speak to his father. And at the end of the said days a man came who told them they wanted to proceed, that the father truly wanted it, and he gave her to drink, and she drank with her mother's consent, and he gave her an écu. And on this a brother of his arrived who said the contrary, and that the said Cristofle's father truly wanted it. And the Burgundian, La Rava's son-in-law, Master Claude de La Tor, D'Orsiere, Jaques Sçavua, knew that the said Cristoble's father truly wanted it then.

Jehan Chautems says they should have spoken about the marriage, and he answered that he did not care about the marriage.

The said Crestoble says about the conflict that it does not please his father or him, and his father told him not to do it. And as to the first proposals, if his father did not consent, answers that the girl never gave him a term to consider, and he offered some words that his father had spoken to him, which he had not done, and his father never consented to her. And he did not drink, and he gave her an écu before her mother.

Romanestoz, brother of the said Cristoble, says he could not do it, and because he was lodged there and the girl's mother urged the said Cristoble and her father told him that he wanted to give him his daughter, who showed him the écu the said Cristoble had given her, which he knew well. The said Romanesto answers that it will not be proven and that he would never take his words back for any man whatever. He was exhorted not to be evasive in his speech.

Anthoyne Panisso[160] says that he was the first to speak to the said Cristoble's father and that the father never consented to it.

The said Romasto [sic] says that he was never evasive and that no one ever spoke to his father. And he is assured by his father that he told him he would never call them his children if this were done.

The said Cristoble, that he gave an écu for the first time, the coif, the ribbon and four silver rings, and his father never consented, on his conscience, and he does not want to disobey his father. [f. 177v] And his father would repudiate him if he had done it. And Anthoyne Pannissod, his father-in-law, told him that he answered and that Claude made him no response, and about the one who lent him the écu, and that his father said he did not want it. And his father knew well that the said Cristoble had given her the rings, and he had already done it when he spoke to his father. And the girl answered him that she was well assured of her father and mother. And if

160. Antoine Panissod, member of the CC in the *dizaine* of Michel Morel (Rive) in 1541 [R.C. 35, f. 56ᶜv (February 9, 1541)].

he said that his father truly wanted it he failed to tell the truth. And when it was time the fathers would agree well together, and his father never consented, but told him: "Watch out. If you do it, you will not find yourself well off." And his brother was angry with him because I [sic] displeased his father, and they always went there because . . .[161] And he did not want it because his father wanted it, and the girl is a respectable girl. And his father is in Nyon.

The advice is that the father be remanded to Thursday, and that they bring their witnesses of the girl, and that the son not leave if he intends his advantage. And that the abst . . . (?) be taken to find out the facts, and notify the said Cristoble's mother, and that the officer go to summon the father to be here Thursday and bring his son. And that Jehan Conte not name the witnesses to avoid subornation, and the rings given for a marriage gift were returned. Remanded to next Thursday, and let them bring the witnesses they know of who would know that the father truly wanted it. The names of witnesses: Master Claude de l'Escuallaz and Claude Savua and Nycolas Chatron[162] and the son-in-law of Ravaz, Hudri Jaquoz, Petrequin Guygoz, carter.[163]

178] *On the other marriage of Pierre Cristin, Pernete, daughter of the late Jaques Du Crest, merchant of Geneva.*

Answers that she was in Lancy with her sister and that she was summoned for someone from Evian. Answers that he is named Pierre Crestin and that he did not speak to her at all, but to her brother, and she does not know when it was; about ten months ago. And this was in Lancy at the house of her brother, Claude Hugoz,[164] and he brought a cousin of hers, and her brother Jaques told her that this Pierre from Evian wanted her, and she answered that she did not want to go to Evian. And she drank from one glass with the said Pierre, and she did not talk about this affair after supper, and she stayed there until Saturday. And he told her that he indeed wanted to take her for a wife, and then her brother gave him a term of a week to await a response. And she told her brother that she did not want to be married in the papistry. And if she drank, she did not intend this to be in the name of marriage. And she does not have her heart set on him and did not drink with him again. And indeed they wanted to give her a half ducat, which her sister

161. Incomplete sentence.
162. Nycolas Chappuys, called Chatron, was received into the bourgeoisie on May 1, 1543 (*L.B.,* p. 224).
163. Guigoz Martin, called Petrequin.
164. Her brother should be Jaques Du Crest, not Claude Hugoz, who lived in Compesières (see above, March 13, 1544). Possibly Claude Hugoz was her brother-in-law.

told her would do her no injury. And on Friday. And she reserved that it should please her uncles, and she never had him in her heart. And she never wanted to agree and did not intend that this was in marriage, and indeed he said that this was in the name of marriage, and this was on Friday. And she did not receive the ducat, and her sister told her she should take nothing when her uncles were not there.

The advice: that the witnesses be summoned and examined one after another. Pierre Cristin has brought for witnesses: Noble Claude Hugoz and his wife Mychie. Jehan de Prelez received one florin to get someone from Evian. Estienne Conte, citizen of Geneva.

[f. 178v]   The said Estienne Conte says what he knows about the marriage contract. He was in Lancy to make a contract of marriage for the daughter of Jaques Du Crest about six weeks ago, and the other day it was said that Jaques Du Crest, the said girl's brother, would be among the witnesses of Saint Suzanne. Being in Thonon, he was asked to come to Lancy. And this was on Thursday, and he arrived at the house, and it was night. And on Friday to give the word for the said Cristin, and he wanted to complete the contract of marriage with Jaques Du Crest. And he wanted to speak to the girl, and she told him, Pernete did, that she wanted to marry and that she came from Rive, and she was told she would go to a good house, and asked an answer. And they wanted to come, and they were asked to stay by Claude Hugoz. And they went to Compesières to the Red[165] and returned to Lancy and found Robert Collon. And the said Pierre and the girl remained in the kitchen and asked to make a collation, although he did not see them do it. And they sat down and took two glasses and gave each other to drink and touched glasses,[166] and Donne Mychie began to cry. And Robert said it was good news; the said Robert was very happy. And in leaving in the morning to go away they gave each other to drink and he gave her a ducat. And the said Donne Mychie told her, "Don't dry up![167] He does not stay warm. Take him boldly!" And the said Claude said a ducat was little enough, since the girl was worth more. And on Saturday a week later in Evian the said witness notified

165. A Tyvent Volland, called Le Rouge, or the Red, appeared in Consistory on June 29, 1544. There was also a certain Durand, called Red, who took part in the rising of June 6, 1540, that led to the fall of the Philippins (Roget I, p. 249, n. 1). There was also a Pierre Duran, Red, undoubtedly the same, elected to the CC for the Rue du Boule in 1537 [R.C. 30, f. 168 (February 7, 1537)].

166. Translator: Translation uncertain, but logical.

167. Translator: *"Ne t'en seche!"*, an expression whose meaning is not clear. It most likely means "Don't be discouraged, don't give up," or something similar. "Dry" has a number of figurative meanings in French, as in English.

the parents of the said Pierre Cristin that they should come on the designated day. And the said Jaques did not understand that the term had come, and he went to Evian, and they talked about having either money or goods. And Jehan Ferra stayed there, and the [f. 179] witness returned, and they came to achieve the completion of the said marriage. And they came to talk to Jehan Ferra and they were told that they could complete it at the beginning of Lent. And when the said Pierre gave the ducat, the said girl never reserved the will of her uncles, and she said it wittingly.

Noble Claude Hugoz says that he knew that they drank in his house in Lancy about three weeks ago at supper. And Estienne Conte supped, and he does not know what other. And it seems to him Jaques Du Crest. And the said Cristin stayed two nights, that he wanted to have Pernete for a wife, that he did not have charge of her and had to talk to her brothers and uncles and brother-in-law. And they talked together, and the said witness was not there and only heard that it was necessary that Jaques . . . ,[168] and they supped together and presented glasses and drank together. And he had two glasses, and Pernete took the glass on the table, the said Cristin took the other, and they drank together. And one named Jaques, from Evian, was there, and he wanted to give her either a ring or a piece of gold, and he knows nothing else, and he refers to his wife, who knows more than he.

Donne Michie, his wife, says and deposes that it is true that she knew Pierre Cristin about two months ago in Lancy. She does not know what he did there, and he came one Thursday night and they supped together. It is true that after supper they passed the time and the said Conte went to bed and they made a collation, being seated at the table, and he offered drink to Pernete, who refused. And the next day he wanted to give her a piece of gold, which she refused. And her brother answered that in a week they would proceed. Pernete came and went and did not hold still, and the said Pierre offered her drink, and she does not know whether it was in marriage. And Pernete did not like him enough to talk to him alone at all. Indeed she drank in company and took the glass on the table and drank, and never in the name of marriage. And on Friday she did not want . . .[169] [f. 179v] Indeed she believes they supped again the said Friday together, and they gave her a term of a week for a response; it was indeed presented, but she never wanted to take anything. And she believes he wanted to give her a half ducat, and told her, "If you want to do it you can indeed take it." And her brother did not agree that she should take anything. And the said Pierre said, "Pernete does not

168. Words omitted.
169. Incomplete sentence.

like me at all," and this was near the bed where the said witness was already in bed. And the said Pernete never wanted to consent to anything.

Jehan and Jehan Ferraz, brothers.[170] Jehan the elder. That the day of Claude Frant, those from Evian came to him and said that they wanted to have Pernete and he should answer them. And he told them still to wait for a response and ask for the answer in a week. And he wrote him that his niece did not want to go there and that she would be married to another than this Cristin.

Jehan the younger says that he came to Lancy to talk and Jaques came to say that someone wanted to marry Pernete and that they wanted to go to Evian to talk about the said affair. And some words were spoken, that he had spent [money] in the war where he went, and spent fully three hundred écus. And the said Jehan was never in Lancy, and he would not give two sous to this man if he did not bind himself for it.

The advice of the Consistory: that it be learned from the uncles whether they desire and consent that the marriage be carried out or not. That it be remanded to the Council, since the family does not consent, and she reserved [the consent] of her family. The two Ferrats, guardians and uncles, do not want in the least to agree and do not intend at all that it should take place, and the girl does not want it; also she would like better to have a day-laborer in this city than to go to [f. 180] Evian, and it should never be done against the girl's will, and because the said Pierre is a debauched man. Remanded to tomorrow.[171]

Jehan Du Nant, from Groisy, habitant *of Geneva, farm laborer.*

Answers that he goes to the sermons on Sundays, and had the plague for 13 months without going to the sermons. Named many houses that were cleaned of the plague[172] in Saint Jean de Gonville, and he commends himself

170. Jean and Jean, sons of Hudriod Ferrat. Jehan the younger was a member of the CC in 1545, and one of the two was a member of the CC for the Terraillet in 1537 [Galiffe I, pp. 358-359; R.C. 30, f. 167v (February 7, 1537)].

171. On March 24, 1544, the Council decided "that the said girl does not consent to the said marriage, and the relatives, either of one or the other party, did not consent to it; the contract made between them is ordered and pronounced to be null and invalid, freeing both parties to marry elsewhere" (R.C. 38, f. 132v). On April 7 Pierre Cristin asked in Council that Pernete Du Crest be condemned to the expenses of the trial. On April 10 Jaques Du Crest asked "to be freed from this, since he is not guilty of having caused the said expenses and never wanted to consent to the said marriage, and many other things," which the Council in substance granted him (R.C. Part. 1, f. 145 and f. 146).

172. Translator: This is the usual meaning of *"depester,"* the word used, but from the context it may mean "infected with the plague" here.

to God and is helped by the Word of the Lord. And his wife was in this city, who sold bread and wine, and he gave her all he earned and six score florins, and he does not know what she did. And when he told her to help him she insulted him. And he asks justice, and she gave him a promissory note for 25 florins. He does not know what she did, and she has behaved badly, and he has a suspicion that she gave a man 10 écus that he cannot have, because she does not want to tell him. And he has often seen him in his house, and he is from Perly, and he has forbidden her his company, and she always does the opposite. And he has a child by her that he has indeed given her money to support. And he wanted . . .[173] and asks justice, that it should be noted that he cannot have peace with her, and he admonishes his said wife to follow the Word of Our Lord.

Jane, his wife. Jane answers that she does not know the prayer, and knows it only when her husband says it; she speaks after him. And nevertheless she would like to know it, and she did not want to go to the Molard, and she did not want to go except when she went for water. She was exhorted about the devil, whom she invoked one night. Answers that this was for a guest who was at her house, and when her husband was in the house she was angry and could not understand this Pater. And since Michaelmas he has given her money and a *bichet* of wheat, and he has not left her any goods in the house, and he told her she took money. [f. 180v] And she gave 25 florins to some people in Lully that he had ordered her to give them, and she does not know that she has spent anything, except that when she has money she uses it for the house. And he reproaches her for things. Her neighbors know about her behavior, and as far as she knows she has done nothing for which she can be blamed. And she has not spent money except what was put into the household. And there is a village man to whom she lent two écus despite her husband, who has him bake his bread. And her husband told him she should not see him, and he never entered the house except when she lent the said man the two écus. And she never lent money without the consent of her husband except these two écus. If she was formerly, etc., she is not at present, and she paid for the cultivation of the vineyard.

Both together. They were given strong admonitions and remonstrances to frequent the sermons and live in peace together and treat each other well as husband and wife according to the commandment of God. He says that the man who was lent the money should give him a *coupe* of wheat and a *setier* of wine for a year. Term to learn to pray to the Lord: two weeks.

173. Words omitted.

Thursday, March 27, 1544

Lord Syndic Michiel Morel.
Calvin, De Ecclesia, Albert, Genesto, Trippereaulx, Ferrand, Champereaux.
Checand, Vernaz, Pensabin, De Ulmo, Blandin, Veyrier, Vellu, Donzel, the officer Vovrey.

Claude Tappugnier,[174] his wife and Mermet Julliard.

Because of injurious words and [f. 181] superstitions. The said Tappugnier answers that he had some words that Just[175] knows about and Pierre Vernaz, who wanted to make an agreement between him and the said Mermet, and he was summoned before the lieutenant because he had words with a fugitive. And he has endured all the insults he can and has been in prison 18 days, and they have taken a nephew of his to Vienne and have removed him from Lyon where he lived.

All three intended to receive the next Communion at Easter, and they are reconciled with each other. The said Tappugnier says that he has a niece whom his brother came to get and take away, and he wants to live in peace with them, and pardons them the insults given previously, and if they will leave him alone he will leave them alone. They were admonished, and the said Mermet was commanded to make his wife do similarly and treat her uncle Tappugnier and his wife with honor, and that they settle the lawsuit they have together and frequent the sermons.

Amed Andrion[176] and[177] Claude Tappugnier.

Because of a certain conflict they have with the said Tappugnier. The said Amed and Tappugnier say that they wish each other no harm because

174. Claude Tappugnier having been put in prison, on March 14, 1544, "his wife, his parents and associates" presented a supplication to the Council asking the Council to free Tappugnier and "make past events forgotten, for which he offers 30 écus, and as for the words he formerly spoke against the Holy Gospel, he prays to be pardoned for this." The Council freed him from prison, imposing a fine of 20 écus and condemning him to the expenses (R.C. 38, f. 124).

175. Just de l'Olme, member of the Consistory.

176. Ami Andrion, apothecary, native of Cavour, in Piedmont, admitted to the bourgeoisie in 1513, died in 1554. Little interested in the Reform, Andrion left Geneva in 1535, but returned in 1536 on paying a fine of 100 écus. He remained, however, to say the least, tepid toward the Reform [*L.B.,* p. 176 (February 15, 1513); L. GAUTIER, *Médecine,* pp. 20 and 447-448; LAMBERT, "Cette loi"; SORDET, *Dictionnaire,* p. 28].

177. "Claude Chateauneufz" is struck; "and" is written three times.

they have had words with each other. Andrion says it is nothing, and they have done away with all enmity for each other for the honor of God.

Noble Claude Chateauneufz,[178] goldsmith, on the conflict as above with the said Tappugnier. Answers that he intends to say his prayer and receive Communion as is proper, and they have had no business together. The said Tappugnié says it is because of a house that someone wanted to sell him, and it was in Chambéry, where he paid for the said house which he has, and he has a lawsuit about it. And this is the reason why the said De Chateauneufz has a quarrel. The said Claude says that he has done him no harm and has taken the wine of a vineyard they have together that he should have next year, and he should have had the wine one year and the other the next.

181v] They were exhorted to live as good neighbors from now on, in peace and kindness together. They say they have a vineyard together for which one gives the money to the other, and they share the vineyard amiably. The said Claude pardons him all insults, and that the said Tappugnier make his wife be quiet, who is very haughty. They pardoned each other for all offenses.

Anthoyne, wife of Pierre Rosset.

On the case as above of her husband and Bocone[179] and Rosset, her husband. Answers that her maid should be asked how they go on. That her husband is worse than before; he beats her every night, and he beat her again yesterday with a stick, and she does not know what it is about. And he has been lost for two or three nights at a time, and she does not know where he goes or comes from, and she trembles when she sees him. And he arrived on Monday at 8 o'clock, and Bocone has often been with her and she has bathed with her, and she has never slept with her and with her husband. And indeed a man said once that she was the cause of it. And Bocone often came to find her, and her maid carried a letter and money to Bocone, a *teston*. And the next day she gave her three sous, and she told her she would be found behind the Corps Saints.[180] And the said day she waited at

---

178. Claude Chateauneuf, called the Gilder *(dorier)*, or sometimes simply Claude Dorier. He was a councillor in 1529, lieutenant in 1532, and served various functions in the mint between 1535 and his death before May 5, 1545. With many others he was forbidden to leave the city without the permission of the Council for three years after the fall of the Philippins in June 1540 [GALIFFE I, p. 491; DEMOLE, pp. 17 and 30; R.C. 37, folios 133v-134 (June 19, 1543); R.C. Part. 1, f. 68 (June 19, 1543)].

179. Franceyse Bocone.

180. Near the church of St. Gervase, on the present Rue des Corps-Saints.

the Corps Saints and the maid had given her the said three sous because she did not bring them so that the said Franceyse would not go to the said place. And she sent her a shift by Wooden-Feet,[181] and she returned it, that she did not want it. And they argued, and they were in the court, and they were angry because they were jealous. She does not know where Bocon was when her husband was lost for days. And her said husband threatened to cut off her head if she returned to this place of the Consistory. And she was beaten because he had to give six écus to her brother, and many other words that would be very tedious to [write]. [f. 182] The said Anthoyne: to verify the case it would be good to have Bocone's maid and find out about the agreement. She will tell everything, and without this nothing can be known. She fears that Martin the apothecary[182] is helped by the said Bocone. She showed a certain paper written in charcoal, two, that the said Franceyse sent to the said Rosseti, her husband, that Franceyse's maid took to her said husband.

Claudaz, daughter of Amy Rogemond, servant of Pierre Rosset. Answers that sometimes when she comes from fetching the wine he asks whether she has seen Bocone. And last Saturday he gave the said servant three sous to carry to the said Bocone, and she did not take them to her. And he and his wife do not love each other at all, and he beats her as much as he can at night, and not by day. And the three sous were given to her mistress, and she repents it. When her master does not see the said Bocone he is enraged, and when he sees her he behaves well. And on Monday he was lost and did not sleep in the house, and he returned to their table on Tuesday at 8 o'clock. And Bocone has a maid, and she spoke to her yesterday on the Grand Mézel.

The syndic took the papers produced. She was admonished. The opinion of the Consistory is that the fornication of Bocone be dealt with, and her maid [and] Rosset are remanded to the Council for justice. Friday.[183]

181. Anthoyne Wooden-Feet.

182. There is no apothecary of this last or first name mentioned in Geneva at this period in the list of apothecaries in L. GAUTIER, *Médecine*.

183. On March 28, 1544, Calvin declared in Council that it "is entirely certain that the said Rosseti continues in adultery as before with Boccone and that he commits terrible things that are very much against God. And that for such a whore he mistreats his wife." The Council then decided to put them in prison along with Bocone's maid, "who is a pander" (R.C. 38, f. 139v). On April 7 it was reported in Council that Rosset had fled the city, but Bocone and her maid, Claude, daughter of Claude Mestral, remained in prison and denied the affair (R.C. 38, f. 154). The maid was soon freed, but on April 10 Franceyse Bocone was condemned to nine days in prison on bread and water [R.C. 38, folios 156, 158, and 160 (April 8, 10, and 11, 1544)]. Having apparently returned to the city and been

Jehan Chappon and Vincent Fichet,[184] *glover.*

Because of the hatred they have for each other, and the next Communion. The said Chappon answers that he lives according to God and would be very unhappy otherwise, and he wishes no harm to the chambermaid of Noble Jehan Donzel;[185] also about certain merchandise that was for sale.

The said Vincent answers that it has pleased the Council to have them summoned here, and he has done no wrong in dealing, and he is not aware that he has done him a penny's harm. [f. 182v] And they have been great friends. He thinks they are still good friends, and he will satisfy him. If there is anything to be adjusted he is ready to satisfy him, and he protested that he does not mean harm to any merchant.

Chappon said that the said Vincent had friends who helped him to live and that the said Vincent went to Hermance to get skins he had bought that were sold to the said Vincent, and they were promised to him. He was given strong admonitions and remonstrances that he should give up these resentments and that they live in peace and love in order more worthily to receive the next Communion.

Answers about the chambermaid of Lord Jehan Donzel: when he sees her he is sad, and about the last Communion, and the said Donzel always keeps her in check, and he knows well how things are, and that the maid be exhorted about the sermon. And he has a resentment against the said Vincent because of a merchant of Vailly who sold him merchandise. And for this he wishes him no harm. And the said Vincent went and mounted a horse and went to break open their chest, because the merchandise was in Villeneuve. And he wishes no harm to the said Vincent; if anyone else wanted to do him harm he would protect him if he could. So many grudges are not . . .[186]

The advice of the Consistory is that within a week he make the chambermaid come, and himself, to know the decision. On Communion: they are forbidden it if they continue in this way, and that Vincent and he be reconciled. The two, Vincent and Chappon, agreed and shook hands in amity with

---

arrested, Rosset was freed from prison on May 16, 1544, and forbidden to converse with Bocone (R.C. 38, f. 203v). See also R.C. Part. 1, f. 154v and f. 170v (May 2 and July 3, 1544).

184. Vincent Fichet, glover, from Petit Bornand les Glières, was received into the bourgeoisie on October 6, 1551, "gratis, because he resided here in times of war and adversity." He died in the Fusterie on July 3, 1558 (*L.B.*, p. 237; E.C., Morts 2, p. 37).

185. Pernete, daughter of Jaquemaz de Jonvier (see below, April 3, 1544).

186. Incomplete sentence.

each other. Chappon says that he has received Communion, and he repents deeply because he has always held a grudge against the said Donzel's maid. Thursday: Jehan Donzel's maid[187] and Chappon's wife.

[f. 183]   *Jane, wife of Gonet Chevallier.*[188]

And says that her daughters[189] did not come because they have business for their husbands. And she goes to the sermons when she can, and says the prayer and not the confession, because she is ill. And her daughters, one is married[190] and the other not, and she has not yet eaten today. And her daughters curse her. The younger goes to the sermons twice on Sundays. She was admonished that if her daughters do anything to her that she say so, and make her daughter's husband come here. And that the two daughters be summoned for Thursday.

The Red's two sons are remanded to Thursday.[191]

Thursday, third day of April 1544

Lord Syndic Philippin.
Calvin, De Ecclesia, Albert, Tripereaulx, Genesto, Ferrand, Champereaulx. Pensabin, Veyrier, Just, Donzel, the officer Vovrey.

Master Monet Du Citer,[192] *mason.*

Because of sorcery for his wife. Answers that Master Claude Vernaz of Challex. And he never sent for him, because he was summoned by one of his relatives, and he treats the sick with herbs, and he gave him, himself, parsley(?) and spoke only words of Our Lord and gave him a drink of herbs. The said [Monet] drank it, and he was chilled, and his relatives sent for him. And he is called the Good Wizard, as they say. The beginning was when he arrived; he knew nothing about it, and he asked him how he was,

187. Struck: "and Vincent, because they left without permission."
188. Also called Corbet Gonyn Chivallier below, April 8, 1544.
189. Claudaz and Collete Chevallier.
190. Claudaz, wife of Jaques Ravier.
191. Reymond and Claude de La Ravoyre, sons of a woman called "the Red."
192. Monet Du Cetour (de Sertoux, etc.), native of Moëns (GE), received into the bourgeoisie gratis on October 26, 1537, because of his services to the city (he is frequently mentioned in connection with the works of fortification). He died on June 18, 1555, but a Monet Du Certour, possibly his son, is found still living in 1559 [*L.B.*, p. 217; E.C., Morts 1, p. 215; ROGET II, p. 121; R.C. 55, f. 32 (April 14, 1559)].

and he touched the vein in the hand and said that he would be entirely cured. And [f. 183v] he ground herbs in a mortar and gave it to him to drink, and he had brought his herbs in a bag, that he made him drink. It seems to him that he did not say that if he had known about it his wife would have been cured sooner. And he does not know whether the said man is a sorcerer or not, and he did not see him make the cross. And he gave his herbs to Master Franceys the doctor,[193] who planted them in his courtyard. And he felt well when he had drunk the said drink, and he never saw a man whom he would rather have around. And indeed he has heard people say he divines, and he never heard him say that this illness had been given to him, and he does not believe someone gave it to him. And he took this illness near Cornavin when it rained so hard once that his mason's mortar was ruined.

Pierre Furjon,[194] apothecary.

Because of certain words. Answers that he was away and was in Gex and had a quarrel with his brother-in-law three weeks ago, and he does not know how the quarrel happened. And Tappuniere, his wife, came and they insulted him, and he knew their nephew in this city and in Vienne, and he had no business with him. And he bought something from him at a price of 100 écus: lands, meadows, houses; and he is 23 years old and is Tappugnier's nephew, so he wanted to meet him. And then he took the chance of buying from him what he bought, and he does not know the edicts of the city,[195] and the said nephew came to him long afterwards, and he did not swindle him. He does not go to the sermons every day, and he did not know that the said Tappugnier was his nephew's guardian. He was admonished, and he was at the sermon Sunday morning, and Monsieur Calvin preached. Said the prayer.

193. François Chappuis, doctor, from Lyon, received into the bourgeoisie on June 11, 1535, then thirty years old; died of plague on September 13, 1569. He wrote a popular treatise on the plague of which two editions survive [L. GAUTIER, *Médecine*, pp. 22, 37-39, 424 and 516].

194. Pierre Furjon, citizen of Geneva, possibly the son of the apothecary Jaques Frojonis (Latinized form). He was accused with various others in 1556 of having made "false powder" [L. GAUTIER, *Médecine*, p. 453].

195. This refers to the edicts regulating the purchase of the goods of minors, the edict of 1532 having fixed the age of maturity at 25 years [*S.D.* II, p. 293 (November 17, 1532)].

[f. 184] *Pernete, daughter of Jaquemaz de Jonvier,[196] servant of Monsieur Jehan Donzel.*

She answers that she knew Monsieur Jehan Chappon, who lost it. It was about two years ago that it was lost, and the said Jehan Chappon went to the diviner to divine who had the said *peyrnez,[197]* and the said diviner divined that it was she. And she wishes no harm to the said Chappon and says that she always prays to God to remove from the said Chappon the feeling he has against her. She goes to the sermons when she can, on Sundays, and on Sunday she was at the Magdalen after dinner, and it was Monsieur Calvin. Said the prayer and the confession. Remanded to Tuesday.

Noble Pierre Mercier, because of a quarrel he has with Humbert Exerton.

It was about a year ago that he paid a fine of 400 florins for Master Savoex,[198] and he asked for it and they agreed together. And he was patient a little while, and was put in prison and was belied. For which things they are at law, the words and the money the said men have together.[199] And he wishes him no harm for this reason, except that he wants to be paid what they owe him. And he gives 300 écus to the hospital or all his goods, and the said Exerton gives 100 if what he says is the case, that I [sic] asked a larger sum than is due to him. And he does not wish them any harm, but he asks for what is due to him.

Also the said Mercier. Humbert Exerton, his associate, on the quarrel with the said Mercier. Answers that he bears him no grudge and is only waiting for the lieutenant's order, although the said Mercier said certain words which he is waiting for a decision about, and he does not agree that he owes him what he asked for by law, and he has receipts for what he paid the Treasurer.[200] They are exhorted to live in peace to receive Communion. The said Mercier says that if he is [f. 184v] paid what is due to him first he will be a friend afterwards. The said Exerton says that the matter will be tried tomorrow. They are remanded to agree between now

196. Jonvier was at the same time a place name (today Jonzier, H.-S.) and, although fairly rare, a family name in Geneva.

197. Translator: A word of unknown meaning; evidently an object of value. The word is used again in discussing the same case on f. 193 below.

198. Claude Savoex? If this is truly Claude Savoex, it appears that he was still known by his title of Monsieur le Maître [of the Mint], although he was dismissed from this office in 1537.

199. Pierre Mercier and Humbert Exerton at this time held the rent farm of Peney together [R.C. Part. 1, f. 92 (October 1, 1543) and f. 210 (October 10, 1544)].

200. Either Pierre Tissot (treasurer from 1541 to 1543) or Amblard Corne (treasurer in 1544).

and Tuesday. The said Mercier wants only his money, and meanwhile they will agree.

Claudaz, daughter of Gonet Chevallier,[201] wife of Jaques Ravier.

Answers that she has her father and her mother[202] and Collete[203] on the Rue de La Juiverie; her sister is at work. And she goes to the sermon when she can, and she has not been there for a week. And she was not there on Sunday a week ago because she has a small child and cannot come to the sermon with her husband also. And on Sunday if she had been at the sermon there were two children who would have burned themselves, but she saved them. And she said the prayer, and that she is obedient to her father and mother, and she did not curse her mother, and wants to be punished. And she got angry at her mother about three weeks ago, and she never got angry at her, and she did not not [sic] curse her mother with cankers. And may God confound her, and it was her husband who cursed her and not she. It never happened that she cursed her. She was admonished. She wishes no harm to anyone whatever.

Bytry, wife of Jaques Jasse, haberdasher.

Answers that she cannot go to the sermon and cannot hold herself up by either her arms or legs, and therefore cannot go. She liked the Mass well when it was said and likes the sermons well at present and no longer hears the Mass, and she could not go to the Mass any more than to the preaching. And she did not say that this is a bad law at present and that it would not forbid her from hearing the preachers to prevent her from denying the Virgin Mary.[204] And she does not pray to her, and the Virgin [f. 185] Mary has no more value than another woman. And she has a quarrel with a man, Corbet.[205] Said the prayer and the confession, and wishes no harm to any one she knows of. And it was a year and eight months ago, and she became

---

201. The father is also called Corbet Gonyn Chivallier below, April 8, 1544.

202. Jane, wife of Gonet Chevallier.

203. Her sister, Collete Chevallier.

204. Translator: This sentence seems to become rather confused. The sense of course is that she was accused of worshipping the Virgin, and she denied having said that "this present law" would force her to avoid the sermons in order to avoid denying the Virgin.

205. Below, on April 8, 1544, after having written and then struck the name "Corbet," Maillet identifies the man quarreling with Bytry Jasse as Pierre Jaquenoz. Corbet Gonyn Chivallier (alias Gonet Chevallier) follows directly after Pierre Jaquenoz, but has no apparent connection with this case.

weak all at once. And she has had a suspicion of a certain person, a woman whom she owed a sou. And she sent the said sou and asked her to come eat with her. And the said woman lingered in front of her, and the said sou was more than formerly and threatened her, this woman, and the girl who went. She answered her that she would never draw the bolt except for Loys Dufour and her. And she is named Big Jannaz, in the house of Monsieur Claude Hugoz. And another woman told her once that this Jane had said that the said Bytri should die; the other the last day of the month of March. And she has a little suspicion of the said Jane, although she did not hear her threaten.

Claude Clement, called Humbert.

Answers that he has not been in Cranves for six weeks, and he heard the Observant's preaching, and it was on St. John's Day after Christmas,[206] and it was after the Mass. And he heard the preaching but did not hear the Mass, and he heard the preaching in Annecy and Seyssel, and he does not remember more that was said than that gentlemen should hold their swords in their fists to maintain the church. And he went to warm himself when there was preaching, and he told no one that he said that he had returned when he lingered there in Cranves.[207] And touching the sermons, he answers that he has so many lawsuits that he cannot go to the sermons, and the suits he has and sustains cost him more than a thousand écus, and he makes his children go when he cannot go.[208]

Jehan Curtet, baker, son of Claude Curtet, butcher, servant of Paule Tarex for two years.

Answers that he was at the sermon at St. Gervase before dinner and after dinner, and does not know who preached. It was Champereaulx. A lie, it was not Champereaul. Understands his master is content with him, and the said Jehan with his master. And concerning [f. 185v] fornication, gluttony

206. The feast of St. John the Evangelist, December 27.
207. On March 7, 1549, Claude Clement, called Humbert, was "asked whether he has been at the Mass in the last ten years, either in Cranves, Annemasse, Bourg or Vétraz. Answers no, and he was once in Cranves at the hour of vespers because someone said a religious from Cluse would preach, and when he saw he would not preach he returned. And what he deposes he wants to maintain with his life, although the Sieur De Monthouz urged him to do it, and he told him that he would not dare do it without the license of his lords and superiors" (P.C. 2ᵉ sér., 792).
208. We know little about the lawsuits of Claude Clement, but Nycod Floutet at least had a suit against him before the court of the *bailli* of Gex in 1543 [see R.C. Part. 1, f. 66v (June 15, 1543); see also *ibid.*, f. 41v (April 17, 1543)].

and other things, says that those who have spoken such words wish him harm, and his master does not let him run loose. And he does not take girls or women anywhere, and if not [he throws himself] on the mercy. And this Sunday a week ago, it was nothing but his master's service. And he would like to tell the truth if he knew it. And the Seigneurie is badly informed.

And touching counterfeit keys, answers that it is not so, and he does not leave the house at night. And he did not know Jehan Papillier's maid, and he was with Jehan Blanc once at the said baker's house. And said the prayer. He was admonished to frequent the sermons. Pierre[209] was commanded to inquire into the affair because of the fornication committed on Sunday.

Jehan Carrel,[210] cobbler.

Answers that he was at the sermon Sunday twice, once at St. Peter's and again at St. Gervase. And on the marriage, Jehan Faucoz's widow promised him 100 florins, and it was at St. Gervase, and he asked for the money and they did not have it, and he wanted a guarantee. And then they did not want to do it, because they would not give him any money. And he was always ready to do what he should, but only if he was given his money. And he wanted the woman and the child, and he wanted to accept her for a house that he should be given for the marriage, and he indeed wanted the child of her other husband, of Jehan Faucoz. And they had no words. And if they wanted to hold to their promise he would do what he should do. And they remained still at Vernaz's house and after Easter, and he wants to go find his other wife's son in order to have the power of accepting the said marriage. He was given admonitions and remonstrances.

f. 186] *Reymond de La Ravoyre, son of the Red.*

Answers that he was at the nine o'clock sermon, and working days no, because he has to work. And he has a wife and a mother, and his mother lives alone and does nothing but fight with his wife, and he wants to go to stay in Saint Gervays to live and go there so his said mother will not fight any more either with him or with his said mother.[211] And he was in prison once and

209. Probably Pierre de Veyrier, member of the Consistory, present at this session, while Pierre Verna was absent.

210. A Jehan Carrel, from Suze, was received into the bourgeoisie in 1514, but he was a locksmith and not a cobbler like this one. However, he lived in the parish of the Magdalen like Jehan Carrel, cobbler (Rue du Boule in 1543). Jehan Carrel (Quarre), cobbler, died on the Rue du Boule on January 13, 1550 [*L.B.,* p. 179 (October 20, 1514); R.C. 37, f. 84 (May 4, 1543); E.C., Morts 1, p. 2].

211. Presumably he meant to say "wife."

his mother did not give him money and did not help him. And his mother threw him out of the prison, and he wanted to give her everything he had so he could go away to work for his living. And his mother injured herself in the main door of his brother's shop. She became enraged and said that I [sic] had broken her finger.[212] He was admonished.

Tuesday, April 8, 1544

Lord Syndic Philippin.
Calvin, Genesto, Albert, Trippereaulx.
Du Pain, Checand, Vellut, Donzel, Blandin, Justz, Vernaz, Pensabin, the officer Vovrey.

Colletaz, wife of George Mailliet.

She says she will improve from now on. She was admonished.[213]

Monsieur Jehan Guynet, merchant, and his wife.

Because they are always angry at each other. The said Jehan answers. Answers that he does not know that he quarrels with his wife, although sometimes it may be. He confesses that he has an illegitimate child about four or five years old that he was given.[214] The wife says she has been angry about this child and that one may order what one wants; she will do it for the honor of God and will always obey her husband here present and will treat the child as well as she can. They both intend to live in peace together.

[f. 186v] *Pierre*[215] *Jaquenoz, farm laborer.*

Has two children, and one girl five years old; because of the sermons. Answers that he goes to the sermons on Sundays, and not the other days. And he has a quarrel with Bytri,[216] who prevented him from buying some

212. The French is ambiguous. This is the most probable guess at the meaning.
213. The scribe George Maillet shows himself reticent in giving the details of his wife's crimes. One may suppose, however, that she appeared because of some question connected with religion: in 1546 Collette Maillet confessed that three years before she had said that "when the priests were in this city the plague did not last as long as now, and when God was on Earth everything went well" [R.Consist. 2, f. 53v (April 22, 1546)].
214. Jean Guynet, called Taccon, was convicted of adultery and condemned to prison in January 1540 [R.C. 34, folios 1, 24v, 33, 39 (January 5, 13, 16, and 20, 1540)].
215. Struck: "Corbet."
216. Bytry Jasse.

things from Jacobe, and thus he was angry, but at this time they are good friends. Said the prayer and the confession. He prays to the Virgin Mary, Our Lord, and this week and the others are all similar, and he would indeed like to eat meat on Fridays if he had any.

Corbet Gonyn Chivallier,[217] farm laborer, and his wife and Collete, their daughter.

Because of the sermons and blasphemy. Answers no, and that he goes to the sermons on Sunday morning. The said Gonyn's wife and the said Collete do not get angry with each other or with the neighbors, and they go to the sermons twice,[218] and not the other days. Collete said the prayer and the confession, and she does the will of God as well as she can and is not angry with her mother, because she does not live in the house, and she has not cursed her mother either with cankers or other things, and she never thought of cursing her father or mother. They were all given remonstrances and admonitions to live in peace.[219]

Claudaz,[220] wife of Amyez Poentet, farm laborer in Saint Gervais, called Conodaz.[221]

Answers that her husband has been in Meyrin for about a month and that she was with him on Tuesday. She has a child, and because the workers do hardly anything here she lives at Claude Serex' house[222] and goes to the sermons when she can. She cannot go to the works because of her child. She does not know what man was at her house about two weeks ago and she did not see him in the street or elsewhere, and she would say it willingly if she knew him. She knew Anthoyne Darbey because she was his servant. She gives him "good day" and "good vespers," and she does not make the said Darbey's wife misbehave, and he does not frequent her house, nor has she seen or perceived him there.

217. Called Gonet Chevallier above, March 27 and April 3, 1544.

218. That is, twice on Sundays.

219. On April 21, 1544, Gonet Chevallier was reproached with not wanting to work and was ordered to leave the city (R.C. 38, f. 170).

220. Claudaz Rosset.

221. The name "Conodaz," added in the margin, is apparently here in error. Jaquemaz Pontheu, called Conodaz, was accused below of having lodged two prostitutes (see especially April 10, 1544, for the identification).

222. Claude Serex, citizen, tithe collector in 1541 [P.C. 1ᵉ sér., 435 (November 15-22, 1546); R.C. 35, f. 250 (June 30, 1541)]. Like many others he was apparently disgraced at the fall of Jean Philippe and had to ask permission to go outside the city for his business. It was not until May 1543 that he again obtained the right to carry his baton in the company of arquebusiers on the day of the Papegay [see R.C. Part. 1, f. 40 and f. 54 (April 13 and May 15, 1543)].

Anthoyne Darbey.

Because of fornication, not at the sermons, and a quarrel with his wife. Answers that the Consistory is badly informed, and he cannot go to the sermons, and he does not mistreat his wife, and he denies what he is charged with. And he has enough from one wife without [f. 187] having two, and he wants to endure [the penalty]. And he has no quarrel with his wife; sometimes a long time ago. And he knew well the one who left here, and she was his servant, and he was not seen to leave, because false witnesses are not [respectable?] people. And he never entered the said Claudaz's house after the Thonon fair,[223] although he was indeed at Claude Serex' for a bowl. And he has never drunk or eaten with her since she was his servant. He was given admonitions and remonstrances always to live in peace with his wife.

The said Claudaz Poentetaz said it has been about a month or five weeks and he should come today, and she has had no quarrel with her husband. She was given admonitions and remonstrances to frequent the sermons.

Estienne Furjod.

Their lordships of the Consistory advise that the Council be advised to see that he has his wife, in order that there be no divorce in this [case].

And for Pierre Amyaux.

Friday.

Jana, wife of Jehan Du Nant, called Lentilliez.

Answers that she was at the sermon. And as for the money, he is content, and he has never spoken to her, and they have never quarreled since. Said the prayer. She bears no grudge against anyone. She was admonished, and she has abandoned the other Credo for that of the present.

Claude, son of Pierre Pirasset,[224] tavern-keeper, nephew of Charveta in Saint Gervais.

Because of the sermons. Answers that he cannot go there when his mistress goes, nor she when he goes, because they sell many times a day. Said the prayer and the confession. He was given admonitions and remonstrances.

223. The two fairs of Thonon took place on the Thursdays after St. Martin's Day and after Ascension. See the note above, January 10, 1544.
224. Claude Pirasset, native of Geneva, son of the late Pierre Pirasset, was admitted to the bourgeoisie in 1547 and was host of the Eagle in Saint Gervais at the time of his death in 1565 at age 40 [*L.B.*, p. 233 (August 4, 1547); E.C., Morts 6, p. 30 (April 10, 1565)].

Noble Denys Hugoz, citizen of Geneva.

Because of the sermons, blasphemies in execration and other things giving a bad example to people. Answers that he goes to the sermons sometimes, and sometimes he swears and blasphemes in anger. About the quarrel he does not know what to do, since if someone wants to insult him he cannot suffer it, and he would like to hear those who have made the report, and he will answer. And he does not ask etc. [f. 187v] About mistreating his wife and the management of his household, he was admonished to make an agreement with the one with whom he is involved whom he struck. And says he has not wasted the goods of the children of this city. And at this remanded to next Thursday.

The quarrel of Pierre Mercier and Humbert Exerton.

Because the said Mercier did not appear, as was ordered last Thursday. They are remanded to Thursday after the sermon. Thursday after the sermon at the Magdalen.

Thursday, April 10, 1544

Lord Syndic Philippin.
Calvin, Champereaulx, Genesto, De Ecclesia, Albert, Tripereaulx.
Checand, Pensabin, Just, Vellu, Vernaz, Blandin, Donzel, Du Pain, the officer Vovrey.

Noble Anthoyne Lectz, because of a quarrel with Noble Denys Hugoz.

Answers that it is true that he had a quarrel with him, and the said Hugoz had a baton and his sword. He pardons him the wrong for God's sake. And if he had had his baton he might have injured his affairs and those of the said Hugoz. And he is content to do as a respectable man should do, since the other wronged him, and it is not his trade to hang around taverns.

The said Denys Huguez answers that he was abroad and could not go to the sermon. And why he struck the said Lectz at his house. And if one were well informed, possibly he did not do so well, and he had spoken some words against the said Hugoz. And he would not know how to endure the words the said Lectz said to him then, and he wanted to maintain his honor. He was exhorted to be reconciled with the said Lect to receive Holy Communion. And says he could well receive Communion without being reconciled, since he wishes no harm to any person whatever. He is ready to do what will please the Seigneurie, and wishes him no harm, except that he wanted to insult him, and he is ready to do his pleasure and service.

[f. 188] The two together, Lectz and Denys. They both wish to be friends with each other and do any service for each other, and everything should be forgotten, and they will be more sensible in the future than they have been in the past, and they shook hands in friendship. The said Anthoyne Lectz because of blasphemy: he was given remonstrances and proper admonitions to frequent the sermons.

Gonyn de Monthouz, carter.

Answers that he was in Bernex and Challex for a sword that had been lost in the said Bernex that belonged to a captain of mercenaries. And he was promised two *testons* for going to find Glaude Vernaz in Challex, which Vernaz he brought to this city. And the said Vernaz answered [the] captains that he knew nothing about this matter, only about curing horses of certain illnesses. And they gave the letter to the said Vernaz, and the said Vernaz cooked some herbs he brought, which was written in the said Bernex. And Pierre Blanch showed the said Vernaz to the said captain and wanted to have an écu. And he came to the inn of the Angel[225] and immediately left, and the said captain gave him another *teston*. And he had never seen the said Verna until that time, since he did not know that someone wanted him, and he wanted nothing else, except that he gave him the letter, saying two captains who came from the war had sent it to him. And this was Tuesday, and he returned to Bernex to get the wine he had bought, and he went to Challex to earn money. The advice of the Consistory is that he be given strong remonstrances not to meddle again in such things, and be admonished and asked about Conodaz of Saint Gervais.[226]

Asked mercy of God and the Seigneurie for his offenses. Answers that he knew Conodaz well, and he no longer lives in Saint Gervays. He answers that he did go to see some girls at the said Conoda's house. She has had a bad reputation all her life in her house, and he has often been seen there, and he perceived that people went there and that she gave drink and food to those passing by and that she would be reprimanded for it by the Seigneurie. And he saw two girls leave there one Sunday morning, and therefore he removed himself from there and left. [f. 188v] And he saw Pauloz's servant leave there

225. The inn of the Angel, kept by Claude de Lavonex in 1540 (ROGET I, pp. 233 and 234, n. 1).
226. Jaquemaz Pontheu, called Conodaz.

who is named Jehan Curtet.[227] He was given admonitions and remonstrances.

It was proposed that one of the ministers go to Jehan Chappon and his wife to admonish them.

Jaquemaz, daughter of Claude Pontheu, wife of Bernard Joly, farm laborer, tavern-keeper, selling wine by the glass.

And they lodge only a few people they know. And there were two girls from the Vaud country one day, one Sunday. And they left and returned on Sunday and were there only briefly and did not sleep. And no one was with them except Paule's servant[228] and one other, the son of Pierre Curt, cobbler,[229] and he did not . . .[230] And she told them to go, and the girls wanted to drink before going, and this was about nine o'clock in the morning. And when they had made a fricassee they left. And they spoke together at the table and held no other conversation. They dined and then left. And she does not know whether they were wicked or not, and she believes they were from Fribourg. She has never been informed that she should not do thus, except Gonyn Floutet told her once that she would be reprimanded for it, and she only wanted to behave well. And they went to bed at Coppet's and returned to drink at the house of the said Jaquemaz. She has never sheltered a haberdasher.[231] Also asked if . . .[232] That Jehan Curtet be summoned, who was here last Thursday and denied everything, and the son of Pierre Curt, cobbler.

Jehan Teysiez,[233] miller of this city.

Is married and his wife is there and he has been ill of fever, and they made him drink water and a spider and herbs. And he does not know who taught his wife about what was put on his neck, and he is cured, thanks be to

227. Jehan Curtet, servant of Pauloz Tarex.
228. Again Jehan Curtet, servant of Pauloz Tarex.
229. Claude Curt, son of Pierre Curt called Choupin.
230. Incomplete sentence.
231. The Small Council condemned Jaquemaz Pontheu, called Conodaz, from Saint Gervais, to prison for procuring [R.C. 38, f. 168v (April 21, 1544)].
232. Incomplete sentence.
233. Jehan Teysiez, miller, was imprisoned with other millers for not having respected the established prices and for having ground wheat "outside the prohibitions" [R.C. 38, folios 299v, 320, 327v (July 25, August 11 and 15, 1544)]. A Jean Theysier, citizen, lived on the Rhône Bridge, but he was an apothecary [see P.C. 2ᵉ sér., 800 (July 12-23, 1549), regarding a fight between Theysier and Antoine Darbey].

God. Donne Jane, wife of Claude Savoex, did give him one, and he was told that Claude Vernaz, if he were in this city, would have cured him quickly. And the son of Monsieur Girardin de La Ryvaz[234] gave him drink, a drink that was red. And when he put the . . .[235] on his neck he told him nothing, and it was a spider that was between two walnut shells,[236] and he kept them . . .[237] [f. 189] days. And as for the sermons, one should be well informed; he goes there when he can.

Jana, wife of the said Jehan Teysiez. Answers that her husband was cured of fever, and thanks be to God. She took a spider that she enclosed between two walnut shells and attached it to his neck and gave him no drinks except what she was given by Donne Savoex, and she does not know how many days he carried it. And the spider was taken on Tuesday or Wednesday, and it is necessary to make sure it is alive, since while it lives it draws the venom. She herself carried one nine days, by which she does not know whether she was cured or not. Her mother taught it to her. Lord Loys saw the animal and does not know whether it was alive or not. Also touching the sermons she answers that she goes often. Said the prayer and the confession. She was given admonitions and remonstrances.

Noble Pierre de Joex.

Because of the resentment between him and Goddet's widow. Answers that they have had a lawsuit between them for a long time, and he wants to live in peace, since they have been in the suit for nine or ten years, and they should have already settled it. He is ready to behave as a respectable man, and Monsieur Girardin[238] should have already brought them to an agreement. And he would like to be in agreement. He pardons her with a good heart, except that he does not want to lose his own, having made a settlement of the suit. Wants to live as good friends with her, and it is not his fault. He was ordered to have Monsieur Girardin and Sillimandi[239] summoned, and it will be

234. Girardin de La Rive, himself an apothecary, had at least two sons who were apothecaries: Thomas (member of the CC in 1532, elected guard of the mint in 1546) and Jean (member of the CC in 1563) (CHOISY, *G.G.*, pp. 41-42; DEMOLE, p. 17).

235. Word omitted.

236. A spider enclosed in a walnut shell and carried as an amulet, a traditional remedy for fever (see OPIE and TATEM, p. 369; see also HOFFMANN-KRAYER VIII, col. 279-281).

237. The scribe fails to state how many days.

238. Girardin de La Rive. It should be noted that this case must have begun before Girardin de La Rive, lieutenant, between November 18, 1533, and November 15, 1534 (*R.C.* XII, pp. 382, 384-385, and *R.C.* XIII, p. 96).

239. A Claude Sillimandi was admitted to the bourgeoisie on September 20, 1530

done promptly, and he is ready to do and support what they, their two arbiters, will do.

Goddet's widow because of the said Pierre de Joex. Answers that she has a barn in the village that she lent him and he appropriated it to himself, and she has had to sell some property to carry on the said suit. And it is forbidden, and she made him come here before the Consistory, and he is close to destroying her. She does not know how it happens that it lasts so long, and she has no money to carry on the said suit. [f. 189v] And the said De Joex has beaten her in the said barn when she told him it belonged to her and he was doing wrong to receive Communion in such discord. And the said De Joex had the house built for 200 florins and 10 écus. Said the prayer and the confession. They were exhorted to make an agreement in order to receive Holy Communion more worthily, and also to find arbiters to settle it for them. She wants to pardon all ill will. Both together to live in peace, to put down all hatreds and grudges; she and he pardon each other, leaving the business in hope of settlement, also with his sister.[240]

Jehan Curtet

Answers that he ate at Conodaz's[241] house with two girls, and Pierre Curt's son[242] was there, and the girls are from Lausanne. And they were at Conodaz's, and after breakfast they went to the sermon; this was on Sunday. And they went to find them in a barn, and it was before the preaching, and they ate a fricassee, and it was before the sermon, about 9 o'clock. And he was not there on Saturday. And after dinner they went to find the said girls at the house of the said Conodaz. He does not know that Cognode knew what it was about, and she did not send for them, and they did not think the said girls were there. And they had seen them pass by there, and they came from the city, and they did not see them except on Saturday and Sunday. One slept at Conodaz's and the other left. And on Sunday the other returned in the

---

(*L.B.*, p. 207). Savion says that in September 1535 "those in Geneva who were the richest and had large holdings in the country of Savoy were plundered, like . . . Silmandy," to whom Geisendorf gives the first name Claude, taken from the R.C. (GEISENDORF, *Annalistes*, p. 447 and index).

240. The Council had already investigated this quarrel between Goddet's widow and Pierre de Joex many times without ever resolving their dispute, having sent it at first to arbitration and finally before the lieutenant. See in this connection R.C. 35, f. 144v (April 5, 1541); R.C. 36, folios 7v, 11, 23, and 29 (May 9, 12, 26 and June 2, 1542); *ibid.*, f. 214v and f. 225 (January 16 and 30, 1543).

241. Jaquemaz Pontheu, called Conodaz.

242. Claude, son of Pierre Curt.

morning, and no one had slept with her at the said Conodaz's. Pierre Curt's son was there, and no other, and they stayed there in the barn after dinner until the evening, and he told someone else that he was married and should leave: Jaques Pratiqua[243] is his name. And they slept in the barn, and on Monday morning they returned, and it was in Pauloz's barn.[244] And they brought supper to the said girls in the said barn. And the said Pratiqua wanted to stay, and the said Jehan [told] him: "Go away, you are married."[245] And he knows nothing else. And they kept them from two o'clock until the morning, when the girls returned, and he does not know where [f. 190] they went afterwards, and he has never seen them since. And this was on Sunday at six o'clock in the morning. The said Curt knew well that they were at the said Conodaz's.

Claude Curt, son of Pierre Curt, cobbler. Has always lived in this city. And he knew the said Jehan, Pauloz's servant, well, and on Sunday two weeks ago he was at Conodaz's with two girls, and they did not know whether they were there, and they found them and breakfasted and paid for them on Sunday at six o'clock at Conodaz's. And her husband[246] was there, and he does not know whether the girls slept there or not, and he does not know what agreement they made with them. And they wanted to drink with the girls and the girls with them. And they made no other stop, and he was not there at two o'clock in the afternoon and he did not speak to them until after dinner. And he was never in this barn to do anything wrong and he never slept there and he wants to have his head cut off. And Pratiqua did not ask for a share, and he supped in his father's house, and he did not carry or pay for supper in the barn with the girls. And he did not know that they were at the said Conode's. And he breakfasted with Jehan Curtet at Conodaz's and there were two girls there and they paid the bill for them. And he never took them to the barn and did not enter it, and he may be made to say it in front of . . .[247] Confesses.[248] And they returned after dinner and were in the barn, and he never slept at Conoda's, and he does not know whether either of these girls slept at the said Conodaz's. And he found them there on Sunday; the one came from the city and went to find the other girl at the said Conodaz's. And Jehan Curtet told him: "I think that this girl slept here last night." And

243. Jaques Pinget or Pinguet, called Pratiquaz, baker.
244. Paulo Tarex, master of Jehan Curtet.
245. Assuming she is the same, Jaques Pinguet, called Pratiquaz, was married to a certain Pernette, who died on March 2, 1553 (E.C., Morts 1, p. 95).
246. Bernard Joly, husband of Jaquemaz Pontheu, called Conodaz.
247. Incomplete sentence.
248. "Confesses" is added in the margin.

they were in the said barn, the said Jehan and he, and Pratiquaz told them that the watch were watching to take them, and they were entirely alone in the said barn with the said Jehan. And a man told them, "Watch out for yourselves; the watch are on the lookout." And Jehan Curtet said he was married, that he would return, that he was married and that they would be taken if the watch saw them enter there. And the said Conodaz knew well what merchandise it was, and he only had breakfast with the girls. And he had the older girl, and he only knows that Conodaz was the procuress. [f. 190v] The one had slept at Pierre Guyron's and the other at the said Conodaz's.

The said Conodaz was examined to tell the truth, and that neither of the girls slept there. Indeed she found her on a bed that had neither mattress nor cushion, and her company found her about six o'clock, since they wanted to sleep at her house, and the other went away to sleep in the city, and they were there and breakfasted together and ate a fricassee between eight and nine o'clock, and left after dinner. And the said boys returned to lunch, then went elsewhere. She saw only the one who slept, and the other found her in the morning, and she has only two beds at her house and a bench for the workmen who come. And she saw one on the straw, and she does not know whether she slept there or not. And she did not sleep there to do anything wrong. She did not hear any agreement they made and does not know where they went. She does not know where they were from. And on Monday the girls left and on Sunday they went away to sleep elsewhere, and she gave them nothing for supper. They had no money to pay her what they owed her. They left her a . . .[249] of theirs for a pot of wine. Said the prayer badly, and the confession she does not know how to say. She was at the sermon Wednesday and knows well who preached.

The advice of the Consistory is that since the thing is verified and she is remanded to the Council tomorrow, that the affair proceed and all three be confronted. As for the boys, the case merits punishment. That they be punished and admonished more sharply here and remanded to the Council before Communion. That he be confronted with Paule's servant.

All three together. Jehan Curtet says they were in the barn and he did not stay long and he left the said Claude Curt in the said barn, and he had said in the stable to the said Pratiquaz that he should withdraw, and one of the girls said she had slept at Conodaz's. The said Conodaz answers that she knows nothing about it, and the said Curtet received the two girls' money, and he came to find them after dinner and took them to the barn, and the said Conoda heard everything, and she did not know that they would return.

249. Word omitted.

[f. 191] Conodaz answers that they should have returned. The two boys were asked what they gave and paid, for the two, eight sous each. They were given admonitions and remonstrances to be . . .[250] They asked mercy of God and of justice. Indeed they said that the younger slept at the said Conodaz's house. The said Conodaz denies that she knew they would return to her house. The older did not tell her where she had slept the evening before, which was Saturday. All three are remanded to the Council.[251]

Pierre Berthet, called Thallabard.

Because of certain words with Syndic Morel. Answers that about a week ago he told Lord Mychiel Morel that he had a man lodging in his house. And then the said Mychiel Morel told him he did not want to lodge a fornicator or pimp. And then the said Berthet was very angry, and it was in front of Naviode's house, and Jehan Martin was present and was very angry. And he said he would pardon him, waiting for him to give up the rod of justice, and afterwards he would have it in for him. And he was admonished by Monsieur Pensabin, and he says he pardons him with a good heart and wants to be punished and was not angry. Also he has no other grudge except that he called him a pimp, and for this he wants to be punished if he did not say it. And if it were anyone else it would not be passed over in this way. And he pardons him and everyone else also, and he wants to do him service. He was admonished, and he wants to be ready to obey, and that he be given strong remonstrances.

The mother of De Ripha.[252]

Because of knowing how to pray to the Lord. She says the prayer as last time, not very well, and the confession only as formerly, and no longer prays to the Virgin Mary, and wants to behave like a respectable woman. Goes to the catechism and the other sermons. She has not said "Accursed be so many preachers," and it will not happen to her again, if it pleases God.

[f. 191v] *Pierre Mercier and Humbert Exerton.*

They were reported to be in agreement, and let them be there tomorrow after the sermon. Neither the one nor the other was there on Friday or Saturday. After the sermon tomorrow, Friday.

---

250. Incomplete sentence.

251. Their fornication earned Jehan Curtet and Claude Curt three days in prison on bread and water [R.C. 38, f. 168v (April 21, 1544)].

252. Ayma, widow of Jehan de Ripha. Although omitted at her first appearance before the Consistory, normally "de" is part of this name.

Claude Tappugnier and Pierre Furjon.

Because of their previous quarrel. They were admonished. Tapponier indeed pardons, and he has been done so much wrong that he will never see him with a good heart and he will never have faith in his friendship, and he has done wrong to endure so much, and he has already often pardoned him. He was given strict admonitions to abandon all hatred and discord. He intends to pardon him if the said Furjon wants to pardon him, reserving the rights of his ward.

Pierre Furjon, who was given remonstrances and admonitions and who is ready to do service to the said Tappugnié, and they pardoned each other.

The appearances in the Consistory from the 14th of February until the 10th of April 1544.

Lord Syndic Philippin	VIII	XVI	ss.
Lord Michiel Morel	I	II	ss.
Checand	VII	XIIII	ss.
Du Pain	IIII	VIII	ss.
Vernaz	VII	XIIII	ss.
Molard	IIII	VIII	ss.
Pensabin	VIII	XVI	ss.
Veyrier	VI	XII	ss.
Blandin	VII	XIIII	ss.
Loermoz	IX	XVIII	ss.
Vellut	VI	XII	ss.
Donzel	IX	XVIII	ss.
Peronet	II	IIII	ss.
The officer Vovrey	IX	XVIII	ss.
The scribe Maillect	IX	III	ff.

Total: 17 florins 6 sous.

[f. 192] *The ordinance for the Holy Communion of Our Lord for next Easter, Sunday, 13th day of the month of April 1544.*

And first for the two Communions in the temple of St. Peter: Lords Pernet de Fosses, Mychiel Varod, Pierre d'Orcieres and . . .[253]

For the Communion at the Magdalen: Jehan Chautemps, Pierre Vernaz, Jehan Pensabin.

253. Incomplete sentence.

For the two Communions at St. Gervase: Claude Du Pain, Loys Dufour, Mermet Blandin, Amed Gervaix.

And throughout a lord syndic.

[f. 192v]   **Thursday, 17th of the month of April 1544**

Lord Syndic Philippin.

Calvin, Albert, Genesto, Trippereaulx, Ferrand, Champereaulx, De Ecclesia. Checand, Vellut, Vernaz, Just, Donzel, Blandin, the officer Vovrey.

Case of marriage. Pierre, son of Gonyn de La Combaz,[254] *from Jussy.*

Says that Monsieur Henri, preacher of Jussy, has remanded him to the Consistory, and he wants to marry a girl, Françoyse, daughter of Jehan Favre. And Johente, wife of the said Jehan Favre, mother of the said Françoyse. The said Françoyse absent. The said Johente said that she gave the said Françoyse to the said Pierre, and that there is a relation between the women, and they are relations-german; their grandmothers were sisters and their daughters cousins.[255] The said Pierre was asked whether he has anything to say. Answers no, and that there have been no murmurs about the two of them, that no one has said a word. And he never had a wish of committing fornication. The advice of the Consistory is that, concerning the relationship, they may be delivered from this difficulty and that the said marriage not be broken for this. They go to the sermons. He goes to the sermons sometimes. Said the prayer. The mother also said the prayer.

Jehan Chappon and his wife Pernete.

Because of discord with the maid of Monsieur Jehan Donzel[256] and Communion. Answers that he did not celebrate Communion except in bed, because he was ill, as the Consistory has been informed. Answers that he does not carry a grudge except because she should return him what his wife [f. 193] gave to the maid of the said Monsieur Jehan Donzel and that a judg-

254. A Gonin de La Combaz, citizen, had a son named Pierre, member of the CC in 1573, who made his will in 1625; but considering the dates this is probably a coincidence of names (GALIFFE, III, pp. 169-171; SORDET, *Dictionnaire*, p. 400).

255. Translator: I assume the phrase used *(reunies de germain)* is intended to mean cousins-german *(cousins-germain),* but this is not the usual modern definition of cousins-german in either French or English, which use the term similarly. I am told the correct French term is *"cousins issus de germains."*

256. Pernete de Jonvier.

ment should be made promptly between them and he should be restored what they are in conflict about. And his wife who is here will tell how she gave her the *peyrnez*[257] that he asks for that he lent to the said Donzel by the hands of his maid. And the said Noble Jehan Donzel answers that is not so except as they will make appear. And they will do it.

Pernete, his wife, answers that she does not know about the diviner, and it is not so, and she never spoke to any diviner, although the said Donzel's maid told her that it would be good to have him and where he was. Numerous insulting words were spoken by the said Jehan Chappon against the Donzels and their maid, always hoping that the *peyrnez* would be found. However, he did not want to permit anyone else to do it for them; he would have forbidden it with all his power, and he does not wish them any harm. They were given advice, with admonitions and remonstrances from Monsieur Calvin.

Claude de La Ravoyre,[258] called Dondin.

Because of certain words and mistreatment of his mother,[259] and concerning the sermons. Answers that he is obedient to his mother and holds her in honor and reverence. And his brother[260] had a little anger against his mother, and he does not want to disobey her, and he goes to the sermons on Sundays, since he has to work for himself and his children.

Pierre Mercier and Exerton are in agreement.[261]

---

257. Translator: Word of unknown meaning; see also f. 184 above.

258. Claude de La Ravoyre and his sons Guillaume and Jean were admitted to the bourgeoisie on January 6, 1562, "because he has already lived twenty-five years in the city" (*L.B.*, p. 270).

259. The mother of La Ravoyre, called the Red.

260. Reymond de La Ravoyre.

261. Possibly under pressure to find funds to pay Exerton his share of the rent farm of Peney, on April 24, 1544, Mercier was reprimanded in Council for having "commanded a peasant not to leave Geneva without paying him a debt" (R.C. 38, f. 173v). In a case that was possibly linked to this farm, on May 15, 1544, the Council ordered Mercier, Exerton, and [Anthoine?] Panissod, debtors to the city, "to post a bond to satisfy their obligation or be made prisoners" (R.C. 38, f. 200). Apparently the resolutions of the Consistory and Council did not suffice to put an end to this dispute: in the register of January 22, 1545, there is mention of a "supplication presented by the Exertons against the Merciers, mentioning that the lieutenant does not want to make them pay 60 sous, alleging that they have made a disturbance and violated the proclamations. On which ordered that the lieutenant should obtain information, and that the one found at fault should make satisfaction and show it to them; this will be proceeded with" (R.C. Part. 1, f. 246).

Pierre Truffet.

Because of the sermons and games. Answers that he has to have fun, and he gambles only for drinks. He is married and has his wife and children.[262] And he has not gambled higher than one florin at a time. And he only gambles on Sundays. He was given admonitions and remonstrances.

[f. 193v]
Thursday, April 24, 1544

Lord Syndic Philippin.
Calvin, Champereaulx, Trippereaulx, Albert, Genesto, Ferrand.
Checand, Molard, Pensabin, Blandin, Peronet, Vellut, Donzel, the officer Vovrey.

Claude Durand, miller.

Because of fornication committed with his maid. Answers that something has happened to him that displeases him and has offended God and the Seigneurie; he has fornicated with his chambermaid since Martinmas, and he believes she is pregnant, and he is married. He was tempted by Satan and begs mercy of God and of justice. He freely confessed the sin himself.

Pernete, daughter of Françoys Milliaud of Jussy, servant of Claude Piazguex.[263] Has lived with him for three and a half years. Answers that she has had his company since Martinmas, and begged mercy of God and the Seigneurie. She went at a late hour of the night, and she has been pregnant since the said time of Martinmas when she began. And she has felt the child for about a month. And she has no other but herself, and she has been promised in marriage since Sunday. And he knew nothing about it, and they cannot be separated. She is a poor orphan girl. The advice of the Consistory: that the said Claude be summoned to learn how much they fornicated together and that both be admonished and remanded to the Council.

The said Durand says that it was not earlier than he said that he fornicated with the said Pernete, because she went late at night to the mill. And he confesses having greatly offended. He was given remonstrances and admonitions and remanded to next Monday to the Council, and let him take the said Pernete to the side and find out what will become of her fruit.

262. A Claude, wife of Pierre Truffet, barber, living on the Rhône Bridge, died on July 24, 1555 (E.C., Morts 1, p. 290; L. GAUTIER, *Médecine*, p. 482).
263. Claude Durand, called Piazguex [R.C. 38, f. 177 (April 28, 1544)].

194]   The said Pernete was at the sermon Sunday morning. She cannot go there because there are five children in her master's house, and she believes her mistress is pregnant. Said the prayer, and the confession not very well. Said that her engaged husband[264] was willing to have the child she carries only if he was given 40 florins, and her master wanted to give them, but only if someone wanted to prepare her said husband. And after she was engaged the said husband knew she was pregnant and then repented, and she does not know now what he will do.

She was admonished to govern herself and the fruit she carries well. And was remanded to the Council to Monday after the sermon in the [City] Hall before the Council.[265]

Lyonard Fontanel.

Because of Holy Communion and the sermons. Answers that he rarely goes because of poverty, and he works, and cannot till the soil. He has two sous a day, and promises to go to the sermons every day. Said the prayer and the confession, and that he has made the sign of the cross twice, and does not mean to do wrong and did it with good intentions.

Thursday, first day of May 1544

Lord Syndic Philippin.
Calvin, De Ecclesia, Albert, Trippereaulx, Genesto.
Checand, Molard, Pensabin, Blandin, Vellu, Donzel, Du Pain.

Jehan Bollié, miller, living at Claude Humbert's mill.

Says he has promised himself to a girl who has committed a fault who is named Pernon, servant of the miller Piazguex,[266] whom he does not want because she [is] pregnant, and therefore he has not agreed with her. Asks to be separated, and was solicited to take her, and for how much he would leave the said Piazguex, for which he asked 80 florins, and he did not want to give him so much, only 40 florins. And if he were given that much now he would be content and the child would be his during her confinement, and to give

264. Jehan Bolliet.
265. The Council ordered that Claude Durand be put in prison for nine days on bread and water and pay a fine. The Council remitted the punishment of Pernete Milliaud until after her confinement [R.C. 38, f. 177 (April 28, 1544)]. On May 2, 1544, Durand's wife asked the Council for clemency for her husband (R.C. 38, f. 184v).
266. Pernete Milliaud, maid of Claude Durand, called Piazguex.

the child to its father. And that she return him what he gave to Pernete. And his mother does not want to consent that he [f. 194v] have a share. And he did not know that she was pregnant when he swore faith to her. Said the prayer, and almost nothing of the confession. The advice of the Consistory is that the girl be summoned and the boy's mother and he himself to learn what agreements have been made among them and the master who is in prison, for Thursday. Was remanded to Thursday.

Egrege Jehan Buctin.[267]

For certain words spoken by him in the Bishop's Palace. And what he said was just a manner of speaking, and that the devil has no power except as much as God gives him.

Bernard Prodhom, butcher.

Because of a certain diviner and the sermons and papistries. And on the purse he had lost which he found. And his nephew found it, and he did not remember where he had put [it]. And he had put it in a wall in the barn when he thought he had the pox, and his nephew found it in taking care of the animals, and his nephew gave it to him. And they have business together and are not in conflict and are in good accord. Touching the sermons, he was there twice on Sunday. Answers that he finds himself as well off under this present law as the other, and the one who is in the heavens must be adored. And he says the Pater as at present. And when he has no business he goes to the sermons. And said the prayer and the confession.

Jaques Pinget, called Pratiquaz, whose [son he is(?)] he does not know, baker, on a certain suspicion.

He knows Conodaz[268] and has not been there for half a year, and does not know, that he was in Pauloz's[269] barn several times in right and honor, and he saw no one other than Pierre Curt's boy[270] and Pauloz's servant,[271] and he saw no person other than the one he told them of. And there was no girl there. That he did not search or look for one. Jehan Curtet asked him what he was there for and said that he should go, that he was married. And then he left, and

267. Jehan Buctin was received into the bourgeoisie gratis on June 7, 1538, "because of the wages he might be owed because he exercises the office of judge of Trois Château and has much to do" (*L.B.*, p. 218).
268. Jaquemaz Pontheu, called Conodaz.
269. Pauloz Tarex.
270. Claude Curt.
271. Jehan Curtet, servant of Pauloz Tarex.

understood that there was some reason . . .[272] And he goes to the sermons when he can. And he has not been seen gambling with the others because he is not a gambler. Said the prayer and the confession. [f. 195] The advice of the Consistory: that he deserves admonitions and remonstrances here, and that he watch out another time that he is not remanded to the Council afterwards.

Jana, daughter of Tyvent Vuy, from Satigny.

And she was never married. And Monsieur Jaques Bernard made her come here because she had a child by someone from Chevrier who was a servant with her at Jehan Let's house. And the child is dead, and he promised to take her, and when she was pregnant he left. And she had another child by someone else. She has two children. She has no father or mother or house, so they live where they are sheltered for the love of God. And she has a child in Bourdigny 12 years old, at its father's house, who is married and poor. She does not fornicate any more. Begged mercy of justice, and she fought with a woman who does nothing but fight and has been banished from this city and is named Guilliama Betesie. She was led through this city about six or seven years ago and had had a child which she brought to this city, for which she was banished.

The advice of the Consistory: since her repentance is seen and she confesses, that one have pity on her and that she be given admonitions and remonstrances. And Master Jaques Bernard may reconcile them, and that her faith and religion be inquired into. Answers that the said Guillama indeed comes here and was here recently. She never called her a witch, although her nephew Pierre Rolet [did]. And she told her she had had a devil and not a child, and the child did not live. It was well formed and died suddenly, and nothing was done to it but what God did. And a woman from Satigny named Genon delivered it, and she is married to one named Claude Vuy, her brother, who shelters her. And she works as much as she can, and will not turn to her sin again. Said the prayer and the confession.

Thursday, May 8, 1544

Lord Syndic Philippin.
Calvin, Trippereaulx, Ferrand, Genesto.
Checand, Pensabin, Justz, Blandin, Donzel, Vernaz, Peronet, the officer Vovrey.

---

272. Incomplete sentence.

Jehan Bolliet; Pernete, wife of Jehan Bolliet;[273] *the mother of the said Jehan Bolliet, miller.*

Because the said son promised himself to a woman. Answers that this is not a possible thing because he was never told anything about her having misbehaved. And afterwards they did not tell him, and he asked 80 florins, and the said Durant[274] wanted to give him 40. And indeed before the said day he swore faith, and they wanted to give him, as they said, 80 florins, and afterwards he was told she was pregnant and wanted to make an agreement with him. And at supper at Pierre Damour's house they spoke of the 40 florins, and afterwards found out that he did not want her thus and only stayed for the money. The mother answers that he may do what he wishes and that they tried to marry her to someone else. The said Jehan answers that he does not want her and that he has reconsidered since, and if they had been content to give him money he was content, and now he would rather abandon everything than take her, and he was content then for 40 florins to have the woman and the child.

On these responses the Consistory advises that, since he was agreeable in the first place and afterwards consented, that he not be compelled. And as for the 40 florins, if the marriage could be confirmed to avoid scandal, if he has not obtained a guarantee of the 40 florins, unless he wants to come of his own good will.

Pernete, daughter of François Milliaud of Jussy, his promised wife, Durand's servant. Answers that she does not know how much she promised him, and it was at her master's at supper, and her master, and her brother and sister were present. She had spoken to her said master and no one had spoken to him. She told her master that this Bolliet would be good for her in order to hide her shame. And at [f. 196] this supper she swore faith to him and her brother gave him 80 florins. And if it pleases God and the Seigneurie she would like him well, and he would mistreat her afterwards and spend the money he would be given.

The advice of the Consistory is that the said Jehan be recalled. If he intends to take her let him say so, and let her master and her and the husband, Bolliet, be summoned. The said Bolliet answers that it is not possible for her to be his and his heart is not in her, and even if he were given twice as much he would not want her. And if he were forced he would leave the place and would leave her to herself. And therefore it is ordered that he does not want it and that all four be summoned. Claude Durant, Bolliet and the said Pernete.

273. Pernete Milliaud, promised wife of Jehan Bolliet.
274. Claude Durand, called Piazguex, master and lover of Pernete Milliaud.

Their lordships of the Consistory advise that they be remanded to Monday to the Council. The said Claude Durant answers that he informed the said Jehan Bolliet, and he wanted to give her at supper and the said Bolliet did not want her, and she was pregnant when he spoke to him, and the said Pernete urged him to swear faith to her. All three are remanded to Monday.[275]

Pernon, wife of Anthoyne Valloz, farm laborer, daughter of . . .[276]

Answers that her husband is not in this city because he was ill and then went to Lyon to see his sister. And he went with Jehan de Vovrey, and there is nothing she has done involving bad behavior, and that nothing remained to them in the sickness they had. And she received Communion this . . .[277] St. Peter's with Monsieur Velluti's maid at the first sermon. She will send to him on St. John's Day and he may come, or she will send to him or go, and she will be helped by respectable women. And she cannot say how long she was in Plan Les Ouates, except when there was a cold spell three years ago. She knew Clement de La Tire and served him there two years and did not leave there except for two months when she went to la Sémine, and she cannot say how long. And since Easter she has not spoken with him and he has not been in her room, and one should find out about it, and she wants to be punished as a wicked woman. [f. 196v] And no one goes to her room except her brother, and no other. She wants to be shown mercy. Her brother lives in Saint Gervais and is a baker. She goes to the sermons when she can, and she is a poor woman and works for her living when she can. And said the prayer in Latin, and she would like to know it, and has received Communion. She believes in God who made and shaped her. Said the whole prayer in Latin. She says she does not know how to say the Ave Maria, and just as her father and mother taught her. She has good intentions in praying to God after the preacher and receives Communion as it should be received. And she was at the first sermon on Sunday and did not recognize the one who preached, and said the prayer. The advice of the Consistory: that she be given a term of two weeks to learn to pray to the Lord and that the procurator general[278] inquire into her behavior.

275. On May 12, 1544, Jehan Bolliet asked the Council to annul his promise of marriage with Pernete Milliaud, denying at first having known that she was pregnant by Durand and then confessing he did not want to marry her because Durand could not give him the 40 florins he had promised him. The Council acknowledged the validity of the marriage and named two arbiters to resolve "amiably" the question of the 40 florins (R.C. 38, f. 196v).

276. Incomplete sentence.

277. There is probably an omission. Possibly "this Easter at St. Peter's."

278. Claude Roset was named procurator general in place of Pierre Vandel on April 18, 1544 [R.C. 38, f. 167v; also R.C. Part. 1, f. 38 (April 9, 1543)].

Jehan Papillier, baker.

For the anger between him and his wife. Answers that he goes to the sermons sometimes and sends his servants there. And it displeases him, and he must be believed in his house, and she has her mother nearby and goes about with her and carries whatever she wants of his to her mother. And sometimes he strikes her and she gives him the stick to be put down [with]. And it is not his fault that they have no peace at his house and he does not hit her with a stick except an occasional blow. And he does not chase her outside, but she wants to go there. And when it is night he shuts his door after her, and he will not be subjected to his wife, and he has often pardoned her for the love of the neighbors and of Monsieur Françoys Chamoex. He was admonished. The . . .[279]

Vincent Millet, farm laborer, living in Saint Gervais.

Stated that Jehan Caliat told him to return his cloak he had taken on the day of Easter, which cloak he found on his bench. He said the prayer and the confession.

[f. 197]

Thursday, May 15, 1544

Lord Syndic Philipin.
Calvin, Champereaulx, De Ecclesia, De Genesto, Pupin, Trippereaulx, Ferrand.
Checand, Molard, Pensabin, Blandin, Donzel, Du Pain, Justz, the officer Vovrey.

Jaquemaz, wife of Jehan Papilliez; Pernete, widow of Dominique Dance,[280] mother of the said Jaquemaz.

On the behavior of her husband and his treatment of his household and because of the sermons. Pernete answers that she goes to the sermons on Sundays; the other days she has to work for her living. And she is not sheltering her daughter because she has not entered her house for fully three years because her husband wanted to throw her through the window

279. Incomplete sentence.
280. Dominique Dance, tailor, admitted to the bourgeoisie on January 22, 1518. Pernette, his wife, was among the baker women authorized to sell bread in Saint Gervais in 1545. She died on May 12, 1565, living then on the Rhône Bridge, aged 70 [*L.B.*, p. 187; CHOISY, *G.G.*, p. 13; R.C. 40, f. 184 (July 16, 1545); E.C., Morts 6, p. 40].

into the Rhône. And then when she saw that her daughter wanted to throw herself down she began to cry out against the said Papillier that he did wrong to treat his wife so, and she never insulted him except when he beat her daughter.

The said Jaquemaz answers that she cursed her husband when he beat her and gave him the lie sometimes, and her said mother . . .[281] And he wanted to beat her every day, and she did not give him the rod to be beaten, and . . .[282] And in winter he threw her out of his company pregnant. He threw a bucket of water on the fire so she would not get warm and so she might die. And he beats her more often when she is pregnant than other times, and he often goes to the sermon, and he wants his wife to stay home. She does want to go, but he wants to go there. They were given remonstrances and admonitions.

Jehan Caliat, cobbler, habitant *from Saint Gervais.*

Because of a cloak he lost last Easter and because of Communion. Answers that he received Communion at St. Gervase, and he wore Jehan Roman's robe when he was at Communion because he had lost his own robe. And on Sunday morning he asked a woman whether she knew where his cloak was, and this woman insulted him and spoke villainously to him. [f. 197v] And a butcher, Monet,[283] at Ballesser's[284] returned it to him the next Tuesday and did not want to tell him who had given it to him, and he asked for wine, and said the woman must have had it. And he thought the said woman had hidden it and her husband, since he had business with the workers and did not remember his cloak and therefore left it and did not . . .[285] Answers regarding the sermons that he goes to the sermons when he can, and he does not gamble, because he only gambled once, with the officers and Monsieur . . .[286] The argument in his household was about a chambermaid he had whom he sent, and he profited, since he gained fully six score florins he would have lost if he had not gone to court. And he gives drink to those who serve him well. He has good accord now in his household. He was given remonstrances and strict admonitions.

281. Incomplete sentence.
282. Incomplete sentence.
283. Claude Monet.
284. Possibly Claude Ballessert (Balexert, Ballexert, etc.), or rather one of the Claude Ballesserts. At least one of them was a butcher in Saint Gervais. See GALIFFE II, pp. 50 and 53; GEISENDORF, *Annalistes,* p. 445.
285. Incomplete sentence.
286. Name or title omitted.

Thursday, May 22

The Consistory was not held because of a certain obstacle.

Tuesday, May 27, 1544

Lord Syndic Philippin.
Calvin, Genesto, Albert, Trippereaulx, Ferrand.
Molard, Vellut, Blandin, Pensabin, Peronet, the officer Vovrey.

The Honorable Jaques Symond, merchant.

On the papistry. Answers that it is not so and he wants to maintain the contrary and that he has not spoken against religion and the words were invented and he has never spoken against the [new] law and has said nothing about it. And he wants to live according to the rules of the city, and Geneva has not changed its God, and he has never adored images, and he has done honor to images. Asked whether he would do honor to an image for the honor of God. Answers no, and what was done in the past was with good intentions, and he changes his opinion 24 times a day. Adoration is for God, and he does not presently adore any image and does not want to [f. 198] adore them and does not do them honor. And if he prays to the saints, do not . . .[287] And he adores only God, and he takes Communion like a respectable man.

Monsieur Calvin says he will not give him Communion if he does not respond better about his religion. The opinion of the Consistory: in view of his evil speech that he be admonished for the words he spoke and recognize his fault and answer, and that he be given the catechism and admonished not to be thus and asked where he received Communion at Easter and be instructed in his faith. He was admonished not to come to the next Communion if he is not better versed in religion, and he alleges passages of Holy Scripture. Remanded to another time to be confronted with the one who said that he, to whom he had spoken, that he had not done well to come to this religion, leaving the Mass, which is so good and beautiful.

Pernon Contesse; Jane Du Puys, Brand's widow.

Contesse's accuser says that the said Pernete said that the said accuser had stolen a piece of meat, and asks for justice and her honor, and it belonged to Loys Gardet. Contesse says that it is not so, that the woman sold

287. Incomplete sentence.

the meat, a piece she had hidden under[288] her apron. And the said Jana says it was a bone that she was taking to the mill and two girls, and asked that her honor be restored to her. And Contesse says they pardoned each other and shook hands in sign of peace.

Claude Monet, butcher.

Because of the cloak that was lost before Easter. Answers that he is a neighbor of the one who lost it, and he got up in the morning and found the cloak, which he picked up, and he was told that he had lost his cloak, and the said Monet told him he had it and he should pay for the wine. And the said accuser had the said cloak that had been proclaimed by the crier. And on Monday morning the said accuser told the one who had lost the cloak, and it was in front of the house of the one who had lost it, and he gave it to him. And on Sunday the said accuser told the said man that he should not look for the cloak any more; the cloak that was lost was found. And his wife did not know that it was found and the said accuser was told that the said cloak had only been lost in his imagination. And touching the sermons, he rarely goes there because his trade holds him down and he has a thick head. Said the prayer, "His name be done," [f. 198v] very poorly as it appears, and knows nothing else except that he has a thick head and will learn to pray. Remanded to Thursday to learn to pray to the Lord. He was at the preaching at St. Gervase before dinner and does not know who preached.

Michiel Cochet, carpenter, from L'Eluiset, habitant *of Geneva, and Françoyse, his wife, from Grand Bornand.*

The wife answers that they have been together for six years, and she has a child six weeks old, and it was baptized at the Magdalen seven days ago. She has had four children by him and Jo . . .[289] Touching her infirm mother. And in going to her mother she was pregnant and wanted to die, and she had the child there. When the child had left her body she did not want it baptized in the said place, and if the said child was baptized there she knows nothing of it. And the said child was baptized in this city, and she does not know that it was ever baptized there. She does not know that it [was] baptized except in this city, and the godfather who carried it is faithful and is from Viry. The said husband did not want at all to baptize his said child where it was. They both said their prayers and their confession. Because the wife did not want to baptize her child in the papistry she has none of her mother's goods.

---

288. Maillet forgot to strike the word "over" when he added the correction "under."
289. Incomplete sentence.

Pernete Bordaz.

Has been summoned four times. Answers that she appeared last Thursday. And on the quarrel, answers that otherwise she has only . . .[290] And once recently she said that she told Julian Bordon the devil should carry him off if he did not pay her. And the said Jullien answered that he did not owe her anything. She presented a written letter with her request in it. She was given admonitions and remonstrances about her wicked words. He reproached her that she was a whore and everyone knew at what fire she warmed herself.

[f. 199]   **Thursday, May 29, 1544**

Lord Syndic Philippin.
Calvin, De Ecclesia, Genesto, Albert.
Du Molard, Vernaz, Pensabin, De Loermoz, Donzel, Peronet, Blandin, the officer Vovrey.

Jehan Galliard[291] and Claudaz, his wife, and Pierre Roufi, drummer.[292]

Because of certain insults spoken by the said Pierre Rofi. And first Jehan Galliard says that the said Roffi blamed him, saying that he kept a synagogue.[293] The said Pierre answers that it is not so, and he has small children about a year old, and says a wind blows like a horn[294] and makes a noise there and howls. And sometimes he goes to the children, takes them by the neck and various other

290. Incomplete sentence.
291. Jehan Galliard, called Damouz, apparently ranged himself on the side of the Philippins and was condemned like the others not to leave the city without the permission of the Council: on March 15, 1541, he is found asking two days of leave to go on his business, which was granted him on condition of not speaking "with our enemies" (R.C. 35, f. 116). He was later imprisoned with Anthoine Darbey on suspicion of having had contacts with the enemies of the city, in other words the partisans of Jehan Philippe. He was rehabilitated on February 25, 1544, by the Small Council (confirmed on February 29 in the Council of Two Hundred) [R.C. 37, folios 197v, 198, 207, and 216v (August 18, 20, and 28 and September 7, 1543); R.C. 38, f. 86 and f. 94v (February 25 and 29, 1544)].
292. Pierre Ruffi, drummer and, apparently, cobbler (on April 9, 1529, the register of the Council speaks of "*Petrus Ruffi, timpanatarius, et magister Henricus Martini, condurerii* {Petrus Ruffus, drummer, and Master Henricus Martinus, tailors}" [R.C. XI, p. 237]). Not to be confused with Pierre Ruffi, secretary of the Council.
293. Translator: A dialect term for an improper assembly, especially a witches' coven.
294. Translator: This phrase, "*qu'il court ung vent et ung cort,*" does not make sense in French. The meaning given here is a guess. Apparently he was accused of misbehaving in some way that involved noise.

things, telling them to refrain from so much fighting and noise at night. And the crossbowmen asked the said Pierre to go sleep with them, and that night the said noise came to his children. And if it is desired that they come let them be summoned. And also he said they were sorcerers. And Pierre said it is not so and that he did not tell them they were sorcerers. The wife of the said Galliard presented an affidavit of legality. Said the prayer and . . .[295] And the said Galliard said similarly, and they do not know how to say the confession.

The advice of the Consistory is, in view of their ignorance, that they do not know how to pray, that they be given a term to learn their prayers. And that Pierre the drummer be spoken to firmly and that the ignorance of the others be considered, and that the said drummer be given strict remonstrances, and that the others be given a term of one month to learn to pray. Jehan Galliard and his wife pardoned Pierre the drummer.

199v] *Franceys Cheynellat.*[296]

Because of a child. That he has had a child by some girl or woman, since . . .[297] Answers that he does not believe he has any child except by his wife. It has been five or six years and he has had none given to him except by his own wife, and he wants to respond if the contrary is proven. The opinion of the Consistory: that the one who carried it to baptism be asked about it.[298]

Jehan Favre, butcher, from Longemale.

Because of some red wine that he gave at the baptism of the last. Answers that he has three children and does not know which time it was, and he did not have a midwife there, because she had gone elsewhere. And the water was carried to the Magdalen, and it is not his office to carry the wine, since Boniface[299] had delivered the child. And he does not know who carried this wine unless it was Jehan Collomb's wife, and he saw(?) nothing of it.

Franceyse, wife of Jaques Mauris, miller.

Because of Masses and other actions and words that they did not do right to . . .[300] Answers that she never spoke these words and has never carried

295. Struck: "the confession."
296. François, son of Etienne Chenellat, husband of Françoise Goule and 20 years old in 1535 (GALIFFE II, p. 117).
297. Incomplete sentence.
298. In the margin: "Investigation."
299. Possibly Boniface Vovrey, wife of the officer of the Consistory and apparently a midwife. See R.Consist. 2, f. 74 (August 12, 1546).
300. Incomplete sentence.

her rosary in the last eight years. And she has not said her rosary for more than eight years, and she always says the Pater as it is said at present. She offered to say it. And let her be told the words spoken that were spoken about Masses. She never spoke to anyone about it, and she says her prayer at St. Gervase. She wants to be punished severely if she ever said anything in Latin. No one comes into their house. And said the prayer and the confession very correctly. She wants to live and die in the law and religion of the present. Also she wishes no harm to anyone whatever. She was given remonstrances and admonitions.

Pierre de Faignant.

Presented a supplication and had it read to the Consistory.[301] The advice of the Consistory: that he be made to come to hear how he behaves and that the said Pierre be admonished to live with his wife. Answers that he will never live with his wife, or he will make it appear against those who have blamed him, and he asks the restoration of his wife's honor and 100 écus for his wife's dishonor. He [f. 200] will live with his wife if he is given justice, and she has been abandoned by everyone. The advice of the Consistory: that he ask justice of those whom he accuses and that he should live with his wife, and if he does not want to live with his wife that he be remanded to the Council tomorrow before Communion is given, and he was admonished as to this. Answers that he will never take her back unless he is given justice on the accusers, and they have formed a party against her. Says again that he will do nothing if he does not have justice. And he wants her as a respectable woman, as when he took her.

Franceyse, his wife. Answers that she lives at her mother's and he has not been there since she left the prison, and he spoke with her in the evening, asking her whether she had been summoned to the Consistory and telling her he did not want to be around her because she had been in prison. And he has not slept with her since the said time. She indeed wants to agree with her said husband, and he does not drink or eat with her, and he does not go to see her except to get angry with her. The advice of the Consistory is that they be perceived to be in good accord in their house and that the mother of the said Franceyse be exhorted.[302]

301. The text of this supplication is found below at the end of the present session.

302. On April 1, 1544, Alexandre Davonex presented a request to the Council on behalf of Pierre de Faignant to be allowed to return to the city and pay his creditors (R.C. 38, f. 145). On May 2, 1544, Françoise, wife of Pierre de Faignant, "submitted that she was charged with fornication for which she was detained and found innocent, and for the restoration of her honor she asks to be told the names of her accusers in order to pursue them at law before the Ordinary," which was refused her (R.C. Part. 1, f. 154v). However,

Claude Monet, butcher.

Was remanded to today to learn to pray to the Lord to receive Holy Communion. Answers that it is too short a term to learn to pray to the Lord, and he thanks God that he lets him earn his living and that of his children. And he knows the Pater well in Latin and he does not know how to say it and desires to know the one that is said at present. And he said it in Latin, and the Ave Maria, also the Credo in a general way. He was admonished that he will be forbidden Communion and that he frequent the catechism, and one month to learn to pray.

Gonyne, daughter of Claude Michaud, servant of Monsieur Jehan Pensabin.

Because of the white wine he found in a pot full of white wine. Answers that she has served Monsieur Pensabin. She knows he had words with Jehan Achard two weeks ago because of certain wine that was drunk in her master's house. And Jehan Achard's maid drew a *quarteron* of wine in two pots that she carried to Pensabin's. And she does not know whether this maid drew it several times. And the said Jehan Pensabin told the wife of the said Achard,[303] [f. 200v] and that her master tested the pots. And this was last Thursday, and Monsieur Piere Baux came to the said house of Pensabin, and he went to supper with Pierre Baux and carried the wine in an urn(?). And some people from Evian came who drank of this wine, and they had no servant except the said Achard's nephew. And she only drew on the said wine twice in her master's house. Said the prayer, and the confession half way. She begged mercy of God and of justice for the offense she committed. She was commanded to appear here in a week and learn to pray to the Lord and the confession, and to beg mercy of Jehan Achard.

In the absence of Pensabin. The Consistory is of opinion that strict remonstrances be given to the said Jehan Pensabin that he should dismiss

---

her husband subsequently presented a request for divorce in Council [R.C. 38, f. 229 (May 30, 1544)]. On July 4, 1544, the Council accused Pierre de Faignant and his wife of having engaged Thomas Genod to write a release for Claude Philippe "for having known her carnally for the sum of four écus, a document received by De Ripha about three weeks ago" (R.C. 38, f. 275v). Following his persistent refusal to return to live with his wife, De Faignant was condemned to nine days in prison for having consented to the adultery of his wife and for having received money for it. Freed from prison on July 28, he asked permission the next day to leave the city, "since he has no means of living in Geneva." The Council ordered that first of all he receive his wife, "and as for going away to find work, there is no wish to prevent him" [R.C. 38, folios 278, 280v, 292v, 301, and 303v (July 7, 8, 18, 28, and 29)]. He died in Geneva on July 21, 1552 (E.C., Morts 1, p. 72).

303. Bartholomie d'Orsières, more often called Bartolomie Richardet.

his maid. And that Jehan Achard and Pensabin be found tomorrow after the sermon.

Pernete, wife of Master Henri Martin,[304] tailor.

Because of suspicion of fornication. Answers that she knows why she was summoned here, and she always goes to the sermons when she has leisure; on working days no, because she cannot. And she would indeed like to go there if her husband wanted it, and that inquiry be made whether she has ever done anything wrong, and that she be punished if she has done anything bad or dishonest. And when she came the other time her husband swore by the body [of Christ], and she stayed too long. And if her said [husband] says so she goes to the sermons, and she wants to do what she should. And sometimes someone has spoken words to her, and he once named a young man who had been with her and presented a dagger to her belly to kill her. And she is innocent of such a thing if she ever thought of it, and she would not want to do anything dishonest. Asks the Consistory to tell her who the one is who has had this opinion of her. And her husband visits a neighbor woman's house where he spends his money, and he often does this, and this woman who entertains him and he . . .[305] She was admonished.

Advised concerning Breganton to forbid him Communion, and also to Nycolas.[306] And that the case of Jehan Chappon against the Donzels be considered. And of Henri Martin, tomorrow.

[f. 201]   *Pentecost.*

On the ordinance of the Holy Communion of Pentecost, just as at Easter.[307]

---

304. An Henri Martin was guard of the Porte Tartasse and also a member of the CC for the Juiverie in 1542. A Pernete Martin died in the Hospital on April 29, 1573 [R.C. 35, f. 489 (February 7, 1542); R.C. 36, f. 201v (December 27, 1542); E.C., Morts 12, p. 45].

305. Incomplete sentence.

306. This probably refers to Claude Soultier, called Briganton, and Nycolas de Mollie. They were imprisoned several times over the years for being "out of their senses"; Briganton was also shut up to prevent contagion from the plague because, "out of his senses," he visited the sick. The two were freed on September 19, 1543. For Briganton see R.C. 36, folios 39, 53, 69v, 92, 104v, and 128v (June 13 and 26, July 14, August 10 and 28, and September 25, 1542); R.C. 37, folios 106v, 116v, 153, and 223v (May 25, June 5, July 13, and September 19, 1543). For Nycolas de Mollie see R.C. 36, folios 47v, 66v, and 69v (June 22, July 11 and 14, 1542); R.C. 37, folios 121, 123v, 219, and 223v (June 9 and 11, September 11 and 19, 1543). Claude Soutier, called Briganton, butcher, died on April 30, 1554 (E.C., Morts 1, p. 157).

307. See above, April 10, 1544. Two days after the present session Henri de La Mare

Contents of the supplication produced today by Pierre de Fagniant.

Most honored lords, Pierre de Fagnyan, citizen of Geneva, humbly states it to be true that Franceyse Bernarde was long detained in the prison of our magnificent lords, as Your Excellency is amply informed. And it was for the offense of adultery, which is a thing greatly defaming to the said suppliant and to the said Françoyse Bernarde. For which reason the said suppliant asks to be separated and a divorce to be made between the said suppliant and the said Franceyse, since the name and fame is that the said Franceyse has committed adultery, and this thing is against God and his commandments. And the said suppliant never intends to live with her. For which reason the said suppliant claims to be owed good and prompt justice. And he will pray God for the preservation of Your Noble Excellency, whom may God wish to preserve for his grace.

[f. 201v]
Thursday, June 5, 1544, first Thursday after Pentecost

Lord Syndic Philippin.
Calvin, Champereaulx, De Ecclesia, Genesto, Albert, Ferrand.
Checand, Du Molard, Vernaz, Pensabin, De Loermoz, Vellut, the officer Vovrey.

Hugonin Floutet in the name of his brother.

Because of the Italians that his said brother conducts to the sermons, and he goes with them. He was commanded to tell his said brother not to leave until the sermon is done and finished.

Bernard Marcet, hosier.

Because of his wife. Answers that he did not have her summoned otherwise, and he is in great discord with her and does not know where she lives and cannot find a room for her, she is so perverse. He cursed(?) her once and has started a suit that has cost him a great deal and is still not at peace with his wife. He cannot prove the reasons, which are in her. And if she is brought to him by force he will be forced to leave the place. He will prove clearly that she is a thief, and if she manages things so that she lives in the house where he lives . . .[308]

"revealed that in Jussy the plague reigns, and asks whether it would be good to put off Communion. Ordered that he not fail to hold Holy Communion, but that the castellan command that no infected person should mix with the others" [R.C. 38, f. 230 (May 31, 1544)].

308. Incomplete sentence.

Pernete, his wife, daughter of Jehan Recouz. Answers that she has been with her husband often, and she went to her brother's. And the said Bernard says that he never beat her since he was imprisoned, and that he, Anthoyne Bernard, wanted her. Says also that she stole everything she found in the said Bernard's room and left and only wanted to mock him. And she drank a pot of wine, and that he should not meddle in her affairs, and since then she did something which will be proven at the bench, and they would not let her stay or live in the house where he is staying. And she took him by the nose. And she says that she . . .[309] [f. 202] The said Pernon. In the absence of the said Bernard she was given strong admonitions and remonstrances. Answers that she will behave as a respectable woman and that she wants to stay with her [husband].

The Consistory is of the opinion that she should beg mercy of him and do better than she has done in the past, and that they live together, and that the said Bernard be told that if she does something she will be remanded to the Council. And they should live together as respectable people should do. The said Bernard wants to verify everything, since he has reconsidered. Nevertheless he consents that she return to him, but only if she refrains from doing him any harm and from quarreling with the neighbors or with him, because he fears she will hardly stay with him, not two weeks. The said Pernete begged mercy of God and justice and her husband and said she would behave like a respectable woman.

Thursday, June 12, 1544

Lord Syndic Philippin.
Calvin, Viret,[310] Genesto, Ferrand, Champereaulx, Albert.
Checand, Vernaz, Blandin, De Luermoz, Donzel, Pensabin, the officer Vovrey.

Claude Morel,[311] *mason, called Malateste,* habitant *of Geneva on the Rue du Boule.*

Because of blaspheming the name of the Lord and the sermons. Answers that he goes on all the feasts, he goes to the sermons, and he came

309. Incomplete sentence.
310. Pierre Viret arrived in Geneva on June 10, 1544. On June 13 he told the Council he had to return to Lausanne, but the Genevans proposed that he make his excuses to the Council of Bern and that the Genevans send another minister to Lausanne in his place [R.C. 38, f. 243v and f. 247v].
311. Not to be confused with Claude Morel, saddler, bourgeois of Geneva and a *dizainier* in Longemale.

from Cologny for the works, and on Sunday he was at the sermon and Calvin preached. Does not know what he said at the sermon and could not say it, and this was at the morning sermon, before dinner. And he prays to God as he has said, and does not know how to say the prayer. And is very happy that he was summoned. And said thus, "Our Father," two words, and in Latin the whole Pater, Ave Maria, Credo, etc. In view of his poverty the Consistory is that he be given a month to learn to pray to the Lord; otherwise he will come every Thursday until he knows how to pray. And his son similarly, and that the father admonish his son. And on Sundays to the four sermons.

202v]   *Aymoz Pilliod,[312] haberdasher.*

For his difference with Loys Franch.[313] Answers that he does not know that he has one, and he would like to do him any service in his power. And he received the last Communion, using someone to make him talk, and he is threatened by him. And he would have gone into the fields if it had not been for the said Loys Franc, who bears him a grudge, and if he comes across him he means to be revenged on him. The Consistory is that, in view of the good will of the said Pilliod, that one wait until the coming of Loys Franch and they can be brought to good accord and peace, and that the said Pilliod, on seeing Franc, do honor to the said Franch.

Jana, wife of Richard Garmese,[314] baker.

Answers that she has five children at her house and she has a little girl who is her sister's who has been in the Low Countries since the year of the destruction of the *faubourgs*[315] about eight years ago. She has given one out

312. Aymo Dufour (Amedeus de Furno), called Pilliod, from Avouzon (Ain), was admitted to the bourgeoisie on December 4, 1515. On Thursday, March 5, 1545, he was in prison "because he opened his shop yesterday" (the day of prayer). The Council "ordered that there is no harm, that he be freed" (*L.B.*, p. 183; R.C. Part. 1, f. 16v).

313. Already in 1541 Pilliod complained in Council about Domaine Franc (Franch), father of Loys, but we do not know whether there was any connection between the two disputes [R.C. 35, f. 363v (October 18, 1541)].

314. Richard Garmese, from Foncenex (H.-S.), was admitted to the bourgeoisie on July 7, 1524 (*L.B.*, p. 201).

315. The demolition of the *faubourgs* of Geneva began slowly in 1530 and reached its peak between 1534 and 1536. The work was not completed until 1540. This was an event of the first rank in the urban history of Geneva. Although admitting that the historians say little about it, Louis Blondel says that "the material life of the city was as much overturned by these demolitions as its intellectual and moral life had been by the Reformation" [BLONDEL, *Faubourgs*, p. 2 (citation) and pp. 16-23].

to nurse that belongs to a man from the village of Allemogne and is being nursed in Gy, and her nephew's wife is keeping it. And it was brought to this city, and she does not know whether she was baptized. And it was baptized in Gy by Lord Henri[316] and was in Foncenex. Cannot name the father of the said child and has not seen the girl by whom he had the said child. And she had 18 florins, of which she gave four florins to the nurse, but she did not know its name. And she does not know who is the mother of the said child, and the said father brought the child in a small basket under his robe. She sent to tell the nurse to bring a cradle to put the said child in. Otherwise she would know who the father and mother are. Answers that she already had the child and sent by her son to Gy for someone to bring a cradle. She says she will make the father come to speak to the lords. Does not know whether the father is married or not. She did not ask whether the said child was baptized or not. The advice of the Consistory is: since she is guilty and merits reprehension, that she make the father come and come herself as often and when [summoned], and that she have the father arrested and not respond for her to guard and guarantee her; otherwise she will be remanded to the Council.

[f. 203]   The said Jane answers that he is named Pierre and she does not know his surname, and he is a young journeyman and is not married.[317] She claims she will make him come, and he is a rather old journeyman and looks well and is neither very tall nor very short, and his age she does not know. She has not seen his mother and she has never been at his house, and she offers to bring the father here in a week. And she moved the said child and gave the rest of the money to her boy who gave him the said money. And she will make the nurse and the other nurse come. And she gave four florins to the former because he did not want to keep it, and the other nurse went to Gy to get the child, and she gave her four like the other. The nurse brought the cradle and she gave her all the other supplies and took the blanket from Exerton's and the shirt from Remillier's. And the said child was wrapped in a cloth in a basket,[318] and the said father gave the money. She goes to the sermons on the feasts and not on working days and was there Sunday; did not recognize the one who preached. Said the prayer and the confession. Reminder to have the nurse summoned who has the said child to know better. And that the child of the said Jane who is in Gy be summoned for Thursday by Master Henri.

316. Henri de La Mare, minister of Jussy, near Gy.
317. This was Pierre Nycolas.
318. Translator: This is a guess for a word of unknown meaning, "*piex*," based on the reference to a basket above.

Thursday, June 19, 1544

Lord Syndic Philippin.
Calvin, Champereaulx, Albert, Genesto, Ferrand, De Ecclesia.
Checand, Vernaz, Molard, Pensabin, Peronet, Justz, Vellut, Blandin, the officer Vovrey.

Tyvent Voland, called Red, baker.[319]

Does not know why he was summoned, and he is rarely absent on Sundays and he is a seller of oxen and mares. He sold a mare to his nephew called Prodhon and sold two oxen the other day to someone from Cruseilles and had 54 florins, and they cost him 40. And he gave him a term for half to Michaelmas, and the rest at Christmas. And he sold them the next day, and he did not know the one who sold them, and the one who bought them is named Jehan Galliard. And he brought them from Cruseilles, and he does not know the one who sold them to him. And he is not from Mornex, and he sold them [for] 55 [florins]. And the box-maker[320] bought them. The one who sold them [f. 203v] lives on the Rue des Chanoines, and he should be paid in cash, and he had never dealt with the said box-maker. And he will give all his goods if the said box-maker did not sell them to him. And never any other dealings than this, he never dealt with him. He does not know to whom the said oxen belonged, and he asked him if he wanted to buy oxen, and indeed he believes that the man from La Muraz to whom he sold them, and he was from La Muraz and owed the said box-maker the money, and . . .[321] The opinion of the Consistory is that he be admonished whether he recognizes his fault and given a term, and that the box-maker on the Rue des Chanoines be summoned, and if he does not recognize his position that he be remanded, and the box-maker will tell something more about it.

Jane, wife of Richard Garmese, and the father of the child she had baptized, Pierre Nycolas, from Arbusigny, and he lives in Allemogne and is a farm laborer.

Has been married and is a widower and has a child by his dead wife, and they are in Arbusigny, and he has them looked after for money. And he made linen and cloth in Allemogne, and he has known her since Saint Léger,

---

319. A Thivent Voland (Voullant), citizen, merchant, living in Saint Léger, died on March 19, 1568, aged 80 [E.C., Morts 9, p. 6 (see also *ibid.*, p. 3, *ad diem*)].
320. Claude Guychard, box-maker.
321. Incomplete sentence.

and she gave him bread. And says that a little after Christmas he asked the said Jehanne whether she wanted to do him a favor, that he had a pregnant girl whom he did not want to get a bad reputation. And a little before Candlemas he brought the small child in a little basket, and she had found a nurse, and he gave her 18 florins, and it was not yet baptized. And it was Wednesday night. And on Thursday he brought it to the said Jehanne and she sent for her. He was in Annecy when it should have been baptized. And he did not tell her the name of the said girl, who is not married and is not from Allemogne. And he would have wanted to marry her if she had not been removed to . . .[322] some were taken to Avignon, and he is very unhappy about it.

The said Jane, baker, says he did not name the person to her and that she had found him a nurse who carried the child. And she sent to Gy to get the nurse to come get it to nurse it. She knew him since he was in Saint Léger at Recameysaz's house, and she does not know what his trade was, and she never saw him work. And the same one brought her the said child, and he did not tell her whether it was baptized or not, and Master Henri [f. 204] baptized it at . . .[323] The Consistory is that she is a liar, and that the second nurse and the nurse and the godfather be made to come, and that one learn about the 18 florins and the name of the girl and where she is from and from what house.

The said Pierre was asked where the said girl is from. Answers that he does not know where she is and she was from the Conté. Does not know where she was from, and he paid her expenses and she was brought to bed in Murcier la Servita(?). And he carried the child through the Porte de Saint Anthoine and did not tell the said Jane where he brought the said child from and he said [sic] the baker woman the said child and gave her 17 florins to nurse it. And he promised nothing to the said Jane, and she had the said child nursed in Monnetier in the Conté. And he does not know where she had it nursed, and it was not he who went to get the said child. And the son of the said baker woman went to get it, and the nurse has kept it since the first Monday in the month of May, and it is in Gy, and the child is named Martin. She gave four florins to the first nurse and four to another, and on Sunday when he came she returned him six florins. And for the blankets and things he gave her 18 *gros*,[324] and he had made a contract for a year, and they did not nurse it the whole time. And from now on he

322. Words omitted.
323. Name of place omitted.
324. Note: she had just said (or Maillet had just written) "17 florins."

will give the nurse what he must give, because he was afraid of the girl, of her family. And he spoke to the girl's relatives, and he did not want to expose the girl. And he told them he wanted to have her in marriage, and they did not want to consent. And he does not know where she is. If it were near here there would be a good reason to inquire. And he had a child by this girl, and it was not baptized twice. The baker woman sent to him often, and that she had already changed to another nurse. The girl was never at the baker woman's, and it is six or seven years since he was in Allemogne and he is from Arbusigny, him. And the baker woman asked him where he came from and he answered that he came from Allemogne. And the said girl was never there and the said baker woman never sheltered her, and he did not fornicate in this city, and he is from Arbusigny.[325] And he knew Monsieur Pierre Vandelle who has property in Arbusigny. And he is a poor journeyman and earns his living here and there, and he never knew where she is from. And she had her child at the house of Claude Boytouz of Murcier, and he was not always with her. And he thinks she has neither father nor mother, and her uncle never wanted him to have her to wife. And when she left he was in Annecy, and he found her in the said Murcier. [f. 204v] And he was present when she had the child, and it is a year and a half since he fornicated with her. And she came and went with him, and she knows well how to make linen like him. And she worked in this city at Le Mouroz's house. He does not know whether she is in Avignon or not. And he says she, the baker woman, did him a favor and she heard in right and honor that he had a child he wanted nursed. And he wants to answer for the baker woman rather than that she be in trouble. And he will show where she was brought to bed and pay what he should pay.

The said baker woman answers that the said man never named the girl and said the child was his and asked whether she knew a nurse. And she did know one, for pay. And he took it to her the Thursday after Candlemas and she sent for her niece, who kept it as long as the money lasted she had given her. And then she returned it and went to Gy, and they found the nurse when they came to get the child, and he had given 11 florins, of which she had spent 8 florins, and 10 florins remains, and she gave him six florins on Sunday, and she has four florins left that she wants to turn over to him. And she bought the swaddling clothes and the blanket from her money, and he gave her 18 florins and 18 to have the said child nursed. Does not know whether he told her when he brought the said child that he brought it from

325. The text says: "and is De Rey of Arbusigny." We think he began to write "De Reygnier," then wrote "of Arbusigny" without striking the former.

Allemogne(?) or Arbusigny or elsewhere. And she said it just as he told her; when he brought her the child, that he said that he had had it from a girl, and nothing else. And in the money he gave her there were no écus or *testons*, but *quarts* and other money.

The said Pierre answers that the girl is from the Conté and he has indeed seen one of her uncles and does not know her name. And the said girl is named Aymaz and her uncle is named Jehan. He gave *quarts*, sous and *testons*. And the six florins, she gave him a *teston*, as he had given her before. The cradle is not his and the nurse borrowed it who nursed it, and this from Gy, to this nurse from Gy, the cradle. And the baker woman sent for the nurse, and he spoke to her uncle in Murcier and La Roche. The Consistory has decided that they be left alone until more is known, and she until she is summoned, until Master Henri is spoken to, who will tell everything.

[f. 205] *Jehan Curtet, servant of Pauloz Tharex.*

Answers that he has been married for two weeks and is engaged to the millstone-cutter's maid,[326] and he knew her because she often came to his master's barn. And he found her a good girl and proposed to have her, and he did not know her before he promised himself to her. And her father established the marriage, and her father is named Humbert de La Palluz, of Cruseilles, and was his master. And he does not know that she was pregnant before he was engaged to her. Maclamo[327] and her father made the said marriage, and God inspired him to take her to wife. And he has always talked with her in front of his master's house. The opinion of the Consistory is that both be remanded to Thursday and that the said girl's mistress, the millstone-cutter's wife,[328] be summoned. All three Thursday, the maid and the mistress. The said Curtet gave a half-*berlingue* to the said Pernete, daughter of Humbert de La Pallu of Cruseilles. He never spoke to his master or his mistress. He says they never met for anything else, although he always said he would never have another than her. She came once to find him in the stable, and immediately his master and Maclamod were immediately there with them.

326. Claude Falquaz's maid.
327. Maclamo was reprimanded several times in Consistory for fornication and for having assisted pilgrims of St. Claude and for other things [R.Consist. 2, folios 88, 95, and 95v (November 4, December 2 and 9, 1546)]. In 1557 a Pierre Falca, called Maclamo, was called to the Consistory, but he did not appear [R.Consist. 12, Ann. f. 9 (October 14, 1557)].
328. Henriette, wife of Claude Falquaz.

Claude Guychard,[329] box-maker.

Answers that he goes to the sermons when he can, and he has attacks of fever and has not had business with the Red.[330] Once he gave the Red two oxen for 40 florins, and he then sold them to someone else who gave him 56 florins. And he bound the one who bought them there for the money, and the one who sold them was from over by Mornex. And he had nothing else to do with him. And two weeks earlier he said he had no money, and they drank to the deal at Jehanton Burdet's in Saint Léger. And the one who bought them was short of money and he saw that he found it and made him guarantee it, and he wanted to have 55 florins. And the oxen were still in the house, and De Domo of Bourg du Four received the bond. In view of the said Tyvent's lies, that the Council make the decision, and let the said Tyvent be remanded to Monday to the Council.

205v] The said Tyvent says they led out the oxen and De Domo received the bond, and the oxen were not in this city but at their house, and one of the brothers bought them and the other bought them, and they were bought for 40 florins and were sold to the brother of the seller for 55 florins.

The said Pierre Nycolas.

He still has not stated where the said girl is from or who her father is, and he will bring those who nursed the said child.

Thursday, June 26, 1544

Lord Syndic Philippin.
Champereaulx, Genesto, Albert, Ferrand.
Checand, Molard, Vernaz, Pensabin, Blandin, Just, Velluti, the officer Vovrey.

Noble Loys Franch.

Because of the quarrel with Aymoz Pilliod. Answers that the said Pilliod made him crippled and ill, and may God pardon him. And he did nothing to him, and let him mind his business and he will mind his own, and he has no hatred against him and no grudge against him and does not look for him and leaves vengeance to God. And may the said Pilliod not come before his eyes, because he is crippled through the said Pilliod. And indeed he

---

329. Claude Guychard, box-maker from Bougy (Vaud), became a bourgeois of Geneva on July 28, 1534 [*L.B.*, p. 211].
330. Tyvent Voland, called Red, or the Red.

would like to lose this memory, but he cannot take away his courage, and he does not seek his injury. And he says that his said enemy Pilliod still, after the quarrel, again came to show him his arquebuse when he got up and went to Cologny, and he is crippled. Aymod Pilliod because of the quarrel between him and the said Loys Franch, and what the said Franc stated here was repeated to him, with his last statement here. The Consistory asked Monsieur Jehan Du Mollard and Blandin to urge again the said L[oys] Franc to correct his heart and pardon the said Pilliod.

[f. 206]   *Petremandaz Corbaz, Janna Coudreaz, and Mennech.*

Because of the feasts and Corpus Christi. Answer that they were at the sermons last Sunday, and they cannot go because they must prepare their herbs to sell. Janna de Coudrea. Petremandaz answered that her colleague was ill the day of Corpus Christi. Menneche says that Corpus Christi was created by the city. The advice is that their religion be learned and whether they still have some faith that the feasts they keep are salutary to them or have some scruple in their consciences, and about the Mass. They were given strong admonitions and remonstrances to frequent the sermons.

*Franch and Pilliod.*³³¹ *Pardoning.*

The assigned elders³³² state that they are in good accord. Monsieur Loys Franch says that the thing is very serious for him, but he is content to pardon him for the honor of God and of justice. The said Pilliod, who was given severe admonitions and remonstrances, begged mercy and pardon of him, throwing himself on the ground, and the said Noble Loys Franch pardoned him.

*Henriete, wife of Claude Falquaz, millstone-cutter.*³³³

She was [at the sermon] Sunday, and very little the other days. Saint John's Day was Tuesday, and she went to Petit Saconnex. She does not have her maid; her father took her away two weeks ago. And she went to Cruseilles, and she had finished her time. And she was married without our consent and took Pauloz' servant. And she found he talked to her, and Pauloz says she withdrew, that someone wanted to speak to her maid. And she was seen to behave badly, and they wanted to give her the said servant

331. Loys Franc (Franch) and Aymoz Dufour, called Pilliod.
332. Jehan du Mollard and Mermet Blandin.
333. This concerns the matrimonial case between Jehan Curtet, servant of Paulo Tarex, and Pernete de La Palluz, servant of the Falquaz family.

of Pauloz in marriage, and Pauloz said she was seen to behave badly. And they made her swear faith to him. And on Saturday her father[334] came to Pauloz's and they made her swear. The Juggler[335] went into the courtyard and went to the cows and cried "Pernete." And she was from somewhere, and they made her promise three score florins. And the husband wanted everything, and the father is poor and does not have enough to marry her or pay for her. [f. 206v] And she never saw that the said girl behaved badly. The opinion is that one wait until the girl comes and that her mistress make her come with her to the Consistory, and then the whole of her behavior will be learned from the girl. Another method is that the mistress be told to make the girl tell the truth about everything. Another is that if one can know that she lives with her father it can be learned whether she [is] pregnant or not.

The said Henriete does not know when they should come to make an agreement. And the poor man wanted to give her 20 florins, and they dismissed her, and she should have gone to the preaching, and she went to the barn in the morning and at vespers and stayed all day in the stable, and therefore they wanted to dismiss her. And she hopes that on Saturday [she will be] here, and she will bring her to Monsieur Calvin or Syndic Philipin who will speak to her and tell her something for her profit.

Thursday, July 3, 1544

Lord Syndic Philipin.
Calvin, De Ecclesia, Genesto, Albert, Ferrand.
Checand, Vellut, Donzel, Pensabin, Just, the officer Jehan the hunchback, the watchman.

Jehan Bornant, baker.

Because of his wife who does not live with her [sic]. Wants to be paid the rest of his wife's marriage [portion]. Answers that he does not want to have any more to do with his wife's father and wants his father-in-law to pledge and give him a bond for what remains of the marriage; was ordered. Again he does not want to have any more to do with his father-in-law, and it is not his fault, since if he had his money . . .[336] He was given severe remon-

334. Humbert de La Palluz.
335. Aymoz Vulliet, called the Juggler.
336. Incomplete sentence.

strances by the lords. The said Jehan wants them to agree together between now and next Saturday.

[f. 207]   *Egrege Claude Veneri, procurator.*

Does not know why he was summoned here; because of the sermons. Answers that he wants to do his duty to the church, and he goes to the sermons. Has three children and is a poor man. Concerning the law, he is being done wrong because of words he did not intend to say, and he asks for his opponent who accused him of those words. Touching the wife of Denis Hugue,[337] answers that he will explain it. He has a wife who does not know how to do anything and has children by her, and someone on the bench contradicted him with words in the case of Françoys Bordon. Denys Hugue's wife came with letters, and there are respectable people, and says that if his wife knew anything he would not have said these words, for it is said that the husband takes care of the bread and the wife of the meat. And if he is wrong he says he wants to be punished for it, and he demands his rights against his accuser. And what he said he did not say from bad intent but through ignorance, and he did not intend to say anything wrong. And if it is found that he did something he wants to be punished for it, asking for the law.

Gonynaz, wife of Franchoys Planche, called Moctu, butcher.

Answers that she was at the sermon Sunday in the morning and at vespers and she has no scruples about religion and did not keep St. John's Day or Corpus Christi.

[Bocone]

Monsieur Calvin said something about Bocone,[338] who prayed him that an end be put to her affair, that it is a serious thing that her husband is not ordered to take her back with him.[339]

---

337. Jane Exchaquet.
338. Franceyse Bocone.
339. The case of adultery between Pierre Rosset and Franceyse Bocone dragged on for several more months. On October 13, 1544, the Consistory remanded Rosset to the Council, this time also accusing Franceyse Bocone of adultery with [Jean Gabriel?] Monathon (R.C. 35, f. 5v; minutes of the Consistory lost).

Pernete, daughter of Loys Magnin, from Viry.

Was brought up in this city, was a servant of Monsieur Jehan Gurguigni who died, and lives near the Magdalen. Does not know why she was summoned here. Answers that she goes to the sermon willingly. She works for her living, and worked on the said days of Saint John and Corpus Christi. And she works, and has nothing to live on. Has sold two of her shifts to live. And does not know how to pray to the Lord. She came to her house on Christmas. She has lived in her house four or five years, and was at the sermon on St. John's Day, and was like her neighbors, and thinks she kept the feasts, in that she resisted. She broke her arm three weeks ago, and she does not know how to pray to God. She does not know who preached or what he said. She does not know who preaches in Viry; does not know whether he is old or young. She says the Pater in Latin as she knows how to say it, Ave Maria Virgo, the *Credo in deum,* [f. 207v] *Sanctum, sanctum, sanctorum,*[340] *Commem. remissio*(?),[341] and she indicates there Taberte's wife, a boatman's wife. She was given two weeks to learn to pray to the Lord and frequent the sermons.

Petremand Pellouz.

Because of his hatred for his enemy Claude Philipe. Answers that he did not receive Communion because his enemy is here and his opponent mocks him, and he knows well that it was he himself who wounded him, and he cannot work at his trade for his living and that of his children. And he had a good trade and is allowed to do the best he can. And when he sees his enemy he is deprived of his senses and does not know what he does. And it would have been better for the said Pellouz if his enemy had killed him rather than done as he did. And Monsieur Amed Bandiere and Monsieur Hudriod Du Molard tried once to make them compromise. And he had to stay in bed five months on the occasion, and they suffered a fine of 500 écus. And he has already answered here once. And he denounced the mockery of his said enemy at the bench, and that . . .[342]

Noble Claude Philippe because of the argument and quarrel with Petremand Pellouz, and where he last received Communion. Answers that he did not receive the last Communion because of a grudge he has against him, and he was struck by him in front of his own house. And this is the reason

---

340. Uncertain reading. The first word could also be *suum.* In that case the prayer would probably be the *Suum Sanctum Spiritum* (see WIECK, p. 163 under *terce,* Hours of the Holy Spirit), but the third word does not support this reading.

341. Again, the reading is uncertain, and we know of no prayer commencing thus.

342. Incomplete sentence.

why he did not receive the last Communion. He was admonished. Answers that he wishes him no harm and he will make the contrary appear, that he did not strike him and it was not the said denouncer. And what the Council commands him to do he will do. And that it will not be proven that he was ever struck by him, and he has not been before arbitration for it. Again the said person deposes that the said Pellouz has said that the said denouncer would never die except by the hand of the said Pellouz, which is something that disturbs him greatly. And the said Pellouz struck the said denouncer.

The opinion of the Consistory is that they can make a compromise and pursue the case at law, or that they be brought to peace in order to receive Communion. And that they be given inhibitions and prohibitions not to deal with each other in any way, and that they be exhorted to agree. The syndic is of opinion that they be remanded to the Council if they do not want to agree. [f. 208] The said Petremant answers that if he could do him any service he would do it willingly and that the said . . .[343] and he has his examination in which he has faith, and he knows that he has business and that the Council has not given him any prohibitions, and he would not know how to pardon him. The opinion is that they be remanded to the Council on Monday on leaving, since they do not want to agree, on the part of the said Pellouz.

The attendances at the Consistory of Geneva.

Made by the members assigned and deputed by the most dread Lords our superiors Syndics and Council of Geneva, from Thursday, April 17, until July 3 inclusive. And first the said Thursday, April 17, Thursday 24 of the said month, Thursday first day of May, Thursday 8, Thursday 15, Tuesday 27, Thursday 29 of the said month of May, Thursday 5 of June, Thursday 12, Thursday 19, Thursday 26 of the said month of June and Thursday third day of the month of July inclusive, of the present year 1444 [sic], which are in number 12.

First:

Lord Syndic Philippin	XII	II	ff.
Nobles: Anthoyne Checant	X	XX	ss.
Claude Du Pain	II	IIII	ss.
Pierre Vernaz	VII	XIIII	ss.
Jo. Du Molard	VIII	XVI	ss.
Jo. Pensabin	XI	XXII	ss.
M[ermet] Blandin	X	XX	ss.
Just de Loermoz	IX	XVIII	ss.

343. Name omitted.

G[uillaume] Vellut	VIII	XVI	ss.
Jo. Donzel	VIII	XVI	ss.
Jo. Peronet	V	X	ss.
The officer Vovrey	XII	II	ff.
The scribe Maillié	XII	III	ff.[344]

Total: 20 florins.[345]

344. Writing irregular. In principle the scribe received four sous per session (there-fore, in this case, four florins for the twelve sessions). If he received four florins, however, the total should be 21 and not 20 florins.

345. Here end the minutes of George Maillet, who died a few days later. The regis-ter of the Council for July 17, 1544, says that "on the decease of Egrege George Malliet it was advised to establish another secretary, and Karoli, Cuvacti, Johan Porral, De Domo, Magnin and De Ripha have been put forward. And the loudest voice fell on De Ripha; nevertheless he has still not been accepted." The next day Jean Porral was chosen as the new secretary (R.C. 38, f. 291 and f. 292v). As for the history of the present volume, on September 25, 1544, "Jehan Porral, secretary of the Consistory . . . asked that the registers of the Consistory of the late Georges Malliet, former secretary of the said Consistory, be delivered to him. Ordered that such registers be deposited at the City Hall" (R.C. 38, f. 388v).

Appendices

1. The Establishment of the Consistory: The Ecclesiastical Ordinances of 1541

From *R.C.P.* I, pp. 6-7, 11-13, without variants. The complete text of the Ordinances can be found in *R.C.P.* I, pp. 6-13 or *S.D.* II, pp. 377-390.

The third order follows, that of the elders, who will be assigned or deputed by the Seigneurie to the Consistory.

Their office is to watch over the life of everyone, to admonish gently those they see at fault and leading a disorderly life, and where it is proper make a report to the Company who will be assigned to make fraternal corrections, and then make them in common with the others.

As this church is set up it will be good to elect two from the Narrow Council, four from the Council of Sixty and six from the Council of Two Hundred,[1] men of good life and honest, without reproach and above all suspicion, above all fearing God and having good spiritual discretion, and they should be so elected that there will be one in each quarter of the city in order to have their eyes everywhere, which we want to be done.

---

1. In fact during these years a syndic and two others were elected from the Narrow Council and nine were elected from the Council of Two Hundred. See above for February 15, 1543, and January 31, 1544.

On the manner of electing them

Likewise we have decided that the manner of electing them should be thus: let the Narrow Council suggest the names of the most proper men who can be found and the most adequate; and to do this, summon the ministers to communicate with them about it; then let them present those they have suggested to the Council of Two Hundred, which will approve them . . .

On the order that should be followed regarding adults to maintain good discipline in the church

The establishment of a day for the Consistory

That the aforesaid deputies who have been spoken of assemble once a week with the ministers, that is on Thursday, to see that there is no disorder in the church and decide together on remedies when there is need.

Because they will have no authority or jurisdiction to compel, we have decided to give them one of our officers to summon those to whom they wish to give some admonition.

If anyone from contempt [refuses] to appear, their office will be to inform the Council so it can supply a remedy.

There follow the persons the elders or deputies should admonish and how they should proceed.

If there is anyone who dogmatizes against the received doctrine, let him be summoned to confer with him. If he conforms let him be sent back without scandal or defamation. If he is opinionated let him be admonished several times, until it is seen that greater severity will be necessary, and then let him be forbidden Communion and denounced to the Magistracy . . .

[Similarly for the one who is "negligent in coming to church" or a "despiser of the ecclesiastical order," for the one who is guilty of "secret vices" or "notorious and public vices . . . if these are faults that merit only admonition . . ."]

When there are crimes that do not merit only remonstrances in words, but corrections with punishment, if anyone has fallen into these, according to the needs of the case it will be necessary to order him to abstain for some time from Communion to humble himself before God and better recognize his fault . . .

And nevertheless let all this be so measured that there is no rigor by which anyone will be grieved and so that the corrections will be merely medicines to bring back sinners to Our Lord.

And let all this be done in such a way that the ministers have no civil jurisdiction and use only the spiritual sword of the Word of God, as Saint Paul orders them, and that this Consistory does not derogate from the authority of the Seigneurie or the ordinary courts, but that the civil power remain in its entirety. And where there is need of giving some punishment or compelling the parties, the ministers with the Consistory, having heard the parties and given such remonstrances and admonitions as will be desirable, must report everything to the Council, which will decide from their account to command and judge according to the needs of the case.

That this discipline be not only for the city, but also for the villages depending on the Seigneurie.

2. Bonivard Describes the Consistory

Bonivard, *Police,* pp. 153-155, written at the end of the 1550s (partially modernized).

You have first seen civil discipline still enduring in the times of trouble;[1] but there was still no ecclesiastical [discipline] to censure morals, although there were many respectable people who desired it and tried to bring it to Geneva, as it was in the other evangelical cities of the country of the Leagues; but the quarrelers fearing correction did not want to consent to it, alleging to sustain their arguments that this would be to reestablish a papacy, giving such jurisdiction to the ministers as the Pope and the bishops had formerly; and therefore the ecclesiastical authority and its Senate could not be established until after the death of Johan Philippe,[2] pastor of the quarrelers, since at that time the sheep were astray; and it was established thus: of the four syndics one would always be judge of the Consistory and its chief, with the assistance of certain laics, both of the Narrow Council and the CC, and of the preachers, who would be censors of morals, before the correction went before the temporal court, and also of marriages, just as it was in the court of the bishops before; but still, in order that despite their associates the ministers not take too much authority, the said Consistorial Senate would not have power to judge, with or without a vote, but only to admonish, if it was a light case; also it would not have the power to administer an oath; if it was a case of importance, it would be returned before the Narrow Council to judge it the next Monday, since this was done on Thursday. They would have a jurisdiction to excommunicate, depriving those obstinate in their sin of Communion, and for this purpose, where the papists before receiving their Sacrament are compelled entirely to confess their sins orally to a priest, these do not wait until someone presents himself to them, but each one knows the government committed to him by the public, which is divided in various *dizaines;* they go accompanied by the *dizainiers* from house to house, asking all those of a household for an explanation of their faith, and afterwards whether they feel there is any disorder in the house, and in general and in particular admonish

---

1. That is since the beginning of the struggle for Genevan independence, but especially during the events leading to the fall of the Perrinists in 1555.
2. This was the party of Jean Philippe, the "Philippins," who were opposed to the party of the "Guillermins," partisans of Guillaume Farel and John Calvin. Philippe and his party lost their credit at the time of the affair of the Articulants or Artichauds in 1540, when it was found that the Genevan ambassadors had yielded too much to the Bernese. It was the downfall of the Philippin party that permitted the recall of Calvin to Geneva.

them to repentance so they will not receive the Sacrament unworthily. This is the former authority of the Consistory; it has recently been given authority to administer an oath.[3]

3. The Consistory obtained the right to administer oaths in 1556. See *R.C.P.* II, p. 68 (July 30, 1556), and *S.D.* III, p. 32 (July 24, 1556).

3. Roll of Persons Called by the Consistory, 1543-1544

A.E.G., P.C. 2e série, 602 (1543-1544). Original in the hand of Georges Maillet. The words in italics are found in the margin of the text. The names in italics refer to the minister or elder who denounced the person to the Consistory. In general the dates in italics refer to a first appearance before the Consistory, often the date of excommunication. In place of giving all references to the text of the first register in the notes, we give the complete name only where it is needed so the reader can find it in the index. An asterisk (*) marks passages erased in the original. Often, but not always, the scribe struck out a name when the person appeared before the Consistory. Therefore the names of those persons mentioned below who did not appear before the Consistory are not struck out, but frequently Maillet forgot to strike the names of persons who did appear.

[f. 1] The names of those who must be called to the Consistory in the present year 1543, before the lords assigned by the Great Council of Two Hundred.

The wife of Domeyne Franch,[4] who carries her rosary.
See. Mathieu Canard because of murmuring.
*Jehan L'Ostoz, weaver.
*The wife of De Myribello[5] because of murmuring.
*The widow of Jullian Recouz who cursed the Gospel and those who maintain it.
*The host of the Savage[6] and his maid.[7]
*Marquot in the Pellisserie because of an image.[8]
Reminder to the Council to post wardens at Jussy.
Sarpollet[9] because of ill will, and Des Vignes.[10]

4. Clauda de Fernex, wife of Domaine Franc.
5. Pernete de Miribello.
6. Jean Curt.
7. Guillermeta Martin.
8. Marquiot de Villa?
9. Jehan Jaquard, called Sarpollet.
10. Pierre Des Vignes.

Those who must be summoned for
Thursday, February 22, 1543

First:

*Maurisaz Talluchetaz remanded to give an explanation of her confession.
*Pierre Gerod, who is said not to know how to pray to the Lord: to say the prayer.
*Jehan L'Ostoz, weaver, why he left his wife in Lyon.
*The wife of Domeyne Franc[11] because she carries her rosary.
*The wife of De Miribello[12] because of murmuring at the sermons.
*The widow of Jullian Recouz because she cursed the Gospel and those who maintain it.
*The host of the Savage another time because of the sermons and papistry, and his maid[13] also.
*Pierre Des Vignes, bath-house keeper.
*And Sarpollet[14] also who wish each other harm, and they are enemies of each other.

See.

For Thursday two weeks

De Miribello.[15]

For Thursday, March 1

To have the woman summoned who worships the Virgin Mary.[16]
*Jehan Clement because he has dismissed his wife.
Henri. Françoyse, wife of a tailor in Saint Germain.
Henri. And Jana, widow of Glaude Bron, in Saint Germain, who are insulted and called sorcerers.

11. Clauda de Fernex.
12. Pernete de Miribello.
13. Jean Curt and Guillermeta Martin.
14. Jehan Jaquard, called Sarpollet.
15. Claude de Miribello.
16. Probably Pernon Contesse.

Henri. *Mermeta,[17] maid of Deleta, who keeps Lent and feasts; honors the Virgin Mary.

Orsieres. *Claude,[18] farm laborer, and Collete, his wife, who live at Chappuisi's house near the New Church of Our Lady, who beat each other.

Orsieres. *Madame the Mistress of the Mint,[19] for idolatry.

Oriseres. *The wife of Berteracti.[20]

Oriseres. *The widow of Richardet, wife of Achard.[21]

Master Henri. *Belletaz.[22]

*XXX Cote.[23]

*The mother of George Lombard.[24]

*Tybauldaz and her mother,[25] who have the company of Bellete,[26] who always observe the papistic commandments.

*Pierre Des Vignes and Sarpollet.[27]

*The wardens of Satigny and of Jussy.

*Reminder for the baths for Monday.[28]

*Richardetaz.[29]

*Bertheratie.[30]

For Thursday, March 8

*De Miribello.[31]

*Mathieu Pratinez(?).[32]

*The wife of Tyvent Chenu.

17. Mermete de La Chavanne.
18. Claude Corniez.
19. Mye Nergaz, wife of Henri Goulaz, master of the mint.
20. Guillauma Bertherat.
21. Bartholomée d'Orsières, widow of Claude Richardet, wife of Jehan Achard.
22. Janne, widow of Pierre Aprin, called Belletaz.
23. Trente Cote, or possibly Christophe Cote (see the note above in the main text, May 26, 1542).
24. Mermaz Plantens, mother of Georges Plantens, called Lombard.
25. Probably Thibauda Arpin and Pernete Torniez.
26. Janne, widow of Pierre Aprin, née Bellet.
27. Jehan Jaquard, called Sarpollet.
28. See above at the end of the session of January 25, 1543.
29. Bartholomée d'Orsières, widow of Claude Richardet.
30. Guillauma Bertherat.
31. Claude de Miribello.
32. Read: Mathieu Gathiner (Gathsiner)?

*The daughter of Contesse,[33] near . . .[34]
*Dominique Du Gerdi, his maid[35] and his wife.[36]
*De Miribello and his wife[37] were remanded.
*Perriar,[38] tailor. Solliet[39] and his wife.
*Arthaud and Floutet.[40]

2v] For Communion next Easter
Those who were remanded before receiving Holy Communion at Christmas.

The first:

December 28. *Jehan Bornant, granary worker, and his wife.[41]
Maurisaz Talluchetaz.
December 28. Jehan Corajo and his wife,[42] who went to the village.
See what Grand Pierre[43] stated to the Consistory.
*Whether the syndic's mother will be summoned for now, Pertemps,[44] before Communion.
Whether Jaques and Robert[45] the pack-saddlers will be summoned.
January 4. *Whether Claude Valloz and Du Mur and their wives[46] will be asked whether they are in accord.
January 25. *The wife of Master Michiel the saddler,[47] whether she has learned to pray to the Lord.
*Whether the children of De Pane[48] have done with their mother what the Council ordered last.

33. Pernon Contesse.
34. Name of place omitted.
35. Clauda Blandet.
36. Pernete Du Nant.
37. Claude and Pernete de Miribello.
38. Pierre Dumont, called Perriar.
39. Thivent Solliet.
40. Probably Claude Arthaud and Hugonin Floutet.
41. Françoyse Bornand.
42. Jehan Corajod, called Du Nant, and Jane, his wife.
43. Pierre Rugoz?
44. Jane Pertenne, née Bonna, mother of Claude Pertemps.
45. Jaques Emyn and Robert Breysson.
46. Claude and Girarde Vallouz and Michel Du Mur and his wife.
47. Clauda, wife of Michel Julliard.
48. Pernete Du Pain, née Roget, and her sons Amblard, Amied, and Pierre Paulo Du Pain.

427

March 8. Mathieu Gathiner was remanded to appear once before Easter.

Calabri, who did not appear when he was summoned, who was remanded to the Council with Arthaud.[49]

The Court of Appeals discussed the two Curtet[50] brothers because of Communion.

[f. 3]   *Lucresse Curtetis

*The daughter of Vullietaz,[51] who is angry with her mother.

*Polleti and his maid.[52]

*Anthoyne de Crouz for disorder in his house.

*Loys Piaget, sheath-maker, who keeps Lent and holds to papistry.

Frochet. *Angelline de Crouz, who does nothing but get angry at her daughter-in-law[53] and does nothing but insult her every day.

*Pierre the shearer,[54] who was remanded on February 1 and has not appeared. See the said day.

February 8. *The wife of Pernet the shearer,[55] who was remanded to frequent the sermons and pray to the Lord.

Also it would be good to consider a butcher in the Grande Boucherie who engaged himself to a woman and then engaged himself to another, agreement being made between them.[56]

Jehan Bennard should be summoned because of a child he presented for baptism.

[f. 3v]

For Thursday, March 22

The wife of Jehan Bornand,[57] granary worker of Longemale.

The wife of Jehan Corajod.[58]

49. Pierre Calabri and Claude Arthaud.

50. Jean and Claude Curtet.

51. Marie Du Nant, daughter of Jean Du Nant, called Vulliet.

52. Pierre Guillermet, called Pollet, and Nycolarde Perrissod.

53. The wife of Anthoine de Crouz, son of Angelline de Crouz.

54. Pierre Rugoz.

55. Jaquemetaz, wife of Pernet Guex.

56. This concerns the marriage case of Tyvent Prodhon, Jehan Gardet's maid, and another woman.

57. Françoyse Bornand.

58. Jane, wife of Jehan Corajod, cobbler.

For Thursday, April 5

Jehan Fassoret and his wife.[59]
Donne Pernete, widow of Michiel Du Pain, because of Communion.
Thomassaz Mabuectaz.
Petremand Pelloux, for usury and Communion.
The names of the marriage at Prodhom's to get information. And first Loys Gardet, Hugoz from the house of Ludriaz(?), the maid of Monsieur Lorant[60] who is named Glaudaz, Mermet Blandin, the wife of Tyvent Chenu.
Gonyn de Soubz-le-Crest, armorer.
Donne Ayma Balletaz.[61]
Guillaume Villars, barber.
Buc[l]ini and his wife and sister, who never go to the sermons but remain inside when there is preaching, kept Lent and celebrated the novena of Saint Felix because of an illness. The said Buclin was ill.
*Next Monday: Jehan Favre, butcher.

For next Thursday, April 12, 1543

4]

Maurisaz Talluchetaz.
Janne, wife of Jehan Corajoz, at the Golden Lion.
Claudaz, who lives with Anna in the house of De Vegio.[62]
Pierre Paulo Du Pain and his wife.
Ayma Du Chabloz, wife.
Pernete the Adventuress[63] of the Molar because of the cross made on the body of Fran[çoys] Conste.
Pierre Lossier of Chêne because of Claude Combaz, [from] Versoix, who cures horses, as is in the information at the bench.

---

59. Jehan Fassoret and his wife are not mentioned in this volume.
60. Laurent Symond, called the Picard.
61. We have not found this woman in the first volume.
62. Claude Joct and Anne de La Ravoyre.
63. Pernete de Mengoz, called the Adventuress.

For Thursday, May 3

The son of Colleta Chabodaz,[64] who is disobedient to his mother.
Bonbrelez, to learn where his wife's daughter had her child.[65]
Claudaz, wife of Colin Pollier.[66]
The two daughters of Rolete de Pari.[67] See April 19; they were remanded.

For Tuesday

Jehan Villiet, son of the ironmonger.
Pierre Guillermet, tailor, called Guillermet.[68]
The wife of Girard Le Mugnier.[69]
Pernete, who was a servant of the little doctor.[70]

[f. 4v] *Pensabin.* Aymoz Marquet and his wife[71] and her sister on the Rue de la Pellisserie.

Morel. Bonivard and his wife, widow(?);[72] City Hall.

For Tuesday, August 28, 1543

Noble Bartholemé, widow of Richardet, wife of Noble Jehan Achard.[73]
Donne Pernete, wife of Monsieur Lyonard de Bouge.[74]
The servants of the inn of the Sun.

64. Jehan Chaboz.
65. Jean Grissaney, called Bonbrilliez, and Tybaudaz Le Guex, his wife.
66. Claudaz, wife of Jehan Collin, called Pollier.
67. Boniface and Mermete de Pary.
68. Sic. This is Pierre Guillermet, called Pollet.
69. Madelayne, wife of Girard Le Mugnier.
70. Pernete, daughter of Pierre Mathieu, servant of Master François [Chappuis], doctor.
71. Loyse Querlaz.
72. François Bonivard and Jane Darmeis, widow of Pierre Corne.
73. Bartholomée d'Orsières, widow of Claude Richardet, wife of Jehan Achard.
74. Pernete Vuychard, wife of Lyonard de Bougier.

For next Thursday

Humbert Exerton and his sister Janna.

The lieutenant has turned in these:

*The daughter of Martinaz Richel of Saint Gervais, who has left her husband for a long time and lives here fornicating.

Jehan the Braggart[75] because he was at the Mass in his own country.

Mauris Savua, boatman, and his wife, who do not live together, and she is said to fornicate and does not sleep with her husband. They have left.[76]

Thursday, October 4, 1543[77]

Alexandre the watchman[78] announces having summoned Jehan de L'Arche to the Consistory.

*Reminder of the widow of Tyvent Tissot[79] on the Rue de Saint Anthoine because she cursed the Gospel and those who brought it and maintain it and preach it; and papistic ceremonies.

*Marguerite,[80] wife of a farm laborer who lives at Gruetz' house because of her small child she left to die, which strangled itself in the cradle, and she did not bother to go see it all day, and the neighbors told her she should go to her child and she answered that it was asleep, and it slept so much that she found it strangled.

Jehan Biolley, brandy dealer, for papistry.

Claude Moyron, farm laborer who fornicated and kept a mistress with his wife, who died recently, and the mistress[81] is pregnant and lives with him and his daughters. Because his wife died of distress only five or six weeks ago.

Claude Moyron should be asked:

Whether he is married.

Whether he did not keep with his wife and his daughters a respectable girl who fornicated with him.

Whether he did not often beat his wife to effusion of blood because she was sad.

75. Jehan Renault, called the Braggart.
76. That is, they left Geneva before appearing.
77. There are no minutes of the Consistory for this day.
78. Probably Alexandre Davonex.
79. Françoyse, widow of Tyvent Tissot.
80. Marguerite Falcat.
81. Jane, future wife of Claude Moyron.

Whether he did not threaten to beat his daughters if they said anything about it.

Whether he has not threatened those who spoke about it.

Whether his mistress is not pregnant.

Whether he did not go to recover the rest of the marriage [portion] of his late wife, recently dead.

[f. 5v]   *And whether she did not remain always with him and with his daughters in his house.

Whether he does not want to marry her.

Whether he has not spent the rest of the money from the marriage of his other dead wife with his said maid, the fornicator.

And other things, as it will be good to ask and as will please Your Mag[nificence?].

A decision must be made about the clerks who do not frequent the sermons except on Sundays, who should set an example.

De Compesio.[82]

Martin from the house of Anessi(?).

The son-in-law of De Compesio.[83]

Martinaz Richiere.[84]

*Loys the sheath-maker[85] because he did not want to receive the last Holy Communion in the temple of St. Gervase from the hands of the minister but waited until the end when the minister was gone and then received it from the hands of Don Jaques de Bonis. It must be known whether it was better from the hands of Don Jaques than from the hands of the minister. And it is said that the said Don Jaques is the calendar of the feasts in Saint Gervais for the papists.

[f. 6]   Moreover it was suggested once to summon Dominique Dentant because his brother died of plague by his fault, by the negligence of the said Dominique who never wanted to give him help in his illness.

Jo. Du Mollard. *The two Du Bochets from Petit Saconnex who wish each other harm to the death and their neighbors.[86]

*Cholex the tailor, who has a German woman whom he beats and chases outside every day through the streets, and she does not know where she should shelter. And if it were not for some neighbors she would have run into the fields; therefore it would be good to summon them both.

82. Claude de Compois.
83. Aymoz Choupin.
84. Probably Martinaz Richel.
85. Loys Piaget.
86. Claude Du Bochet and his wife and their neighbors Claude and Loyse Davaulx.

Next Monday[87]

*Reminder to the Council for Monday: the Pitards of Jussy, who seized the temple to bury their father in the temple.

*Also on the Ardins of Ponto, who buried Jehan Fran[çoys] Ardin in the temple.

For Thursday

Viennesiaz.[88]

The two daughters of Guyotz the armorer.[89]

Amed the draper[90] at Monsieur Grossi's(?) the gentleman and the wife of Collombz.[91]

[f. 6v]

For Thursday, December [13]

Tyvent, haberdasher.[92]

The mother of Amblard Cornaz.[93]

The woman whom Vincent Brolion made pregnant[94] in(?) the bed(?) at Rosse's house, and his advice.

Vincent Brolion.

Thomas Genod.

The wife of Mychiel the saddler[95] and his maid, and that the servant once beat the maid and the valet.

Pierre de Joex and his wife[96] for the sermons.

The maid of Roz Monet[97] must be considered, who is pregnant and keeps herself hidden, saying she has a bad foot, trying to go away and perhaps

87. We have found no reference to the two following cases in this volume.

88. Anthoyne Viennesaz.

89. On November 15, 1543, there in fact appeared before the Consistory three daughters of Guyot Vuydat: Pernete, Jane, and Oddete.

90. Amed Servex, weaver?

91. Loyse, wife of Pierre Joly, called Collomb?

92. Probably Tyvent Mathe, weaver.

93. Jane Darmeis.

94. Ayma Gallaz.

95. Claudaz, wife of Michel Julliard.

96. Berthe de Joex.

97. Berthe Moyron.

lose the child or make it be brought here to be put in the hospital. And the one by whom she is pregnant is married and lives on the Rue de Saint Anthoine. Little robe.[98]

Noted for Communion: those who have been forbidden to receive it since last Christmas.

First:

The wife of Master Michel,[99] who did not know how to pray to the Lord at Easter.
March 29. The wife of Jehan Corajod, cobbler, similarly.[100]
April 26. Thibaude, wife of Bonbrilloz, because of praying to the Lord and to know where her daughter gave birth(?).[101]

For Thursday

The wife of Don Hugoneri and Hugoneri her husband.[102]
Monsieur De Saint Victeur.[103]
The wife of Pierre Amyaulx and the said Ameaulx.[104]
[f. 7] Jana, wife of Glaude Pignard, purse-maker.
Anthoyne, maid at the house of Pierre Baux,[105] and Claude, servant of Monsieur Françoys Philibert.
Choupin, son of Decompesio.[106]
The maid of the lieutenant.
Lois the sheath-maker and his wife.[107]

98. Translator: This seems to be a nickname.
99. Clauda, wife of Michel Julliard.
100. Jane, wife of Jehan Corajod, cobbler. He was forbidden Communion on March 29, 1543.
101. On April 26, 1543, Thibaudaz Le Guex, wife of Jehan Grissaney, called Bombrilli, was given "a term to learn to pray and to learn where her daughter gave birth," and she was forbidden Communion.
102. Jehan Hugonier and Marie Bertherat, his wife.
103. François Bonivard.
104. Benoyte Jacon and Pierre Ameaux, her husband.
105. Anthoyne Blanc and Claude Martignin from Briod (Jura, F), servant of Jehan Philibert (not Françoys Philibert) Bonnaz.
106. Aymoz Choupin, son-in-law of Claude de Compois.
107. Loys Piaget and his wife.

Rolet the barber.[108]
Rosset and his wife.[109]
Belliaz.[110]
Jehan Favre and his wife.[111]

For Thursday

Ayma, the mother of Jehan Ripha, for religion.
The wife of Pierre de Fagniant.[112]
Wooden-Feet, wage-laborer.[113]

For Thursday, March 20, 1544

Cristobloz Pillisiaz(?),[114] boatman, at the instance of Jehan Conte, inhabitant of Nyon, Nycolardaz his daughter and Jaquemaz her mother, wife of the said Jehan. Remanded by Jehan Saubre.
Command of Syndic Philippin, referred at the instance of the said Jehan Conte.

7v]   ## For Thursday

Claude Clement, [called] Humbert.
Jaques Carrel,[115] cobbler in Longemale.
The old(?) children.
Blandin. The servant of Paule,[116] Jehan Curtet.
Denys Hugue.
Bytri.[117]

108. Rolet Galliard.
109. Pierre and Anthoyne Rosset.
110. Belletaz? Janne, widow of Pierre Aprin, called Belletaz.
111. Johente Favre.
112. Françoyse de Fagniant.
113. Anthoyne Wooden-Feet.
114. Cristoble Favre, son of Pierre Favre, boatman. See above in the main text, March 20, 1544.
115. Called Jehan Carrel above, April 3, 1544.
116. Paule Tarex.
117. Bytry Jasse.

Master Monet the mason.[118]
Collete, wife of George Gonet Chevallier.[119]
Conodaz[120] in St. Gervais, who follows an evil course.
Claude de La Ravoyre.
Pierre de Joex and the widow of Goddet.
Anthoyne Darbey and Clauda[121] his mistress.
Jehan Guynet and his wife.

For Thursday

Anthoyne Lect.
Tappugnier.[122]
Pierre Furjon.

For Thursday, May [1]

Bernard Prodhom, butcher, because of the diviner who divined his money
   which he found.
Some from Cologny and Chêne who follow an evil course and fornicate.
And those from Champel.
Monet[123] the butcher at Ballessert's, because of a cloak of Jehan Calliat's,
   cobbler.
Jehan Favre, butcher of Longemale, because of the red wine he gave [f. 8] to
   baptize his child which Monsieur Albert[124] baptized at the Magdalen.
Jaques Symond, that he played some part in the Mass at Easter.
The hostess of the Sun in St. Gervais.

118. Monet Du Cetour.
119. Called variously Gonet Chevallier and Corbet Gonyn Chevallier; he was a
farm laborer by trade.
120. Jaquema Pontheu, called Conodaz.
121. Claudaz Rosset, wife of Amy Poentet.
122. Claude Tappugnier.
123. Claude Monet.
124. Abel Poupin.

Index of Names of Places and Persons

Place names in this index appear in **boldface** type. Places mentioned only in the notes are not in the index. Numbers followed by an asterisk (for example, 251*), indicate pages where the person is mentioned only as one of the members attending the day's Consistory meeting. People whose first names only are known are entered in the index under X (for example, X, Jean). Those whose last names only are known are entered as though their first names were X (Dupont, X). Last names beginning with "de" or "d'" are alphabetized under the name itself. Names beginning with "des," "du," "le," "la," "l'," or "les" are alphabetized under "des," etc., as though part of a single word; thus "Du Puys" comes between "Dupra" and "Durand."

437

CPSIA information can be obtained at www.ICGtesting.com
Printed in the USA
BVOW021714280413

319261BV00003B/24/A